BAPTISM
ITS MODE AND SUBJECTS

BAPTISM
ITS MODE AND SUBJECTS

by

Alexander Carson

Biographical Sketch

by

John Young

KREGEL PUBLICATIONS
Grand Rapids, Michigan 49501

Baptism: Its Mode and Subjects by Alexander Carson. Published by Kregel Publications a division of Kregel, Inc. All rights reserved.

Library of Congress Cataloging in Publication Data
Carson, Alexander, 1776-1844.
    Baptism: Its Mode and Subjects.
    Reprint. Originally published: Baptism in its mode and subjects. 5th American ed. Philadelphia: American Baptist Publication Society, 1853.
    1. Baptism.   I. Title.
BV811.C27   1981   234'.161   80-8067
ISBN 0-8254-2324-4   AACR2

CONTENTS

Chapter 1

BURDEN OF PROOF

Chapter 2

MODE OF BAPTISM

MEANING OF THE WORD *BAPTO:*—DIFFERENCE BETWEEN *BAPTO* AND *BAPTIZO*

vi / Contents

Chapter 3

SUBJECTS OF BAPTISM

Chapter 4

DEFINING GREEK WORDS

Chapter 5

PHILOLOGY OF BAPTIZO

Chapter 6

A FULLER STUDY OF BAPTIZO

Chapter 7

EARLY NEW TESTAMENT BAPTISMS

x / Contents

Chapter 8

FURTHER STUDY OF MODE

Chapter 9

SPRINKLING? POURING? IMMERSION?

Chapter 10

IS IMMERSION BAPTISM?

Chapter 11

PURIFICATION OR BAPTISM?

xii / Contents

Chapter 12

CHURCH FATHERS SPEAK

President B. complains of the severity of Dr. Carson's attack on his theory with respect to the meaning of *baptizo* : Grounds on which the charge of want of discrimination on the part of President B. is founded, 487.—President B. makes *baptismos* and *katharismos* synonymous, 487.—The testimony of the Fathers, 488.—The three immersions practised by the ancients in the performance of the rite, 491.—Canon as to impossibility, 492.—Meaning of the preposition *ek*, 493.—Meaning of *louo*, 493.—Meaning of *klizo*, 494.—President B.'s complaint with regard to the manifestation of a bad spirit by Dr. Carson, 494.— Six special advantages brought forward by President B. as recommendations of the Pædobaptists' mode of attending to the ordinance, 495.

PREFACE

Nothing can be farther from the intention of the following Work than to widen the breach among Christians of different denominations, or to minister to the increase of a sectarian spirit. There are two extremes which I wish to avoid—on the one hand, a spirit of liberalism that supposes the Christian his own master, and hesitates not to sacrifice the commandments of God to the courtesies of religious intercourse—on the other, that sort of dogmatism that finds all excellence in its own party, and is reluctant to acknowledge the people of the Lord in any denomination but its own. Liberality of sentiment is not a phrase which I admit into my religious vocabulary; for though I love and acknowledge all who love the Lord Jesus, I hold myself as much under the law of God in embracing all the children of God, as in forming the articles of my creed. My recognition of all Christians I ground on the authority of Jesus. To set at nought the weakest of Christ's little ones, I call not illiberal, but unchristian. To disown those whom Christ acknowledges, is antichristian disobedience to Christ. But while I gladly admit, that many who differ from me with respect to baptism, are among the excellent of the earth, I cannot, out of compliment to them, abstain from vindicating this ordinance of Christ. This would show greater deference to man than to God. "Every plant," says Jesus, "that my heavenly Father hath not planted, must be plucked up." To permit the traditions of men to pass for the ordinances of God, is injurious to the edification of Christians, and disrespectful to Christ.

Some are diverted from the examination of this subject, by considering it as a thing of small moment, and that time is better spent in schemes of general usefulness. That baptism is a thing of small moment, is an opinion that is not likely to have been suggested by the accounts of it in the Scriptures. It is an ordinance that strikingly represents the truth that saves the soul; and is peremptorily enjoined on all who believe. But were it the very least of all the commandments of Jesus, it demands attention and obedience at the hazard of life itself. Nothing that Christ has appointed, can be innocently neglected. To suppose that schemes of general usefulness ought to take the place of the commandments of God, is a direct affront to the wisdom and power of Jehovah. Saul alleged that he had substantially obeyed the word of the Lord, though he spared Agag, the king of Amalek, and a part of the spoil for a burnt-offering; but the answer of the prophet ought for ever to deter from the exercise of a discretionary power, with respect to the commandments of God : " Hath the Lord as great delight in burnt-offerings and sacrifices, as in obeying the voice of the Lord? Behold, to obey is better than sacrifice ; and to hearken, than the fat of rams. For rebellion is as the sin of witchcraft, and stubbornness is as iniquity and idolatry : Because thou hast rejected the word of the Lord, he hath also rejected thee from being king."

Many seem alarmed at controversy, and shrink from it as opposed to the spirit of the Gospel. It is, no doubt, a grievous thing, that controversy should be necessary ; but as long as error exists, it is impossible to avoid controversy, except we value peace more than truth. Can we forget that the whole life of Christ and his apostles was a scene of never-ending controversy ? He who was love itself, contended constantly against the errors of his time. There is not a truth or an ordinance of the Gospel that Christians can hold without opposition. From the manner of revelation, it seems evidently the design of God to manifest what is in man ; and to leave an opening to discover the opposition to his wisdom in the minds even of his own people, as far as it exists. The arguments that are opposed to the truth on any subject of revelation, have their effect on the mind, not from their intrinsic weight, but from their adaptation to the corruptions of the heart. We yield to them, because what they are designed to establish is more agreeable than that to which they are opposed. Of this we have a remarkable example in the disobedient prophet at Bethel. When he was sent to denounce the judgments of the Lord against Jeroboam's altar, he was forbidden to eat or drink in the place. Yet, after refusing the hospitality of the king, he suffered himself to be deceived by another prophet. " Come home with me, and eat bread. And he said, I may not return with thee, nor go in with thee ; neither will I eat bread nor drink water with thee in this place. For it was said to me by the word of the Lord, Thou shalt not eat bread, nor drink water there, nor turn again to go by the way that thou camest. He said unto him, I am a prophet also, as thou art, and an angel spake unto me by the word of the Lord, saying, Bring him back with thee into thine house, that he may eat bread and drink water. But he lied unto him. So he went back with him, and did eat bread in his house, and drink water." Many things might be plausibly said to justify or excuse this unhappy man. But the Lord did not excuse him. " Thus saith the Lord, Forasmuch as thou hast disobeyed the mouth of the Lord, and hast not kept the commandment which the Lord thy God commanded thee, but camest back, and hast eaten bread, and drunk water, in the place of the which the Lord did say to thee, Eat no bread, and drink no water ; thy carcase shall not come unto the sepulchre of thy fathers." It behoves those who change the mode and the subjects of baptism, to consider this awful example. If Christ has commanded his disciples to be baptized on their belief of the truth, who can change it into the baptism of infants ? If he has commanded them to be immersed, who can change it into pouring or sprinkling ?

In stating the evidence on my own side, and in refuting the arguments of my opponents, I have from first to last proceeded as if I were on oath. I have never allowed myself to use artifice, or to affect to despise an argument which I found myself unable to answer. This is a resource in many controversialists, that is both disingenuous and mean. I have not used one argument to convince others, that has not with myself all the weight which I wish it to have with them. I am not conscious of forcing one line in the word of God. I have no temporal interest to serve, by establishing my views of baptism. Interest and reputation are both on the other side.

False first principles, and false canons of interpretation, lie at the bottom of most false reasoning and false criticism. This is remarkably verified in the reasonings and criticisms of my opponents, which I have examined. The reader will find innumerable instances in which I substantiate this charge. Criticism can never be a science until it founds on canons that are self-evident. When controversy is conducted on both sides in this way, truth will soon be established. My dissertation on the import of the word *baptizo*, I submit with confidence to the judgment of the really learned. If I have not settled that controversy, there is not truth in axioms.

I earnestly entreat my brethren to consider the subject with patience and impartiality. Though it may injure the temporal interest of many of them, yet there is a hundred-fold advantage in following the Lord. It would give me the greatest pleasure in being the means of leading others to correct views on this subject. But I know human nature too well to be sanguine. Something more than the strength of argument is necessary to bring even Christians to understand the will of their Lord. However, should I not make a single convert, I shall not be disappointed. My first desire is to approve myself to my Lord. If I please him, I hope I shall be enabled to bear not only the enmity of the world, but the disapprobation of Christian brethren. I expect my reward at his appearing. The motto I wish to be engraven on my heart is " Occupy till I come."

PUBLISHER'S PREFACE

For further examination of the use of the word *Baptizein* in secular and sacred sources, we refer you to *The Meaning and Use of Baptizein* by Thomas Jefferson Conant, reprinted by Kregel Publications in 1977.

THE PUBLISHER

INTRODUCTION

As in the baptismal controversy I have taken the side opposed to interest and popularity I could have no temptation to become a Baptist. Knowing the strength of prejudice on the other side, and the odium attached to truth on this question, I have, from the commencement of the examination of the subject, acted with the utmost caution and deliberation. I have no pleasure in reproach or persecution. To me, it was a very serious sacrifice to change my views on this question. All the other points in which I differ from the dominant sects of this country, do not give so much offence to the world, as does the difference on the subject of baptism. I anticipated the end, I counted the cost, and I am daily paying the instalments. In the present work, I have, at great length, laid the evidence before my readers, both in proof and refutation. In both I have acted with integrity and candour. I have, in every line, written as in the sight of God, and with the full impression that I shall give account. It is no light matter to attempt to influence the views and conduct of the Lord's people as to any part of his will. Nothing I wish more to avoid than, in the day of God, to be found to have led his people away from his truth and ordinances. I have not used an argument which has not the weight on my own mind, which I wish it to have on my reader's. I have not overlooked a single objection from a conviction of its difficulty, nor given it an evasive or sophistical answer. If truth is my client, I shall not affront her by an unworthy defence. I despise sophistry on all subjects: when employed on the work of God I loathe and abhor it. I am not indifferent to the approbation of honest and sound-minded men; to these I confidently appeal. But my ambition is, to be recognised by Jesus as the defender of his truth, "when he shall come to be glorified in his saints, and to be admired in all them that believe."

I have thought it necessary to premise some observations on the nature of the burden of proof. If they are sound they will be of immense importance on any subject. It is a thing on which controversialists appear to be universally mistaken. As it is essential to the manifestation of truth, it is not possible that it can be either optional or conventional.

The nature of the testimony of the Fathers, with respect to the meaning of the word which designates the ordinance, I have pointed out. It is only as they testify as to the meaning of the word in the time of the Apostles, that they can be called in as witnesses. The word might have received any number of secondary meanings after this period without affecting the question at issue. To speak of meaning conferred by progress of ideas after the institution of the ordinance, as being applicable for proof on this subject, is at the utmost verge of absurdity.

In order to make the work more agreeable and useful to the English reader, I have not printed a single Greek word: and there is hardly a criticism which men of a sound mind without learning may not understand and estimate. My canons and my criticisms generally apply to all languages, and require nothing in the reader but patience and a sound judgment. The only thing which I regret in following this plan is, that it prevents me from using much valuable evidence supplied to me by my friends from the testimony of modern Greek, &c.

To a highly respectable individual who sent me his views against the *perpetuity* of Baptism, I reply, that I had originally intended to treat on this point, but, on consideration, I found that it did not lie before me, and would require to be treated in a separate work.

I give a similar answer to many other friends who have suggested points which they wished to be handled. I wish to avoid anything but what is essential to my main object. A writer who attempts to do every thing at once, will do nothing well.

Some of my antagonists speak as if I were a most bigoted and intolerant Baptist. In replying to them I have taken no notice of this. I despise misrepresentation; in the end it can do no injury. So far from fostering a sectarian spirit, no one can more thoroughly abhor it than I do. It mars the progress of the truth, which with every Christian ought to be paramount to all things; it dishonours Christ and his people; and it does injury even to the cause which it is designed to favour. While I defend what I consider truth, with respect to this ordinance, I cordially embrace every lover of the Lord Jesus, and concede to him the same privilege that I take to myself. In my mind it is a heinous sin to despise the very weakest of all the children of God; and if ever Christian union was important, it is so in the present time, when all the machinations of the Prince of darkness are employed in combination to destroy the truth. I am as warm an advocate for Christian union as I am for Baptism. I am fully convinced that, if Christian union were fully understood and acted on by Christians in general, right views of Baptism would soon prevail. Among all the causes that prevent Christians from impartial and earnest inquiry, a sectarian spirit is the chief: it shuts them out from confidential intercourse with one another, and disinclines them to think of the subject.

Many seem to think that zeal for any of the things in which Christians differ, is inconsistent with zeal for Christian union. Accordingly, while some, on the one hand, from zeal for their peculiarities, are unfriendly to Christian union, others, on the other hand, from zeal for Christian union, think themselves bound to undervalue and neglect the things in which Christians differ. Nothing can be more unfounded and dishonourable to truth than this. On the contrary, the greatest zeal for a particular opinion is quite consistent with the utmost regard for Christian union. Christian union is not founded on perfect agreement with respect to all the will of God, but agreement about the truth that unites them all in one body in Christ. No difference consistent with this, can really separate them. I press my views on my brethren: if I succeed, I do them service; if I fail, I discharge my duty, but have no cause of complaint against them. They are not accountable to me, and it is the essence of popery to assume any authority but that of argument. In the field of battle, I strike in earnest, but even then it is the arguments, or the talents, or the harmony of my opponent, at which I aim. I never judge the heart! I am united in heart with all who are united to Christ.

BIOGRAPHICAL SKETCH

of

Alexander Carson

BIOGRAPHICAL SKETCH

THOSE who undertake to record the lives of literary men, often complain of a want of stirring incidents, such as enliven the histories of warriors and statesmen. The man of letters is compelled, by the very nature of his pursuits, to spend much time in retirement, and in labours which, however useful, possess but little interest in narration.

The beloved individual, of whom we are now to give an account, was peculiarly fond of seclusion, and passed nearly all his time in the bosom of his own flock, without ever attemping to urge his way into the bustle of the great world. Yet his life is by no means destitute of important events, which, if properly presented, cannot fail to interest at least the christian reader. He was a fearless warrior, who fought, not for an earthly, but a heavenly crown; and whose victories were gained, not by destroying, but in labouring to save his fellow men. He was a profound and skilful statesman, expounding the laws, not of fleeting human governments, but of that divine and spiritual kingdom, which is the last and noblest work of the Creator. Shall bloody conquerors have their annalists, while the soldiers of Immanuel are forgotten? No! never. The names and memorials of God's people must live, when earth's empires have perished, and oblivion shall cover all their glories.

---

*In attempting the preparation of the following article, the writer feels that an apology is due from him to the public. The lamented death of Dr. Carson, occuring just as his work on Baptism was about to be republished in this country, seemed to require that a brief sketch of his life should accompany it; in order that American readers might know something of the character of a man whose productions they so highly prize. At the request of the Publication Society, the writer, with much diffidence, consented to perform this service. He had no materials for the purpose on hand; and time could not be afforded him to procure them from Ireland. He has described the events from recollection, and the testimony of others. He has aimed to give a faithful picture. If inaccuracies should be found, he hopes they will be pardoned, as incidental to the circumstances in which he was placed.

The scene of Dr. Carson's labours, for a period of nearly fifty years, was Tubbermore, a small town in the north of Ireland, containing about 2,000 inhabitants. The place is so mean in appearance, and so unimportant, that geographers and travellers—those universal describers—have scarcely deigned to notice it. Its principal buildings consist of two meeting-houses and a post-office. The rural scenery around it is much disfigured by the vicinity of a large Irish bog, on one side of which, fronting towards the miry waste, stands the white-washed cottage of Alexander Carson. As the traveller passes from Tubbermore in the direction of Derry, his eye rests only upon a vast extent of mountain land, thinly covered with stunted heath, over which he may toil the livelong day amid the solitudes of nature, uncheered by any abode of man, except one miserable hut in the middle of the wide expanse.

The inhabitants of the north of Ireland are a mixed race, the majority being of Scottish origin, whose ancestors fled thither from prelatical persecution, because they could there enjoy their beloved Presbyterianism, unharassed by the soldiers of the English king. Into their new home they carried, not only their stable religious principles, but their sober industry, and careful attention to all the arts of civilized life. By the practical application of the steadiness and intelligence, so characteristic of the land from which they sprung, the north of Ireland has been made to differ as widely from the rude and uncultured south, as if they were not both parts of the same green isle. Almost every thing in this region is Scottish. Three fourths of the people are Presbyterians; a few, consisting chiefly of the gentry and their dependants, belong to the Episcopal or established church; the remainder are Roman Catholics. The Scottish population are readily distinguished by the broad Scotch dialect, which has crossed the water, and still continues among them; while the original inhabitants are equally well marked by their ruddy complexions, sandy hair, Irish brogue, and strong Roman Catholic superstitions. Education has made considerable progress in this part of the country; and it may safely be asserted, that the working classes, and especially those engaged in agriculture, are much better instructed and more intelligent, than the same classes in England. The people of Tubbermore partake largely of the characteristics both of the north and west of Ireland. Their little village lies almost upon the boundary line between Popery and Protestantism, where the two races and religions meet and mingle on somewhat equal terms. In this community, some fifty years ago, Mr. Carson was settled as Presbyterian minister. His birth was in a place about twelve miles distant, called Artrae. He had received his education in the University of Glasgow, at the same time with a large number of other students, who have since become eminent in the religious world. His preparatory classical course was of the most thorough kind; and the closeness of his application, during his residence at the University, was evinced by his graduating, with the first honours, in a large class, containing, among others afterwards distinguished, such men as Dr. Wardlaw of Glasgow, and Dr. Brown of Langton. It is remarkable, that his published works contain replies to some productions of each of these his former classmates.

On his entrance into public life, he speedily manifested that a solid foundation had been laid for future eminence. Among his earlier writings, was a work on the figures of speech, in which he developed those self-evident principles in the philosophy of language, by the aid of which he has since been able to clear his way through all the sophistries that had entangled and obscured the imagery of Scripture. This work has been regarded as a standard one on the subject of which it treats.

As a Presbyterian minister, he was highly esteemed by his brethren, and generally considered one of the first minds connected with that body in Ireland. It is very creditable to both parties, that, although he left their connection, and has since been much engaged as a controversialist, dealing heavy blows upon all who will not fully obey the institutions of Christ; yet the Presbyterians, both ministers and people, still speak of him with the greatest respect as a christian of devoted piety, and award to him as a scholar the highest rank in the country. The writer has often heard them express their regret that Mr. Carson did not remain in their communion, as in that case he would probably have been appointed to the Professorship of Moral Philosophy in the Royal College of Belfast, as the best qualified man in Ireland for that situation.

At the period of Mr. Carson's induction into the christian ministry, religion had sadly declined in Ireland. The ministers, who first planted Presbyterianism there, were men of burning zeal and holy devotedness. They had lost all for religion, and for its sake were exiles from their native land. They, therefore, knew well how to value it; and they infused the same spirit into the congregations which they gathered. Filled with a first love, those churches then stood forth " fair as the moon, clear as the sun, and terrible as an army with banners." Their steps were free; for, although the government of the country was against them, still they were not persecuted, and were amenable only to King Jesus. Courting not the smile of the world, and fearing not its frowns, they gave their whole hearts to the work of the Lord.

But, alas! in an evil day for Ireland, Satan, unable to destroy the men of God by the flood which he cast after them, laid a plan to entrap them in the deceitful snare of riches, and to paralize their zeal by the withering influence of secular patronage. The Irish Presbyterians were supposed to be unfriendly to the existing form of government; and cunning statesmen, well instructed by the prince of darkness, saw that the most effectual way of gaining them over to toryism, was to pension their clergy. Overtures were accordingly made to them; and almost all the ministers of the Synod of Ulster became at once voluntary stipendiaries of the government, receiving an annual gift from the public treasury, termed " Regium Donum."

This device had the effect which its authors intended. The ministers soon ceased to bear testimony against the evils and corruptions of the age. They became worldly-minded, and spent their time in cultivating their fine farms, instead of faithfully preaching the gospel, and laboriously tending the vineyard of the Lord. Religion was soon allowed to take care of itself. Church discipline fell into neglect. Evangelical truth gave place to moral essays, and often to absolute socinianism, in which the whole scheme of human redemption was neutralized. Regeneration, and holiness of heart and life were scouted as unnecessary and fanatical. The church-courts became arenas for angry debate between the Orthodox and the Arians; and true piety almost abandoned the land.*

At this juncture, Mr. Carson entered upon the ministerial office at Tubbermore. In the general disregard of religion which prevailed, the people of his charge were not behind their neighbours. Horse-races, cockfights, and other forms of sinful diversion were frequent, and were numerously attended even by professing christians. The soul of this pious servant of God was deeply grieved. He knew well the heaven-born excellence of christianity, and clearly understood what should be " the fruits of the Spirit;" but he beheld around him only the works of the devil. He rode into the throng that crowded the race-course, and there saw the members of his own church flying in every direction to escape from his sight. What was he to do? He had preached the truth fully—had warned the offenders of their danger, and set before them the terrors of the Lord. But now he felt that there was another step to be

---

* Since the period here referred to, the state of the Presbyterian churches in Ireland has greatly improved. The separation of the Unitarian congregations from the Synod of Ulster, and the introduction of Sunday schools, have effected a very delightful reformation in that body. They are now as evangelical in doctrine, and as zealous for the spread of the gospel, as any class of Presbyterians in the world.

taken. This was the exercise of Scriptural discipline upon those who would not live as christians ; a task easy in thought, but which he found most difficult in execution. These people had been introduced into the church just eight days after their entrance into the world. They had drank in their religion with their infant nourishment. They had been permitted to approach the sacramental table as soon as they possessed the important qualification of being able to repeat the " Shorter Catechism." They paid the stipend regularly—had their own pews in their meeting-house—and felt that, while they attended divine service on Sunday, brought forward their children for baptism, and committed no gross immorality, they had an unquestioned right to the privileges of the church, and ought not to be placed " *ex cathedra* " for such trifling matters as vain amusements, and a worldly life. In short, they held themselves perfectly independent, and spurned all the restraints of discipline. Aid was then sought by Mr. Carson from the higher court, the Presbytery. Here certainly he might expect, that delinquents would be dealt with according to their merits. Here lay the great statute-book of the kingdom of the clergy —the Westminster Confession of Faith. Here also was the lesser light, the " Code of Discipline," containing the enactments, partly of the Bible, and partly of the Church, with all the legal rules of proceeding in cases of " fama clamosa." And here were the Reverend, the Clergy, lords of God's heritage, ready to execute the laws. Surely, could he once put this mighty machinery in motion, his infected flock must speedily be purified from unworthy members. But no! far from it. This vast system of church-laws had not been framed to regulate the conduct of a spiritual body, like the primitive churches—for whose government the rules of the Bible would have been sufficient—but to hold together, in a state of religious formalism, the unnatural and discordant amalgam of saint and sinner, the wheat and the tares, the church and the world. Now this was precisely the condition of the people at Tubbermore. They had the " form of godliness," but were destitute of its power ; and the legislation of a formal church could supply no remedy.

Abandoning his hope of church improvement from the workings of ecclesiastical courts, Mr. Carson now gathered around him all that had been written upon church government, and toiled his way through the heaps of rubbish by which he was encompassed ; until, casting aside all human teaching, and guided only by the light of inspiration, his eye rested on the simple, scriptural model, of a congregation of spiritual men, governing themselves solely by the word of God. Then did he, for the first time, perceive the real difficulties in which he had been placed. His

church was composed of worldly people, whom neither force nor persuasion could bring into subjection to the laws of Christ. The work thus
extended before him into one of awful magnitude, and in it vain was the
help of man. The building was to be laid anew of lively stones—of
members, fitted by a renovated nature, to have place in the temple of the
Lord. The well defined outline of the house of God—the beautiful ex-
emplar of New Testament christianity—now rose before him, in all its
harmonious proportions, and radiant with its first loveliness ; concentrat-
ing upon itself his most ardent affections, and strengthening his faith, that
he might be able fearlessly to execute the task of developing it before his
fellow-men.

One of his first objects was to regain his religious freedom by abandoning the Synod. In a work which he published at this time, entitled
" Reasons for leaving the Synod of Ulster," he sets down this as his
second reason for taking that important step. " I cannot," he says, " be
a member of the General Synod, without renouncing my christian liberty,
and submitting my conscience to be ruled and lorded over by man. I am
not allowed to be directed by my own conscience in the service of my
Master. I must not act on my own conviction of what is right and
wrong ; but according to the caprice of others ; nay, of those whom I
esteem the decided enemies of the Lord Jesus."

In this production, he maintains, with great force of reasoning, the primitive independence of the churches. From his argument on this point,
we extract a few passages, in order to show the principles by which he
was actuated in this interesting crisis of his history.

" That form of church government which is capable of the least abuse,
is the most likely to be divine. Now, unquestionably, this is Indepen-
dency. If a particular church on this plan degenerates, becomes erroneous, or indifferent, it has no power to injure others, or draw them into its
errors. If all the independent churches of a nation were to degenerate
except one, that one cannot be compelled or overawed to follow their example. But it is quite contrary with Presbyterianism. I know, indeed,
it is said, that the Presbyterian system is better calculated to prevent error
from creeping into congregations, by the power which the majority claims
over the minority. But how should one man, or one congregation, keep
another from error ? By compulsion, or persuasion ? I apprehend there
is no lawful means for one church to keep another from error, but by re-
monstrance and exhortation. If these fail, pains, penalties, imprison-
ments, confiscations, and death, would be useless. Force may make hypo-
crites, but can never make a christian. But let the history of Synods

vouch their utility and efficiency in restraining error, and preserving vital religion. They may for a time preserve orthodoxy in *the letter*, but midnight darkness may reign with an orthodox creed. ‘The natural man cannot know the things of the Spirit of God, because they are spiritually discerned.’ Vital religion seems in a great measure extinguished, even among those who make the highest pretensions to orthodoxy. A violent, wrathful spirit of party, and an ardent zeal for human forms and human creeds, seem pretty generally substituted for spirituality, and catholic christian love.”

“Again, that form of church government which cannot preserve purity of doctrine without human expedients, is not so likely to be the scripture model, as that which can attain and preserve the highest possible degree of vital religion, as well as purity of doctrine, without admitting, in any instance, the devices of the wisdom of man. Now it is generally acknowledged by Presbyterians themselves, that it is impossible to maintain uniformity of opinion among them, without a formula, or Confession of Faith, to be publicly recognized by all the members. But it must be evident to every unprejudiced person, that there is no formula in the Scriptures. That constitution, then, which requires one to maintain purity, is not likely to be of God.”

“ Lastly, that form of church government which leads us most to the Scriptures, and requires in church members the greatest acquaintance with them, is the most likely to be that of the New Testament. Now, without an intimate acquaintance with the Bible, Independents cannot advance a step in church affairs. I might speak from what I have witnessed of the knowledge of the Scriptures among Independents. But I speak only of its necessity, arising from the constitution of their churches. With them it is absolutely essential, not merely in church rulers, but in private members. The Bible is their code of laws ; they have no other confession or book of discipline. They can do nothing without it; it must be continually in their hands ; the rulers rule only by the word of God. But a man may be a Presbyterian all his life, either pastor or private member, with a very slender acquaintance with the Bible. A knowledge of forms and of ancient usages, of ecclesiastical canons and books of discipline, is the chief qualification necessary for a Presbyterian judicatory.”

Influenced by views such as these, and strong in the conclusions to which he had arrived, Mr. Carson threw up his government salary, and removed from the farm he had formerly occupied, that he might devote himself more entirely to his ministerial work. It was deemed at the time a most astonishing occurrence, that a man high in public favour, of splendid talents, and elevated piety, should abandon a church in what was

called the zenith of its glory, to take up his abode with poverty and contempt. Little could the people comprehend the power of christian principle by which he was impelled. Hence they concluded with respect to
him, as Festus did concerning Paul, that "much learning had made him
mad;" and his presumed insanity was received by many, as the only
rational explanation of a course of conduct so far above the wisdom of
this world. He was then married, and had a rising family. His wife
was the daughter of a Mr. Leidly, a linen-bleacher of wealth and respect-
ability, residing in the same county. On hearing the sad tale of the heresy
of his son-in-law, Mr. Leidly immediately visited him, and spent a long
time in endeavouring to persuade him to return to the Synod. Tired of
his importunities, and well knowing what would be the result, Mr. Carson told him that he would leave the whole matter to the decision of his
wife. With renewed hope the father betook himself to his daughter:
placed before her the good that might be done, and the comforts which
they might enjoy, by retracing their steps; and, on the other hand, set
forth, in gloomy colours, the poverty into which they would be thrown
by continuing in their present position; declaring the firm determination
to which he had come, never, in that case, to relieve them; and assuring
her that her children would soon be starving for bread. But how full of
serene faith and pious confidence was her reply! "Father," said she,
" God feeds the young ravens when they cry unto him; and I cannot
believe, that, while we are striving to do his will, he will let the young
Carsons starve." Thus did that noble woman sustain and cheer on her
husband in his trying hour, and forsake, not only houses and lands, but
father and mother, in obedience to the commands of Christ. From that
day, she was to her parents as a stranger. What a sublime spectacle is
it, to behold the christian struggling, by the sacrifice of all that earth holds
dear, to free himself from the domination of his fellow men, and from the
customs of the world—not that he may enjoy a licentious liberty, and
walk after the imagination of his own heart; but that he may bring his
soul into more complete subordination to the statutes of Heaven's King,
and devote his life more unreservedly to the service of God—that thus
God may be "all in all!"

For some years after his secession from the General Synod, Mr. Carson continued to occupy his former place of worship, and to preach to
the congregation as before. But he had now embraced a principle which
contained within it the germ of yet further reform. He had recognized
the Bible as the only law-book in the kingdom of Christ; and had taught
those members of his church who still adhered to his ministry, to rise

above human authority and human customs in religion, and bring all things to the Word and Testimony of God. It was by losing sight of this radical principle, that early Christianity degenerated into Romish superstition. Ecclesiastical authority laid the foundation, and worldly policy raised the superstructure of that mass of abominations, which is to be destroyed by the brightness of the Lord's coming. The partial application of this principle shook the Papal hierarchy, and brought forth the Reformed churches from its dark embrace. And it is to its full, fearless, and faithful application alone, that we are to look for a complete emancipation from the trammels of will-worship, and from the various admixtures and perversions by which men have corrupted the simplicity of the Gospel. This use of the Bible as the only law-book, and the rejection of ecclesiastical authority, carried Mr. Carson and his congregation to results, of which, in the beginning, they little dreamed. Of such progress, however, they are far from being solitary examples. The history of religious reformations demonstrates, that in all cases where this single elemental truth has been clearly developed, and wisely brought into exercise, it has uniformly led in the same direction; and, consequently, has produced a new basis of christian union, differing widely from any which human systems have ever afforded. In the Baptist Memorial of July, 1844, we find an account of the rise and establishment of the Baptist church in Sturbridge, Massachusetts. The narrative informs us, that, in the preaching of Whitfield and the Tennants, a principle was held forth and inculcated, which led to conclusions that they themselves neither adopted nor contemplated. " They taught that the Bible, and the Bible alone, is the religion of Protestants. The consequences of this position, however, those excellent men did not follow out in their full length. But others, guided by the light which this sentiment sheds upon the mind, began vigorously to inquire, not only what are the great fundamental truths of Christianity, but also what are the ordinances of Christ's house. The result was, that many of the converts of those days, became Baptists. Taking the Scriptures for their only guide, they arrived by a plain and direct course of reasoning at this result. This was the origin of the Baptist church in Sturbridge. At first they believed in and practised infant sprinkling. The fact that this is not an ordinance of Scripture, had probably never entered their minds. But still the other principles which they had adopted, especially that of making the Bible the supreme arbiter in religion, prepared the way for their giving up that unscriptural ceremony."

About the time that Mr. Carson left the Presbyterians in Ireland, a

mighty movement towards primitive christianity also took place in Scotland
The Haldanes, together with Wardlaw, Ewing, and Innis, had become
alive to the unscriptural character of worldly churches ; and were busy in
organizing christian societies upon the Bible only, with the sincere determination to regulate all the ordinances of Christ's house in accordance with
the plain dictates of Revelation. They adopted the congregational order,
and weekly communion, throughout Scotland ; but were not Baptists. ,

In the year 1807, James Haldane, after having sprinkled an infant, was
accosted by his little son, a child of six years old, with the pertinent question, " Father, did that child believe ?" " No," said the surprised parent,
" why do you ask me such a question ?" " Because, father, I have read
the whole of the New Testament, and I find that all, who were baptized,
believed. Did the child believe ?" It was enough. God's simple truth,
which had been hidden from the wise and prudent, was revealed to the
babe. The strange question, " Did the child believe ?" haunted the mind
of that father, until, after a thorough examination, he renounced his former errors, and was publicly immersed. His brother Robert soon followed his example. Whole churches saw the light of this ordinance
flashing upon them ; and thousands of the most devoted men of Scotland,
who had taken the Bible as their sole directory, reformed their " Tabernacle Reformation," and followed the Lord fully.

Now it is certain that when Mr. Carson withdrew from the Presbyterian connection, he had no idea of becoming a Baptist. Indeed, several
of his flock were before him in discovering the fact that believers only
are the proper subjects of baptism. For when the question was first
mooted among them, and some became convinced that infant sprinkling
was never instituted by Christ—although he did not attempt to interfere
with their obedience—yet he took ground against the novelty ; and, as he
himself says, " defended the citadel, while he had any ammunition in the
store-house." But the mind of Carson could not but advance to right
conclusions. His reasoning powers had been too thoroughly disciplined,
for insufficient evidence long to satisfy him—especially now, when the
laws of the church could no more settle the matter, but the appeal must
be made directly to the Bible. Truth was his fortune—his delight—his
all ; and for the truth of God he was ready to suffer trials even greater
than had yet fallen to his lot. It is deeply to be regretted that there is in
the religious world so little real love for truth ; or rather, we should say,
so little inclination to enter upon those inquiries which might issue in its
attainment. Heathen sages, by calm and candid investigation, were able
to rise far above the superstitious customs of their countrymen ; and for

such scattered rays of divine light as fell on the mind of a Socrates, were willing to lay down their lives. But now the painful fact cannot be concealed, that, while the glories of Heaven's Revelation are beaming upon us, we suffer prejudice to retard our researches, or fear of consequences to prevent us from doing our duty. Mr. Carson deserves no praise. He only did what every christian ought to do. He received and he obeyed the truth. But what vast multitudes, with the truth shining clearly before them, refuse to follow where it leads!

The object, moreover, for which Mr. Carson was striving, could not be gained without the surrender of infant church-membership. He saw around him manifold evidences of the fearful danger which resulted to the souls of men, from allowing those, who had nothing of christianity but the name, to share the privileges of the church relation. He had renounced the Synod, in order that he might enjoy a purer communion, and be guiltless of the blood of all men. This noble purpose led him directly to the inquiry, in what the qualifications for church-membership consisted. He perceived that the house of God was designed to be wholly spiritual, composed of lively stones united to Christ, the living Head. From that inspired volume, to whose teachings he implicitly bowed, he learned, that the true members of the christian family were sons, born not of blood, nor of the will of the flesh, nor of the will of man, but of God—begotten by him through the incorruptible seed of his truth which abideth forever; that faith is indispensable to a union with the body of Christ; that faith cometh by hearing, and hearing by the word of God; and that, consequently, infants, incapable alike of hearing and of believing, and growing up with all the manifestations of a carnal nature, were not lawful subjects for admission into the brotherhood of the renewed. Could he introduce these unregenerate offspring of Adam into the church of Christ, on the right of their natural birth, and in the vague anticipation that they might afterwards be born again? And if he did thus mingle the seed of men with the sons of God, could he expect to guard against the tendencies in such a society to a merely formal religion?" Could he admit the children of believers to religious privileges along with believers themselves, and yet have a pure, regenerated church, qualified for spiritual communion with its Lord? No; this was more than he could accomplish; and never will the ingenuity of man, with all its multifarious devices, be able to effect it. It is impossible! The very attempt is an absurdity whose folly and hopelessness all history and all experience have conclusively demonstrated.

When it was found that Mr. Carson, so far from being likely to return to the Synod, was proceeding yet further in his course of reform, the hostility of the disaffected portion of his own church could no longer be restrained. Vigorous efforts were now made by the Presbyterians to dispossess him of the meeting-house. A party was organized, whose business it should be to eject him by force. While he was preaching, on a Lord's day, to a large congregation, they entered, and announced their intention of thrusting him from the pulpit. He quieted the rising tumult, and requesting the intruders to wait until the close of his discourse, assured them that he would then voluntarily retire. They accepted the proposal, and remained. After the services were concluded, as he descended from the pulpit, and was passing out, one of his deacons lifted the Bible from the desk, swung it upon his shoulder, and taking up his march in the rear of his pastor, exclaimed, " *let all who wish to follow the Bible come this way.*" The house was instantly emptied. A vast mass congregated in a green field near by ; and there, guided by the Bible, as by a Shekinah of glory, a little band, sixteen in number, partook, with hearts joyful amid their tribulations, of the emblems of their Redeemer's love. This was the feeble beginning of greater things—the chrysalis from which was to spring a glorious gospel church, walking in the ordinances of Christ blameless, and pouring a flood of light upon the surrounding region. From that period, the Lord has been constantly adding unto them the saved, insomuch that their present number approaches 500, although very many baptized into their fellowship have removed from the district. They have also had the happiness of seeing other churches rising up around them, on the same apostolical model, and, animated by a kindred spirit, observing and promoting a strict obedience to the requirements of the Saviour.

After they had left their meeting-house, they assembled for worship, during summer, in the open air ; and in winter, in an old barn kindly lent them for the purpose. Thus they continued to meet, until the shell of their new house was erected. We say the *shell*, for their means enabled them to do little more than to put up the walls and enclose the building. For many years they occupied that house, and saw it crowded by large congregations, although only an earthen floor supported them, and the eye was permitted to scan the rude frame-work of a roof unrelieved by an ornamented ceiling. Latterly, they have considerably enlarged it to accommodate their increasing numbers ; and we believe that the improving taste of the age has been evinced in removing some of its more glaring architectural defects. Still, however, the English visitor is apt to return to his own more favoured Isle, with his imagination filled with strange pictures of Irish ruralness and simplicity. Yet humble as that building is, that can be said of it which was never true of many a gorgeous cathedral—that for many years a pure gospel has resounded there ; and that there the living word has been the power of God unto salvation to a multitude of souls, who, though some of them are scattered far from their native village, will ever remember the hallowed spot which witnessed their birth into an everlasting kingdom.

The situation of Mr. Carson, at the period when he thus went forth from his old connections, was peculiarly trying. His regular means of subsistence were now all gone. He had thrown himself upon the voluntary offerings of God's people ; they were willing to do what they could ; but that was little, as the more wealthy of his former congregation had remained by " *the stuff.*" Another minister was called to occupy the pulpit which he had vacated; and the men of means and influence soon rallied around the standard of *the things that had been.* For, at all times, as in the time of Jesus of Nazareth, the question goes, " Have any of the rulers believed on him ?" Unfortunately it occurs, that our little, petty aristocracies can hardly ever find their way to truth, unless truth happens first to find its way to popular favour, by the help of God and the poor. Then, indeed, when it has become fashionable, they will awake as from a dream, and graciously patronize it. Thus did the respectable citizens of Tubbermore abandon in his difficulties a man whom the world will admire, and elect to themselves another christian teacher who will scarce ever be heard of beyond his own two-mile circle. Nobly, however, have the people of the district since redeemed their character, by flocking around the banner of Bible truth which Mr. Carson unfurled. Never did a man more fearlessly trust the promises of God, and never were those promises more faithfully verified than in his case. He has at no time received from his people more than $250, per annum ; and for a long period subsequent to the events we have been narrating, the support which they were able to afford him was far less. Yet he has always lived in comparative comfort ; has been blessed with a numerous family ; has educated them well ; and placed them in respectable situations of usefulness to themselves and to society. To this result, the extensive sale of his valuable writings has no doubt materially contributed.

Mr. Brown, the minister who was installed in the Tubbermore church after Mr. Carson's secession, was a man of rather combative propensities ; and, mistaking his vocation, he considered himself as placed in a sort of dangerous pass, for the defence of the faith as it is in Presbyterianism. Hence he has been frequently engaged in hostile demonstrations, which, if he had more correctly estimated his own abilities, and the strength of his cause, he would have studiously avoided. After the publication of Mr. Carson's work on " The Mode and Subjects of Baptism," an attempt at reply was made by Mr. Brown, and a rejoinder was also published by the author. This little controversy finally extended to perhaps two pamphlets on each side. In the present revised edition of his work, Mr. Carson has embodied nearly all the pamphlets which he previously issued in answer to the criticisms of various eminent men both in Great Britain and America ; but he has shown his sense of the futility of Mr. Brown's reviews, by omitting altogether his refutations of them. This Tubbermore discussion, although not worthy of being handed down to posterity in the following immortal work, yet served to convince many in that immediate vicinity, that their previous practice was not so capable of defence as they had fondly hoped. The consequence was, that Mr. Carson's church began rapidly to increase ; and the people, laying aside their former notion of his insanity, now listened to him as one more competent to expound the Scriptures than the men by whom he was surrounded.

The church at Tubbermore became Baptist by degrees. Some of the members were baptized before the pastor. Owing, probably, in part to this circumstance, they have never regarded an obedience to this ordinance as an indispensable condition of admission to the Lord's supper. Indeed, they have carried the principle of open communion to the utmost extent, by receiving members into their body simply upon evidence of their conversion, with but little inquiry whether they agreed with them on the subject of Baptism, expecting that whenever they became convinced of their duty to be immersed, they would attend to it.

To the great majority of Baptists it will appear, that this practice, together with their open communion, was not in accordance with the example of those primitive churches, which, in other points, it was Mr. Carson's delight to imitate ; and that its tendency must be to throw into the shade an ordinance prominent in the New Testament, and to dissever baptism from the gospel of which it is so expressive an emblem. Certain it is, however, that Mr. Carson believed this plan to be consistent with the will of the Lord ; and this fact, while it may seem to show that his views of gospel order were not, in all respects, precise and clear, is, at the same time, a strong proof of his extreme liberality and kindness of disposition. It ought, therefore, to bespeak for his writings a very favourable attention from those who are so loud in their complaints of the want of charity among Baptists. He was as charitable as their hearts could wish; and was ever more ready to hold fellowship even with those Pedo-baptists, who otherwise taught a pure gospel, than with such Baptists as he might conceive to have departed from genuine orthodoxy.

He united, in a wonderful degree, an enlarged charity with the holiest boldness in defence of truth. In all the intercourse of private life, he eminently displayed the humility and gentleness of the christian charac-ter. Indeed, he seemed simple and childlike even to a fault. Yet his productions are remarkable for the boldness and originality of the thoughts, the strength of the arguments, and the severity of the rebukes, which they contain. Many have conceived a most erroneous impression of his whole character from the apparent harshness of his criticisms. This, however, arises, in a great measure, from a mistake as to the origin of what may be called " *the attic salt* " in writing. The author of Junius was proba-bly a very goodnatured man, although his writings are fearfully severe. He knew that the disease which he had to treat, required a powerful re-medy; and he applied a caustic one. No man of ill temper can write keenly. As the razor, when its edge becomes ruffled, will not cut freely; so angry passion weakens the force of argument, and prevents criticism from taking effect. The man who would criticise with vigour, must possess the power of self-control in a large degree. Coolness will enable him to polish his shafts, and direct them to the best advantage. Anger and wrath evaporate in abuse. But no one will find this applied by Mr. Carson to his opponents. True, he will not allow impertinent quibblers, who, to support the system of their own party, continue still to argue against the clearest demonstrations of Scripture, to pass without re-buke. And where is the ardent lover of truth, who will not say that such ought to be rebuked and made to retire ashamed, that the public mind may no more be darkened by their perversions? We frankly confess that the more we read on the Baptismal controversy, the more our charity compels us to struggle against the conviction which forces itself upon us, that, on this subject, it is not light that is most wanted—but *religious honesty*.

If, beyond this, it should still be supposed that there are, in Mr. Car-son's writings, instances of unwarrantable severity, we would submit, in alleviation, the national character. The Irish people are remarkable for vigorous conceptions and strong feelings, which they express with very little attention to softness and suavity of language; and when this Irish vehemence is united with an ardent love of truth, and dislike of subtle perversions, it may give to their publications an appearance of unkindness which is really very foreign to the writers themselves. Certain it is, that

Mr. Carson has been most favourably known as a peace-maker; and when troubles have arisen in some of the little churches of Ulster, his presence and prudent counsels have generally contributed to settle their difficulties, and to calm their agitations.

As a preacher, he was very remarkable. He possessed all the solid qualifications of an orator, without any of the pomp and display usually attendant upon those who are regarded as good speakers. His manner was natural and graceful. His illustrations were very abundant, but never learned or far-fetched. The scenes of rural life supplied him with a rich fund of incidents and analogies, that enabled him to make truth plain to the weakest capacity, and which told powerfully on the unsophisticated sympathies of human nature. His usual course was, not to sermonize, but to expound the word of God, by passing regularly through its successive portions. This plan afforded him full opportunity to bring out all the latent resources of his mind, and to apply his vast learning to the important practical purpose of solving the various difficulties which his hearers might encounter in their reading; while it enabled him completely to avoid that petty ingenuity which is too often exercised in building a discourse upon some insulated or perverted sentence.

The results of expository teaching have always been of the most delightful kind. It was the invariable custom of Scottish preachers, in former times, to employ the forenoon of every Lord's day in the exposition of a chapter. This they denominated lecturing; and so highly did the people value this exercise, that, in calling a young minister to a parish, the great question was, not how he could preach, but how he could *lecture*. Of these congregations, as compared with those of our own time, we believe it might almost be said, "There were giants in those days." The fact is, that the great mass of professors in this age, though evidently displaying a more enlightened and christian liberality than their forefathers, are far behind them in familiar acquaintance with their Bibles; and must, we fear, remain so while the practice continues of making preaching consist mainly in uninstructive appeals to feeling. In religion, as in every thing else, the judgment ought to be the regulator both of the affections and the conduct. The great facts of Bible history form a solid foundation on which Christianity rests, plain to every mind, and speaking to every heart. The piety that is built upon an intimate knowledge of these, and a cordial faith in them, can weather all storms; while that which depends upon the changing eddies of human emotion, can withstand nothing, and is entirely delusive.

Under the mode of teaching above described, the church over which

Mr. Carson presided grew exceedingly in scriptural intelligence, and a comprehensive understanding of divine things. In this particular, the writer regards them as having surpassed any christian society with which it has ever been his lot to mingle ; and his opportunities for observation have not been limited within a narrow circle. Among them, many young men have been trained up, who are now scattered abroad, labouring in the gospel, either as city missionaries, or as pastors of churches. The high state of intelligence to which this people have been brought, may also be partly owing to the abundant opportunities afforded the members for the exercise and cultivation of their gifts. It has generally been their custom to allow such brethren as were skilled in the word of righteousness, to speak to their fellow men in the public assembly, in accordance, as they believe, with the direction of the Apostle. " Let us wait—him that teacheth on teaching, and him that *exhorteth* on *exhortation.*"

This practice, it must be admitted, has been carried by the Scotch Baptists to a most extravagant length. Many of them have concluded that the members of a church have a right to talk, whether it be to the edification or the annoyance of others. As those least qualified to speak well, are often most fond of hearing their own voice, the custom, when thus licentiously indulged, has invariably banished the congregation, and left the would-be orator to address himself to empty benches. It has also contributed to destroy the regular ministry which Christ has instituted, by leading the members of churches to suppose that it was better for them to do the work of christian teaching by turns, than to sustain any one man as a constant preacher of the gospel. These are some of its abuses. But what good thing may not be abused ? It must, we think, be obvious to every mind, that all which is to be done for the spread of the gospel in a congregation, was never intended by the great Head of the Church to be thrown upon the shoulders of one man ; but that all the members of the body should bear their part, each in his appropriate sphere, and in that department of duty to which he is best adapted. In this way, by a prudent and judicious employment of the gifts which God has bestowed, the talents of the church may be brought out, and many a christian fitted for usefulness, whose capacity for doing good might otherwise have remained comparatively hidden and unknown.

The congregation at Tubbermore was also divided into districts ; and in each locality meetings were held, which were addressed, with great effect, by a band of brethren who gave themselves diligently to the study of the Scriptures ; and who were competent, from their knowledge and piety, to act as preachers in almost any situation. Thus the word of the

Lord had free course and was glorified; while the pastor had leisure to make full preparation for his public duties.

Every Lord's day, for the last forty years, has this church commemorated the Saviour's death by the breaking of bread, regarding it as binding upon them to do so, as often as the return of hallowed time calls them to remember his resurrection. This is a universal practice amongst all the Congregational and Baptist churches both in Scotland and Ireland. As authority for it, they appeal to Acts xx. 7: "And upon the first day of the week, when the disciples came together to break bread, Paul preached unto them." From this they infer that one of the most prominent objects for which the churches met on that day, was the breaking of bread. In their belief that such was the primitive custom, they consider themselves sustained by what is known of the manner in which christian institutions were observed for many years after the death of the Apostles. On this point, they cite the testimony of Justin Martyr, who, in his Second Apology for Christianity, says, " On the first day of the week all christians, in the cities and in the country, are wont to assemble together, because it is the day of the Lord's resurrection. They then read the sacred writings; listen to an oration from the bishop; join together in prayer; partake of the Lord's supper; and close by a collection for the widows and poor." This may be viewed as an interesting picture of Apostolical order in its native simplicity, before the rude hand of corruption had marred its fair proportions.

The increasing frequency with which this ordinance is observed, among most evangelical denominations, is a pleasing feature of the present day; and we cannot but regard the extensive change from annual communion—a custom derived from the superstitions of Easter—to its monthly celebration, as a cheering approach to primitive example.*

Mr. Carson's church were accustomed to partake of the supper in the

---

* NOTE BY THE COMMITTEE OF PUBLICATION.—In admitting this account of the peculiarities of their Scotch and Irish brethren, the committee wish not to be understood as favouring all the views and practices described, or as encouraging their propagation in this country. They believe that mixed communion, and the admission of unbaptized persons to church-fellowship, are in direct violation of scriptural authority; that public exhortation by laymen in Lord's day assemblies, is an irregularity, tending to produce disorder, and many other evils; and that Christ has given us no express precept for the *weekly* observance of the supper—but has simply required that, " *as often* as we do it, we should do it in remembrance of him." Yet as the object of this memoir is not to *defend* particular points of doctrine or order, but only to sketch the history of a most eminent and beloved minister, it was deemed advisable to keep back none of the facts necessary to throw light on the circumstances in which he was placed, and the course which he pursued.

public assembly, during the morning service, believing that, in this manner, they made it an instrument of really showing forth the Lord's death, and proclaiming, by visible emblem, the great facts of his Gospel; and deeming the ordinance far more lively and impressive when thus administered in the midst of surrounding spectators, than when observed, as is often the case, in the general absence of the congregation.

The peculiarities of church order to which we have now alluded, served, for a long period, to keep up a sort of denominational distinction between the churches in Scotland and the north of Ireland, and the English Baptists. It was thought by the former, that too little attention was paid, on the part of the latter, to the scriptural model of church government; while, by the churches of Scotland especially, a narrow-minded and unlovely spirit was manifested towards all who did not practise like themselves. In 1840, Dr. Maclay of New York visited Ireland, spent some time in Tubbermore, admired the harmony, doctrinal soundness, and efficiency of the church, and was deeply grieved that minute points of difference should continue to separate brethren, who ought to be uniting their energies for the advancement of Zion. On passing to London, he represented the state of the Tubbermore church to some of the ministers there, informed them of the great liberality of Mr. Carson's disposition, and advised them to seek a plan of mutual co-operation with him. This opened the way for his introduction to the English churches.

For several years, a missionary society, sustained and managed by the Baptists in England, had been labouring to evangelize the dark portions of Ireland. Schools were established, bible-readers employed, and ministers sent forth to itinerate among the destitute population. At length it was determined that a change in the mode of the society's operations would be expedient. Many believed that some of the places, on which large sums had been expended, were so completely immersed in Popish darkness, and, withal, so unimportant as centres of influence, as not to present the best points for missionary effort. The conclusion, therefore, was, to occupy in future, as far as possible, the more commanding positions in that country, and from these to extend their colonies by degrees into other and darker sections. From this time, the attention of the society was directed to the north of Ireland, which had been hitherto overlooked; and the writer of this article, being a native of that region, was the first missionary appointed to the field. The little churches previously existing there, seemed to the society to present favourable beginnings for more extended labours; while the only obstacle in the way of con:ert with them, arose from the little peculiarities of their church order

This the society, with a liberality much to be commended, removed, by allowing their missionaries to organize churches upon any plan which might seem to them and their people most in harmony with Scripture. Thus all appearance of estrangement is vanishing among the Baptists of Ireland. The New Testament is universally taken by them as their only guide, and they endeavour scrupulously to follow its example. They are neither Scotch nor English Baptists distinctively, but catholic christians, extending their fellowship to both. The result of union in this instance, has been truly an accomplishment of the dying prayer of Jesus, that his followers might be one, that the world might know that the Father had sent him. Interesting churches are now rising up throughout the northern counties. One was organized at Bangor, near Belfast, by the writer, which continues to prosper. Another has been gathered at Coleraine, to which a son of Mr. Carson ministered, until he was removed from opening usefulness by an early death. It is now under the care of a missionary. In both these places convenient houses of worship have been erected. The writings of Mr. Carson are every where preparing the way for much wider success than has yet been realized. A Presbyterian minister, and two or three students for the ministry, have forsaken the General Synod, and are now setting forth, not only the doctrines of Christ, but his ordinances, in their original simplicity. Thus, by the labours of Mr. Carson, and the union effected between him and the English brethren, a wide and effectual door has been opened for the introduction of a pure Gospel into Ireland.

In 1840 the degree of LL. D. was conferred on Mr. Carson by Bacon College, in the State of Kentucky. To an American college belongs the credit of having done justice to a man, who deserved the highest honours which literary institutions can bestow, but who was shut out from receiving the merited reward of his scholarship in his own country, by his faithful adherence to primitive example.

During the last three years of his life, Mr. Carson was induced occasionally to visit England, and take part in the missionary meetings of London and Bristol. He appeared before the congregations of the British metropolis, not with studied and artificial eloquence, but in the most simple and natural manner, illustrating the word of God by plain allusions to the events of rural life ; yet enkindling the hearts of his hearers with his own holy devotedness, and stirring them up to greater zeal in the work of the Lord.

The first edition of his unrivalled Treatise on Baptism having become exhausted, he was requested to enlarge it, and prepare it anew for publication. The English churches, with their accustomed liberality, determined to raise such a subscription list, as would compensate him for his arduous researches, and show their high estimate of his character and labours. Without any solicitation on his part, a numerous list of subscribers was immediately obtained in Great Britain and Ireland ; and the American Baptist Publication Society, in adopting and issuing the work in this country, resolved to afford its author a share of the profits arising from his mental toils.

From the midst of these delightful tokens of the esteem of his brethren, he has been suddenly called to an imperishable reward in heaven. His mission is accomplished. His literary career has now terminated—but not before his great task was done. Death could not touch him, until he had put the finishing hand to this masterly production, in which his name and his memory shall live through all future time. He who, like Dr. Carson, has vindicated and rendered prominent an ordinance of Jesus Christ, by disentangling it from the web of human sophistry and perversion, has done better for the world, than if he had founded a kingdom ; and has reared for himself a monument more lasting than pillars of marble.

The solemn and painful circumstances of his death, we shall lay before our readers, by presenting them with the following extracts from a letter written by a gentleman who was studying with him, to Dr. Maclay of New York.

" Dear Sir,

Your letter of the 5th of July last to the late Dr. Carson lies before me. As his hand is cold in death, and his sons are greatly afflicted, it devolves on me to acknowledge your favour.

Knowing that you, and many others of our American brethren, will be anxious to learn when and how he died, I shall endeavour to furnish you with a true, though brief account.

He went over to England in July, to advocate the cause of the Baptist missionary society. For this purpose, he travelled through many parts of England, and, I believe, most of Wales. When on his return, about the end of August, he was waiting in Liverpool for the sailing of the Belfast steamer. It was night fall ; and in taking out his watch to ascertain the hour, he approached unawares to the edge of the dock, and was immediately precipitated into the water, where it was twenty-five feet deep. Providentially, there were persons near at the time, who, with the aid of a ladder, succeeded in rescuing him from a watery grave. His shoulder having been dislocated by the fall, he had it set, and was conveyed on board the steamer. During the passage he became dangerously ill; and though, on his arrival at Belfast, he had the aid of the physicians there, together with that of his son and son-in-law, Doctors Carson and Clarke of Coleraine, it was all in vain; he must go to his rest, and receive what he often termed the reward *of grace.* On Saturday morning, August 24th, 1844, he departed in peace, aged 68.

His remains were taken for interment to his residence at Tubbermore. Oh, what tears were shed, and what voices of lamentation were heard, over the dear departed warrior! Never was there such an exhibition of sorrow in this country before. It would have pierced the soul of any one, to have beheld the anguish of the old veterans who had stood by him for the last forty-five years. They looked for their captain, but he was gone! they sought their general, but he was no more! Having supplied his pulpit, most of the time during his absence, it became my painful duty to do so on the first Lord's day after his departure from our world. But such a house of weeping hearers I never saw before, and hope I never may again.

You may be able, in some measure, to calculate the loss which the churches of Christ have sustained, when I tell you of what he intended to accomplish. After the death of his beloved and excellent wife, he told me that he never intended to take another holyday in this world. "I will," said he, "leave them all for heaven." At another time, he said, "My head is full of books; I will write on till I empty myself." One of the first which he intended to have given us, was a Treatise on the Atonement. Would that he had been spared to execute it. But God's purposes must be fulfilled. The eyes of all the Presbyterians of this country, with a part of the Scotch church, as well as many of other denominations, were on him for some time, expecting this work. At length he consented to satisfy their wishes. He had the subject thoroughly studied—the plan formed—authors read—notes taken—and the book itself all but written. When lo! he was not, for God took him. He intended also to write a book, *on the best mode of teaching the Churches.* He thought that ministers in general were lamentably deficient in this matter. When I think of all he designed to do, and which he could do so well, I am almost overwhelmed with sorrow. You will be glad to learn that he has left a good deal behind him yet unpublished. He had just completed a work on " *The characteristic style of Scripture,*"—showing its purity, simplicity, and sublimity, and contrasting the God of the

Bible, as therein displayed, with the gods of the Heathen, as described by their poets. He has also left commentaries on the Epistles to the Galatians, and to the Hebrews, with many smaller articles.

How irreparable is his loss! How successful and brilliant has been his course! What labours has he undergone, what results has he achieved, what privations and sacrifices has he endured! How like was he to the apostles and primitive disciples! He preached the Gospel, through good report, and evil report. Nothing could cool his zeal. Onward! was ever his motto. When Christ was to be served, his laws obeyed, or his truth defended, no force of opposition could discourage or intimidate him. Many an Alps has he crossed. His arm was mighty when fighting the battles of the Faith.

> "He was a warrior in the Christian field,
> Who never saw the sword he could not wield."

What shall I say of his assiduity? For the last fifty years or more, he was never known to be idle one day. He laboured hard for knowledge. What shall I say of him as a scholar and a critic? Viewed in this light, he was far above either praise or censure. The grand peculiarity of his mind was *critical acumen*. He always saw to the bottom of any subject which he undertook to handle. The foundations of his reasonings were laid, either in self-evident truths, or in explicit statements from the Holy Scriptures; while his honesty of heart would not allow him to deviate a single iota from truth, to accomplish any sectarian object. What shall I say of him as a Christian? Only this, that with all his classical, philological, and philosophical acquirements, he had especially learned the humility of his lowly Master. With the colossal stature of a giant, he possessed the meekness and simplicity of a child. May we all in this respect imitate his example. What shall I say of him as a theologian and a minister? Nothing. Let his works and his church speak for him. Might I not safely challenge the world to produce such a church? In knowledge and understanding of the Scriptures, its members could teach many a minister. And is it possible that such a man can ever be forgotten? Never, till the last trumpet sounds. He himself once said of Luther, "It requires an age to produce a great man in some departments." But a Carson is not to be found once in a millenary. Who is so blind as not to see that God made him expressly for his work? Had not the fire of God kindled his soul, would courage so romantic, have led him to attack the hosts of the "Man of sin," in their strongest entrenchment? His faith was bold as that of Jonathan, when, with his armour-bearer alone, he assailed the thronged ranks of the Philistines. Of him may be said that which was once said of Robert Hall :—" He is gone, and has left the world without one like him."

Yours truly,

G. C. MOORE.

Tubbermore, Sept. 27, 1844."

How mysterious are the ways of Divine Providence ! It might naturally have been expected that this eminent servant of God, whose habits were so retiring, that he scarcely ever passed beyond the bounds of his own flock, except at the imperative call of duty, would have been permitted to breathe his last amid the quiet scenes which he so fondly loved, and which had witnessed his sacrifices and his toils. And yet, in a journey undertaken to promote the Redeemer's triumphs, and while far away from the spot in which were concentrated all the objects of his earthly affection— he is summoned suddenly away, and borne, as in a chariot of fire, to glory. But the Christian is prepared for all events. At home or abroad, in safety or in peril, he is alike enfolded by the arms of a faithful God. Carson dies in peace. How could it be otherwise ? He had eminently served his generation, and made it his highest joy to do the will of his Heavenly Father. For Christ's sake he had suffered the loss of all things. His Lord declares it is enough—and the messenger comes quick from the celestial realm, to bear him to that bright world, where he shall rest from his labours, and wear forever the crown of those " who turn many to righteousness." Well may it be the ambition of every Christian minister to die, like him, on the field of battle, flushed with conquest, girded with heavenly armour, wielding the sword of the Spirit, and leaving it recorded over his grave, that his last work on earth was preaching the Gospel of the kingdom to perishing men.

He was peculiarly happy in his family. His wife was truly a companion and helper, cheering him on in his toils, sustaining him in his trials, and taking upon herself the entire management of his domestic concerns. She was also useful to him in his studies, by finding the quotations he required, and reading them while he wrote. She has gone to the world of spirits a little before him. He was exceedingly careful to train up his children in the nurture and admonition of the Lord. He conducted their education himself, and experienced, in their subsequent character, the literal fulfilment of the divine promise, that those who have been early instructed in the fear of God, will not, in after years, depart from it. His was a happiness that falls to the lot of few parents. He lived to see all his children, thirteen in number, converted to God, and openly professing their faith in Christ, by following him into the baptismal grave. He was also called to experience the sorrows of a father, and the joys of a Christian, in the happy death of some of them. His son, Dr. Carson of Coleraine, died of brain fever, just as he was about to be ordained to the pastoral office, and only two weeks after he had written a memoir of his two sisters, who were removed within a short time of each other, by consumption. They departed in the triumphs of faith. One of them, when expiring, said, " Father, grieve not for me. I am only going before." It was even so! Father, mother, son, daughters, have now united their hallelujahs before the throne of God and the Lamb. For such mercy bestowed upon fallen humanity, let God have all the praise.

1

BURDEN OF PROOF

EXAMINATION OF THE DOCTRINE OF ARCHBISHOP WHATELEY ON THE SUBJECT OF THE BURDEN OF PROOF, WITH A VIEW TO ITS BEARING ON INFANT BAPTISM, EPISCOPACY, AND RELIGIOUS RITES

I ENTIRELY agree with the present distinguished Archbishop of Dublin, that, in the discussion of any question, it is of immense importance to ascertain with precision on which side lies the necessity of proof. But I utterly disagree with his Grace, in his doctrine on this subject. I shall, therefore, as the question of infant baptism is concerned in the decision, devote a few pages to the examination of what has been advanced by this learned writer.

" It is a point of great importance," says the Archbishop, " to decide in each case, at the outset, in your own mind, and clearly point out to the hearer, as occasion may serve, on which side the *presumption* lies, and to which belongs the [*onus probandi*] *burden of proof*. For though it may often be expedient to bring forward more proofs than can fairly be demanded of you, it is always desirable, when this is the case, that it should be *known*, and that the strength of the cause should be estimated accordingly." This passage expresses the substance of what I have often advanced, and what I have always practised. Controversy cannot be skilfully conducted without a perfect acquaintance with the laws which regulate this matter. But in what follows this quotation, I differ from his Grace in almost every step. " According to the most correct use of the term," says the author, " a presumption in favour of any supposition means, not (as has sometimes been erroneously imagined,) a preponderance of probability in its favour, but such a pre-occupation of the ground as implies that it must stand good till some sufficient reason is adduced against it; in short, that the *burden of proof* lies on the side of him who would dispute it."

Now I do not think that this account of the most correct use of the word *presumption*, in the phrase to which he refers, is at all a just one.

And he has given no examples from use to justify what he approves, or to condemn what he censures. Mere assertion is no proof; and nothing but instances from the language can have a right to a hearing on this question. In opposition to his Grace, I contend that the phrase " *a presumption* in favour of any supposition," always implies that there is something which renders such supposition probable, previously to the examination of the proof, or independently of it. In proof of this, I might allege innumerable examples. " If one opinion is universally prevalent," says Zimmerman on Solitude, " it amounts to a *presumption* that no one has a sentiment of his own." Does this imply no degree of antecedent probability?

Dr. Johnson assigns as the strict meaning of this word, " an argument strong, but not demonstrative,—a strong probability." As an example he quotes the following passage from Hooker : " The error and unsufficience of their arguments doth make it, on the contrary, a strong *presumption*, that God hath not moved their hearts to think such things as he hath not enabled them to prove." Here the word imports probability.

I may here observe, incidentally, with respect to the strict meaning assigned to this word by Dr. Johnson, that it is an instance of what I have asserted with respect to the caution necessary in taking secondary meanings from lexicons and dictionaries. This greatest of lexicographers alleges the passage from Hooker as using the word *presumption* for a *strong* probability. But the idea of strength is not in the word *presumption ;* the epithet *strong* is added to it,—" a strong presumption."

But where does this writer find any passages in which the word *presumption* signifies *pre-occupation of the ground?* I can think of none either in vulgar or in correct use. I appeal to the universal practice of the language. When we say that there is " a presumption in favour of any supposition," we always mean that there is something which makes it probable antecedently to the consideration of the direct conclusion,— never that it has such a pre-occupation of the ground, as casts the burden of proof on the side of him who would dispute it.

With respect to *the burden of proof*, I shall submit the following observations :

First,—If the *burden of proof* lies on one side of every question, it is self-evident that there must be a self-evident principle to determine, in every case, on which side it lies. It is often said, that controversy has no end ; but if there is not in every case a self-evident principle to determine on which side lies the *burden of proof*, controversy could have neither beginning nor end. Discretionary laws can have no place, because they have no authority.

Second,—Is it self-evident that *pre-occupation*, which may be accidental, necessarily casts the *burden of proof* on the other side? It is not self-evident. It is a mere arbitrary figment, totally destitute of self-evident authority.

Third,—It is self-evident that pre-occupation of ground does not cast the burden of proof on the opposite side, for this might establish error rather than truth.

Fourth,—If *proof* is a *burden,* it is still more clearly self-evident that there must be a self-evident principle, in all cases, to determine the bearing of this burden. Nothing can be more absurd, than to suppose that a *pre-occupation*, implying no probability, could confer such a prerogative.

Fifth,—Even the highest antecedent probability affects not the *burden of proof*.

Sixth,—It is self-evident that in every question the *burden of proof* lies on the side of the affirmative. An affirmation is of no authority without proof. It is as if it had not been affirmed. He who denies has nothing to do till proof is advanced on the other side. Can he refute evidence till it is advanced? Does not his Grace himself not only admit but assert this when, in his censure of those who do not avail themselves of the privilege of casting the *burden of proof* on the opposite side, declares that in such a case there is "absolutely nothing in the other scale?" If, then, there is absolutely nothing in the opposite scale, can it be necessary to fill the other scale to outweigh nothing?

This may be brought to the most decisive test. Let the combatants disagree as to the side on which lies the *burden of proof*, and both perversely refuse to commence the encounter; the person who affirms, in every instance, loses his cause. If he submits no arguments in proof, there is no evidence of its truth, and it cannot rationally be received. The negative, without speaking a word, has all it needs: if nothing is alleged in proof, there can be no necessity to disprove. This law of controversy has always appeared to me perfectly self-evident; and it is one of great importance. For nothing can be more true than what is asserted by the Archbishop, on the importance of knowing and respecting the law with respect to the *burden of proof*. When a man engages to prove, in a case in which proof lies on his antagonist, he always injures his cause, and in some cases he may bring it unjustly into suspicion, or even destroy it. For sometimes the negative may be capable of no other proof, than that the affirmative is not proved; and this is perfectly sufficient.

The burden of proof must necessarily lie on the side that needs the proof. This, surely, is the side that cannot subsist without an exhibition of its evidence. If one side remains safe as long as the other proves nothing, it cannot be necessary for that side to undertake proof. For if neither attempts proof, the negative is proved. If I assert a doctrine, I must prove it; for until it is proved it can have no claim to reception. Strictly speaking, it exists only on its proof, and a mere affirmation of it is only an existence on affirmation. If I obstinately refuse proof, I leave my doctrine without foundation, and a simple denial of it is sufficient. No man can be called on to disprove that which alleges no proof. What is disproof, but the refutation of proof? And what has no proof needs no refutation.

It must be observed, that though the *burden of proof* always lies on him who holds the affirmative, yet when he has alleged his proof, the objector is bound to proof. That is, the objection must be proved before it can be admitted against the evidence. An objection can have no force till it is proved. In fact, till it is proved it does not properly exist as an objection. He who objects, must affirm something to be inconsistent with that to which he objects. If he refuses to prove, his objection ceases to exist. It is perfectly the same thing as if he did not object. If a man must prove his doctrine, an objector must prove his objection. Every man must bear his own burden. He who affirms must bear the burden of proving his affirmation : he who objects must bear the burden of proving his objection. This is a rational, clear, and self-evident law. Indeed, the very phrase, *burden of proof*, or if the Latin is more edifying, the *onus probandi*, necessarily refers to *proof*, and not to *refutation*. It is absurd to suppose that the *burden of proof* should lie on him whose only business is to disprove. The burden of proof, as to different things, lies on both sides of any question. The holder of the doctrine is bound to submit the evidence on which his doctrine is founded : the objector to the doctrine must prove anything that he alleges as an objection. Every man must prove that which his cause requires. If I do not prove my doctrine, it falls : if my opponent does not prove his objections, they fall. Here each of us must affirm, and each must prove what belongs to himself, but neither of us is to prove that which belongs to the other. How different is this law from the erroneous principle employed by this great logician, to regulate the matter in question. I proceed not a step but with the torch of self-evidence in my hand!

My view of this subject is, I find, similar to that taken by the learned Lord Chancellor King, in the following passage from his " Enquiry into the Constitution, Discipline, Unity, and Worship of the Primitive Church," p. 41. Part II. 1691 :

" Now this being a negative in matter of fact, the bare assertion of it is sufficient proof, except its affirmative can be evinced. Suppose it was disputed whether ever St. Paul writ an epistle to the church of Rome, the bare negation thereof would be proof enough that he did not, except it could be clearly evidenced on the contrary that he did. So unless it can be proved that the ancients had fixed liturgies and prayer-books, we may very rationally conclude in the negative, that they had none at all."

I will admit the law which I here lay down, to be equally binding in all inquiries after truth. When I contend with the Archbishop, I am bound to proof: my opponent has nothing to do but to refute my proof. He is bound to prove all his objections; and a merely possible solution of a difficulty is sufficient to refute the objection. So also with respect to every doctrine, and every institution that pretends authority from the word of God. There is another observation of great importance on this subject. The procedure is the same with respect to every individual, were there no one in the world to dispute with him. I believe it is very generally supposed that a man may safely retain such institutions as he believes to have the privilege of casting the *burden of proof* on the side of those who dispute them, till he is forced by his opponents. This is a monstrous mistake. Were there no one to dispute with us about any of our doctrines or ordinances, we are equally bound to the proof of what we receive. And in considering objections, we are to admit none that are not proved. We are fairly to act the part of both parties. In this way only can we legitimately expect to arrive at truth.

The Archbishop refers to the procedure at law for a confirmation of his doctrine. "Thus," says he, "it is a well known principle of the law, that every man (including a prisoner brought up for trial,) is to be *presumed* innocent till his guilt is established. This does not, of course, mean that we are to *take for granted* he is innocent; for if that were the case, he would be entitled to immediate liberation: nor does it mean that it is antecedently *more likely than not* that he is innocent."

Upon this I observe; First, though his Grace is the first logician of the age, he here confounds two distinct meanings of the word in question, and considers them as one. When it is said that a prisoner is to be *presumed* innocent till he is proved guilty, the word *presumed* signifies *supposed, considered, treated in law:* that is, he is not to be *legally judged as guilty*, till his guilt is established. In fact, neither guilt nor innocence is properly presumed. If innocence is *presumed*, it must be on account of something that makes guilt unlikely: if guilt is *presumed*, it must be from something that makes guilt more likely than innocence. The law anticipates nothing as to his guilt or innocence; it pronounces no judgment till it hears the proof.

But the word *presumption* in the phrase, "a presumption in favor of any supposition," has a very different meaning, both in common use, and according to his Grace's definition of it. Accordingly, while the prisoner is to be legally considered innocent, there may be the strongest *presumption* that he is guilty. He cannot, then, in the same sense, be *presumed* both innocent and guilty. Besides, the prisoner's being legally considered as innocent, till he is proved guilty, is never designated as "a presumption in favor of the innocence of the prisoner." There is not, then, even a legal use of the phrase, in his Grace's sense. In any case in which it is said that there is "a presumption in favor of the prisoner," it will be understood by both learned and unlearned, both by the court and by the crowd, that there is something that renders innocence probable.

Second,—His Grace here confounds a law regulating those who judge in civil matters for others, with a law that respects every individual in regulating himself, as to his views of divine things. A jury, whatever may be their opinion, are not to find a man guilty, but on evidence submitted in court; but the prisoner himself is not to form his judgment by this standard.

Third,—The prisoner is to be legally considered innocent, till he is proved guilty, but this is not from a *pre-occupation of the ground.* There is nothing here that can be like pre-occupation.

Fourth,—The treatment of the prisoner is grounded on self-evident truths. If he did not commit the crime, he is actually innocent of it; and if it is not proved that he committed it, he is legally innocent of it. If there is no proof of guilt, why should he be accounted guilty? Here the *burden of proof* is regulated by the same self-evident principle. The accuser must affirm and prove his affirmation. If he refuses, the charge falls. It is the accuser who needs the proof. The want of proof of guilt, is legal proof of innocence. If there is no affirmation of guilt, there is no pretence for trial: if the affirmation of guilt is not proved, there can be no legal conviction. All this is in perfect harmony with my doctrine.

The author next gives an example from possession as to property. "Thus again," says he, "there is a presumption in favor of the right of any individuals or bodies corporate to the property of which they are in actual possession. This does not mean that they are, or are not, *likely* to be the rightful owners; but merely that no man is to be disturbed in his possessions till some claim against him shall be established.'

On this I observe, First,—It is true that the *burden of proof* lies on him who disputes the right of the present possessor; but it is not true that this is called a "presumption in his favor." It is true, also, generally speaking, that there is a presumption in favor of the possessor; but the sense in which this assertion will be generally admitted, is not the sense in which it is defined by the writer, but the sense which he disclaims. It will universally be understood to mean some degree of probability that the possessor is the rightful owner of the property. It is never employed to designate merely that the burden of proof lies on the side of him who disputes the right of the possessor.

Second,—The principle on which the law proving possession as to property, must undoubtedly be founded on an opinion of previous probability, otherwise it would be most unjust and absurd.

Third,—There is actually an antecedent probability on the side of possession as to property. There are a million of cases against one, in which the possessor is the legal owner. The law, then, is founded on self-evident truth. There is the soundest reason directing the procedure of the law in this instance.

Fourth,—To put the proof on the possessor would unhinge property, and be most evidently unjust. Many rightful possessors might not be able to give any other evidence of their right than possession. But with respect to religious doctrines and institutions, there is no antecedent probability that those in existence at any time are actually in Scripture. The vast majority of religious rites used under the Christian name are the mere invention of men; and not a single institution of the Lord Jesus, as it is recorded in the New Testament, has been left unchanged; and it is no injustice to put each of them to the proof, because, if they are in Scripture, proof is at all times accessible. There is no similarity between religious ordinances and property. As to a man's right to retain his faith and practice, it not only continues till his doctrine and rites are disproved by Scripture, but equally after this as before it. He is to be left in the undisturbed possession of his religion after the clearest demonstration of its falsehood and its absurdity.

Fifth,—The civil law actually establishes the procedure as to possession in property: the Scriptures nowhere recognise the claims of possession as to doctrines or institutions.

His Grace, after some very just and appropriate observations on the importance of deciding on which side lies the *burden of proof*, and having illustrated them with suitable examples, speaks of him who neglects it as leaving out " *one, perhaps, of his strongest arguments.*" Now how does this consist with the assertion, that the *presumption* referred to implies not a previous probability? Can anything be an argument which has no evidence? If there is no evidence in this *presumption*, what gives it so much weight?

" The following," says the author, " are a few of the cases in which it is important, though very easy, to point out where the presumption lies.

" There is a presumption in favour of any existing institution. Many of these (we will suppose the majority) may be susceptible of alteration for the better; but still the ' burden of proof' lies with him who proposes an alteration; simply on the ground that, since a change is not a good in itself, he who demands a change should show cause for it."

With respect to civil institutions, there is, in the common sense of the term, a presumption that they were agreeable to the wisdom of the legislature when they were enacted. There can be no reason to alter them, except they can be improved. But even with respect to a civil law, the moment that the legislature consents to bring it into discussion, it must prove its utility or perish: proof of this lies on its friends. It is self-evident that the advocates of a law must show the arguments that support it. If these are refuted, it perishes without further assault. If it is a useless law, why should it be law?

But with respect to existing religious institutions, there is no presumption in their favour, in any sense of the term. Their present existence is a presumption that they were agreeable to the wisdom of the institutor, but not that they are of Divine origin. He who holds them must prove them. He who assails them has only to refute what is alleged from Scripture in their support. The question is not whether the institution is useful or injurious, but whether it is founded in Scripture. Had an institution existed from the time of Noah, it has not the smallest authority from its age. It must prove its origin to be from God. " To the law and to the testimony : if they speak not according to this word, it is because there is no light in them."

" Every book again, as well as person," says the author, " ought to be presumed harmless (and, consequently, the copyright protected by our courts,) till something is proved against it. It is a hardship to require a man to prove, either of his book or of his private life, that there is no ground for any accusation ; or else to be denied the protection of his country. The burden of proof in each case, lies fairly on the accuser."

" The *burden of proof*, in the cases referred to, certainly rests justly, as his Grace determines ; but not from a *presumption of innocence*, nor from a *pre-occupation of the ground*, but from self-evident truth. Nothing could be more self-evidently unjust than to oblige a man to prove his own innocence. He might be innocent, yet quite unable to prove it. What other proof could he justly be called on to give of his innocence of a crime, but that there is no evidence he did it? In some cases he is able to do more, as when he proves an *alibi;* but more is not necessary. If he is not proved guilty, he is innocent of course. His accuser, then, must affirm guilt, and prove it.

And how could he prove that his book is innocent, but by denying that it is guilty, and challenging his opponent to proof? Instead of going over every sentence, and showing that it is innocent, he challenges his adversary to prove guilt in any sentence. If all this proceeds on the foundation of self-evident truth, why lodge it on the slippery ground of presumption of innocence, and pre-occupation? It is an abuse of terms.

"There is a presumption," says his Grace, "against every thing *para-doxical*, i. e., contrary to the prevailing opinion : it may be true ; but the burden of proof lies with him who maintains it ; since men are not to be expected to abandon the prevailing belief till some reason is shown."

The burden of proof lies indeed with him who holds anything contrary to the prevailing opinion ; but not more so than with him who holds what is in accordance with the prevailing opinion. Every opinion is to be supported by the holders of it, with the arguments on which it rests ; and the business of him who rejects it is to disprove these arguments. If a man is not to be expected to abandon the prevailing belief till some reason is shown, neither is he rationally to be expected to adopt or retain the prevailing belief till he has a reason that convinces himself, though he is not bound to convince others. As to the burden of proof, there is not the slightest difference between the wildest singularity and the most prevailing faith. Every thing that claims belief must submit its evidence, else it cannot be rationally received. Every thing believed must rest on evidence, else it cannot be rationally retained. The burden of proof lies necessarily on the side of the opinion believed : the burden of disproof, or of showing that the arguments alleged in proof do not prove, lies on the other side. Each side has its own peculiar proof.

It is not only a fantastic, but an absurd and pernicious principle, that relieves the prevailing faith of the burden of proof. If it is the prevailing opinion that the Man of the Moon has a beard down to his knees, am I obliged to make an expedition to that planet to determine the question by actual measurement ? Proof lies on the opinion, not on its opposers. Besides, the very fact that his Grace gives a reason why men should not be expected to abandon the prevailing belief till some reason is shown, destroys his doctrine : for, if he gives a reason, then he rests not on a mere pre-occupation without evidence.

Again, if mere pre-occupation determines the burden of proof, then the holder of the most singular opinion should not give it up till some reason is shown ; that is, he may cast the burden of proof on the side of the prevailing opinion, for the singular opinion has pre-occupation in regard to him.

Still further, if the prevailing opinion enjoys this prerogative, it will, in many cases, be a contest which is the prevailing opinion. The doctrine of his Grace, on the burden of proof, is perfectly absurd.

I have another observation. His Grace says : "There is a presumption against every thing paradoxical." Now I ask every reader, what is the sense that the English language naturally assigns to the word *presumption* in this sentence? Is it not a degree of antecedent probability ? But this is not his Grace's meaning. He means merely that the burden of proof lies with him who holds the paradox, without expressing any opinion of probability. If my observation is just, his Grace has unnecessarily chosen to express himself in phraseology that is not English in the sense in which he uses it. The expression is *paradoxical.*

If it were not foreign to the present controversy, I would dispute his Grace's application of the word *paradoxical.* He says, " Correct use is in favour of the etymological sense. It is my opinion, that correct English never uses the word for what is merely contrary to the prevailing belief. Indeed in this respect there is no difference between vulgar and classical usage. The word is never used, either by scholars or the illiterate, in the sense in which it is explained by this writer. In its best sense, it always implies something at first sight incredible, or apparently false, or contradictory,—never simply that a thing is contrary to the prevailing belief. It is said, that his Grace has an opinion on the sabbath, contrary to the prevailing belief; but I should consider it calumnious, to assert that he holds a *paradoxical* opinion with regard to the sabbath. The most singular opinions are not *paradoxical,* simply from their singularity ; I know, indeed, that one of the meanings assigned to this word by Dr. Johnson, coincides with that given by his Grace ; but he has given no example for proof; and he gives the others which this writer denies. *Paradox,* Dr. Johnson explains as " a tenet contrary to received opinion; an assertion contrary to appearance ; a position in appearance absurd." From correct use, he exemplifies all but the first : that he does not exemplify, and I cannot think of an example in the English language. It is given merely on the authority of etymology, which is no authority at all. Mere contrariety to the prevailing opinion, is not a *paradox* in the sense of the English language. This is another proof of the necessity of caution in using the authority of lexicons. If Dr. Johnson is guilty of such an inaccuracy in the account of the meaning of an English word, what may we not fear from lexi ographers in dead or foreign languages? Nothing but examples from a language can be ultimate proof of the meaning of words. The authority of lexicographers and critics is only secondary.

"Accordingly," says his Grace, " there was a presumption against the Gospel in its first announcement." In the English sense of the term, there was no presumption against the Gospel on its first announcement. But I admit that proof lay on that side. This, however, is not from any pre-occupation of ground on the other side; it was on the common, self-evident principle, that every doctrine or opinion must show its proof, else it must cease to have a rational existence. He who denies it has nothing to do but refute what is alleged in its favour. This holds universally. Indeed, his Grace himself rests his assertion on the nature of the thing, and the self-evidence of the case, not on pre-occupation. " A Jewish peasant," says he, " claimed to be the promised Deliverer, in whom all the nations of the earth were to be blessed. The burden of proof lay with Him. No one could be fairly called on to admit his pretensions till He showed cause for believing in Him." Here the author does not rest on the authority of an arbitrary principle, but gives a reason for his assertion. And if it is true, that " no one could be fairly called on to admit his pretensions till He showed cause for believing on him," it is on the same ground, then, that no one can be fairly called on to believe anything till evidence is presented.

"*Now*," continues the writer, "the case is reversed. Christianity *exists* : and those who deny the Divine origin attributed to it, are bound to show some reasons for assigning to it a human origin."

This indeed is a most chimerical principle. The same doctrine is at one time bound to proof, at another it has the privilege of casting the burden of proof on the other side; from the mere circumstance of *existence*. Nothing can be more absurd. If at first it is bound to proof, but as soon as it is received, it can cast the burden of proof on the other side, its reception must be evidence of its truth, or the ground of its reception is irrational and insufficient. Now the presumption for which his Grace contends, is not of the nature of evidence at all.

This doctrine is utterly without foundation. Christianity is as much bound to proof this day, as it was the first day of its publication. Its opponents are not " bound to show some reasons for assigning to it a human origin." If they refute the arguments on which Christianity rests, they have done their business. The establishment of Christianity considered in connexion with its nature and means of propagation, is indeed evidence of its truth, but no reason to cast the burden of proof on its enemies.

On what does such an arbitrary principle rest? Do the Scriptures teach that as soon as any doctrine or position is established, or received, proof lies on the side of those who dispute it? No such thing is pretended. Is it a self-evident truth? Instead of this, the author himself denies this presumption to be even a previous probability. Every ultimate reason must be self-evident. But here we have an ultimate reason that has not even the nature of evidence.

His Grace rests on the *simple existence* of Christianity. But did not Christianity *exist* from the first day of its reception by the first individual who received it? According to this doctrine, then, with respect to all who from the first moment received it, proof lay on the other side. Besides, with respect to infidels and all who have not received Christianity, proof must still lie on it. They must not give up their old systems till proof is submitted. There is nothing but concessions on this principle of settling the burden of proof. Christianity on the ground of its *existence* rests the burden of proof on those who dispute it; yet all who dispute it have the same reason to cast the burden of proof upon it. Their belief had, with respect to themselves, a previous existence. If each has a right to cast the burden of proof upon the other, they never can contend.

The author himself forsakes his own principle, and in the following passage, gives a reason why the burden of proof should now lie on the opposers of Christianity. " The burden of proof," says he, " *now* lies plainly on him who rejects the Gospel ; which, if it were not established by miracles, demands an explanation of the greater miracle, its having been established in defiance of all opposition, by human contrivance." Here instead of relying on simple existence, he relies on miraculous propagation, in defiance of all opposition. This indeed is an argument in proof of the truth of Christianity—not a reason to relieve it from the burden of proof.

"The burden of proof, again," says the Archbishop, "lay on the authors of the Reformation : they were bound to show cause for every *change* they advocated; and they admitted the fairness of this requisition, and accepted the challenge. But they were not bound to show cause for *retaining* what they left unaltered. The presumption was, in these points, on their side; and they had only to reply to objections. This important distinction is often lost sight of, by those who look at the ' doctrines, &c., of the Church of England as constituted at the Reformation,' in the mass, without distinguishing the altered from the unaltered parts. The framers of the Articles kept this in mind in their expression respecting infant baptism, that it ought by all means to be *retained*. They did not introduce the practice, but left it as they found it; considering the burden to lie on those who denied its existence in the primitive church, to show *when* it did arise."

The burden of proof did not lie on the Reformers. They who held the established doctrine and rites at that time, were bound to show that they are the doctrines and rites of the New Testament. The business of the Reformers was to refute any arguments from Scripture alleged in support by their opponents. What is the thing controverted? Is it not whether certain doctrines and rites are instituted in Scripture? If this protestant Archbishop receive the common protestant maxim, *the Bible, the whole Bible, and nothing but the Bible*, he cannot controvert this. And if this is the controversy, is it not necessarily the business of those who hold them to be in Scripture, to produce the proof that they are in Scripture? The business of the other is to refute the alleged evidence. This is a self-evident truth. If any doctrine, or rite, declines to show its proof, from the admitted standard, it necessarily falls to the ground for want of proof. To deny it is to disprove it. If it will not bear the burden of proof, it is unproved. The opposers of it have nothing to do. They cannot refute proof that is not submitted to them. If pre-occupation is rested on, that pre-occupation must either be evidence, or the thing is believed without evidence. But pre-occupation is not proof, and the Archbishop himself does not make it even probability.

Besides, as soon as the Reformers had received their new system, that system, with respect to themselves, had pre-occupation. It was in possession, and according to the Archbishop's doctrine, they had a right to cast the burden of proof on the other side. There is a confusion in the Archbishop's doctrine, which I am surprised to find in the views of so great a logician. *Pre-occupation* he at one time applies with reference to the date of the doctrine or institution; at another with reference to the reception of the doctrine or rite by individuals. He grants the privilege of *pre-occupation* to every man with respect to his own system, or the system of his party. There is nothing akin in these two pre-occupations.

The distinction on which the Archbishop rests all the rites retained by the Reformation, is indeed a very important one, but it is a distinction that has not the shadow of a support either in Scripture or in self-evident truth. If a man is bound to show cause for every *change*, he is equally bound to do so, with respect to every thing which he retains. He must submit evidence for every thing which he holds, or be charged with the absurdity of believing without evidence. If the Reformers renounced *extreme unction* because it was not instituted in Scripture, why did they retain infant baptism, or any other human invention?

How could the Reformers disprove what they rejected? Was it not by proving that the rejected doctrines and rites were not taught in Scripture? And was not this as easily to be done with respect to many things which they retained, as it was with respect to those which they rejected? And how was this to be done with respect to either, but by denying that they are in Scripture, and challenging their opponents to proof? Were they to quote the whole Scriptures, sentence by sentence, showing as they proceeded that the rejected doctrines and rites were not there? This absurdity is imported in the doctrine that proof lay with the Reformers. It is a truth clear as the light of the sun, that, in every instance, proof lies with the affirmative, or with the holders of the doctrine or rite.

But even if proof of the rites and institutions retained by the Reformers, lay with their opponents, what is it they have to prove? Is it not merely that the things objected to, are not instituted in Scripture? But the Archbishop unjustly calls for the proof of a very different thing, a thing that in no case can be demanded. He demands of the opponents of the rejected rite, or institution, " to show *when* it did arise." I care not when it arose. It is perfectly sufficient for my cause, that it is not in Scripture. Let its friends trace its genealogy. This demand is arbitrary, unscriptural, irrational. You might as well demand the author of the rite as the time of the introduction of the rite. Do the Scriptures teach that every rite in existence is to be continued, unless the time of its introduction shall be ascertained? Is it a self-evident truth that every thing ought to be retained as divine, which cannot be traced to its origin? Here is a forged bank note that has passed over half the kingdom, imposing on the best judges, but is at last rejected by the bank; will the Archbishop think himself bound to receive it in payment, unless he can trace it to its origin? This bank note has *pre-occupation*, yet I will engage that his Grace will shift the burden of proof from his own shoulders. His demand is not founded on any self-evident principle of evidence, but has been first invented for the very purpose of giving a sanction to the circulation of human forgeries in the kingdom of God.

" The case of Episcopacy," says his Grace, " is exactly parallel; but Hooker seems to have overlooked this advantage : he sets himself to *prove* the apostolic origin of the institution, as if his task was to *introduce* it. Whatever force there may be in arguments so adduced, it is plain they must have far *more* force if the important presumption be kept in view, that the institution had notoriously existed many ages, and that consequently, even if there had been no direct evidence of its being coeval with Christianity, it might fairly be at least supposed to be so, till some other period should be pointed out at which it had been introduced as an innovation."

The case of episcopacy is, indeed, exactly parallel with that of infant baptism; and equally groundless. Hooker showed his judgment in declining a mode of defence which is so completely irrational. Episcopacy, and every doctrine and institution, must submit their proof, or be charged as being without proof. To prove an existing institution o be scriptural, and to introduce, as scriptural, one which has been neglected, demand the same process. The question to be discussed is, whether the institution is in Scripture, not whether it is in practice among any denomination. What is the ground on which this distinction rests? Do the Scriptures teach, that an institution in practical existence, has a pre-occupation that entitles it to be received as Divine, until it is convicted of human origin? Is it a self-evident truth? No such thing: it is a figment forged to sanction the doctrines and traditions of men.

But even if proof did lie on the opposer of episcopacy, what is he to prove? Surely nothing more than that it is not in Scripture. Yet the Archbishop puts him to another proof. He obliges him to *point out a period at which it arose as an innovation.* I resist such a demand, as unscriptural, irrational, and without countenance from self-evident truth. No man, in order to disprove error, is obliged to hunt after its origin. If I knew the pedigree and the birth of episcopacy to a moment, I would not make use of my knowledge, without a caution that the thing is not necessary to my case.

What is *presumption* in the explained sense of his Grace? It is a *pre-occupation of the ground,* that does not *take the thing for granted,* or mean that it is *more likely than not.* But what is this presumption about episcopacy? It is a *presumption* by which "it might fairly, at least, be supposed to be so, till," &c. Does not this *take the thing for granted,* till contrary proof is submitted?

In the foregoing extract it is assumed that if episcopacy existed at a certain period, it must be of Divine origin. This I deny. Were I writing against episcopacy, I would trample on the evidence with regard to its date. I care not if it was coeval with Adam, if it is not appointed in the Scriptures. It is also insinuated that there is some degree of direct evidence for episcopacy. Does this mean Scripture evidence? Will the very learned and liberal Archbishop of Dublin venture to assert, that the Scriptures make the bishop an officer superior to the presbyter?

It is here supposed that the fact that episcopacy notoriously existed many ages, is ground to believe that it is coeval with Christianity, unless the period can be pointed at which it had been introduced. The writer is universally acknowledged as the first logician in Europe; yet this is not logic. It might be coeval with Christianity, and not be Christian: it might have existed many ages, and not be coeval with Christianity, even although the period of its introduction could not be pointed out. Freemasonry has existed for many ages. Are we to believe the brotherhood that it is of Divine origin, or that it was instituted by Hiram the great architect of Solomon, unless we are able to trace its origin?

" In the case of any *doctrines,* again," says the writer, " professing to be essential parts of the Gospel revelation, the *fair presumption* is, that we shall find all such distinctly declared in Scripture."

Here, it seems, his Grace abandons his defined sense of the word *presumption*, and uses it in the sense which he condemns—the common English sense, importing a degree of probability. I ask every reader whether this is not the sense in which he understands the words last quoted. Does he not mean that the thing referred to, is more probable, or *more likely* than the contrary? It respects not the burden of proof, nor pre-occupation of the ground; but the antecedent probability of the thing asserted. Why is the thing to be *presumed?* Is it not because of its probability?

With respect to the assertion itself, while it is not only probable, but self-evidently true, that every thing revealed by God, will be revealed with a sufficient degree of clearness, and that every thing is revealed which he commands to be believed or practised, yet as to the manner and degree of clearness of the revelation, there can be no just anticipation. Here the anticipations of human wisdom have always failed. How a thing is to be revealed, we learn from the revelation, not from our own anticipations. It is sufficient if a truth, or duty, is revealed in any manner. Has the Archbishop a design of protecting, by his *presumption*, disbelief of certain doctrines, as not being *essential parts of revelation*, because their opponents may allege that they are not *distinctly declared* in Scripture?

" And again, in respect of commands or prohibitions, or to any point," says the author, " delivered by our Lord or his apostles, there is a presumption that Christians are bound to obey." Why speak of this as a *presumption?* Can anything be more certain than that all the commands and prohibitions delivered by our Lord and his apostles, are to be obeyed by those who profess subjection to him?

" If any one," continues the writer, " maintain on the ground of tradition the necessity of some additional articles of faith (as for instance that of purgatory) or the propriety of a departure from the New Testament precepts (as for instance in the denial of the cup to the laity in the Eucharist) the burden of proof lies with him."

In such cases, instead of calling for proof, I would assert that the things supposed are incapable of proof. It is assumed that the things referred to are not in Scripture; but are additional articles of faith. Now, if the Scriptures are the only standard, how can anything not in the Scriptures, be proved from the Scriptures? If any man adds *tradition* to his standard, we have not a common standard, and cannot reason as to the conformity or nonconformity of certain doctrines to our standard. We must dispute, not about doctrines, but about the standard of our doctrines. If any one, professing to be guided by the New Testament, asserts the propriety of a departure from New Testament precepts, I would not call on him for proof; I would assert that the thing is absurd. How can a standard teach that it is not a standard?

" It should be also remarked, under this head," says the author, " that in any one question the presumption will often be found to lie on different sides, in respect of different parties—*e. g.*, In the question between a member of the Church of England and a Presbyterian, or member of any other church, on which side does the presumption lie? Evidently, to each, in favour of the religious community to which he at present belongs. He is not to separate from the church of which he is a member, without having some sufficient reason to allege."

In the Archbishop's sense of the word *presumption*, this appears to me a *paradox* in the worst sense of the word. It is impossible that two parties can have previous possession of the same thing. One may have pre-occupation of one part of the disputed property, and another of another; but unless they are as clever as St. Dennis, who kissed his own head, they cannot be both put in possession of the same thing.

And the paradox is obviously founded on a confounding of things that are different. The presumption of the episcopalian is not the presumption of him who holds the bishop and the presbyter to be the same officer. The *pre-occupation* of the episcopalian, as the Archbishop formerly stated, is a present occupation preceded by a previous occupation of notoriously many ages' duration. But here the pre-occupation respects present possession, that is, to have authority with none but themselves respectively. In this kind of pre-occupation, the episcopalian is only on a footing with his opponent. And this is a most useless pre-occupation that equally belongs to all opinions, and is to have influence only on those who hold them. This cannot affect the burden of proof. The pre-occupation in which episcopacy glories, is not the pre-occupation here recognised.

If this is *presumption*, and if *presumption* has the privilege of casting the burden of proof on the other side, then every man has a right to decline defending his own opinions, and to cast the burden of proof upon those who dispute them. Can anything be more monstrous?

" It is worth remarking," says the author, " that a presumption may be *rebutted* by an opposite presumption, so as to shift the burden of proof to the other side : *e. g.*, Suppose you had advised the removal of some *existing* restriction : you might be, in the first instance, called on to take the burden of proof, and allege your reasons for the change, on the ground that there is a presumption against every change. But you might fairly reply, True, but there is another presumption which rebuts the former : every *restriction* is in itself an evil; and therefore there is a presumption in favour of its removal, unless it can be shown necessary for prevention of some greater evil; I am not bound to allege any *specific* inconvenience; if the restriction is *unnecessary*, that is reason enough for its abolition : its defenders therefore are fairly called on to prove its necessity."

It is true that a presumption may be rebutted by an opposite presumption, if the word is taken in its common English sense. But I cannot see how this is true according to the sense in which the word is explained by the Archbishop. If one thing pretends pre-occupation, how can it be rebutted, as to pre-occupation, but by proving that its pretensions to pre-occupation are false? If by pre-occupation it has the privilege of casting the burden of proof on its opponent, how can this burden be cast upon it, except it is proved not to have the pre-occupation which it pretended? One of them only can have pre-occupation, and consequently that one only can have presumption. Can each of them be before the other? This would be like the seven ladies, who were each of them handsomer than another.

A change is in itself neither good nor evil; it is good or evil according to the nature of the thing changed: consequently it cannot be a sound, just principle that " there is a presumption against every change." A presumption, in the English sense of the word, that lies against a change, must be founded on the supposition that the thing sought to be changed, was at first the result of wisdom, or at least of deliberation. This is the case with respect to all laws. But mere pre-occupation has not the smallest authority. And though when a legislator calls for the change of a law, it is implied that he considers it either bad or useless, yet in all cases the defender of the law is bound to prove the utility or innocence of the law : his opponents have nothing to do but to disprove his arguments and show that he has failed to prove its innocence, or its utility. If they succeed, the law is justly dead.

What does the learned author mean by *presumption* when he says that " there is a presumption in favour of the removal of every *restriction,* unless it can be shown necessary for the prevention of some greater evil ?" If every *restriction* is in itself an evil, can certainty be more certain than that it should be removed, if unnecessary ? Here *presumption* turns out to be *self-evidence,* and the *restriction* being *unnecessary,* is never enough for its removal. Here presumption is more than *probability,* and rests on self-evident truth.

But does not the Archbishop here abandon his own doctrine? Has not the *restriction* pre-occupation? According to the author, then, the burden of proof falls on those who dispute it. Yet he puts the burden of proof on those who defend the restriction, on the ground of self-evident truth. " Its defenders," he asserts, " are fairly called on to prove its necessity." If so, pre-occupation has no authority.

The following passage, quoted by the writer from Dr. Hawkins, is entirely in harmony with my doctrine. " In no other instance perhaps besides that of religion, do men commit the very illogical mistake of first canvassing all the objections against any particular system whose pretensions to truth they would examine, before they consider the direct arguments in its favour." Now, if the arguments in favour of a doctrine, or system, are first to be considered, who is it that is obliged to state these arguments? Must it not be the person who holds the doctrine or system? How can the objector reply to arguments that are not laid before him? And it is perfectly the same thing with a man examining his own system, or doctrine : he must first consider the arguments in proof, and afterwards the objections : for it is an important truth that is stated by Dr. Hawkins, that " there may be truth, and truth supported by irrefragable arguments; and yet at the same time obnoxious to objections, numerous, plausible, and by no means easy of solution." I go farther; there may be truth liable to objections that to us may be unanswerable, while the proof is irrefragable.

But the next quotation is not in accordance with this. He adds, " that sensible men, really desirous of discovering the truth, will perceive that reason directs them to examine first the arguments in favour of that side of the question where the first presumption of truth appears. And the presumption is manifestly in favour of that religious creed already adopted by the country." Reason directs to begin the inquiry as to the truth of any religion, by examining the evidences alleged in its favour, whether antecedent probability be favourable or unfavourable. But it is monstrous to suppose that there is a "presumption of truth" in favour of the religion of a man's country. What relation to truth has the relation of a man to his country? According to this doctrine there is a presumption of the truth of every religion in the world. What is the value of that presumption in favour of any religion, which is equally a presumption in favour of every other religion?

Upon the whole, the doctrine of the learned and scientific Archbishop, on the subject of the burden of proof, is neither scriptural nor philosophical: it is self-evidently false. *Presumption* is not *pre-occupation* of the ground, and *pre-occupation* decides not the privilege. The burden of proof cannot be directed by any arbitrary principle, but must be determined by self-evidence from the nature of the theory. The side that affirms needs the proof; and the side that needs the proof must produce it. Infant baptism, then, and *episcopacy*, and all religious rites, must show their authority in Scripture, or perish with the other human inventions discontinued at the Reformation. "Every plant which my heavenly Father hath not planted, shall be plucked up."

I will close my observations on his Grace's doctrine, with stating a *presumption*. I appeal to every man of candour, is there not a vehement presumption against the supposition that infant baptism is in Scripture, when so eminent a scholar as the Archbishop of Dublin labours so hard to find it a slippery foundation in pre-occupation? Were it in Scripture, Dr. Whatley is the man who could defend its title against every opponent.

2

MODE OF BAPTISM

Meaning of the word BAPTO—*Difference between* BAPTO *and* BAPTIZO

SECTION I.—The word BAPTO, from which is formed BAPTIZO, signifies primarily, to *dip;* and, as a secondary meaning obviously derived from the primary, it denotes to *dye.* Every occurrence of the word may be reduced to one or other of these acceptations. It has been said, that it signifies also to wash; but, though this is given by the lexicographers as one of its meanings, and is admitted by many Baptist writers, it is not warranted by a single decisive example, either in the Scriptures, or in the classical authors. It has also been said that it is a generic word, and, without respect to mode, or inclusive of all modes, denotes any application of water. So far from this, the idea of water is not at all in the word. It is as applicable to every fluid as to water. Nay, it is not confined to liquids, but is applied to every thing that is penetrated. The substance in which the action of the verb is performed, may be oil, or wax, or mire, or any other soft matter, as well as water. Except when it signifies to dye, IT DENOTES MODE, AND NOTHING BUT MODE.

BAPTO and BAPTIZO are considered by most writers as perfectly identical in their signification. On the other hand, there are writers on this subject, on both sides of the great question, who have assigned a difference of meaning, which is merely fanciful. Some have alleged, that the termination *zo* makes *baptizo* a diminutive; but utterly without countenance from the practice of the language. Others have erred as far on the other side, and equally without authority make *baptizo* a frequentative. The termination *zo* has no such effect as either class of these writers suppose; and the history of the word, both in sacred and classical use, justifies no such notion. It is true, indeed, that early church history shows that Baptism was performed by three immersions; but it is equally true, that this is neither scriptural, nor indicated by the termination of the verb. Even had Christ appointed trine immersion, the frequency could not have been expressed by this word. We should recollect that the word was not formed for this religious ordinance; but, being taken from the language, must be used in the common sense. The termination *zo* does not make a frequentative according to the practice of the language in other words; and the verb *baptizo* is not used as a frequentative by

Greek writers. It could not become such, then, in an ordinance of Christ. When Tertullian translates it by *mergitare*, he might wish to countenance the trine immersion; but it is strange that he should be followed by Vossius and Stephens. It is strange, also, to find some Baptists still speaking of *baptizo* as a frequentative verb, since they cannot suppose that it is such in the ordinance of baptism. It is a sufficient induction from the actual history of a language, and not speculations from theory, that can settle a question of this kind.

The learned Dr. Gale, in his Reflections on Mr. Wall's History of Infant Baptism, after giving us a copious list of quotations, in which *bapto* and *baptizo* are used, says: "I think it is plain, from the instances already mentioned, that they are exactly the same as to signification." As far as respects an increase or diminution of the action of the verb, I perfectly agree with the writer. That the one is more or less than the other, as to mode or frequency, is a perfectly groundless conceit. Yet there is a very obvious difference in the use of the words, and a difference that naturally affects the point at issue. This difference is, BAPTO IS NEVER USED TO DENOTE THE ORDINANCE OF BAPTISM, AND BAPTIZO NEVER SIGNIFIES TO DYE. The primitive word *bapto* has two significations, the primary to *dip*, the secondary to *dye*. But the derivative is formed to modify the primary only; and in all the Greek language, I assert that an instance is not to be found in which it has the secondary meaning of the primitive word. If this assertion is not correct, it will be easy for learned men to produce an example in contradiction. That *bapto* is never applied to the ordinance of baptism, any one can verify, who is able to look into the passages of the Greek Testament, where the ordinance is spoken of. Now, if this observation is just, it overturns all those speculations that explain the word, as applied to baptism, by an allusion to dyeing; for the primitive word that has this secondary meaning is not applied to the ordinance; and the derivative word, which is appointed to express it, has not the secondary signification of *dyeing*. BAPTO has two meanings; BAPTIZO in the whole history of the Greek language has but one. It not only signifies to dip or immerse, but it never has any other meaning. Each of these words has its specific province, into which the other cannot enter; while there is a common province in which either of them may serve. Either of them may signify to dip generally; but the primitive cannot specifically express that ordinance to which the derivative has been appropriated; and the derivative cannot signify to *dye*, which is a part of the province of the primitive. The difference is precise and important. Most of the confusion of ideas on both sides of the question, with respect to the definite meaning of the word baptism, has arisen from overlooking this difference. Writers, in general, have argued from the one word to the other, as if they perfectly corresponded in meaning.

To show that derivatives in *zo* are equivalent to their primitives, Dr. Gale gives us a number of examples. Now, in every thing essential to his purpose, this is perfectly true; and in innumerable instances, no variation may be capable of being traced. Yet I apprehend that such derivatives were not introduced merely to vary the sound, but that they were originally designed to modify the action of the primitive verbs. The termination *zo*, when employed to form a derivative, appears to me to have served some such purpose, as the Hebrew causal form, and to denote the making of the action of the verb to be performed. Mere speculation is of no value. The most ingenious theory, not confirmed by the use of the language, ought to have no authority. To ground any-thing on conjectures, with respect to a subject that concerns the faith or obedience of the people of God, would be not only unphilosophical but impious. But that my observation is just, may be fully verified by examples. There cannot be the smallest doubt, that the Greeks did form derivatives on this plan. Could I produce no other instance, the following from Ælian's Varia Historia, would be sufficient to establish my doctrine. It occurs in the anecdote he relates with respect to the beneficence of Ptolemy Lagides. "They say that Ptolemy, the son of Lagus, took great delight in enriching his friends. He said that it is better to enrich others than to be rich," 197.* Here *ploutoo* is to be rich, and *ploutizo*, to make rich.

We have another instance in Heraclides, "of whom he provided many with a supper." *Deipneo* is to *sup; deipnizo* signifies to give a supper.

Such, then, indubitably was originally the use of derivatives with this termination, though in many cases they and their primitives may be interchangeable; and although in some the distinction cannot at all be traced.

In this view *baptizo* would signify originally to make an object dip. Its use then, would be to apply to the dipping of things too heavy to be sustained by the dipper. Its use in classical occurrence, I think, will accord with this. Compared with its primitive, its occurrence in profane writers is very rare, and it generally applies to objects that are too heavy to be lifted or borne by the dipper. It applies to ships which are *made to dip* by the weight of the lading. As to the general idea of dip-ping, the primitive and the derivative are interchangeable. The primi-tive may be used with respect to the largest body that can be immersed; but it will not express the modification denoted by the derivative. The derivative may be applied to the smallest object that is dipped; for it is evident, that if we dip an object in any way, we cause it to dip or sink. I shall illustrate this observation further when examples actually come before us. In the mean time I observe, that whatever may originally have been the modification of the termination in question, the difference in the use of BAPTO and BAPTIZO is clearly established. To ascertain a difference, and to account for that difference, are two very different things. In the former our success cannot be doubted, whatever may be thought with respect to the latter.

From some instances in the application of this word, Dr. Gale was induced to suppose that it does not so necessarily express the action of putting under water, as that the object is in that state. But this is evidently inconsistent with the essential meaning of the word; and not at

---

* See my former edition for the original of *all* my translations.

all demanded by the examples on which he founds it. "The word *baptizo*," says he, "perhaps does not so necessarily express the action of putting under water, as in general a thing being in that condition, no matter how it comes so, whether it is put into the water, or the water comes over it." Now, were this observation just, every thing lying under water might have this literally applied to it. But every one acquainted with the Greek language must acknowledge that the word has not literally such an application. In any particular instance when this word is applied to an object lying under water, but not actually dipped, the mode essentially denoted by it is as truly expressed as in any other instance of its occurrence. Indeed, the whole beauty of such expressions consists in the expression of a mode not really belonging to the thing expressed. The imagination, for its own gratification, invests the object with a mode that does not truly belong to it; and if that mode were not suggested to the mind, the expression would lose its peculiar beauty. Common conversation exemplifies this mode of expression every day; and mere children understand its import. When a person has been drenched with rain, he will say that he has got a *dipping*. Here *dipping* does not lose its modal import, but immediately suggests it to the mind, and intends to suggest it. But were the English language one of the dead languages, and this expression subjected to learned criticism, it would be alleged that the word *dipping* does not denote mode, but *wetting*, without reference to mode.

The very example alleged by Dr. Gale is formed on this principle. It is brought from the works of Aristotle. " The Phenicians who inhabit Cadiz relate, that, sailing beyond Hercules' Pillars, in four days, with the wind at east, they came to a land uninhabited, whose coast was full of sea-weeds, and is not laid under water at ebb; but when the tide comes in, it is wholly covered and overwhelmed." Now, though the water comes over the land, and there is no actual exemplification of the mode expressed by this word, yet it still expresses that mode; and the word has been employed for the very purpose of expressing it. The peculiar beauty of the expression consists in figuring the object, which is successively bare and buried under water, as being dipped when it is covered, and as emerging when it is bare. In the same style we might say that, at the flood, God immersed the mountains in the waters, though the waters came over them.

No example can more clearly disprove the notion, that this word denotes to pour or sprinkle a little water on an object. The thing here supposed to be baptized was wholly buried under water. The beach is said to be baptized when the tide comes over it. Can any child, then, be at a loss to learn from this, that baptism means to lay under water ? Should we say that God baptized the earth at the flood, we should use an expression exactly like the above. Who, then, can be at a loss to know the meaning of the word baptism ?

This example tends to confirm my observation with respect to the peculiar import of derivatives in *zo*. This was a large object, that was not supposed to be taken up and dipped, but to be caused to dip, as it were by sinking.

The distinction which I have observed between the use of *bapto* and *baptizo*, will enable us to refute the interpretation of the word baptism by Mr. Robinson of Cambridge. "The English translators," says he, "did not translate the word baptize, and they acted wisely; for there is no one word in the English language which is an exact counterpart of the Greek word, as the New Testament uses it, containing the precise ideas of the evangelists, neither less nor more. The difficulty, or rather the excellence of the word is, that it contains two ideas, inclusive of the whole doctrine of baptism. Baptize is a dyer's word, and signifies to dip, so as to colour. Such as render the word dip, give one true idea; but the word stood for two, and one is wanting in this rendering. This defect is in the German Testament. Matt. iii. 1 : 'In those days came John *der* *Tauffer*, John the Dipper;' and the Dutch: 'In those days came John *der* *Dooper*, John the Dipper.' This is the truth, but it is not the whole truth. The Saxon Testament adds another idea, by naming the administrator, John *le* *Fullubtere*, John the Fuller. The Icelandic language translates baptism *skirn*, scouring. These convey two ideas, *cleansing* by *washing*, but neither do these accurately express the two ideas of the Greek baptize; for though repentance, in some cases accompanies baptism, as it does prayer, yet not in every case. Jesus was baptized in Jordan, but he was not cleansed from any moral or ceremonial turpitude by it, nor was any repentance mixed with his baptism. Purification by baptism is an accident; it may be, it may not be,—it is not essential to baptism. The word, then, conveys two ideas, the one literal, *dipping*, the other figurative, *colouring ;* a figure, however, expressive of a real fact, meaning that John, by bathing persons in the river Jordan, conferred a character, a moral hue, as dyers, by dipping in a dyeing vat, set a tinct or colour; John, by baptism, discriminating the disciples of Christ from other men, as dyers, by colouring, distinguish stuffs. Hence John is called, by early Latins, John *Tinctor*, the exact Latin of Joannes Baptistes, John the Baptist."

Mr. Robinson was a man of talents and of extensive reading; but whatever other accomplishment he might possess, the above specimen shows that he was no critic. Such a combination of the primary and secondary meaning of a word, is unphilosophical; and, I am bold to say, that in no language was it ever really exemplified. It is a mere speculation, and a speculation that no man at all acquainted with the philosophy of language could indulge. Did Mr. Robinson suppose that *baptizo* had this double import in common and classical use? If he did, he must have paid no attention to the various occurrences of the word; for in no instance is his observation verified. Did he suppose that the word, in its appropriation to the ordinance of baptism, received this new meaning? If he did, he supposes what is absurd, and what cannot be exemplified in any word in the Bible. If words could receive such an arbitrary appropriation in Scripture, the Book of God would not be a revelation. Words must be used in Scripture in the sense in which they are understood by those who speak the language, otherwise the Bible would be a barbarian both to the learned and to the unlearned. "Baptize," he says, " is a dyer's word." Baptize is not a dyer's word. *Bapto*, in a

secondary sense, signifies to dye; but *baptizo* never does. IT IS STRICTLY
UNIVOCAL. What a ridiculous thing to suppose that, by immersion in
pure water, Christians received a discriminating hue, like cloth dipped
in the dyer's vat! What mark does it impress? Are we to take the
explanation of the import of an ordinance of Christ from the creations
of genius, rather than from the explicit declaration of the Apostles?
Such a meaning the word in question never has. Such a combination
of primary and secondary meaning no word in any language could
have. Such a meaning has nothing in the ordinance to verify it. It
is infinitely more important to resist such explanations of baptism, even
though their authors should agree with us with respect both to the
mode and subjects of that ordinance, than to combat the opinion of
our brethren who on these points differ from us. It is the truth itself,
and not any ritual ordinance, that our Lord has appointed to be the
bond of union among his people. A disproportionate zeal for baptism
may sometimes lead to danger of seduction from the Gospel, by frater-
nizing with its corrupters, from agreement with them in a favourite
ordinance.

"Not long before the death of Professor Porson," says Dr. Newman,
"I went, in company with a much respected friend, to see that celebrated Greek scholar at the London Institution. I was curious to hear
in what manner he read Greek. He very condescendingly, at my request, took down a Greek Testament, and read, perhaps twenty verses
in one of the gospels, in which the word *bapto* occurred. I said, 'Sir,
you know there is a controversy among Christians respecting the meaning of that word.' He smiled and replied, 'The Baptists have the
advantage of us! He cited immediately the well-known passage in
Pindar, and one or two of those in the gospels, mentioned in this letter;
I inquired, whether, in his opinion, *baptizo* must be considered equal
to *bapto*, which, he said, was to tinge, as dyers. He replied to this
effect; that if there be a difference, he should take the former to be
the strongest. He fully assured me, that it signified a *total immersion.*
This conversation took place August 27, 1807."

I should like to know in what respect this eminent scholar considered
baptizo to be a stronger term to denote *immersion*, than its primitive
bapto. I wish we had his opinion more in detail on this subject. As
expressive of mode, the derivative cannot go beyond its primitive. As
to *totality of immersion*, the one is perfectly equivalent to the other.
But, as I observed before, *bapto* has two senses, and *baptizo* but one;
and therefore, in this respect, the word used, with respect to the ordinance of baptism, is stronger in support of immersion, as being univocal.
Perhaps this was the meaning of the professor. The additional modify-
ing meaning, which I pointed out in the derivative, adds nothing to the
strength of signification as to mode, though it sufficiently accounts for
the use of the derivative to the exclusion of the primitive, in every
instance, with respect to the ordinance of baptism.

The just and most obvious method of ascertaining the meaning of a
word, is to examine its origin and use in the language. It may wander
far from its root, but if that root is known with certainty, the connexion

may still be traced. The derivative, however, may reject ideas contained in the primitive, or it may receive additional ideas, which can be learned only by being acquainted with its history. That BAPTIZO is formed from BAPTO is a thing beyond dispute. But as I have shown that they are not perfectly coincident in their application, I shall examine them separately, contrary to the general practice of writers on both sides of the question. I shall give a copious list of examples, as it is from this that my readers will be enabled independently to form their own judgment. This method will, doubtless, appear tedious and uninteresting to many; but it is the only method entitled to authority. For a writer on controverted subjects to give merely his own opinion of the import of his documents, accompanied with a few examples as a specimen of proof, would be the same as if an advocate should present a judge and jury with his own views of evidence, instead of giving them all his facts and circumstances in detail, to enable them to decide with knowledge. A work of this kind is not for amusement, but requires patience and industry in the reader, as well as in the writer. If the one has ransacked documents to most readers inaccessible, to collect evidence, the other should not grudge the toil of examining the evidence, seeing it is only by such an examination that he can have the fullest conviction of the truth. Is the meaning of this word to be eternally disputed? If one party says that it has this meaning, and another that, while a third differs from both, and a fourth is confident that all three are wrong, what method can legitimately settle the controversy, but an actual appeal to the passages in which it is to be found? These are the witnesses, whose testimony must decide this question; and consequently the more numerous and definite the examples, the more authoritative will be the decision. And as it is possible to tamper with evidence, the witnesses must be questioned and cross-questioned, that the truth may be ascertained without a doubt. Instead, therefore, of making an apology for the number of my examples, and the length of the observations that ascertain their meaning, the only thing I regret is, that I have not every passage in which the word occurs in the Greek language. Never was the meaning of a word so much disputed: no word was ever disputed with less real grounds of difficulty.

SECTION II.—As it has been supposed by some to be a generic word, signifying every application of water without any respect to mode, I shall first give a specimen of examples, showing that it not only signifies mode, but that the idea of water is not in the word at all. The nature of the fluid is not expressed in the verb, but is expressed or understood in its regimen.

Near the end of the Sixth Idyl of Theocritus, the word is applied to the dipping of a vessel in honey. "Instead of water, let my maid *dip* her pitcher into honey-combs."

Here such abundance of honey is supposed, that in the morning, the maid-servant, instead of going to draw water, will dip her pitcher into honey-combs. Not water, then, but honey, is the substance, with respect to which the verb in question is here applied. And that dipping is the mode there can be no question. It would be absurd to speak of pouring, or sprinkling, or washing, or wetting an urn into honey-combs. Aristotle also applies it to the dipping of hay into honey for the curing the flux in elephants. "Dipping hay into honey, they give it them to eat."—Hist. Animal. lib. viii. 26. Though it would be possible to sprinkle hay with honey, yet it would be absurd to speak of sprinkling or pouring hay *into* honey. The preposition *eis*, with which the verb is connected, forbids it to be translated by any other word but *dip*, even were it possessed of different significations.

The same author, in his Treatise on the Soul, applies the word to wax. "If one dip anything into wax, it is moved as far as he dips."—Lib. iii. 12. This surely is not an application of water. Nor can the mode be any other than dipping. Neither pouring nor sprinkling, washing nor wetting, can be imported here.

In the last line of the First Idyl of Moschus, the word is applied to immersion in fire. Speaking of the gifts of Cupid, it is said, "For they are all dipped in fire." This is a baptism in fire, and, beyond dispute, dipping was the mode.

Ælian applies the word to ointment: *Stephanon eis muron bapsas.*— Lib. xiv. cap. xxxix. "Having dipped a crown into ointment."

The learned friend who writes the Appendix to Mr. Ewing's Essay on Baptism, translates this example thus: "Having tinged (imbued or impregnated) with precious ointment a crown (or garland),—the crown was woven of roses." This translation, however, is not made on sound principles of interpretation. It rests on no basis. The author has not produced one instance in which the word *bapto* incontestably and confessedly must signify to *imbue*, except in the sense of *dyeing*. To *tinge* a crown of flowers, is not to imbue it with additional fragrance, but to colour it. The author violates both the Greek and the English. When we speak of the *tinge* of a flower, we refer to its colour, not to its perfume. To *tinge with ointment* to give a fragrant smell, is not an English expression. The translation labours under another disease. *Eis muron* cannot be translated *with ointment*, but must be rendered *into ointment*. To *tinge into ointment* is a solecism. The verb then cannot here be translated *tinge*, or *imbue*, or *impregnate*, even though it had these significations in other places. The expression cannot bear any other translation than—"He dipped the crown into ointment." The learned writer thinks it improbable that a crown of roses would be dipped in viscid oil in order to improve its fragrance. I admit that it would not be to my taste. But does the gentleman forget that it was the oddity of the thing that induced the historian to mention it? Had it been a common thing, it would not have had a place in Ælian's anecdotes. The person to whom it was presented, observed that he accepted it as a token of the good-will of the giver, but that the natural fragrance of the flower was corrupted by art. It is no improvement to gild a statue of exquisite workmanship. Shall we, therefore, force the words of the historians, that assert this of a certain Roman emperor, to assume another sense? Shall we say, that, as it was no improvement to the statue to be gilded, the language must signify merely that it was washed? To proceed on such principles of interpretation, would render the precise meaning of language utterly unattainable. It is absurd and chimerical in the highest degree. In some points of view, I respect this writer very much. But he reasons without first principles, and therefore, has no basis for his conclusions. He is extensively acquainted with Greek literature; but had he all the writings of the ancients in his memory, he cannot be a critic, so long as he multiplies the meanings of words in an arbitrary manner, according to his view of particular exigencies. In his very next example, he makes the word *bapto* signify to *purify*, from a different exigency. Jamblichus, in his Life of Pythagoras, relates, as one of the directions of the philosopher to his disciples,—*oude eis perirranterion embaptein*, which the writer of the Appendix translates, " not to *purify* in the perirranterion." Here, again, he proceeds without first principles. He has not alleged one instance in which the verb must signify to *purify*. He has, then, no ground-work on which to rest this assumption. And the preposition *eis*, occurring here both separately and in conjunction with the verb, determines that the action of the verb was directed *into* the perirranterion, or basin. Besides, as a matter of fact, they did not purify *in* it, but *out* of it. Persons sprinkled at the door of a Roman Catholic church are not said to be purified *in* the vessel that contains the holy water. But the writer alleges that the perirranterion was too small. for *dipping*. Very true, if it is meant that it was too small to dip the body in; but it was not too small to dip the thing that is here understood to be dipped, that is, the sprinkling instrument. Had the writer considered that the phrase is elliptical, as referring to a thing so well known that the regimen of the verb is understood without being expressed, he would have had no necessity for giving a new and an unauthorised meaning to the word *bapto*. In the next direction given by Jamblichus, we have a similar ellipsis. "Nor to bathe in a bath," that is, nor to bathe the body in a bath. We ourselves use the same ellipsis. Pythagoras prohibited these things to his disciples, because it was not certain that all who had fellowship with them in the perirranterion and bath were pure. *Do not dip in the perirranterion;* do not use the perirranterion; do not dip the sprinkling instrument in order to purify. Nothing can be more unphilosophical than the conduct of this writer. As often as he meets a difficulty, he gives a new meaning to suit the situation. Now, though I could make no sense of the passage at all, I would resolutely refuse to adopt any meaning but one that the word confessedly has in some other place. It is not enough to say that such a translation will make sense; it must be the sense that the word is known to express.

Another difficulty with respect to a passage in Suidas de Hierocle, induces this writer to translate *bapto*, to *wet*. He might as well translate it, to *dry*. A person was scourged before the tribunal, " and, flowing with blood, having wetted the hollow of his hand, he sprinkles it on the judgment seat." The word, however, never signifies *to wet;* and even this translation does not suit the writer's own commentary. He explains it as referring to the catching of the blood flowing from his wounds, or letting the pouring blood fill the hollow of his hand. To *wet* is far enough from representing such a process. There can be no doubt that the word *bapsas* is here to be translated in its usual sense. " And having *dipped* the hollow of his hand, he sprinkles the tribunal." It may be difficult to conceive the process, but of the meaning of the expression there can be no doubt. If the blood was flowing down his body, he might strike the palm of his hand on his skin, and gather up the blood in the hollow of his hand. Whatever was the way in which the operation was performed, the writer calls it a *dipping* of the hollow of his hand.

In the Nubes, Aristophanes represents Socrates as ludicrously dipping the feet of a flea into wax, as an ingenious expedient to measure its leap. " Having melted the wax, he took the flea and dipped its feet into the wax." Here the liquid is wax, and the mode can be nothing but dipping. Such an instance determines the meaning of the word beyond all reasonable controversy.

But, though the word is most usually and properly applied to fluids, it is often applied even to solids that are penetrated. Dionysius of Halicarnassus applies it to the thrusting of a spear, *bapsas*, between the ribs of a man. In like manner, we might say that a soldier *plunged* his sword into the bowels of his enemy.

In Matt. xxvi. 23, the action of putting down the hand into a dish is expressed by this word, when the hand was not actually immersed in the fluid at the bottom. " Who dippeth his hand in the dish." Now, it is true that, according to ancient manners, the fingers were actually dipped in taking up food from the dish; yet it is quite proper to speak thus of the action of putting down the hand in the inside of a bowl or dish. An excise officer might be said to *dip* a vessel even when empty : and we speak of *plunging* into a wood. Miners also speak of *the dip* of a rock as being north or south, by referring to the direction of its *sinking* or *slope*.

Lycophron represents Cassandra, foretelling the death of Clytemnestra by the hand of her own son, as saying, " with his own hand he shall *dip* his sword into the viper's bowels."

Here the word is applied to the penetrating of solids, in the sense of thrusting or piercing. In like manner, we speak of *burying* a weapon in the bowels. *Pouring, sprinkling, washing,* have no countenance here, but are entirely excluded.

Ajax is represented by Sophocles as *dipping* his sword into the army of the Greeks. In all such instances, there is a figurative stretch of the word with a fine effect on composition ; but the whole beauty of the expression consists in the reference to the proper and modal meaning of the term.

SECTION III.—Having proved the application of the word to mode, without respect to the nature of the fluid, I shall now at random produce examples.

In the Thirteenth Idyl of Theocritus we have an example of it, in the account of the drowning of the boy Hylas, who went to a fountain to draw water for the supper of Hercules and Telamon. " The youth held the capacious urn over the water, hasting to *dip* it," &c. Can anything be more definite than this? Can any one be at a loss to know how a pitcher is filled with water at a fountain? Can an unprejudiced reader demand a clearer example than this, to show the modal meaning of *bapto*? Even the unlearned reader may judge for himself in this matter. Indeed, from the connexion in which the word is found, he may, in almost all the examples, judge whether the translation of the term is natural or forced. I hope, then, the unlearned reader will not pass over even this part of the subject as altogether beyond him.

The word occurs in the Hecuba of Euripides. "Take a vessel, ancient servant, and having *dipped* it in the sea, bring it hither."

Dr. Gale informs us, that the explanation of the word in this place, by one of the Greek scholiasts, is—"*Baptein* signifies to let down anything into water, or any other liquid." Can we wish for better authority for the meaning of a Greek word?

Aristophanes, in the play entitled Eirene, affords us an example of the word: "Bring the torch, that I may take and dip it."

Dr. Gale observes, that the Greek Scholiast and Florent. Christianus, preceptor to Henry IV. of France, refer this to the manner of purifying among the Greeks, by dipping a lighted torch in water, and so sprinkling the persons or things to be purified. This explains the Pythagorean precept, quoted in Mr. Ewing's Appendix.

Dr. Gale has given us some fragments of this author, preserved by Harpocratian, where the general meaning is more obscure, but in which the peculiar meaning of this word is not at all doubtful. "When I have *dipped*, I will cite the strangers before the judges." "This passage would have been very obscure," says he, "and I do not know whether anything would have given light to it, if Suidas had not attempted it; for I take this to be the passage he refers to, when he says, 'when I have *dipped* the oar,' &c., which helps us to the sense of the word *bapsas*, in this place, though it does not clear up the whole. Or, perhaps," says he, "it may be a metaphor taken from the dyers, who say, for instance, I will dip it, and make it a black." Athenæus has preserved two other fragments of the same author, in which the word occurs; one is, "what a wretch am I, to be thus dipped over head and ears in brine, like a pickled herring!" We have, therefore, the authority of Suidas, that *baptein* applies to the dipping of an oar in the water.

Aristotle, speaking of a kind of fish, says: "They cannot bear great changes, as the *immersion* of them into cold water, even in summer." Can anything be more decisive? We could not speak of *sprinkling*, or *pouring*, or *wetting* a fish *into water*.

Speaking of the remedy for the bite of a certain kind of snake in Africa, he says: "Of which the remedy is said to be a certain stone, which they take from the sepulchre of a king of ancient times, and, having *immersed* it in wine, drink it." Here the virtue of the stone is supposed to be extracted by the wine in which it is *dipped*. They do not *sprinkle* the stone with wine, nor *pour* wine upon it, but they *dipped* the stone, and then drank the wine in which it was *dipped*. Even the unlearned reader can be at no loss with respect to the mode imported by the word in this process.

The same author applies the word to the immersion of animals in a pool of Sicily, which had the property of resuscitating them when put into it after suffocation. What can be more satisfactory than this? If anything can be more decisive, it is an example from the same author, in which he tells us, that it is the custom of some nations to *dip* their children into cold water, soon after birth, in order to harden them.

Herodotus decisively fixes the meaning of this word, when he applies it to the Scythian ceremony of dipping certain things in a mixture of blood and water, in concluding an alliance. " The Scythians, in concluding a league with any one, make it in the following manner :—Having poured wine into an earthen vessel, they mingle with it the blood of the parties, making a slight incision in the body by a knife or a sword. After this, they dip into the vessel a scimitar and arrows, a hatchet and a javelin. When they have done this, they utter many imprecations; and they who make the league, with the most distinguished of the company, drink the mixture." The phrase *apobapsantes es ten kulika*, can mean nothing but *dipping in the bowl. Pouring, sprinkling, washing, wetting*, and all other fancies, are entirely excluded.

The setting of a constellation is termed, by Aratus, *dipping in the sea*. Is there any doubt with respect to mode in this example? When the sun, moon, and stars descend below our horizon, when we stand on the shore, they appear to *dip* in the sea. All nations speak in phraseology that imports this. We have some beautiful examples in Virgil. The same author applies the word, just in our manner, to the setting sun : " If the sun *dips* himself, without a cloud, into the western sea." Again he says : " If the crow dips his head into the river." Can any one need a commentary to point out the mode imported by the word here?

" Constantine," says Dr. Gale, " observes, from an epigram of Hermolaus, *He dipped his pitcher in the water.* The mysterious Lycophron affords us an instance ·parallel to this in Callimachus : *dipping* with strange and foreign buckets." And again, to this may be added what Aristotle says in his Mechanical Questions : " *The bucket must be first let down*, or *dipped, and then be drawn up again*, when it is full." Can anything be supposed more specifically to express *dipping*, than *bapto*, in these instances?

Homer employs the word in the Odyssey, in a situation where the meaning cannot be doubted. He compares the hissing of the eye of Polyphemus, when bored by a red-hot stake, to the hissing of the water when a smith dips his iron in order to temper it.

> " As when the smith, an hatchet or large axe,
> Tempering with skill, *plunges* the hissing blade
> Deep in cold water. (Whence the strength of steel.)"
>
> COWPER.

No one who has seen a horse shod will be at a loss to know the mode of the application of water in this instance. The *immersion* of the newly formed shoe in water, in order to harden the metal, is expressed by the word *baptein*. An instance of the same kind we have in the Apocryphal Book of Ecclesiasticus, where iron heated in the furnace is said to be tempered by immersion in water. The note of Didymus on the place is: "the dipping of red-hot iron in cold water hardens it."

Anacreon, in his Ode on the Arrows of Cupid, represents them as forged by Vulcan, and *dipped* by Venus in honey, into which Cupid put a mixture of gall.

The manner of poisoning arrows by dipping their points in the poisonous matter, sufficiently explains this. Here we see, also, that this word applies to honey, and even to gall—to poisoning as well as to washing.

Herodotus, speaking of a custom of the Egyptians, employs this word in a sense entirely analogous to the use of *baptizein*, in the ordinance of baptism. He applies it to a ceremonial or religious purification of the person and garments, by immersion in a river after defilement. " The Egyptians consider the swine so polluted a beast, that if any one in passing touch a swine, he will go away and *dip* himself with his very garments, going into the river." Here is a religious baptism, for the purpose of cleansing from defilement; and it is by immersion, expressed by *baptein*. Can any one require a more definite example? The person dips himself; therefore it is *bapto*, to dip, and not *baptizo*, to cause to dip. All the occurrences of the word in the Septuagint are confirmatory of this view of its meaning.

Ex. xii. 22. " And ye shall take a bunch of hyssop, and dipping it in the blood which is at the door," &c. The effect of the thing done is not *washing :* it is *smearing.* The mode is not pouring or sprinkling, but dipping.

Lev. iv. 6. " And the priest shall *dip* his finger in the blood, and *sprinkle* of the blood," &c. Here we have the action both of *dipping* and *sprinkling;* and *bapto* applies to the former, while *raino* applies to the latter. Can anything be more decisive than this?

Lev. iv. 17. " And the priest shall *dip* his finger in the blood of the bullock, and *sprinkle* it," &c.

Lev. ix. 9. " And he dipped his finger into the blood." He could not sprinkle or pour his finger *into* the blood.

Lev. xi. 32. "It must be put into water." Literally, " It shall be dipped into water." This cannot admit even of plausible evasion.

Lev. xiv. 6. " And shall dip them and the living bird in the blood," &c.

Dr. Wall has asserted that the word *bapsei* here, cannot be understood dipping all over; *for the blood of the bird in the basin could not be enough to receive the living bird, and the cedar wood, and the scarlet, and the hyssop, all into it.* To this the answer of Dr. Gale is perfectly satisfactory. The blood of the slain bird was received in a vessel of running water, in which mixture, as appears from verse 51, the things were to be dipped. It may be added, that this makes the figure have a beautiful allusion to the double efficacy of the blood of Jesus Christ It washes as well as atones; and though this might be exhibited by separate dippings, yet the union is seen more clearly in the combination of blood and water. But that the word *baptein* is employed when only a part of an object is dipped, is most freely admitted; and the same thing may be said of the very word *dip* itself. Thus we speak of dipping a pen in ink, when only the point of the pen is dipped. What should we say of the foreigner who should allege that the English word dip, when applied in the expression, *They dipped the man in the river*, does not necessarily imply that they dipped him all over, because he finds from the expression, *dip a pen in ink*, it is applied sometimes when only a part is dipped? Yet grave doctors, when they criticise in a dead language, make themselves such fools! and their folly is concealed only by the circumstance, that the language is dead with respect to which they make their silly observations. Every person at all accustomed to philosophise on language, knows that such a figure is quite common; but that it never alters or affects the proper meaning of the word. The figure, in fact, is not in the verb, but in its regimen. In all such expressions, both *bapto* and *dip* have their proper and entire significations, and express mode, as fully as when there is no figure. The expression, *dip a pen*, determines mode as clearly as when the object is sunk to the bottom of the sea, never to arise. A writer must be perverse indeed, who indulges himself in such quibbles; yet some of the gravest and most learned writers have urged this objection. It must be observed, that Dr. Wall, though he is a friend to infant baptism, is decidedly in favour of immersion. With respect to all such elliptical phrases, I observe, that they are used only about common operations, when the part to be dipped is so well known as to prevent obscurity. But granting to the authors of this objection all their demands, I hope we shall find them dipping at least a part of the body of the person baptized. It is strange to find Christians arguing that the word, though it signifies to immerse, may be applied when only a part is dipped; yet in their own practice, *dipping* neither in whole nor in part, but substituting *pouring* or *sprinkling* in its place.

Lev. xiv. 16. "That the priest shall dip his right finger in the oil that is in his left hand, and shall sprinkle of the oil with his finger seven times before the Lord." Here, also, we see the characteristic distinction between *dipping* and *sprinkling*. The action of putting the oil on the finger is expressed by *bapto;* that of applying it to the object, by *raino*. The word occurs again in the 51st verse, with reference to the same process as that described in verse 6.

Numb. xix. 18. "And a clean person shall take hyssop, and *dip* it in the water, and sprinkle it upon the house."

Deut. xxxiii. 24. "Let him *dip* his foot in oil." Here the great abundance of oil is expressed by representing the possessor as *dipping* his foot in it. The unlearned reader may perceive, that in all these instances the meaning of the word in question is so clear and definite, that even our translators, who were no practical immersers, render it as we do. Can it then admit a doubt, that this is the proper rendering?

Josh. iii. 15. "And as they that bare the ark were come unto Jordan, and the feet of the priests that bare the ark were *dipped* in the brim of the water."

Ruth ii. 14. "*Dip* thy morsel in the vinegar."

1 Sam. xiv. 27. "And Jonathan heard not when his father charged the people with the oath; wherefore he put forth the end of the rod that was in his hand, and dipped it in a honey-comb." Here the mode is

most determinately fixed. He stretched forth his rod, and *dipping* the point of it, ate the honey off the rod.

2 Kings viii. 15. " And it came to pass, that on the morrow he took a thick cloth, and *dipped it in water*."

Job ix. 31. What our translators render, " yet shalt thou plunge me in the ditch," &c., in the Greek is, *Thou hast dipped me deeply in filth.* Here we not only have the mode signified by this word, but evidence that the word is as applicable when the object of *dipping* is to *defile*, as when the object is to *wash*. It denotes the mode only, without any reference to the intention with which it is used.

Psalm lxviii. 23. " That thy feet may be *dipped* in the blood of thine enemies, and the tongue of thy dogs in the same." Here the person is supposed to wade through blood, to denote the great slaughter.

In 2 Mac. i. 21, the word is used to signify the drawing of water from a deep pit (compare verse 19) : "He ordered them to draw," literally *dip*.

The use of the word in the New Testament is exactly the same as in the examples which have been quoted from other writers. Matt. xxiv. 23, has already been referred to. The same transaction is related Mark xiv. 20 : " It is one of the twelve that dippeth with me in the dish." John xiii. 26, relates the fact, omitting the circumstance that the betrayer was dipping with him in the dish, and giving a circumstance omitted by Matthew and Mark, namely, that Jesus pointed out the betrayer by giving him a sop, after he had dipped it. The word here refers to the dipping of the bread in the bitter sauce. Neither pouring nor sprinkling could have any place here.

Luke xvi. 24. " And he cried and said, Father Abraham, have mercy on me ; and send Lazarus, that he may *dip the tip of his finger in water*, and cool my tongue."

Rev. xix. 13. " And he was clothed with a vesture dipped in blood." The glorious Redeemer is here represented as going forth to the destruction of his enemies, and, as an emblem of his work, he is figured as clothed with a vesture *dipped in blood*. This gives the most awful image of the approaching slaughter. Dr. Gale, indeed, has alleged some reasons, to prove that we have not here the genuine reading. " The authority of Origen," says he, " whose writings are older than any copies of the Old Testament we can boast of, and therefore that he described from more ancient copies, must be more considerable than any we have. Now he, in his Commentary on St. John's Gospel, cites these words from ver. 11, to ver. 16, inclusively, almost verbatim as they are in our edition, but reads *sprinkled*, instead of *dipped;* which makes this passage nothing to our purpose. However, I should not think this single authority of Origen sufficient to justify my altering the word; but I have likewise observed that the Syriac and Æthiopic versions, which, for their antiquity, must be thought almost as valuable and authentic as the original itself, being made from primitive copies, in or very near the times of the apostles, and rendering the passage by words which signify to sprinkle, must greatly confirm Origen's reading of the place, and very strongly argue, that he has preserved the very same word which was in the autograph." These reasons, however, do not in the least bring the common reading into suspicion in my mind, and I will never adopt a reading to serve a purpose. Misapprehension of the meaning of the passage, it is much more likely, has substituted *sprinkled* for *dipped.* The warrior is represented as going out, and not as returning, and the garment is emblematically dyed to represent his work before it was begun. Dr. Cox's reply to Mr. Ewing's observations on this verse, is a triumphant refutation of the objection which misconception has founded on this passage, and must silence it for ever.

SECTION IV.—Before I proceed farther, I shall advert to some examples in which *bapto* has been supposed to signify to *wash;* but in all of which it retains its own peculiar meaning.

Aristophanes applies the word to the cleansing of wool in warm water ; must not *wash* or *cleanse*, then, be one of its meanings? By no means. Let us examine his words : " First they dip the wool in warm water, according to ancient custom." What is asserted is, that they *dip*, or *immerse*, or *plunge* the wool into warm water. Washing is the *consequence* of the operation, but is not the thing expressed by the verb. It might be rendered by *wash* in a free translation ; but this would be to give the sense, not an exact version of the words. Had he used the word *pluno,* then the *washing* would have been expressed, and the *dipping* would have been necessarily supposed. Both these words might be used for the same thing in many situations ; still each of them would have its peculiar meaning. Accordingly, Suidas and Phavorinus interpret *baptousi* here by *plunousi*. It argues very shallow philosophy, however, to suppose, that on this account the words are perfectly synonymous. We could, even in our own language, say indifferently, that *sheep are dipped in the river before they are shorn*, or *sheep are washed in the river before they are shorn*, yet this does not make *dip* and *wash* synonymous in our language.

Words may be so far equivalent, as in certain situations to be equally fitted to fill the same place, when each continues even in such situations to have its characteristic meaning. Ignorance of this important principle in the application of words, has led writers into the greatest absurdities, in determining the meaning of terms in a dead language. Whenever they find one word used in explanation of another, or where another would serve the purpose, they think the words are synonymous. This is a false first principle, and all reasonings founded on it must be unsound. Yet this is the most plausible argument that Dr. Wall and others can find to prove that *bapto* signifies to *wash.* Suidas and Phavorinus explain it by *pluno*, therefore they think it must signify to *wash.* To convince the unlearned reader of the fallacy of this principle, let him open an English dictionary, and try if all the words given in explanation are strictly synonymous with those which they are used to explain. Yet on this principle, it is supposed to be irresistibly evident that *bapto* signifies to *wash*, because baptism is referred to in the expression, " having your bodies washed with pure water," Heb. x. 22. When a person is *dipped* in pure water, he is *washed ;* still *dipping* and *washing* are two different things. Baptism is a *washing*, not from the meaning of the word itself, for as far as that is concerned, it might be a defilement; but because it is an *an immersion in pure water.*

The passage from Herodotus, in which he represents swine as an abomination to the Egyptians, coincides entirely with this doctrine. If an Egyptian touches a swine, he runs immediately to the river and dips himself. That he dips himself, is the thing expressed; but as the purpose of the dipping is cleansing, or religious washing, the same fact might be substantially reported by saying, that *he washed, or cleansed, or purified, or bathed himself in the river.* Yet *bapto* no more signifies to *wash* or *purify* here, than it does in the translation of the LXX., with respect to Job, when applied to plunging in filth. The word has here its own peculiar meaning, and makes not the smallest intrusion into the province of *louo.* Mr. Ewing's remarks on this passage is truly surprising. The Egyptian, it seems, performed this operation on himself, but the Christian is baptized by another. And can Mr. Ewing really think that this is anything to the purpose? Was it ever supposed that it is from the verb *bapto* that we are to learn whether a believer is to dip himself, or to be dipped by another, in the ordinance of baptism? It is enough that the word informs of the mode : other things must be learned from their proper sources. From Herodotus, in the story of the Egyptian, we may learn the meaning of the word; but from Scripture, we must learn whether the operation is to be performed to the believer by himself, or by another. Was ever anything so unreasonable, as to expect a perfect coincidence between an ordinance of Christ, and a superstitious custom of heathens? The meaning of the word is quite unaffected, whether the person dips himself or is dipped by another. Does Mr. Ewing doubt whether *bapto* can apply when the operation respects a thing different from the agent? This cannot be his meaning, for almost all the examples of its use refer to such cases. Does he mean, that among the innumerable things which are said to be dipped, as expressed by *bapto*, a human being is not to be found, except in the case of one performing the operation for himself? If this is his meaning, it is not to the purpose ; for though an example could not be found in which one person is said to dip another, the command of Christ warrants the practice, and the word *bapto* will apply to one thing as well as another. But, as Dr. Cox has observed, there is an example in the case of the drowning of Aristobulus, which we shall afterwards consider : and we have already seen an example in the Scythian custom of immersing their new-born infants. But I will never consent that any such example is necessary. The demand is founded on a false principle of criticism. A passage from the Hymns of Callimachus, in which this word is misunderstood by some, is set in its proper light by Dr. Gale. "My opinion," says he, "is confirmed also by Callimachus, in his Hymns, when he says : 'Ye Grecian watermen (they furnished private houses with water, as some do among us), dip not your vessels in the river Inachus to-day.' The hymn was made on the solemnizing the festival of washing the statue of Pallas; which ceremony was performed by persons set apart for that purpose, in the river Inachus, a little before day ; from this river the inhabitants were usually supplied with water, which makes the poet, in veneration to the goddess, charge the watermen here not to dip their pitchers in the river on that day."

This, however, is of importance, rather for the understanding of the poet, than for ascertaining the meaning of the word in question. For whether the purpose of the waterman was to wash their pitchers by *dipping* them, or to fill them by *dipping* them, *dipping* is the only thing expressed by the word *bapto.*

In Dan. iv. 30, and v. 21, this word is rendered by *wet* in our version, which may seem an insuperable objection to the uniformity of its signification of mode. This instance is thought to support their opinion, who assert that *bapto* is a generic word, denoting the bringing of anything into a state of wetness. But there is here no exception to the peculiar meaning of the word. The term *wet* gives the general sense of the passage well enough, but it is by no means a translation of the word in the original, nor of that employed by the Septuagint. It ought to have been rendered according to the usual modal meaning, which, instead of being harsh, would have found corresponding expressions in all languages. By employing a general word, our translators in this instance have lost the peculiar beauty of the original, without in the least adding to the perspicuity. The words of the Septuagint are, " His body was *immersed* in the dew." In the translation, " His body was *wet* with the dew," the general effect is the same, but the eloquence of expression has evaporated. But a soulless critic will reply, " there was here no literal immersion; the word cannot then be used in that sense." Were we to pass through the poets, conforming their language to this observation, what havoc should we make of their beauties! How dull and lifeless would become their animated expressions! I have seen no explication of this passage that appears to develop the principle of this application, though the general sense of the passage is well enough understood. As the theory of generic meaning in *bapto,* including every application of water without reference to mode, has no other plausible foundation but the common version of this passage, it will be of importance to settle the question, though it should occupy some pages.

Dr. Gale affords us many materials to prove that the word has here its ordinary sense; but I think he fails in his attempt to analyze the expression. His observations on the copiousness of the eastern dews are much to the purpose; a part of which I shall transcribe. " Philosophically speaking," says he, " the hottest climates and clearest skies naturally abound most with dew, which is also confirmed by constant experience. It is commonly known to be so in her Majesty's Leeward Islands in America,—where one season of the year, when they have no rains for a considerable time together, the fruits of the earth would be burned up, were it not for the dews that fall plentifully in the night. That incomparable mathematician, Captain Halley, observed, when making some experiments in St. Helena, that the dews fell in such abundance as to make his paper too wet to write on, and his glasses unfit for use without frequent wiping. And as to Africa, in particular, where part of Nebuchadnezzar's dominions lay, Pliny tells us the nights were very dewy Egypt has little or no rain; but is fed by the overflowing of the Nile, and by constant nocturnal dews; and Nebuchadnezzar kept his court in a country of near the same latitude, and consequently of the like temperament."

This is very useful as a ground-work for the analysis of the expression; but it does not in the least give a reason why a *wetting* with a copious fall of dew is called an *immersion*. Had this monarch been wet even by a shower-bath, why is his *wetting* called a *dipping?* If all the water in the ocean had fallen on him, it would not have been a literal *immersion*. The *mode* would still be wanting. Our opponents, if they know their business, may admit this, and still deny the consequence which this writer draws from it. Nor does this gentleman succeed better in analyzing the expression. "Hence it appears very clear," says he, "that both Daniel and his translators designed to express the great dew Nebuchadnezzar should be exposed to, more emphatically, by saying, he should lie in dew, and be covered with it all over, as if he had been dipped; for that is so much like being dipped, as at most to differ no more than being in, and being put in; so that the metaphor is easy, and not at all strained." But Daniel does not say that Nebuchadnezzar *should lie in dew, and be covered with it all over*. Had this been his expression, it would have been quite literal. Dr. Gale absurdly supposes that *bapto* means to cover with water without reference to mode, and at the same time metaphorically alludes to *dipping*. Neither Daniel nor his translators say, that Nebuchadnezzar should be as wet as if he were dipped; for if that had been the expression, there could have been no dispute about it.

Dr. Cox's reply to Mr. Ewing, with respect to the analysis of this expression, appears to me not quite satisfactory. "It was," says Mr. Ewing, "*popped upon*, not even by *effusion*, but by the gentlest *distillation* that is known in nature." "To this it has been generally replied," says Dr. Cox, "and I think satisfactorily, that a body exposed to eastern dews would be as wet as if plunged into water." Now, this is valid, as proving that the body ought to be completely *wetted* in baptism; but it leaves the mode unaccounted for. Mr. Ewing might grant this, yet still insist, from this passage, that mode is not contained in the word. Many persons do plead for a copious effusion of water in baptism; and they might yield to the above reasoning, still contending that the mode is not essential, or that it is not *immersion*. The most complete wetting by dew or rain is not *dipping* literally. If we would fairly meet this passage, we must show, not merely that Nebuchadnezzar was completely wetted, but that a wetting in one mode may be figuratively designated by the words that properly denote a wetting in another mode. I will not hide one particle of the strength of our opponents' cause, nor an apparent weakness in our own. Let Christianity itself sink, rather than use one insufficient argument.

Dr. Cox continues: "The passage, however, merits a little more detailed explanation. The verb is used in the passive voice, in the second aorist, and the indicative mood, implying consequently that the action was past, and indefinite as to time." It does not seem to me, that the voice, tense, and mood of the verb, have any concern in this debate.

In all voices, tenses, and moods, a verb must have its characteristic meaning. "It does not," continues Dr. Cox, "imply the *manner* in which the effect was produced, but *the effect itself;* not the mode by which the body of the king was wetted, but its *condition*, as resulting from exposure to the dew of heaven." Without doubt, the verb expresses mode here as well as anywhere else. To suppose the contrary gives up the point at issue, as far as mode is concerned. This in fact makes *bapto* signify simply to *wet*, without reference to mode.

Dr. Cox gives an illustration, but unfortunately it can give no relief, as it fails in an essential point of similarity. "Suppose," says he, "by way of illustration, we select another word, and put it into the same voice and tense; as *eblabe upo sou*, 'he was hurt by you.' It is obvious that this representation might refer to an injury done long ago, and would predicate nothing of the *manner* in which it was inflicted," &c. Very true. Nothing of *manner* is here expressed, and for an obvious reason, *nothing of manner* is expressed by the verb *blapto*. But will Dr. Cox grant that this is the case with the verb *bapto?* If he does, about what is he contending? *Bapto* not only necessarily implies mode, but literally expresses nothing but mode. Instead of literally denoting *wetting* in any manner, it does not literally include *wetting* at all. This is as true in this passage, as it is in any other. Mode is as much expressed here, as it is in the commission of our Lord to the apostles. The difference is, that the thing that is here called an immersion was so only figuratively. I claim this passage as much as I do the plainest example in the New Testament.

That the word in question ought here, as in all other places, to be rendered *immerse*, is necessary from the following reasons:

1. It is utterly unwarrantable to give a meaning to the word which it cannot be shown to have in some unquestionable examples. To assign a meaning not so justified, is to reason without first principles—to build without a foundation. This suits the visionary, but can never be the resource of true criticism. Now, the whole history of the word does not afford a single example in which it must signify to *wet*. Whatever, then, may be the principle on which this *wetting* of Nebuchadnezzar is called *immersion, immersion* it is called.

2. This is confirmed, as Dr. Cox has observed, by the original. The word in the original signifies to *dip;* if so, why should not the Greek word by which it is translated have its own peculiar meaning? How can mode be excluded, if it is in both the original and the translation?

3. The Syriac version, as Dr. Gale remarks, renders the original in the same manner as the LXX. "The authors of the ancient and valuable Syriac version," says he, "who were of the neighbourhood of Babylon, and well enough acquainted with the large dews in those parts, and endeavored to give an exact literal translation, have shunned this error." If, then, the Syriac translators have rendered the original by a term that signifies *to dip*, why should not *bapto* in the translation of the LXX. have the same meaning? To me the reasoning of Dr. Gale is entirely satisfactory.

4. The expression is intelligible and beautiful in our own language,

and, I have no doubt, might be exemplified in all languages. Alluding to the flood, we might say, that God *immersed the world in water ;* or of a rock when covered by the tide, that it is *immersed* in the sea. Do we not every day hear similar phraseology? The man who has been exposed to a summer-plump will say that he has got a complete *dipping.* This is the very expression of Daniel. One mode of wetting is figured as another mode of wetting, by the liveliness of the imagination. The same figure meets us almost in every page of the poets. Virgil will supply us with instances in abundance :—

> " Postquam collapsi cineres, et flamma quievit ;
> Relliquias vino et bibulam lavêre favillam.''

> They washed the relics, and the warm spark, in wine.

Who *washes* ashes, and bones, and embers? On the principle of Mr. Ewing's criticism, we might, from this passage of Virgil, deny that *lavo* properly signifies to *wash,* and assert that it denotes to *drench,* to *quench,* to *wet,* to *moisten,* &c. What avails it, then, to tell us that Nebuchadnezzar was *wet* with the gentlest distillation in nature? The effect of that gentle operation may be so like that of another more violent operation, that the language of the imagination may designate the more gentle by the characteristic denomination of the more violent. A *wetting* by dew may, in the language of animation, be called a *dipping.* Language violates the laws of natural philosophy, as well as of logic, without scruple ; or rather it does not at all own subjection to them. It owes allegiance only to the laws of mind. Things most absurd, if explained according to the laws of natural philosophy, and most untrue, according to the laws of logic, are true and beautiful when tried by their proper standard. Why did Virgil make such an application of the word *lavo* here? Was it for lack of proper terms to express his ideas? Of these he had abundance. Was it to deceive or puzzle? Neither ; for his meaning appears at a glance. He uses *lavo* for the same reason that the Holy Spirit, by Daniel, used the word signifying to immerse, when speaking of the wetting of Nebuchadnezzar by the dew, to enliven the style. Every reader must observe that much of the beauty of this passage in Virgil is owing to the use of the word *lavo* in this figurative, catachrestic sense. Literal accuracy would have been comparatively tame. And had not the word *bapto* been a term whose meaning affects religious practice, the above expression of Daniel and the Septuagint, instead of tormenting commentators and controversialists, would have been admired as a beauty in composition. " Wetting by the gentlest distillation in nature," would the critic say, " is here, in the most lively and imaginative language, figured as an *immersion.*" But what is an elegance in the classics, is a ground of never-ending quibble to theologians, who, instead of seeking the laws of language in the human mind, subject the words of the Spirit to the laws of logical truth. No doubt, were Virgil of authority in religion, and were rites and ceremonies to be determined by his writings, the above expression would have been as variously interpreted as that in Daniel. Many a time we should hear, tha* *lavo,* from this example, does not signify to wash, but to *wet,* to *moisten,* to *drench.*

Virgil affords us another example in the same word:

> " Illi alternantes multa vi prælia miscent
> Vulneribus crebris : *lavit* ater corpora sanguis."

In the encounter of the two bulls, *the black blood washes their bodies.* Here it might be said, in the spirit of Mr. Ewing's criticism, the black blood could not wash; nay, it would defile the bodies of the contending animals. *Lavo,* then, cannot signify to *wash,* but to *smear.* But every one must see that the word *lavo* has here its peculiar signification, and that the whole beauty of the expression depends on this circumstance. Every man who has a soul at all, knows well that *lavo* is here much more beautiful, than if the poet had chosen a term literally signifying to smear. That which was a real *defilement* is called a *washing,* to express figuratively the copiousness of the blood that flowed from the mutual wounds of the contending bulls. This gives a feast to the imagination, where literal expression would afford no food. *Audire habenas,* to hear the reins, signifying to *obey the bridle,* is an expression of the same kind. Indeed, it is impossible to open the poets without being presented with examples of this phraseology.

SECTION V.—Having examined those examples in which this word has been supposed to signify to *wash* or to *wet,* but in each of which it is to be explained according to its characteristic meaning, I shall now proceed with other examples. The word occurs, as might be expected, very frequently in the writings of Hippocrates : and as, in medical use, there is occasion to refer repeatedly to every mode of the application of liquids, in the voluminous writings of this great physician, there can be no doubt but we shall find the characteristic meaning of *bapto.* Accordingly, we do find it in numerous instances; and in all these, I do not recollect any but one, in which it has not the sense of *dip.* In that one, it signifies *to dye,* according to its secondary import.

The first occurrence of it which I have observed in this author, is in his treatise De Superfœt. p. 50, edit. Basil. " Dip the probes in some emollient."

At the bottom of the next page, we have another example : " *Dipping* the rag in white sweet-smelling Egyptian ointment."

In the treatise De Victus Ratione, p. 104, the following example occurs : " Let the food be cakes *dipped* hot in sour wine."

In the treatise De Usu Humidorum, we have the following example : " But for the sake of cooling the wound, wool is either sprinkled with the sour wine, or put into it, or it may be *dipped* into the coldest water."

In continuation from the last words, the following immediately succeed, p. 113 : " As a cooler, black wine is sprinkled on wood, whereas beet-leaves and linen are for the most part *dipped.*

In the treatise De Morbis, we have the following examples, lib. xi. p. 145 : " Dipping sponges in warm water, apply them to the head."

In the next page, at top, we have the following example : " As an

external application, dipping sponges into warm water, let them be
applied to the cheeks and jaws. A similar example occurs near the
top of the next page : " Dipping a sponge into warm water, apply it."
Page 149 : " Give garlic, *dipping* it into honey."

In page 151, we have the following example : " Let him not sup soup,
nor even dip his bread into it." In the Appendix to Mr. Ewing's Essay
on Baptism, written by a friend, we find a very odd view of this passage.
I shall quote his observations at large. " Hippocrates (de Morb. lib. ii.)
uses *baptesthai* to denote the application of a liquid to the skin ; *zomos
de me phoreito me de baptesthai*, 'neither sip, nor *pour* (or sprinkle)
broth ;' using *baptesthai* in this sense, I suppose, from the idea that the
application of the liquid would strongly affect the place to which the
application was made ; at all events, it would require no small ingenuity
to discover in this passage the idea of immersion." In this criticism there
is a complication of errors and false principles. 1. Why does the author
translate *baptesthai* by *pour* or *sprinkle?* Is there one instance in which
it confessedly must have this meaning in the whole compass of Greek
literature? If not, to apply such a meaning in any particular emergency
is to reason without first principles. 2. If the author read the whole of
the works of Hippocrates, as I am convinced he did, must he not have
found a multitude of examples in which the word *bapto* unquestionably
has the meaning *dip?* He might reply, such a meaning could not apply
here. But even if he could not find any view in which the usual meaning of the verb could apply in this instance, would it not have been more
candid to grant the usual signification of the word, and confess a difficulty, than to assign a meaning altogether at random, without a shadow
of authority either from the word or the context? 3. How does he
bring the *skin* of the patient into requisition in this place? Where does
he find this? Neither in the expression, nor in any usual ellipsis. He
might as well have supposed the feet or the head. 4. Is it a fact that
broth or soup would have such a mischievous effect on the skin? The
solution of this surpasses my medical knowledge. 5. It requires no ingenuity to find here the proper meaning of the word *baptesthai*, as importing to *dip*. It is well known that at table the ancients dipped their
bread into the soup, or other liquid which they used as a seasoning.
What, then, can be so natural as to fill up the ellipsis with the bread
which was dipped? An ellipsis of the regimen in things so common
was quite usual. The evangelist uses the same ellipsis, where he says,
" he that dippeth with me in the dish," that is, he that dippeth *his hand*
with me in the dish, as another evangelist expresses it; or "he that
dippeth *his bread* with me" might, with equal propriety, be supplied as
the supplemental matter. 6. The elliptical matter must be supplied by
the connexion. In an ellipsis we are never left to wander abroad to look
for the thing that is wanting. It is always omitted, because it is so obvious
that it cannot be missed. This is the principle on which ellipsis is used,
and on no other is it justifiable. Were it otherwise, all language would
consist of riddles. This is the reason why ellipsis is so common in conversation, and about the most common things. What is omitted is
omitted because every hearer will instantly supply it. We say of

man, that he is a great drinker—drinker of what? Drinker of water? No Drinker of milk? No. But, without the smallest hesitation, we understand it to be *drinker of ardent spirits.* Just so in the present passage. The elliptical matter must be supplied from the connexion, and this leaves no doubt what it is. The writer was giving direction about the food of his patient. In the words immediately preceding, he prescribed boiled mutton, fowl, gourd, and beet. In the passage quoted, he forbids him to eat broth, or even *to dip*—dip what? *Dip* his bread, or his food, whatever it was, in the broth. What else could he mean? In this view, the passage has a natural and a rational meaning. In some cases, a patient might be forbidden to partake freely of broth, when he might be permitted to season his morsel by dipping it in the savoury liquid. But in this case, it seems, even this indulgence was not permitted. But upon what principle could the skin of the patient be supplied as the supplemental matter? It is not in the connexion, and is as arbitrary as if we should supply the *coat* of the patient. It may be added, that, in the immediately succeeding connexion, the patient is permitted to eat fish. The whole passage speaks of diet. 7. Whatever is forbidden in a medical prescription, must be a thing that is likely to be done, if not forbidden. No physician would act so absurdly as to prohibit what there is no probability his patient would do. Now, there was no probability that the patient here would sprinkle broth on his skin, had the physician been silent on the subject. I never heard of any such custom; and against even accidental sprinkling he was sufficiently guarded, by the circumstance that he was not permitted to use the fluid as food. There was surely no danger of sprinkling his skin with broth, if he was not permitted to eat broth. This gloss is one of the wildest that I ever met.

The word occurs again in the same book, p. 153. "*Dipping* linen rags into water, apply them to the breast and back."

Lib. iii. p. 163. "A livid blister rising on the tongue, as of iron *dipped into oil.*"

P. 164. "Having *dipped* a piece of fine linen into moist Eretrian earth, well pounded and warm, cover the breast round with it."

In the treatise De Internarum Partium Affectibus, we have the following examples from the same author:—

P. 193. "*Dipping* beet in cold water, apply it to the body, especially to a new pain; or *dipping* rags in cold water, after wringing out the water, apply them."

In the same page we have another example: "Let him eat green marjoram, for the most part *dipping* it into honey."

P. 199. Having prescribed a variety of things to be eaten by his patient, he adds: "These are of a very dry nature; and let him not *dip* them into the broth." This passage is a decisive commentary on the ellipsis which Mr. Ewing's friend has so strangely misunderstood. The different kinds of food here mentioned are prescribed on account of the quality of dryness, and the patient is expressly forbidden to *dip* them in the soup or broth, as was usual. He is not forbidden to *sprinkle* his skin with broth, which no man ever thought of doing; but he is forbidden, in the eating of the things prescribed, to *dip* them in the soup, which he was likely to do, had he not been forbidden.

P. 202. " Burn it with spindles of box-wood, *dipping* them into boiling oil."

P. 203. " Let him use radish and parsley, dipping them into vinegar." In the treatise De Natura Muliebri, p. 119 : " *Dipping* (the flies) into the oil of roses."

P. 226. " *Dipping* the softest wool in a pipkin."

P. 228. " *Dipping* the balls into the juice of the fig-tree."

P. 231. " *Dipping* (the plaster) into white Egyptian oil." In the treatise De Morb. Mul. the following examples occur :

P. 249. " Taking a sponge, or *dipping* soft wool into warm water." And in the next line : " Then *dipping* again the sponge, or the wool, into pure wine."

P. 250. Speaking of a number of things boiled together, he says : " Then *dipping* wool into this."

P. 254. Speaking of a certain mixture, he says : " After this, having *dipped* it into the oil of roses, or Egyptian oil, let it be applied during the day." In the same page, we have another example : " After supper, let her eat onions, *dipping* them into honey."

P. 257. When a blister is too painful to the patient, he orders it to be taken away; and " *dipping* wool into the oil of roses, let her apply it."

P. 258. " Having boiled nitre with rosin, and forming them into a ball, *dipping* it into the fat of a fowl, apply it."

P. 261. " *Dipping* the ball into white Egyptian oil." " Having *dipped* nut-gall into honey, or the gall of a bull into Egyptian oil, let it be applied."—*Ib.* " Make an oval ball, and *dip* it into white oil."—*Ib.*

P. 262. " Then put a fine rag about it, in wool, *dipping* it into Egyptian oil." " *Dipping* (the thing prescribed) into white Egyptian oil."—*Ib.*

P. 263. " Having rolled a bit of galbanum the size of an olive into a piece of linen, and having *dipped* it into cedar-oil."

P. 264. Having prescribed different kinds of flesh to his patients, he directs, " Cooked without pepper, *dipping* it into vinegar."

P. 269. Speaking of wool rolled round a quill : " *Dip* it either in white oil, or," &c. And within a few lines : " *Dip* the feather in vinegar "

P. 273. " *Dip* the leaden instrument into cold water."

P. 279. " Apply the fat of the deer, melted, *dipping* soft wool into it."

P. 279. " *Dipping* wool into ointment."

P. 280. " Put this mixture into clean soft wool, and let her *dip* it in white Egyptian oil."

P. 284. " *Dipping* the unscoured wool in honey."

P. 288. " Form it into a ball, and *dip* it into some liquid." " Roll around a quill the gall of a bull, rubbed ; and *dipping* it into Egyptian oil, apply it."—*Ib.* " Or cyclaminus, the size of a die, with the flower of brass ; or a head of anemone, bruising it with meal, and putting the mixture into white wool, around a quill, *dip* it," as directed above. For *eirion*, some read *elaion; dip it into white oil: oleo albo intingito.—Ib.*

P. 289. " Having pounded finely a drachm of the fibres of flax with the stalks, steep them thoroughly for the night in the sweetest white wine; then, having strained and warmed it, *dip* the softest wool in it." Literally, *dip in it with the softest wool;* just as we might say *dip the liquor with the wool,* instead of dip the wool in the liquor.

P. 290. " Mixing myrrh and rosin together, and putting them in wine, *dip* a piece of linen in the mixture, and apply it."

De Steril. p. 292. " *Dip* the probe in the unguent."

P. 293. "Working them into a little ball, roll it in wool, except the top; then having *dipped* it in the sweetest oil, apply it."

P. 297. Speaking of a mixture the size of a nut-gall, he says: " *Dipping* it in the ointment of fleur-de-luce."

P. 299. "Taking lead and the magnetic stone, rub them smooth, and tie them in a rag; then having dipped them in breast milk, apply them." " Dipping unwashed wool into honey."—*Ib.*

De Morb. Pass. Grass. p. 339. Speaking of a shoemaker who was killed by the prick of his awl in the thigh, he says, " The instrument dipped about a finger's length."

P. 362. " Dipping sponges."

De Ratione Victus Acutorum, p. 383. " *Dipping* hot cakes in black wine and oil."

Coacæ Præcognitiones, p. 435. "If a livid blister rise on the tongue at the beginning, as of iron *dipped* in oil, the cure becomes the more difficult."

De Ulceribus, p. 514. "The other things being the same; but in place of the wine, take the strongest vinegar of white wine. *Dip* into this the most greasy wool." " *Dip* the wool in the smallest quantity of water possible; then *pouring* into it of wine a third part, boil it to a good thickness."—*Ib.*

P. 522. " Dipping the raw liver of an ox in honey."

Thus we have seen in what a vast multitude of examples Hippocrates uses this word to signify *to dip;* and that quite irrespectively of the nature of the fluid. Indeed, he not only uses it so frequently in this signification, but he uses it in no other signification, except once in the sense of *to dye;* and it is the only word which he employs to denote the mode in question: for I have intentionally omitted no instance in which the word occurs in all his works. Besides, we have in this writer the words which signify every application of water, and other fluids, from the gentle distillation from the nipple, to the bathing of the whole body. He uses *raino, aioneo,* &c., for *sprinkle,* and for *pour* he uses *cheo* with its compounds, which occurs times innumerable. For *wet, moisten, soak, steep,* he uses *deuo, brecho, teggo,* &c.: the first of which meets us in almost every page; the second is often used; and of the last there are several examples. For bathing the whole body, he constantly uses *louo,* and he makes a very free use of the bath, both hot and cold: for washing a part of the body, he uses *nipto,* with its compounds; and occasionally the compounds of *pluno.* If it is possible to settle the meaning of a common word, surely this is sufficient to fix the meaning of *bapto* beyond all reasonable controversy. *In the works of the father of medicine, in which he has occasion to treat of every mode of the application of liquids, and which consist of no less than five hundred and forty-three closely printed folio pages, all the words of mode are applied, and* bapto *invariably is used when he designates immersion.*

SECTION VI.—Having established the meaning of this word, as significant of mode, I shall now show that it signifies also *to dye.* That it has this signification, I believe, is not doubted by any. But while one party contends that this is its primary signification, the other errs as far on the opposite side ; contending that this meaning is only by consequence, and that the word, when it relates to *dyeing*, always denotes *dyeing* by dipping, as the mode. Now, while I contend that *dyeing* is the secondary meaning of this word, I contend also that this is a real literal meaning, independent of consequence. Although this meaning arose from the mode of *dyeing* by *dipping*, yet the word has come by appropriation to denote *dyeing*, without reference to mode. Were this a point of mere philological accuracy, I would pursue it no farther ; but as it is of material importance in this controversy, I shall establish it by a number of examples that will put the fact beyond question. One truth can never injure another ; and if it has the appearance of doing so, we may depend that there is something about the matter which we do not understand. The advocates of truth often labour in the proof of what cannot be proved, the proof of which their cause does not require, and which sometimes would be injurious rather than profitable. That *bapto* signifies *to dye in any manner*, is a truth which, instead of being against us, serves to solve difficulties that have been very clumsily got over by some of the ablest writers on this side of the question. Indeed, one of the most plausible objections is by this fact removed to a demonstration.

Nothing, in the history of words, is more common than to enlarge or diminish their signification. Ideas not originally included in them are often affixed to some words, while others drop ideas originally asserted in their application. In this way, *bapto*, from signifying mere mode, came to be applied to a certain operation usually performed in that mode. From signifying to *dip*, it came to signify to *dye by dipping*, because this was the way in which things were usually *dyed*. And afterwards, from *dyeing by dipping*, it came to denote *dyeing in any manner*. A like process might be shown in the history of a thousand other words. Candlestick originally denoted a *stick* to hold a candle, but now the utensil employed to hold a candle is called a candlestick, even when it is of gold.

The only instance in which I have observed the word *bapto* in this signification, in the works of Hippocrates, he employs it to denote dyeing by *dropping* the dyeing liquid on the thing *dyed :* " When it *drops* upon the garments, they are *dyed.*" This surely is not *dyeing* by dipping.

There is a similar instance in Arrian's Expedition of Alexander the Great, the only one in which I have found the word at all in that work. " Nearchus relates that the Indians *dye* their beards." It will not be contended that they *dyed* their beards by immersion.

We meet this word, or its derivatives, several times in Ælian, in the sense of *dyeing*, and sometimes when the process was not by dipping. Speaking of an old coxcomb, who endeavoured to conceal his age by dyeing his hair, he says, "He endeavoured to conceal the hoariness of his hair by *dyeing* it." *Baphe* here denotes *dyeing* in general; for hair on the head is not dyed by dipping. In the title of this anecdote, the old man is styled : "The old man with the *dyed* hair." Lib. vii. c. xx. Speaking of a lady whose yellow locks were not coloured by art, but by nature, he uses the word *baphsais*. Lib. xiii. c. i.

Nicolas of Damascus, speaking of parasites as obliged to flatter their patrons, says, "Does a patron affect to be younger than he is? or does he even *dye* his hair?"

Æschylus, in the Choëphoræ, p. 85, uses the word in the same way : "This garment, *dyed* by the sword of Ægisthus, is a witness to me." The garment must have been *dyed* by the blood running down over it.

These examples are sufficient to prove, that the word *bapto* signifies to dye in general, though originally and still usually applied to *dyeing* by *dipping*. Having such evidence before my eyes, I could not deny this to my opponents, even were it a difficulty as to the subject of the mode of baptism. In a controversialist nothing can compensate for candour ; and facts ought to be admitted, even when they appear unfavourable. It is an unhallowed ingenuity that strains to give a deceitful colouring to what cannot be denied, and cannot ultimately serve a good cause. Truth will be sooner made to appear, and will sooner be received, if on all sides there is openness and honest dealing, without any attempt to conceal, or to colour. To force through difficulties, employ insufficient evidence, refuse admissions that integrity cannot deny, and by rhetorical artifice cut down whatever opposes, is the part of a religious gladiator, not of a Christian contending earnestly for Divine institutions.

On the subject of this application of the word *bapto*, I cannot but blame some of the most distinguished writers on both sides of the question. On the one side, supposing it to be necessary, or at least serviceable, to prove that, when the word relates to *dyeing*, it is always dyeing by *dipping*, they have evidently strained, and have employed false criticism. With respect to the other side, to say nothing of the straining to squeeze out of the word the several significations of *sprinkling, pouring, washing, wetting*, &c., for which there is not any even plausible ground, the obvious fact, that it signifies *dyeing* by any process, has been uncritically pressed to prove, that when it relates to the application of pure water it denotes all modes equally. There is neither candour nor philosophy in such attempts. It manifests little acquaintance with the history and philosophy of the signification of words. In reality this admitted fact is nothing in their favour, as it is perfectly agreeable to the history of the meanings of a numerous class of words. Use is always superior to etymology as a witness on this subject. A word may come to enlarge its meanings, so as to lose sight of its origin. This fact must be obvious to every smatterer in philology. Had it been attended to, Baptists would have found no necessity to prove that *bapto*, when it signifies to *dye*, always properly signifies to dye by *dipping*; and their opponents would have seen no advantage from proving, that it signifies *dyeing in any manner*. The word candlestick applies now as well when the material is gold, as when it is timber. He would not, however, be worth reasoning with, who should from this circumstance deny that the name points out the materials of which candlesticks among the Saxons were originally made.

The observations of Dr. Gale on this subject fall in some degree under the above censure. "The Grecians," says he, "very frequently apply the word in all its various forms to the dyer's art, sometimes perhaps not very properly, but always so as to imply and refer only to its true natural signification *to dip*."

What does this learned writer mean when he expresses a doubt of the propriety of this usage? Does he mean that such an extension of the meaning of words is in some degree a trespass against the laws of language? But such a usage is in strict accordance with the laws of language; and the history of a thousand words sanctions this example. Language has not logical truth for its standard; and therefore against this it cannot trespass. USE IS THE SOLE ARBITER OF LANGUAGE; AND WHATEVER IS AGREEABLE TO THIS AUTHORITY, STANDS JUSTIFIED BEYOND IMPEACHMENT. *Candlestick* is as properly applied to gold as to timber; *bapto* signifies *to dye by sprinkling*, as properly as by *dipping*, though originally it was confined to the latter.

Nor is he well founded when he asserts, that the word in such applications always implies and refers to its primary signification only. On the contrary, I have produced some examples, and he himself has produced others, in which candour cannot say that there is any such implication or reference. From such examples it could not be known even that *bapto* has the meaning of *dip*. They relate *to dyeing* wholly without reference to *dipping*; nay, some of them with an expressed reference to another mode. This is a fact, and were it even against me, I could not but admit it.

Nor are such applications of the word to be accounted for by metaphor, as Dr. Gale asserts. They are as literal as the primary meaning. It is by extension of literal meaning, and not by figure of any kind, that words come to depart so far from their original signification. The examples of this kind which Dr. Gale produces, cannot be accounted for by his philosophy. "Magnes, an old comic poet of Athens, used the Lydian music, *shaved his face, and smeared it over with tawny washes.*" Now, surely *baptomenos* here has no reference to its primary meaning. Nor is it used figuratively. The face of the person was rubbed with the wash By anything implied or referred to in this example, it could not be known that *bapto* ever signifies *to dip*.

Ornis baptos, a coloured bird. This expression is indeed figurative. But the figure has no reference to *dipping*, the primary meaning of the word, but to *dyeing*. The bird is said to be *dyed*, though its colours were natural. By the same figure we should say a *painted bird*, though its colours were not conferred by the pencil. This example strongly confirms my view of the word in Daniel. Here even in the verbal (*baptos*) of the very word *bapto*, we have the same figure which I have pointed out in the use of the word in the above contested passage. The colours of a bird are said to *be dyed*, by a beautiful figure founded on like-ness; just as, in Daniel, Nebuchadnezzar was said to be *immersed in dew*, though literally the dew fell on him. What a Goth should we reckon the critic who would philosophize on such expressions as *painted bird*, on the principle of the objection to *dipping* as the meaning of the word in the expression used by Daniel! "The plumage of the bird," says the philologist, "is natural, and not conferred by either painter or dyer. The word *painted*, therefore, and the word *dyed*, when applied to birds, designate properly natural colours. *Baptos*, therefore, in the expression used by Aristophanes, does not signify *dyed*, but denotes colour, whether artificial or natural." A foreigner, on the same principle, might show the depth of his philosophy on the phrase *painted bird*. "Here," says he, "a bird is said to be *painted*. Now we know that the colours of a bird are not given by the pencil, but by the Creator. The proper sense, then, of the English word *painted*, is not *coloured by the pencil*, but coloured in any way." This might appear to have great depth and justness to people as little acquainted with the language as himself, and who should not venture to dip into the philosophy of the criticism. But a mere child who speaks English would laugh at it. Yet it is the very criticism employed by celebrated scholars on the passage in Daniel. If theologians had as much taste as they have ingenuity and learning, it would save themselves and their readers an immensity of useless labour.

The *pictæ volucres* of Virgil is a perfectly similar example in the Latin language. Aristophanes speaks of *dyed birds*, Virgil of *painted birds*. Let the criticism on the passage in Daniel be applied to the phrase of Virgil. "Here," says the critic, "instead of colours laid on by the pencil of the painter, the colour is given by the invisible hand of nature. *Pictæ*, then, cannot signify *painted*, or have any allusion to *painting*, but must denote properly *natural colouring*." This is the very essence of the criticism on the passage in Daniel. Nebuchadnezzar, they say, was not *immersed* in dew,—therefore the word *bapto* must here signify the *distillation of dew*.

Our own Milton uses the same figure when, speaking of the wings of the angel Raphael, he says, *colours dipped in heaven*, though he does not mean that they were either *dipped* or *dyed*. The foreigner, who, from this authority, should argue that the English word *dip* does not signify the mode which we understand by it, would find his justification in the criticism on the above passage in the book of Daniel.

Dr. Gale gives us another passage from Aristotle, which is as little to his purpose, namely, to prove that the word, when it signifies *to dye*, has always a reference to dipping, and implies it. "If it is pressed, it dyes and colours the hand." Surely there is no reference to dipping here; the hand is dyed by pressing the thing that dyes. Here, also, the critical eye will see a confirmation of my view of the principle that operates in the application of the word *bapto* in the passage of the book of Daniel. Things are said to be *dyed* by nature, on the same principle that Nebuchadnezzar was said to be immersed in dew.

Having found, beyond reasonable doubt, that *bapto*, in its secondary sense, is employed *literally and properly* to denote *dyeing*, even when there is no *dipping*, we are now prepared to examine the occurrence of the word in the Battle of the Frogs and Mice, which has been so obstinately contested; and which hitherto has been the most plausible resource of those who have laboured to prove that at least one of the meanings of the word is to pour. The blood was poured into the lake, therefore it is thought *bapto* must signify *to pour*. But in reality, the passage favours neither the one party nor the other. It expresses neither *pouring* nor *dipping*, but *dyeing*, without reference to mode. If *bapto*, as we have proved, signifies to *dye in any mode*, there is no occasion for the advocates of immersion in baptism to find immersion in the word, as it signifies *to dye*. This simple fact settles the controversy about this passage forever.

" He fell, and breathed no more, and the lake was tinged with blood;" or, according to the translation of Cowper,

> " So fell Crombophagus, and from that fall
> Never arose, but *reddening* with his blood
> The wave," &c.

To suppose that there is here any extravagant allusion to the literal *immersion* or *dipping* of a lake, is a monstrous perversion of taste. The lake is said to be *dyed*, not to be *dipped*, nor *poured*, nor *sprinkled*. There is in the word no reference to mode. Had Baptists entrenched themselves here, they would have saved themselves much useless toil, and much false criticism, without straining to the impeachment of their candour, or their taste. What a monstrous paradox in rhetoric is the figuring of the dipping of a lake in the blood of a mouse! Yet Dr. Gale supposes the lake dipped by hyperbole. "The literal sense," he says, " is, the lake was *dipped in blood*." Never was there such a figure. The lake is not said to be *dipped* in blood, but to be *dyed* with blood.

They might have found a better commentary to this passage in the battles of Homer's heroes in the Iliad. The expression evidently alludes to one in the beginning of the twenty-first book of the Iliad, with respect to the slaughter of the Trojans by Achilles in the river Xanthus:

> "The waters as they ran *reddened* with blood."—COWPER.

In allusion to this, in the burlesque poem, from which the disputed passage is taken, the whole lake is said to be *dyed* with the blood of a mouse, which fell in battle on its edge.

The monthly reviewers, as quoted by Mr. Booth, understood the expression in this paradoxical sense. " In a poem attributed to Homer," they say, " called the Battle of the Frogs and Mice, it is said a lake was baptized with the blood of a wounded combatant—a question hath arisen in what sense the word *baptize* can be used in this passage." This should never have been a question; for this lake is not said to be *baptized*. The word BAPTO, not BAPTIZO, is used. Again, the lake was not dipped, as these friends of dipping, or at least of profuse *pouring*, assert. The expression is literal, and has not the smallest difficulty.

SECTION VII.—The derivatives of this word, both in the primary and secondary meaning, prove that it denotes immersion. *Bamma, sauce* or *soup* into which bread or other food is dipped in eating; also *a dye* into which the thing to be *dyed* is *dipped*, as distinguished from *chroma*.

Baphe, immersion, &c., Soph. in Ajace: "I who endured horrible things, as iron *dipped* in water." *Baphe siderou* is also used for the edge of iron; because the edge, or sharpness, is given in the tempering by immersion in water.

Bapsis, the act of dipping: as *bapsis chalkou kai siderou, the tempering of brass and iron;* quoted by Scapula from Pol. ex Antiphonte. Now metal is tempered in water by immersion.

Baptisis, a laver, or *bathing place,* used by Lucian.

Dibaphos, dyed by being twice *dipped;* just as dyers with us speak of giving their cloth one *dip,* or two or three *dips.*

Oxubaphos, oxubaphon, and *oxubaphion,* quoted by Scapula from Athen. lib. ii.: *the small vessel which was used to hold the vinegar with which they seasoned their food.* This the ancients did by dipping. To this, doubtless, our word *saucer* owes its origin, however differently it is used at present. This is an instance of the process by which words extend their signification beyond the ideas originally contained in them. The word *saucer,* from signifying a small vessel for holding *sauce,* now signifies one for cooling tea. This is a fine illustration of the process by which *bapto,* from signifying to *dip,* came to signify *to dye by dipping,* and at last dropping the mode, *to dye in any manner.* The foreigner who should allege that the English word *saucer* cannot signify a small vessel for tea, but must always denote one for *sauce,* would reason as correctly as those who attempt to force *bapto,* when signifying to dye, always to look back to its origin.

This compound, mentioned above, is also used as the name of a measure, doubtless because this vessel was at first used as the measure of the quantity so designated. At last, however, it would come by a natural process to denote the measure, without any reference to the vessel.

In medical language, this compound was also applied to the deep cavities or *cups* in which bones turn in the joints—doubtless taking the name from the shape. Here the *socket of a joint* is called *a vinegar cup.*

Opsobaphon, taken also by Scapula from Poll. lib. vii. denotes the small vessel in which these things were served up, which were eaten with bread, and which were always used by dipping. Xenophon represents the hands of the king of Media, as smeared in this operation.

The verbal *baptos, to be dipped,* or *that may be dipped,* we have already seen in the passage quoted from Euripides in justification of the translation of a passage in Hippocrates. The negative *abaptos* may also be alleged as confirmatory of the application of the root in the sense of dipping. *Abaptos sideros* is untempered iron, literally *undipped iron,* for iron is tempered by *dipping.*

Abaptistos also signifies *that cannot be immersed,* and is applied by Pindar, as Scapula observes, to cork. This fact is perfectly decisive. There can be no doubt that the property of cork, not to sink in water, is referred to by Pindar.

Abaptiston, a *trepan,* a surgical instrument, so called because it was so formed as not *to sink too deeply*, lest it should injure the membrane of the brain. This shows that the word from which it is derived signifies *to dip*.

In ascertaining the meaning of *bapto*, it may be of assistance to us to examine also some of its compounds, and also the prepositions with which it is construed. In composition, we find it sometimes joined with prepositions that point to the meaning for which we contend, and which will not suit the meaning attached to it by our opponents. Besides, it admits no preposition in composition or construction with it, which cannot be accounted for on the supposition of this meaning. If this position can be made good, it will afford the strongest confirmation to our doctrines.

We have seen, in the numerous examples quoted, that it admits both the prepositions *eis* and *en* to be compounded with it, as well as to construe with it in regimen. A mere glance at the examples may convince any one that this would not suit either *pour* or *sprinkle*, from the consideration of the things which are the subjects of the operation of the verb. We could not, for instance, say, *pour or sprinkle wool in or into the river*. If, then, the word signified *pour* or *sprinkle*, it could not admit these prepositions either in composition or in regimen, with respect to many things that are the subject of the operation of the verb. Both the prepositions *eis* and *en*, in composition with this word, have the same form. *Embapto* is the compound word with respect to both. The regimen, however, is different. If *em* is put for *eis*, the verb is construed with the accusative of the thing in which the operation of the verb is performed, either without, or more generally with the preposition itself repeated before it. *Embapto eis to udor.* When *em* is put for *en*, the verb is construed with the dative of the thing in which the operation of the verb is performed, either with the same preposition repeated before it, or without it.—*Embapto en to elaio.*

When *eis* is used either in the compound or before the substantive, there can be no question that all idea of *pouring* or *sprinkling* is excluded. And though *en* may sometimes be translated *with*, it never has this acceptation in composition. Indeed, this form is so decisive, that the celebrated Dr. Owen asserts, that it is this that makes the verb signify to *dip*. " *Baptizo*, says he, " does not signify properly to *dip* or *plunge*, for that, in Greek, is *embapto* and *embaptizo*." This observation is not worthy of the learning of that great and good man. If the verb *bapto* did not of itself signify to dip, the preposition in question could not give it that meaning. Dr. Owen's criticism is well exposed by the cool good sense of Mr. Booth. " Besides," says he, " I appeal to the learned whether Dr. Owen might not as well have asserted, that *mergo* does not properly signify to *dip* or *plunge*, for that, in Latin, is *immergo?* Nay, does not the Dr. himself, in the same discourse, acknowledge, that ' the original and natural signification of the word imports to *dip*, to *plunge*, to *dye*, to *wash*, to *cleanse?*'"

Embamma signifies sauce, or any liquid into which food *is dipped* in order to be eaten—*something to be dipped into*. This compound could not suit either *pouring* or *sprinkling*. *Embaphion*, a *saucer* or vessel to hold the liquid for seasoning food, which was used by *dipping*. It came also to denote a certain measure,—no doubt from the circumstance that this vessel was employed as a measure. In this sense, Hippocrates uses it several times.

Katabapto signifies, literally, to dip *down*, that is, to dip deeply, or thoroughly. The preposition is designed to increase the action of the verb. Accordingly, *katabapton* signifies a *dyer*.

Epibapto, to dip *upon*. We find this compound once used by Hippocrates, and, although it affords us no evidence, it takes none from us.

The use of *apo* with this word may appear more strange, but it is explicable. It is used both in composition and following the verb; and sometimes it is used in composition when *eis* follows the verb. *Apobapto* appears to designate *to dip*, as intimating the departure of the thing dipped from the thing in which it is dipped. When *apo* follows *bapto*, it respects the point from which the finished dipping has proceeded. *Bapto apo tou aimatos. I dip it from the blood.* The blood is the point from which the thing dipped proceeded, after the operation.

The preposition *ek* is also construed with *apobapto*, in one of the examples taken from Hippocrates. This makes it still more evident, that *apo*, in construction with this verb, denotes the point *from* which the dipping was effected. *Ek* views the thing dipped as proceeding *out of* the thing in which it was dipped.

Scapula seems to think that *apo* in composition with this word, is designed to intimate the gentleness of the operation, as he translates it, immergo leniter, *I dip gently;* and refers to Dioscorides, lib. v. *apobapsai eis udor.*

But though it may be used with respect to the gentlest *dipping*, it cannot intimate this. But whatever may be the peculiar effect of this preposition in composition with *bapto*, and on whatever principle its use is to be accounted for, the fact that the compounded word is sometimes used in construction with *eis*, removes all appearance of objection to our view of the meaning of the verb.

SECTION VIII.—Let us now take a glance at a few passages in which *bapto* is used figuratively, as this also may cast some light back upon its literal meaning. Aristophanes says : " *Lest I dip you into a Sardinian dye.*" The figure is but low, and is just the same as if a pugilist with us should say, *I will dip you in vermilion.* It is an allusion to the dyer's art, and means, *I will beat you, till you shall be covered all over with your own blood.* It would be to no purpose to allege, that, when a man is beaten, he is not literally *dipped* in his blood, but the blood runs over him. This would indicate a total misconception of the figure. The likeness does not consist in the *manner*, but in the *effects*. As the reference is to the art of *dyeing*, so the expression must be suited to the usual mode of dyeing. *I will dip you in vermilion*, is exactly the expression of the poet in English. He would be a sorry critic, who, from this, should allege that the English word *dip* signifies to *run over*, as blood from the wounded body. In fact, *pour* and *sprinkle* are as little applicable here, in a literal sense, as *dip* itself. When a man is beaten, there is no *pouring* or *sprinkling*, more than *dipping*. The blood is not put on the beaten person by the beater, *in any manner*.

Marcus Antoninus Pius speaks of the man of virtue as *bebammenon*, dipped or *dyed* in justice. I would not explain this with Dr. Gale, " dipped as it were in, or swallowed up with justice." *Justice* is here represented as a colouring liquid, which imbues the person who is dipped in it. It communicates its qualities as in the operation of dyeing. The figure can receive no illustration from the circumstance, that "persons given up to their pleasures and vices, are said to be immersed or swallowed up with pleasures." The last figure has a reference to the primary meaning of the word *bapto*, and points to the *drowning* effects of liquids; the former refers to the secondary meaning of the word, and has its resemblance in the colouring effects of a liquid dye. The virtuous man is dipped to be *dyed* more deeply with justice; the vicious man is drowned or ruined by his immersion. Perfectly similar is the figure in an observation of the same writer, where he asserts that the thoughts *are tinctured* by the mind. We use the word *imbue* in the same way. He uses the same word also when the *dye* injures what it colours. He cautions against bad example, *lest you be infected*.

We see, then, that the use of this word in a figurative sense, is not only always consistent with my view of the meaning of this word, but that it frequently illustrates its primary import.

Section IX.—That *bapto* signifies *to dip* is strongly confirmed by the circumstance, that *dyeing*, which it also imports, was usually performed, both among the Greeks and Romans, by immersion. If the word originally denoted to *dip*, it might, by a natural process, come to signify to *dye*, which was performed by dipping. But if the word originally signified *to pour* or *to sprinkle*, no process can be supposed by which it would come to denote *to dye*. Upon our view, there is a connecting link which joins these two meanings together, notwithstanding their great diversity. They are seen by our doctrine as parent and child. On the view of our opponents there is no relation. The two meanings cannot have any consanguinity. Now, that *dyeing* anciently was commonly performed by dipping, and that it still is so, admits no reasonable doubt. Dr. Gale has well observed this, and has given evidence of the fact, should any be so perverse as to deny it. After producing some passages, he observes, " I will only observe, you will please to consider *dipping* as the only probable and convenient way; and in every respect perfectly agreeable to the nature of the thing, as well as to that sense of the word, which is very considerable. We see it is the only way with us; and, which carries the parallel still farther between the ancient Greeks and us, as they used *bapto*, we used the word *dip*, both among the workmen in the shop, and in ordinary conversation; for what is more common than to talk of such or such a thing *dipped*, meaning in the dyer's copper, or in some colours?" " Besides it is observable, that the Grecians made a difference between *dye*, and other colouring matter. Thus Plutarch distinguishes between *chromata* and *bammata*; and Pollux does the same; *bammata* signifying only that sort of colouring-matter into which anything is dipped, according to the sense of the word, as I see Stephens also has remarked. And there is a passage in Seneca very clear to this purpose. ' Interest quamdiu macerata est, crassius medicamentum an aquatius traxerit, sæpius mersa est, et excocta, an semel tincta.' *There is a difference also, how long it lies infused; whether the dye be thick and gross, or waterish and faint; and whether dipped very often and boiled thoroughly, or only once tinctured.* And Phavorinus and Pollux use, *katabapton*, which on all hands is allowed most emphatically to signify *dipping, plunging, immersing*, as a synonymous word for *bapton* and *chronnus*, in English, *a dyer.*"

" This makes it necessary to suppose they dyed by *dipping*; as well as another word used by them in these cases, namely, *epsein*, to boil: *they boiled it in kettles*, says Aristotle; *and when the flowers are boiled long enough together, at length all becomes of a purple.*"

A most decisive passage to the same purpose, he thus translates from Plato de Republica, lib. iv. p. 636. " *The dyers, when they are about to dip a quantity of wool, to make it of a purple colour, cull out the whitest of the fleece, and prepare and wash it with a world of trouble, that it may the better take the grain; and then they dip it. The dye of things thus dipped is lasting and unchangeable, and cannot be fetched out or tarnished, either by fair water, or any preparations for the discharging of colours. But things which are not dyed after this manner, you know what they are; no matter what dye they are dipped in, they never look well; without this preparation they take but a nasty colour, and that is easily washed out too. And thus in like manner our choosing soldiers, and instructing them in music, and those exercises which consist in agility of body, you must imagine our design is only to make them the better receive the laws, which are a kind of dye,—that their temper being formed by a proper discipline, may be fixed and unalterable by terror, &c., and their tincture may not be washed out by any medicaments of the most powerfully expelling nature; as pleasure, which is stronger to this effect than any dye, as is likewise grief, fear, or desire, and the like.*"

Here is the most complete evidence, that both among the Greeks and Romans *dyeing* was usually performed by *dipping*. Indeed, nothing but perverseness can make a question of this, though there was no evidence of the fact from history. There is no other way in which fluids can be extensively applied in dyeing, but by dipping.

The truth of this fact is not in the least affected by the observation of Mr. Ewing, that *dyeing, staining*, and *painting* were originally similar operations, having been first suggested by the accidental bruising of fruits, &c. Though this were a fact recorded, instead of a conjecture, it could be of no service on this subject. Arts are not necessarily conducted in the way in which they were originally suggested. Whatever was the origin of *dyeing, dipping* was the common way of performing it as an art. It is the usual mode of performance, and not the accidental mode of discovery, that could give its name to the art. Dr. Cox's answer to this objection is quite satisfactory. " In reply to this," says he, " it might be sufficient to say, that in whatever manner the process was primarily discovered, the correct meaning of the term which expresses it, involves the idea of immersion, and did so at the very period when the contested words were in colloquial use. Pliny states, 'the Egyptians began by *painting* on white cloths, with certain drugs, which in themselves possessed no colour; but had the property of abstracting or absorbing colouring matters; but these cloths were afterwards *immersed in a diluted dyeing liquor*, of a uniform colour, and yet, when removed from it soon after, that they were found to be *stained* with indelible colours, differing from one another, according to the nature of the drugs which had been previously applied to different parts of the stuff.' In this passage, we are favoured with an intelligible distinction between *painting, immersing* (or the art of dyeing), and *staining;* yet we are required to admit that they were *one*.

Agreeably to the above view of the connexion between the secondary meaning of this word and the primary, we have a great number of the branches which have the same double import, from the same connexion. *Bamma*, sauce into which food is *dipped*,—and a *dye* into which things are to be dipped. *Baphe, dipping* and dyeing stuff, or the tincture received from dyeing. *Baphikos*, both *dipping* and *dyeing*,—and *baphike*, the dyer's art. *Baptos*, to be *dipped*, and to be *dyed*, &c. &c. In all these, there is no other common idea but mode : this is the link that connects these two things that are altogether different. If the same word has the same double meaning in so many of its branches, there must surely be at the bottom some natural relation between these meanings.

This view of the primary meaning of *bapto*, and the secondary, is greatly confirmed by the analogy of other languages. The same primary and secondary meanings are found in the corresponding word, in many other languages. The Septuagint translation gives *parabapta*, in Ezek. xxiii. 15. The Hebrew, to which this corresponds, signifies *dyed raiment*. Here we see that the Hebrew, which, as Dr. Gale observes, every one must own, signifies to *dip*, is used also for *dye*. This analogy is complete, and must arise from the same cause, namely, that among the Hebrews, as well as the Greeks and Romans, *dyeing* was commonly performed by *dipping*. The same word, in the Chaldee also, as Dr. Cox has observed, signifies both to *dip* and to *dye*.

In the Latin, also, the same word, *tingo*, signifies to *dip* and to *dye*. To this Mr. Ewing replies, that " *Tingo* is the Greek *teggo*, [pron. *tengo*,] which is very properly translated in the Lexicons, *madefacio, humido, mollio; I moisten, wet, soften,* or *mollify.*" That *tingo* is derived from *teggo* is undoubted; but to assert that it has all the significations of its parent, and that it has no other, would be as unphilological in theory, as it is inconsistent with fact. *Teggo* does not signify to *dye; tingo*, its derivative, has this signification. Where did it find it? *Teggo* signifies to moisten, &c.; *tingo* has not this signification. I am aware that *wash* is given as one of its meanings in the dictionaries, but I have seen as yet no authority for this from the classical use of the word. Besides, *wash* is not the same as *moisten, wet,* &c. I grant, indeed, that the word may be used when *washing, wetting, moistening, softening,* &c., is the consequence of the *dipping*. Still, however, this is not literally contained in the expression. Though any of these words might be given in certain situations as a translation, yet such a translation would not be literal. *Tingo* expresses appropriately *dipping* and *dyeing*, and these only.

Indeed, the meaning of *tingo* is to be learned from its use in the Latin language, and not from the use of its root in the Greek. When this is ascertained, then the philologist may look into its origin, to discover a correspondence. It may be expected that the root will contain some idea which has been a foundation to its use in the derived language. But a correspondence in all their meanings would often be looked for in vain. The derived word often drops every meaning of the root but one, and takes others that the root never possessed.

Does Mr. Ewing deny that *tingo* signifies to *dip?* If he does, the classical use of that word will contradict him. The *dipping* of the sun, moon, and stars, in the ocean, as we should express it, is in the language of the Latin poets expressed by *tingo.* If he does not deny this, his assertion in the above extract is nothing to his purpose.

If there was any need of authority with respect to the meaning of *tingo*, we have it in Tertullian. He understood the Latin language, and he uses *tingo* for *dip.* It is well known that he believed that proper baptism consisted in three immersions; and he translated the Greek word by *tingo.*

The same analogy is recognised by our own language; and though I would not say with some, that *dip* has *dye* as a secondary signification, yet in certain circumstances it may have this import by consequence,— "*colours dipped in heaven.*" Since, then, the analogy of so many languages connects *dipping* and *dyeing* by expressing them by the same word, why should not the same thing be supposed in the Greek? and *bapto*, as it has the secondary meaning of *dye*, have also the primary meaning of *dip?* It may be added, that we have the authority of the Latin poets, to translate *bapto* by *tingo*, in the sense of *dipping.* As the Greek poets apply *bapto* to the setting of a constellation, or its *dipping* in the ocean, the Latin poets express the same thing by *mergo* and *tingo.*

SECTION X.—Having viewed *bapto* in every light in which it can assist us on this subject, I shall now proceed to exhibit the examples of the occurrence of *baptizo* itself, which, to the utter exclusion of the root, is applied to the Christian rite. BAPTO, the root, I have shown to possess two meanings, and two only, to *dip* and to *dye*. BAPTIZO, I have asserted, has but one signification. It has been formed on the idea of the primary meaning of the root, and has never admitted the secondary. Now, both these things have been mistaken by writers on both sides of this controversy. It has been generally taken for granted, that the two words are equally applicable to baptism; and that they both equally signify to *dye*. Both of them are supposed, in a secondary sense, to signify to *wash* or *moisten.* I do not admit this with respect to either. I have already proved this with respect to BAPTO; the proof is equally strong with respect to BAPTIZO. My position is, THAT IT ALWAYS SIGNIFIES TO DIP; NEVER EXPRESSING ANYTHING BUT MODE. Now, as I have all the lexicographers and commentators against me in this opinion, it will be necessary to say a word or two with respect to the authority of lexicons. Many may be startled at the idea of refusing to submit to the unanimous authority of lexicons, as an instance of the boldest scepticism. Are lexicons, it may be said, of no authority? Now, I admit that lexicons are an authority, but they are not *an ultimate authority*. Lexicographers have been guided by their own judgment in examining the various passages in which a word occurs: and it is still competent for every man to have recourse to the same sources. *The meaning of a word must ultimately be determined by an actual inspection of the passages in which it occurs, as often as any one chooses to dispute the judgment of the lexicographer.* The use of a word, as it occurs in the writers of authority in the English language, is an appeal that any man is entitled to make against the decision of Dr. Johnson himself. The practice of a language is the House of Lords, which is competent to revise the decisions of all dictionaries.

But though it is always lawful to appeal from lexicons to the language itself, it is seldom that there can be any necessity for this, with respect to the primary meaning of words. Indeed, with respect to the primary meaning of common words, I can think of no instance in which lexicons are to be suspected. This is a feature so marked, that any painter can catch, and faithfully represent. Indeed, I should consider it the most unreasonable scepticism, to deny that a word has a meaning, which all lexicons give as its primary meaning. On this point, I have no quarrel with the lexicons. There is the most complete harmony among them, in representing *dip* as the primary meaning of *bapto* and *baptizo*. Except they had a turn to serve, it is impossible to mistake the primary meaning of a word commonly used. Accordingly, Baptist writers have always appealed, with the greatest confidence, to the lexicons even of Pædobaptist writers. On the contrary, their opponents often take refuge in a supposed sacred or scriptural use, that they may be screened from the fire of the lexicons.

It is in giving secondary meanings, in which the lines are not so easily discovered, that the vision of the lexicographers is to be suspected. Nor is it with respect to real secondary meanings that they are likely to be mistaken. Their peculiar error is in giving, as secondary meanings, what are not properly meanings at all. The same objection that I have to lexicons, with respect to this word, I have not with respect to it alone, but with respect to almost all words to which they assign a great variety of meanings. I do not exclude Dr. Johnson himself from this censure.

It may appear strange to some, that the most learned men can be imposed upon in this matter; and with respect to words which they find in use in what they read, think that they have meanings which they have not. But a little consideration of the nature of the mistake will explain this matter. I admit that the meaning which they take out of the word, is always implied in the passage where the word occurs. But I deny that this meaning is expressed by the word. It is always made out by implication, or in some other way.

To explain this point more clearly, I shall lay down a canon, and by this I mean a first principle in criticism. That which does not contain its own evidence is not entitled to the name of a critical canon. I do not request my readers to admit my canon. I insist on their submission

—let them deny it if they can. My canon is, THAT IN CERTAIN SITUA-
TIONS, TWO WORDS, OR EVEN SEVERAL WORDS, MAY, WITH EQUAL PRO-
PRIETY, FILL THE SAME PLACE, THOUGH THEY ARE ALL ESSENTIALLY
DIFFERENT IN THEIR SIGNIFICATIONS. The physician, for instance, may,
with equal propriety and perspicuity, say either "dip the bread in the
wine," or, "moisten the bread in the wine." Yet this does not import
that *dip* signifies to *moisten*, or that *moisten* signifies to *dip*. Each of
these words has its own peculiar meaning, which the other does not
possess. *Dip the bread* does not say *moisten the bread*, yet it is known
that the object of the dipping is to *moisten*. Now it is from ignorance
of this principle that lexicographers have given meanings to words which
they do not possess; and have thereby laid a foundation for evasive
criticism on controverted subjects, with respect to almost all questions.
In Greek it might be said with equal propriety, *deusai en oino*, or *bapsai
en oino*, "moisten in wine, or dip in wine;" and from this circumstance
it is rashly and unphilosophically concluded that one of the meanings
of *bapto* is to *moisten*.

Let it be remembered that my censure lies against the critical exactness of lexicographers, and not against their integrity, or even their
general learning and ability. I go farther,—I acquit them of misleading
their readers with respect to the general meaning of the passages, on the
authority of which they have falsely assigned such secondary meanings.
The ideas which they affix to such words, are implied in the passage,
though not the meaning of the words out of which they take them. But
this, which is harmless with respect to most cases, is hurtful in all points
of controversy, as it gives a foundation for the evasive ingenuity of
sophistry in the defence of error. It may be of no importance to correct
the lexicographer, who, from finding the expressions *deusai en oino* and
bapsai en oino employed for the same thing, asserts that here *bapsai* signifies to *moisten*. But it is of great importance when the error is brought
to apply to an ordinance of Christ. Besides, it introduces confusion into
language, and makes the acquisition of it much more difficult to learners.
The mind must be stored with a number of different meanings in which
there is no real difference. What an insurmountable task would it be
to master a language, if, in reality, words had as many different meanings as lexicons represent them! Parkhurst gives six meanings to
baptizo. I undertake to prove that it has but one; yet he and I do not
differ about the primary meaning of this word. I blame him for giving
different meanings, when there is no real difference in the meaning of
this word. He assigns to it figurative meanings. I maintain, that in
figures there is no different meaning of the word. It is only a figurative
application. The meaning of the word is always the same. Nor does
any one need to have a figurative application explained in any other
way, than by giving the proper meaning of the word. When this is
known, it must be a bad figure that does not contain its own light. It
is useless to load lexicons with figurative applications, except as a concordance.

Polybius, vol. iii. p. 311 ult. applies the word to soldiers passing
through water, *immersed up to the breast*. Here surely the word cannot

mean *pouring or sprinkling*. The soldiers in passing through the water were *dipped* as far as the breast. Strabo also applies the word to Alexander's soldiers marching a whole day through the tide, between the mountain Climax and the sea, (lib. xiv. p. 982,) *baptized up to the middle*. Surely this baptism was *immersion*.

Plutarch, speaking of a Roman general, dying of his wounds, says, that having *dipped* his hand in blood, he wrote the inscription for a trophy. Here the mode of the action cannot be questioned. The instrument of writing is *dipped* in the colouring fluid.

Diodorus Siculus, speaking of the sinking of animals in water, says, that when the water overflows, " many of the land animals, *immersed* in the river, perish." This baptism also is *immersion*. The whole land was overwhelmed with water. This itself, upon a principle before explained, might be called a baptism or immersion, in perfect consistency with the modal meaning of the word. However, it is not the land, but the land animals, that are here said to be *baptized*. These would at first swim, but they would soon *sink*, and be entirely *immersed*. There is here then no catachrestic extension of the word, as in the cases which I have illustrated in another place. The *sinking* of animals in water is here called *baptism*. What then is *baptism* but *immersion ?* Upon the principle of giving secondary meanings to words, which has been resisted by me, *drown* might be given as an additional meaning to *baptizo*, from the authority of this passage. As the animals were *drowned* by immersion, this immersion might be called *drowning*.

Lucian uses the word in a like case, and with circumstances that explain the former example. Towards the end of the dialogue, he makes Timon, the man-hater, say, that if he saw a man carried down the stream, and crying for help, he would *baptize* him—" *If in winter, the river should carry away any one with its stream, and the person with outstretched hands should beg to be taken out, that he should drive him from the bank, and plunge him headlong, so that he would not be able again to lift up his head above water.*" Here is a *baptism*, the mode of which cannot be mistaken. Timon's *baptism* was certainly *immersion*. To resist such evidence, requires a hardihood which I do not envy. Having such examples before my eyes, I cannot resist God, to please men. To attempt to throw doubt on the meaning of the word *baptizo*, is as vain as to question the signification of the word *dip*. The latter is not more definitely expressive of mode in the English, than the former is in Greek. The only circumstance that has enabled men to raise a cloud about *baptizo* is, that it belongs to a dead language. There never was a word in any language, the meaning of which is more definite, or which is capable of being more clearly ascertained.

The sinner is represented by Porphyry, (p. 282,) as *baptized* up to his head, in Styx, a celebrated river in hell. Is there any question about the mode of this *baptism?*

Dr. Gale gives some striking examples from Strabo. " Strabo," says he, " is very plain in several instances: Speaking of the lake near Agrigentum, a town on the south shore of Sicily, now called Gergenti, he says, *things which otherwise will not swim, do not sink in the water of the lake, but float like wood.* And there is a rivulet in the south parts of Cappadocia, he tells us, *whose waters are so buoyant, that if an arrow is thrown in, it will hardly sink or be dipped* into them." "In another place, ascribing the fabulous properties of the asphaltites to the lake Sirbon, he says, *the bitumen floats atop, because of the nature of the water, which admits no diving; for if a man goes into it, he cannot sink, or be dipped, but is forcibly kept above.*" Now, in these several passages, the modal meaning of the word is confirmed in so clear, express, and decisive a manner, that obstinacy itself cannot find a plausible objection. Things that sink in other water, will not sink or be baptized in the lake near Agrigentum. This is mode, and nothing but mode. It is immersion, and nothing but immersion. *Sprinkling,* and *pouring,* and *popping,* and *dropping,* and *wetting,* and *washing,* and *purifying,* and *imbuing,* and *dedicating,* and *devoting,* and *consecrating,* with all the various meanings that have ever been forced on this word, are meanings invented merely to serve a purpose. And if the sinking of an arrow in water is called its baptism, what can baptism mean but immersion? If, when the buoyancy of water will not suffer a person to sink, the idea is expressed by *baptizo,* what can baptism be but an operation of the same nature with *sinking* or *diving,* which are used here as nearly synonymous terms with that which signifies to baptize? It may as well be said that *sprinkling* or *pouring,* is *sinking* or *diving,* as that it is baptism.

Two Greek critics are quoted by Dr. Gale, as applying the word in exhibiting the beauty of Homer's representation of the death of one of his heroes : *"He struck him across the neck with his heavy sword, and the whole sword became warm with blood."* On this, Pseudo Didymus says, that the sword is represented as *dipped* in blood. And Dionysius says, *"In that phrase, Homer expresses himself with the greatest energy, signifying that the sword was so dipped in blood, that it was even heated by it."*

"Heraclides Ponticus," says Dr. Gale, "a disciple of Aristotle, may help us also in fixing the sense of the word; for, moralizing the fable of Mars being taken by Vulcan, he says, *Neptune is ingeniously supposed to deliver Mars from Vulcan, to signify, that when a piece of iron is taken red hot out of the fire, and put into water (baptizetai,) the heat is repelled and extinguished, by the contrary nature of water.*" Here we see that the immersion of hot iron in water, for the purpose of cooling it, is denominated *a baptism.*

Themistius, Orat. IV. p. 133, as quoted by Dr. Gale, says, "The pilot cannot tell but he may save one in the voyage that had better be drowned, sunk into the sea." Such a baptism, surely, would be immersion.

The word occurs in the Greek translation of the Old Testament, and is faithfully rendered *dip* in our version. 2 Kings, v. 14. *Naaman went down, and dipped himself seven times in Jordan.* Here bathing in a river is called *baptism.* What more do we want, then, to teach us the mode of this ordinance of Christ? If there was not another passage of Scripture to throw light on the institution, as far as respects mode, is not this, to every teachable mind, perfectly sufficient? But it seems, we are crying victory before the field is won. This passage, which we think so decisive, has a far different aspect to others. On the contrary, it is made to afford evidence against us. Well, this is strange indeed; but ingenuity has many shifts. Let us see how artifice can involve the passage in a cloud. Nothing is more easy. Does not the prophet command Naaman to *wash?* if, then, he obeyed this command by *baptizing* himself, *baptizing* must signify *washing*. For the sake of argument, I will grant this reasoning, for a moment. If then, this is so, go, my brethren, and wash the person to be baptized, as you think Naaman washed himself, from head to foot. This will show that you respect the example. In what manner soever the water was applied to Naaman, he was bathed all over. If the word signifies to wash the whole body, who but the Pope himself would take on him to substitute the sprinkling of a few drops, in the place of this universal washing?

But I do not admit the reasoning, that, from this passage, concludes that *baptizo* signifies to wash, although no instance can be produced more plausible in favour of that opinion. This passage is a complete illustration of my canon. The two words, *louo* and *baptizo*, are here used interchangeably, yet they are not of the same signification. Not of the same signification! it may be asked, with surprise. Elisha commands him to *wash;* he obeys by *baptizing* himself; must not *baptizing*, then, be *washing?* I think none of my opponents will wish a stronger statement of their objection than I have made for them. But my doctrine remains uninjured by the assault. The true philologist will not find the smallest difficulty in reconciling this passage to it. The words *louo* and *baptizo* have their own peculiar meanings even here, as well as every where else, without the smallest confusion . To *baptize* is not to *wash;* but to baptize *in a river or in any pure water*, implies washing, and may be used for it in certain situations. If Naaman *dipped* himself in Jordan, he was *washed*. It comes to the same thing, whether a physician says, *bathe yourself every morning in the sea*, or, *dip yourself every morning in the sea*, yet the words *bathe* and *dip* do not signify the same thing. We see, then, that we can make the very same use of our modal word *dip*, that the Greeks made of their *baptizo*. No man who understands English, will say that the word *dip* and the word *bathe* signify the same thing, yet, in certain situations, they may be used indifferently. Persons at bath may ask each other, did you *dip* this morning? or did you *bathe* this morning? To *dip* may apply to the *defiling* of any thing, as well as to *washing*. It expresses no more than the mode. It is the situation in which it stands, and the word with which it is construed, that determine the object of the application of the mode. To *dip* in pure water, is to wash; to dip in colouring matter, is to dye; to dip into mire, is to defile. None of these ideas, however, are in the word *dip* itself. No word could determine mode, according to the principles of criticism employed by writers on this subject.

The error in this criticism is that which I have before exposed. It supposes that, if in any circumstances two words can be used interchangeably, they must signify the same thing; and that controversialists are at liberty to reciprocate their meanings, as often as the necessity of their cause demands it. This is a source of error more fruitful in false criticism, than any other of its numerous resources. There is a speciousness in it that has imposed on lexicographers, critics, and commentators. They have universally, so far as I know, taken as a first principle, that which is a mere figment.

The Sibylline verse concerning the city of Athens, quoted by Plutarch in his Life of Theseus, most exactly determines the meaning of *baptizo*.

"Thou mayest be dipped, O bladder! but thou art not fated to sink."

The remark of Vossius and Turretine upon this is: "Hence it ap pears that *baptizein* is more than *epipolazein*, which is to swim lightly *on the surface*, and less than *dunein*, which is *to go down to the bottom*, so as to be destroyed." In the latter part of this distinction, they are certainly mistaken, as to both verbs. *Baptizein* may be applied to what goes to the bottom and perishes; and *dunein* very frequently applies to things that sink without destruction. It is the usual word applied to the setting of the sun, or its apparent sinking in the ocean; and it is the word which Homer applies to the sinking of the marine deities who live in the bottom of the sea. Indeed, the word has no more destruction in it than *baptizo* itself, which is occasionally applied to the sinking of ships. The matter of fact is, that whether the sinking object is destroyed or not, is learned from neither word, but from the circumstances in which it is used. If *baptizein* is applied to a ship going to the bottom, its destruction is known without being expressed by this word: if *dunein* is applied to Neptune, Thetis, or a sea nymph, it is in the same way known that there is no destruction. The obvious and characteristic distinction between the words is, that *dunein* is a neuter verb, signifying to *sink*, not to cause something else to sink. But a thing that sinks of itself, will doubtless *sink to the bottom*, if not prevented; and if it is subject to destruction by such sinking, it will perish. It is therefore characteristically applied to things that *sink to the bottom*. But *baptizein* signifies merely to dip, without respect to depth or consequence, and is as proper to the immersion of an insect on the surface of the deepest part of the ocean, as to the sinking of a ship or a whale in the same. Both words might in many cases be applied to the same thing indifferently, but in their characteristic meaning, as in the above verse, they are opposed. The expression in this verse is allegorical, literally referring to a bladder or leathern bottle, which, when empty, swims on the surface: if sufficiently filled, will dip, but will not sink. In this view, it asserts that the Athenian state, though it might be occasionally overwhelmed with calamities, yet would never perish. There is another sense which the expression might have, which is very suitable to the ambiguity of an oracle. "You may yourselves destroy the state, otherwise it is imperishable." A leathern bottle might be so filled as to force it to the bottom, though it would never sink of itself. Nothing can more decisively determine the exact characteristic import of *baptizein*, than this verse. It is *dip*, and nothing but *dip*.

Mr. Ewing's learned friend, in remarking on this word, falls into an error opposite to that of Vossius and Turretine. They make the word denote to *dip*, without going to the bottom: he makes it to *dip*, so as to continue under water. "Our Anti-pædo-baptist friends," says, he, " when they contend, that from the examples adduced by them, *immersion* is the only sense in which *baptizo*, in its literal acceptation, was employed, do not seem aware that almost all of these examples imply not a mere *dipping*, or immersion immediately followed by an emersion, but a continued and permanent immersion, a continuance under water." Now upon this I remark, first, that if there is one example in which it applies to an immersion, followed by an emersion, it is as good as a thousand to determine that it may apply to such immersions. I observe in the second place, that not one of the examples implies a continuance under water. When the word is applied to a drowning man or a sinking ship, it no more implies the permanence of the immersion, than when Plutarch uses it to signify the dipping of the hand in blood. The word has no reference to what follows the immersion; and whether the thing immersed lies at the bottom, or is taken up, cannot be learned from the word, but from the connexion and circumstances. It is a childish error to suppose, that we must have a model for Christian baptism in the meaning of the word that designates it. But if this argument had any foundation, what does the gentleman mean by it? Does he think that baptized persons ought to be drowned? This is surely very perverse. When it cannot be denied that the word denotes to *dip*, they endeavour to make it more than dipping. Then by all means let them have baptism in their own way. When we have brought them under the water, perhaps they will not make conscience of lying at the bottom.

The example referred to by Hammond is also irresistible. It is said of Eupolis, that being thrown into the sea, he was *baptized*. This baptism surely was immersion. This example shows us also, that the word may be applied when the object is destroyed, as well as when it is raised again out of the water, though in general, things dipped are taken immediately up after the dipping. The baptism spoken of by Plutarch, must also be immersion,—*Baptize yourself into the sea.*

The expression quoted by Hedericus from Heliod. b. v. is equally decisive, *to baptize into the lake.* And that from Æsop, *the ship being in danger of sinking.* If a ship sinking in the ocean is baptized, baptism must be immersion.

But the language of no writer can have more authority on this subject than that of Josephus. A Jew who wrote in the Greek language in the apostolic age, must be the best judge of the meaning of Greek words employed by Jews in his own time. Now this author uses the word frequently, and always in the sense of immersion. He uses it also sometimes figuratively with the same literal reference. Speaking of the purification from defilement by a dead body, he says, " and having *dipped* some of the ashes into spring water, they sprinkled," &c. Here we see the characteristic distinction between *baptizo* and *raino.* The one is to *dip*, the other to *sprinkle*. Antiq. l. iv. c. 4, p. 96.

On this example, Mr. Ewing's friend remarks :—" Now, upon looking into the Levitical law upon this particular point, (Numb. xix. 17,) we find the direction was, ' They shall take of the ashes, *and running water shall be put thereto.'* Here, then, the *putting running water to ashes,* is expressly termed *baptisantes tes nephras.''* Let the gentleman look a little more closely, and he will see that his observation is not correct. It is true that Numb. xix. 17, and the above passage from Josephus, refer to the same thing; but they do not relate it in the same manner. The Septuagint directs, that water shall be poured upon the ashes into a vessel; Josephus relates the fact as if the ashes were thrown into the water. Now this might make no difference as to the water of purification, but it was a difference as to the mode of preparing it. Nothing, then, can be farther from truth, than that the putting of the water on the ashes, according to Numb. xix. 17, is called by Josephus, *the baptizing of the ashes.* If Josephus speaks of the *baptizing* of the ashes, he represents the ashes as being put into the water, and not the water as being poured on the ashes. He uses the verb *eniemi* as well as *baptizo.* According to Josephus, then, the ashes were dipped, or put into the water; though, according to the Septuagint, the water was poured out into a vessel on the ashes.

Speaking of the storm that threatened destruction to the ship that carried Jonah, he says, " when the ship was on the point of *sinking,* or just about to be *baptized.''*—l. ix. c. 10, p. 285. What was the mode of this baptism?

In the history of his own life, Josephus gives an account of a remarkable escape which he had in a voyage to Rome, when the ship itself foundered in the midst of the sea: " For our ship having been baptized or immersed in the midst of the Adriatic sea," &c. Is there any doubt about the mode of this baptism? p. 626.

Speaking of the murder of Aristobulus, by command of Herod, he says, " The boy was sent to Jericho by night, and there, by command, having been immersed in a pond by the Galatians, he perished." Jewish War, Book I. p. 696. The same transaction is related in the Antiquities in these words: " Pressing him down always, as he was swimming, and *baptizing* him as in sport, they did not give over till they entirely drowned him." Can anything be more express and exact than this? Here the baptizers drowned the baptized person in the pool, where they were bathing. p. 458.

Describing the death of one Simon by his own hand, after he had killed his father, mother, wife, and children, lest they should fall into the hands of the enemy, he says, " He baptized or *plunged* his sword up to the hilt into his own bowels." The mode here is not doubtful; the sword was dipped in his body. We have previously seen *bapto* used in like circumstances, and *ebapse* would have been equally proper here, according to the observation already made, that words which have a characteristic distinction, may, in certain situations, be interchangeable. *Ebaptise, he caused it to dip,* may denote a greater effort than *ebapse, dipped it.* Jos. Bell. Jud. l. ii. p. 752.

A little afterwards, he applies the word to the sinking of a ship: " After this misfortune of Cestius, many of the Jews of distinction left the city, as people swim away from a *sinking* ship." Here a *sinking* ship is supposed to be baptized by *sinking.* p. 757.

He applies the word to the immersion of the ships which carried the people of Joppa, after being driven out of the city by the Romans: "The wave high raised, *baptized* them." Here is a sublime baptism. The surge, rising like mountains over the ships, immersed and sunk them to the bottom. The surge is the baptizer, the ships are baptized, and this baptism is the sinking of them to the bottom. Joseph. Jewish War, Book III. p. 737.

Towards the end of the same book, he thus speaks of those who perished in the lake of Gennesareth, having fled from the city of Tarichæ: "They were *baptized* or *sunk* with the ships themselves. p. 792. Here the Roman soldiers were the baptizers; and in executing this duty, they sunk both ships and men.

Hippocrates uses this word sometimes, and always in the sense for which I contend. We have seen that he uses *bapto* very often : I have not found *baptizo* more than four times. This circumstance sufficiently proves, that though the words are so nearly related, they are not perfectly identical in signification. The first occurrence of it is in p. 254 : " Dip it again in breast-milk and Egyptian ointment." He is speaking of a blister which was first to be dipped in the oil of roses, and if when thus applied, it should be too painful, it was to be dipped again in the manner above stated. The first dipping, as we have seen from a preceding quotation, is expressed by *bapsas*. This shows that, in the radical signification of dipping, these words are perfectly of the same import; and that though they have their characteristic distinction, there are situations in which they are interchangeable, where the characteristic difference may be expressed, but it is not necessary.

The same writer gives us the clearest insight into the meaning of this word, by twice comparing a peculiar kind of breathing in patients, to the breathing of a person after being immersed : " He breathed as persons breathe after being baptized." p. 340. The same comparison occurs again, p. 357, in the following words : " He breathed as persons breathe after being baptized." Surely unbelief must be obstinate, if this does not remove it. The breathing of persons under the disease referred to, is like the breathing of a person after baptism. Can anything, then, be more obvious, than that baptism is an immersion in water, even an immersion over head, so as to stop the breath till it is over?

Hippocrates applies the word also to a ship sinking, by being over-burthened : " Shall I not laugh at the man who baptizes or immerses his ship, by overlading it; then complains of the sea, that it ingulfs it with its cargo?" p. 532. What sort of baptism was this? Is it possible that a mind really thirsting for the knowledge of God's laws, can resist such evidence? Here we see *baptizo* not only most definitely signifying to immerse, but contrasted with another word, which signifies this with additional circumstances. *Baptizo* is used to denote that immersion that takes place when a ship is weighed down by its burthen, so as to be completely under water : *katabuthizo* signifies to make to go down into the abyss. Yet we have more than once met with instances in which *baptizo* itself is applied to a ship going to the bottom. But as I observed in such cases, it is not from the word itself that it is known that the ship goes to the bottom, but from the circumstances. It does not, by virtue of its own intrinsic meaning, denote going to the bottom, but to dip or immerse, without reference to depth. It may, then, be applied when the operation is extended to the bottom, as well as when it is confined to the surface. But when it is so applied, it does not definitely distinguish the idea of depth. When this is intended to be expressed, another word, as in the present case, is employed: *katabuthizo* definitely expresses *going down into the abyss.*

This word is found in Polybius, in circumstances that leave no doubt of its signification. He applies it to soldiers wading through deep water, and expressly limits its application to that part of the body which was covered with water: "The foot soldiers passed with difficulty, baptized or *immersed* up to the breast." Polyb. iii. c. 72. Does not this decisively determine the meaning of *baptizo?* They were not, indeed, plunged over head; but for this reason, a limitation is introduced, confining the application of the word to that part of the body which was under water. That only was baptized which was buried.

The same author gives us another example equally decisive: "They are of themselves baptized or immersed, and sunk in the marshes." v. c. 47. Here *baptizomai* is coupled with *kataduno*, as a word of similar import, though not exactly synonymous: the former denoting simple immersion; the latter, the sinking of the immersed object to the bottom.

Dio also affords evidence decisive of the same meaning: "They are entirely baptized, sunk, overwhelmed, or immersed." xxxviii. p. 84.

He applies it, as we have seen it employed by others, to the sinking of ships: "So great a storm suddenly arose through the whole country, that the boats were *baptized* or *sunk* in the Tiber." xxxvii. What, then, is baptism but immersion?

He applies it in the same way, l. 492: "How could it escape *sinking,* from the very multitude of rowers?" We see, then, that the classical writers in the Greek language, without exception, know nothing of this word in any other signification than that of *immersing.* They never apply it to any other mode. They no more apply it to *pouring* or *sprinkling,* &c. than to *warming* or *cooling.* Such significations have been conjured up by profane ingenuity, endeavouring to force the words of the Spirit of God into agreement with the long-established practices of men, in perverting the ordinances of God.

Porphyry applies the word to the heathen opinion of the baptism of the wicked in Styx, the famous lake of hell: "When the accused person enters the lake, if he is innocent, he passes boldly through, having the water up to his knees; but if guilty, having advanced a little, he is *plunged* or baptized up to the head."—De Styge, p. 282. The baptism of Styx, then, is an immersion of the body up to the head. The part not dipped is expressly excepted.

Diodorus Siculus applies the word to the sinking of beasts carried away by a river: "The most of the land animals being caught by the river, *sinking or being baptized,* perish; but some escaping to the higher grounds, are saved."—I. p. 33. Here to be *baptized,* is to sink in water. This example also confirms my observation, that though when *sinking to the bottom,* or *sinking in the great deep* is designed to be distinguished from simple immersion, *baptizo* could not suit the situation; but another word, such as *kataduno, katabuthizo, katapontizo,* &c., is used : yet *baptizo* will apply to the deepest immersion, and to destruction by immersion, when there is no contrast, and when the depth and destruction are known from other words or circumstances in the connexion. *Baptizo* denotes simple immersion, yet it may be used in circumstances when that immersion is certainly known to *be going to the bottom,* and *being destroyed.*

Section XI.—There are instances in which the word is by some translated *wash,* and in which the general meaning may be thus well enough expressed in a free version. Still, however, the word, even in such situations, does not express the idea of washing, but has its own peculiar meaning of *mode,* the idea of *washing* being only a consequence from the *dipping.* There are some cases in which it is pretended that it must apply to purification by sprinking, &c. Now, as I am pledged to show that the word does not signify to *wash in any manner,* I am still more bound to show that it does not denote purification by *sprinkling.* I shall therefore now attend to this part of the subject.

In Ecclesiasticus xxxiv. 30, it is said, " He that washeth himself because of a dead body, and toucheth it again, what availeth his washing?" Now as *baptizomenos* is the word here used, and as from Numb. xix. 18, we learn that such a person was to be purified by sprinkling, does it follow that *baptizo* must signify to sprinkle, or to purify by sprinkling? He that wishes to see this objection honestly stated in all its strength, and refuted in the most triumphant manner, may consult Dr. Gale's Reflections on Dr. Wall's History of Infant Baptism. But the answer must be obvious to every person who consults Numb. xix. 19, which shows that sprinkling was but a part of that purification, and that the unclean person was also *bathed in water.* It is this *bathing* that is effected by *baptism.* The passage in question ought to be translated,—" He that *dippeth* or *baptizeth* himself because of a dead body, and toucheth it again, what availeth his *dipping* or *baptism?*" The word *baptizo* has here its appropriate meaning, without the smallest deviation.

Besides, had there been no immersion or bathing of the whole body enjoined in Numbers, I should utterly despise this objection. Though God had not made bathing of the body a part of this purification, might not the traditions of the elders have made the addition? And would not this have been sufficient authority for the author of this apocryphal book to make a ground of his reasoning? When I have proved the meaning of a Greek word, by the authority of the whole consent of Greek literature, I will not surrender it to the supposition of the strict adherence of the Jewish nation, in the time of the writing of the Apocrypha, to the Mosaic ritual. We know that they made many additions, and that these were esteemed as of equal authority with the rites of Moses.

For a very full and interesting discussion of Luke xi. 38, and Mark vii. 4, let the reader consult Dr. Gale, p. 125. Here he will find a triumphant answer to every quibble from Dr. Wall. But as the text itself is perfectly sufficient for my purpose, I shall not swell my volume with quotations from that learned writer. In our version, Luke xi. 38, *ebaptisthe* is translated wash. " And when the Pharisee saw it, he marvelled that he had not first washed before dinner." The objection is, does not *baptizo*, then, sometimes denote *to wash*? Nay, farther, as the Jews washed the hands by having water poured on them, and as this passage respects the washing of the hands, is there not here evidence that the word in question sometimes signifies *to wash by pouring*? This surely is as strong a statement of their objection as our opponents can wish. Yet, in all its plausibility, I despise it. Even here, the word signifies *to dip*, and not *to wash*. Dipping is the thing expressed; *washing* is the consequence, known by inference. It is dipping, whether it relates to the hands or the whole body. But many examples from the Jews, and also from the Greeks, it is said, prove that the hands were washed by pouring water on them by a servant; and I care not that ten thousand such examples were brought forward. Though this might be the usual mode of washing the hands, it might not be the only mode, which is abundantly sufficient for my purpose. The possibility of this is enough for me; but Dr. Gale has proved from Dr. Pococke, that the Jews sometimes washed their hands by *dipping*. People of distinction might have water poured on their hands by servants, but it is not likely that this was the common practice of the body of the people, in any nation. The examples from Homer cannot inform us with respect to the practice of the common people.

But I say this without any view to my argument in this place, for it is evident that the word does not here refer to the washing of the hands. It may apply to any part, as well as to the whole; but whenever it is used without its regimen expressed, or understood in phrases much used, it applies to the whole body. When a part only is dipped, the part is mentioned, or some part is excepted, as is the case with *louo*. The passage, then, ought to have been translated,—" And when the Pharisee saw it, he marvelled that he was not immersed before dinner." The Pharisees themselves, on some occasions, would not eat till they had used the bath, and this Pharisee might expect still more eminent devotion from Jesus. Indeed, to use the bath before dinner, was a very common practice in eastern countries; and the practice would be still more in vogue with those who considered it a religious purification. But there is no need to refer to the practice of the time, nor to ransack the writings of the Rabbins, for the practice of the Jews. We have here the authority of the Holy Spirit for the Jewish custom. He uses the word *baptizo*, and that word signifies *to dip*, and only *to dip*. If I have established the acceptation of this word by the consent of use, even an inexplicable difficulty in this case would not affect the certainty of my conclusions. But the difficulty is not inexplicable. What should hinder the word to have here its usual import?

Mark vii. 4, our translators render, "except they wash, they eat not." Now, my opponents may say, does not *baptizo* here signify to wash? I answer, No. Dipping is the thing expressed; but it is used in such circumstances as to imply *washing*. The *washing* is a consequence from the dipping. It ought to have been translated, "except they dip themselves, they eat not." In the preceding context, we are told that usually they do not eat without washing their hands. Here we are told that when they come from market, they eat not till they are *dipped or baptized*. Dr. Campbell's notion, that *nipto* and *baptizo* here both refer to the hands, the one to washing by having water poured on them, and the other by dipping them, I do not approve. For, though *baptizo* will apply to the dipping of the hands, as well as to the dipping of the whole body, yet when no part is mentioned or excepted, the whole body is always meant. His view of the matter I consider nothing but an ingenious conceit, without any authority from the practice of the language. *Nipto* cannot denote a peculiar mode of washing, in distinction from another mode. Besides, to wash anything by mere dipping, is not so thorough a washing as may be expressed by *nipto*. Now, if the words both refer to the washing of the hands, the first will be the best washing, which is contrary to Dr. Campbell's supposition. Dr. Campbell, indeed, with Pearce and Wetstein, understands *pugme* of a handful of water. But they produce no example in which *pugme* has this signification, and therefore the opinion has no authority. Indeed, there is a self-contradiction in the opinion of these learned writers on this point. *Pugme* they properly consider as signifying the fist, or shut hand; and from this, suppose that the word here denotes as much water as may be held in the hollow of the hand, with the fingers closed. But a fist will hold no water; and the hand with the fingers closed so as to hold water, is no fist. With as little reason can it be supposed to signify, as Dr. Campbell suggests, that *pugme* denotes the manner of washing, with reference to the form of the hands when they wash each other. In such circumstances, neither of them is a fist, but still less the washing hand. In this operation the hands infold one another, and if there is anything like a fist, it is the two hands united. Dr. Campbell quotes, with approbation, the remark of Wetstein : "*baptizesthai* est modus acquæ immergere, *niptesthai* manibus affundere." But the former does not signify to dip *the hands*, except the regimen is expressed ; and though the latter applies to pouring water on the hands, it will equally apply to washing out of a basin. Parkhurst, indeed, translates the phrase ; "*to wash the hands with the fist*, that is by rubbing water on the palm of one hand, with the doubled fist of the other." This distinguishes the infolded hand as the rubbing hand, but, as a matter of fact, I believe that, though both hands may be said to rub on each other, yet the infolding hand is distinguished as the rubbing hand. *To wash the hand with the fist*, is not an expression which would be likely to be chosen to express the operation of washing the hands. The palm of one hand is applied to the palm of the other ; and when the palm of one hand is applied to the back of the other, the intention is to cleanse the latter, and not by the latter to cleanse the former. Besides, the inside hand is seldom closed into a fist. I prefer, therefore, the explanation of Lightfoot, which is both most agreeable to the meaning of *pugme*, and to the Jewish traditions. He understands it as denoting *the hand as far as the fist extended*. This is agreeable to the definition of the word by Pollux : "If you shut your hand, the outside is called *pugme :*" and it is agreeable to the Jewish traditions, one of which he shows enjoins such a washing. The contrast then, here, is between the washing of the hands up to the wrist, and the immersion of the whole body. Dr. Campbell, indeed, remarks, that "it ought to be observed, that *baptisontai* is not in the passive voice, but the middle, and is contrasted with *nipsontai*, also in the middle; so that by every rule, the latter must be understood actively as well as the former." But though I understand *baptisontai* in the middle voice, I do not acknowledge that this is necessarily required from a contrast with *nipsontai*. Let the meaning of this passage be what it will, the active, passive, and middle voices, might be so associated. I know no rule that requires such a conformity as Dr. Campbell here demands. It might be said of Christians, *they eat the Lord's supper, and they are baptized.* The contrast between *nipsontai* and *baptisontai* in the passage referred to, does not require the same voice. *Nipsosi*, the active itself, might have been used, and *baptisontai* in the passive. I understand it in the middle, not because *nipsontai* is middle, but because in the baptism referred to, every one baptized himself. Had it been as in Christian baptism, I should understand it in the passive.

Mr. Ewing translates the passage thus : "For the Pharisees and all the Jews, except they wash their hands oft, eat not, holding the tradition of the elders. And *even when they have come* from a market, unless they baptize, they eat not," &c. But the word *oft*, as a translation of *pugme*, is liable to the objections of Dr. Campbell, which I need not here repeat. Mr. Ewing surely should have obviated them. Besides, neither Mr. Ewing, nor any person, so far as I know, has produced one example, in which *pugme* confessedly signifies *oft*. Without this the translation has no authority. Mr. Ewing translates *kai, and even,* for which there is no authority. That particle often signifies *even*, but never *and even*. Mr. Ewing's translation makes their baptism after the market, inferior to the washing before mentioned. But this certainly reverses the true meaning. Defilement certainly was understood to be increased by the market. Mr. Ewing indeed endeavours to give a turn to this, but it is a complete failure. "And in order to show how strictly they hold this tradition," he says, "they observed it, not merely on their more solemn occasions, but even when they had just come from places of public resort, and from the ordinary intercourse of life." But where did Mr. Ewing find *their more solemn occasions?* This is apocryphal, and, like the Apocrypha, it contradicts the genuine Scriptures. The evangelist declares, that *except they wash their hands, they eat not.* This implies, that they never sat down to table, even at their ordinary meals, without washing. The baptism, after market, then, must have been a greater or more extensive purification. Mr. Ewing supposes that the word *baptize* is used here to show that the washing was not for cleanliness, but was a religious custom. But this is shown sufficiently, if *baptize* were not used. It is directly stated, that this washing was obedience to the tradition of the elders. I observe farther, that if the washing was not by other circumstances known to be a religious custom, this would not have been known by the word *baptizo* more than by *nipto*.

Besides, *baptisontai* does not here explain or limit *nipsontai*. If the latter could not, with the words construed with it, be known to designate a religious observance, it can receive no assistance from the former. Mr. Ewing understands both words as referring to the same thing, washing the hands by water poured on them. Why, then, is *nipto* changed for *baptizo?* Surely the change of the word intimates a change of the meaning in such circumstances. "They eat not, except they wash their hands. And after market they eat not, except they *baptize.*" Surely no person, who has not a purpose to serve, would suppose that *baptize* here meant the very same thing with *wash the hands.* But if it is insisted that *baptize* here is distinguished from *nipto* as a religious washing, then how will it determine that *nipto* here refers to a religious washing? If it is here so distinguished from *nipto*, then the washing denoted by *nipto* cannot be a religious washing. This would import, that the washing of the hands first spoken of by *nipto* was not a religious washing; and that the latter washing was distinguished from the former by this. The meaning then would be : " Except they wash their hands, they eat not; and when they have come from the market, they eat not until they have washed their hands religiously."

But as respects my argument, I care not whether *baptisontai* here refers to the hands or the whole body; it is perfectly sufficient for me, if it here admits its usual meaning. Let it be here observed, and never let it be forgotten, *that with respect to the meaning of a word in any passage, the proof that it has such a meaning always lies upon him who uses it in that meaning as an argument or objection; for this obvious reason, that if it is not proved, it is neither argument nor objection.* Now if I choose to bring this passage as an argument, or as additional evidence, I must prove its meaning. In this way I have viewed it as having weight : but if I choose to give up its evidence, and stand on the defence, my antagonist is bound to prove his view of it as a ground of his objection, and my cause requires no more of me than to show that the word in such a situation is capable of the meaning for which I contend. For it is evident, that if it may have such a meaning, it cannot be certain that it has not that signification. Many a passage may contain the disputed word in such circumstances as to afford no definite evidence. It cannot, in such a passage, be used as proof: it is enough, if it admits the meaning contended for. This is a grand law of controversy, attention to which will save the advocates of truth much useless toil; and keep them from attempting to prove, what it may not be possible to prove, and what they are not required to prove. It will also assist the inquirer to arrive at truth. Now, in the present case, except Mr. Ewing proves that *baptisontai must* here signify the *pouring of water* upon the hands, or that it cannot refer to the dipping of the hands or the body, he has done nothing. I bring passages without number, to prove that the word *must* have the meaning for which I contend. No passage could be a valid objection against my conclusion, except one in which it *cannot have* that signification. These observations I state as self-evident truth : the man who does not perceive their justness, cannot be worth reasoning with.

But why should it be thought incredible, that the Pharisees immersed themselves after market? If an Egyptian, on touching a swine, would run to the river and plunge in with his clothes, is it strange that the superstitious Pharisees should *immerse* themselves after the pollution of the market?

Dr. Gale, however, on the authority of the Syriac, Arabic, Ethiopic, and Persic versions, is inclined to understand the passage as relating to the dipping of the things bought in the market. But as I decidedly prefer the other sense, I will not avail myself of this resource. I abhor the practice of catching at any forced meaning that serves a temporary purpose, at the expense of setting loose the meaning of God's word. I do not wish to force a favourite mode of baptism on the Scriptures, but I will implicitly submit my mind to the mode that God has appointed. I have not a wish on the subject, but to know the will of Christ.

What our version, Mark vii. 4, calls the *washing*, &c., the original calls, *the baptisms* of cups, pots, &c. It may then be asked, does not this imply that this word signifies washing? But I answer, as before, that though these things were *dipped* for *washing*, yet *dipping* and *washing* are not the same thing. The *washing* is not expressed, but is a mere consequence of the *dipping*. The passage, then, ought to be translated *immersions*. The purification of all the things specified, except the last, was appointed by the law, Levit. xi. 32, to be effected by being put under water. But with respect to the *klinai*, or beds, Mr. Ewing asserts that the translation *dippings* would be manifestly absurd. Now what is manfestly absurd cannot be true. If this assertion, then, is well founded, Mr. Ewing has opposed a barrier, which the boldest cannot pass. But why is this absurd? Let us hear his own words. " The articles specified in ver. 4, are all utensils and accommodations of the Jewish mode of eating, about which the evangelist was speaking; from the ' cups, pots, and brazen vessels' of the cook and the butler, to the ' beds' of the *triclinium*, or dining-room, for the use of the family and their guests. There were three only of these beds in one room. Each was commonly occupied by three persons, and sometimes by five or even more. Three such beds probably accommodated our Lord and his disciples at the last supper. They must have been of such a size, therefore, as to preclude the idea of their being immersed, especially being frequently immersed, as a religious ordinance." Now I will admit this account in every tittle, yet still contend that there is nothing like *an absurdity* in the supposition that the *couches* were immersed. The thing is quite possible, and who will say that the superstitious Pharisees might not practise it? It would indeed be a very inconvenient thing, but what obstacles will not superstition overcome? It would be a foolish thing; but who would expect anything but folly in will-worship? Such religious practice was indeed absurd, but it is an abuse of language to assert that it is *an absurdity* to say that the Pharisees immersed their couches. Let Mr. Ewing beware of using such language. If the Holy Spirit has asserted that the Pharisees *baptized* their couches, and if this word signifies *to immerse*, Mr. Ewing has asserted that the Holy Spirit has asserted an absurdity. This is no light matter. It is an awful charge on the Spirit of inspiration.

Dr. Wardlaw is equally rash on this point. He supposes that it is incredible that they *immersed* their beds. How is it incredible? Is the thing impossible? If not, its credibility depends on the testimony. But whether or not the Holy Spirit gives the testimony, depends on the meaning of the word. If from other passages we learn that it has this meaning, this passage cannot teach the contrary, if the thing is possible. Upon the principle of interpretation here recognised by Mr. Ewing and Dr. Wardlaw, we might reject every thing in history not suited to our own conceptions; or explain them away by paring down the meaning of words. This is the very principle of the Neological explanation of the Scripture miracles. The things are thought absurd in the obvious meaning of the words; and therefore the language must submit to accept a meaning suitable to the conceptions of the critics. Mr. Robinson thinks the common view of the exploit of Samson in killing such a multitude with the jaw-bone of an ass incredible, and he takes away the incredibility of the scriptural account, by explaining it of the tooth of a rock which Samson pulled down on his enemies. Dr. Wardlaw says, with respect to the immersion of beds, " he who can receive it, let him receive it." I say, he who dares to reject it, rejects the testimony of God. This is a most improper way to speak on the subject. If *immersion* is the meaning of the word, it is not optional to receive or reject it. Whether or not this is its meaning, must be learned from its history, not from the abstract probability or improbability of the immersion of beds. If the history of the word declares its meaning to be immersion, *the mere difficulty of immersing beds, in conformity to a religious tradition, cannot imply that it has another meaning here.* The principle, then, of this objection, and the language in which these writers state it, cannot be too strongly reprobated. If adopted on other questions respecting the will of God, it tends to set us loose from the authority of his word.

I will here reduce my observations on this point to the form of a canon. WHEN A THING IS PROVED BY SUFFICIENT EVIDENCE, NO OBJECTION FROM DIFFICULTIES CAN BE ADMITTED AS DECISIVE, EXCEPT THEY INVOLVE AN IMPOSSIBILITY. This is self-evident, for otherwise nothing could ever be proved. If every man's view of abstract probability were allowed to outweigh evidence, no truth would stand the test. The existence of God could not be proved. The Scriptures themselves could not abide such a trial. If my canon is not self-evident, let no man receive it; but if it is just, it overturns not only this objection, but almost all the objections that have been alleged against immersion in baptism. Besides, there is hardly any point of theological controversy in which it may not be useful. Many who are willing to admit it on the subject of baptism, may act contrary to it on other subjects. Indeed, there are few who do not in things of small moment overlook this principle.

In tracing the history of Jesus, we shall see how much of the opposition to his claims was founded on the principle which my canon reprobates. When he said that he was the bread that came down from heaven, the Jews murmured, and replied, " Is not this Jesus, the son of Joseph, whose father and mother we know? How is it then that he saith, I came down from heaven?" John vi. 42. Here was a difficulty that they thought insuperable. " We are sure he was born among us —he could not therefore have come from heaven." But there was a solution to this difficulty, had their prejudices permitted them to find it. It was possible, that though born on earth, as a man, he might come from heaven, as he was God. But they were glad to catch at the apparent inconsistency; and their prejudices would not allow them to attempt to vindicate themselves. This in fact is the very substance of one common objection to the deity of Christ. The Arians still collect all the passages that assert the human nature of Christ, and take it for granted that this is a proof that he is not God. Let our brethren take care that it is not on the same principle they allege this objection to immersion in baptism. Were there no wish to find evidence on one side only, would it be supposed that it is *absurd* or *incredible* that the superstitious Pharisees *immersed* even their couches?—Another striking instance of objecting on this principle we have, John vii. 41, 42. " Shall Christ come out of Galilee? Hath not the Scripture said, that Christ cometh of the seed of David, and out of the town of Bethlehem, where David was?" This would appear to them a noose from which he could not extricate himself—a difficulty that he could not solve. *The Scriptures assert, that the Christ will come out of Bethlehem, but this man has come out of Galilee.* Had they been as willing to see evidence in his favour, as evidence against him, they might have perceived that the agreement of these apparent contradictions was not impossible. The knowledge of his real history would have given the solution. But it was not a solution they wanted. In reading the history of Jesus also, it is not uninstructive to remark, that many things which appear to his enemies decisive evidence against him, had no weight at all with his friends. This discrepancy shows how much our sentiments are under the influence of our feelings, and consequently the guilt of unbelief, with respect to any part of the Divine counsel which we reject. Though we have no right to judge one another, we have a right, when God has given a revelation, to ascribe all ignorance of it to sin. I make this observation not merely with respect to the point now in debate, or to criminate my opponents. The observation applies to every error; and as no man has attained in every thing to truth, it applies to us all. I make the observation to incite my brethren on both sides of this subject, to search without prejudice— to inquire under the influence of an impression of great accountableness.

I will state farther, THAT IN PROVING THAT A THING IS NOT IMPOSSIBLE, THERE IS NO OBLIGATION TO PROVE THAT ANY OF THE POSSIBLE WAYS OF SOLUTION DID ACTUALLY EXIST. THE BARE POSSIBILITY OF EXISTENCE IS ENOUGH. This also is self-evident, and may be stated as a canon. Yet from inattention to this, the opponents of immersion are constantly calling on us to prove, that there were, in such and such places, things necessary for dipping. Mr. Ewing gauges the reservoirs and wells of Jerusalem, to show their insufficiency for immersion. He may then call on me to find a place sufficient to immerse a couch. But I will go on no such errand. If I have proved the meaning of the word, I will believe the Spirit of God, who tells me that the Pharisees baptized their beds, and leave the superstition and industry of the devotees to find or make such a place. Let the demand which our opponents in this instance make on us, be conceded to the infidel, and the Bible must be given up. In replying to difficulties started by the deist, the defender of Christianity thinks he has amply done his duty, when he shows that the solution is possible, without proving that the possible way of solution did actually exist. Indeed, many of the defenders of Christianity undertake too much, and lay too much stress on actual proof, with respect to the way in which difficulties may be removed. When such proof can be got, it is always right to produce it, more clearly to confound the infidel. But it is extremely injudicious to lay such a stress on these solutions, as if they were actually necessary. It ought always to be strongly stated, that such proof is more than the defence of truth requires. When writers think themselves remarkably successful in this way, they are not disinclined to magnify the importance of their discoveries, and are willing to rest a part of the evidence on their own success. This discovers more vanity than judgment, and more desire for the glory of discovery, than for the interests of the truths defended. When this happens, it is not strange that infidels are emboldened to make the unreasonable demand, which their opponents have voluntarily rendered themselves liable to answer. If I could prove that there was at Jerusalem a pond that could immerse the High Church of Glasgow, I would certainly bring forward my proof; but I would as certainly disclaim the necessity. To give an example. In opposition to Dr. Campbell's opinion, that Mark vii. 4, refers to the dipping of the hands, Mr. Ewing, as his proof, alleges, that " as far as he has observed, there is only one way of washing either the hands or the feet in Scripture, and that is, by pouring water upon them, and rubbing them as the water flows." Now, were I of Dr. Campbell's opinion on this passage, I would grant Mr. Ewing all this, yet abide by my position. It is very possible that all the other instances of washing the hands that are mentioned in Scripture may be such, yet a different way have been in existence on some occasions. And if the expression were *baptisosi tas cheiras*, this I would suppose not only possible, but undoubtedly true. No number of examples of one mode of washing the hands can prove that no other mode was ever practised. It is of vast importance in every controversy, to know what we are obliged to prove, and what is not necessary to our argument. From inattention to this, Mr. Ewing thinks he has defeated Dr. Campbell, when he has never touched him. His weapons fall quite on this side of the mark. Now, on this last point I differ from Dr. Campbell. I do not think that *baptisontai* refers to the dipping of the hands. Yet I would not use Mr. Ewing's arguments to disprove this. Indeed, were Dr. Campbell alive, he would not be so easily defeated. Mr. Ewing discredits his authority on the subject of *immersion* as the scriptural mode of baptism, by representing him as resting his opinion on Tertullian among the ancients, and Wetstein among the moderns. Nothing can be more unfair. He merely refers to Tertullian, to show the sense in which the word *baptizo* was understood by the Latin fathers, and quotes the opinion of Wetstein, with a general approbation of him as a critic, certainly beyond his deserts, and with respect to a criticism which I believe to be false. But Dr. Campbell was not a man to found his views on such authority. When he says, "I have heard a disputant of this stamp, in defiance of *etymology* and *use*, maintain that the word rendered in the New Testament *baptize*, means more properly to sprinkle than to plunge; and in defiance of all *antiquity*, that the former method was the earliest, and for many centuries the most general practice in *baptizing*," does he not found it on his own knowledge of *etymology* and *use*—on his own knowledge of *antiquity?* Will Mr. Ewing venture to say that Dr. Campbell was not well acquainted with the *etymology* and *use* of the word in question? From what modern must he receive instruction with respect to the antiquities of church history? It may be true, indeed, that Dr. Campbell has not done all for this subject that he might have done. But did he fail in what he attempted? Who would expect that in his situation he could have done more? Nor is his candour in confessing a mode of baptism to be primitive, which he did not adopt, to be ascribed to a vanity of patronising what he did not practise. Like many others, he may have thought that the mode was not essential to the ordinance. And I have no hesitation in affirming, that such an opinion is far less injurious to the Scriptures, than the attempt of those who will force their favourite mode out of the Scriptures, while even on the rack they will not make the confession. Such persons are obliged to give a false turn to a great part of Scripture, totally unconcerned in the controversy. Nay, they are obliged to do violence even to the classics. Popery itself is not obliged, on this point, to make such havoc of the word of God. It has a happy power of changing Scripture ordinances, and therefore, on this point, can confess the truth without injury to its system.

I am led to the defence of Dr. Campbell, not from a wish to have the authority of his name on my side on this question. In nat point of view, I do not need him. I consider myself as having produced such a body of evidence on this subject, that I am entitled to disregard the mere authority of names. I have appealed to a tribunal higher than the authority of all critics—TO USE ITSELF. I do not hold up Dr. Campbell as universally successful in his criticisms. Many of them I am convinced are wrong; and those who have in all things made our version of the Gospels conform to his, have done no service to the cause of Christ. His judgment is always to be respected, but often to be rejected. On some points of Christian doctrine, he was evidently but partially enlightened, and against some he has made his translation and criticisms to bear. But as a man of integrity—as a candid adversary—as a philosophic critic, he has few equals. With respect to the philosophy of language, he is immeasurably before all our Scripture critics. I bow to the authority of no man in the things of God, yet I cannot but reverence Dr. Campbell. I respect him almost as much when I differ from him, as when we are agreed. He looks into language with the eye of a philosopher, and in controversy manifests a candour unknown to most theologians. Mr. Ewing's censure of Dr. Campbell involves the great body of learned men : it is too notorious to need proof, that the most learned men in Europe, while they practised sprinkling or pouring, have confessed immersion to be the primitive mode.

But with respect to Mark vii. 4, though it were proved that the couches could not be immersed, I would not yield an inch of the ground I have occupied. There is no absolute necessity to suppose that the *klinai*, or beds, were the couches at table. The word, indeed, both in Scripture and in Greek writers, has this signification; but in both it also signifies the beds on which they slept. Now, if it were such beds that the Pharisees *baptized*, there is nothing to prevent their immersion. They were such that a man could take up from the street, and carry to his house, Matt. ix. 6.

Besides, as it is not said how often they purified in this manner, we are at liberty to suppose that it was only for particular kinds of uncleanness, and on occasions that did not often occur. Mr. Ewing, indeed, says, "there was, no doubt, a complete observance of the 'baptisms' of cups, and pots, and brazen vessels, and beds, at the feast of the marriage in Cana in Galilee." There is no doubt that at that feast there was a purification of all things, according to the custom of a wedding: but where did Mr. Ewing learn that it was *during the feast* that the couches were purified? The water-pots were, no doubt, for the purification usual at a wedding: but this does not indicate all Jewish purifications. The hands and the feet of the guests were washed, and very likely also, the vessels used at the feast: but that the couches were purified is not said, and is not likely. It is not necessary, even, that all things purified at a feast, should have been purified out of these water-pots. It is enough that they were suitable for the purification of some things. If there was anything to be purified which could not be purified in them, it may have been purified elsewhere. It is not said that all things were purified in these water-pots. Besides, it is not said that these water-pots were but once filled during the wedding feast. We may therefore fill them as often as we find necessary. I do not, therefore, find it at all necessary, with Mr. Ewing, to gauge these water-pots, in order to settle this question.

Mr. Bruce informs us, that in Abyssinia, the sect called Kemmont "wash themselves *from head to foot*, after coming from the market, or any public place, where they may have touched any one of a different sect from their own, esteeming all such unclean." Is it strange, then, to find the Pharisees, the superstitious Pharisees, immersing their couches for purification, or themselves after market? I may add, that the couches might have been so constructed, that they might be conveniently taken to pieces, for the purpose of purification. This I say, only for the sake of those who will not believe God without a voucher. For myself, it is perfectly sufficient that the Holy Spirit testifies that the Pharisees baptized themselves before eating, after market; and that they baptized their couches. It is an axiom in science, that no difficulty can avail against demonstration; and with me it is an axiom, that no difficulty entitles us to give the lie to the Spirit of inspiration.

In Heb. ix. 10, the word *baptismois* is translated *washings*. Is not this proof that the word signifies to wash? The reply to this has already been given, in showing the difference between *dip* and *wash*. The translation ought to be " different immersions," not " different washings." *Dipping* is the thing expressed, *washing* is a consequence. But Dr. Wardlaw observes, "that amongst the 'divers washings' of the old dispensation, referred to Heb. ix. 10, must surely be included all the various modes of Jewish purification; and consequently the *rantismata*, or *sprinklings*, which were the most numerous," p. 172. But how is this certain? Why should it be supposed that the *baptisms* under the law contained all the purifications required by the law? This is not said here, nor anywhere else in the Scriptures. There is no necessity to suppose that every thing enjoined in the law must be included in the things here mentioned. The apostle designs to illustrate merely by specification, not to give a logical abstract. But even were the *sprinklings* to be included in one or other of the things mentioned, it may be in the *carnal ordinances*. It is a very convenient way of proving any-thing, to take it for granted. Dr. Wardlaw here takes for granted the thing to be proved. The phrase "divers baptisms," must indicate the *sprinklings;* therefore baptism must signify sprinkling, as one of its meanings. But we deny that the "divers baptisms" include the *sprinklings*. The phrase alludes to the *immersion* of the different things that by the law were to be *immersed*. The greatest part of false reasoning depends on false first principles. Dr. Wardlaw's first principle here, is like that of Nathaniel with respect to Christ: "Can any good thing come out of Nazareth?" If it is granted that no good thing could come out of Nazareth, the proof was undoubted, that Jesus was not the Christ. To refute such reasoning, we have only to demand the proof of the premises.

Judith xii. 7, is another passage which may be alleged to prove that *baptizo* sometimes signifies to wash; but from what has frequently been observed on the like use of the word, with how little reason, will appear in a moment: "And she went out in the night, and baptized herself in the camp at a fountain." This ought here to have been translated *she dipped herself*. Washing was the consequence of dipping in pure water. Homer speaks of *stars washed in the sea*, (Il. E. 6;) and Virgil, express-ing the same thing, speaks of the constellation of the bear, as fearing to be *dipped* in the ocean, (Georg. i., 245.) Now, though exactly the same thing is referred to, the expressions are not exactly equivalent. By the word *washing*, Homer fixes our attention, not on the mere dipping, but on the effect of it,—the washing of the stars by being dipped. Virgil fixes our attention, not on the washing of the stars, but on their dipping, with reference to the danger or disagreeableness of the operation. We may say either *fill the pitcher*, or *dip the pitcher;* but this does not imply that *dip* signifies to *fill*. In like manner, the word *baptizo* is used when persons sink in water, and perish. Whiston, in his version of Josephus, sometimes translates it *drown*. But does this imply that *baptizo* signifies to *drown*, or to *perish?* The *perishing*, or the *drown-ing*, is the consequence of dipping in certain circumstances. The per-son, then, who so perishes, may be said to be drowned. But this is not a translation; it is a commentary. I have already pointed out the fallacy of that position, which is a first principle with most critics; namely, the supposition, that words are equivalent, which in any circumstances are interchangeable. It is an error plausible, but mischievous. Yet, on no better foundation does Dr. Wall, and innumerable others after him, argue that *baptizo* must signify to wash in general. The verb *louo* is applied to baptism ; therefore *baptizo*, it is thought, must signify to wash, as well as *louo*.

Mr. Ewing, indeed, says, "In this case, the washing could not have been by immersion, being done at a spring or fountain of water." But what sort of impossibility is this? Was it utterly impossible to have a conveniency for bathing near a fountain? On the contrary, is it not very probable that stone troughs, or other vessels, were usually provided at fountains for bathing and washing clothes? We find such a provision at two fountains near Troy, mentioned by Homer, lib. xxii. 153 :

> "Two fountains, tepid one, from which a smoke
> Issues voluminous, as from a fire ;
> The other, ev'n in summer's heats, like hail
> For cold, or snow, or crystal stream frost-bound.
> Beside them may be seen the broad canals
> Of marble scooped, in which the wives of Troy,
> And all her daughters fair, were wont to lave
> Their costly raiment, while the land had rest," &c.
> COWPER.

We find also a like provision at a river in Phæacia, in the Odyssey, lib. vi. 86 :

> "At the delightful rivulet arrived,
> Where those perennial cisterns were prepared,
> With purest crystal of the fountain fed
> Profuse," &c.　　　　COWPER.

Why, then, may not such a provision have been at the fountain referred to, especially as it was in a camp? Is it likely that in such a place there would be no convenience for bathing? Indeed, nothing is more common in our own country, than where there is no river, to have a vessel, or contrivance of some kind, for bathing, near a well. But I produce this evidence as a mere work of supererogation. Nothing more can be required of me than to show that the thing is not impossible. Even were it certain, that at this fountain there was no such provision, might not some person have supplied her with a vessel? To argue as Mr. Ewing does here, is to reason without first principles. He takes it for granted, that a thing is impossible, which is so far from being impossible, that it is not improbable. Were this a lawful mode of reasoning, it would be easy to disprove every thing.

SECTION XII.—I shall now try what evidence can be found to determine the literal meaning of the word *baptizo*, from its figurative applications. When a word is used figuratively, the figure is founded on the literal meaning ; and, therefore, by examining the figure, we may discover additional evidence with respect to the literal meaning. And here I would first observe, that some instances of figurative use may not be decisive, as well as some instances of literal use. It is enough that every instance of both literal and figurative use will explain fairly on the supposition of the meaning for which we contend, when other instances irresistibly and confessedly imply it. Our opponents contend, that in some of its figurative occurrences the allusion is to *pouring.* " In this sense of *pouring upon,* and *pouring into,*" says Mr. Ewing, " till mind and body are *overwhelmed, impregnated, intoxicated,* and the circumstances are oppressive, or even destructive, the word is very frequently used in profane writers." In opposition to this, I assert that not one of all Mr. Ewing's examples necessarily refers to *pouring upon,* or *pouring into.* In many of them, the translation may be *overwhelm;* but in this term, the reference is not to water *poured upon,* or *poured into,* but to water coming over in a current, like the tide overwhelming the beach. This is strictly and characteristically expressed by *kluzo.* To this, some of the figurative occurrences of *baptizo* have a reference; and here there is a real immersion. The *overwhelming* water *baptizes* or *sinks* the person or thing baptized. Some of the instances in which the word is translated *overwhelm,* may well enough be so rendered, as a free translation; yet as there is no allusion to water *coming over,* but to sinking in water, the translation is not literal. I observe again, that whether the water is supposed to come over the object, or the object is supposed to sink in the water, there is not a single figurative occurrence of the word, which does not imply that the object was completely covered with the water. Now, this kind of baptism would be little relief to Mr. Ewing. The man who is covered by the tide, while he lies on the shore, by the edge of the sea, is overwhelmed; and he is as completely covered, as if he had gone into the sea, and dipped himself. Even were Mr. Ewing to *pour* or *sprinkle* the water in baptism, till the person baptized should be entirely *drenched,* it would afford no relief from immersion. Not one, then, of the examples of figurative use adduced by Mr. Ewing, countenances his own favourite mode of baptism.

Let us now take a look at Mr. Ewing's examples, in which the word is used figuratively : " To have been *drenched* with wine." I have no objection to the translation *drench,* as it may imply that the object is *steeped* or *dipped,* so as to be *soaked* in the fluid. But as a thing may be drenched by *pouring* or *sprinkling,* the translation is not definitely exact. Literally, it is *immersed in wine.*

In order to determine whether *pouring* or immersing is the ground of the figure, let us examine what is the point of likeness. It must be a bad figure, if the point of resemblance in the objects is not obvious. Now, let it be observed, that there is no likeness between the *action* of drinking, and either the *pouring* of fluids, or *immersion* in them. Were this the point of resemblance, the drinking of one small glass might be designated a *baptism,* as well as the drinking of a cask ; for the *mode* is as perfect on the lowest point in the scale, as on the highest. Every act of drinking, whether *wine* or *water,* would be a *baptism.* Mr. Ewing, indeed, supposes that there is *an excessive pouring,* but as this cannot be included in mere mode, it cannot be included in the word that designates this, but must be expressed by some additional word. Besides, if the word *baptizo* signifies *excessive pouring,* it must do so in baptism, which condemns Mr. Ewing's *popping* a little water on the face. If it is supposed that there is *pouring* in the drinking of a drunkard, which is not in drinking moderately, and that the design of this application of the word *baptizo* is to designate this; I reply, that the mode of drinking a small glass is as much *pouring*, as the drinking of the cup of Hercules. Indeed, there may be something of pouring in the action of putting a small quantity of liquid into the mouth, which is not in drinking a large goblet. But if the word *baptizo*, in expressing drunkenness, refers to the mode of drinking, there is then no figure at all in the expression, for between *pouring* and *pouring* there is no resemblance. This is identity. Indeed, Mr. Ewing does not treat these expressions as figurative. He speaks as if he considered that the word *baptizo* was taken in them literally. He supposes that there is a "*pouring upon* or a *pouring into*, till mind and body are overwhelmed," &c. The wine then is poured into the person till he is intoxicated. This might be true, if the wine was put into him as men administer a drench to a horse. But the drunkard administers the wine to himself. What is the sense of the expression *he is poured with wine*, which on this supposition is the literal meaning?

But when *baptizo* is applied to drunkenness, it is taken figuratively; and the point of resemblance is between a man completely under the influence of wine, and an object completely subjected to a liquid in which it is wholly immersed. This is not only obvious from the figure itself, but from the circumstances with which the figure is sometimes conjoined. Clemens Alexandrinus, employing the same figure, says, *baptized into sleep*, through drunkenness. Now, *baptized* into sleep, is exactly our figure *buried in sleep*, which is an immersion; and burial is the thing represented by Christian baptism. Is there any likeness between *pouring* and *sleeping*? Is not the likeness between complete subjection to the influence of sleep, and the complete subjection of an object to the influence of a liquid when immersed in it? The same father applies the word to those who give themselves up to fornication. This is just our own figure when we speak of *plunging* headlong into debauchery.

This view is fully confirmed by the same figure in other languages. All figures that are founded on nature, and obvious to the observation of all nations, will be in all languages the same. Figurative language is a universal language. Now, when we examine this figure in the Latin language, our view of it is put beyond all doubt. Virgil says of the Greeks taking Troy,

"Invadunt urbem somno vinoque sepultam."
They invade the city *buried* in sleep and wine.

Here *burial* is applied both to sleep and wine. *Baptized*, therefore, into sleep and wine, as used in the Greek language, must be the same as *buried* in sleep and wine in the Latin. Surely if the expression in the Greek needed a commentary, this must be an authoritative one. There can be no pretence for taking *pouring* out of *burial*. This must be immersion.

Lactantius, as Gale remarks, employs the phrase *vitiis immersi*, *immersed* or *plunged in vice;* and Origen, in his commentary on John, uses the same figure. The expression of the former, therefore, must be the best commentary on that of the latter. Vices are not supposed to be *poured upon* the vicious person, but he *sinks in them.* We ourselves speak in this manner. We speak of a man who *sinks in vice.* Martial's figure—" Lana sanguine conchæ ebria"—wool *drunk* with the blood of the shell-fish—also affords a commentary on the Greek figure. Here, wool *dipped* in a liquid is said to be drunk with that liquid from being completely soaked with it. Schwarzius, indeed, supposes that Shakspeare's figure, " then let the earth be *drunken* with our blood," countenances the supposition that *baptizo,* though it primarily signifies to dip, sometimes signifies *pouring* or *sprinkling.* But what is the ground of this opinion? Why, it is this. *Baptizo,* sometimes, is figuratively applied to *drunkenness,* and *drunkenness* is sometimes figuratively applied to the earth *drenched with blood.* Therefore, since the earth is drenched with blood by *pouring* or *sprinkling, baptizo* must sometimes signify *pouring* or *sprinkling.* This states the evidence as fairly as any can desire. But there is a multitude of errors here. If one word may figuratively be applied to an object literally denoted by another word, does it follow that they mark the same mode? Is there any likeness between the mode of drinking, and that of the falling of blood on the earth? The earth is here said to be drunk with blood, not because there is a likeness between the manner of drinking wine, and that of the falling of blood, but from being completely drenched with blood, without any reference to the manner in which it received the blood. Indeed, as there is no likeness between the falling of blood on the earth, and the mode of drinking, the above expression is the clearest proof that the expression *baptized with wine* does not refer to the same mode. It might as well be said, that the expression, Deut. xxxii. 42, " I will make mine arrows drunk with blood," implies a proof that *baptizo* signifies to dip; because arrows are besmeared with blood by being dipped in the body. But this would be false criticism. God's arrows are supposed to be drunk with blood—not from the manner in which arrows are usually covered with blood, but from the abundance of the blood shed by them.

These observations will apply to all the examples in which this word is applied to drunkenness. I need not, therefore, examine them particularly: but I must refer to one or two, to show how ill Mr. Ewing's explication will apply to them. " *Oino de pollo Alexandron baptisasa,*"— having immersed Alexander in wine,—that is, having made him drunk with wine. This, according to Mr. Ewing's explication, would be, " having poured Alexander with much wine," not " having poured much wine into Alexander." This would be pouring the man into the wine, instead of pouring the wine into the man. " Baptized into insensibility, and sleep under drunkenness." Now, a *baptism into sleep,* we have already seen, is an *immersion. Immersed,* or *buried* in sleep, is a phrase that is warrantable; but what is the meaning of being *poured* into sleep and insensibility? Here it is not supposed that sleep is poured out on the person, but if *bebaptismenon* signifies pouring, the person must have been *poured out into sleep.*

The words, *dunamis bebaptismene en to bathei tou somatos*, Mr. Ewing translates, " a force *infused into* (or *diffused in*) the inward parts of the body." This translation, however, is not only unwarranted by the original, but is as unsuitable to the supposition that *baptizo* signifies *to pour*, as that it signifies *to immerse*. To *infuse into* would not be *baptizein en*, but *baptizein eis*. Does Mr. Ewing mean to say, that the parenthetical words are explanatory, and that *diffused in* is equivalent to *infused into?* or does he mean that they are two different meanings, of which the text is equally susceptible? A strange thing, indeed, if the same phrase can equally signify *infused into* and *diffused in!* In English these things are very different. Greek, it seems, has a wonderful fertility of meaning. When a controversialist indulges himself in a license of this kind, he may indeed very easily prove or disprove anything. He has nothing to do but make the text speak what he wants. This gives *baptizo* a new meaning, *to diffuse*. This is the most wonderful word that was ever found in any language. It can with equal facility in the very same phrase denote *opposite* things. To *diffuse* is surely the opposite of *infuse*. It is very true, that the same word compounded with different prepositions may do so, as is the case with *infuse* and *diffuse;* but let it be observed that it is the very same phrase that Mr. Ewing makes equally susceptible of these opposite meanings. This surely is philological legerdemain. Let it be observed, also, that Mr. Ewing supposes that the word *baptizo* itself in these examples signifies *to pour upon*, or to *pour into*. Now where does he find the force of these prepositions in the Greek word? If it signifies to *pour*, it does not signify to *pour into*, or to *pour upon*. The additional idea which varies the word so materially, must be got by a preposition prefixed or following: the literal translation of the above example is, " a force or power immersed in the depth of the body." *To immerse in the depth* is a congruous expression, but to *pour in the depth* is altogether incongruous.

The example from Plutarch will suit my purpose well enough in Mr. Ewing's translation; "for as plants are nourished by moderate, but choked by excessive watering, (literally *waters*,) in like manner the mind is enlarged by labours suited to its strength, but is *overwhelmed* (Gr. *baptized*) by such as exceed its power." Mr. Ewing says, " the reference here to the nourishment of plants, indicates *pouring* only to be the species of watering alluded to in the term." But in this figure there is no reference at all to the mode of watering plants. The reference is to the quantity of water. The mode is not mentioned; but even were it mentioned, it would be merely a circumstance to which nothing corresponds in the thing illustrated. What critic would ever think of hunting after such likenesses in figurative language? There is actually no likeness between the mode of watering plants, and the proportioning of labour to the mind of a pupil; and Plutarch is not guilty of such absurdity. To Plutarch's figure it would be quite the same thing, if a pot of plants was dipped into water, instead of having the water poured into it. The pot itself might be dipped in water, without any injury to the plants. The plants are injured when the water is suffered to lie about them in too great abundance, in whatever way it has been applied. The

choking of the plant corresponds to the suffocation in baptism, or immersion. The *choking* of the powers of the mind is elegantly illustrated
by the *choking* of the vegetable powers when a plant is covered in water.
There is a beautiful allusion to the suffocation of an animal under water.
Were Plutarch to rise from the dead, with what indignation would he
remonstrate against the criticism that makes him refer to the *mode* of
watering plants, in a figure intended to illustrate the bad effects of too
much study! How loudly would he disclaim the cold, unnatural
thought! Is it not possible figuratively to illustrate something by a
reference to the mountains buried under snow, without referring to the
manner of its falling, and pursuing the resemblance to the *flakes of fea-
thered snow?* So far from this, I assert, that this manner of explaining
figures is *universally improper.* No instance could be more beautifully
decisive in our favour than the above figure of Plutarch. Mr. Ewing
makes him compare the *choking* of one thing to the *overwhelming* of
another. But the author himself compares the *choking of a plant,* or
the extinction of vegetable life, to the *choking or the extinction of the
mental powers;* and in both there is an elegant allusion to the choking
of an animal under water.

But even on Mr. Ewing's own system, his explanation of this example
is most fatal to his *popping. Baptizo* here he makes to signify death by
too much water, as opposed to the moderate application of water. If
this is the distinctive meaning of *baptizo,* it cannot also denote *the
smallest application of water.* It cannot surely designate the opposite
extremes.

The word is frequently applied to overwhelming debt, or oppressive
taxation: " *tous de idiotas dia ten ek touton euporian, ou baptizousi tois
eisphorais.*" This Mr. Ewing very well translates, " on account of the
abundant supply from these sources, they do not oppress (or overload,
Gr. *baptize*) the common people with taxes." But neither the original
nor the translation will bear to be explained by the assertion that they
are brought to support, namely, that *baptizo* sometimes signifies to *pour
upon* or *pour into.* Taxes are not supposed in this figure to be *poured
upon,* or *poured into,* the people who pay them; and overwhelming taxes
are not supposed to be *poured,* while small taxes are dropped on the
people. The people might rather be said to *pour* their taxes into the
treasury. If *baptizousi* here signifies to *pour upon,* or *pour into,* as
Mr. Ewing supposes, the translation, when literal, will be, " They do not
pour the common people with taxes," or rather, " they do not *pour into,*
or *pour upon,* the common people with taxes." If any man can take
sense out of this, he will deserve the praise of invention. But in this
figure, the rulers are supposed to immerse the people, through the instrumentality of the oppressive taxes. The literal translation is, " They do
not *immerse* the common people with taxes." The people, in the case of
oppressive taxation, are not in such figures supposed either to have the
taxes *poured upon them,* nor themselves to be *immersed in the taxes,* but
to sink by being weighed down with taxes. The taxes are not the
element in which they sink, but are the instrumental *baptizers.* They
cause the people to *sink* by their weight. This suits the words: this

suits the figure : this suits the sense : this suits every example which refers to debt: this suits the analogy of all other languages. We say ourselves *dipped in debt, drowned in debt, sunk by debt,* or sunk in debt. *To sink in debt* figures the debt as that in which we sink. It is a deep water in which we sink. *To sink by debt* figures the debt as a load on our shoulders, while we are in deep water. In this view, it is not the drowning element, but the *baptizer* or *drowner.* To be dipped in debt, supposes that we owe something considerable in proportion to our means. But we may be *dipped* without being *drowned.* The last cannot be adequately represented by *baptizo,* except when circumstances render the meaning definite. The Latin language recognises the same analogy. Were we at any loss with respect to the meaning of the figure in Greek, the *Ære alieno demersus* of Livy is a commentary. This supposes that the debtor is *plunged* or *sunk* in debt. A man struggling for his life in the midst of deep water, and at last sinking by exhaustion, is a true picture of an insolvent debtor. When *baptizo* occurs in such a situation, the meaning is substantially given in English by the word *oppress,* or *overload ;* but neither of them is a translation. They convey the meaning under the figure of a *load ;* the other gives the idea under the figure of immersion.

The same observation applies to the next example, which Mr. Ewing quotes from Josephus, p. 302, translated by Mr. Ewing, " those, indeed, even without (engaging in) faction, afterwards *overburdened* or *oppressed* (Gr. *baptized*) the city. The original is stronger than the translation. It asserts that the robbers ruined, or *sunk* the city. The passage is translated by Whiston, " although these very men, besides the seditions they raised, were otherwise the direct cause of the city's destruction also." The reference is to a ship sinking from being overburdened, and ill-managed in the storm, from the dissensions of the crew. In this view, the figure is striking and beautiful. But how can Mr. Ewing accommodate even his own translation to his definition of the meaning of the word *baptizo* in such examples? In them, he says, it is used in the sense of *pouring upon* and *pouring into.* What did the robbers pour *upon* or *into* the city? Besides, there is neither *upon* nor *into* here. If the word *baptizo* signifies *to pour,* the translation literally will be, " they poured the city." This will not accommodate to Mr. Ewing's own definition of the meaning of the word, more than ours. Again, even according to Mr. Ewing's own translation of this passage, the word *baptizo* here denotes *something in excess.* What aspect has this towards the popping system? A few drops of water is not an oppressive load.

Josephus uses the same figure on another occasion. Speaking of Herod's sons, he says, " *touto osper teleutaia thuella cheimazomenous tous neaniskous epebaptisen,*" p. 704. This is a commentary on the preceding example, and limits the figure to a ship sinking. In the former case, the ship was overburdened, and there was a mutiny among the sailors. Here the ship is attacked by repeated storms, and at last is sunk by a hurricane. The word *cheimazomenous* imports, that the young men had a winter voyage, in which they were attacked by many storms, and at last were plunged into the abyss by an overwhelming blast. Whiston, who has no purpose to serve, translates it thus: "and this it was that came as the last storm, and entirely sunk the young men, when they were in great danger before." What has *popping* or *pouring* to say here?

The very next example which Mr. Ewing quotes in the sense of *over-whelming* by being *overburdened*, definitely refers to *sinking* in water: "I am one of those who have been overwhelmed by that great wave of calamity." Now, what allusion is there here to *pouring upon*, *pouring into*, or *pouring* of any kind? Yet this is one of the examples brought by Mr. Ewing, to prove that the word sometimes signifies to *pour upon*, and pour into, till mind and body are overwhelmed. What was *poured upon* or *poured into* this person? Is it supposed that the wave gradually poured on him till it sunk him? Nay, verily. He is said to be baptized *under* the wave. Indeed, a wave does not cover by *pouring*, but by *flowing*, *dashing*, or *sweeping* horizontally. In the overwhelming by a wave, there is no likeness to pouring or popping, and the object is as completely covered by the wave, as when it is dipped. Besides, the person is here supposed to be forced down into the water below, by the weight of the superincumbent wave. The wave is the baptizer, not the thing in which he is baptized. He is baptized *under* the wave. And can there be a stronger proof that baptism is immersion? Let Mr. Ewing perform baptism according to his own translation of this passage, and he will act as differently from his own mode as from ours. Let the baptized person be overwhelmed with water, and he will be buried in water.

Another example of this figure from the same author, is entirely decisive in our favour. Liban. Ep. 310. "He who bears with difficulty the burden he already has, would be entirely overwhelmed (or crushed) by a small addition." Is it possible to squeeze the idea of *pouring* out of the word in this occurrence? A burden is not *poured* on the shoulders. Besides, it is not the putting of the burden on the man, that is here called baptism. The baptism is effected by the burden after it is put on. The burden causes the man to *sink*.

The example which Mr. Ewing quotes from Plutarch, is already decided by the evidence produced with respect to the allusion when the figure respects debt: "Oppressed by a debt of 5000 myriads." This debt was not *poured upon* him, nor *poured into* him; but, oppressed by it as a load, he *sunk* or became insolvent. The figure does not represent the mode of putting the debt on him, for in this there is no likeness. It represents the debt *when on him* as *causing him to sink*.

The example from Heliod. Æthiop. lib. iv. can, by no ingenuity, be reconciled to the assertion which Mr. Ewing brings it to support: "And overwhelmed with the calamity." If *baptizo* is supposed to signify to *pour*, this passage must be translated, "and *poured* by or with the calamity." The calamity is not poured upon him, but the calamity *pours* him. But to be *immersed*, or to *sink*, by calamity, is good sense, and a common form of speech. This also is baptism by immersion, and can be nothing else. What is more common than to speak of *sinking* under misfortunes?

In like manner Gregory Thaumaturgus, p. 72, speaks of persons as delivered from the difficulties in which they were *immersed*. But the observation of Schelhornius, renders the reference in this figure entirely definite. After quoting a number of examples in which the word is applied figuratively to calamities, he observes, with great sagacity, that the same sentiment is expressed in the same author by the word *buthizesthai*, which determines his meaning when he uses the word *baptizo* to express the same thing. " Sunk into the deep by a greater wave or tide of misfortunes." Now, that *buthizo* denotes *to cover, to sink in the abyss,* there can be no doubt. It is a verb formed from the appropriate name of the great abyss. *Baptizo*, then, as expressing the same thing, must agree with it in the general idea, though it characteristically differs from it in strength of expression. In some circumstances, they may both refer to the same thing, while in others they have a characteristic difference. No evidence can be more satisfactory in determining the meaning of a word than this. It is indirect, and would be hid from the ordinary reader ; but when sagacity points it out, no candid mind can reject it. This also confirms an observation which I have made on another example, namely, that to be *baptized by a wave*, does not import that the baptism was *in* the wave, but *under* it; and that the wave is the baptizer, or power that sinks the baptized person under it. Here the great wave not only covered the person itself, but sunk him *below itself* into the deep.

The Septuagint renders Isaiah xxi. 4, " iniquity immerses me," translated by Mr. Ewing, " iniquity *overwhelms* me." " Here," he says, " the idea of *plunging into* is excluded. The subject of baptism is viewed as having something *poured* or *brought upon* him. He is not *popped into* the baptizing substance, but it *pops upon* him." And pray, Mr. Ewing, who *pops* this iniquity upon the baptized person ? Is iniquity itself the popper ? Is not iniquity the thing with which he is *popped* ? Is it both *popper* and *popped* ? But if iniquity *pops* him with itself, does not this represent sin as coming on the sinner of itself? But Mr. Ewing most manifestly mistakes the meaning of this phrase. The expression, " iniquity baptizeth me," does not mean that iniquity comes on him either by *popping* or *dipping*, either by *pouring* or *sprinkling ;* but that his sin, which originated in himself, and never was *put on him in any mode*, *sunk* him in misery. Our iniquities cause us to *sink* in deep waters. This example is, with all others in which the word occurs either in its literal or figurative use, completely in our favour. Iniquity is the baptizer, and, instead of *popping* the subjects of its baptism, would *sink* them eternally in the lake that burneth with fire and brimstone, were they not delivered by that which is represented in the baptism of Christians. Upon the whole, there is not one of all the examples of the figurative use of this word, which will not fairly explain in perfect accordance with the literal meaning which we attach to it, while many of them can bear no other meaning. So far from all explaining with an allusion to *pouring*, there is not one of them, taking all circumstances together, will fairly explain in that meaning. There is not one instance in which Mr. Ewing can show, that the reference must necessarily be to pouring. All languages employ corresponding words in the same figurative meaning for which we contend in the above examples. No evidence can be more entirely satisfactory.

The figurative baptism of our Lord is quite in accordance with those examples in which the word is used for afflictions. Matt. xx. 22; Mark x. 37. In accordance with this view, also, he is represented in the prophetical parts of the Old Testament, as *immersed* in deep waters. " Save me, O God, for the waters are come in unto my soul. I sink in deep mire, where there is no standing; I am come into deep waters, where the floods overflow me." Psa. lxix. 1, 2, 14. In like manner, the afflictions of the church are represented by this figure. " Then the waters had overwhelmed us, the stream had gone over our soul: then the proud waters had gone over our soul." Psa. cxxiv. 4, 5, &c. The enemies of the Lord, also, and of his people, are represented as destroyed by immersion in deep waters. " Then will I make their waters deep, and cause their rivers to run like oil, saith the Lord God." Ezek. xxxii. 14.

The baptism of the Spirit is a figure that has its foundation in immersion, by which the abundance of his gifts and influences, and the sanctification of the whole body and soul, are represented. That which is immersed in a fluid is completely subjected to its influence, as wool is said to be drunk with the blood of the shell-fish. So the sanctification of the believer by the Holy Spirit, through faith in the atoning blood of Christ, is figuratively called an *immersion* or a *baptism*. But this and the preceding figure I shall meet again, in the examination of the theory of Mr. Ewing.

SECTION XIII.—EXAMINATION OF MR. EWING'S SYSTEM.—Having considered the evidence for the meaning of this word from its occurrences in Greek writers, I shall now examine the new theory proposed by Mr. Ewing. This writer pretends to have discovered the signification of *bapto*, by reducing it to its radical letters; and by interchanging labials and vowels, he forms the word *pop* from the sound. For an admirable exposure of this fancy, I refer the reader to Dr. Cox. But the very attempt is absurd and ludicrous. It could not succeed on any subject, or with respect to any word. It is entitled to no more consideration, than an attempt to decide by an appeal to the cry of birds. The tnought of settling a religious controversy about the meaning of a word in a particular language, by speculations with respect to its radical letters, as applying to all languages, is certainly one of the wildest conceits that has been broached in criticism since the birth of that art. Upon this theory, I shall do no more than make a few observations.

1. It applies etymology utterly beyond its province. Etymology, as a foundation for argument, can never proceed beyond *the root existing as a word in the language*, whose meaning can be learned from its use. To trace a word to a more remote ancestry, is to relate fable for history.

2. When etymologists go farther, they do not pretend to give a meaning to a word which it is not found to have by use, nor to reject any meaning which use has assigned. They do not pretend to regulate

language by assigning meanings from origin, but, from a comparison of actually ascertained meanings, to assign a probable root. The value of their discoveries is not from their authority in settling controversies about the meanings that use has actually assigned to the words which they analyze, but from the light which they reflect on the philosophy of language, and the science of mind. So far from having authority in theological controversy, their researches have no authority in criticism, with respect to the use of words in classical writers. Classical writers are an authority to the etymologist, but the etymologist cannot give law to the classics. The etymologist must collect, and from use ascertain, the various meanings of a word,—on the authority of which he may venture a conjecture of an origin higher than that of any word now in the language. By a comparison of these meanings, he may discover a common idea, and thereby be enabled to determine the primary meaning. But without this authority, the primary meaning can never be ascertained by the mere sound of radical letters. It may be true that particular radical letters are found in words that designate a common idea; but that this is the case, and how far it is the case, depends on ascertaining from use the actual meaning of the words. If the meaning of words may lawfully be ascertained from the radical letters which they contain, instead of the tedious process of reading the classics, and acquiring the meaning of words from their use, we may at once proceed to reduce them to their radical sounds, and determine their import by this philological chemistry. Mr. Ewing not only fails in this instance of analysis, but utterly mistakes the true object of etymological researches. His attempt is not calculated to throw light on the philosophy of language, nor illustrate the processes and relations of human thought, but converts etymology into a sort of philological alchemy.

3. Were the origin of *bapto* to be traced, even with the utmost certainty, to some other word or words in the language, its meaning in the language must be determined by its use in the language, and not by its origin. Words often depart widely in their use from the meaning of their root. They may drop some idea that was at first essential, or they may embrace ideas not originally implied.

4. In analyzing any word, the etymologist must be guided not merely by the consideration that the letters that compose it have the appearance of indicating a certain origin, but, especially as a ground-work, that such an origin corresponds to its known and acknowledged meaning. And when we have found such an origin to a word, it is of no authority in argument, as it takes the meaning of the word for granted. If *pop* were the ascertained and acknowledged meaning of *bapto*, the etymologist might employ his art to reduce the one word to the other. But even then, the evidence that the one was the parent of the other, would depend on the fact that the meaning was ascertained by use, and could not rest on the coincidence in sounds. That *rain* comes from *raino*, to sprinkle, and plunge from *pluno*, &c., depends on the fact, that the meaning of the one word is known by use to correspond to the meaning of the other. Were there no such correspondence in known

signification, the correspondence in sound would be no foundation for derivation. Many words correspond as nearly in sound, which have no relation. In deriving a word, therefore, by reducing it to its radical letters, the etymologist, if he acts agreeably to the sound principles of his art, must have all the meanings of the derived word previously ascertained, as a ground-work for his conclusions: they are data which in his process must be taken for granted. But if the meanings of a word are taken for granted in this process, the object of the process cannot be to ascertain a doubtful meaning. If the word *bapto* has not from use all the meanings which Mr. Ewing assigns to it, no etymological process can give any of these meanings to it, for they must be all taken for granted, as a foundation for his deductions.

5. This theory assigns to *bapto*, as its primary meaning, a signification which use has not given it in a single instance. Indeed, though the author endeavours to conform the examples to this primary acceptation, he does not pretend to have derived it from the examples. He concludes that the primary meaning of this word is *pop*, from the sound, and from its correspondence to the other meanings. That *bapto* has such a primary meaning there is no evidence. If *pop* really embraced all the significations assigned by Mr. Ewing to *bapto*, he might allege, that it is probable that the word once signified to *pop;* but this would not be proof that it had any such signification during the period to which the writings now extant in the Greek language belong. This could be proved only by examples from these authors. Whatever is the origin of the word *bapto*, it never signifies *pop*.

6. To prove that any meaning is sanctioned by use, it is not sufficient that there are examples of its occurrence which will explain on this meaning. There is no word of frequent occurrence, which in some situations might not bear a false translation, or explain in a sense which it really never has, without making nonsense. Nay, a false translation of a word may, in many situations, make good sense, and even express a scriptural truth, though not the truth of the passage. Before the authority of use, therefore, can be pleaded for a meaning, a passage must be produced in which the word *must* have the meaning assigned. This is self-evident. I state it, therefore, as a canon, or first principle of criticism, THAT IN CONTROVERSY A WORD OCCURRING FREQUENTLY IN THE LANGUAGE IS NEVER TO BE TAKEN ARBITRARILY IN A SENSE WHICH IT CANNOT BE SHOWN INCONTESTABLY TO HAVE IN SOME OTHER PASSAGE. An acknowledged sense is necessary as a foundation on which to rest the supposition, that in the contested passage it may have the signification assigned. There is no ground to allege that the word has a signification in the contested passage, which it is not proved to have in some other place. It may have this authority and fail; but without this it cannot succeed. A meaning not so proved has no right to be heard in controversy. I have limited the canon to controversy, but, in fact, it extends in some measure to matters in which men do not find an inducement to dispute. Many of the beasts and fishes and fowls and plants mentioned in the Old Testament, cannot be now exactly and confidently ascertained by us, for want of this criterion ; and although there is no warm

controversy about these things, it is because there is no temptation from the subject. If a word occurs so seldom in what remains of any language, and in such circumstances as cannot definitely determine its meaning, nothing can be legitimately rested on it in controversy. Now this canon sweeps away not only Mr. Ewing's theory, but all other systems that give a meaning to *baptizo*, different from that for which we contend. There is not one instance in all the Greek language in which it necessarily signifies to pour, sprinkle, &c. Our opponents have not an acknowledged foundation on which to rest the opinion, that, with respect to the ordinance of baptism, the word *baptizo* may have the meaning for which they contend; for in no instance can it be proved to have such a meaning. On the contrary, even Mr. Ewing himself, the boldest of all the critics on that side of the question, does not deny that this word sometimes signifies to dip; nay, he himself gives many examples in which it must have this signification.

7. I will state another canon equally self-evident, and equally fatal to the doctrine of Mr. Ewing, and all our opponents: A WORD THAT APPLIES TO TWO MODES CAN DESIGNATE NEITHER. The same word cannot express different modes, though a word not significant of mode may apply to all modes. *Wash*, for instance, may refer to the action designated by it, in whatever mode it may be performed. Whether it is done by dipping or by pouring, the word *wash* does not assert. It is indifferent as to mode, although even here one mode is more common than another. *Stain*, in like manner, asserts nothing of mode, but applies to all modes. A thing may be stained by sprinkling, by pouring, or by dipping. *Wet* also applies to all modes. A thing may be wetted by *dipping*, by *pouring*, by sprinkling, by the insensible distillation of the *dew*, by *damp*. The word expresses the effect only, and says nothing of the mode. But it would be both false and absurd to say that these words signify all these modes. They express nothing of mode. Modes are essentially different from one another, and have nothing in common. One word, then, cannot possibly distinguish them. The name of a mode is the word which expresses it as distinguished from other modes. But it is impossible for the same word to express the distinction of two modes. It might more reasonably be supposed, that the word *black* may also be employed to signify the idea denoted by *white*, as well as the idea which it is employed to designate, because black and white admit of degrees; but there are no degrees in mode. Without reference, then, to the practice of the language, on the authority of self-evident truth, I assert that *bapto* cannot signify both *dip*, and *pour* or *sprinkle*. I assert, that *in no language under heaven can one word designate two modes*. Now we have the confession of our opponents themselves, that *baptizo* signifies to *dip*. If so, it cannot also signify to *pour* or *sprinkle*.

8. The various meanings that Mr. Ewing assigns to this word, will not derive from *pop*. His theory, then, has not the merit even of consistency, which a false theory may have. He asserts, indeed, that all the meanings which he admits may easily be reduced to this word; and that each holds of it, independently of all the rest. But how does he make out this assertion? By making as many compounds of *pop*, as

bapto is supposed to have meanings. In each of these meanings, it becomes, in fact, a different word. *Pop in, pop out; pop up, pop down; pop backward, pop forward,* &c., are different compound words, as much as diffuse is different from infuse. Now, if the word *bapto* signifies merely to *pop*, it cannot signify to *pop up*, to *pop down*, &c., by its own power. It must have something added to give it such a meaning. It is false, then, to say that *bapto* has all these significations. But if *bapto* signifies to *pour*, it does so without the aid of any other word: if it signifies to *sprinkle*, it must do so by itself. It signifies to *dip*, without the aid of any other word. It is true, indeed, that *baptizo* admits composition with prepositions, but this is not to enable it to signify *to dip*: for if this were the case, it could never have that signification without the preposition in composition. But it has this signification where there is no such composition. Indeed, there are but few of its occurrences in which it admits the composition. It was indeed a conceit of the great Dr. Owen, that *baptizo* cannot denote to dip, except in composition with *en* or *eis*. But this is contradicted by use, and by the analogy of other words, as is well remarked by Mr. Booth. Besides, if *bapto* signifies to *pop*, and if *pop* can apply to none of the meanings which *bapto* is said to have, without the aid of a preposition, then it cannot be said that *bapto* signifies to *pour* or *sprinkle*. It only signifies a part of that idea.

Again, when the compound is formed, it will not produce the meanings contended for. To *pop upon* does not signify to *sprinkle*, for there may be a *popping upon*, when there is no sprinkling, though *sprinkling* may be performed by *popping upon*. In the very example alleged by Mr. Ewing, there is *popping upon* without *sprinkling*. "A fellow finding somewhat prick him, popped his finger *upon* the place." Did he sprinkle his finger upon the place? But if there is *popping upon* without *sprinkling*, then *popping upon* will not signify sprinkling without something to limit it still farther. Granting, then, that *bapto* signifies to *pop*, for this very reason it cannot signify to *sprinkle*.

In the same manner it may be proved, that if *bapto* signifies to *pop in* or *into*, it does not signify to *pour;* for there may be *popping in* or *into* without *pouring*. Mr. Ewing's own example proves this:

> "He that kill'd my king,
> Popt in between th' election and my hopes."

There was no pouring here. But a word that does not necessarily imply *pouring*, cannot signify *pouring*.

Even with the addition of the word *water* itself, the idea is not made out. If we substitute *water* for finger in the above example, we shall fail in the attempt to express *sprinkling*. The fellow might pop *water* upon the place without *sprinkling*. In like manner, there may even be *popping* into water, without immersion. When a boy *pops* a duck into the water, she does not sink. Mr. Ewing, then, has failed in every point of view. Even the expression, " he popped water into his turned up face," Mr. Ewing's favourite expression for *baptizing*, does not express either *pouring* or *sprinkling*. So far from necessarily implying that the water was *poured* or *sprinkled*, it naturally implies that the water was cast by a *jerk* or *slight dash,* and not by *drops,* or by *a stream.* Instead, then, of accounting for all the meanings attached by Mr. Ewing to the word *bapto,* it does not account for any one of these meanings.

Still less will this derivation account for *dyeing* as a meaning of *bapto.* How is it possible, that if *bapto* primarily signifies to *pop,* it could also receive the signification *to dye?* Mr. Ewing answers this, by supposing that a thing may be dyed, by having the colouring liquor popped upon it, and by the supposition, that the art of *dyeing* was suggested by the accidental staining of things by the juice of fruits. But this account is totally unphilosophical. All this may be true, yet be insufficient to account for the fact. Accidental and infrequent union cannot originate a meaning founded on such union. It is not priority of the mode of doing anything, but the frequency of doing in a mode, that will confer the name of the mode on the thing effected in such mode. This is the voice both of philosophy and of fact. Thus, *cano,* to sing, came to signify to foretell, because prophets uttered their predictions in song. This principle operates very extensively in language. I have already exemplified the thing in many instances. *Bapto, to dip,* comes naturally to signify *to dye,* from the frequency of *dyeing* by dipping. But there never was such a frequency of *dyeing* by *sprinkling,* as would, on philosophical principles, give the name of the mode to the thing effected in that mode. Besides, if *bapto* primarily signifies *to pop,* and if it came to signify *to dye,* because *dyeing* was usually performed by *popping,* then *dyeing* must have been performed neither by pouring nor sprinkling, for *popping,* as I have shown, is different from both. It is impossible philosophically to account for *dyeing* as a meaning of *bapto* on any other principle, than that this word primarily signifies to *dip.*

Again, if *bapto* came to signify to *dye,* because that the art of dyeing was suggested by the accidental stains from the bruising of fruits, why did not *pop* accompany its relative in this signification? Why did not Milton say, " colours *popped* in heaven," instead of " colours *dipped* in heaven?" There is no end to the absurdity of this fantastic theory; it is a mine of inconsistency that never could be exhausted. This is the necessary condition of all false theories. However plausible they may be made by the ingenuity of their inventors, they must contain inconsistency that will sometimes *pop* out its head, and show itself even to the most indolent readers. But truth is consistent; and, although many apparent difficulties may at first sight occur, they will gradually disappear, as light is cast on the subject by inquiry. Even when its defenders, by inadvertency, couple it with something extrinsic, that tends to obscure and mar its evidence, the ingenuity of opponents will only have the good effect of separating the chaff from the wheat.

But no absurdity can vie with that of supposing that a word of so peculiar and restricted a meaning as *pop* is represented to be, should be accounted so generic, that it becomes the liege lord of innumerable different significations, that do not arise the one out of the other, but hold immediately of itself. Nay, according to Mr. Ewing's philosophy, it might become the liege lord of half the language. Instead of originally representing a very generic idea, it is supposed primarily to signify a particular sound,—a small smart quick sound. It is said to be a word "formed from the sound." All its applications agree to this; and *pop* itself never came to have the acceptations that Mr. Ewing supposes *bapto* to have. We never find this word applied to any things, but such as are of a trifling or playful nature. We never hear of a shipwreck as a popping of the ship into the deep. This would be ludicrous. *Pop*, instead of being a generic word, is as specific a word as can be imagined, and never was actually extended to serious or important things, except to burlesque them. Indeed, instead of being a liege lord, conferring ample and separate territories on many great vassals, it is so very confined in its own territory, that it has a domain hardly sufficient for a walk, to give it an airing. To enable it to go a little into the world, it is obliged to take assistance from the prepositions. Mr. Ewing himself cannot send it abroad without escorting it with *up* or *down*, *backwards* or *forwards*, *in* or *into*, *off* or *upon*, &c. A word so limited in its own territories is ill fitted to become, as liege lord, proprietor of a great part of the language,—nay, of every language; for Mr. Ewing's chemistry must extract the same thought from all languages. The author, indeed, while he declares that each of the vassals is independent of all the rest, and holds immediately of the liege lord, inconsistently gives it a process from the particular sound originally denoted by it, to "the noise caused by the *agency of body in motion upon body*, and that *in any direction whatever*." Here we have a process that by gradually dropping particularities, and encroaching on territories not originally included in its kingdom, gives it a generic meaning. Here every step in the process is connected with that which precedes and depends on it. But let us look at the generic meaning which we have found by this process. It is so generic, as to disclaim all kindred with *pop*, according to the use of that word in the English language. Mr. Ewing's definition assigns this word to express "the noise caused by the agency of body in motion upon body." Now, has *pop* actually so generic a meaning? If so, we may speak of the *popping of a cart*, when we mean to express the *creaking* of its wheels; for this is "noise caused by the agency of body in motion upon body." In short, every noise from motion may be called *popping*. But with all the impudence of this little playful word, it has never had the boldness to *pop* itself into such a province.

Again, if *bapto* signifies primarily to *pop*, and if *pop* signifies primarily to make "a small smart quick sound," and if all the various meanings of *bapto* hold of it in this signification, then they must all be reducible to the primary signification, namely, "a small smart quick sound," without any relation to one another. The signification *to dye* must be referred immediately to this particular sound, and not to the accidental bruising of fruits. Mr. Ewing inconsistently makes the various meanings hold of *pop* in its generic meaning, acquired by process, instead of its primary, particular motion. Nay, he absurdly makes the various meanings of *bapto* hold of the English *pop*, and that in a meaning far removed from its primary meaning. No matter that it was as true that *pop* had the generic meaning acquired by process from a particular one, as it is manifestly false; this would say nothing to the processes of *bapto*. Instead of tracing the progress of *pop* from "a small smart quick sound," to a "sound caused by the motion of body in motion on body," let Mr. Ewing trace the progress of *bapto* itself. It is with this the controversy is concerned, and not with the mutations in the meaning of an English word. Let him show such a primary meaning in *bapto*, and then let him trace it through all the rivulets derived from the fountain. Can anything be more obvious, than that if *bapto* primarily signifies *to pop*, and if *pop* primarily signifies *to make a small smart quick sound*, *bapto* cannot be admitted as proprietor of any other territory, till it is proved by use to possess it? Is the harmony between *bapto* and *pop* like that of the monads of the soul and body, according to the system of Leibnitz, that the one must necessarily accompany the other in all its most fantastic movements? Can anything be more absurd, than to squeeze *pop* out of *bapto*, on the authority of sound and primary acceptation, yet in the theory founded on this, to reason not from the primary meaning of *pop*, but from a meaning acquired by process? Can anything be more absurd, than to pretend to determine the different meanings of a Greek word, by the mutations of meaning in the English word derived from it?

9. If *pop* originally denoted "a small smart quick sound," as is very likely, then there is no reason to extract *pop* out of *bapto*, for *bapto* never denotes such a sound,—nor any sound. Mr. Ewing himself does not pretend to allege one example in which *bapto* has the meaning which *pop* originally implied. On the authority, then, of the coincidence of primary meaning, no relation can be found between them.

10. The construction of the words in connexion with *bapto*, in many of its occurrences, contradicts this theory. Mr. Ewing says, "a person or thing may be either *popped into* water, or may have water *popped upon* or *into him*." Very true, but the same syntax will not *pop him* into water, that will *pop* water *upon* or *into him*. According to Mr. Ewing, to *pop into* water is to dip. If so, the examples of *dipping*, as denoted by this phrase, are innumerable. Let any person examine the number which I have produced. But can Mr. Ewing produce out of all Greek literature, a single example of the phrase *popping water upon a person or thing*, when the verb is *bapto*? *Baptizing water upon* a person or thing, is a phrase that never occurs. This would be the baptism of the water, not of the person. *To pop water upon a man*, in Greek, would be *baptein udor ep anthropon*, if *baptein* is the Greek word for *pop*: but such a phraseology is not to be found in all the Greek language.

11. The many examples in which *baptizo* is applied to great, serious, and terrific objects, contradict this theory. Mr. Ewing, indeed, has foreseen this *storm*; and to prevent his theory from being *overwhelmed* by it, has invented a groundless distinction between what he calls the *proper* and *lax* sense of the word. "It is a word," he says, "which properly denotes operations on a small scale, and of a gentle nature: it is in a secondary sense that it comes to be applied to the vast and the terrible." But can it apply to the vast and the terrible, if it does not either include the vast and the terrible in its primary meaning; or, by forsaking its primary meaning, has it, by philosophical procedure, advanced to

new territories? Words often advance to meanings very distant from their roots; but when they do so, they give up their first acceptation, and take the new meaning as their proper acceptation. *Candlestick,* for instance, at first denoted a utensil of wood; it now denotes the utensil, without respect to the material of which it is composed: but it has forsaken its ancient meaning altogether. It cannot be said that it properly signifies an implement made of wood, for holding a candle; and in a secondary sense, the same utensil of any materials. It now as properly signifies the utensil when it is made of metal, as when it is made of wood; of gold, as when it is made of an osier.

In this every thing is natural, and the philosophy of the progress is intelligible to the child: but let Mr. Ewing point out any philosophical principle that would lead *baptizo* from such a primary sense as he contends for, to the secondary sense which he here assigns. Is there any principle to conduct the operation in extending the word pop-gun to signify a cannon? He does not pretend that this process has been verified in the term *pop*. To employ *pop* in this way, would be ludicrous. The same must be the case with *bapto,* if it signifies *to pop*.

But if there were any principle to lead to this process, when it had taken place, the first meaning must be given up; for they are utterly irreconcilable. Let Mr. Ewing point out any principle in the human mind that would naturally conduct this process. Let him point out any example in any language, in which a word at the same period of its history has such primary and secondary meanings. Can anything be more extravagant than the supposition, that this word properly denotes operations on a small scale, and, as a secondary meaning, things of a vast and terrific nature? If it has the one meaning it cannot have the other. There is no philosophy in this distinction. What a wild thought, that the noise of a pop-gun, and destruction by the overwhelming torrents of boiling lava from the crater of a burning mountain, may be expressed by the same word! Mr. Ewing, indeed, acknowledges that it is not usual in English to say, " he popped upon me with an overwhelming flood." But he might have added, that this could not be said in any language, employing a word corresponding to *pop*. This word cannot apply to such things, from the inconsistency between them and the ideas which it denotes: and there must be the same inconsistency with respect to the words that correspond to *pop* in all languages.

Mr. Ewing calls this *secondary* sense, " *a figurative,* an *exaggerated* rather than a proper and natural sense." But if it is a *secondary* sense, it is not a *figurative* sense, for a *secondary* sense is a *proper* sense; and a *figurative* acceptation of a word is no sense of the word at all. When a word is used hyperbolically, it still retains its proper sense, and from this circumstance the figure has its beauty. When the Psalmist represents the mountains as *leaping,* the word leaping still retains its proper meaning, but the motion of a mountain in an earthquake is elegantly figured as *leaping*. The word *leap* does not here come by exaggeration to denote the motion of a mountain in an earthquake. In like manner, when a wild Irishman says that he was *killed* when he had received a severe beating, the word *kill* is not diminished in its meaning, but what is not *killing* is, by a lively imagination, so called for the sake of energy. It is absurd to speak of the *exaggerated* or diminished meaning of a word. The *exaggeration* or the *diminution* is not in the words at all.

I have already pointed out the true distinction between BAPTO and BAPTIZO. The former signifies to *dip*, the latter to *cause to dip*. Now these significations equally apply to small objects and to great; but while the latter may be applied to the smallest object, it is peculiarly fitted to denote the immersion of objects greater than can be lifted in the hand. Accordingly, we find that *baptizo*, while it is sometimes applied to the smallest objects, is much more usually than *bapto* applied to large objects. It more exactly applies to the immersion in baptism, because the baptized person is not taken up by the baptizer, but caused to sink into the water by the force impressed. It is *baptizo*, also, as any one may see by a look at the examples which I have quoted, that is applied to the sinking of ships, and the destruction of things not lifted out of the water. This is a distinction philosophical, intelligible, useful, and agreeable to fact. Mr. Ewing's distinction has nothing to recommend it but the necessity of his theory. Josephus speaks as literally when he designates the sinking of a ship by the word *baptizo*, as when he speaks of the *immersion* of the smallest object.

12. Mr. Ewing mistakes the effect that prepositions have in composition with the verbs. He seems to suppose, that they always modify or give direction to the action of the verb as simply as the English prepositions. But a slight examination of this subject will convince any one that they have a variety of power unknown to our language. Let us take one or two examples: *eita thermous artous ex oinou melanos kai elaiou apobapton.* Here it is obvious *apo* does not direct its force in conjunction with the verb, upon the object of the verb; but marks the departure of the object from the thing in which the action was produced. The latter is without doubt the effect of the preposition after the verb, *ex oinou, out of wine.* It is not " dip the loaves into the wine," but " dip them *out of the wine.*" The point to which our attention is here called by the expression, is the departure of the object out of the thing in which the action of the verb was produced. This implies that it was in the wine, but does not express it. Now, the preposition in composition may unite with the preposition after the verb, as is frequently the case, when the same preposition that is used in composition is also used after the verb, as *embaptizo eis thalassan,* and our own phrases, *the tyrant was expelled out of the kingdom,—he* INfused *courage* INTO *the soldiers,* &c. &c.

Whatever is the meaning of the participle in the above example, the preposition in composition with it cannot exert its influence on the object of the verb. We could not say, *popping from the loaves out of the wine.* The expression is on the same principle that operates in the phrase, " shall dip his finger *from* the oil," Lev. xiv. 16; and "from the blood," Lev. iv. 17.

Eis and *en* occur very frequently in composition with this verb; but their effect is quite obvious: *apo* is less frequent because it is only on the above principles that it applies. *Epi* is still less frequent. It does not imply that the baptizing substance was put upon the thing baptized, but that the thing baptized was put upon the baptizing substance. " Dipping a piece of fine linen into moist Eretrian earth," &c. Here the linen was baptized upon the earth, and not the earth upon the linen. Now, this is Mr. Ewing's favourite compound for denoting *poptism.* *To pop upon* must mean to pop the water on the person. But let the verb be translated as he will, it cannot comport in this example with this view. The Eretrian earth was not to be *popped upon* the linen, for it was a mass of moist earth; and it is not said that the linen was to be *baptized upon* with the earth, but *into the earth.* Now, Mr. Ewing supposes that when the verb is compounded with *epi,* the baptizing substance is preceded by *with.* " He popped upon me with an overwhelming flood." But this is not the syntax in any of the examples in which this compound word occurs. It is not *baptize with,* but baptize *in* or *into.* This is a capital mistake, and the detection of it leaves him without aid from his favourite compound. To *baptize upon,* in the construction in which it always stands, is as inconsistent with *popping,* as *into* would have been. Indeed, *into* is in this example expressly used before the baptizing substance. If the linen was to be baptized *upon* moist earth, it was also to be baptized *into* the earth.

The expression in Josephus in which this compound is used, to which Mr. Ewing seems to refer, is as little in unison with his doctrine : " This, as the last storm, immersed the young men," &c. Here the storm is not the *baptizing substance,* but the *baptizer,* and it did not *pop itself upon them,* for the verb is in the active voice. If, then, it signifies to *pop,* the *popper* must *pop* something on them. What is it, then, that the storm *pops on them different from itself?* To express Mr. Ewing's meaning, the syntax must be quite different. Some *popper* must " pop the young men with a storm," &c., or it must be, " the young men were popped upon *with* a storm." But instead of this the storm itself is the *baptizer,* and as their *baptism* was their destruction, it must have been *immersion.* *Epi,* then, cannot here import, as Mr. Ewing's doctrine supposes, that the baptizing substance was *popped upon* the baptized; for the baptizing substance was the sea in which they perished, and the storm was the baptizer that sunk them. Mr. Ewing's own translation of the passage cannot give him relief. " This, as the last storm, *epibaptized or overwhelmed* the young men, already weather-beaten." Now what did the storm baptize *upon* them? With what did it *overwhelm* them? With itself, Mr. Ewing may say. I answer, No. The verb is in the active voice, but to express this meaning would require the middle. If the storm *popped* them, it must have popped them with something different from itself. Besides, the allusion is evidently to a ship *sinking* in the sea by a storm. The sea is the baptizing substance, the storm is the baptizer, and the effect of such a baptism is destruction. *Epi,* then, is evidently intended to mark the violence of the pressure of the storm on the ship, as the force of the agent in effecting the action of the verb.

Again, if *epibaptize* signifies to *pop upon,* how is it that it here imports to overwhelm? Can any two ideas be more inconsistent than that of *popping upon*, and that of overwhelming? Can two extremes meet? How does *overwhelm* hold of *pop*? I have already shown that no process can account for two meanings so discordant, and that no figure will justify it. This is contrary to a canon as clear as any in language,— THAT WHICH DESIGNATES ONE EXTREME, CANNOT AT THE SAME TIME DESIGNATE THE OTHER. As I have observed in another place, many words may apply to both extremes, but this can never happen except when they designate neither. *To dip*, for instance, applies to an *immersed world*, and it applies to an immersed insect. But it designates neither. How ludicrous is the expression, the storm *popped upon* the young men! Even were we to grant for a moment, that *pop* should enlarge its signification so as to apply to the most violent storm, still it would express only the force of the storm, and not its effect. The translation would then be, "the storm rushed on them with tremendous violence;" but this would not import the effect of the storm, as issuing in their destruction. In many ways they might escape from the greatest storm ever known. Jonah was even cast into the sea, and yet escaped. Even when the *whistle* becomes a *tempest*, it will not serve Mr. Ewing.

The same observations will apply to the other example from Josephus: "That he would *baptize* or *sink* the city." How is it that Mr. Ewing has translated this as if the verb was in the passive voice, and as if Josephus himself was not supposed the *baptizer*? "For the city," says Mr. Ewing, "must be *epibaptized* or *overwhelmed*." Do not the people, in their expostulations with Josephus, in order to dissuade him from leaving them, tell him, that if he should depart, he would himself *sink* or epibaptize the city? His desertion of the city would be the means of its ruin. He is then represented as doing the thing that would be the consequence of his departure.

But how is this, as Mr. Ewing says, an overwhelming *by rushing* or *pouring upon*? Did Josephus, by *popping off from* the city, *pop upon it* with such violence as to overwhelm it? This surely implies the mysteries of transubstantiation. Josephus *popped* nothing on the city by leaving it, nor did he rush or pour on it with violence by flying from it. *Epi*, then, in this compound, can afford no countenance to the supposition, that in baptism the water is popped or poured upon the baptized person. To suit the example to this purpose, Josephus must have been represented as pouring the baptizing substance on the city.

Upon the whole, Mr. Ewing labours under a capital mistake with respect to the effect of the prepositions prefixed to this verb. The Greek prepositions have a much more extensive and varied power in composition than ours have, in such compounds as *pop in*, *pop out*, &c. *Epibaptize*, which he supposes expressly to imply that the water is poured on the baptized, does not in one instance occur in syntax suitable to his interpretation, even although the meaning of the verb were doubtful.

13. In this theory of Mr. Ewing, we have the strongest evidence that our opponents are not themselves satisfied with any mode of defence hitherto devised. We have Mr. Ewing's own virtual acknowlegment, that the ground on which pouring has till his time been held for bap-

tism, is not firm. Can there be a more certain sign that he himself was dissatisfied with the usual view of the subject, than his having recourse to so extravagant a theory? If he has taken to sea in this bark of bulrushes, must he not have considered the ship which he left as being in the very act of sinking? I call on the unlearned Christian to consider this circumstance. What must be the necessities of a cause that requires such a method of defence! This theory is not only unsound, and unsupported by the Greek language, but it is ludicrous in the extreme. Since the heavens were stretched over the earth, there has not been such a chimerical scheme embodied under the name of criticism. The thought that the ordinances of Christ could be squeezed out of the radical sounds contained in words, or that the actual meaning of words may be authoritatively determined by such a species of etymology, is frightfully fanatical. Sober criticism can lend no ear to such dreams. What, then, must be the desperate situation of that cause that takes aid from such a theory as that of Mr. Ewing!

The passages which Mr. Ewing brings forward in support of his theory are already mostly considered. I shall, therefore, only touch on a few of his observations on them. There is one rule of interpretation which Mr. Ewing prescribes to us, at which I am beyond measure astonished. Though he does not formally state it as a canon, yet he reasons on the supposition, that we are obliged to find an exact parallel for immersion, with all its circumstances, in the purifications of the heathens or of the Jews. Having quoted the passage from Herodotus, which is so decisive in our favour, he endeavours to lessen its value in the following words: "After all," says he, "there is one very manifest point of difference. The person who adopts this summary method of purification, performs the operation for himself. The immersion of one person by another, for any purpose except that of medical treatment, or that of murder, I can discover in no writings whatever, sacred or profane." And does Mr. Ewing really think that any such authority is necessary to determine the meaning of this word? Must we seek for a model for Christian baptism, either among Jewish or heathen rites? I care not if there never had been a human being immersed in water since the creation: if the word denotes *immersion,* and if Christ enjoins it, I will contend for it as confidently as if all nations, in all ages, had been daily in the practice of baptizing each other. Whether I am to immerse myself in baptism, or be immersed by another, I am to learn from the Scripture accounts of the ordinance, not either from the meaning of the word, or the practice of nations. The demand of Mr. Ewing is unreasonable beyond anything that I recollect to have found in controversy. If it could not be accounted for by the strength of prejudice, it would indicate a want of discernment that no man will impute to Mr. Ewing. The man who demands, in order to the proof of immersion in baptism, that a complete model of the ordinance be found in Jewish or heathen purifications, must either labour under the influence of the strongest bias, or be strangely deficient in the powers of discrimination. " *For any purpose except that of medical treatment, or that of murder ! ! !*" And is not any of these cases as authoritative as an *immersion for purification?* Is not the immersion of a man for medical purposes, as much an *immersion*, and as authoritative to show the meaning of the word, as an *immersion* for superstitious purposes? Examples are useful to settle the meaning of the word, not as a model for the ordinance. The dipping of the flea's foot in Aristophanes, is as authoritative as the immersion of a Pharisee for purification. But what heightens the extravagance of this demand is, that while Mr. Ewing calls for a complete model for Christian immersion in the purifications of Jews and heathens, he is so easily satisfied with evidence on his own side of the question, that he has found *popping water on the turned up face* to be the baptism of the New Testament. Here he has the eyes of a lynx, for he has seen what I believe no other man ever pretended to see in the Scriptures.

But it seems, that even a complete model in heathen purifications would not serve us. Nay, if we have been condemned for want of a heathen pattern for baptism, we are also condemned for having it. "There is also," says Mr. Ewing, " a point, not of difference, but of resemblance, between this example and an anti-pædobaptist's baptism, which seems to have very much astonished the historian, namely, the person's plunging himself, ' with his very clothes on.' It was evidently regarded as a singular and monstrous sort of purification by this heathen writer ; and we shall meet with abundant evidence that it was never so seen in Israel." Here we are condemned for observing baptism according to the model, as we were before condemned for coming short of the model. Surely I may answer such reasoning in the language of Christ : " We have piped unto you, and ye have not danced ; we have mourned unto you, and ye have not lamented." As long as the mind is in a state to make such objections, it would not yield though one should rise from the dead. A heathen thought purification with the clothes on, singular and monstrous. Must Christ's ordinance conform to heathen notions of purification ? But, Mr. Ewing, how can you assert that Herodotus regarded this as monstrous ? There is no such thing said, nor implied. The historian does not mention the circumstance as monstrous, or in any degree improper, but as an evidence of the abhorrence that the Egyptians have for swine, and the deep pollution contracted by their touch. The thing that was singular and strange is, that the person touching the swine supposed the pollution to affect his very garments, or that it was as necessary to baptize them as himself. The polluted Egyptian baptized himself, with his very clothes, that he might purify his clothes, which he considered to be defiled as well as himself. The Christian is baptized with his clothes on, not indeed to imitate the example of the Egyptian, but for the sake of decency. Had Christian baptism been like Egyptian baptism, an ordinance in which every believer was to baptize himself, there would have been no need to baptize with the clothes on. The thing, then, that is strange and singular in the Egyptian baptism, is not strange in Christian baptism. It would be strange if persons bathing alone in a retired place should encumber themselves with a bathing dress ; but it would not be strange to find them using a bathing dress on a crowded strand. A little discrimination under the influence of candour would have taken away all monstrosity from this

example. There is nothing in the historian that in the remotest degree gives ground for Mr. Ewing's assertion. Is this a candid or a Christian way of representing evidence? If men will indulge themselves in such liberties with the documents on which they found their report of antiquity, no credit could be given to history. Mr. Ewing here represents Herodotus as regarding the circumstance as *monstrous*, without the smallest authority from his words. Is not this bearing false witness? The intention, I am convinced, is not to misrepresent evidence. Yet evidence is misrepresented, where nothing but bias could discover the supposed meaning. Well may a Roman Catholic see all the doctrines of popery in the Scriptures, when Mr. Ewing can find the circumstance of bathing with the *clothes on*, designated as monstrous in this language of Herodotus. If, in all the passages which I have considered, I have made one such misrepresentation, let me be put to shame. I may mistake the meaning of my author, but a mistake that indicates a bias, I hope no man will be able to find in my criticism. I would let baptism and the Bible itself sink, rather than force evidence. What I demand from my antagonist, I will grant him in return. I will not lay down one law for him, and walk by another myself. I will do all in my power to save the Israelitish spies; but if this cannot be done without a falsehood, let them perish.

The same uncandid and unreasonable mode of reasoning is again resorted to in the following language. Formerly he had complained that the examples implying immersion, do not respect cases in which one person baptized another, but each baptized himself. " Here," he says, " it must be confessed, that in some of the cases, there are *dippers* as well as *dipped*." Now, if there is, in any instance, the model he requires, why does he complain, that in some instances it is not to be found? Does he suppose that every instance must contain the full model, or that one instance is not sufficient for the purpose, even were it necessary to produce such a model from heathenism? If, in one case, he finds a *dipper*, is it not enough to show that the word may be applied to the ordinance of Christian immersion? But whether a person *dips* himself, or is *dipped* by another, has no more to do with the meaning of this word, than the name of the baptized person has. Nor can an example from heathen or Jewish purification, that would coincide in every particular with the external form of the ordinance, be of more authority as a model, than an example of plunging a pick-pocket in the mire. To speak in the above way, then, is totally to misconceive the nature of the evidence on which a just conclusion can be founded.

Mr. Ewing complains, that " the other cases also, are not those of voluntary plunging, but of fatal sinking." But is not immersion *immersion*, whether the immersed person rises or sinks? We want no aid from these examples but what they can give, what they cannot refuse to give, and what our opponents admit that they give. The examples in which the word applies to sinking, prove that the word implies *dipping*. This is all we want from them. That the baptized person is not to lie at the bottom, but to rise up out of the waters, we learn not from the word, but from the accounts of the ordinance. We wish no model in heathenism, as an authority for the ordinance of baptism. This we have in the Scriptures. We are indebted to the heathen writers only for the meaning of the word. It is altogether astonishing that a man like Mr. Ewing can indulge in such trifling. If all his requirements were necessary, no ordinance of Christ could be proved. But happily his requirements are only for his opponents. They do not regulate his own conduct. He relaxes from his rigour, wherever his *popping* scheme comes to the trial. If one instance could be brought, in which this disputed word necessarily signifies to pour or sprinkle, though it related to a person sprinkling himself, what would he say, should I object that this was no authority for one person to sprinkle another? Very true, he would doubtless say, but it proves that the word signifies to sprinkle. I have other ways of learning whether baptism is a sprinkling of one's self, or a sprinkling of one by another. In like manner, the examples of involuntary immersion prove to me the meaning of the word. From Christ and his apostles I learn that Christian immersion is neither involuntary nor fatal. It is a grievous thing to be obliged to notice such reasoning.

Mr. Ewing exclaims, " Is this the pattern of *baptizers* and *baptized?*" No indeed, Mr. Ewing, this is not the pattern, and I never heard of any who made this a model. But these examples are authority to show the meaning of the word. Had Mr. Ewing produced one instance in which the disputed word signifies to *sprinkle* or *pour*, and that instance referred to bespattering with filth, what would he say were we to exclaim, " Is this the pattern of baptism by sprinkling?" Would he not pounce upon us with the reply : " This determines the meaning of the word, which is all any examples from heathen writers can do. That pure water is to be used in baptism, we learn from the Scriptures." And why does he not use common sense in his objections?

" Shall we illustrate the office of John the Baptist, and of the apostles and evangelists of Christ," says Mr. Ewing, " by the work of providential destruction, or that of murderers?" We shall determine the meaning of the word by such examples. Nothing more can be done by any examples from antiquity. Nothing more do we want. I put it to every candid reader,—I put it to Mr. Ewing himself, whether he would make such an objection, if the examples were in his favour. Nay, we have the answer virtually expressed in the authority which he gives to the example of heathen and Jewish purifications. While he complains of us for establishing the meaning of the word by documents that apply the word to involuntary and fatal immersion, his mode of reasoning in other places gives an authority to heathen models of purification that they do not possess.

" These examples imply," says Mr. Ewing, " not a mere *dipping* and *up again*, an *immersion* immediately followed by an *emersion ;* but a continued and permanent immersion, a remaining under water." Now, is not this mode of reasoning perverse and unjust? If some examples are found, in which this word is applied to the dipping of things taken immediately up, is not this sufficient to establish the propriety of its application to the ordinance of baptism? Can it be necessary that all the examples refer to things taken up? Will Mr. Ewing never learn that we are seeking, from these examples, not an authoritative model for baptism, but the meaning of a word? If the disputed word, in some instances, applies to things taken immediately up, and in others to things never taken up, a true critic, nay, common sense, will learn that the word itself can designate neither *taking up* nor *lying at the bottom*. One instance in which the word applies when the thing is taken up after dipping, is as good as ten thousand.

But though some examples of the occurrence of this word imply a permanent immersion or destruction, the word *baptizo* never expresses this. Whether the thing is taken up, or is allowed to remain, is not expressed by the word, but is implied by the circumstances. The word, without one exception, signifies simply *to dip*.

In the following extract, the reasoning is more plausible. The author seems to think that it is demonstration. However, when it is dissected, it has no muscles. " Some may think," says Mr. Ewing, " it was not necessary to use a word directly to express the *emersion*, because if *immersion* really was enjoined, the *emersion* must be understood to follow of course, from the necessity of the case. This is a perfectly natural thought, but it cannot help the cause of anti-pædobaptists. According to their views, baptism is a *twofold* symbol, representing *two* things of distinct and equal importance. The *immersion* and the *emersion* are both of them parts of this symbol ; the first representing the *death*, and the second the *resurrection* of Christ. Now, if this be the case, the word *baptizo* is a name for *the one half only* of their ordinance of baptism. It entirely fails them as to *the other half*. A word may have various meanings, but it cannot have two of them at the same time. If, therefore, this word *pops them down*, it certainly cannot give any warrant, or suggest any literal or figurative meaning, for their *popping up again*." Now, how can we deliver ourselves out of this tremendous gulf? Nothing can be more easy. Distinguish the things that are different, and place every thing on its proper evidence, and all difficulty vanishes. The word *baptizo*, even applied to baptism, expresses *immersion* only. Yet I contend, that in baptism there is a *two-fold* symbol. How is this? I learn the meaning of the word from its use ; and I learn the meaning of the ordinance, not from the word, but from the Scripture explanation of the import of the ordinance. If there was nothing said in Scripture about the import of baptism, I should learn nothing on the subject from the word that designates it. I should learn as little of its being a symbol of the death of Christ, as of his resurrection. I learn neither from the word ; for it is possible that this word might have been used, without teaching anything on the subject. I learn both from the Scripture explanations of Christ's institution.

But it may be said, if the word signifies immersion, it may be a symbol of Christ's burial ; but it is not fitted to be such a symbol, unless it also signifies to *emerge*.—Now, as far as depends on what is actually expressed by the word, I grant that this is the case. But as in the ordinance of baptism, the *emersion* is as necessary as the *immersion*, there is nothing to prevent the institutor to make the *emersion* symbolical as well as the immersion. If the institutor had not made it symbolical, if it was not explained as pointing to Christ's resurrection and ours, I would as soon anoint with oil and spittle, as deduce it from the meaning of the word, even though the word had expressed both *immersion* and *emersion*. The ordinance is as fit to represent *emersion* as *immersion*, though the word baptism expresses the latter only. *The symbol consists in the thing, not in the name.* There is no necessity that the name should designate every thing contained in the ordinance. But even granting that this is necessary, what would follow? Not that baptism is not *immersion*, but that baptism is an emblem of burial only. This would do Mr. Ewing little service. If we can once persuade him to have himself *popped into the water*, it is not likely that he will be so obstinate as to reject the half of the edification of the ordinance.

Mr. Ewing says, "Now if this be the case, the word *baptizo* is a name for *the one half only* of their ordinance of baptism." But why should the name of any ordinance designate every thing that the ordinance is explained by the institutor as containing? This is not necessary; nor do Scripture ordinances at all recognise the authority of such a principle. Is it not strange that Mr. Ewing should have forgotten one of the names of the Lord's supper which is liable to the like objection? It is called *the breaking of bread;* yet it includes the drinking of wine. Such are the effects of intemperate zeal. It requires, in one instance, what it overlooks in another.

SECTION XIV.—ON THE BAPTISM OF THE SPIRIT.—The baptism of the Spirit is a figurative expression, explicable on the principle of a reference to immersion. This represents the abundance of the gifts and influences of the Spirit of God in the enlightening and sanctification of believers. That which is immersed in a liquid, is completely subjected to its influence and imbued with its virtues; so *to be immersed in the Spirit*, represents the subjection of soul, body, and spirit, to his influence. The whole man is sanctified. It is objected that the Holy Spirit is said to be *poured out*, and therefore, to represent the pouring of the Spirit, baptism must be by *pouring*. This is the grand resource of our opponents, and is more specious to the illiterate than anything that has been said. A very considerable part of the language of Scripture, in the representation of the gifts of the Spirit, is founded on the figure of *pouring;* and readers who have no discrimination, or who are under the influence of bias, at once conclude that this *pouring* is the baptism of the Spirit. This argument is drawn out in formidable array by Mr. Ewing; and is relied on with the utmost confidence by Dr. Wardlaw. But it is nothing but a careless confusion of things entirely distinct, and is founded on an egregious blunder, as the reader will perceive from the following observations.

First, The word in its literal sense must guide all its figurative applications. The explanation of the figure must conform to the literal meaning, but the literal meaning can never bend to the figurative. The latter, indeed, may assist us in ascertaining the former; but when the former is ascertained, the latter must be explained in accordance with it. But the literal meaning of this word is ascertained to be that of *immersion,* by a strength of evidence, and a multitude of examples, that cannot be exceeded with respect to any word of the same frequency of occurrence. This is a fixed point; and in the examination of the reference in the baptism of the Spirit, nothing can be admitted inconsistent with this. *The baptism of the Spirit* must have a reference to *immersion*, because baptism is *immersion*, and in its literal sense never signifies anything else. When we come to the examination of this figure, or any other of the same word, we must ground on this ascertained fact. As there is not one instance in the literal use of the word, in which it must signify *pouring*, or anything but *dipping*, the pretensions of *pouring*, as the figurative baptism, do not deserve even a hearing. They cannot legitimately even go before a jury, because true bills are not found. There is no ground of trial, because there is nothing in the allegations that can at all excite a doubt. *Pouring cannot be the figurative baptism, because baptism never literally denotes pouring.*

Secondly, This opinion is founded on the egregious and blasphemous error which teaches that God is material, and that there is a literal pouring out of his Spirit, which may be represented by the pouring of water. Our opponents understand the baptism of the Spirit to be a literal baptism, and the pouring out of the Spirit to be a literal pouring out of Him who is immaterial. But though there is a real communication of the Spirit, there is no real or literal baptism of the Spirit. Let the reference in the baptism of the Spirit be what it may, it cannot be a literal baptism, because God is not material. We cannot be literally either *dipped* into God, or have him *poured* on us. *Pouring,* then, in baptism, even if *baptism* were *pouring,* could not represent the *pouring* of the Spirit, because the Spirit is not literally *poured.* Baptism, whatever be the mode, cannot represent either the manner of conveying the Spirit, or his operations in the soul. These things cannot be represented by natural things. There is no likeness to the Spirit, nor to the mode of his operations. It is blasphemy to attempt a representation. It would be as easy to make a likeness of God creating the world, and attempt to represent by a picture the Divine operations in the formation of matter, as to represent by symbols the manner of the communication of the Holy Spirit, and his operations on the soul. If Christians were not infatuated with the desire of establishing a favourite system, such gross conceptions of God could not have so long escaped detection. This error is as dishonourable to God, as that of the Anthropomorphites. It degrades the Godhead, by representing it as a *material* substance.

When the Spirit is said to be *poured*, it is a figurative expression, to which there is nothing resemblant in the manner of the Divine operations. What, then, it may be asked, is the resemblance? Why is the Spirit said to be *poured*, if the *pouring* of water does not resemble it? The foundation of the figure is the very reverse of what is supposed. The Spirit is said to be *poured out*, not because there is any actual *pouring*, which is represented by *pouring out* water in baptism, but from the *resemblance between the effects of the influences of the Spirit and those of water.* Between the Spirit itself and water there is no resemblance, more than between an eye or a circle and the Divine nature. Nor is there any resemblance between the mode of the operations of the Spirit, and that of the influences of water. The Holy Spirit is said to be *poured*, because his influences or effects are like those of water, and because he is supposed to dwell above. The Holy Spirit is represented as poured out, on the same principle on which God is said to have come down from heaven, or to look down from heaven, or to have hands and arms. It is in accommodation to our ways of thinking and speaking, not as expressive of reality. The Holy Spirit is figured as water, not to represent any likeness in him to water, just as God is figured as a man. If the Anthropomorphites blasphemously perverted this language to degrade God, as supposing that it teaches that he has actually the human form, it is no less a blasphemous perversion of the language in question, to suppose that it imports a real *pouring out* of the Spirit. The Holy Spirit is said also to be as *dew*. Does this imply that there is a likeness to the falling of dew and the manner of the communication of the Holy Ghost? Our Lord represents the Spirit as a *well*, the waters of which spring up, John iv. 14. Is there also a likeness in the manner of the communication of the Spirit to water *rising up* out of the ground, as well as to water *poured out* from above? The Holy Spirit is also represented as a river whose streams make glad the city of God. Is there also a likeness between his operations and the *running* of water? In all these figures, the Spirit is represented in accommodation to natural things, and natural things are not accommodated to it. *The effects of the one resemble the effects of the other; but as to manner, there is no likeness.* A particular *manner* is given to the operations of the Spirit, to suit the *manner* of the communication of the natural object. Therefore it is that the Spirit has ascribed to him all the various modes mentioned above. The Spirit, in every figure, takes the *manner* of the resembling object, but the resembling object never takes the *manner* of the Spirit, because nothing is known of his manner. Of this there must not be—cannot be any likeness. If the manner of the communication of the Spirit could be represented, one only of these modes must be employed. If his manner is *pouring*, it cannot be like *dew*, nor like *rain*, nor like a *river*, nor like a spring-well. But if the likeness be merely between the *effects* of the Spirit and the *effects* of water, then the Spirit may be represented as *dew*, or *rain*, or a *river*, or a *spring-well*, just as the water is supposed to be applied. It is absurd to suppose an ordinance to be appointed to represent the mode of the Spirit's communication; and as it is spoken of under all these modes, each of them might claim an ordinance as well as pouring. Baptism might as well represent water *rising out of the earth, distilling in dew, running in a stream*, or *falling in rain*, as *pouring out of a cup*. Each of these represents the blessings of the Spirit, by conforming the language about the operations of the Spirit to a particular state of the water; none of them represent the mode of these operations. The Holy Spirit is said to fall; why, then, should not baptism represent falling? The Holy Spirit is represented as wind; why, then, is there no *blowing* in baptism? The Holy Spirit is represented by *fire;* why is there no fire used in this ordinance? The gift of the Spirit was represented by the *breathing* of Jesus on the apostles; why is there no *breathing* in baptism? The influences of the

Spirit are represented by *oil;* why is not *oil* used in baptism? The reception of the Holy Spirit is represented by *drinking water;* why is there no *drinking* in this ordinance?

In like manner, curses are represented as *poured out* by God on his enemies, or put into their hands as a cup to be drunk. Drinking is equally an emblem of blessings and curses, because it is the one or the other according to the qualities of the liquid. In the judgments of God on the wicked, there is no likeness to the manner of the Divine operations. Why, then, should such a likeness be supposed when pouring respects blessings? Baptism, then, cannot be either *pouring* or *dipping,* for the sake of representing the *manner* of the conveyance of the Holy Spirit; for there is no such likeness. *Pouring of the Spirit* is a phrase which is itself a figure, not a reality to be represented by a figure. Baptism is a figure, not of the mode of any Divine operation, to which there can be no likeness, but *of the burial and resurrection of Christ,* which may be represented by natural things, because it respects the objects of sense. In this reference it has a real application, a true likeness, and the most important use. Of the *immersion of the Spirit,* I will say the same as of the *pouring of the Spirit,* that it cannot represent the operations of the Spirit, or the mode of his conveyance. Believers are said to be *immersed* into the Spirit, not because there is anything like *immersion* in the *manner* of the reception of the Spirit, but from the resemblance between an object immersed in a fluid, and the sanctification of all the members of the body, and faculties of the soul. The common way in which the *pouring* of the Spirit has been explained, is inconsistent both with sound taste and with sound theology. It mistakes the nature of figurative language, and converts the Godhead into matter.

But though the baptism of the Holy Spirit is a figurative baptism, to which there cannot be a likeness in literal baptism; yet as respects the transaction on the day of Pentecost, there was a real baptism *in the emblems of the Spirit.* The disciples were immersed into the Holy Spirit by the abundance of his gifts; but they were literally covered with the appearance of wind and fire. The place where they met was filled with *the sound as of a rushing mighty wind,* and *cloven tongues as of fire* sat over them. They were then completely covered by the emblems of the Spirit. Now, though there was no dipping of them, yet as they were completely surrounded by the wind and fire, by the catachrestic mode of speech which I before explained, they are said to be *immersed.* This is a process exemplified with respect to innumerable words, and the principle is quite obvious, as well as of daily application. The shepherd, when his sheep are covered with snow in a glen, says that they are *buried* in the snow. When a house falls upon the inhabitants, we say that they are *buried* in its ruins. A general will threaten to *bury* the inhabitants in the ruins of their city. The word *bury* with us, strictly conveys the notion of digging into the earth, as well as of covering over the dead. Yet here it is extended to a case in which the former does not take place. Burial usually is performed by both operations, but here the thing is performed by one; and therefore the word that designates both, is elegantly assigned to that which serves the purpose of both. Just so with respect to being covered with a fluid. *Immersion* denotes that the thing *immersed* is put into the *immersing* substance; yet when the same effect is produced without the manner of the operation, the usual name of the operation is catachrestically given to the result. Virgil's expression, " Pocula sunt fontes liquidi," Georg. iii. p. 529, is an exact parallel. " The liquid fountains are their cups," &c. Now, *fountains* are not *cups*, more than the thing referred to is *immersion*, yet they are called cups, because in the instance referred to they serve the purpose of *cups*. This poet supplies innumerable examples of the operation of the principle here illustrated.

Let it not be supposed that the principle which I have now illustrated is at all akin to that unfounded fancy of Mr. Ewing, with respect to the supposed *exaggerated* meaning of *baptizo*. Mr. Ewing in this gives two meanings to a word, at variance with each other, and while he calls it figurative, he makes it literal; and agreeably to his doctrine, it must, in the hyperbolical meaning, hold directly, and immediately, and independently, of the primary meaning. The principle which I have explained is not of this paradoxical kind. I give but the one meaning to the word; and, even when there is no literal *immersion*, I maintain that the word never drops its characteristic meaning. Indeed, the beauty of the figure is that the word suggests its own peculiar meaning, even when it does not literally apply. It professedly calls a thing by a name, which literally does not in all respects belong to it, to gratify the imagination. Why does Virgil call *fountains* by the name of *cups?* Not because they were really *cups*, or because *cup* signifies *fountain* literally, but because the human mind by its constitution is delighted in certain circumstances by viewing a thing as being what it is not, but which in some respects it resembles. The process for which I contend, I can vindicate by the soundest philosophy,—I can trace to its origin in the human mind,—I can illustrate by parallels without number. Mr. Ewing has not attempted to illustrate his figure, nor is it in his power to show its foundation in the human mind, or to sanction it by corresponding examples.

Mr. Booth, with a truly critical judgment and correct taste, illustrates this mode of speech by alluding to the electrical bath, "so called," says the writer whom he quotes, " because it surrounds the patient with an atmosphere of electrical fluid, in which he is *plunged.*" Here the writer to whom he refers, scruples not to say that the patient is *plunged* into the fluid which is brought around him. Indeed, the very term electrical bath is an exemplification of the operation of the same principle. *Bath* properly refers to a vessel of water in which persons are *bathed:* but by a catachresis, this term is given to a vessel filled with a fluid, which fluid is not for the purpose of bathing.

Thirdly, There is another grand fallacy in this argument. *It confounds things that are different.* Water is *poured* out into a vessel in order to have things put into it. But the *pouring* out of the water, and the application of the water so poured out, are different things. Water is poured into a bath in order to immerse the feet or the body, but the *immersion* is not the *pouring*. Now, our opponents confound these two things. Because the Spirit is said to be poured out in order to the baptism of the Spirit, they groundlessly conclude that the *pouring* is the baptism. A foreigner might as well contend that, when it is said in the English language, " Water was *poured into* a bath, and they *immersed* themselves," it is implied that *pouring* and *immersing* are the same thing.

> ———"Then taking the resplendent vase
> Allotted always to that use, she first
> Infused cold water largely, then the warm.
> .   .   .   .
> She, then, approaching, ministered the bath
> To her own king."—Cowper, *Odys.* xix.

The *pouring* out of the Spirit is as different a figure from the *baptism* of the Spirit, as the *infusion* of the water into the bath is different from the application of the water to the object in the bath.

Now, let us apply these observations to Mr. Ewing's reasoning. Dissection is not a pleasant work, either to the operator or the spectators; but it is impossible to make an anatomist without it. General observations must be applied to the subject in detail, that all may thoroughly understand their application, and perceive their justness. It is tedious, but the business cannot be effectually done without the knife.

Speaking of water, air, and fire, Mr. Ewing says. " which are all considered in Scripture as elements of baptism." Air and fire were elements of the baptism that took place on the day of Pentecost, but they are not elements in the standing ordinance of Christ. In the baptism of the day of Pentecost there was no water at all. They who were baptized on that day in wind and fire, had been baptized before. This was not the ordinance of Christian baptism, nor an ordinance at all. Christ himself was the administrator, and it is called baptism only in an allusive sense. If it was baptism as an ordinance, it would prove, that after the baptism of water, there ought to be another baptism into wind and fire.

" And in this connexion," continues Mr. Ewing, " these elements are uniformly represented as *poured, inspired, and made to fall from above.*" Very true, but is this *pouring, inspiring, falling from above,* called baptism? Never—never.

Mr. Ewing asserts, that these emblems of the work of the Spirit are an allusion to the creation of man. But how does he find the fire in that work? Why, was there not " *the fire of life?*" But the *fire of life* is no element. This is only a figurative expression. It is mere fanaticism to take such mysteries out of the Scriptures. Is it not strange that Mr. Ewing will allow himself to indulge so wild a fancy in deriving emblematical instruction from his own creations, and that he so obstinately refuses to take that edification from the import of baptism, which is obviously contained in the apostolical explanations of the ordinance?

He says that baptism " consists in a representation of all the elements employed in our first creation." I have remarked that there was no fire employed in our first creation; and Christian baptism has no representation either of fire or air. Nor has the water of baptism any allusion to the water that moistened the clay in the creation of man. These mysteries are akin to those that the Romish church so piously finds in the oil and spittle used in baptism.

He says that the promise of the baptism with the Holy Spirit and with fire " was given to all the disciples." Then the promise has not been fulfilled. Wind and fire are not used in the baptism of all disciples. This baptism was peculiar to the day of Pentecost. This promise cannot be supposed as literally applying to all disciples. He says, " it belongs to them, both as it regards gracious influence, and as it regards miraculous inspiration." But the baptism of the day of Pentecost could not respect the spiritual birth, else there would be two baptisms representing the same thing. The persons baptized on the day of Pentecost were previously baptized into water as being born again. It could not respect their progressive sanctification, else it might be repeated as often as the Lord's supper, and every disciple would equally need the *wind and fire* literally. Nor have all disciples the promise of miraculous gifts. *Miraculous inspiration* he understands as applying to all believers only in the sense of their being " built on the foundation of the apostles and prophets; that is, their faith is founded on the authority and energy of that Spirit by which the apostles and prophets were inspired." What an abuse of words is this! A man is miraculously inspired, because he believes the doctrine of an inspired person!!!

Mr. Ewing derives another argument for pouring, from the expression, " *born from above*," John iii. But *from above*, merely designates that God is the author of this birth, without respect to any emblem appointed to represent it, though baptism is, in ver. 5, referred to as its emblem. Born *from above*, is perfectly synonymous with *born of God*.

As little can be built on the emblem, John xx. 22. The *breathing* on the disciples was not a *baptism*, nor is it called a *baptism*.

Mr. Ewing says, that " the mode of the baptism, Acts i. 5, is explained ver. 8." But ver. 8 says nothing of the mode of that baptism : " But ye shall receive power, after that the Holy Ghost is *come upon you*." The *coming* is not the *baptism*. The influence of the Spirit when *come*, not the *coming* of the Spirit, is the baptism.

The author observes, with respect to Acts ii. 2, " that ' the sound' of the wind was heard *descending* from heaven, and filling the house." Yes—but the *descending* is not the *baptism*. The wind *descended* to fill the house, that when the house was filled with the wind, the disciples might be baptized in it. Their baptism consisted in being totally surrounded with the wind, not in the manner in which the wind came. The water must be brought from the river or fountain, to fill the vessel for immersion. Does this say that the conveyance of the water is baptism?

Mr. Ewing says, that " distributed flames of fire appeared like tongues, and *sat down* upon every one of them." Though this translation is warranted by the learned Bishop Pearce, it is by no means justifiable. The common version is perfectly exact. It is not fire cloven, or distributed into tongues, but cloven tongues. There were not only many tongues, to denote many languages; but the tongues were cloven, to denote that the same individual could speak different languages. The fire *sat down* upon each of them. The baptism did not consist, as Mr. Ewing supposes, in the *sitting down*, or the mode of the *coming of the flame*, but in their being *under it*. They were surrounded by the wind, and covered by the fire above. They were therefore buried in wind and fire.

It is quite obvious, indeed, that even the mode in which the house is said to have been filled with the wind on the day of Pentecost, is no more *pouring* than it is *dipping*. The wind is not said to be *poured into* the house, but to come *rushing* with a mighty noise; or the sound that filled the house, was like the sound of a *rushing* mighty wind. If literal baptism has any allusion to this, the mode ought to be that of a *rushing wind*. If the manner of the coming of the emblem is the *baptism*, then baptism is neither *pouring* nor *immersion*, but *rushing*.

But even if the Pentecost baptism were, for argument sake, allowed to be pouring, this would not relieve Mr. Ewing. The whole house was filled with the sound of the wind—the emblem of the Spirit. This was not *popping* a little water with the hand on the turned up face. When Mr. Ewing pours water on the baptized person, till the latter is covered completely with it, he will give as much trouble as if he were to immerse at once. In whatever way the water in baptism is to be applied, this passage teaches us that the baptized person must be totally covered.

Speaking of our Lord's baptism, Mr. Ewing asserts, " the meaning of the ordinance, and the very mode of its administration, confirmed the truth that the Holy Spirit was about to be given." But how did the meaning and mode of Christ's baptism confirm this truth? Does not this take for granted that Mr. Ewing's meaning of the mode and import of this ordinance is just? If the very thing in debate is granted to Mr. Ewing, no doubt he will prove it. He refers to John vii. 39, and Acts xix. 2, 3. But neither of these passages asserts what he teaches. He speaks also of the influences of the Holy Spirit, " visibly *descending from on high*, and *abiding upon him*." The influence of the Holy Spirit did not *visibly* descend. It was the emblem of the spirit that descended *visibly*. The appearance of a dove *descended visibly* and *abode upon him*. But was this Christ's baptism? The baptism was over before the emblem descended. Besides, the *descending* of the Spirit could not be the baptism of the Spirit. Jesus is not here said to be baptized with the Spirit. This baptism was literal baptism. This extraordinary communication might indeed have been called a baptism, just as in the case of the disciples, but it is not so called here; and if it were so called, it would not be the *descent* of the Spirit, that is the baptism, but the communication of it after its descent. If the baptism consisted in the *descent*, the baptism was over when the dove reached Jesus. Is it possible that there is any one who has so little of the powers of discrimination, as not to be able to distinguish between bringing water from a fountain, and the use of that water when it is brought—between pouring water into a bath, and bathing in the bath? Yet every one who concludes from the *pouring* of the Spirit, that baptism must be *pouring*, either wants this discrimination, or is unwilling to use it.

Another passage alleged by Mr. Ewing on this subject, is Psal. xlv. 2, "Grace is *poured into* thy lips," &c. What has this to do with baptism? The Spirit, indeed, is here said to be poured, but did any man ever deny this? But let it never be forgotten, that such language does not imply the blasphemous notion, that there is any literal pouring in the giving of the Spirit, or that an ordinance is appointed to represent this pouring. It is quite useless, then, to refer to each of the passages which Mr. Ewing alleges to prove a descent. The *descent* is not the *baptism*, and cannot represent any real movement in the Spirit. The same answer will serve for all. But Mr. Ewing says, that " John supposed Jesus to receive the symbol of the Holy Spirit's descent, and presently he was seen, by miracle, to receive the reality." And is it possible that Mr. Ewing can say, that what was seen after the baptism of Christ was the reality!!! The appearance of a dove seen to light on the head of Christ, the reality of the communication of the Spirit!!! Surely, surely, the dove itself was but the emblem, not the reality represented by an emblem of baptism.

But was the dove *poured out* of heaven? Is not she Spirit said to *descend* from heaven, in conformity to the dove, the emblem? *This shows that the descent of the Spirit is spoken of in language always suited to the emblem under which he is represented.* When water is the emblem, his descent is spoken of as pouring, or as falling like dew, &c. When the dove is the emblem, the descent is spoken of, not as pouring, but as the descent of a bird. Such varied language is suited to the various emblems, and not to any reality in the manner of the communication of the Spirit. Let any Christian attend to this observation, and he will be ashamed of the childish, or rather heathenish explanation of this language, that implies that the Godhead is matter. Pouring is most frequently used for the sending of the gifts of the Spirit; but I have shown that the same thing is spoken of with reference to a fountain springing up—a running stream,—the rain that is said to fall,—or the dew that distils. And here the same thing is exhibited as the descent of a bird, in conformity to the dove, which is the emblem employed. Let us hear no more, then, of baptism as *pouring*, in order to represent the *pouring* of the Spirit. We may as well make baptism a *flying*, to represent the descent of the dove; or a *blowing* and a *blazing*, to represent the wind and fire on the day of Pentecost; or a *stream*, to represent the river that supplies the city of God; or a *jet*, to represent the springing of a fountain; or a *distillation*, to represent the gentle falling of the dew; or a *shower-bath*, to represent the falling of the rain.

But if we are so obstinate as to resist the passages which Mr. Ewing has alleged above, the most incredulous will doubtless surrender to the "view expressly given (Acts ii. 16—21, 33, 38, 39,) of baptism with water, in consequence of the performance of the promise of baptism with the Spirit." "I will *pour out* of my Spirit," &c. "He hath *poured out* this, which ye now see and hear." "For as yet he was *fallen upon* none of them." "The Holy Ghost *fell upon* them all." The reply I have given will equally apply to this. The *pouring* is not the *baptism*, though the Spirit was *poured out*, that they might be *baptized* in it. The *descent* and the *pouring* are over, *before* the baptism takes place. But it may be alleged, Is it not said (Acts xi. 15, 16, 17,) that the Spirit's falling on them brought to remembrance the promise of the baptism of the Spirit? Does not this import that the baptism of the Spirit is the same thing with the falling of the Spirit?— It implies, indeed, that the baptism of the Spirit fulfilled the promise; but it does not imply that the baptism was the *falling*. The *falling* preceded the *baptism*. Rain *falls* to *moisten* the earth. The *moistening* of the earth is not the *falling* of the rain; the falling is a previous process. Suppose that in a drought, a man skilled in the signs of the weather, should foretel that *on to-morrow the earth will be moistened with water*, should we not consider the prophecy fulfilled when we saw rain falling? Yet *falling* is not expressed by the word *moistening*. Just so with *the pouring* and *the baptism of the Spirit*. Let my opponents bring to the subject a small portion of discrimination, and they will instantly discern that the *falling* of the Spirit on the disciples, fulfilled the promise of the baptism of the Spirit, though *falling* and baptism are two very different things. Is not *falling* itself different from *pouring*? They are modes as different as *pouring* and *dipping*. But every thing will serve Mr. Ewing that *pops down*. Yet strange, though he argues with equal confidence from every mode of *descent*, he comes at last to the confident conclusion, that no mode of descent will answer, but that of pouring. Though *falling* and *flying* will serve him in opposing immersion, yet he unceremoniously dismisses them all, when through their means he has gained the victory. Even decent and innocent *sprinkling*, that has held joint and unquestioned possession with its sister *pour* for so long a period, he turns out of doors with every mark of indignity.

But with respect to the *falling* of the Spirit on the disciples in the house of Cornelius, how did Peter and the rest perceive the descent? Was there anything visible? No; they knew that the Holy Spirit fell on them, because they saw the effect of his influences. Acts x. 46. The influences, then, of the Spirit, and not *the falling*, were the baptism of the Spirit.

Mr. Ewing concludes with all the confidence of demonstration : "Is it credible," says he, "that a word which signifies the motion of body upon body, in any direction, should, when applied to represent both the figure and the reality of a DESCENT FROM ABOVE, be meant to be understood of motion in an OPPOSITE DIRECTION?" &c. Stop a little, Mr. Ewing. You have said that the disputed word signifies the motion of body upon body, but you have not proved this. Nor is this word employed to represent the *descent from above* in any instance which you have brought forward. Why does Mr. Ewing substisute the word *baptize* here for the word *descend?* In his premises, the words are *pour, descend, fall*, &c.; in his conclusion, they become *baptize*. This is a trick in sleight of hand which we will not admit. It is utterly unlawful to reason from words that denote descent, and then draw the conclusion from *baptizo*. So far from its being fact that *baptizo*, in the passages referred to, is applied to represent both the figure and the reality of a descent, the words that are pplied for this purpose do not represent the baptism, but a process previous to the baptism. Whether the water, or the wind, or the fire, descends from above, or ascends from below, is nothing to the baptism. The baptism is the same, in whatever manner the baptizing substance is conveyed to the place of baptizing.

The authority of Milton is utterly valueless on this subject. I notice it merely to show the boldness and the rashness of Mr. Ewing's criticism. "Because Milton speaks of baptism as dispensed in a river," says Mr. Ewing, "it has been supposed that he favoured the mode of immersion; but I am inclined to think this is a mistake. He says, indeed, of our Saviour's commission to his disciples,

> " 'To them shall leave in charge
> To teach all nations what of him they learned,
> And his salvation ; them who shall believe
> Baptizing in the profluent stream, the sign
> Of washing them from guilt of sin to life
> Pure ; and in mind prepared, if so befall,
> For death, like that which the Redeemer died.' "

Well, reader, what do you think of this? What was Milton's view of the mode of baptism? If our Saviour commanded them to baptize disciples *in the profluent stream*, must not baptism be immersion? What hardihood must that man possess, who will dare to criticise in this manner! But, says Mr. Ewing, "According to this account, baptism is the sign of, not *immersing*, but *washing* in a river." What egregious trifling! *Baptism* is not the sign of *immersing*! That is, *immersing* is not the sign of *immersing*. Very true; for how could a thing be the sign of itself! Well, of what is baptism a sign, according to Milton?— Of *washing in a river!* So then Milton makes baptism a sign of washing in a river! Then the sign and the thing signified are the same. *Washing in a river* is the sign of *washing in a river!* Alas, poor Milton! here thou hast a fool's cap. Illustrious bard! perhaps thou wast a heretic, but certainly thou wast not a fool. Immersion in a river, thou hast said, is the sign of washing from guilt. O that thou hadst known the reality as well as thou didst know the figure! Hadst thou known the Saviour as well as thou hast known the mode of this his ordinance, thou wouldst have been great indeed!

Speaking of the baptism of the Spirit, Milton indeed uses the phrase "on all baptized." But this may be accounted for by his using the word baptize as it is generally used in English. Using the word in its most common acceptation, I would not scruple to say, *baptized with the Spirit,* when there was no need for accuracy of distinction. Milton, also, from not closely considering the phraseology, might fall into the vulgar error, that the baptism of the Spirit was pouring, because the Spirit is said to be *poured out*, though water baptism was by immersion. This way of explaining the apparent inconsistency, I believe, is not uncommon. I hope I have made it unnecessary to have recourse to this resource.

Mr. Ewing quotes a passage from which it has been concluded that Milton was opposed to infant baptism, but from which Mr. Ewing himself concludes that the poet was a friend both to pouring and the baptism of infants. I need not quote the whole passage; the marrow of it is found in the expression, "When ye had laid the purifying element upon his forehead." Now, both this and the whole passage may agree with either of the opinions, and consequently can neither prove nor refute either. Mr. Ewing is well founded in supposing that the disparagement may not respect the sprinkling; but he has no authority to conclude that Milton approved either of sprinkling as the mode, or of infants as the subjects of baptism, because he calls the water laid on the foreheads of infants, *a purifying element*. Water is a *purifying element*, even when applied in the holy water of the Church of Rome. The nature of the water is the same, whether it is used superstitiously, or according to the appointment of God. But Milton might have gone much farther, without giving ground for Mr. Ewing's inference. Many protestants would speak of the baptism of the Church of Rome, with all its trumpery, as true baptism. I am not sure that Mr. Ewing himself would re-baptize a convert from popery. I refer to this note with respect to Milton,— not from any desire to have him on my side, but to manifest the utter unreasonableness of Mr. Ewing's criticism. No evidence could withstand the torture of such an inquisitor. I doubt not but Mr. Ewing could make Milton as orthodox on the subject of the Trinity as on baptism, if he would as zealously set about the work.

We have a delicious morsel of criticism in Mr. Ewing's explanation of the figurative baptism that was fulfilled in the sufferings of Christ. Mr. Ewing is at no loss to find edification in his mode of this ordinance. He does not need the apostles as commissaries to find provision for the house of God. He gives us much edification in his explanation of this ordinance, not to be found in the Scriptures. "We are led to conceive of baptism," says Mr. Ewing, "as the pouring out of water from a cup on the turned up face of the baptized; and whether he be adult or in infancy, it may thus not only wet the surface as a figure of washing, but be drunk into the mouth, as the emblem of a principle of new life, and of continual support and refreshment,—of a source of spiritual and heavenly consolation, and of a willingness given, or to be given, to the baptized, to receive whatever may be assigned them as their portion." Here surely is a discovery. Here is edification unknown to all former ages. Had the ancients perceived this in the import of *sprinkling* or *pouring*, there would have been no need of the honey and milk at baptism. Mr. Ewing can obtain the same thing from the manner of putting the water on the face. Mr. Ewing considers the *drinking* of part of the water poured on the turned up face, as an emblem. If so, then this drinking is essential to true baptism; and if any baptized person happen not to receive a part of the water into the mouth, he is not properly baptized. He wants something that belongs to the ordinance. If this is the case, a very great number are not truly baptized. Nay, it is not only essential to receive some of the baptismal water into the mouth, but it is necessary to drink it. If the child by suffocation makes an involuntary effort to throw out the water, it is unbaptized. I think the probability is, that not one of a thousand actually drink any part of the water. I am convinced also, that very many who baptize by pouring water on the face, so far from being aware of the virtue of drinking a part of the element, endeavour to avoid giving pain to the child by pouring the water into the mouth. If this is a part of the emblem of baptism, the nature of the ordinance is yet unknown to the great body of those who practise infant baptism, and the bulk of those called Christians are unbaptized.

But this *drinking* is not only an emblem, it is an emblem pregnant with mysteries. An emblem of a principle of new life—of continual support and refreshment—of a source of spiritual and heavenly consolation—of a willingness given—ay, and of a willingness to be given, &c. What a striking emblem of this willingness, is a child screaming and coughing to eject the water that falls into its mouth! With what a keen appetite does its thirsty soul drink down this agreeable beverage! What pity that the apostles were ignorant of all these mysteries in baptism! What pity that Mr. Ewing's book was not written till the nineteenth century!—Ah, shame! Can it be possible that the minister of an Independent church, should indulge his fancy in finding mysteries in an ordinance of Christ, which are nowhere explained by the apostles as included in it? Where is the passage of Scripture that explains baptism as containing these mysteries? Where is this drinking found? The very foundation of these mysteries is not once mentioned in the word of God. Where is the turned up face? For anything that the Scriptures contain on the subject, it might as well be the turned up foot. Another might find mysteries in the foot, as well as Mr. Ewing has found them in the face.

Mr. Ewing, however, says, " We are led to this conception of baptism, by various passages of Scripture which it will be found to explain." But to justify such an explanation, it is not enough that it will illustrate the various passages of Scripture. Some passage of Scripture must explain the ordinance in this sense. There is no rite of superstition that might not, by a wild imagination, be alleged to illustrate some passage of Scripture.

We are not yet at the end of the mysteries in the mode of baptism. " The cup," says Mr. Ewing, " which I refer to, is the cup of nature, that is, the hollow of the human hand." Though the word of God says nothing at all about the hand in the administration of this ordinance, Mr. Ewing finds it under the designation of a cup. He gives us the full process in the following words : " From this cup, the baptizer so pours it out on the baptized, that it shall run down his face, as the ointment did from the head of Aaron, and even to the skirts, rather to the upper border or collar of his garment. Psa. cxxxiii. 2." Not only, then, must some of the water be received into the mouth, some of it must also run down on the garments. What nice adjustment is necessary in the position of the person to be baptized, that all these mysteries may be accomplished? Would it not be an improvement if a little oil was added to the ceremony?

Mr. Ewing next proceeds to caution against taking offence at the simplicity of oriental manners, and to justify, by examples, this drinking out of the cup of nature. But all this is unnecessary. Could Mr. Ewing show from Scripture that we are to drink water out of the hollow of the baptizer's hand, we would submit without a murmur. He himself might have a lesson from his own admonition. It is very applicable to his objection to immersion. But because it was customary to drink out of the hollow of the hand, does it follow that baptism must be such a drinking? There is no connexion between the premises and the conclusion. Let us not, however, be too rash in asserting that Mr. Ewing has no Scripture for his mysteries. He alleges several passages. Was ever the Church of Rome at a loss for Scripture allusions to countenance its rites and mysteries? In no instance is it less successful than Mr. Ewing. He alleges, 1 Cor. xii. 13, " baptized into one body;" and " made to drink into one Spirit." But does this imply that *baptizing* and *drinking* are the same emblem? Does it imply that these two figures are taken from a process in baptism? What reason is there to suppose that the last respects that ordinance? The two figures are totally unconnected,—as unconnected as any two figures that in conjunction are applied to the same object. That the last has a reference to drinking in baptism, is as arbitrary a conceit as anything in the mysteries of popery.

Mr. Ewing adds, "There is perhaps a more intimate connexion between a ' cup' and a ' baptism,' as belonging to *one* allusion, than some readers of Scripture have as yet remarked, Matt. xx. 22," &c. These figures both respect *one* object, but they have not, as Mr. Ewing asserts, *one allusion.* They are figures as independent and as distinct, as if one of them was found in Genesis, and the other in Revelation. One of them represents the sufferings of Christ as a cup of bitterness or poison, which he must drink; the other represents the same sufferings as an immersion in water. When the Psalmist says, " the Lord God is a *sun and shield*," is there one allusion in the two figures? Both the figures represent the same object, but they have a separate and altogether independent allusion. The *sun* is one emblem, a *shield* is another. In like manner, when the Psalmist says, " we went through *fire* and through *water*," have the *fire* and the *water one* allusion? This criticism is founded on a total misconception of the nature of figurative language.

Again, if the *drinking of the cup* and *the baptism* have *one* allusion, that is, if they both allude to the ordinance of baptism, why are both expressions used? Is not this the same as to say, *Are you able to suffer as I suffer, and to be baptized with my baptism?* It gives not two illustrations of the same thing, but merely two names. If drinking the cup is baptism, then there are not two figures. We might as well say, the *son of Philip king of Macedon, and Alexander the Great.* But if the *drinking of the cup* and the *baptism*, conjointly, represent the same object, each exhibiting a part, then it follows that the *baptism* is not *baptism*, but is part of baptism, which is completed by the drinking. Besides, this view places the last part of the figure first; the *drinking* is before the *pouring out of the cup.*

It may be remarked, also, that if sufferings are represented as the drinking of a cup, in allusion to the cup of nature in baptism, then the ordinance of baptism represents *sufferings* as well as *blessings.* The drinking in baptism represents not only the reception of the Spirit, but the suffering of afflictions. The figure of drinking a cup, is equally calculated to represent either. But both cannot be contained in the same cup. Afflictions might be represented by the drinking of a cup, but not by the cup of Christian baptism, which represents the blessings of the Gospel.

The expression, " I have a *baptism* to be *baptized* with ; and how am I straitened till it be finished," Luke xii. 50, Mr. Ewing explains thus : " I have a cup to drink of, and how am I straitened until it be finished." But it is utterly without authority to say, that *baptism* is a *cup*. This is a new meaning given to the word, with as little foundation as to say that *baptism* is a *sword*. Mr. Ewing refers to Matt. xxvi. 39, for support to this explanation. But this gives him not a shadow of countenance. The cup there spoken of, refers indeed to the sufferings of Christ, but the cup is not called a baptism. These figures respect the same thing, but they do not respect the same likeness. What a wild idea, to suppose that two independent metaphors cannot in conjunction illustrate the same object ! A hero is a *lion*, is a *tower*, is a *rock*, is a thousand things ; without supposing any identity or relation between the lion, and the tower, and the rock, and the thousand things that represent him. It is really sickening to dissect such criticism. Proofs and illustrations are brought forward and exhibited with an importance that intimates them quite decisive, which have not the most distant bearing on the point in hand. The passages in which the sufferings of Christ are spoken of, under the figure of *drinking a cup*, are all mustered and paraded, as if the fact that this phrase refers to the same thing with the figurative baptism of Christ, is proof that they are the same figure, or must both refer to baptism. What should we think of the critic who should argue that the phrase *sun* and *shield*, in the eighty-fourth Psalm, is one allusion, because they both refer to God ? This is the very crticism of Mr. Ewing.

Mr. Ewing very justly observes, that in the Old Testament, the punishment of the wicked by God is represented by their being *compelled* to drink a cup. But, surely, there can be nothing corresponding to this in baptism. We are not compelled to drink a cup of poison, when we drink of the influences of the Holy Spirit.

" This simplicity, and this littleness of the sign," says Mr. Ewing, " mark its resemblance to all the other symbolical ordinances of God, and distinguish it from those clumsy and unseemly additions, which a superstitious dependence on means, or rather on the show of wisdom in will-worship, has rendered men so prone to adopt." If any man adopts immersion from a dependence on means, or as an inventon of will-worship, I will give him up to Mr. Ewing's most indignant reprobation. It is the commandment of God I am searching after ; and if I find this, I will never use any reasoning to make the sign either less or greater than it is. " I have as little faith," continues Mr. Ewing, " in the compromise of *copious* pouring, as in the enormity of immersion baptism." But according to some of the precedents alleged by the author himself, he is not at liberty to have little faith in copious pouring. Even granting that the Pentecost baptism was pouring, it was an immensely, it was an *enormously copious* pouring. It was a pouring that filled the whole house. It is Mr. Ewing's business to reconcile this precedent with his *popping*. But Mr. Ewing gives us reasons—Scripture reasons, for his having little faith in *copious* pouring. " A small quantity of blood sprinkled once a year," says he, " by the high priest, with one of his fingers, on a little gold-plated seat, was, for ages, the sign to Israel, of the acceptance in heaven of the sacrifice of Christ for the whole church." Very true, because a small quantity was sufficient to perfect the figure. A small quantity of water cannot suffice for the exhibition of the likeness of a burial and resurrection, which are declared by God to be the import of baptism. Had God commanded to sprinkle with a few drops of water, or to pour a little water on the turned up face, for a purpose that such an emblem is calculated to serve, it would have been impious to change this into another ordinance to represent a burial and resurrection. A little blood served the priest for sprinkling; but a little water did not serve him for his bathing. A " little gold-plated seat" served to receive the sprinkling of the blood; but a little water did not serve to fill the brazen sea. "A small morsel of bread, and a sip of wine," &c. No doubt of it; but this small quantity is as fit to represent the thing figured, as a baker's shop and a wine cellar would be. " The handful of water," says Mr. Ewing, " on the face of the polluted sinner, confirms the good news of the washing of regeneration," &c. If *washing only* were intended to be represented, this might be true : but the Spirit of inspiration has declared, that this ordinance re- presents the burial and resurrection of Christ, and our fellowship with him in these, by faith in which we are washed. Had not God instituted immersion, and explained its meaning, man could not do either. I disclaim all ordinances of will-worship, and all human explanations of Scripture ordinances. God only can institute. God only can interpret. If Mr. Ewing claims the right of inventing mysteries in the signification of baptism, I believe he will not find a fellow among those on the other side of the question.

The passage of the children of Israel through the Red Sea is figura- tively called a baptism, from its external resemblance to that ordinance, and from being appointed to serve a like purpose, as well as to figure the same thing. "Moreover, brethren, I would not that ye should be ignorant, how that all our fathers were under the cloud, and all passed through the sea; and were all baptized unto Moses in the cloud and in the sea," 1 Cor. x. 1. Here they are said to have been baptized. There can be no doubt, therefore, that there is in their passage through the sea, something that resembles both the external form, and the purpose of Christian baptism. It was a real *immersion*—the sea stood on each side, and the cloud covered them. But it was not a literal *immersion in water*, in the same way as Christian baptism. It is, therefore, figuratively called by the name of the Christian ordinance, because of external similarity, and because of serving the like purpose, as well as figuring the same event. The going down of the Israelites into the sea, their being covered by the cloud, and their issuing out on the other side, re- sembled the baptism of believers, served a like purpose as attesting their faith in Moses as a temporal saviour, and figured the burial and resurrection of Christ and Christians, as well as Christian baptism. If Christian baptism is a representation of burial and resurrection,—and if the passage of the Israelites is called a baptism, we are warranted in supposing that both have the same figurative meaning. It has been argued by some, that the Israelites were baptized by the rain from the cloud, and the spray from the sea. But this is quite arbitrary; for there is nothing said about rain from the cloud, or spray from the sea. It is not in evidence that any such things existed. On the contrary, as they would have been an annoyance, there is reason to believe that they did not exist. The baptism of the Israelites in ver. 2, is evidently referred to their having been under the cloud, and having passed through the sea, as stated in the first verse.

Dr. Wardlaw asks in astonishment, "Are our brethren not sensible of the straining that is necessary to make out immersion baptism here?" Not in the least sensible of any straining, I can assure Dr. Wardlaw. But we do not strain to make out a literal baptism, as respects an ordinance to be performed as an appointment of God. Surely there is no straining, to see in this fact something that may darkly shadow a burial. There is no straining to find in it something corresponding to Christian baptism, though in all things it does not identify with it. However ridiculous this *conceit* may appear to Dr. Wardlaw, it is the very thing asserted by the Holy Ghost. The Israelites, by being *under* the cloud, and passing through the sea, were baptized into Moses. By venturing to enter into the sea, they professed and exhibited full confidence in Moses as sent of God to lead them out of Egypt to Canaan.

"A dry baptism!" exclaims Dr. Wardlaw. Be patient, Dr. Wardlaw: was not the Pentecost baptism a dry baptism? Christian baptism is not a dry baptism; but the baptism of Pentecost, and of the Israelites in the Red Sea, were dry baptisms. Immersion does not necessarily imply wetting : immersion in water implies this. " Would our brethren," says Dr. Wardlaw, " consider a man duly baptized by his being placed between two cisterns of water, with a third over his head?" Certainly not. Nothing is Christian baptism, but the immersion of a believer in water, in obedience to the command of Jesus. Every thing that can be called *immersion* is not *baptism* as an ordinance of Christ. Strange, indeed, that Dr. Wardlaw should suppose that every thing is Christian baptism, which can be denominated an immersion. To be spotted with blood is a *sprinkling:* would Dr. Wardlaw consider this true Christian baptism? In an ordinance of Christ there is something more than mode. Would Dr. Wardlaw consider a man duly baptized, when he is sprinkled with rain, or wet with dew? The Spirit of God calls the passage through the Red Sea a baptism; a likeness then it must have to the Christian ordinance of baptism, to which there is an undoubted reference. Surely it requires less straining to find this likeness from the facts stated, than from fancies supposed. The passage through the sea as much resembles baptism, as the manna does the bread in the Lord's supper. They are figures of the same thing, and therefore, though different, are similar.

SECTION XV.—Having examined the testimony of the figurative applications of the word *baptizo*, I shall now try what light can be obtained from its syntax, and the circumstances in which it is found. Matt. iii. 11 : " I baptize you *in* water." It may be surprising that, after all that has been said on the subject, I should still lay any stress on the preposition *en, in.* I may be asked, Do you deny that it may be translated *with?* I do not deny this, yet I am still disposed to lay stress on it. A word may be used variously, yet be in each of its applications capable of being definitely ascertained. Were not this the case, language would be incapable of conveying definite meaning. To ascertain its meaning here, I shall submit the following observations : 1. *In* is its primary and most usual signification. Even in the instances in which it is translated otherwise, it may generally be reduced to its primary meaning, although it is more usual with our idiom to employ other prepositions. There are instances, indeed, in which we cannot trace the primary idea. This, however, is nothing but what happens with our own preposition *in,* and with all prepositions. If the Greeks say, *en cheiri ischura,* (in a strong hand,) we say, *they went out in arms. En* is so obviously the parent of *in,* that Mr. Ewing says, that " it can hardly be called a translation." He considers it merely a change of alphabet. It may be true, that this was the case in the formation of the derived word, but it certainly is a translation in as full a sense as any one word is a translation of another. It is not like *baptize,* which was not a word of our language. *In* is an English word, as truly as *en* is a Greek one. It is given as an equivalent to *en,* not because it was formed from it, but because in meaning it coincides with it. We adopted the word and its meaning also.

2. As the instances in the acceptation of this preposition in which the primary idea cannot be traced are extremely few, so it cannot be admitted in a signification inconsistent with this idea, except when necessity demands it. If the words in connexion admit the primary and usual meaning, it is unwarrantable to look for another. Such a use would render the passage inextricably equivocal. The passages in which it is translated *with,* are, without exception, of this cast. They would not make sense in our idiom, if *en* were translated *in.* Without such a necessity, no translator would ever think of rendering *en* by *with.* What is more usual than to find, when *en* is translated *among,* &c., critics explaining it as being " *literally in?*" Now, in the instance alluded to, all the words in connexion admit the primary and usual meaning of *en.* Even the most extravagant of our opponents admit, that *baptizo* signifies to *dip.* If, then, the word also signifies to *pour,* to use *en* in connexion with it, would render it altogether equivocal. We could not from the passage determine its meaning. I contend, then, that though *en* may sometimes be translated *with,* yet it cannot be so used here. For if *baptizo* is allowed to denote *dip,* and not *pour,* *with* is rejected as incongruous : if *baptizo* is supposed to signify either *dip* or *pour,* then to use a preposition after it which usually signifies *in,* but here in the sense of *with,* which is rare, would inevitably be equivocal, or would rather lead to a false meaning. It is absurd to suppose,

that such an equivocal expression could be used with respect to the performance of a Divine ordinance, which is to be a precedent for all ages.

3. I have produced innumerable examples in which *en* is construed with this verb incontestably in the sense of *dipping*. If, then, we have found the disputed phrase in a situation in which our opponents must admit our meaning of it; if the examples of this meaning of the phrase are numerous; and if no example can be produced in which the phrase is used in a situation in which we must confess that it refers to *pouring*, or any other thing but *dipping*,—all the laws of language forbid the supposition of *pouring*. What can forbid the phrase to have its usual meaning? What can authorise a meaning which the phrase has not necessarily in any other passage?

4. Even Mr. Ewing's translation of *baptizo* will not construe with *en* in the sense of *with*. He would not say, *I pop you with water*, but *I pop upon you with water*. Now, there is no *upon* in the verb. Mr. Ewing, indeed, supposes himself at liberty to vary his word *pop* by any preposition he chooses to subjoin to it. But he cannot do so without something in the original to justify the variation. I have shown that *to pop, to pop upon, to pop into*, &c., are all different words. To consider them all as contained in *baptizo* and in *pop*, is to say that a *halfpenny* is a *guinea*, because in a guinea there is a portion of copper,— or that *copper* is *brass*, because brass contains copper as a part of its composition.

5. Any translation that can be given of *en* is inconsistent with the supposition that *baptizo* signifies to *pour*. We could not say, " I *pour* you with water." *Pour* must be immediately followed by the thing *poured*, and not with the person on whom anything is *poured*. It is not *I pour you with water*, but *I pour water upon you*. The syntax, then, of the word, as well as its acceptation, forbids *pouring* as the mode of baptism.

What I have further to observe on this passage, will occur in my remarks on Mr. Ewing's attack on Dr. Campbell's note.

In admitting that *en* may sometimes signify *with*, Dr. Campbell appears to ground the fact on a Hebraism. In this sense Mr. Ewing understands him; in which he coincides. " That the phraseology to which the Dr. refers," says Mr. Ewing, " does not restrict the sense to *in*, but absolutely recommends the sense of *with*, appears from the occasional omission of the preposition, the use of it in such phrases being entirely a Hebraism, corresponding with the Hebrew *beth*, which, as the Dr. owns, signifies *with* as well as *in*." Now, in opposition both to Dr. Campbell and Mr. Ewing, I maintain that *en* in this use is not a Hebraism, either in its meaning or use. It signifies *with* in classical Greek, as well as in the Septuagint or New Testament; and just in the same circumstances. It is also as frequently used with this verb in the heathen authors, as in the Scriptures. To convince any one of this, it is necessary only to look over the examples which I have produced, both with respect to *bapto* and *baptizo*, which perfectly coincide in their syntax. Was Hippocrates a Hellenistic Jew?

Indeed, to enlarge the meaning of a Greek preposition, that it may correspond with a Hebrew preposition, is a thing which, though the conceit has been sanctioned by Dr. Campbell, and many great names, is a pure absurdity. To do so, would not be to speak the Greek language. To do so, would be to mislead all the Greek nations. There is not one instance in which such a thing is done in the word of God. If the apostles used the Greek prepositions, not as the Greeks themselves used them, but as the Hebrews used theirs, they have not given a revelation of the will of God. This view of the Hebraism of the New Testament is one of the worst things in Dr. Campbell's translation. Whatever may be the extent of the Hebraisms of the New Testament, they cannot, consistently with the honour of revelation, be supposed to affect the sense. This supposition is the resource of those who wish to corrupt the Gospel of Christ, or, in some way, to modify a disagreeable doctrine.

Equally groundless, and even equally absurd, is Mr. Ewing's assertion, that the fact that the preposition is sometimes omitted, recommends the sense of *with*. If that preposition is sometimes written, and sometimes left out, it is as clear as an axiom, that the passages in which it is omitted, must agree with the passages in which it is written, and must be translated just as if it were present. The meaning of the passages, then, in which it is omitted, must be determined by those in which it is written. When it is not expressed it must be understood. Such an omission, then, can cast no light on the subject.

Mr. Ewing alleges, that " our English translators, at least, being friends of immersion, would have been led by their system to have patronised the Dr.'s translation. But this is a fallacious argument. It is true, as Mr. Ewing says, that on this question our translators were " directly opposed" to him. But what sort of friends were they to *immersion?* Just such as Professor Porson, and the thousands of learned men who have the candour to confess the truth, though, as they think the matter of little importance, they practise the contrary. There was then no temptation to induce them to testify for immersion. There was the strongest temptation to induce them to accommodate their translation to the practice of their church, not to their views of the original mode of baptism. Dr. Wall was so far a friend of immersion, that he would have preferred it; yet how has he laboured to prove that it is not necessary! Mr. Ewing's friend's strictures, then, on Dr. Ryland, have no weight, for they view the subject in a false light. The authority of our translators in our favour, is the authority, not of friends, but of practical opposers; and, as Dr. Campbell has shown, real opposers, in every case, that could, in their judgment, admit pouring or sprinkling.

Dr. Campbell has censured our translators as inconsistent, in rendering *en udati* " with water," while they rendered *en to Iordane* " in Jordan." How does Mr. Ewing vindicate them from inconsistency? Why, by alleging that the former refers to the ACT and ELEMENTS of baptism, and the latter to the PLACE! Now, this might vindicate Mr. Ewing, but it does not vindicate our translators. Mr. Ewing forgets that the conceit that *Iordane* is not the river, but the district in the neighbourhood of the river, is of his own invention. Our translators evidently understood it of the river itself, as every sober reader must do. Our translators, then, remain under Dr. Campbell's censure, for anything that Mr. Ewing has done to relieve them.

But let us see if he can justify himself in this business. I admit that "a difference of connexion" will justify us in "understanding the same word in a different sense." But I see no difference of connexion here. On the contrary, the word Jordan, in the sixth verse, as evidently means the river Jordan, as *water* in the eleventh verse means *water*. The Jordan never signifies, as Mr. Ewing supposes, *the plain of Jordan*, the *valley of Jordan*, or *Jordan-dale*. This is a figment formed for a particular purpose. Can Mr. Ewing justify this explanation by a single corresponding example, in which a similar phrase must be so understood? Were we to read in the newspapers that certain persons in Glasgow were *baptized in the Clyde*, should we understand that it imported merely that they were baptized in Clydesdale? This is a daring perversion of the words of the Holy Spirit. It requires a hardihood that every heretic does not possess. An Arian or a Socinian does not require more. No Neological gloss is more extravagant. The Spirit of God tells us that our Lord did many miracles ; the Neologist forces him to say that there was nothing miraculous in the Saviour's works. The Spirit of God tells us that the people of Israel were baptized by John *in the Jordan* ; Mr. Ewing forces him to say that it was not in Jordan, but in Jordan-dale. What a system is it that compels its abettors to take such liberties with the word of God! I view such conduct, not only with disapprobation, but with horror.

But Mr. Ewing says that an Evangelist explains the thing in his sense. This is high authority indeed. I will ask no better. If this is made good, I will bow with submission. "That it was not the *water* of the river, but the *country* on its banks, is evident from the fuller and more particular account of the apostle John. What Matthew calls, *in Jordan*, John calls, *in Bethabara*, and expressly says, it was beyond Jordan."

I admit the premises; I deny the conclusion. Let the two evangelists refer to the same thing, yet what the one calls Jordan, the other does not call Bethabara. Matthew speaks of the *river* in which John was baptizing; John of the *town* in which he was baptizing. John is more particular as to the part of the river in which the Baptist was baptizing; it was in the town of Bethabara. Matthew is more particular with respect to the water in which he was baptizing; it was the Jordan. Corresponding to this, with respect to the same person, one writer might say, "he was baptizing in the Clyde ;" another, "he was baptizing in Glasgow." Mr. Ewing himself, in asserting that John's account of this matter is more particular than that of Matthew, virtually admits that it is not necessary that Jordan should be perfectly equivalent to Bethabara; for if one account may be more particular than another, Bethabara may axpress the place or part of the river, while Jordan expresses the water in which John baptized

Let it, however, be supposed that the expression of the one evangelist exactly corresponds to that of the other, what follows? As *Jordan* signifies Jordan-dale, so *Bethabara* must not denote the town, but the whole district supposed to be called Jordan-dale. According to Mr. Ewing himself, these two words do not correspond. He makes the one to denote the whole country; the other, one town situated in the country.

Still it may be said, if the two accounts refer to the same thing, as John is said to be baptizing in Bethabara, and as this town was beyond Jordan, so he could not be baptizing in the river, which was on one side of the town. Mr. Ewing will let us come to the margin of the stream, but the phrase, he says, will not carry us " one jot farther." This is hard enough. I will try to advance a little into the river. This I am enabled to do with the sanction of the usual phraseology in similar cases. The limits of a town, in speaking in a general way, are not confined to the ground occupied by the houses. Suppose, for instance, that a man is charged with having committed a breach of the peace, on a certain day of the month, in Glasgow. In proving an *alibi*, he alleges that he was on that day in the town of Belfast. Opposite counsel cries out, " My lords, and gentlemen of the jury, he is a perjured rascal, for I can prove that he was the whole of that day in a ship in *Belfast harbour*. He never once entered the town that day." What will the judge and jury think of such a mode of proof? Surely he was in Belfast when he was in the port of Belfast. And is it not the same thing with the town and port of Bethabara? When Mr. Ewing changes his views on the subject, and comes over to Belfast to baptize his brethren in that town, it will be asked by some of the people of Glasgow, Where is Mr. Ewing? The reply will be, " He is in Belfast, baptizing the independent church of that town." This reply will be made without any reference to the situation of the water. Might it not also be said, that the people of Glasgow go down to Gourock or Helensburgh to bathe? Yet the place of bathing is in the sea. Might it not also be said, that such a person was drowned in Port-Glasgow while he was bathing in the Clyde? In like manner, it might have been added to John's account, that the Baptist was baptizing in Jordan. *John was baptizing in Bethabara in the Jordan.* Now, Mr. Ewing, say candidly, am I not now entitled to step a little distance from the margin into the river? Have I not demolished this strong hold?

But I have many other resources, had it been necessary to employ them on this point. A small bend in the river, or hollow in the bed on one side, might have formed a basin, so that houses might actually have been nearer to the centre of the river, than some parts of the basin. A bare possibility is all that is necessary to obviate a difficulty. But sober criticism could never dwell on such things. The common forms of speech utterly condemn such a mode of opposition. Indeed, the houses do not generally extend to the margin of the sea or river. If a town was limited by the houses, the quay itself would often be no part of it. The harbour has as good a title to be included in the town as the quay.

But there is another awkward situation in which our view, it seems, places John the Baptist, out of which I must endeavour to deliver him. Mr. Ewing asserts, that if John the Baptist baptized in Bethabara, standing in the water of the river, then he must have been in that situation when he bore his testimony to the priests and Levites. Now, it is a hard thing to keep the poor man in the water during this discourse. I will endeavour, then, to put him on dry ground. The argument is, that in John i. 23, all the things previously mentioned are said to have been done *in Bethabara, where John was baptizing.* Therefore, if he was standing in the water when he spoke to the priests, all the things are said to be done in the same place. The answer is, all the things were indeed done in the same place, that is, in Bethabara, but this does not imply that they were done in the same part of Bethabara. When Mr Ewing comes to baptize his brethren in Belfast, it is likely he may have a fierce encounter with the Arians. The Glasgow newspapers will say, " these things happened in Belfast, where Mr. Ewing was baptizing.' Will the people of Glasgow understand that the engagement with the Arians was when Mr. Ewing was actually baptizing? Ah, Mr. Ewing! what shall I call such a mode of opposing immersion? Shall I call it childish? Or shall I call it perverse? Were it in reality asserted, that John gave his testimony to the priests while he was baptizing, I would implicitly believe it. The thing is not impossible. There is not, how-ever, the smallest appearance of such an assertion.

That Jordan denotes the river, and not the country in the neighbour-hood of Jordan, is not only obvious from the word of God, it is expressly asserted to be the river by Mark i. 5, where the word *river* is joined to it. "And there went out unto him all the land of Judea, and they of Jerusalem, and were all baptized of him in the river of Jordan, confess-ing their sins." Nothing can limit the word more clearly than this, *in the river Jordan.* As if the Holy Spirit had anticipated Mr. Ewing's perversion of the word Jordan, by converting it, without any authority, into Jordan-dale, the word *river* is added to it by Mark. Mr. Ewing, indeed, says, that if John i. 28, Matt. iii. 6—13, John x. 40, are con-sidered, they will explain Mark i. 5, in his sense. But I hope I have shown that these passages have no bearing on the point. It would be a strange explanation that would explain the *river Jordan* not to be the *river Jordan,* but something else. This would be a Neological expla-nation. There is in the passage under consideration, other evidence that baptism was performed by immersion. It is said that Jesus, when he was baptized, went *up* straightway *from* the water. I admit the proper translation of *apo* is *from,* and not *out of;* and that the argument from the former is not of the same nature with that which is founded on *ek, out of.* I perfectly agree with Mr. Ewing, that *apo* would have its mean-ing fully verified, if they had only gone down to the edge of the wa-ter. I shall not take a jot more from a passage than it contains. The Bible is orthodox enough for me as it is. How then can I deduce *dip-ping* from the phrases *going down,* and *coming up from?* My argument is this.—If baptism had not been by immersion, there can be no ade-quate cause alleged for going to the river. Can sober judgment, can can-dour suppose, that if a handful of water would have sufficed for baptism, they would have gone to the river? Many evasions have been alleged to get rid of this argument, but it never will be fairly answered. I have strong suspicions that these evasions are scarcely satisfactory, even to those who make them. I am much mistaken if they are not perplexed with the circumstance of John the Baptist's great predilection for the neighbourhood of Jordan, and other places, where the water is the very reason assigned for the preference. There is no spot on the earth in which a human being can be found, that without any inconvenience will not afford a handful of water. Even in a besieged town, with a scarcity of water, what would sprinkle the whole inhabitants would not be felt as a sensible loss.

Mr. Ewing attempts to account for the above phraseology, by the fact that fountains and rivers are generally in hollow places. This, indeed, accounts for the *phraseology*, but does it account for this *fact!* Whether the river was in a hill or in a valley, why did they go to it, when a handful of water would have sufficed. Mr. Ewing himself says, " I believe, indeed, that John frequented the banks of the Jordan, as the most convenient place of the wilderness, not only for multitudes to attend him, but also for having water at hand with which to baptize them." But was there any place in Judea in which he could not find a supply of water for *popping* or *sprinkling?* The greatest crowd that ever assembled might be *popped* at a small fountain. Besides, however many the persons were who went to his baptism, there is no foundation to suppose that immense crowds were always with him. The account itself does not imply that there ever was at any time an immense crowd. All Judea and Jerusalem are said to be baptized by him; but they are not said to have been with him at once, or even in crowds at any one time. Why should they be supposed to have staid with him any considerable time?

But our argument on this passage is not only that they frequented the banks of Jordan; but that, being there for the performance of baptism, they went down to the water. Now, if an army encamped on Glasgow Green in a time of war, were all to be baptized by *popping*, would they bring the water from the river, or would they all go to the very edge of the water? Why did Jesus go down to the water, when the water might as well have been brought up to him? Does Mr. Ewing take the infants to the edge of the Clyde when he is *popping* them? This answer, then, is but an evasion. No reason has ever been given, or ever will be given, to account for this fact, on the hypothesis of baptizing with a handful of water.

Mr. Ewing observes that this phraseology is confined to baptisms out of doors. Very true, but in Mr. Ewing's baptism, why were there any baptisms out of doors? If they are *popped upon* with a handful of water, any number might successively be *popped* in the same house with equal convenience as out of doors. When a conveniency for baptism was found within doors, there was no recourse to a river ; and then there could be no *going down* nor *coming up*. When a person was baptized in a bath, the baptizer was not in the water at all.

Mr. Ewing says, " Rebekah went down to the well—and came up." " Does this imply that she immersed herself? No. She went down to the well, and filled her pitcher, and came up." Very true. But are the cases parallel? Do they not differ in the very point in which it is essential for Mr. Ewing's argument that they should agree? This illustration favours us, and refutes Mr. Ewing himself. If Rebekah went down to the well, she had a good errand to the well—an errand that is not left to be supplied by conjecture, but is expressly specified, namely, to fill her pitcher. Can Mr. Ewing show such an errand in going to the edge of the river *for popping?* Even the idiot that followed the Armagh coach to Dublin, to see if the great wheels would overtake the little ones, had an errand. But if popping is baptism, there could be no errand to the river for the performance of the ordinance. " Gideon," says Mr. Ewing, " brought down the people unto the water." " Was it to immerse them? No; it was to give them an opportunity of drinking." And could there be a better refutation of Mr. Ewing than what he gives himself? Gideon did not lead the people to the river for no purpose. The object is expressed. Let us have such a reason for John's baptizing at Jordan, and it will suffice us. Mr. Ewing entirely mistakes the jet of this argument. I observe also, that Matt. iii. 6, Mark i. 5, cannot admit *pouring* as the sense of *baptizo.* *Ebaptisanto en to Iordane* cannot be rendered *they were poured in Jordan,* nor *with Jordan,* nor *in Jordan-dale.* The water is poured, not the people. If the clumsy expression *poured upon* could be admitted, it is not to be found. The *upon* is wanting. *The people were poured upon in Jordan-dale,* would be a very awkward expression. Yet shabby as such an auxiliary would be, even that is not to be found.

Let us next examine the baptism of the eunuch, Acts viii. 36. " And as they went on their way, they came to a certain water : and the eunuch said, See, here is water ; what doth hinder me to be baptized? And Philip said, If thou believest with all thine heart, thou mayest. And he answered and said, I believe that Jesus Christ is the Son of God. And he commanded the chariot to stand still : and they went down both into the water, both Philip and the eunuch ; and he baptized him. And when they were come up out of the water, the Spirit of the Lord caught away Philip," &c. This is as correct and as literal a translation of the words as can possibly be made ; and surely it is so plain that the most illiterate man can be at no loss to discover from it the mind of the Lord on the subject. I have written some hundred pages on the mode of this ordinance, yet to a mind thirsting to know the will of God, and uninfluenced by prejudice, this passage without comment is in my view amply sufficient. The man who can read it, and not see *immersion* in it, must have something in his mind unfavourable to the investigation of truth. As long as I fear God, I cannot, for all the kingdoms of the world, resist the evidence of this single document. Nay, had I no more conscience than Satan himself, I could not as a scholar attempt to expel *immersion* from this account. All the ingenuity of all the critics in Europe could not silence the evidence of this passage. Amidst the most violent perversion that it can sustain on the rack, it will still cry out, *immersion, immersion!*

Philip, in preaching, had shown that believers were to be baptized immediately, yet the eunuch never speaks of being baptized till he came to water. Now, this implies immersion. Had a handful of water been sufficient, this might have been found in any place. Had it been even a desert without water, there can be no doubt that the eunuch would have a supply of water with him.

When they came to the water, instead of sending down one of the retinue to bring up a little water, they went down to the water. Mr. Ewing supposes that our argument is founded on the mere *going down* and *coming up*. But it is upon the circumstance that no reason can be given for the *going down* but the *immersion*. What would take them to the water, when the water could be more conveniently brought to them?

But they not only went down to the water; they went *into* the water. What would take them *into* the water, if a handful of water would suffice?

Let it be observed, also, that there is something very peculiar in the account of their going into the water. It is not only said, "*they* went into the water;" our attention is fixed on the fact that they *both* went into the water. This, we might think, would suffice. Yet the Holy Spirit marks the circumstance still more precisely. He adds, *both Philip and the eunuch*. Can any one imagine that such a precision, such an apparent redundancy of expression, is not designed to teach something that the Spirit of Inspiration foresaw would be denied? Had the water been deep enough at the edge, the eunuch only might have been in the water. But in this case both the baptizer and the baptized went *into* the water. Now, this determines that the preposition *eis* must be rendered *into*, and not *unto*, as Mr. Ewing would have it. Had the account related merely to the going down to the edge of the water, there would be no use in saying that they both went down. Could it be necessary to inform us that Philip, the baptizer, went to the place of baptism as well as the person to be baptized? What would take the one down without the other? There is good reason, however, to inform us that *they both* went *into* the water; because, in certain circumstances, it would have been necessary only for one of them to be in the water;· and the relation of the fact takes away the ground of perversion.

It is not only said that they went into the water, but their return is called a coming up *out of* the water. They could not come *out of* the water, if they had not been *in* it. This is more precise than the account of our Lord's baptism. There it is said that he came up *from* the water. Here it is *out of* the water.

Let us now see how Mr. Ewing attempts to evade the evidence of this passage. Let my readers put their invention to work, and try what they can think of to darken this evidence. Mr. Ewing, I engage, will go beyond them. His ingenuity is unparalleled. He destroys our doctrine even by demonstration. Demonstration! Ay, demonstration! Jesus is said, Matt. iii. 16, to have gone up *from* the water, not *out of* the water as our version renders it. "Now," says Mr. Ewing, "it surely will not be said that Philip had any occasion to go farther with the Ethiopian nobleman than John did with our Saviour, in order to the administration of baptism. It is reasonable, then, to understand the *eis* and the *ek* of Acts viii. 38, 39, as signifying precisely what is indicated by the *apo* of Matt. iii. 16." Now, is not this demonstration? I may as well think to pierce the divine shield of Achilles as this argument. **But I will strike.** Truth is stronger than sophistry. The helmet of Goliath could not resist the pebble from a sling. I deny the first principle on which this argument is founded. It is taken for granted that *apo* can reach no farther than the edge of the water. Now, while I admit that this is all that is necessarily imported in this preposition, I contend that it can apply to the centre of the water, or even the farther edge of the water, as well as the edge on this side. *Apo* signifies the point of departure from an object, but that point may be in any part of the object to which there is access. Whether the point of departure be the edge or the centre, or the nearer or the farther edge, depends not on the word, but on the circumstances, or other information. If the point of departure be an impenetrable object, it must be from the edge; but if the object be penetrable, the departure may be from any part in it. If a fowl on the opposite side of the river, or in the middle of it, takes wing, and, flying across, alights on a hill, we say, *it flew from the river*, just the same as if it had commenced its flight on this side. This is the distinction between *apo* and *ek*. The former denotes the point of departure, in whatever part of the object that point is found; the latter always supposes that the point of departure is within the object. Of course *apo* cannot serve us in Matt. iii. 16, but as little can it injure us. It is indefinite as to the situation of the point of departure. In this case, then, it is not necessary to suppose that Philip and the eunuch went farther than John and our Saviour. Though *apo* does not imply that the latter were *in* the water, it is not inconsistent with this, if other evidence demands it. Besides, it might be on some occasions necessary to go farther into the water than on this. At some places, baptism may be performed at the edge; in others, it may be necessary to advance to the centre.

But if *apo* could not reach one inch into the water, I should find no difficulty in refuting Mr. Ewing's argument. If our Lord and John were *in* the water, in returning they must have come from the edge of the water. They would then have come from the edge of the water, and from beyond. Though the account commences with the edge, it does not deny that there was a previous point of departure. When I say, *this friend has come from Edinburgh*, all I assert is, that the point of his departure was Edinburgh. It might be the very edge; but it might be also from the very centre. On the other hand, when I say, my friend is *out of* Edinburgh, it expresses that he was within the city. We might also fix a point of departure, which will apply only to a certain point, and reach no farther. Yet this will not deny a previous point of commencement of departure. *We started at such an hour from Prince's-street, and at such an hour we arrived in Glasgow.* Now, this point of departure cannot be extended an inch, yet it is quite consistent that we might have had a previous point of departure from Duke-street.

Though I have thus proved, that for anything to be found in *apo*, our Lord might have been baptized in the middle of Jordan, yet since *apo* necessarily implies no more than the edge as the point of departure; since we are not otherwise informed that John and He went into the water previously to baptizing, as we are informed with respect to Philip and the eunuch, I think there is no reason to believe that John the Baptist usually went into the water in baptizing. The striking difference between the accounts of these two baptisms, leads me to conclude that John chose some place on the edge of the Jordan that admitted the immersion of the person baptized, while the baptizer remained on the margin. The place of baptizing the eunuch did not admit this,—most providentially, indeed, because it affords an example that cannot be plausibly perverted. If the above distinction is well founded, there is no ground for the jest, that John the Baptist was an amphibious animal. There is no necessity at all to suppose that *eis* and *ek* are limited in Acts viii. 38, 39, by *apo* in Matt. iii. 16.

"I am far from saying," says Mr. Ewing, "that *eis* does not often signify *into*, and *ek*, *out of*." And I am as far from denying that *eis* sometimes signifies *unto*. Its most usual signification, however, is *into;* and in general applies when the thing in motion enters within the object to which it refers. There are instances, however, in which the motion ends at the object. It is, therefore, not of itself definite. But it is evident that there must be some way of rendering it definite in each of its occurrences, else language would be unintelligible. We are not to suppose that when a word is in itself indefinite, we are at liberty, in every occurrence of it, to understand it as we will. The sound critic is able, on all occasions, to limit it by the connexion, or by circumstances. I observe, then, that as this word usually signifies motion to a place ending within the place, so it is always to be understood in this sense, except circumstances forbid it. I believe the few examples in which the motion does not end within the object towards which the thing in motion is directed, are all of this kind. They are such as cannot cause a moment's hesitation. But if it had such a meaning here, it would evidently be equivocal. It would as readily lead astray as inform. Agreeably to this, in the very examples produced by Mr. Ewing, from Gen. xxiv. 16, Judges vii. 5, where the motion ended at the margin of the river, this preposition is not used. It is not *eis*, but *epi ten pegen;* not *eis*, but *pros to udor*.

This observation is confirmed by the circumstance, that *eis* is applied to the river Jordan, when the motion ceases on the banks, in an instance that can create no doubt. 2 Kings vi. 4 : " And when they came to (*eis*) Jordan." Here the object of the journey determines the extent of the meaning of the preposition.

But I utterly deny such an indefiniteness in the meaning of *ek*. In opposition to Mr. Ewing's assertion, I say that it always signifies *out of.* I say this while my eye is upon all the examples alleged by him and his learned friend.

" Now," says Mr. Ewing, " wherever *eis* and *ek* correspond to each other, the extent of the one must measure the extent of the other. The point of departure to return, cannot be different from the point of arrival in going. In other words, if *eis* signify *to*, then *ek* must, in the same connexion, signify nothing more than *from*." What can be more mathematical than this? It is as clear as that twelve inches and a foot

denote the same measure. The demonstration is perfect, *if* the axiom
on which it is founded be granted. The demonstration is drawn from
the hypothetical proposition, " if *eis* signify *to*." But I deny that in this
instance it signifies *to*. Mr. Ewing himself admits that it often signifies
into. Why, then, is it taken for granted that it cannot so signify here?
To do Mr. Ewing any service, *eis* must always signify *to*. It cannot be
employed to measure *ek*, if it is itself indefinite. It is very true that
the progress *into* the water cannot be less than the progress *out*. All
depends on the distance advanced. Now, though *eis* might be used, if
the advance was only to the margin; yet as it can be used, if the advance were to the centre, it cannot restrain *ek* to its own lowest extent.
On the other hand, I will reverse the demonstration, on the principle
that *ek* always signifies *out of*, which I will prove. If *ek* always signifies
out of, as one of these prepositions, when they correspond to each other,
must measure the other, then, though *eis* is in itself indefinite, *ek* renders it definite in this instance. As *ek* signifies *out of*, *eis* must here
signify *into*. Now, I defy ingenuity to refute my demonstration. If
an elastic chain is twelve inches at the stretch, but only ten when
relaxed; and if the same measure is called a foot, in the same connexion,
then we are to make the *foot* determine the extent of the chain, in the
instance referred to, and not the chain to determine the number of
inches in the *foot*. The definite must limit the indefinite.

Dr. Wardlaw concurs with Mr. Ewing, in thinking that nothing can
be learned from *en*, and *eis*, and *ek*, the prepositions usually construed
with *baptizo*. " It is truly surprising," says he, " that so much stress
should be laid on the frequently vague import of a Greek preposition."
I ask Dr. Wardlaw, what preposition in any language is perfectly
univocal? Are there many words of any part of speech, except those
expressive of mode, which are perfectly univocal? Are the above
prepositions more vague than the prepositions that correspond to them
in our language? Does it follow from a word's having two significations, that no stress can be laid on itself, in determining on the evidence
of its meaning in any particular situation? If a word is sometimes
used in a sense different from its usual one, are we at liberty to understand it in such unusual signification at random, as often as it may suit
our argument? Were this the case, every sentence we utter would be
a riddle. Every time we open our lips, we use words which are as
vague as any Greek prepositions, yet the most ignorant are not misled
by the circumstance. It is only when the observation applies to dead
languages, that it imposes on those who do not trace arguments to first
principles. *En* may sometimes be translated *with;* but there must be
laws that regulate this matter, else human language could not be sufficient for testimony. *Eis*, in rare cases, may be translated *unto;* but
if this will justify us in assigning this meaning to it when it suits our
purpose, nothing could be definitely expressed in human speech. Yet
this is the resource of Dr. Wardlaw, in evading the evidence of immersion;—a resource which, if used with respect to English, would expose
the critic to derision. I have pointed out some of the laws that determine in such cases; and whether I have been successful or not, such

laws must exist, if human language is an adequate evidence of human thought. This I hold as an axiom. But I will venture to appeal still farther to the common sense of my readers. Admitting all that is demanded for this supposed vagueness, is it not utterly incredible that, with respect to this ordinance, each of these three prepositions should assume, as it were in concert to deceive us, its most unusual signification? Can we ascribe such a miracle of delusion to the Spirit of truth? Now, that *in* is the most usual signification of *en*; *into*, the most usual signification of *eis*; and *out of*, the most usual signification of *ek*, I suppose no one will be hardy enough to deny. I could easily prove that the exceptions to this, with respect to the two former, are much fewer than they are generally supposed; and when I come to Mr. Ewing's Appendix, I will show that, with respect to *ek*, there is no exception at all. But I am here taking for granted all that our opponents demand; and allowing the vagueness to be as great as they suppose, is it not absurd to suppose that the Holy Spirit would use the three prepositions all in an unusual sense, when there were other prepositions better suited to the purpose? The absurdity is still heightened by the consideration that these prepositions are used in connexion with a verb, which the hardiest of our opponents cannot deny as importing, at least in one of its senses, *to immerse*. The usual sense of the whole three prepositions is in our favour: the verb admits our meaning, even according to Mr. Ewing; but according to the great bulk of the most learned of our opponents, this is its primary meaning: judging, then, even from their own admissions, is it credible that the Holy Spirit would use language so calculated to mislead? Could there be any reason to pitch upon such phraseology, except to deceive? *If pouring or sprinkling had been appointed, there were words which univocally denote these meanings.* Why, then, should the Holy Spirit pass by these words, and pitch upon a word that, according to our opponents, has perhaps a dozen of significations? If there are prepositions that would, in their usual acceptation, express the meaning our opponents attach to the three prepositions in question, why should the latter be employed in an unusual sense? There never was a greater specimen of Jesuitism, than that which Dr. Wardlaw here charges on the Holy Spirit.

But this mode of reasoning carries its condemnation in its very face. If the controversy were in a language of which we were entirely ignorant, and on a subject to which we were utterly strangers, we might hold it as a self-evident truth, that the man who screens himself under the vagueness of words, and argues at random, on the supposition that on any emergency it is fair to take a word in any signification that in any situation he may find attached to it, has either a bad cause, or does not know how to defend a good one. As no one will charge our opponents with the latter, the cause which they defend must be incapable of a sound defence.

But after we have beaten them down the hill, and pushed them to the very verge of the stream; nay, after we have driven them into Jordan up to the chin, these obstinate enemies of immersion will not *pop down* their heads *into the water*, but will *pop* the water upon the head. Both of these writers declare resolutely that they would not surrender, even in the midst of the river. " Let it be supposed," says Mr. Ewing, " that the baptizer led the person to be baptized, not only to the water, but into it; the question returns, what did he do with him there?" Dr. Wardlaw also expressly refuses to submit, even were it granted " that the parties were *in* Jordan when the ceremony was performed." What shall I do now? Of what service is all my criticism? Can I put them under the water either by the verb or by its syntax? I will first try to discipline them a little with common sense; for if I cannot succeed on this point, it is in vain to appeal to the laws of language. I admit that it is possible to sprinkle or pour water upon a person in a river, as well as in a church or parlour. But in the awful presence of the living God, I ask Mr. Ewing and Dr. Wardlaw if they think it credible that John the Baptist would take into the water the multitudes whom he baptized, for the purpose of pouring a little on their faces? If they can answer this in the affirmative, I have no more to say on that point. I must appeal to the common sense of mankind. What other purpose could there be in going *into* the water, but to be *immersed*? Turks, Jews, and Infidels, declare your judgment. Every other mode might have been observed, with much greater convenience, out of the water than in it. I know it is possible for Mr. Ewing and Dr. Wardlaw to take every infant baptized by them, with all the nurses and attendants, *down into* the river Clyde, and pop them there; but verily, if I read in the newspapers, that they did this, I should be convinced that they were deranged. Madness or fanaticism would universally be supposed to be the cause. Upon such evidence, could the Lord Chancellor refuse an act of lunacy against them? And shall they ascribe to John the Baptist and the Saviour, conduct that in Great Britain would prove lunacy? It is useless to reason with persons so obstinate. Neither argument nor criticism can reach such extravagance. As Dr. Campbell, in reference to the class of first principles which he ascribes to common sense, says, that to deny them, does not imply a contradiction,—it implies only lunacy; so to assert that John the Baptist led the multitudes into the river Jordan, in order to pour a little water into their faces, does not imply an impossibility,—it implies only that they were all mad.

However, as I have now, by their own admission, got them into the water, I will try to force them under it, before I let them out. Dr. Wardlaw asserts that *eis ton Iordanen* may be translated *at* or *in* Jordan. To this I reply, 1. *At* and *in* are not senses of *eis*. 2. There is no reason to bring them to the water, or place them *in* the water, but the intention of immersing them into the water. 3. A multitude of examples might be produced, in which *eis* is construed with *baptizo*, in which the signification is without doubt *immersion*. I appeal to those I have given. No one example can be produced in which *eis* in construction with the verb, signifies either *at* or *in*. The phrase, then, cannot be supposed to have a signification here different from its usual signification; and which there is no single proof that it ever has. I will force them down, then, by the verb and the preposition separately, and by both united as a phrase. I defy them to produce, out of Greek literature, one instance in which the phrase has the meaning contended for by them.

Dr. Wardlaw partakes with Mr. Ewing in his astonishment, that an argument should be drawn from *going down* and *coming up*. If my astonishment had not been entirely exhausted with the Jordan scene, I should be mightily astonished that both these writers so far mistake the jet of the argument. The *going down* and the *coming up* are not supposed to refer to the act of immersion. As pouring water into a bath is necessary in order to immersion in the bath; so going down to the river is necessary in order to dipping in the river. We do not confound the going into the water with the immersion in the water. This would show the same want of discrimination that confounds *pouring* with baptism.

But Mr. Ewing overturns all our arguments and criticisms with a difficulty. " If the *act* of baptizing," says he, " had consisted of immersing the subject in water, there would surely have been some allusion to the lowering of his body in that supine direction, which is, I believe, commonly observed for the purpose of bringing it under the surface : some allusion, also, to that stooping attitude, which is at the same time necessary on the part of the immerser. But there is nothing of this kind to be found in all the Scriptures, either in the accompanying phraseology, or, as we have seen, in the name of the ordinance itself." Now, if the *surely* was a real *surely*, the conclusion would be undeniable; for I do not know a single reference of the kind demanded. But what makes this *surely* necessary? Why, it is necessary to keep Mr. Ewing's theory from *sinking*, but this is its only necessity. If no information is given about the way of putting the body under water, then no part of the meaning of the ordinance depends on one way more than another. We are then at liberty to do it in the most convenient way. But this requirement is very strange in one who maintains baptism to be a popping of a handful of water out of the cup of nature, or the hollow of the hand, upon the turned up face of the person baptized. Each of these things is a necessary part of baptism, yet I am so stupid as to be unable to see a glimpse of any of them in the Scriptures.

I shall now examine the example in Mr. Ewing's Appendix, alleged to prove that *ek* sometimes signifies merely *from*, as perfectly synonymous with *apo*. I have admitted that *en* may, in certain circumstances, be translated *with*, and that *eis* sometimes denotes motion to a place, that ends on this side of the object, without occasioning any confusion or ambiguity. But I have denied that *ek* is ever used when the object *departing* is not supposed to have commenced its departure *within* the object from which it departs. Now, Mr. Ewing's very learned friend, who writes the Appendix, in reply to some observations by Dr. Ryland, steadily abides by his first position ; and by a number of instances alleges, with the utmost confidence, that the use of the Greek language proves the supposed laxity in the use of *ek*. The general acquaintance of this gentleman with Greek literature, entitles his opinion to the highest respect; and I am willing to allow him to be in all respects what Mr. Ewing represents. I take the utmost liberty in exposing false reasoning and false criticism, even in those whom I respect. God's truth is a paramount object, and whatever tends to pervert it must be cut down. The extensive reading in Greek writers, which this gentleman possesses, is a qualification of indispensable importance to a critic; and that he is conversant in the philosophy of language, is obvious at a glance. I stand upon ground too firm to make me fear the talents of my antagonist, and I should feel ashamed were I conscious of under-rating these talents through dread of them. No man unjustly disparages the abilities of his opponent, who is not conscious either of having a bad cause, or of his inability to defend a good one.

The learned writer of the Appendix says: "The truth is, that though *apo* and *ek* were originally distinct, in the progress of the language they came to be used indiscriminately, and while *apo* encroached on the province of *ek*, *ek* in return usurped part of the territories of *apo*." Now, on the very face of this observation, I pronounce it unphilosophical; and I would confidently do so, had the assertion respected a language of which I do not know the letters. It is contrary to the first principles of language, that prepositions appointed to express different relations, should be used to express the same relation. Were this the case, the prepositions would be two only in sound; one of them would cumber rather than enrich the language. There is a sense in which one word may be said to encroach on the territories of another; that is, it may be used in a situation which another usually fills. But this is not properly an encroachment. So far as it properly goes, the territories are its own. The territory occupied by both, belongs exclusively to neither. It is common, and either may be used at pleasure. But consistently with this joint reign, either may have a peculiar territory, into which it is usurpation in the other to enter. Were it true, according to the learned writer, that *apo* and *ek* at random usurp each other's territories, it would be impossible for criticism to ascertain anything from their use. Language would be incapable of definite meaning. From my account of them, it is clear that in a vast multitude of instances, they may be used in the same place, optionally. But even here, it is possible to discrimi-nate them. Each of them has in every instance its own distinctive meaning. I may say in English, this friend is *out of* Glasgow, or *from* Glasgow, yet *out of* and *from* are not the same. The one expression denotes that the point of departure was *in* the city; the other may have its point of departure either *in* or *at* the city. There are cases also in which the English preposition could not be used in the same situation. In a besieged city, the expression, "this soldier has come *out* of the city," is very different from "this soldier has come from the city." I assert, then, that the fact that these prepositions may be used often in the same situation, is no evidence that they have not their characteristic meaning; and far less is it evidence that they are in all things indiscriminate. While they have a common territory, each has a province of its own. Even when *apo* is used where *ek* might be used, there is this difference, that the former is not definite, and does not mark the idea which the use of the other would have marked. I call the attention of critics to this distinction as one of vast importance, and one which has been universally overlooked. It has been hitherto taken for granted, that if two words are interchangeable in any situation, they may, at the pleasure of the critic, be supposed interchangeable. I maintain that two words with meanings characteristically distinct, may have in other things a common province, while there are laws to ascertain the extent of the common province, and to limit each within its peculiar boundary. I maintain even farther, that in the common province each expresses its own meaning. They reign without interference even over the common territory. Now, if I am well founded in these observations, they will be of vast advantage in ascertaining definitely the import of language. Instead of being a nose-of-wax, as critics in general have made the Scriptures, temerity will not be able to deface their features.

With respect to the prepositions *apo* and *ek*, though they may often be used interchangeably, yet the latter always implies *intusposition;* the former the point of departure in general. But the writer of the Appendix has alleged a number of examples to prove, " that *ek* may be, and often is, made use of to express removal, distance, or separation, merely where previous intusposition neither was, nor could be in view." Now, if his examples prove this, let him have it. That none of them do so, I am quite confident.

His first example is from Thucydides. Speaking of a promontory, he says, " which was steep *from* the sea, and not easily attacked *from* the land." The example has not the colour of opposition to our doctrine. Were I lecturing on the passage to students, I should remark as a beauty, the distinctive import of *ek*, which this writer's criticism teaches him to overlook. The promontory is supposed to rise *out of* the sea below, as a tree grows *out of* the ground. The imagination views the object *commencing* at the bottom of the sea, and rising a vast height above its surface. Do we not ourselves speak of a rock rising *out of* the ocean ? There is nothing here said in Greek, but what we ourselves say in English, yet *out of* with us is never *from*. As to the example alleged, there is no real motion, or point of departure, whether *apo* or *ek* is used. The point of departure is merely in the view of the imagination. While examples of this kind still preserve the original distinction, yet examples most decisively to the point must be taken from real motion, and a real point of departure. It is with these that *apo* and *ek* are connected on the subject of baptism. The writer remarks : " The historian surely never meant to convey the idea, that the steep part of the rock had formerly been within the rock." The *surely* is granted, but the observation is *surely* so absurd as to need no answer. When we say that " a rock rises boldly *out of* the sea," do we mean that the top of it rose from the bottom? But there is here an *intusposition :* the rock commences below the water.

But if we are able to manage the first *ek*, he asks us what we will do with the second. This he thinks altogether refractory. However, it cost me no more trouble than the first. A glance discovers its bearing. " Would Dr. R. maintain," says the writer, " that Thucydides meant that the promontory, if attacked on the land side, must then be understood as having come *out of* the land ?" No, indeed, Dr. R. could not make such an assertion,—nor is any such assertion needed. It is not the promontory that comes out of the land ; it is the assault that comes out of the land. When attacked on the land side, does not the assault come from the interior of the land? I am surprised at such an observation from such a writer. What is most strange is, that the same question might as well be asked if *apo* had been used. In that case, would the writer suppose that the promontory was represented as coming *from* the *land*? The promontory is not, as this writer absurdly supposes, here represented as the point of departure, whether *apo* or *ek* is used. The promontory is the point of arrival. The assailants come out of the country on the land side, and direct their assault, not *from* the promontory, but *upon* it. Never were witnesses farther from serving the cause of the party who summoned them.

The next example is, "The road *from* Abdera to Ister." I say, literally, "the road *out of* Abdera to Ister." The road is supposed to commence *within* Abdera. Does the road *out of* Edinburgh to Leith commence at the extremity of the city? There might be as much of the road within the city as without it. This example is clearly on my side.

But what shall I do with Alexander's mound? Surely I cannot bring it *out of* the continent. Yes, I will bring a machine that will force it *out of* the land. Let us see the words of the author, "he resolved to carry up a mound *from* the continent to the city." I say, literally, "*out of* the continent." "But," says the writer, "the rampart never had been within the continent, but merely commenced at it." I say the rampart, according to Arrian, commenced *within* the continent. The point of commencement was not without the land, but within it. As the foundation of a house is more secure when it commences underground, so a mound is more secure when it commences within the land. I was not, it is true, present on the occasion when Alexander commenced this work; but I know where Arrian fixes the commencement. We could say that the mound of Edinburgh runs out of Bank-street into Prince's-street. The point of commencement is *within* the street above, the point of ending is *within* the street below. Mr. Locke, in one of his letters to Mr. Molyneux, speaks of his letters written *out of* Holland. The letters were written *in* Holland. What sort of a critic would he be, who should say that this implies that Mr. Locke was not in Holland when he wrote the letters? Yet this is the principle on which many criticise on dead languages. My opponents are in error in their canons of criticism.

The next example is,—"a line is said to be drawn *from* the pole of a circle." "It is impossible," says our author, "for a line to be within a point." Very true; and did not the writer see that it was equally impossible for the whole line to be at a point? And if its point of commencement could be at the edge of a point, might it not also be within the point? This is the thing said. The line is supposed to commence within the pole. The author adds: "in other propositions of the same book, *apo* is made use of to denote precisely the same idea." Say, is made to fill the same situation. This is quite in accordance with my doctrine. We ourselves do the same thing with *from* and *out of*, yet they do not signify precisely the same idea.

Another example is,—"She led him *from* the gate to the inner apartment." "Though he came from the gate," says the writer, "he could never be supposed to have come *out of* it." Certainly not *out of the wood or metal* of the gates, but as certainly *out of* the gates. Who is so ignorant as not to know that *gates* denote, not merely the gates strictly, but the place in which they stand, and that whole assemblies are said to meet and sit in the gates? We speak in like manner of a door. *He stood in the door*—he came *out of* the door—he came *from* the door. But *out of* the door is not perfectly the same as *from* the door. There is not the shadow of difficulty in such examples.

Another example brought by this writer is: " Who forming men *from* the extremity of the foot, making a statue." The writer remarks, "forming *out of* the extremity of the foot, would convey either no meaning at all, or a very absurd one; *ek* in this passage is completely synonymous with *apo.*" To suppose that the upper parts of the statue proceeded out of the foot, would indeed be absurd. And to suppose that they proceeded *from* the foot, would be no less absurd. But if the meaning is, as without doubt it is, that the foot was the point of commencement in the making of the statue, it may as well be said that this point was *within* the foot as *at* the foot, and that the work commenced *out of* the foot as *from* the foot. Nay, it seems to be the very intention of the expression to include the foot; for if he made the statue only *from* the foot, he did not make the foot. The expression is not only intelligible on the supposition of the peculiar meaning of *ek*, but is more definite than it would have been had *apo* been used.

The next example alleged is from the Periegesis of Dionysius : " From the Sicilian mountains the sea is extended far to the east." " No one," says the writer, " I think, will contend that *ek* here implies anything but the point of departure,—certainly it was not meant to denote, that the sea was ever *within* the mountains." Nothing, indeed, but the point of departure, or rather the point of commencement. But that point is within the mountains, either really or in the imagination. Is not the sea *within* the mountains in every bay formed by mountains? What is meant by " the sea *within* Lybia?"—an expression used by Dionysius, a few lines above the passage quoted by this writer. But in this place I do not understand the point of commencement, as respecting the place where the sea touches Sicily, but the place of the spectator. When viewed *out of* the Sicilian mountains, the sea of Crete extends far to the east. On no supposition, however, has the expression any appearance of opposition to my doctrine, with respect to the distinctive meaning of *ek*.

Another example is,—" Rising from her seat." " Not out of it, certainly," says the writer. *Yes, out of* it, *certainly*, say I. Thrones or chairs of state were of such a construction, that persons were said to sit down *into* them, and to come *out of* them,—just as we should say that a gentleman comes *out of* his gig. Indeed, we might say ourselves, that the old man rose *out of* his arm-chair. This is a most unfortunate example for our author. The phrase in Matt. xx. 21, is elliptical; and its explication depends on a knowledge of ancient customs, which may not now be attainable. The word thrones, or seats, or places, may be understood, and from their construction and situation the application of *ek* might have arisen. But of this I am not bound to say anything

I observe, however, that in some way the idea of *out of* must have been implied, because *ek* is used. Every professor of Greek, in speaking on these phrases to his pupils, if he was not a disgrace to his chair, would say, " literally, *out of* right hand (seats), and *out of* left hand (seats),—*on* my right hand, *on* my left hand, are our phrases, but they are not a translation." But did not the gentleman perceive that these phrases are as hard to be accounted for, on the supposition that *ek* signifies *from*, as on the supposition that it signifies *out of?* Could we say, " to sit *from* my right hand," more than " to sit *out of* my right hand?" If it is said, that the point of the sitting commences *at* the right hand, I reply, that it may also commence *within* the *right hand places*. We are at liberty to supply any word we please, for it is evident that the substantive to which *dexion* is related, is not *hand*. It is possible to sit *within* right hand places, or right hand seats.

The phrase, *from* my youth, has no difficulty. The commencing point is *within* his youth. It did not commence in the outer verge of youth, or at the very edge of youth, but within it, far within it. Philosophically, then, as well as literally, it is *out of* my youth. In like manner, *from* the beginning, is literally *out of* the beginning. The commencing point is supposed to be *within* the beginning, not where the beginning ended. He knew it *in* the beginning. The distinctive meaning of *ek* is visible even in these phrases. It is no proof of the contrary, that in some of them we have no idioms to correspond to them. If all languages had corresponding phrases perfectly alike, what would be meant by idiom? There is not one of the phrases alleged by this writer, in explaining which, a Greek scholar would not say " *literally out of.*" In some of them, our idioms may be *from;* the Greek idiom is not *from* in any of them.

I have followed the writer through all his examples, and have wrested them out of his hands. But this was more than my cause required. There is not one of the examples that corresponds to the subject of our debate. Our contest respects a case in which there is *real motion*, and a change of position from one point to another. It respects departure and arrival. Now there is no example to the purpose in which there is not a change of place. The preposition *ek* might be used with respect to other things in which the primary idea could not be discovered; while, with respect to real change of place, the distinction might be universally preserved. But there is not one of the author's examples that respects cases similar to the case to be illustrated. Not one of them relates to real motion, either *from* or *out of*. These are the examples that must decide the matter. Though I could not analyse one of the examples brought by this writer, I would still contend that *ek*, as signifying point of departure, or motion *from* one point to another, is more definite than *apo*, since it always implies that the point of departure is *within* the object, and not *without it*. From this there not only is no exception, but there is no colour of exception.

I conclude, then, with all the authority of demonstration, that Philip and the eunuch were *within* the water, because they came *out of it*. I have already observed, with respect to other examples in which *baptizo* occurs, that it will not construe with the signification *pour*. I observe the same thing with respect to Acts viii. 38: " What doth hinder me to be baptized?" It could not be translated, " what doth hinder me to be poured?" It is not the baptized person, but the water, that is *poured* in the observance of this ordinance by pouring. Philip baptized the eunuch. If the word, then, signifies to pour, it was the eunuch he poured, and not the water on the eunuch. Now the same thing may be observed, with respect to all the passages in which this word occurs. Not one of them will construe on the supposition, that it signifies to *pour*. The same thing is true to a certain extent, with respect to *sprinkle*, and every other meaning that has been given to this word. Some of the passages may construe on that supposition; but many of them will not. I need not waste time in going over all the examples, and applying to them all the meanings that have been given to the word in question. This has been done by many, and must, at a glance, be obvious to all. It merely may be stated as a canon, that WHATEVER THIS WORD SIGNIFIES WITH RESPECT TO THE ORDINANCE OF BAPTISM, WILL TRANSLATE IT IN EVERY PASSAGE IN WHICH IT REFERS TO BAPTISM. There can be no exception to this, even though it should be supposed to admit a different syntax, in other meanings; yet, as referred to the same ordinance, it must, without doubt, have the same meaning. This canon, then, excludes the pretensions of *pour* and *sprinkle*, and every other meaning that invention has given to it. *Immerse* or *dip* is the only word that can stand this ordeal. This I have shown can bear the test, not only with respect to this ordinance, but with respect to every instance in which the word is used. Can there be any rational doubt, then, in determining on the pretensions of the different claimants? Let the unlearned reader prove this, by running over the passages in which the word is found, and applying the various words which have been given as translations of the original.

The reason alleged, John iii. 23, for baptizing in a particular place, implies, that baptism is immersion. " And John also was baptizing in Ænon near to Salim, because there was much water there; and they came, and were baptized." But when Mr. Ewing reads this, he " can see nothing concerning immersion." Strange, indeed, that the same object should have an appearance so different to different eyes. Mr. Ewing sees here, with every one else, that the Holy Spirit assigns a reason for John's baptizing in Ænon, and that this reason is, the circumstance of the convenience of water. As to my purpose, I care not whether it is translated " much water," or " many waters." Does not this imply, that the water was for the purpose of baptizing? The people came there, and were baptized, because of the suitableness of the place for baptizing. This is the meaning that undoubtedly will present itself to every candid reader, who has no system in his mind as to the mode of baptism. Let the language be submitted to persons utterly unacquainted with Christianity, and among a thousand there will be but one judgment. Instead of being difficult to be discovered here, I venture to say, that there is scarcely any mind that has not some difficulty in keeping itself from seeing it. This is the labour : this is the difficulty. A person having made up his mind on the mode of baptism, when he comes to this passage, may succeed in satisfying himself with some view of the matter which has been created by his own fancy; but I am much mistaken, if it is not always with some difficulty. That the water was for the purpose of baptism, is to my mind the very testimony of the Holy Spirit. When I say, that in such a district, there are *many bleach-greens*, or *many grist-mills*, because there is there a fine river, would not every person understand that the water was necessary for the bleaching, and for turning the wheels of the mills? What would be thought of the critic who should deny this, and argue that the water was not necessary for the mills, or for the bleaching, but for the accommodation of the persons who are employed about them? Just such criticism is it, that denies that this passage makes the water here mentioned, necessary for baptism; and finds out some other use for the water.

But if Mr. Ewing will not see what these words so evidently imply, he makes ample amends by his quicksightedness in seeing here what is not here at all. He sees here " a plain reason why two large companies, which it was not the intention of God ever to unite together, except in the way of gradual transference, should nevertheless have been attracted to the neighbourhood of each other, where they might act without interference, while separately engaged in making the same religious use of water." Here Mr. Ewing can see very clearly, that the water referred to, was not for baptism, but for the Jewish purifications. He sees then what is neither said nor suggested. It is not in evidence at all, that Jewish purification was an object of this water. Mr. Ewing sees two large companies. I cannot see one large company in the passage, nor in all the history of John the Baptist. Mr. Ewing sees two companies not uniting. I see no such thing among the Jews. Nor can I see such a separation between the disciples of John or of Christ, and other Jews. But that this reason exists only in Mr. Ewing's imagination, is clear from the fact, that Jesus went every where, and every where was attended with crowds immensely great. I care not what were the crowds attending John; much water was not necessary for the purpose of accommodating hearers. This invention of Mr. Ewing is nothing better than that of his predecessors, who employed the water in giving drink to the camels.

Mr. Ewing thinks that the expression refers not to Ænon only, but also to the land of Judah. If there were such a plenty of water in all the land of Judah, it would be no loss to us. But it is as plain as language can be, that the *many waters* spoken of were in Ænon only.

Having considered the syntax and connexion of the word *baptizo*, I shall next proceed to ascertain how far any light can be obtained from the Scripture explanations of the ordinance, and the occasional allusions to it. It is a most providential circumstance, that the mode of this ordinance is determined not only by the word that designates it,—by its syntax, and words in construction with it,—but also by direct explanations.

SECTION XVI.—EVIDENCE FROM THE SCRIPTURE EXPLANATIONS OF THE ORDINANCE.—*Examination of Rom.* vi. 3.—The apostle Paul, having strongly and fully stated salvation to the guiltiest of men, through grace reigning through righteousness unto eternal life by Jesus Christ our Lord, anticipates, in the beginning of the sixth chapter of his epistle to the Romans, the objection that in every age has been made to his doctrine: " Shall we continue in sin, that grace may abound?" He refutes this objection by the fact, that from our union with Christ by faith, we have died along with him. And that we have died along with Christ, he proves from our baptism. " Know ye not, that so many of us as were baptized into Jesus Christ, were baptized into his death?" Something is here supposed to be implied in baptism, of which no Christian should be ignorant; and that thing is, that all who are baptized, are by that ordinance exhibited as dead along with Christ. To be baptized into Christ's death is not merely to be baptized into the faith of his death, but of our own death with him. For if our death along with him is not implied in being baptized into his death, then this would be no proof at all of our own death. But it is our own death with Christ, that the apostle is proving by our baptism into Christ's death. The third verse would be no proof of what is asserted in the second verse, if our baptism into Christ does not imply our death in his death.

" Therefore we are buried with him, by baptism, into death." As in Christ's death, we have died with him; so in baptism, we are figuratively put into the grave along with him. Words cannot more plainly teach anything than these words declare, that *in baptism we are buried with Christ*. Baptism, then, must not only contain a likeness to burial, but that likeness is emblematical. There may be resemblance between two objects, and to exhibit that likeness in words is a beauty in language. But if the likeness is merely accidental, it is only a figure of speech, and can teach nothing. To found an argument on such ground, would be the extravagance of fanaticism. Homer compares the falling of his heroes headlong from their chariots, to the diving of water-fowl. But this resemblance is merely accidental, and the victor had no intention of giving an emblem of *diving;* nor could any argument be grounded on the likeness. When a person *dips* in bathing, he might be said to be *buried* in the water; and there would be as good a likeness in this to Christ's burial, even as in baptism. But the likeness is only accidental, not emblematical. No argument could be drawn from this, to prove a dying with Christ. This would be a metaphor. But baptism is not a figure of speech; it is an emblematical action. The likeness is intentional, and the action performed is symbolical. Were it not so, the apostle might as legitimately argue from the *bath* as from *baptism*. This distinction is self-evident, and we shall find that it is of decisive importance. From not understanding it, some have said that we have as good a right to find in the meaning of baptism, something corresponding to planting, as to burial. *Planting* is a metaphor; there must then be a likeness, but no emblematical import.

"That like as Christ was raised up from the dead by the glory of the Father, even so we also should walk in newness of life." Here we see that baptism is an emblem also of the new life of the Christian. He dies with Christ to sin; he rises with him to a new life of holiness. There must, then, be something in baptism, that is calculated to be an emblem of a resurrection, as well as of a burial. Immersion is a mode that answers both; and immersion is the only mode that can do so.

"For if we have been planted together in the likeness of his death, we shall be also in the likeness of his resurrection." In our baptism, then, we are emblematically laid in the grave with Christ, and we also emblematically rise with him. It is designed to point to our own resurrection, as well as the resurrection of Christ. In baptism, we profess our faith in the one as past, and in the other as future. What simplicity, what beauty, what edification is contained in this ordinance! How have all these been overwhelmed by the traditions of men! How clearly does this ordinance present the truth that saves the soul! How admirably is it calculated to recall the mind to a view of the ground of hope, that is calculated to silence unbelief! How is it that a vile sinner can escape the wrath of God, and obtain eternal life? How is it that Christ's work is available for him? Why, when Christ paid our debt, we ourselves have paid our debt, for we are one with Christ. We have died with Christ, and have risen with Christ; Christ's death is our death; Christ's burial is our burial; Christ's resurrection is our resurrection; Christ's sitting in heavenly places, is our sitting in heavenly places.

This clear testimony of the Holy Spirit, Mr. Ewing endeavours to set aside, by a mode of criticism certainly the boldest and most violent that I recollect ever to have seen from the pen of a man of God. The grossness of the perversions of those who know not God, is not astonishing. The extravagance even of Neologists, may be accounted for. But that one who knows and fears God, should take such liberties with his word, is more than I was prepared to expect. Indeed, there is nothing more extravagant in Neologism, than in the manner in which Mr. Ewing explains the burial of Christ. Had I been informed merely of the result, without knowing anything of the author, I should have at once concluded that it was the offspring of Neology. But the character of Mr. Ewing, as well as the document itself, gives full evidence that it is the work of sincerity. Indeed, while I must say that it is one of the most mischievous perversions of Scripture that I have ever met from the hand of a Christian, I am fully convinced that the author considers that he has conferred an important benefit on the world, by his discovery in criticism. His wild conclusions are speciously drawn from premises hastily adopted, and utterly unsound.

He begins by saying, that "the great, and, as it appears to me, the only original reason why baptism has been thought to imply immersion, is the expression which occurs in Rom. vi. 4, and Col. ii. 12." I shall not answer for the dead, but for my own part, the word by which the ordinance is designated, is perfectly sufficient for me, without a particle of evidence from any other quarter. Yet I am disposed to set as great a value upon the evidence of these passages as any writer can do. I value the evidence of these passages so highly, that I look on them as perfectly decisive. They contain God's own explanation of his own ordinance. And in this, I call upon my unlearned brethren to admire the Divine wisdom. They do not understand the original, and the adoption of the words *baptize* and *baptism* can teach them nothing. Translators, by adopting the Greek word, have contrived to hide the meaning from the unlearned. But the evidence of the passages in question, cannot be hid, and it is obvious to the most unlearned. The Spirit of God has, by this explanation, enabled them to judge for themselves in this matter. While the learned are fighting about *baptizo*, and certain Greek prepositions, let the unlearned turn to Rom. vi. 4, and Col. ii. 12, &c.

Mr. Ewing, speaking of the reasoning of the apostle in this passage, says: " He then infers, that since baptism has so immediate a reference to the death of Christ, it must, by consequence, be connected also with his resurrection; and that, as in the former view, it teaches the regenerated the abandoning of the old life of sin, so, in the latter, it equally teaches them the habitual, increasing, and permanent pursuit and progress of the new life of righteousness." By no means, Mr. Ewing. This inference is not legitimate. Baptism might have a reference to burial, without being by consequence connected with his resurrection. Has not the Lord's supper an immediate emblematical reference to Christ's death, without any emblematical reference to his resurrection? These two things are quite distinct; and it is possible for an ordinance to represent the one, without representing the other. The Lord's-day is a memorial of Christ's resurrection, but is no emblem of his burial. If there was nothing in baptism that is fitted to be an emblem of resurrection, baptism does not become an emblem of resurrection by consequence from being an emblem of burial. But baptism is here explained as an emblem of resurrection, as well as of burial; there must, therefore, be something in the emblem, that will correspond to resurrection as well as to burial. There is such a thing in *immersion*, but there is no such thing in *pouring*; nor is there any such thing in applying water as an emblem of sepulchral rites. This, then, overturns Mr. Ewing's system altogether. He confesses virtually in this quotation, that the apostle infers that baptism is connected with the resurrection. If so, as there is nothing in sepulchral rites, that is, in washing and embalming the dead, that corresponds to resurrection, washing and embalming the dead cannot be the burial referred to,—and pouring water as an emblem of washing and embalming the dead, cannot be baptism. Nothing can be more decisive than this. Indeed, so far from arguing that resurrection must be implied in baptism, because that baptism represents Christ as dead, we could not know that either death or resurrection was referred to in that ordinance, had not inspiration given the information. It is possible that an ordinance, performed either by *immersion* or *pouring*, might have had no instruction in mode. The instruction might have been all in the water. That there is any meaning in the mode, we learn merely from the inspired explanation. Here Mr. Ewing takes the half of his edification in this ordinance, from a source that does not contain anything on the subject. There is nothing in the emblem, according to his view of it, that corresponds to a new life, or resurrection. Has washing the dead any likeness to resurrection? Have sepulchral rites, or embalming, any likeness to resurrection? Mr. Ewing was so tender in the conscience, that he scrupled to give the name to this ordinance from *immersion*, if it also denoted *emersion*, though these two things are necessarily connected, and both explained as belonging to the ordinance. He does not scruple to make the emblem of death, an emblem of life by consequence.

"It is a common remark," says Mr. Ewing, "that the apostle is treating in this passage, not of the form of baptism, but of its object, its design, and its actual effects." Let its form be what it may, this passage treats of its object as known from its form. "On this account," says he, "many are of opinion that no inference can be drawn from his language, concerning the form of baptism at all." No inference is necessary. The apostle has drawn the inference himself. We could not have drawn the inference which the apostle has drawn. Had not the apostle explained this ordinance, we should have had no right to do so. But even if baptism had not here been explained as a symbolical burial,—had it been alluded to as a burial merely in metaphorical language, it would have been equally decisive of form, though not of meaning. If baptism is a burial merely by a figure of speech, there must be a likeness between baptism and burial, to justify that figure.

"Perhaps," says Mr. Ewing, "it would be more correct to say, that he is here treating of the connexion between the justification and the sanctification of Christians." True—but he is treating of these things as they are implied in baptism. He is treating also of more. He incidentally treats of the resurrection of believers as implied in their baptism. "And that in doing so," says Mr. Ewing, "he makes three distinct allusions, to baptism, to grafting, to crucifixion." He makes no allusion to *grafting* at all; and whatever is the meaning of the phrase *planted together*, it refers to baptism. Crucifixion does not allude to baptism.

We come now to the examination of Mr. Ewing's account of "the scriptural meaning of 'being buried.'" Here we shall find the mysteries of the critical art. By a learned and laborious process, Mr. Ewing endeavours to prove that Christ was not *properly* buried at all; and that *burial* in Scripture is not burial, but *washing* or *embalming* the dead. Now, on the very face of this allegation it contains its own condemnation. *Burying*, in the Scripture meaning, must be the same as *burying* in the common meaning, otherwise the Scriptures are not a revelation. This is a canon—a canon which is self-evident. If the Scriptures do not use words in the sense in which they will be understood by those who speak the language, they do not instruct, but mislead. I overturn the whole system, then, by taking away the foundation on which it rests. It assumes what is not true in any instance.

"By burying," says Mr. Ewing, "we commonly mean the lowering of the dead body into the grave, covering it with earth, and so leaving it under ground." This, indeed, is in general our way of burying. But we should apply the term to burying in any way. We should say that a person *was buried in a vault*, where he would lie exactly as Christ lay, —without lowering, without a covering of mould, &c. If a person was deposited in all respects as Christ was deposited in the tomb, we should say that he was *buried*. The difference is merely in circumstances; the things are essentially the same. Besides, the immersion of a believer, is equally suited to all kinds of burial. No part of the figure depends on any peculiarity in any age or nation.

"In Scripture," says Mr. Ewing, "*to bury*, not only includes all the preparations of the body for interment, but is the expression used in cases where our method of interment was not practised, where no interment followed at the time, and where no final interment followed at all." Neither in Scripture nor any where else, is the word used for preparatory rites alone, or where the body was not truly and properly interred.

What does Mr. Ewing mean by final interment? Does he mean that Christ was not finally interred, because he rose on the third day? Then none of us will be finally interred; for we shall all rise again. Does he mean that the disciples did not consider him as truly interred, and that they designed to bury him better? They had no such design. They intended to cover him with more spices, but not to take him from the place where he was buried. He was as truly buried as if he had been in the ground till the resurrection. What does Mr. Ewing mean? Does he deny that Christ was truly buried? If he was not buried, the Scriptures are false. And if he was truly buried, though he had lain but a moment, our baptism may be an emblem of his burial.

But it seems Mr. Ewing has Scripture proofs for the meaning that he assigns to *burial*. Let us then take a look at these. In Gen. i. 26, where the Hebrew says, *they embalmed* Joseph, "the Septuagint," says Mr. Ewing, "has *ethapsan, they buried him*." Very true. But does this imply, that by *ethapsan* the translators understood embalming? No such thing. Had they used the word in this sense, they could not have been understood by those who spoke the Greek language. This translation is not a proof either that the Septuagint understood *embalming* to be the meaning of *burial*, or that they did not understand the true meaning of the original. It is only proof of what occurs in this translation a thousand times, and what occasionally occurs in every translation, namely, careless and loose rendering. Their text said, *he was embalmed:* they content themselves with saying, he was buried.

"The rites of burial were," says Mr. Ewing, "from the very commencement, a proof that the attending friends had ascertained the fact of the decease." Indeed, it is obvious enough, that they would not commence these rites till after the death of the person; but these rites never were designed as proof of this. Above all, the Scriptures do not require such a mode of ascertaining the fact of decease. He adds, "and that among all believers of revelation, the zeal and the solemnity with which these rites have ever been performed, ought to be considered as the effect, not merely of personal attachment, but of religious principle, and particularly of the hope that God will raise the dead." Whatever may have been the origin of these rites, nothing can be more certain than that they were used by persons who had no notion of resurrection, —nay, by many who denied it. Above all, these rites were not a Divine appointment for reminding of the resurrection. Nothing can be built on this.

"It is our happiness to know," says Mr. Ewing, "that our blessed Saviour never was finally interred." By *finally interred* here, Mr. Ewing must mean that he was raised again, and did not lie like the other dead. For, as far as concerns our salvation and comfort, he might as well have been kept in a common grave for the period of three days, as have been buried in a rock. But may he not have been truly buried, though he had risen in a moment after being deposited?

"Preparations of his body for burial were made," says Mr. Ewing, "both by anticipation, and after the event of his death had taken place. In both cases they are called 'his burial.'" How can Mr. Ewing say so? The preparatory rites are never called *burial.* The passages referred to have not the smallest appearance of confounding *embalming* with *burying.* John xii. 3 represents Mary not as burying our Lord by the act of anointing him, but as having anointed him as preparatory for burial. She *anointed* him by anticipation; but she did not *bury* him by anticipation. Is it said that she buried him? The woman, Matt. xxvi. 12, is represented as doing what she did, not to bury him, but to *embalm* him, or prepare him for burial. She did to him, when alive, what is usually done to persons after death. She embalmed him by anticipation. *Entaphiazo* is used for embalming, but *thapto* never.

"After our Lord had given up the ghost," says Mr. Ewing, "the rites of burial were renewed by Joseph of Arimathea, and Nicodemus." This was strictly and properly the embalming. But is this called a burial? Had they done nothing but this, Jesus would not have been buried; and the Scriptures would not have been fulfilled. He adds, "and were intended to have been finished by the women which came up with our Lord," &c. These rites, then, were not *finished;* and if they are *burial,* Jesus *was not buried.*

Mr. Ewing, then, has utterly failed in his attempt to prove, that in Scripture, preparatory rites are called burial. Not one of his examples has a shadow of proof. I will now make some general remarks on this strange opinion.

First, The word *thapto* signifies *to bury,* and is never applied exclusively to preparatory rites. This is as true, with respect to Scripture use, as it is with respect to the use of the classics. Mr. Ewing gives a meaning to this word, not confirmed by use, but merely to suit his purpose. In like manner *sunthapto,* the word here used, signifies to *bury one thing or person with another,*—never to embalm one thing with another. The opinion, then, does not deserve even a hearing.

Secondly, Thapto applies to all kinds of burial. No doubt, originally, in all countries, burial was by digging a pit, and covering the dead with the mould. But when repositories were built for the dead, or were scooped out of rocks, the same word was still used. This, in fact, is the case with our own word *bury.* We apply it to the depositing of a body in a vault, as well as the common burial. This process in enlarging the meaning of words, may be exemplified in a thousand words. The idea that is common to all *burying,* is that of covering the dead, or surrounding them with something to keep them from violation. It is quite a waste of time, then, for Mr. Ewing to discuss the situation and peculiarities of our Lord's sepulchre. He was buried as many others are buried; and to this burial there is a likeness in our baptism, when we are buried in water.

Thirdly, Burial and embalming are often distinguished as quite different things. Josephus speaking of the magnificent manner in which Herod buried Aristobulus, says, "And as for his funeral, that he took care should be very magnificent, by making great preparation of a sepulchre to lay his body in, and providing a great quantity of spices, and *burying* many ornaments with him," &c. Here the *embalming* and the *burying* are distinguished. It was the laying of him in the sepulchre that was the burial. It may be noted also, that here is a magnificent sepulchre, built as a house for the dead, in which the corpse lay on a bier or couch; yet the person is said to be buried. If Christ was not truly buried, Aristobulus was not truly buried. We have here, also, not only *sunthapto*, but *sugkatathapto*. The ornaments that were *buried together* with Aristobulus, were deposited in the tomb with him,—not washed along with him by preparatory rites. These ornaments were *buried down with* him, although he was laid, like Christ, in a sepulchre above ground. Yet this is as truly burying as the common way of burying; though the sepulchre should have been on the top of the highest mountain in the world, the corpse is buried under a covering, as truly as if it were deposited in the centre of the earth.

Moschus, describing a funeral, represents the burial as taking place after all the rites were finished. Meg. i. 35.

Patroclus, notwithstanding all the embalming he received, appears to his friend Achilles, and calls for *burial*. *Thapte me,* "*bury me.*"

The dead body of Hector was washed regularly by the maids of Achilles, yet it was not *buried* till long after.

The passage produced by Dr. Cox from Herodotus, is most decisive. The *embalming* is designated by *taricheuo*, the *burying* by *thapto*. But it is useless to be particular in disproving a thing that has not even the colour of plausibility to support it. No two things can be more distinct than *washing* or *embalming* the dead, and *burying* the dead. Indeed, in the burial of Jesus itself, these two things are distinguished. They first rolled him in spices, which was the *embalming :* then they laid him in the sepulchre, which is the burying. What is laying in a sepulchre, but burying? But Mr. Ewing says, that the body of Christ "was never finally deposited in the tomb; but, after being wound up with about an hundred pounds weight of spices," &c. No matter how short a time it was in the tomb; in the tomb, it was buried like any other dead body. The disciples had no intention of ever removing it from the tomb. The women who came with more spices, had no intention to unbury it, or take it elsewhere. To give more spices, was not to complete the burying, but to complete the embalming. Were a person in Edinburgh to visit the grave of a friend every day, and even open both grave and coffin, to ascertain whether the body was removed, this would not affect the burying. Why should preparatory rites be called the *burying* of Jesus, seeing he was actually laid in the sepulchre? No fancy can be wilder than this.

Fourthly, The representations of Scripture suppose Jesus to have been truly buried. "For as Jonas was three days and three nights in the whale's belly; so shall the Son of man be three days and three nights in the heart of the earth," Matt. xii. 40. Mr. Ewing himself allows that this was fulfilled by his being laid in a sepulchre. And what is laying in a sepulchre, but burying? Besides, this removes all Mr. Ewing's objections with respect to the situation of the tomb of Jesus. In this sepulchre, Jesus was in the heart of the earth. It is usual for a ridge of rocks to have earth on the top. The Saviour was under the earth here as well as if he had been buried in a pit at the bottom of a valley. Again, Christ's being buried, is taught as a part of the gospel, 1 Cor. xv. 1. To allege, then, that he was not truly buried, is to call in question the truth of the gospel. " Moreover, brethren, I declare unto you the gospel which I preached unto you, which also ye have received, and wherein ye stand; by which also ye are saved, if ye keep in memory what I preached unto you, unless ye have believed in vain. For I declared unto you first of all, that which I also received, how that Christ died for our sins, according to the Scriptures; and that he was buried, and that he rose again the third day, according to the Scriptures." Here, what was in the evangelist called *three days in the heart of the earth*, the apostle calls being *buried;* for he is said to have risen on the *third* day. The third day from what? The third day from his being buried. He is here considered as being three days buried, for he rose on the third day from his being buried. His resurrection here, is also opposed to his being buried; it must then be burying, in the proper sense of the word.

Fifthly, The very basis of this doctrine is a mere assumption, namely, that the dead body of Jesus was washed. It is not in evidence that he was washed at all; and nothing can be deduced from a mere supposition. Mr. Ewing, indeed, endeavours to supply what is wanting in the history. He alleges, what no one will deny, that it was usual to wash the dead. But does it follow from this, that Jesus must have been washed? We should not have known that he was embalmed, had not the history given us the information. It is not necessary that the dead body of Jesus should receive all the usual rites, nor any of them, except those that prophecy foretold. The proof, then, that it was usual to wash the dead, is no proof that Jesus was washed. Indeed, I perfectly agree with Dr. Cox, that it is probable Jesus was not washed at all. So far as the history goes, this is the obvious conclusion. I acknowledge, indeed, that many things might have taken place, that are not mentioned in the history. If any other part of Scripture said, or implied that Jesus was washed, as well as embalmed, I would argue that the omission of the fact in the history is no evidence to the contrary. But if the washing is not recorded, nothing can be built on it; because it might not have taken place. The washing of Jesus is an apocryphal washing, of no more authority than the story of Tobit and his dog, or of Bel and the Dragon. I admit no argument but what is founded either on Scripture, or self-evident truth. Had Mr. Ewing been obviating a difficulty,—had he been proving that some part of Scripture asserts that the dead body of Jesus was washed, and had any one alleged the silence of the history as evidence of the contrary, I would take part with Mr. Ewing. The silence of history is not to be alleged against proof. To remove a difficulty, it is sufficient that the thing alleged is possible; to be an argument, the thing alleged must be in evidence. This distinction is self-evidently obvious, when it is considered; yet it is a thing that lies hid from most controversial writers.

But Mr. Ewing says, " as far as the preliminary process went, we are told it was conducted, as the manner of the Jews was to bury." No, Mr. Ewing, we are not told this. Had this been said, it would settle the question ; for undoubtedly, it was the manner of the Jews to wash the dead. But we are not told that, as far as the preliminary process went, all the usual rites were observed. It is the winding in the linen cloth with the spices, that is said to have been, " as the manner of the Jews is to bury."

Mr. Ewing alleges the state of the body, covered with blood, &c., as making washing necessary. All this, however, is no evidence that it was done. Had it been necessary to fulfil anything in Scripture, there is no doubt it would have been done. But there is no necessity to fulfil national customs. The burying of Jesus with his blood unwashed, marred not his sacrifice, nor left any prophecy unfulfilled. It was customary for all friends to escort the body to the grave; it was customary to keep the corpse some time after death, yet Jesus was carried imme- diately to the grave without any funeral pomp.

Sixthly, Is it not above all things absurd to suppose, that an ordinance in the church of Christ should be instituted as an emblem of a thing that is never once mentioned in his history? If the washing of the dead body of the Saviour was a thing of so much importance, is it credible that it would not have been mentioned? How is it that the spices are mentioned, yet the washing, which was the principal thing, omitted?

Seventhly, Mr. Ewing supposes, that the washing, as a part of the embalming, is put for the whole. Why does he make such a supposition? Was there not a word to signify embalming? Why then use a word that denotes only a part of the thing? Can he produce any instance to give authority to such a supposition? Was it usual to denote the whole process of embalming by the word *wash?* If not, why does Mr. Ewing make the arbitrary supposition? Again, the *washing* was no part of the embalming. It was a part of the rites of burying, and as such, when embalming was used, washing of course first took place. But it is evident, that the washing and the embalming were different things. Besides, many were washed who were not embalmed. If so, it was impossible to designate embalming by washing. This would have im- plied, that all who were washed were embalmed ; whereas multitudes were washed who were not embalmed. This theory, then, is not only founded on an arbitrary supposition ; but that supposition may be proved to be false. It is an axiom, that washing cannot stand for embalming, if many who were washed were not embalmed.

Eighthly, This theory makes baptism an emblem of the embalming of Christ. This is a new view of the import of baptism, that must be as unexpected to those who baptize by pouring, as to the friends of immersion. From the days of John the Baptist to the present hour, was ever such a thing heard of but from Mr. Ewing? If this is true, there has not been one properly baptized till the time of the author. For this discovery, Mr. Ewing is undoubtedly entitled to a patent. Till his time, the baptized person was never embalmed. This is a new mystery in baptism. But how does this consist with the other mysteries that the author has found in the same ordinance? The baptized person drinks from the cup of nature as emblematical of a host of blessings; and from the same cup he is washed and embalmed for funeral. No popish ordinance can vie with this ordinance of Mr. Ewing, in fertility of mysteries. The mystery of the five wounds has as good a foundation; but it is not so pregnant in multifarious meaning. If all these things are contained in baptism, it is a most heterogeneous ordinance; and I am sure, that of all the millions who practise it, there is not one in every thousand that understands it. The Roman Catholic church has done much better. She has a multitude of mysteries in baptism, but she has a corresponding multitude of emblems. The oil, and the spittle, and the breathing, &c. &c., entitle her to enlarge the meaning of her ordinance. But Mr. Ewing, by the management of one handful of water, contrives to couch the most discordant meanings.

But if washing stands for embalming as a part for the whole, then it cannot, in this situation, stand simply for itself, without the other parts of the process of embalming. In baptism, the water must signify not washing only, nor chiefly, but also and especially the spices, &c. The principal part of the mystery must be in the anointing with oil, and the use of the spices, for these were the principal things in the embalming. Now, Mr. Ewing overlooks all but the washing; which is only the previous step to the embalming. He first makes the embalming the principal thing, that he may have some plausible foundation for getting rid of true burying, by substituting the embalming in its place. Then, when this is effected, as he has no need of embalming, but finds it rather cumbersome, he contrives to dismiss it, retaining only the part that fits him. *Washing* is brought in only in the right of *embalming;* but whenever it *pops* its head into this situation, it takes care to displace its principal. Accordingly, washing is the only thing that is made emblematical. The oil and spices have no mystery. Is not this unjust to the chief parts of the embalming? Surely the anointing ought to have a place in baptism, if baptism is an emblem of embalming. Spices also cannot be dispensed with. Even if they are not used, as they are the chief thing in embalming, they must be chiefly considered in baptism, which is an emblem of embalming. The Church of Rome will thank Mr. Ewing for the oil, which he does not seem forward to use; but the spices, by a very little ingenuity, might serve his system effectually. As embalming preserves the body from putrefaction, so baptism may not only be an emblem of the washing of a corpse, but of the resurrection.

Ninthly, Mr. Ewing complains of the want of likeness between Christ's burial and immersion; yet he makes a handful of water an emblem not only of washing a corpse, but of the whole rites of embalming. Surely there can be nothing more unlike burial rites, than the *popping* of a handful of water into the face of an infant. But the complaint of want of likeness in immersion to the burial and resurrection of Christ, is quite unreasonable. It is as striking as any emblem can be. It ought, however, to be remarked, that the ordinance is merely emblematical—not dramatic. In the former, there is no need of that exact and minute likeness that the latter requires. The former could not be known to be a likeness of something else, if it were not explained to be such. The latter is, by its very appearance, known to be an emblem. The sacrifices of the Jewish law could not, from mere external appearance, have been known to represent the death of Christ. But the dramatic burying of Charles V. declared its own object.

Let it be considered also, that in the emblem of a burial, there is no need of a likeness in the laying down of the body of the person baptized. The emblem is in the actual state of the body as being covered with the water. The likeness to the resurrection consists not in the very manner of being taken up out of the water, but in the rising itself. Nothing could afford a resemblance of the way of the raising of the dead. There was no likeness between the way of killing the sacrifice and the manner of Christ's death. There was no likeness between the manner in which Jonah was swallowed by the whale, and again thrown out, to the way in which Christ was carried into the tomb, and in which he came out of the tomb; yet Jonah in the whale's belly was an emblem of Christ as being three days in the heart of the earth. Surely Mr. Ewing should have attended more to the nature of an emblem, and have distinguished what is the point of resemblance, before he ventured to question the likeness between the baptism of believers and the burial of Christ, which is asserted by the Holy Spirit. If the Baptists set any value on the manner of putting the body of the baptized person under water, in my opinion they come under the same censure. Mr. Ewing's whole dissertation on the Jewish manner of burying the distinguished dead, has no bearing on the subject. Between immersion and burying in any manner, there is a likeness. It is nothing to our purpose to make that likeness dramatic.

Mr. Ewing is of opinion, that verse 5 does not refer to baptism. But whatever is the true meaning of the word translated "planted together," it is evident, that it must have its reference to baptism. It is a distinct figure, and the manner of introducing it, evidently shows that it, equally with *burying*, refers to baptism. "For if we have been planted together in the likeness of his death, we shall be also in the likeness of his resurrection." The conditional statement is here evidently founded on what precedes. "If we have been planted," &c. He does not pass on to a new argument to show that we are dead with Christ, leaving the subject of baptism; but having shown the burial of the Christian in baptism, he goes on to show that resurrection is equally important. If we have been buried with Christ, so shall we rise with him. Had he quitted the subject of baptism, and introduced a new argument, which had no reference to baptism, he would not have stated it conditionally. When he says, "For if we have been planted," it is implied that he had been saying something expressing or implying that *they had been planted.* Whatever is the meaning of *sumphutoi,* it must have a reference to baptism.

Mr. Ewing thinks that *sumphutoi* here signifies *grafted,* and of course can have no likeness to baptism. On the contrary, for this very reason I say that it cannot signify *grafting,* because it is expressly said, that we have been *sumphutoi* in the likeness of Christ's death. If, then, there is in *grafting* no likeness to death, the word cannot mean grafting. Whatever is the meaning of *sumphutoi,* it must suit the supposition of a likeness to death. Even if this word had no reference to baptism, it must refer to a likeness of death. We have been made *sumphutoi* in the likeness of his death.

But independently of the connexion altogether, I maintain that the word does not signify *grafted.* Mr. Ewing produces no authority from use to establish this meaning. When it refers to trees, it does not designate the operation of grafting, or of inserting a part of one into another; but to the planting of trees in the same bed. The trees of a grove are *sumphutoi.* *Grafting* is, indeed, one of the figures employed to represent the union of Christ and his people, and some excellent observations on this subject are contained in Mr. Ewing's dissertation on this verse. But they have no application to this subject. A house, a temple, the human body, the husband and wife, are all figures of this union. But they are not the figures used here. No more is grafting. It is a fine figure in its own place; but it is no likeness to death, and therefore has nothing to do with baptism. If the allusion is here to planting, as it is expressly said to have a likeness to death, and refers to baptism, the resemblance must be found in the burying of the roots of the plants. The likeness is sufficiently obvious to justify a metaphor.

Mr. Ewing's attempt, then, to find in pouring a handful of water on the face, a likeness to the burial of Christ, has utterly failed. It is as forced as anything that the wildest imagination ever conceived. Nothing but the necessity of a favourite system could send a man on such a perilous expedition. It is most astonishing, that any man who allows that Jesus Christ lay three days in the tomb, should attempt to find his burial in the washing or embalming of his body.

This attempt of Mr. Ewing to force a likeness between baptism and the rites of embalming, and to make the burial of Christ, not his being laid in the sepulchre, but his being washed as a corpse, is of great importance as a document on this subject. It testifies in the strongest manner, that in Mr. Ewing's judgment, the evidence from Rom. vi. 3, and Col. ii. 12, that baptism contains a likeness to burial, is so obvious, that he could see no way to explain these passages otherwise. Had any other explanation seemed to him possible, certainly he would not have had recourse to so wild a thought, as that Christ's burial was not his interment, and that *bury* in the Scriptures relates to rites preparatory to interment. It is self-evident, that no man would have fled to such a refuge, who could have found any other. I appeal to common sense for the truth of this observation. Mr. Ewing not only had no temptation to find a likeness to burial in these passages, but his cause would have been much better served, could he have proved that these passages contain no such likness. Since, then, in such circumstances he has confessed a likeness, and since to divert this likeness to another object, he was obliged to have recourse to so violent an expedient, we have a right to say, not only that his judgment is in favour of likeness, but that all his ingenuity could not explain the passages in a manner satisfactory to himself, without the supposition of likeness.

But what Mr. Ewing's intrepidity and ingenuity did not attempt, Dr. Wardlaw has undertaken. He explains the passages on the supposition that baptism has no likeness to burial in any sense. Now, in this we have Dr. Wardlaw's judgment virtually, but clearly pronounced, that Mr. Ewing's attempt is a failure. We have a right then to say, that Mr. Ewing's explanation of these passages is unsatisfactory to the most sagacious of his own party. But Dr. Wardlaw's opinion of the insufficiency of Mr. Ewing's explanation, has the more value, when it is considered, that by refusing to adopt it, he is obliged to have recourse to an expedient as violent, and as wild as that of Mr. Ewing itself. To assert, that there is here no likeness implied between baptism and burial, does as great violence to language as can easily be conceived. If, therefore, Dr. Wardlaw is so convinced of the insufficiency of Mr. Ewing's explanation, that he ventures on one so extravagant, his opinion of Mr. Ewing's failure is entitled to the greater weight. It was his interest to coincide with Mr. Ewing's explanation, had he conceived that it was at all tenable. He would not have ventured to come ashore upon a plank, had he not found Mr. Ewing's leaky boat sinking under him. Dr. Wardlaw complains of the mode of controversy that argues from discrepancies between those on the same side. I admit that the argument may be abused. But if he complain of my argument on this point, he does not see its bearing. Persons on the same side of a controversy, may differ with respect to the explanation of many passages, without any detriment to their common cause. But the difference here is about a thing which must in itself be obvious, namely, whether a certain phrase implies the likeness of one thing to another. About this there cannot in reality be a ground for controversy among those who understand the words.

The difference, also, is of such a nature, that each must look on the other as giving up the common cause. As Mr. Ewing is so fully convinced that it is impossible to deface the likeness, he must look upon those who do not agree with him in finding it in preparatory rites, as giving up the passage to his opponents. As Dr. Wardlaw cannot explain the passages on the supposition of likeness without admitting immersion, he must look upon those who admit likeness, as yielding the doctrine in debate. On the other hand, we may differ about the meaning of *sumphutoi*, without the least danger to our common cause. One may say, it is " *planted together,*" another, that it is " *joined together,*" without overturning the common doctrine. My argument is founded, also, on the extravagancies to which each of these writers is obliged to have recourse, in order to defend his opinion. Each of them must have strong reason of dissatisfaction with the opinion of the other, when, rather than embrace it, he has recourse to an opposite point of extravagance. One sees likeness so clearly, that rather than deny it, he endeavours to find it where sobriety of judgment never could look for it. The other sees the extravagance of this attempt so clearly, that, rather than adopt it, he will deny that the passages contain any likeness.

But let us now take a glance at the process of ejectment by which Dr. Wardlaw has dispossessed likeness out of these passages. " To be ' baptized into Christ,' " says he, " is to be baptized into the faith of him as the Messiah,"' &c. And again, " the simple meaning of the expression evidently is, that by being baptized into the faith of his death, as the death of our surety and substitute, we become *partakers with him in it*." Now, what is here said to be evidently the simple meaning of this expression, is evidently not its meaning at all. We do not become partakers in the death of Christ, by being baptized into the faith of his death. We become partakers in the death of Christ, by faith, before baptism, and without baptism; and should have been equally so, had baptism never been instituted. In baptism, this participation with Christ is exhibited in figure, just as we are said to *wash away our sins* in baptism. Sins are washed away by faith in the blood of Christ, but they are symbolically washed away in baptism. Just so we become partakers in the death of Christ the moment we believe; in baptism, this participation is exhibited by a symbol.

Dr. Wardlaw, by this mode of interpretation, considers *faith in Christ's death*, and *baptism into his death*, as equivalent expressions. But to be " baptized into his death," is more than to " believe in his death." Baptism into his death, not only imports that we believe in him as our substitute, but *marks* our death in his death. To be *baptized into his death*, is the same as to be *buried into death*. In reality, we die with Christ the moment we believe ; but this is not expressed by the phrase, *faith in Christ's death*. It is learned from other parts of the Scriptures. Now, herein lies the importance of the mode of baptism. It marks, in a figure, the way in which we become partakers in the benefits of Christ's death. This is by our being, by a Divine constitution, one with him. His death is a proper atonement for us, because we die with him, so that in reality his death is ours. This is not necessary in all cases of substitution. To have a debt discharged by another, there is no necessity to become one with him. But it is not so in crime. Justice is not satisfied, except the criminal himself suffers ; and by the Divine constitution, that makes all believers one with Christ, they are all considered as having died with him. The criminals have suffered, since he who suffered was one with them. Baptism, then, marks this circumstance. It shows, in a figure, that union with Christ in his death, burial, and resurrection, which we have by faith.

According to Dr. Wardlaw's way of explaining these passages, there was no occasion to mention baptism at all. If the apostle is speaking of the real oneness with Christ, without considering it as exhibited in a figure, he might as well have said, " Know ye not, that as many as have believed in Christ's death, have died along with him?" This would express all that Dr. Wardlaw takes out of the passage; and it would express it definitely. Why, then, does the apostle bring in baptism at all? Again, if baptism implies burial only as implying faith in Christ's death, then the Lord's supper, or anything that implies faith, might have been referred to on this occasion, as well as baptism. We might as well say that we are buried by the Lord's supper as buried by baptism. We might as well say that we are crucified by baptism. But such phraseology is never used in the Scriptures. The only reason, then, that baptism is here brought forward at all, must be that it is a figure of burial.

That baptism has a likeness to death, is put beyond question in this passage, from the phrase, *buried with him through baptism into death.* Here is a burial *by* or *through the means* of baptism. What buries us into death? It is baptism. But the death into which baptism buries us, must be a figurative death. It is faith that buries us truly into Christ's death. But the death and burial here spoken of, are effected, not by faith, but by baptism. This phrase refutes Dr. Wardlaw's assertion, that though a likeness might be fancied between immersion and burial, no likeness to death can be found in it. The phrase, *buried by baptism into death,* imports that we die with Christ in baptism, as well as we are buried with him. Nay, it is by burial we die. We are supposed to be *buried into death.* And the figure is well fitted for this purpose. To immerse a living man, affords an emblem of death as well as of burial. The baptized person dies under the water, and for a moment lies buried with Christ. Christ's own death was spoken of under the figure of a baptism.

Dr. Wardlaw, indeed, asserts that the phrase, *buried with him by baptism into his death,* merely directs the attention *to that into which they were baptized.* But the passage says nothing of the doctrine into which they were baptized, in any other way than as it is contained in the figure. As I observed before, it is by baptism, and not by faith, they are here said to be buried; and, therefore, the burial must be a figurative burial. The phrase in Col. ii. 12, is different, but equally express. It is buried with him *in* baptism. This burial, then, takes place, not in believing, but in baptism. We are buried with him when we are baptized, and *by* the act of baptizing. The two expressions, when taken together, make the thing more definite. One of them expresses that it is *in* baptism that we are buried; the other, that it is *by* baptism that we are buried.

Dr. Wardlaw speaks of this passage, as containing " a beautiful illustration of the spiritual connexion of believers with Christ." Now, how is this an illustration, if it is not by continuing a likeness to the thing illustrated? Is it not absurd to speak of illustrating by things in which there is no resemblance to the principal object? Dr. Wardlaw cannot consistently look on this as an illustration. He sets out with supposing, that the passage refers merely to the participation that believers have in Christ's death, burial, and resurrection, by faith, without any likeness to these things in baptism. Now, if this is the case, death, burial, and resurrection, are here not an *illustration* of connexion, but an *exemplification* of connexion. By calling these things an illustration, the author gives up his doctrine. Indeed, these things are so obviously an illustration—the passage so evidently considers death, burial, and resurrection, as figurative, that it is not easy even for the most determined enemy of immersion, to speak much about the passage, without using language that admits this.

"To be *dead with Christ*," says Dr. Wardlaw, " and *to be buried with Christ*, are the same thing." Certainly not. Death is different from burial, though burial includes death. Were they not different, they would not both have been mentioned here. It is a distinct part of the gospel testimony, that Christ was buried. His burial was as distinct from his death, as his resurrection was.

"The latter of the two phrases," says Dr. Wardlaw, " appears to be used in the fourth verse, chiefly for the sake of *completing the apostle's figure*." This assertion is most injurious to the language of the Holy Spirit, and totally unfounded in the lawful use of figures. I am bold to assert, that there cannot be an instance of what the author asserts, without a serious trespass of the laws of figurative language. It is true, indeed, that in allegory there may be some points in the figure which have nothing to correspond to them in the thing illustrated, because the unity of the resembling object cannot be broken. But to add burial to death, is to add one figure to another without any necessity. If, then, there is no distinct meaning in burial, to add it to death is vicious in taste, and childish in argument. The only reason why burial is mentioned, must be that it has a distinct meaning. To suppose that the apostle would bring it in merely for the purpose of stringing one figure to another, is not only an affront to the Holy Spirit, but would be an impeachment of the good sense of the apostle, if he had written without inspiration. Plato, indeed, goes over the whole human body, and brings out of it a chain of metaphors. He makes the head a citadel, the neck an isthmus, &c. This is sufficiently childish, but it is manly compared with what the apostle is supposed to do. Plato gives some meaning to each of his figures; but the apostle strings one figure to another, not for the sake of additional illustration, but out of the puerile conceit of completing his series of figures. It would have been an improvement, had he inserted the embalming between death and the burial, and added the funeral procession to the series.

But what shall we say of *the apostle's figure?* Is there, then, a figure in the apostle's language? Are this death, burial, and resurrection figurative? If the death, burial, and resurrection in baptism are figurative, they must have a likeness. Is there any figurative death without a likeness? There is a common proverb, that murder will never lie. The murderer will sometimes discover himself even by talking in his sleep. Dr. Wardlaw has murdered this passage most barbarously, and it is no wonder if he informs against himself. While he has assassinated the likeness in baptism to death, burial, and resurrection, he speaks of *illustration*, *figure*, and *resemblance*.

"As it was necessary," says Dr. Wardlaw, "in order to Christ's rising, that he should be *laid in the grave;* so in *the figure,* it is necessary that we should be viewed as *buried with him,* in order to our *rising with him* to newness of life." Certainly, it is necessary that we should be viewed in the figure of baptism as *buried with Christ.* But if the author means that we are buried with Christ by faith in him as a substitute merely by a mode of speaking, it is a most serious error. Does the author say that it is in a figurative way of speaking that the believer dies with Christ? If he does, he has a very inadequate view of the believer's oneness with Christ. The believer is one with Christ, not by a peculiar mode of speaking, or a particular way of viewing the subject, but by a real union. He is one with Christ as truly as he is one with Adam. He dies with Christ as truly as he fell with Adam. Christ's work is his, as truly as Adam's sin is his. By a Divine constitution all Adam's posterity are one in him, and so his first sin is really and truly theirs. By a similar Divine constitution all Christ's people are one with him, and his work is as really theirs, as if they had themselves performed it. When it is said that Christians have died with Christ by faith, there is no more figure than when it is said that they have died in Adam, or that they shall die themselves.

But this view of the subject overturns the apostle's reasoning altogether. Dr. Wardlaw understands the apostle as speaking of the connexion that believers have with Christ by faith; and that they are here said to be dead with him, buried with him, and to be risen with him, not by a likeness to these things in baptism, but merely by faith. Now, if he ascribes to them this death, burial, and resurrection, as a mode of viewing them, or as a figurative way of speaking, he wrests the apostle's argument out of his hands. If this death is the death by faith, and yet nothing but a figure, then our security against living in sin, according to the apostle, is nothing but a figure. A figurative death is no security against sin. An actor will die on the stage to-night, and act to-morrow. If it is only in a certain way of speaking that we rise with Christ by faith, then there is from that figurative resurrection no security of a holy life. The spirit of the apostle's reasoning on this verse would be, "How can they, who are said by a figure to be dead to sin, live any longer therein? Know ye not that as many of us as have believed on Christ, are figuratively viewed as having died with him?" This figure would be a weak security against living in sin. It must be a real death that will secure against sin. Now, how different is the apostle's argument, on our view! "How shall we, that are dead to sin, live any longer therein?" This must be real death, otherwise there is no argument. How then are we dead? By faith in Christ we are dead. But in baptism this truth is exhibited in figure. "Know ye not that so many of us as were baptized into Jesus Christ, were baptized into his death?" To be *baptized into Jesus Christ* imports the being baptized into the faith of his death as our substitute; but to be baptized into his death imports, that by baptism we are exhibited as dying along with him. The death in baptism is a figurative death, founded on the real death by faith. If *baptized into his death* does not import our death with Christ, this verse is not proof of what is asserted in the former;

and if baptism is no figurative burial, it is no proof of death, and therefore would be only an incumbrance in this place. The Christian has a real death, burial, and resurrection with Christ by faith. He has all these also in baptism by figure. Baptism is a proof of death, because it has no meaning otherwise. Hence it is used as an argument here; and hence the great importance of understanding the import of baptism. It gives, by a striking figure, a conception of the union of believers with Christ in his death, burial, and resurrection, that has escaped, we see, the most sagacious Christians who are ignorant of the ordinance.

"The simple meaning," says Dr. Wardlaw, "is this: since, in our being baptized into Jesus Christ, we were baptized into his death,—into the faith of his death as the death of a surety; we may be considered as, by faith, partaking with him in his death." I reply, this partaking is a real—not a figurative partaking. If baptism is not a figure of this, there was no occasion to allude to it at all. The author continues: " as *buried with him;* and that with the special end of our rising with him, in a spiritual resemblance of his resurrection, and 'walking in newness of life.'" But does not Dr. Wardlaw see that we are not here said to be *buried with him by faith*, but *buried with him by baptism into death?* This burial is not merely a burial by faith, but a burial by baptism. The language imports, also, that baptism has a reference both to Christ's resurrection, and our new life. "We are buried with him by baptism into death; that like as Christ was raised up from the dead by the glory of the Father, even so we also should walk in newness of life." This is stated as the end of baptism—not as the end of faith. As baptism does not effect these things, it must be viewed as a figure. Baptism makes us die, buries us, raises us, only in figure; therefore as we are said to die, to be buried, and to rise in baptism, baptism must contain a likeness to these things. It is not said that we are *buried by faith, that we may rise*, &c.; but that we are buried by baptism into death, that we may rise, &c. All these things are connected with baptism. But except as a likeness or figure, it has no connexion with them at all. Any other ordinance might have been equally mentioned. Rather, there was no need for the mention of any ordinance, on the supposition that there is no likeness.

But, that baptism contains a likeness to death, is in this passage expressly asserted: "for if we have been planted together, or united, with him *in the likeness* of his death." Here we see that this death is a symbolical death. It is a likeness to death. Now, the participation in Christ's death, that the believer has by faith, is not a likeness to death, but a real death. It is, by the Divine constitution of the union that subsists between Christ and his people, his own death. How, then, is there in baptism a likeness to death, if that ordinance is not by immersion? Our future resurrection is also figured in baptism: "we shall be also in the likeness of his resurrection." In Col. ii. 12, also, we are said to be risen with Christ: "Buried with him *in* baptism; wherein, or *in which*, also ye are risen with him." Dr. Wardlaw asks, How is it we are said to be "risen with him?" Undoubtedly through faith. Without this there is no rising to new life, nor will there be to glory. But this resurrection is notwithstanding said here to be *in* baptism. It must then be in figure. Dr. Wardlaw supposes that these things are ascribed to baptism; "because it was the first public declaration of the faith of the converts." But baptism is not necessarily a *public* declaration of faith; nor is it necessarily the first public declaration. There may be many instances in which a public declaration of faith is made, before there is any opportunity of being baptized. Besides, this is an apocryphal reason. The Scriptures do not assign it; and as a matter of fact, it is no more connected with salvation than the Lord's supper. It is not in baptism, nor by means of baptism, that we die with Christ really, or are made spiritually alive. This death and this life take place before baptism. Baptism, then, can have these things ascribed to it only in figure. "It is on the same principle," says Dr. Wardlaw, "that they are spoken of as in *baptism* 'washing away their sins.'" All these things are doubtless spoken on the same principle. But that principle is, that baptism is a figure. Baptism washes away sins, not because it is the first ordinance, but because it is an emblematical washing of the body with water. Does not Dr. Wardlaw hold, that baptism is an emblem of washing away sin? How then does he explain the phrase, *washing away sin in baptism,* on the principle of baptism being the first ordinance? We wash away sins in baptism, just as we eat the flesh of Jesus in the Lord's supper. "The cup of blessing which we bless, is it not the communion of the blood of Christ? The bread which we break, is it not the communion of the body of Christ?" How is the cup the communion of Christ's blood? How is the bread the communion of his body? In figure. And when the figure is observed in faith, the real communion is effected. Just so baptism washes away sin. Just so in baptism we die, we are buried, and we rise. But the truth of the emblem is effected, not by baptism in any sense, but by faith of the operation of God. It is absurd and ridiculous to suppose, that an ordinance can wash away sin in any other than a figurative sense. Was it not in this way that Jewish rites were said to make an atonement and to cleanse from sin? The first ordinance observed, has no more to do with these things than the last. The death, burial, and resurrection, which are ascribed to baptism, take place *in baptism,* and *by means of* baptism. The washing away of sins, ascribed to baptism, is effected by baptism. This washing, this death, this burial, and this resurrection, then, cannot be the washing, death, burial, and resurrection, which are effected by faith, and which take place before baptism. If the washing away of sins, the death, burial, and resurrection, ascribed to baptism, were effected previously, and by other means. the Scriptures are not true, that speak of them as effected in baptism, and by baptism. The reality has already taken place, but it is represented in figure as taking place in the ordinance, and by means of the ordinance.

"In Rom. vi." says Dr. Wardlaw, "the language of the whole passage is figurative." And what suppose it were figurative? Would this imply that there is no likeness? When death, burial, and resurrection, are used figuratively, they must of necessity have a likeness. Will Dr. Wardlaw show what kind of figure he supposes to exist here?

Will he show any figure that will justify the ascription of the washing away of sin, of death, burial, and resurrection to an ordinance, because it is the first ordinance observed? This figure he will look for in vain, either in the writings of rhetoricians, or the practice of any language. The principle on which I hold that these things are ascribed to baptism, I have verified by example, and justified on principle. But will Dr. Wardlaw recollect, that this death, burial, and resurrection, he has, in setting out, considered as effected by faith? He cannot, then, speak consistently of this language as figurative. But though he talks of the *simple meaning* of the passage, there is evidently a jumble in his own conceptions of this meaning. There never was a paragraph farther from simplicity, than that which he has employed to show the simple meaning of Rom. vi. 1.

The fact, however, is, that in the expression *wash away sin by baptism, death, burial, and resurrection in baptism*, there is no figure. It is a figurative action, not a figurative expression. A symbol is not a figure of speech. And I have shown, that as Dr. Wardlaw has in the commencement explained death, burial, and resurrection, as the death, burial, and resurrection which we have by faith in Christ, dying as our surety, to speak of these things now as figurative language, is to overturn the apostle's argument, and to deny real union with Christ in his work. We are not one with him by a Divine constitution, as we are one with Adam, but merely one with him in a figurative way of speaking. Dr. Wardlaw, then, ejects immersion out of Rom. vi. only by virtually overturning the Gospel, or denying real oneness with Christ.

"The same principle of interpretation," says Dr. Wardlaw, " according to which the expression '*buried with Christ*' is explained, as referring to the representation of interment by the immersion of the body under water, should lead us also to understand the phrase which immediately follows, '*planted together in the likeness of his death*,' as referring to an emblematic representation of *planting*, which, accordingly, some have stretched their fancy to make out." If the word *sumphutoi* is to be translated *planted together*, there must indeed be a likeness between baptism and planting ; and it requires no stretch of fancy to discover a likeness between the burying of the roots of plants and immersion in water. But even on this supposition, the word is metaphorical, and while it equally with a symbolical action requires likeness, it does not imply that baptism is an emblem of planting. Let Dr. Wardlaw consider the difference between a figurative word and a figurative action, and he will withdraw this objection. Baptism is here explained as a symbolical action, representing death, burial, and resurrection. The likeness to planting is illustrative, not symbolical. The phrase, *planting together*, proves the mode of baptism ; but it does not imply that there is in it anything emblematic of planting. Dr. Wardlaw continues, "or the phrase, *crucified with him*, to some similar exhibition of crucifixion." But does not Dr. Wardlaw perceive that we are not said to be crucified with Christ in baptism? We are indeed crucified with him— really and truly crucified with him—not in baptism, but by faith in his cross. We were nailed to the tree, when he was nailed, because by the Divine constitution we are one with him. But, according to Dr. Wardlaw's explanation of this passage, we might as well be said to be crucified in baptism, as buried in baptism. If there is no allusion to burial in baptism, more than to crucifixion, why are we not said to be crucified in baptism? If we are really crucified with him by faith in his cross, why might we not, on Dr. Wardlaw's principle, be said to be crucified in baptism, and by means of baptism, because it is the first ordinance in which we profess faith in the cross of Christ? But there is no such absurdity of expression in the Scriptures.

After all the labours of Mr. Ewing and Dr. Wardlaw on this passage, I could safely rest my cause on a candid reading of it by the most unlettered good sense. To a reflecting mind, nothing can more strongly prove the impossibility of diverting these words from giving their testimony in favour of immersion, than that one of these learned and ingenious writers could find no other way to effect his purpose, but by forcing burial to denote embalming or washing the dead ; and the other by denying that the passage implies any likeness between baptism and burial. These extravagances are so enormous, that every sober mind may see that the cause that requires them is desperate. I ask any man who fears God and trembles at his word, is Christ's burial merely the washing of his corpse, and not his being laid in the sepulchre? I ask, does the phrase "buried with baptism by death" import no likeness between baptism and burial?

Dr. Wardlaw observes, "according to our Baptist brethren, washing or cleansing, so far from being the exclusive, is not even the principal, but only a secondary meaning of the rite." In this he is mistaken. Death, burial, and resurrection, we do not consider as the primary meaning of baptism; and washing away sin, as a secondary meaning. It takes both together to make one meaning. The ordinance has one meaning only. It not only signifies washing away sin through faith in the blood of Christ, but denotes that such sins are washed away by our fellowship with him in his death. Washing away of sin is the thing which it always signifies : but this is not the whole of its meaning. It is then to no purpose that Dr. Wardlaw insists that sprinkling and pouring may be an emblem of cleansing. They are no emblems of death, burial, and resurrection, which are figured in baptism.

Another passage that favours our view of the mode and import of baptism, is 1 Cor. xv. 29. "Else what shall they do which are baptized for the dead, if the dead rise not at all? Why are they then baptized for the dead?" There must be an argument here, and this object of baptism must be a scriptural object, otherwise it could not be an argument. Indeed, though to us the passage may be difficult from difference of circumstances with respect to those immediately addressed, yet it is evident that the apostle considers the argument as very obvious and convincing. Now, to consider the expression to be a reference to the mode and import of baptism, as implying an emblem of the resurrection of believers, will afford a natural meaning to the words, and an important argument to the apostle. Baptism is an ordinance that represents our burial and resurrection with Christ. We are baptized, in the hope that our dead bodies shall rise from the grave. Now, if there is no resurrection, why are we baptized? On that supposition, there is no meaning in baptism. It is absurd for any to be baptized, baptism being a figure of a resurrection, if they do not believe in a resurrection. Heb. x. 22, is on both sides allowed to have a reference to baptism; and to me it appears evident, that the whole body was covered with water. "Let us draw near with a true heart, in full assurance of faith, having our hearts sprinkled from an evil conscience, and our bodies washed with pure water." Here the heart is said to be sprinkled in allusion to the application of the blood of the sacrifices; and the body, in allusion to the bathings under the law, is said to be washed in pure water, referring to the ordinance of baptism. Now, the pouring of a little water in the face is not a washing of the body. I admit, that sprinkling a little water on any part of the body might be an emblem of purification; but this would not be called a washing of the body. The passage which Mr. Ewing brings to justify his view of this verse, is not parallel. "For, in that she hath poured this ointment on my body, she did it for my burial," Matt. xxvi. 12. "This instance," says Mr. Ewing, "of calling what was poured on the head, a pouring on the body, illustrates what is said of baptism which is in itself a pouring on the face only, but which, being a figure of washing, is called a washing of the body." Our Lord's expression is quite literal, and has no emblem. The smallest quantity of water poured on any part of the body, is as truly poured on the body as if the whole body was covered. Water is literally poured on the body, if poured on any part of the body. But when the body is said to be washed, it implies that the whole body is washed. Washing a part of the body, is not washing the body. Let us have an example in which the pouring of a little water on a part of an object, is called the washing of the object. The bodies of the priests were washed on entering on their office. Shall we say that this may have been the pouring of a little water on their head? Though I do not agree with Dr. Campbell, that *louo* cannot be applied to a part, yet it is so generally appropriated to the bathing of the whole body, that in medical use it is employed without a regimen in that sense. If any part is not to be bathed, it must be expressly excepted, as *except the head.*

"Except a man be born of water and the Spirit," John iii. 5, is another expression which is admitted to refer to baptism; and has its explanation most intelligibly in emersion out of the water in that ordinance. To emerge out of the water, is like a birth; and to be *born of water*, as distinguished from being *born of the Spirit*, is to be born of the truth represented by the water. We are regenerated both by the word and Spirit. We are born into the kingdom of God by the agency of his Spirit, through the belief of the word that testifies the death, burial, and resurrection of Christ, and our death, burial, and resurrection with him. Christ, therefore, is said to have given himself for his church, that he might sanctify and cleanse it with the *washing of water by the word*, Ephes. v. 26. The washing of water is by the word, which is figuratively done in baptism. In like manner, we are said to be saved "by the washing of regeneration, and renewing of the Holy Ghost," Tit. iii. 5.

We are also said to be " washed and sanctified," 1 Cor. vi. 11, in reference to the cleansing from sin by faith in the blood of Christ, as well as to the renewing of our hearts by the Holy Spirit.

SECTION XVII.—STRICTURES ON MR. EWING'S MISCELLANEOUS RE-MARKS ON THE HYPOTHESIS OF IMMERSION.—I have, in a great measure, anticipated anything that I judge necessary on Mr. Ewing's Miscellaneous Remarks on the Hypothesis of Immersion. I cannot, however, dismiss the subject without more expressly entering my protest against the grounds of his reasoning in this part of his work. They appear to me both false and dangerous. Immersion he considers as indecent and indelicate, and in several cases he attempts to prove its impracticability. "The immersion of one person by another," says Mr. Ewing, "except in cases of necessity or mercy, seems to be contrary to decency, and to the respect which we owe to one another." Mr. Ewing commences very properly, by saying, "I feel it incumbent on me to enforce my conviction on others, by every consideration which the examination of the Scriptures on the subject has suggested to my mind." By all means, let us have every thing that the Scriptures suggest on this subject. Pray now, Mr. Ewing, was it the Scriptures that suggested this objection? This is an appeal to our pride against the law of Christ,—an appeal, however, that is likely to have more weight with some, than an appeal to the word of God. But is there more dignity and delicacy in pouring water into a person's turned up face, out of the hand, so that some of the water must be swallowed? Had Mr. Ewing, however, established this from the Scriptures, he would have heard no objection from me on this ground. I would not take the responsibility of this argument for all the wealth of the city of Glasgow. Let Mr. Ewing take care that he is not enlisting the corruption of the Christian's heart against the appointment of Jesus. Does not Mr. Ewing see that the respect we owe to one another has no concern in the question? If it suits the wisdom of Christ's appointments that one person should be immersed by another, even were it a real humiliation, it is to Christ we stoop. That God's institutions cannot foster any of the corruptions of our nature, is self-evident; but that they should consult our sentiments of dignity and delicacy, is a thing that no one acquainted with the Scriptures ought to assert. Has Mr. Ewing never read the Old Testament? Did he never hear of such a thing as circumcision? Has he forgotten the transaction in Abraham's house on the institution of that ordinance? Was there more dignity in that operation, with respect to the father of the faithful, and the males of his house, than there is in immersion in water. What shall we say of the transaction at the Hill of Foreskins? What shall we say of many parts of the law of Moses? What shall we say of many parts both of the Old Testament and the New? Try them by Mr. Ewing's test, and they must be expunged from the book of God. Infidelity here may have a plausible handle, though no just ground of objection. But in immersion, with respect both to males and females, there is none. Mr. Ewing's caricature of the immersion of females, is so much in the spirit of the means by which the Church of Rome keeps the higher ranks from reading the

Scriptures, that I have no language strong enough to express my feelings of abhorrence. "Shall you permit your wives and daughters," say the enemies of the Scriptures, "to read the indelicate statements of the Bible?" It is said that there is no more usual argument to dissuade the higher classes in France from reading the Scriptures than their indelicacy. They are told that the Bible, on this account, is the very worst of books that can be put into the hands of youth. And shall the man of God blow the trumpet of Satan in the camp of Israel? If immersion is an ordinance of Christ, it is a fearful thing to oppose it by such an engine. It is not the first time, however, that Jesus has been rebuked as a sinner. In the estimation of the Pharisees, he broke the sabbath; he was charged as a wine-bibber and a glutton; and it is not strange that the wisdom of this world should find indelicacy in his ordinances.

Mr. Ewing thinks himself very strong, with respect to the argument from the scarcity of water; and no doubt he will appear so to a numerous class of his readers. But the argument, instead of having weight, cannot be admitted to a hearing by any one who understands the nature of evidence. All the information that can be collected at this distance of time, cannot assure us that there were not other resources of water, of which we have no account. Mr. Ewing may say that the pool of Bethesda may have been sufficient only for one person to go down at a time. Well, if my cause obliged me to prove that it admitted two, I grant that I could not prove it. But I am not bound to proof. I may say that it may have admitted a hundred to go down at once, and the bare possibility is enough to remove the objection. Neither of us can prove the dimensions of it. If, then, there had been no water in Jerusalem but this pool, I am at liberty to suppose that it might have sufficed. The pool of Siloam may have been only sufficient to wash the eyes, but it may have been sufficient to float a ship. This is quite enough for me. If immersion is not impossible in some of the places where baptism was performed, no man who understands reasoning will object on this ground.

Were I engaged with Mr. Ewing, even in an historical controversy, with respect to the supply of water in Jerusalem in the days of the apostles, I could easily show that his conclusions are unwarranted. He depends on the accounts of modern travellers. I would admit their statements, and deny the consequence. Must the supply of water be the same now as it was then? Aqueducts and reservoirs may have then existed, of which there are no remains. Herod, at great expense, brought water to the city by aqueducts, from a considerable distance; and the pools, and fountains, and rivers, cannot now be estimated. The supply of water to the city of God, could not be inadequate to the wants of the inhabitants, and to the use of it in legal purifications, which required abundant resources. Shall we judge of the supply of water in the days of the apostles, by that of the present time, when Jerusalem is suffering under the curse? How much depended at that time upon rain? Is there reason to think that the supply is equal at present? Earthquakes alter the course of rivers, and often seal up fountains. In the year 1182, as Goldsmith relates, most of the cities of Syria, and the kingdom of Jerusalem, were destroyed by an earthquake. Mr. Gibbon makes a like objection to the Scripture account of the fertility of Judea The present barrenness of that country, he considers as proof of the falsehood of the accounts of its ancient fertility. This, which may appear to many very sage, is in reality very shallow. There are many possible ways in which the fertility of that country may differ at different times. The peasants of Switzerland draw walls of stone across their declivities, to keep up the mould which industry has brought to the nourishment of their vines. If these were for a few years neglected, the rains would sweep away all their labours, and there would be nothing in the place of luxuriance, but barrenness and naked rocks. Must the brook Kedron have been as scanty as it is now? Mr. Ewing tells us that, like other brooks in cities, it was contaminated. Did the filth run up the stream? and could they not have baptized where it entered the city, or upwards? The very attempt to prove, at this distance of time, that there could not be water in or near Jerusalem for immersion, is absurd. I would hold this, were the question merely an historical one. But if the Holy Spirit testifies that the disciples were baptized on believing the gospel, and if I have proved that th s word signifies to *immerse*, then, though there were real difficulties on the subject, I am entitled to suppose that there must have been in some place a supply of water.

John the Baptist had enough of water in the Jordan; but if there is enough of water, there are, it seems, other wants. "In the course of his ministry," says Mr. Ewing, "he drew his illustrations, like his Master, who came after him, from the objects surrounding him at the time. But he says nothing of the stream, of its depth, of its rapidity, of its strength, of its overflowings, of its billows, of its qualities of purification." Was ever anything so childish put upon paper? Can any mind suppose that there is argument in this? Did ever John the Baptist illustrate his subject by allusions to popping? Is the absence of any such allusions, to be received as evidence that there was not immersion in baptism?

"As a teacher," says Mr. Ewing, "you never find him in the river." Does this say that, as a baptizer, he might not have been in the river? Such arguments are not only unsound, but absurd. Whenever they have any weight, there must be an indistinctness of vision, as to the nature of evidence.

I will not go out of my way to look for water to immerse the disciples of Sychar in Samaria. If Mr. Ewing knows that they were baptized, from the usual practice, I know they were immersed, from the meaning of the word. Had I no other resource, I would make Jacob's well supply me. But as it is not said where they were baptized, I will make them conduct Christ and the apostles on their way, till they come to water. I care not where the water is to be found; if they were baptized, they were immersed.

Mr. Ewing, as well as Dr. Wardlaw, learns from Peter's phraseology, " can any man forbid water?" that the water was to be brought to the place. And if this were certain, it affects not the question. Must the observance of the ordinances of Christ never put us to trouble? But the expression imports no more, than "who can forbid baptism to the persons who have already received the Holy Spirit?" without any respect to mode.

The phraseology of Ananias, it seems, forbids immersion:—"Arise, and be baptized." Where is the proof here? Why, there is no going down to the water, nor coming up from it. Is there any man so frantic as to suppose, that this phraseology must apply to every baptism? Baptism in a bath, is as good as baptism in the Jordan.

But Paul was baptized after a three day's fast, before he had received either meat or strength. "Would this have been done," we are asked, "had his baptism been immersion?" It was done, yet his baptism was immersion. From this, let us learn that baptism is not a thing to be trifled with, but ought to be performed as soon as possible after the belief of the truth. It would give me great pleasure, if Mr. Ewing would make this use of the circumstance. He has certainly delayed his baptism much too long.

But the jailer—How shall we find water to immerse the jailer? "The argument," says Mr. Ewing, "that there was a bath in the jail at Philippi, because there is a very fine tank at Calcutta, and always is one to be found in an eastern jail, may be illustrated in this manner: There was a stove in the jail at Philippi, because there is a very fine one in the jail at St. Petersburgh, and always is one to be found in a northern jail." Does Mr. Ewing suppose that his opponents are bound to prove that there must have been a bath in the jail at Philippi? That there may have been one, is quite sufficient for our purpose. Even this is not necessary. Any vessel that will hold a sufficient quantity of water, will serve us equally well. Besides, for any thing in the narrative, the baptism might have taken place in any part of the town. It is madness to suppose that immersion was here impossible; and if it was not impossible, the objection is not valid. There might have been a thousand ways of obtaining water of which we are ignorant. To suppose that it is necessary to produce, from the history, an actual supply of water, in the case of every baptism, implies a radical error with respect to the first principles of evidence. The jailer and his household were baptized, therefore they were immersed. What sober mind will go in quest of the water, in a foreign country, at the distance of nearly two thousand years.

3

SUBJECTS OF BAPTISM

SECTION I.—HAVING ascertained the mode and the meaning of this ordinance, I shall now inquire who are the subjects of it. If our minds were uninfluenced by prejudice, this inquiry would not be tedious. We have the answer obviously in the words of the apostolical commission: "Go ye, therefore, and teach all nations, baptizing them in the name of the Father, and of the Son, and of the Holy Ghost; teaching them to observe all things whatsoever I have commanded you: and, lo, I am with you alway, even unto the end of the world. Amen." Matt. xxviii. 19. It is well known that the word corresponding to teach, in the first instance in which it occurs in this passage, signifies to *disciple*, or *make scholars*. To disciple all nations, is to bring them by faith into the school of Christ, in which they are to learn his will. The persons, then, whom this commission warrants to be baptized, are scholars of Christ, having believed in him for salvation. If this needed confirmation, it has it in the record of the commission by Mark: "Go ye into all the world, and preach the Gospel to every creature. He that believeth and is baptized, shall be saved; but he that believeth not, shall be damned." Here the persons whom Matthew calls disciples, Mark calls believers. According to this commission, then, none are warranted to be baptized but disciples or believers. But our opponents affect to treat this passage as not at all to the purpose; alleging, that though it commands believers to be baptized, it does not exclude the infants of believers. They consider this as common ground, and as teaching a doctrine which they do not deny, without opposing the peculiar doctrine which they hold. Accordingly, they run over this commission with the greatest apparent ease, and are amazed at the want of perspicacity in their opponents, who see in it anything unfavourable to the baptism of infants. Now, this evidence strikes me in so very different a light, that I am willing to hang the whole controversy on this passage. If I had not another passage in the word of God, I would engage to refute my opponents from the words of this commission alone. Dr. Wardlaw thinks he has shown as clear as a sunbeam, that the words of this commission have no bearing on the subject. I will risk the credit of my understanding, on my success in showing that, *according to this commission, believers only are to be baptized.* It is impossible that a command to baptize believers, can be extended to include any but believers. We need not say that this cannot be done by inference; I say it cannot be done by the most express command or explanation. No command, no explanation, can bring unbelievers into the commission that enjoins the baptism of believers. Even if I found another command, enjoining the baptism of the infants of believers, I should not move an inch from my position. I should still say, this is not included in the apostolical commission. This is another commission, and cannot interfere with the former. This would establish the baptism of infants, indeed; but it would not be according to this commission, nor included in it. It would be another baptism, far more different from the baptism of this commission, than the baptism of John was from that of the apostles. This command to baptize the infants of believers, would not be according to the command to baptize believers. There would then be two baptisms, on quite different grounds; the one on the ground of faith, the other on the ground of descent. Talk not, then, of the Abrahamic covenant, and of circumcision; if a baptism, or any other New Testament ordinance, must be found to correspond to these, it cannot be forced into the baptism commanded in this commission. I would gainsay an angel from heaven, who should say that this commission may extend to the baptism of any but believers. His assertion would imply a contradiction. It would imply that the same persons may be, at the same time, both believers and unbelievers. Here, then, I stand entrenched, and I defy the ingenuity of earth and hell to drive me from my position. THIS COMMISSION TO BAPTIZE BELIEVERS, DOES NOT INDEED IMPLY THAT IT IS IMPOSSIBLE THAT ANOTHER COMMISSION MIGHT HAVE BEEN GIVEN TO BAPTIZE INFANTS, BUT, BY NECESSITY, IT EXCLUDES THEM FOR EVER FROM BEING INCLUDED IN THIS COMMAND. IF INFANTS ARE BAPTIZED, IT IS FROM ANOTHER COMMISSION ; AND IT IS ANOTHER BAPTISM, FOUNDED ON ANOTHER PRINCIPLE.

But not only does this commission exclude infants from the baptism it enjoins: if there were even another commission enjoining the baptism of infants, when these infants, who have been baptized in infancy, according to this supposed second commission, believe the gospel, they must be baptized according to the commission, Matt. xxviii. 19, without any regard to their baptism in infancy. The commission commands all men to be baptized on believing the gospel. Had there been even a divinely appointed baptism for them in infancy, it cannot interfere with this baptism, nor excuse from obedience to the command that enjoins believers to be baptized. The command of Jesus to every believer to be baptized, stands engraven in indelible characters in this commission. Till the trumpet sounds for judgment, it cannot be effaced. I call on all believers, on their allegiance to the Son of God, to submit to this ordinance of his kingdom. Heaven and earth will pass away, before it will cease to be a duty for believers to be baptized. I maintain that it is impossible for any explanation, or any express command for another baptism, to excuse them from this. Is there any power on earth to abrogate this command? Who can alter it, or substitute another baptism for it? Till the end of the world, it will remain a duty for all believers to be baptized. Who is he that dares to substitute infant baptism for the baptism of believers? Whoever he is, he is the man who, by his tradition, makes void the law of God. Our Lord charged the traditions of the Pharisees, not only as the commandments of men in the things of God, but also as making void the commandments of God. He alleged one instance in which the command of God was made void by the traditions of the Pharisees. God commanded the children to support their parents if they needed it; but the Pharisees, by an invention of their own, eluded this command. Just so with infant baptism. It has usurped the place of believer baptism; and, as far as it is received, sets the ordinance of God aside altogether. So it happens, that this great law of the kingdom, that Jesus has connected so prominently with the truth itself; this ordinance, that, in so lively a manner, exhibits that truth in a figure to be observed immediately after its reception, is now generally set aside. Believer baptism is virtually abolished, and expressly explained as fit only for the first reception of Christianity in every country. Why, my brethren, do ye make void the law of God by your traditions?

But Dr. Wardlaw will say, "the reply to this is simple and satisfactory." "Suppose," says he, "the ordinance of *circumcision* had been to continue, and the command had run in these terms:—' Go ye, therefore, and disciple all nations, *circumcising* them in the name of the Father,' &c. Had such language been used, we should have known that children were to be the subjects of the prescribed rite, as well as their parents: the previously existing practice would have ascertained this." I deny it, Dr. Wardlaw. I will not be driven from my position by *circumcision* more than by *baptism*. Had such a commission been given to *circumcise*, it would have excluded infants utterly. Could a command to circumcise believers, include a command to circumcise any but believers? This is impossible. No matter what was the former practice with respect to circumcision. If the apostles are commanded to circumcise believers, they cannot, in virtue of that commission, circumcise any but believers. I will say, also, that if we met in another part of Scripture, a command to circumcise the infants of believers, it would not be included in the apostolical commission. A command to circumcise believers, can extend to none but believers. But Dr. Wardlaw will say, we know that the Jews did circumcise infants. We do indeed know this, but are we to do every thing that was enjoined on the Jews? This commission to circumcise believers, would exclude the circumcision of infants; because it extends to none but believers. The Jewish practice as to circumcision, could not show what must be the Christian practice as to this rite, had it been appointed as a Christian ordinance; and no practice could reduce infant circumcision to a commission enjoining believer circumcision. I stand then to my position as well if a Jewish ordinance is adopted, as if a new ordinance is introduced. A command to believers to observe any ordinance whatever, can never imply any but believers. This is as clear as the light of heaven. It is a first truth. The denial of it implies a contradiction. "Would they," (the apostles) says Dr. Wardlaw, "certainly have inferred from it, that, although the *same rite* was to continue, there was to be a change in the *subjects* of it?" There is no need of any *inference* on the subject. That believers, in such a supposed commission, are the only subjects of the rite enjoined on believers, would be self-evident to all who are capable of understanding the terms. What inconsistency would they see in the continuation of the same rite, while the subjects of it were changed? Had the paschal lamb been continued instead of the Lord's supper, would it imply that all who among the Jews ate the passover, should eat it among Christians?

Suppose the government gives orders to the colonel of a regiment, to fill up a certain company with men six feet high. The colonel sends out his recruiting officers with instructions accordingly. When the recruits are brought to the standard, they are found in general to measure only five feet eight inches. Have the recruiting officers fulfilled their commission? Did not the instructions that mentioned six feet high as the standard, forbid all under that measure to be enlisted? It is not possible to bring into the commission any who come short of that measure. What can justify those who have been guilty of such a neglect of orders? What can screen them from the displeasure of their colonel? They have wasted the king's money, they have suffered the time appointed to elapse, and what is worst of all, they have disobeyed orders. But a flippant recruiting sergeant, instructed by Dr. Wardlaw, stands forward in his defence. "Stop a little, colonel, I will prove to you that our conduct is entirely justifiable. Nay, except you had positively forbidden us to enlist any under six feet, we were warranted to conclude that we were not limited. It is true, that our commission mentions six feet as the standard, but did we not know that in the company for which we were enlisting, there have hitherto always been many men not more than five feet eight? Now, good colonel, were we not bound, in interpreting your instructions, to avail ourselves of our previous knowledge of the practice in the company? I can assure you also, colonel, that we have the sanction of the Independent churches for this way of reasoning, though they profess the strictest adherence to the Scriptures. Mr. Ewing and Dr. Wardlaw explain their Lord's commission to baptize, in the very way in which we have explained our commission to enlist. If they treat the commission of the Lord of heaven in that way, it surely cannot be blameable in us to treat your commission in a similar manner. We reasoned from the former practice, and thought from this, that we were not bound to what was specified in our orders." "You thought, Sir!" says the colonel, "you reasoned! Who authorised you to reason on the subject? Your business, Sir, was to obey. Your orders were so plain that they could not be mistaken. You had no right to reason, whether you would obey them or neglect them. Your conduct is unsoldierly, and would subvert all discipline. Drop your swords, take up your muskets, and return to the ranks." And does Dr. Wardlaw expect a "well done, good and faithful servant," for conduct that would degrade a recruiting sergeant? Cease, Dr. Wardlaw, to pervert the word of the Lord: cease to teach his children how to evade his injunctions: cease to justify as an institution of Christ, the inventions of men : cease to force a commission enjoining the baptism of believers, to sanction the baptism of infants : cease to loose the subjects of Jesus from the first law of his kingdom.

With reference to Mark xvi. 16, Mr. Ewing says, " From this text some infer, that a person must actually believe, else he cannot be baptized. With as much reason they might infer, that a person must actually believe, else he cannot be saved." Certainly; if there were no way of saving children but by the Gospel, this conclusion would be inevitable. The Gospel saves none but by faith. But the Gospel has nothing to do with infants, nor have Gospel ordinances any respect to them. The Gospel has to do with those whc hear it. It is good news; but to infants it is not news at all. They know nothing of it. The salvation of the Gospel is as much confined to believers, as the baptism of the Gospel is. None can ever be saved by the Gospel who do not believe it. Consequently, by the Gospel no infant can be saved. It is expressly, with respect to such as hear it, that the Gospel is here said to be salvation by faith, and condemnation by unbelief. " Go ye into all the world, and preach the Gospel to every creature. He that believeth and is bapti˙ed shall be saved; but he that believeth not shall be damned." Here the salvation and the condemnation respect those to whom the Gospel comes. Infants are saved by the death of Christ, but not by the Gospel—not by faith. Adults are saved by faith, not from the virtue of faith, but it is of faith that it might be by grace. Infants who enter heaven must be regenerated, but not by the Gospel. Infants must be sanctified for heaven, but not through the truth as revealed to man. We know nothing of the means by which God receives infants; nor have we any business with it. The salvation that the Gospel proclaims to the world, is a salvation through the belief of the truth, and none have this salvation without faith. The nations who have not heard the Gospel, cannot be saved by the Gospel, because the Gospel is salvation only through faith in it. They are not condemned by the Gospel; for it is condemnation only to those who do not believe it. To them it is neither a benefit nor an injury. They will be judged, as we are assured in the Scriptures, according to the law written on the heart. I admit, then, that the salvation of the apostolic commission, is as much confined to believers, as the baptism of that commission is confined to such. The man who would preach infant salvation out of the apostolic commission, or attempt to prove that the commission may be explained so as to include it, I should gainsay, on the same ground on which I resist the attempts to include in it infant baptism. None can be saved by the Gospel, but such as believe the Gospel; none can be baptized with the baptism of the Gospel, but such as believe the Gospel. There is no exception to either.

But that believers only can be baptized by this commission, is clear from that *into* which they are said to be baptized : " Baptizing them *into* the name of the Father, and of the Son, and of the Holy Ghost." It is into the faith and subjection of the Father, Son, and Holy Ghost, that men are to be baptized. Surely none can be baptized into the faith and subjection of Father, Son, and Holy Ghost, but adults. Infants cannot believe, nor express subjection. About the glorious doctrine imported in these words, we have no dispute. On this all important point, we have one mind. And I joyfully profess that I embrace as brethren in Christ all who are united with me in that doctrine, and the truths imported in it. While, therefore, I use the surgical knife with an unsparing hand, to remove the morbid parts of the reasoning of my brethren, I love them for their love to that truth; and I cut only to heal. My brethren love the thing imported by baptism, while I lament that they spend so much zeal in endeavouring to establish a baptism not instituted by Christ. In doing so, they injure thousands and thousands of their brethren, and cannot but injure themselves. It is impossible to fight against God on any point, without being wounded. I acknowledge I was long in the same transgression. Many infants have I sprinkled; but if I know my own heart, I would not now pour water into a child's face in the name of the Father, and of the Son, and of the Holy Ghost, for the globe on which I stand. Ah, my brethren! it is an awful thing to do in the Lord's name, that which the Lord has not appointed. Who has required this at your hands? You may explain, and reason, and suppose, but, till the trumpet sounds, you will never force this commission to include your baptism of infants. You may conjure up difficulties to perplex the weak; your ingenuity may invent subterfuges that may cover error; but you will never find an inch of solid ground on which to rest the sole of your foot. Your work will never be done. You are rolling the stone of Sisyphus, and the farther you push it up hill, with the greater force will it rebound on your own heads. The labours of Hercules are but an amusement compared with your task. Ingenuity may put a false system plausibly together; but no ingenuity can give it the solidity and life of the truth. It may satisfy as long as persons do not inquire deeply and earnestly into the question. But it will not satisfy when the mind begins to say, " Lord, what wouldst thou have me to do?"

That believers only are included in the baptism of this commission, is clear also from the command to teach the baptized : " Teaching them to observe all things whatsoever I have commanded you." Here the persons baptized are supposed to be capable of being taught the other ordinances enjoined by Christ. Children then cannot be included.

Never was a commission more definite. Never was a commission violated with less excuse of ambiguity. Yet the arrogance of human wisdom has totally reversed the ordinance here enjoined. It has ordered infants to be baptized, who, by the very terms of this commission, are excluded from this baptism : and it leaves unbaptized, believers whom only Jesus hath commanded to be baptized. Is not this the very spirit of Antichrist? Christians, how long will ye suffer yourselves to be deluded by the inventions of the mother of harlots? How long will you observe the inventions of men as the institutions of God? Will .ne antichristian leaven never be purged out of the churches of Christ? Why will ye deprive yourselves of the edification and comfort to be derived from the true ordinances of your Lord? Why will ye continue to seek evasions with respect to a law that is designed to enrich you? Why tarry ye, my brethren? arise and be baptized, and wash away

your sins, calling on the name of the Lord. As long as ye remain ignorant of this ordinance, much of the treasures of Divine knowledge are
locked up from you. The baptism of John was in two points essentially different from the
baptism of the apostolic commission; but in mode and subjects it was
perfectly coincident. John did not baptize into the name of the Father,
and of the Son, and of the Holy Ghost: he did not baptize into the faith
of Christ as come, but as about to be made manifest. As far, however,
as concerns our subject, the two baptisms correspond. Let us then
examine the evidence to be derived from the baptism of John. "John
did baptize in the wilderness, and preach the baptism of repentance for
the remission of sins. And there went out unto him all the land of
Judea, and they of Jerusalem, and were all baptized of him in the river
of Jordan, confessing their sins," Mark i. 4. Here we see John's baptism
was a baptism of repentance, in order to remission of sins. It could not,
then, include infants who cannot repent, and whose sins, when they die
in infancy, are not remitted on repentance, arising from the belief of the
truth, but through the blood of Christ, applied in a way of which we can
learn nothing from the Scriptures, and with which we have no concern.
Some, indeed, reply, that it is not impossible for God to give faith to infants. Dr. Dwight himself says, that John the Baptist had faith from
the womb. If John the Baptist was a man when he was a child, Dr.
Dwight in this is a child when he is a man. It is astonishing how silly
wise men will become, when they attempt to force the word of God. It
must be a Divine judgment, that when his servants use his word as an
instrument to lead his people astray, the Lord gives them up to speak
foolishly, so as to put them to shame. Infants have faith! Where does
their faith go, when they begin to speak? Can they have faith without
knowledge? And did any one ever hear of the knowledge of infants?
But this observation is founded on deep ignorance. It proceeds on the
supposition, that as faith is necessary to the salvation of adults, it is
necessary in infants also. The necessity of faith to salvation, they must
consider as a necessity of nature, and not a necessity of Divine appointment. They suppose that God himself cannot save infants, without giving them that faith that he requires of all who hear the Gospel. Now,
there is no such necessity. Faith is necessary to those who hear the Gospel, because God has absolutely required it. But it is not at all necessary
to infants, because he hath not required it in infants. The atonement
through the blood of Christ is the same to infants as to believers; but it
is not applied to them in the same way. John the Baptist is not said
to have had faith when an infant. He is said indeed to be sanctified
from the womb, but this was not a sanctification through belief of the
truth. Adults are sanctified by faith, but infants are not sanctified by
faith. If infants believe, we should hear them, as soon as they begin
to speak, talking of the things of God, without any teaching from the
parents, or the Scriptures. Was ever any such thing heard? Can there
be any surer evidence, on the very face of the question, that the Scriptures know nothing of infant baptism, than that the wisest of its defenders should utter absurdities so monstrous in order to prove it? But were

we even to grant that John the Baptist had this infant faith, does it follow that all the children of believers have it also? Is it not mentioned as a thing extraordinary, that John was sanctified from the womb? Let them baptize none in infancy, but such as they have reason to believe are sanctified from the womb. I will go farther. Had God made faith necessary to the salvation of infants, and had he appointed to give faith to dying infants, this would not imply that he gives faith to those who live. Were this the case, they would all be believers before they hear the Gospel. I am sure Christian parents cannot receive such doctrine. They know that their children are ignorant of God, till, by the hearing of the Gospel, he shines into their heart, to give them the light of the knowledge of the glory of God in the face of Jesus Christ. Can any absurdity exceed that of the opinion that infants are baptized on the supposition that they have faith? If it can be fairly made out that the circumstance of being born of Christian parents is evidence that infants have faith from the womb, I have no objection to baptize them. To defend infant baptism on this ground, is virtually to give it up. It acknowledges the necessity of faith in order to baptism; but outrages common sense, in order to find it in infants, when they are born. Christians, is the man worthy of a hearing, who tells you that infants have faith as soon as they come into this world; yea, and before they come into the world? Can such nonsense be worthy of refutation? Were it not that the names under which such absurdities are ushered into the world, have a weight with the public, these arguments would be unworthy even of being mentioned.

The baptism of John was not only a baptism on repentance for remission of sins, it was also a baptism in which sins were confessed. He baptized them in the river of Jordan, *confessing* their sins. Now infant faith will not do without infant confession. Can infants confess their sins? If not, they were not baptized by John. It was the perception of this difficulty that first appointed sponsors, who believe, and repent, and confess for the infant. Unhappily our Independent brethren have not this resource.

The points in which John's baptism differed from that of Christ, may be seen, Acts xix. 1–5: "And it came to pass, that, while Apollos was at Corinth, Paul having passed through the upper coasts, came to Ephesus; and finding certain disciples, he said unto them, Have ye received the Holy Ghost since ye believed? And they said unto him, We have not so much as heard whether there be any Holy Ghost. And he said unto them, Unto what then were ye baptized? And they said, Unto John's baptism. Then said Paul, John verily baptized with the baptism of repentance, saying unto the people, that they should believe on him which should come after him, that is, on Christ Jesus. When they heard this, they were baptized in the name of the Lord Jesus." Here we see that John did not baptize into the name of the Holy Ghost, for they did not know that this distinction in the Godhead exists. Besides, John baptized into the faith of the Messiah about to be manifested: Christ's baptism must confess that Jesus is the Christ. This is an essential difference. Accordingly, "when they heard this, they were baptized in the name of the Lord Jesus." John's baptism did not serve for Christ's baptism. Human wisdom will correct the Scriptures here, and because it cannot see why John's baptism will not serve for Christ's, the words have been tortured to make them say, that they were baptized into Christ by being baptized by John. No ground, however, can be found in the passage for this conceit. No force can extract it from the words. It is man's scripture—not God's.

John's baptism, then, did not serve for Christ's. If so, infant baptism, even if such a thing had been instituted by Christ, would not serve for the baptism in Christ's commission, which is believer baptism. Paul baptized the disciples of John the Baptist, because they had not been baptized into the faith of Father, Son, and Holy Ghost; and because they had been baptized only in the faith of the Messiah to come. Surely then, they who are baptized in infancy upon any pretence whatever, must be baptized when they come to the faith of the Gospel.

But if John's baptism implied repentance and confession of sin, how could Jesus submit to it? This apparent inconsistency struck John himself so forcibly, that he even presumed to forbid him. "But John forbade him, saying, I have need to be baptized of thee; and comest thou to me?" Jesus did not deny this; personally he had no sins to confess; yet still there was a propriety in his submitting to the baptism of repentance. "And Jesus answering, said unto him, Suffer it to be so now: for thus it becometh us to fufil all righteousness." It was necessary for Jesus to observe all the Divine institutions incumbent on his people. But if this was necessary, there must be a propriety in the thing itself. It must not be to Christ an unmeaning ceremony. If he submits to the baptism of repentance, there must be a point of view in which it suits him. And what is that point of view? Evidently that, though he is himself holy, harmless, and undefiled; yet, as one with us, he is defiled. Just as, by our oneness with him, we can say, "who shall lay anything to the charge of God's elect?" so by his being one with us, he can confess himself a sinner. The oneness of Christ and his people, then, is not a figurative way of speaking; it is a solid and consoling truth. By it we die in Christ's death, and are acquitted as innocent; by it Christ is made sin for us, who, in his own person, knew no sin. Christ's baptism, then, is no exception from what is implied in John's baptism. It has the same meaning, as well as the same figure to him as to us. In Christ's being buried in the waters of Jordan, we have a figure of the way in which he was acquitted from the debt he took on him. It represented his death, burial, and resurrection. If we are guilty by being one with Adam, Christ was in like manner guilty by becoming one with us. The object of John's baptism was exhibited in the immersion of Jesus.

It is odd, however, in what a different light the same evidence strikes different people. In the account of the baptism of John, I can see nothing but the immersing of persons professing repentance: Mr. Ewing sees with equal clearness, that the business was done by pouring water on the turned-up face; and that infants were *popped* as well as their parents. Really it is strange, if the words of the Spirit are like an oracle of Delphi, that can be interpreted in two opposite senses.

Upon what ground can Mr. Ewing conclude, from this account, that John baptized infants? Here is the proof, and surely it is demonstration itself! "Consider," says Mr. Ewing, "the very general and comprehensive terms in which the people are said to have come to be baptized, Matt. iii. 5, 6 : 'Then went out to him Jerusalem, and all Judea, and all the region round about Jordan, and were baptized of him in Jordan, confessing their sins.' This account," says he, " most naturally admits the supposition, that the inhabitants of those places, came usually at least, with their families." The account does not import even this. If the whole question depended on the presence of a child, the history could not prove it. But what if it could be proved that children accompanied their parents? Would this prove their baptism? "*The general and comprehensive terms.*" How are the terms general and comprehensive? Are they so general and comprehensive as to include infants? They are not so, Mr. Ewing. However numerous they were, they all confessed their sins. "The disciples," says Mr. Ewing, "there went out to meet John, as the disciples at Tyre did to take farewell of Paul." Who told you so, Mr. Ewing? This is apocryphal. Even this you cannot learn from the history. And if it were expressly stated, it would not serve you. How easily is Mr. Ewing satisfied with proof, when it is on a certain side of the question! The whole Greek language could not produce a phrase that his criticism would admit as conclusive evidence of *immersion*. But that infants were present with their parents at John's baptism, and baptized along with them, he admits without evidence, with the docility of a child. If his obstinacy is invincible on some points, he makes ample amends by his pliancy in others. No man was ever more easily satisfied with proof of his own opinions.

"The same latitude of language," says Mr. Ewing, "is always used respecting the administration of baptism by the disciples of Christ, John iii. 25, 26 : 'There arose a question between some of John's disciples and the Jews about purifying. And they came unto John, and said unto him, Rabbi, he that was with thee beyond Jordan, to whom thou barest witness, behold, the same baptizeth, and all come to him.' John iv. 1—3 : 'When therefore the Lord knew how the Pharisees had heard that Jesus made and baptized more disciples than John, (though Jesus himself baptized not, but his disciples,) he left Judea, and departed again into Gallilee.'" Now, reader, is there anything here about the subject of infant baptism? Is it not mere dreaming, to quote these passages in proof that Jesus baptized infants? Yet, in Mr. Ewing's estimation, this is proof. "The two foregoing passages," says he, " evidently imply that baptism was dispensed in the same extensive manner, by the disciples of Christ, as it was by John the Baptist." There is no doubt but John's baptism and Christ's were equally extensive. But is this proof that either of them extended to infants? The passages import, that a great multitude came for baptism both to John and to Christ; but that infants were brought for baptism, is not hinted. On the contrary, those baptized by John, are baptized on a confession of sin ; and it is said that Jesus made and baptized more disciples than John. The disciples of Jesus, then, baptized while he was with them, *disciples* only.

But not only does Mr. Ewing find infants baptized by John ; he also makes provision for them in the apostolical commission itself. Now, really, if he can do this, I shall not despair of proof for transubstantiation. Well, let us hear him. " We have to add," says Mr. Ewing, " that there is ample room for supposing family baptism to be included in the comprehensive terms of our Saviour's final commission, Matt. xxviii. 18." *Room*, ay, " ample room." I have measured it, and I maintain, that, if there is truth in axioms, there is not room for infants in this commission? How is the language in this commission comprehensive? Does Mr. Ewing find a place for the infants in the *all nations?* I cannot persuade myself that this is the refuge which he has provided for them. Does he deny that it is *disciples* that the commission enjoins to be baptized? Does he make infants *disciples?* Does he deny that the commission, as recorded by Mark, makes the disciples in Matthew xxviii. believers? Why did not Mr. Ewing show how this commission comprehends infants? Why did he pass over this with a mere assertion? If he could do this, he certainly would not have concealed the process by which he has come to the conclusion. That commission commands believers to be baptized; and except both sides of a contradiction may be true, it can never include unbelievers. " When we consider," says Mr. Ewing, " how many things there are which Jesus himself did, which are not written in the Gospel histories, (John xx. 30, and xxi. 25,) we cannot wonder at the brevity of the accounts of the subordinate *practice* of the disciples in dispensing baptism to believers and their houses." But does Mr. Ewing suppose that we are so unreasonable, as to look for long histories of all instances of infant baptism, on the supposition that it was practised? We look for no such thing. Were they included in the commission, we should not look for a single example in practice. And if there was an instance of the baptism of but one newly-born child, we should esteem it as valid as a million; valid, however, not to prove that infants are included in the commission,—for nothing could prove this,—but valid to prove another baptism, not interfering with the baptism of believers. Were a thousand baptisms found in the New Testament, they could not all serve for the baptism of the commission; nor relieve the believer from his obligation of being baptized on the belief of the truth. John's baptism, we have seen, could not serve for the baptism of the apostolical commission.

Though, therefore, no evidence could convince me that it is possible to reduce infant baptism to the commission, I am willing to examine the practice of the apostles, to find whether they used another baptism with respect to the infants of believers. I have no hope that we shall find any such thing; for the apostle tells us that there is but one baptism, as well as one faith. Let us try, then, whether the apostle has told the truth in this matter; or whether his practice gave the lie to his assertion.

How did the apostle Peter preach baptism on the day of Pentecost? Did he preach infant baptism? No, he preached a baptism connected with repentance for the remission of sins. Let us hear the account given of his doctrine on this subject by the Holy Spirit, Acts ii. 38; " Then Peter said unto them, Repent, and be baptized every one of you, in the name of Jesus Christ, for the remission of sins, and ye shall receive the gift of the Holy Ghost." Here baptism is connected with repentance and remission of sins. This baptism, then, cannot extend to infants. If infants have a baptism, it must be essentially different from this,— more different than John's baptism is from Christ's. Well, a number of them did repent, and were baptized. But were any infants baptized with them? Not a word of this. "Then they that gladly received his word were baptized." This does not express infants, nor can it include them. No explanation could make this account extend to infants. It may be said, that it is possible that infants were baptized at the same time. This is possible, just in the same way that it is possible that the apostles administered honey and milk to the baptized persons. It is not in evidence, either expressly, or by implication. Infants are excluded from the number who are said to be baptized; because they only are said to have been baptized, who received the word gladly.

The next account of baptism occurs in Acts viii. 12, "But when they believed Philip preaching the things concerning the kingdom of God, and the name of Jesus Christ, they were baptized, both men and women." Here, also, only they who believed are said to have been baptized. But it is remarkable, that the account specifies *women*. Had the account said nothing of women, yet it would have included them as believers; and the commission would have extended to them. But to make the thing palpably clear, women are not only included, but expressly included. Now, is it not remarkable that the Holy Spirit should be so precise as to women, yet not say a word of infants? This is unaccountable, if they were baptized. How many volumes of controversy would the addition of a word have prevented! How liberal was the Spirit of Inspiration as to the information about the baptism of women! But on the supposition that infants were baptized, how parsimonious with respect to the baptism of infants!

The baptism of Simon proceeded on the supposition of his faith; and though he was not renewed in the spirit of his mind, he was baptized on the same ground with all others. "Then Simon himself believed also : and when he was baptized," &c. The baptism of the eunuch was on the same principle. These examples illustrate the commission, as requiring baptism on the belief of the truth. True, indeed, it is possible that faith might be required in adults and not in infants. But the former is the only baptism included in the commission, and the only baptism that these examples illustrate.

The baptism of Paul, Acts xxii. 16, shows that baptism is a figure applicable only to those who are washed from their sins. " Be baptized, and wash away thy sins." Paul's sins were already washed away, by faith in the blood of Christ. Yet he is commanded here to wash them away in baptism. This shows that baptism is a figure of washing away sins, with respect to those who are already washed. To infants, it can be no such figure. Even if all the infants of all believers, were assuredly to be brought to the knowledge of the truth, yet this is not done in infancy. Infant baptism, then, and believer baptism, are not the same ordinance. To the former, it would be a sign that their sins would hereafter be washed away; to the latter, that their sins were already, by faith, washed away. But who will say that there is any evidence that all the children of all believers will ever come to the knowledge of the truth? But surely the households will settle the business. Here is a word comprehensive enough for including infants. This battery, then, we cannot take. Well, I once talked of the households myself, and sheltered myself here as long as I could fire a gun. But my own conscience obliged me to give up the battery at last. I maintain that it is impossible to defend the cause of infant baptism by this battery. It cannot point one gun on the enemy. Mr. Ewing and Dr. Wardlaw have made the best of it, yet their fire is quite harmless. The noise of their guns may startle the inexperienced soldier; but if he can command as much nerve as will enable him to examine the direction of their fire, he will soon get under it. I shall begin with Dr. Wardlaw.

"In the *first* place, then," says Dr. Wardlaw, "there is one point of fact undeniably clear, namely, that the apostles baptized *households* or *families*." Granted; but it is as clear that these were *believing households*. This fact signifies nothing. A household may include infants, and it may not include them. It cannot, then, give evidence on this point. In such a case, the extent of the baptism must be determined by the commission. Nay, if I were assured that there were infants in every one of the households, I should with equal confidence deny that they were baptized. According to the commission, they could not be baptized; and such phraseology always admits exceptions, with respect to those known to be excluded from the thing spoken of. When I say that such a man and his family dined with me, I am known not to include infants. In like manner, as the baptism of the commission cannot possibly extend to infants, even if they had been present in the families, they are not included among the baptized. I will go a step farther. I will suppose, for sake of argument, that the apostles did baptize infants; even then, I will deny that the infants were baptized according to the commission. It must have been a different baptism, and would not prevent the same infants from being baptized with believer baptism, as soon as they should believe. *If one instance of infant baptism is proved, I will baptize infants; but a million of such examples would not set aside believer baptism.*

"It should be noticed too," says Dr. Wardlaw, "that a man's house most properly means his children, his offspring, his descendants,—and is generally used to denote these even exclusively." This word as properly, both from its origin and use, includes all domestics as children. It properly signifies all the residents in a house. It is capable, indeed, of being limited to descendants, when the connexion or known circumstances require it. It is, therefore, very often used with respect to them exclusively. It is also often used to denote, not only descendants, but ancestors and collateral relations. But in all these instances, it does not mean residents at all. The passages to which Dr. Wardlaw refers, respect descendants without respect to abode, 1 Kings xiv. 10, &c. That it also with equal propriety includes all domestics, is clear from its use, 1 Kings iv. 7; v. 9, &c. It must then be the connexion or circumstances, that, in each occurrence of the word, will declare its extent. I

will allow Dr. Wardlaw to limit it, when, from the connexion or circumstances, he proves his limitation. He must likewise allow me to limit it
by the same principles. If it may, by the connexion of circumstances,
be limited to descendants, it may also be limited to adults, by the necessity arising from the commission.

Dr. Wardlaw, in reasoning on these households, seems to forget the
difference between answering an objection and founding an argument.
It may be so, is enough to establish anything as an answer to an objection; *it may not be so*, is enough to overturn it as an argument. When
I attempt to prove believer baptism, I must produce arguments to establish it; and my opponent will succeed, if he can show that these arguments do not establish my point. In obviating an objection, I succeed,
if I can show that there is any way of understanding it consistently with
my doctrine. Now, with respect to the households, we merely stand on
the defensive. It is our business to reply to the objection grounded on
this fact. As our opponents use the fact as an argument, they must
prove that their doctrine is in it. It is enough for us to prove, that this
fact is consistent with our doctrine. If they do not prove that infant
baptism is necessarily here, the passage is useless to them. If we prove
that infant baptism is not necessarily here, we have all we wish. Now
with respect to *house*, it is enough for our purpose, that the word may
include all domestics; but it is not enough for them to show that the
word may signify descendants exclusively, unless they show a necessary
limitation, from the connexion or circumstances.

But as concerns the point in debate, I care not that it was established
that *house* applies to descendants only. I will still limit it farther by
the commission to adults. Even one of the passages referred to by Dr.
Wardlaw himself, might have taught him this. "One that ruleth well
his own house," 1 Tim. iii. 4. The nature of the thing asserted, determines it to apply to adults only, or at least to children capable of government. Newly born infants are excluded. I require no more, in repelling the objection from the households. *As the ruling of a house cannot
apply to infants newly born, so the baptizing of a house cannot refer to
any in the house but such as come under the commission.* Common sense
every day makes the necessary limitations in such indefinite forms of
speech. It is only the perverse spirit of controversy, that finds any difficulty in them.

"*Secondly*," says Dr. Wardlaw, "To an unprejudiced reader of the
New Testament, it must, I think, be equally clear, that the baptism of
families is mentioned in a way that indicates its being no *extraordinary*
occurrence—but *a thing of course*." The baptism of households was
just as common a thing as the faith of households, and nothing more so.
That the baptism of a household was a matter of course on the faith of
the head of it, without the faith of the family, there is not the slightest
appearance. We are, indeed, informed of the baptism of Lydia's house,
without being informed of their faith. But that they had faith, the
commission leaves no doubt. The narrative tells us that the house of
Crispus believed, but it does not tell us that they were baptized, Acts
xviii. 8. We know, however, that they were baptized, because the

commission enjoins it. In like manner, when we are told that Lydia's house were baptized, we know that they believed, because the commission warrants the baptism of none but believers. Instead of stating that the baptism of Lydia's house was a thing of course on her faith, without theirs, the narrative states, as a piece of important information, that ought to be a lesson to every age, that baptism is so closely connected with the belief of the truth, that not only Lydia herself, but her whole family, were baptized, before she invited the apostle to partake of her hospitality. "And when she was baptized, and her household, she besought us, saying, If ye have judged me to be faithful to the Lord, come into my house, and abide there. And she constrained us. The work of the Lord was first attended to, and then attention to the apostle.

That Lydia had any children, either infants or adults, is not in evidence; and therefore, as her house may have exclusively consisted of servants, the fact can never serve the cause of infant baptism. Indeed, from the way in which she speaks of *her* house, and from her being a stranger on business in that place, there is reason to believe that her family consisted solely of servants. But I will not build anything on even the highest probabilities. I will lay no stone in my building, that time will corrode. I care not that she had no servants; her baptized house must be believers, because the apostle had no authority to baptize others. I care not that she had infants of a week old; they could not be included, and the form of the expression does not require that they should be included. When it is said that a certain nobleman "believed himself, and his whole house," John iv. 53, does it imply that they were no infants in his house? Does it not evidently refer to those in his house who were capable of believing, and to all such in his house? When it is said that Cornelius "feared God, with all his house," is it necessary to assert that there could have been no infants under his roof? Surely not. Why, then, is it supposed that the baptism of households should imply the baptism of infants, who by the commission are excluded?

"*Thirdly*," says Dr. Wardlaw, "Having thus the unquestionable fact of the *baptism of families*,—a fact according with the ancient practice of the circumcision of families, and supported by the use of a word that properly denotes a man's children or offspring; we are warranted to assume, that such was the usual practice."

Here Dr. Wardlaw shifts the ground of his argument, and very conveniently takes for granted the thing to be proved. What is the unquestionable fact in his past observations? *The baptism of families* This is unquestionable, because it is expressly said. But what is the thing that is unquestionable? Why, that the word household is so applied. Is it unquestionable that the household were baptized, not on account of their own faith, but on account of the faith of the head of the family? No; this is not unquestionable; this is the point in debate. But this is what Dr. Wardlaw's third observation takes as unquestionable. If it is not unquestionable in this sense, it is nothing to his purpose. It does not accord with the ancient practice of the circumcision of families. If the household believed and were baptized, it does not accord with the circumcision of a family without any regard to faith. Dr. Wardlaw must take for granted his own sense of the phrase; and when this is granted to him, he will very easily prove his point. If it is granted as a thing unquestionable, that unbelieving families were baptized, as unbelieving families might be circumcised, the debate is at an end. But Dr. Wardlaw must prove his meaning of the phrase, before he takes it for granted.

We are indeed warranted to assume, that it was the usual practice to baptize every family that believed. But from the baptism of a thousand families, we are not warranted to conclude the baptism of every family when the head of it believed. The baptism of one family will prove that all families in the same circumstances ought to be baptized. This is the turning point of the argument. If we read that a man and his whole family were hanged for murder, this will prove that every family that joins with the head of it in committing murder, ought to be hanged. But it will not prove that every family ought to be hanged with the father, when he is guilty of murder. If Lydia's family were baptized on account of her faith, having none of their own, it would prove what Dr. Wardlaw wants; but if this is not in evidence, he cannot take it for granted. Dr. Wardlaw must prove that these households were baptized, not on account of their own faith, but on account of that of the head of the family. This is what he can never do. All the apparent strength of his reasoning depends on the assumption of false principles. No man is more convincing than Dr. Wardlaw, if it is lawful to take for granted the thing to be proved.

Dr. Wardlaw, *in the fourth place*, examines " the principles on which they endeavour to set aside the inference from the examples in question." He thinks that they have not proved that Lydia had no children. And does Dr. Wardlaw think that this proof lies upon us? He is a man of war from his youth; and has he yet to learn the laws of the combat? The proof of the fact that Lydia had children, lies on those who need the assistance of the infants. I maintain that it is not in evidence that she was ever married; and an argument cannot be founded on what is not in evidence. That she may not have had a child is consistent with all that is said here. This is sufficient for my purpose. Before an argument can be deduced from this fact, it must be proved not only that she had children, but infants. Nay, more, I care not that she had infants; the form of the expression does not require that they were baptized, and the commission makes it certain that they were not baptized.

Dr. Wardlaw has a very long, and certainly a very satisfactory discussion, showing that the term *brethren*, in verse 40, may not refer to Lydia's household, but all the believers of the place. Now, if our argument required us to prove, that the *brethren* here must be only Lydia's household, we never could prove it. But our argument requires no such thing. This term can be a proof on neither side, for it is consistent with both.

" Equally futile," says Dr. Wardlaw, " are the proofs adduced, that there were no infant children in the households of the jailer, and of

Stephanas." Now, if there are any on my side of the question who think that it is necessary to prove this, I refer them to Dr. Wardlaw for a most triumphant refutation of their sentiment. But did not Dr. Wardlaw perceive that he was here cutting his own carotid artery? Did he not perceive that the very same arguments which prove that the language with respect to the faith of the households of the jailer and of Stephanas, is consistent with the supposition that there might have been infants in them, equally prove that there might have been infants in them without being baptized? When it is said with respect to the jailer, that Paul " spake the word of the Lord to all that were in his house," I admit that there might have been infants. And when it is said that a family were baptized, infants might have been in the house, without being included in the baptism. The commission as effectually excludes them from baptism, as their infancy excludes them from the number of those to whom the Gospel is preached.

Dr. Wardlaw evidently does not understand the argument that we draw from the above source. We do not attempt to prove that such phraseology is inconsistent with the supposition, that infants were in the families. But we allege these facts, to show that if there were *baptized families,* there were also *believing families;* and that if, in a *believing house,* there may be unbelieving infants, so in a *baptized house,* there may be unbaptized infants. By the very same arguments that our opponents show that there might have been unbelieving infants in *believing houses,* we will show that there might have been unbaptized infants in *baptized houses.* But the facts alluded to are especially important, because they apply to the very houses that are said to be baptized. This not only shows that it was possible that there might be believing houses, but it shows that there were such houses. Two of the three baptized households are expressly shown to be believing households. If this is not said of the house of Lydia, it may have been the same; and the commission requires that it should be so. And if we are informed of the baptism of Lydia's house, and not of their faith, we are told of the faith of the house of Crispus, and not of their baptism. When we are informed of the one, the other is necessarily understood. Why do our opponents speak of their households at all? If the jailer had a baptized house, had he not a believing house? If Stephanas had a baptized house, had he not a believing house? And why may not Lydia have had a believing house. Our cause requires no more than that the baptized houses may have been believing houses. We found here no argument; we merely reply to an objection. But that two of the three baptized houses were believing houses, is actually in evidence. There is here no cover for infant baptism.

"I add," says Dr. Wardlaw, "as a *sixth* observation, the extreme improbability, that a change, which must have been felt so important by those whose minds had been all along habituated to the connexion of their children with themselves in the covenant of promise, should have taken place without the slightest recorded symptom of opposition or demurring." This is a mode of reasoning utterly unwarrantable, and deserves no attention. We learn what God has enjoined from what is written. Even if the fact here stated could not at all be accounted for, it could not be admitted as evidence. A thousand things might account for it, of which we are ignorant. Is every thing recorded that took place in the apostolic labours? Their adult children in unbelief were admitted to all Jewish ordinances; is there any recorded complaint of their exclusion from Christian ordinances? Why should they not complain, that, as all their offspring were admitted to the passover, and all the privileges of the Jewish church, they should be kept from the Lord's table? But, in fact, their zeal was for the law, and nothing would satisfy them in the room of it. Their prejudices were not at all concerned about the extent of Christian ordinances. What offended them, was the giving up of old customs. Of the extent of baptism, whatever it was, they could not be ignorant. Why then should they murmur against the known will of God? Upon the principle of this observation, there were a thousand things of which they might have complained, but of which no complaint is recorded. This takes for granted, also, that there was a spiritual connexion between the Jews and their offspring, which is the thing to be proved,—a thing which is not only not admitted to be true, but which I will prove to be false. This observation proceeds from first to last, on false principles. It takes for granted, that every disagreeable change must have been a cause of murmuring; and if there was murmuring, it must have been recorded. There might have been a disagreeable change, the principle of which might be so well understood as to prevent murmuring; and there might have been great murmuring without any record.

" Another remarkable circumstance," says Dr. Wardlaw, " akin to the preceding, is, that when the Judaizing teachers insisted on the Gentile converts submitting to circumcision, although there can be no doubt that this was done, in every case, *in connexion with their children*, yet, when the doctrine and practice of these perverters of the Gospel came to be discussed in the assembly of the apostles, and elders, and brethren at Jerusalem, no notice whatever is taken of the inconsistency with the spirituality of the new dispensation, of administering *any* sign to *children*, on the admission of their parents into the Christian commonwealth." This is egregious trifling. Are all things recorded that were said on that occasion? Was there any need in that assembly to discuss every error connected with the circumcision of the Gentiles? By cutting off the circumcision of the Gentiles, was not the circumcision of their infants and every error connected with it, cut off also? But such observations, so far from deserving an answer, deserve no mention. Must the apostles give a whole body of divinity, when they denounce a particular error? Dr. Wardlaw, we are willing to listen to anything you can allege from the Scripture in support of your opinion; but such arguments merit no consideration. This observation takes it for granted, that the apostles could not condemn one error, without expressly denouncing every other error connected with it; and that we have, in the records of the Acts, every thing that was said in the celebrated meeting at Jerusalem.

" Let it be further considered," says Dr. Wardlaw, " that we have no recorded instance of the baptism of any person, grown to manhood, that had been born of Jewish converts, or of Gentile proselytes to the faith of Christ." This would try the patience of Job. Is there any need of such an example, in order to show that the children of such persons should be baptized when they believe? What difference is there between such and others? Is not the law of the commission sufficient to reach them? Is it not sufficiently clear? "He ,that believeth and is baptized." "Nor have we," continues Dr. Wardlaw, "in any of the apostolic epistles to the churches, the remotest allusion, in the form of direction, or of warning, to the reception of such children by baptism into the Christian church, upon their professing the faith in which they had been brought up." A very good reason for this. The same law applies to all. There is not the smallest difference between the ground of receiving the child of a heathen, and the child of the most devoted saint. When they believe, they are received equally to every thing.

"This supposition," says Dr. Wardlaw, "let it be further noticed, is in coincidence with the fact of children being addressed in the apostolic epistles to the churches of Christ. Thus, in Eph. vi. 1, ' Children, obey your parents in the Lord, for this is right.' Col. iii. 20, ' Children, obey your parents in all things; for this is well pleasing unto the Lord.' " Now, this argument is deduced from Scripture; and it merits an answer. That answer, however, is easily found. The children here addressed, were believing members of the churches. That they may have been so, is sufficient for my purpose. This will refute an objection. But that they must have been such, is beyond question, from the address itself. Their obedience to their parents, is to be "*in the Lord*," which applies to believers only. The reasons of their obedience, also, show that they were such children as were capable of faith. " *This is right.*"—" *This is well pleasing unto the Lord.*" These are motives quite suitable to believers. As soon as children can evidence that they act from these principles, they ought to be baptized, and to walk in all the ordinances of the Lord.

But Dr. Wardlaw thinks that the children here addressed cannot merely be such adult children as were members of the churches; because it is immediately added, "And ye fathers, provoke not your children to wrath; but bring them up in the nurture and admonition of the Lord."—" Fathers, provoke not your children to anger, lest they be discouraged." Now, as the duty of fathers extends to all their children, Dr. Wardlaw thinks that the children addressed, must be all the children capable of receiving instruction. But if he were not eager in the pursuit of something to defend his system, his powers of discrimination would discern, that in these injunctions, neither the children nor the fathers of the one injunction, correspond to the children or the fathers of the other. In fact, it might happen that not one of either might correspond. When the apostle addresses the children, he addresses all the members of the church who had fathers; but not one of these fathers might be in the church. So far from being necessary to suppose, that all the children of the one address are the same as the children of the other address, it is not necessary to suppose that one of them was the same. When the children are commanded to obey their parents, their obedience is not to be confined to such fathers as were believers and members of the church; but to fathers, whatever they might be. And when fathers are commanded not to provoke their children, &c., the injunction extends to all their children. The fathers addressed may not be the fathers of the children addressed; and the children addressed may not be the children of the fathers addressed. Surely Dr. Wardlaw must be in the habit of teaching according to this distinction. I should not be so much surprised to find this indistinctness of conception in those who make no distinction between the church and the world. In the church in which I labour, there are very many children whose parents do not belong to us; and there are some parents whose children belong to other denominations. Yet these apostolical injunctions are constantly inculcated. Children are to obey their parents in the Lord, even if these parents are infidels; and parents are to train up their children in the nurture of the Lord, though they are not in the church.

"Do our Baptist brethren," says Dr. Wardlaw, "wait till their children are members of churches, before they venture to put their finger on the passages we have quoted, and say, 'This is addressed to you?'" No man who speaks correctly, can say that Ephes. vi. 1, Col. iii. 20, are expressly directed to any but believers. But we can teach the most disobedient children their duty from these passages. Though we cannot tell unbelieving children that these exhortations were originally addressed to such as they are, but to believing children; yet the duty inculcated is equally incumbent on all. The moral duties inculcated on believers, are equally the duty of unbelievers. The duty of obedience to parents is not a new duty, that results from connexion with a church, or with receiving the gospel. What, then, in this respect, is inculcated on believing children, equally shows the duty of unbelieving children. Dr. Wardlaw will not say, that unbelieving fathers are directly addressed in the above injunctions; yet could he not apply the injunctions, so as to make them bear on unbelieving fathers? Could he not urge on unbelieving fathers, their guilt in not training up their children in the nurture of the Lord? Children, from the first dawn of reason, may be taught their duty from such passages, without falsely telling them that they were originally addressed to children as young as themselves. Now, Dr. Wardlaw, of your eleven observations, this is the only one that has even a show of argument; yet I am sure your good sense will admit that it is answered.

"X. The circumstances of the early history of the church, after the apostolic age, are unaccountable on Anti-pædo-baptist principles." So, Dr. Wardlaw, you are returning to your old mode of reasoning from difficulties. Well, then, I will admit, for sake of argument, that the thing is unaccountable. It may be true, notwithstanding. Many things that would cast light upon this point, may be buried in the ruins of antiquity. I am not obliged to account for it. I will not neglect an ordinance of Christ, I will not adopt an ordinance not founded by Christ, from any difficulty arising from church history. My Bible, like that of Mr. Ewing ends with the book of Revelation.

But there is nothing more obvious to a candid mind, than the origin of the early introduction of infant baptism. As soon as baptism was looked on as essential to salvation, infant baptism would naturally follow. Dr. Wardlaw, indeed, says, that we may as well suppose that the *opinion arose from the practice*, as that *the practice arose from the opinion*. It would be easy to show that this is not the case. But that the opinion may have given rise to the practice, is enough for my purpose. I am answering an objection, and anything that will account for the difficulty, is sufficient. *It may have been so*, is quite enough for me. Even thus much I am not bound to give. Infant communion was practised as well as infant baptism. No matter what was the origin of either of them; if one of them is allowed to be an error, the early practice of the other cannot be alleged as proof of its truth. Even were it granted that infant communion was grafted on infant baptism, still, as it was universally received so early without having been from the apostles, infant baptism may have been grafted on some similar stock. It is impossible to argue consistently for infant baptism from the argument of antiquity, and reject the same argument for infant communion. If infant communion was a thing not instituted by the apostles, yet universally adopted so early, why may not any other practice have been adopted universally without apostolic institution? The practice of the earliest antiquity, with respect to the ordinances of Christ, is a matter of much interest; and I am convinced that the subject has never been set in that light, which the remains of antiquity would afford to candour and industry. If God spares me life and leisure, I may yet endeavour to exhibit its testimony. But an ordinance of Christ I will never ground on anything but the word of God. Many things true, may be wholly unaccountable.

"XI. I have only one other particular," says Dr. Wardlaw, "to add to this series. It is the remarkable fact of the entire absence, so far as my recollection serves me, of anything resembling the baptism of *households* or *families*, in the accounts of the propagation of the gospel by our Baptist brethren." Now, at first sight, this has an imposing appearance, but, on reflection, it vanishes into air. There are not now many examples of the abundant success that the Gospel had in the apostles' days. We do not often find that men now believe by households, more than that they are baptized by households. I suppose that the Baptist missionaries have a *baptized household*, as often as they have a *believing household*. They will baptize Krishnoo and his family, if Krishnoo and his family believe. I have never seen three thousand baptized on one day, yet I have no doubt that three thousand believed on the day of Pentecost. However, Baptist writers have produced a number of instances of baptized households. But as there is no argument in the observation, I need not refer to them.

In fact, I have never examined a series of arguments more flimsy than these. The whole chain is no better than a web of gossamer across the high road. It cannot stop the passage of a child. Josephus, on one occasion, took a town by presenting a fleet before it, in which each ship had only four mariners. If any man surrenders to Dr. Wardlaw's fleet, it must be from want of knowing what is in the ships. The man who can satisfy himself with such arguments as these, need never want proof of anything which he wishes to be true.

Let us now take a look at Mr. Ewing's generalship, with respect to the households. "Family baptism," says Mr. Ewing, " as mentioned in the New Testament, is the more remarkable, that no other ordinance, and no privilege of any kind, is mentioned in the New Testament, as given to families." The reason is obvious. Baptism belongs to individuals, and when a household believed, it was baptized on the same footing as an individual. The Lord's supper belongs to Christians, not as individuals, but as a church. It might as well be asked, why is baptism given to an individual, seeing the other ordinances are observed socially? Mr. Ewing gives the answer to himself, in the next sentence. " Mention," says he, " is made of churches in the house of some ; but it is not said that these churches consisted of a believer and his house." To this the reply is obvious. If a believer and his family were not a church, why is it strange that they had not the ordinances that belong to a church? " Neither are a believer and his house," says Mr. Ewing, " ever said to have received the Lord's supper." I reply, If they were only a part of a church, why should they have the Lord's supper? If they were a church, they had the Lord's supper, whether it is recorded or not. There is no necessity for any such record.

" I shall now be asked," says Mr. Ewing, " if all or any of the families of believers, where the family baptism is said to have been practised, can be proved to have contained infants?" Yes, Mr. Ewing, we will ask this question, and notwithstanding all you have said, we will continue to insist on this question. " I answer," says Mr. Ewing, " that ' a house' or family is a term which includes, in its meaning, infants as properly as adult children ; and that, in not one of these families mentioned in connexion with baptism, is any exception made, for the purpose of excluding infants." This is granted fully. But it is more difficult to conceive how such arguments can impose on a sound understanding, than it is to answer them. *House* or *family* includes infants as well as adults—if infants are in them. But from the term itself, this cannot be learned. This is the point, Mr. Ewing. A house may have infants, or it may not have infants ; therefore from the term we can learn nothing on this subject. The eunuch, no doubt, had a house ; and if his house had been said to be baptized, Mr. Ewing would not contend, that his infants were of necessity baptized. We should know, without any intimation, that the term house did not include his children. Just so from the commission, we know that infants are not included among those who were baptized in the households. The commission is as sure a commentary on the households of Lydia, Stephanas, and the jailer, as the state of the eunuch would have been in a like case. But Mr. Ewing says, infants are not excepted in these households. Nor are they excepted in the supposed case of the eunuch. There is no need for the history to except them. They are excepted by that commission that must guide all practice. It is a matter of the highest astonishment to me, that Mr. Ewing and Dr. Wardlaw can see the necessity of an exception in so many other cases to such indefinite phrases, and yet not have the candour to admit the possibility of a like exception here. If the commission does not include infants, are they not of necessity excluded with respect to the households? Can anything be more obvious to common sense, than that as a house or family may or may not have infants, the baptism of a house is no proof that infants were baptized?— Can anything be more obvious, than that as we every day use such phraseology with the supposed exceptions, there may be such exceptions as to the households? Even if infants were proved to have been in those houses, it would signify nothing. The phraseology admits the exception of them, and the commission demands it. The pertinacity with which our opponents continue to rest on the households, is a discredit to their good sense, as well as their candour. There is no axiom in mathematics more clear, than that the households are nothing to the purpose of infant baptism. IF THE TERM HOUSEHOLD DOES NOT NECESSARILY IMPLY INFANTS, THEN THERE IS NO EVIDENCE FROM THE TERM THAT THERE WERE INFANTS IN THOSE HOUSEHOLDS. Again, AS SUCH PHRASEOLOGY IS, IN DAILY CONVERSATION, USED WITH EXCEPTIONS; SO, THOUGH INFANTS HAD BEEN IN THOSE HOUSEHOLDS, THE KNOWN LIMITATIONS OF THE COMMISSION WOULD EXCEPT THEM. This is as obvious as that two and two make four. It is useless to reason with any who are so perverse as to deny what is self-evident; their disease cannot be cured by argument. When Mr. Ewing says, that in the narrative of the households there is no " exception made for the purpose of excluding infants," it is virtually admitted that such phraseology admits exceptions. If so, may not the exception in the commission be as valid as an exception in the history? Nay, the exception of the commission makes an exception in the history perfectly unnecessary. The commission enjoins the baptism of believers, and from that baptism all others are therefore for ever excluded. When a household were baptized according to this commission, they must have been believers. The commission cannot be extended farther. Nay, if a commission had afterwards been given to baptize infants, it could never be reduced to this commission ; it could not have been explained as included in it, nor a part of it. It would be a perfectly distinct commission, containing a quite different ordinance. Till infants are believers, they can never be baptized according to a commission that enjoins the baptism of believers. If there is a commission to enlist recruits six feet high, when we afterwards read that a family were enlisted without specifying their height, we know that none of them were under the standard. Were it not for the strength of prejudice, this form of expression could not for a moment embarrass the weakest of the children of God.

"If a man and his family are degraded," says Mr. Ewing, " does not the degradation include infants? If a man and his family are ennobled, does not the nobility include infants?" It does so, not from the necessity of the phraseology, but from what is known of the laws. Were it said that a man and his family were hanged for murder, his infants would be excluded. Were it said that after a rebellion a man and his family received the thanks of his Majesty for their loyalty, it would not be supposed that the infants had carried arms. "If a man and his family," says Mr. Ewing, " are baptized, does not the language convey a similar meaning, namely, that the baptism includes infants ?" No, Mr. Ewing, because it is known from the commission that infants are not included: whereas in the other cases, it is known that infants are included. In neither case can we learn the extent of the application of the phrase from the phrase itself. It is indefinite, and may include all, or may admit exceptions.

" In calculating," says Mr. Ewing, " as some do, the probability of the case, many confine their attention to the four families mentioned in Acts x., Acts xvi. and Cor. i." Calculating probability ! Is a law of God to depend on a calculation of probabilities ? I would as soon calculate nativities by the stars. " But these," he continues, " are only a specimen of the hundreds and thousands of families, which, in the propagation of the Gospel, were treated in the same way." Who told this to Mr. Ewing ? Has he got it in a dream, or in a vision ? If Mr. Ewing has not facts enough from which he may reason, he can make them. There may have been many other households of the same kind; but that there were so, is not in evidence, and I will not admit it. But I reject it not for the sake of this question ; because, if there were a million of such families, for every one that is mentioned, they were all believing families. The commission leaves no doubt of this. Of the three families mentioned, two of them are expressly represented as believing families.— Why might not the other be so ? I do not profess to have the gift of second sight. I do not know how many hundred families resembled these in their baptism. But I can judge of the evidence before me ; and what number of families soever were baptized, the same number believed.

But it seems there is one baptized household at least, in which it is even certain that there were no believers but the head of the family. " When Lydia was baptized with her house," says Mr. Ewing, " we are made certain that they were none of them believers excepting herself." Whence, reader, can come this certainty ? You will say, I suppose, that Mr. Ewing has received some secret revelation on this point. No, no, I assure you, Mr. Ewing professes to get this evidence out of the narrative itself. The evidence is this : " For she urged Christian character, as the argument for prevailing with Paul and Silas to accept her hospitality. Unquestionably she put her argument as strongly as she could ; yet as it was *her* heart only which the Lord opened, ver. 14, so she could not include so much as one in the family, along with herself as a believer ; but was obliged to use the singular number, saying, " If ye have judged *me* to be faithful to the Lord, come into *my* house and abide.' " Now, this is so shadowy an argument, that it is as difficult to get at it, as it was for Fingal to strike the ghosts. It is as thin as vapour. Had she possessed a thousand servants all believers, would she have spoken in a different manner ? Had there been a thousand the house was *hers*, the hospitality was *hers*, and the ground of the apostles' receiving it must be *her* faithfulness. The household had nothing to do with this invitation ; their faithfulness had no concern in it. At what a loss must the cause of infant baptism be, when such a man as Mr. Ewing is obliged to make such a defence! Must Lydia have been schooled by Sir Roger de Coverley's old butler, that she must say, *our house, our faithfulness*, &c.? The man who can take this for evidence, will never want evidence for anything to his taste. I never met any writer more intrepid than Mr. Ewing, in cutting down opposing evidence; nor more easily pleased with evidence on his own side.

Alexander himself would not more rashly draw his sword to cut a Gordian knot; and in other things Popish credulity itself cannot be more easily satisfied with the proof of the obedience of the church. What Mr. Ewing here considers certain evidence, I maintain is not even the shadow of evidence. If the Scriptures did not furnish me with better arguments for my sentiments, I would let them sink to the bottom of the ocean. Mr. Ewing is right in not surrendering a battery, while it is capable of defence; but why will he keep his flag flying, while it is evident, from his fire, that the ammunition is expended? Mr. Ewing is not at all startled at the consequence of this opinion, namely, that the unbelieving adults of Lydia were baptized on her faith. His boldness is not to be frightened. It requires a more than ordinary audacity to say, in the face of the commission of Jesus Christ, that unbelieving adults should be baptized, if they happen to be in the house of a believer. Jesus Christ has commanded believers to be baptized. Mr. Ewing commands all the unbelievers in every believer's house to be baptized. Christians, whether will ye obey your Lord and Saviour, or Mr. Ewing? How long, Mr. Ewing, how long will you make void the commandment of God by your inventions? Hath not Jesus said, " He that breaketh the least of these my commandments, and teacheth men so, shall be called the least in the kingdom of heaven?" The language of Lydia is consistent with the supposition that there was not an unbeliever in her house. So far is it from implying that her family were all unbelievers.

" The house of Stephanas," says Mr. Ewing, " addicted themselves to the ministry of the saints," 1 Cor. xvi. 15. " Were this a proof that they had among them no infants, we might find a proof that the house of the Rechabites had among them no infants, because in Jer. xxxv. 2—11, they addicted themselves to perform the commandment of their father." Now, this is true: and this is the very argument by which we prove, that, even if the households had contained infants, there is no necessity that they should be supposed to have been baptized. We do not argue, that, because the baptized households were believing households, there could not be any infants in the houses. But we argue, that if there were baptized households, these households were believing households; and that in the household of the jailer and of Stephanas we have direct evidence. We could have known this by the commission, had the narrative been silent. But when the narrative itself shows that they had *believing households*, what difficulty is in the expression *baptized households?* Is not the one commensurate with the other? The importance of the fact of the believing households is, not to show that there could be no infants in those houses, but to show that it is an historical fact that there were in those houses believers to be called a baptized household; and to show that if there were infants in those houses, they may not be included among the baptized, as they certainly are not included among the believing. The fact is very important, for in replying to it, our opponents are obliged to refute themselves. If there may have been infants where a house is said to believe, without supposing that infants are believers, so where a house is said to be baptized, there may have been in it infants who were not baptized. If any man cannot understand the weight of this argument, it is not argument can convince him.

Mr. Ewing asks his opponents, " if they admit the general fact of family baptism, why they do not practise accordingly ?" And do they not practise according to the view in which they admit this fact ? Is there any inconsistency between their practice and their admission ? Are they inconsistent with themselves, because they practise according to their own views, and not according to the views of Mr. Ewing ? Mr. Ewing and Dr. Wardlaw strangely take it for granted that the households were baptized, not on their own faith, but on that of the head of the family, which is not hinted in the narrative, and is contrary to the commission. " To say they baptize whole families when whole families believe," says he, " appears to me to be treating the historical Scriptures as nugatory." But why, Mr. Ewing, does this treat the historical Scriptures as nugatory ? " Any view of this subject," says Mr. Ewing, " would lead us to baptize whole families, or whole nations, if they all believed." Doubtless. And may we not say the same thing of individual baptism ? Is the history of the baptism of the eunuch and that of Paul nugatory, because, if neither of them had been recorded, we should have known from the commission that believers ought to be baptized, and that faith is necessary to baptism ? There may be much use in recording these facts, though they do not bear Mr. Ewing's inference. It is not warrantable to say, that a portion of Scripture must have a certain meaning, because we can see no use in it, if it has not that meaning. " It would not have made the slightest difference in the practice," continues Mr. Ewing, " had no mention been made of family baptism at all." Not the slightest difference. Nor would it have made the slightest difference with respect to the baptizing of individuals, had no example of baptism been recorded. Yet none of the examples is nugatory; the perverseness of Christians requires them all. The family baptisms recorded can warrant no family baptisms but *such* as are recorded ; and two of these are expressly stated as believers, and the remaining third must be according to the commission. " Unless, therefore," says Mr. Ewing, " we admit some peculiar connexion between the extent of a family, and the extent of the administration of baptism, I apprehend that family baptism is a Scripture fact which we do not yet understand." Does not Mr. Ewing perceive that the same thing might be said with as good reason with respect to the house of the Rechabites, and all the examples quoted by Dr. Wardlaw of similar phraseology? On Mr. Ewing's principles, might I not say, unless every infant of the house of the Rechabites was brought into the house of the Lord, and a command given to him to drink wine, the statement of Jer. xxxv. 2—11 is absurd ? Suppose the government issues a commission to raise a number of regiments, and to enlist all men fit for service. In the course of the execution of this commission, we read that they enlisted A and his family, B and his family, C and his family. Should we not know, without a word on the subject, that the enlisted families were men fit for service? There might be infants in the houses, but they were no part of the enlisted families. We should not require to be informed that two of these families were active and brave, in order to convince us that they were not infants or women, but men. It is only the perverseness of Christians in the things of God that requires such illustrations. What shall we say of the person who would observe, that, unless it is admitted, that whenever the head of a family is enlisted, every member of his family, man, woman, and child, are enlisted also; he can see no meaning in the statement of the enlistment of the three families? The fact that three families are enlisted with the heads of the families, does not imply that all families are enlisted with the heads, nor that men, women, and children are enlisted. It is strange that our acute opponents cannot see so obvious a truth. It is only in the things of God that men are children.

Mr. Ewing here takes it for granted, that it is an admitted fact, that all families were baptized with the head, and on the faith of the head, without any faith of their own; nay, except they contradicted and blasphemed. This is not in evidence. The three examples of baptized households state nothing of the baptism of the household on the faith of the head, and the commission forbids the thought. There might be many such families, but how many is not known; nor can the number at all influence the question. How many soever they might be, they must all have been believing households. To justify Mr. Ewing's observation, the commission must have been, *baptize believers and their households.*

"I wished," says Mr. Ewing, "to induce my friends, who have no experience on the subject, to compare their feelings with the feelings of those who have such experience." Feelings have nothing to do with this question, more than with a demonstration in Euclid. This consulting of our feelings is the ground of a great part of our opposition to the word of God. Peter consulted his feelings, and when God said, " Rise, Peter, kill and eat," he arrogantly replied, " Not so, Lord, for I have never eaten anything common or unclean." Shame, Peter, is there anything unclean that God commands to be eaten? What made certain meats unclean to Israel but God's command?

" You keep aloof," says Mr. Ewing, " from this practice, from your apprehension of difficulty with the case of infants." Not so, Mr. Ewing: had the command been to baptize the households of believers on the faith of their heads, we should find no difficulty with infants. We would baptize them, if the command included them, as soon as we would baptize the apostles. " Now, I frankly confess," says Mr. Ewing, " that were anything, after getting a Divine warrant, to deter me from the practice, it would be rather the case of adults." Strange language, indeed! This sounds harshly in my ears. Deter from a practice for which there is a Divine warrant! He must have a scrupulous conscience indeed, who will speak of being deterred from executing a Divine warrant! I would baptize Satan himself, without the smallest scruple, had I a Divine warrant. Give us a Divine warrant, and we have no objection, from our feelings, to baptize infants. But it appears that Mr. Ewing finds some difficulty in the case of baptizing unbelieving adults on the faith of the head of a family. I am glad of it. He may yet be led to see that it is an awful thing to allege a warrant from Jesus to baptize unbelievers, when the apostolical commission includes believers only. " But the truth is," says Mr. Ewing, " infants and adults are precisely on a footing, in regard to the regenerating work of the Holy Spirit, of which baptism is a figure." But are adult unbelievers to have the figure of regeneration which they have not yet experienced? This contradicts every thing exhibited in the figure of baptism, which always supposes that the person baptized is already regenerated. Mr. Ewing says, that " in the original propagation of the Gospel, when the head of a family believes, ' salvation is come to his house,' Luke xix. 9 ; and consequently the whole house may be, nay, ought to be, baptized along with him, (with no exception because some of them may be young,) but except they have grown so old, and so rebellious against both their Father in heaven and their parents on earth, as to refuse the ordinance, and to contradict and blaspheme the truth which it accompanies." This is a most astonishing avowal. Mr. Ewing saw where his doctrine would lead, and he has boldly avowed the consequences. Every unbeliever in the house may be baptized, on the faith of the head, except he refuses. I do not envy the conscience that can receive this without qualms ; I think it will be swallowed with difficulty by many of the Independents. But when Mr. Ewing has avowed this monstrous doctrine, where will he find a warrant? Not in Luke xix. 9. This cannot imply that the moment the head of a family believes, all the members of the family also believe, or are actually made partakers of salvation. If not, it is no warrant to baptize them. But if it does imply that they all actually believe with the heart, then it is believer baptism. Nor does this passage imply that all the members of a believer's house will at last believe, —though even this would be no warrant for their baptism, which implies faith at the time of baptism. Is it a fact that all the slaves, and servants, and children of a believer, will certainly be saved? Let us hear the passage itself: " And Jesus entered and passed through Jericho. And, behold, there was a man named Zaccheus, which was the chief among the publicans, and he was rich. And he sought to see Jesus, who he was ; and could not for the press, because he was little of stature. And he ran before, and climbed up into a sycamore tree to see him, for he was to pass that way. And when Jesus came to the place, he looked up, and saw him, and said unto him, Zaccheus, make haste and come down, for to-day I must abide at thy house. And he made haste and came down, and received him joyfully. And when they saw it, they all murmured, saying, That he was gone to be guest with a man that is a sinner. And Zaccheus stood, and said unto the Lord, Behold, Lord, the half of my goods I give to the poor : and if I have taken anything from any man by false accusation, I restore him four-fold And Jesus said unto him, This day is salvation come to this house, forasmuch as he also is a son of Abraham. For the son of man is come to seek and to save that which was lost." Now, the salvation that came to his house, appears to me to be evidently his own salvation. Zaccheus had been a man notoriously a sinner. The people all murmured, even when Jesus proposed to be his guest. The Lord touched the heart of Zaccheus, and enabled him to give in his confession—the clearest evidence of his conversion. The Lord, therefore, recognises him publicly before the people who murmured, and declared that Zaccheus was not only worthy of being his host, but that he who was among the chief of sinners, was now a member of his kingdom : salvation was now come to that house which the crowd looked upon as so unworthy to receive the Messiah. It was now the house of a saved sinner. Jesus next gave the reason for saying that salvation was come to that house : " He also is a son of Abraham." That he was a natural descendant of Abraham, there was no question ; but now he is a son of Abraham's faith. The Lord Jesus closes with a reason that confirms this view : " For the Son of man is come to seek and to save that which was lost." As if he had said, " Think it not strange that Zaccheus is saved, and that I have called him a son of Abraham. He was a notorious sinner, indeed, but I have come to save such."

Many suppose that the phrase, " Salvation is come to this house," means that others in the house had believed ; or that it was an intimation that they would believe. As far as concerns the question of baptism, I have not the smallest objection to either of these views. My objection is, that they are not the import of the passage. I am quite willing to admit, I am joyful in believing, that when the Gospel comes to a house, it generally spreads. But this is no foundation for baptizing an unbelieving family, and does not seem to be contained in this passage. If salvation comes to a house, let the house be baptized as far as the salvation is known to reach.

But by what authority does Mr. Ewing make the exception, with respect to those who refuse the ordinance, and blaspheme ? Children have no right to refuse ; and slaves may be forced to submit. Those must all be baptized with the household. Ah, Mr. Ewing! is such a household as you represent to be entitled to baptism, at all like the house of the jailer, and the house of Stephanas? How unlike to your commission to baptize, is the commission of Christ! Christ says, " believe and be baptized :" Mr. Ewing says, " baptize all the unbelievers of a believer's house, except they refuse." Is it not a fearful thing to have on record before heaven and earth, a document at such variance with the commission of Christ? I know Christ will forgive the ignorance of his people ; but to teach his children to err from his commandments, is not the way to gain ten cities in the day of judgment.

Was there ever anything so absurd as to stretch the commission to baptize, by the use of an indefinite word in the history of the execution of the commission? Must not the commission limit this indefinite word? Does not Mr. Ewing, does not Dr. Wardlaw, show examples that justify such limitation of indefinite or general language? Why do they contend, that there may be infants in a believing house, though they do not believe; when they will not allow that there may have been infants in a baptized house, without being baptized? None can be baptized, according to the commission, but believers: the phraseology about the households is perfectly consistent with this, according to daily use in all nations: why then conjure up a difficulty when not a shadow of difficulty exists? An infidel, who read the Scriptures, just to learn what was actually the practice on the subject in the apostles' days, would not find a moment's delay from these households. He would at once see that the word household may extend to every individual of the family, or admit of certain exceptions, according to known limitations. The limitation of the households he would find in the commission. He would never dream that the apostles would baptize any but such as are commanded to be baptized.

Let it be recollected, that we stand on the defensive in this matter; and that it is perfectly sufficient for our purpose, if the term household will admit the limitation for which we contend. To serve our opponents, it must be proved that infants were in the families. Even this will not serve them. They might have been in the households, yet not have been baptized. But was it even proved that infants were baptized, it would be a baptism different from that of the commission, and could not stand in its room. Even in such a case, I would call on all who believe to be baptized with the baptism of the commission.

"The case of the little children," says Mr. Ewing, "brought to Jesus, as narrated, Matt. xix. 13—15, entirely agrees with this view," namely, that the disciples of our Lord baptized infants. There must truly be a great scarcity of proof when it is sought in such a passage as this. No view of which this transaction is capable, has any bearing on the subject. We might as well seek a warrant for infant baptism in Magna Charta, or the Bill of Rights. Infant salvation does not imply infant baptism. Baptism is an exhibition of the faith of the Gospel; and of course cannot belong to any but those who appear to believe the Gospel. But infants are saved without the Gospel. These infants are not brought to Jesus for baptism, nor for any ordinance of the Gospel, but to be blessed by him. Can they not be blessed by Jesus without baptism? This passage, then, can have no concern with the subject. "True," says Mr. Ewing, "baptism is not mentioned in the passage, but our Saviour's condescension, which the passage does mention, and which he so beautifully displays both to children and to parents, is by no means EXCLUSIVE of the baptism of the former, but apparently in addition to it." *Our Saviour's condescension, here mentioned, not exclusive of the baptism of infants!* What an argument! Does our Saviour's condescension to children, suppose that they must have been baptized? It is a shame for human understanding to urge such arguments as these. The children taken up into the arms of Christ could speak nothing more childish. Divine truths we must receive like children, but if we receive infant baptism on the authority of such arguments, we must receive it as simpletons. Christ commands us to be like little children, but he never commands us to be idiots. "In malice be ye children, but in understanding be men." The Gospel itself must have evidence ; and we are required to believe nothing without evidence. Is our Saviour's condescension in blessing children any evidence that they ought to be baptized? This passage does not, indeed, EXCLUDE children from baptism ; and many a thousand passages might be quoted, that do not EXCLUDE infants from baptism. But is every passage that does not forbid infant baptism, a proof that infants ought to be baptized? It seems, however, that this passage does more than not exclude infants from baptism, though, in such a lack of evidence, that itself is a great deal. The blessing is apparently in ADDITION to the baptism. Now, how this is apparent, is what I cannot see ; and though I should wear out my eyes in the search, I am afraid I shall never discover it here. The man who can see infant baptism here, may descry the inhabitants of the moon with his naked eye.

Mr. Ewing quotes a passage in his note, that is subtle without penetration. *Of such is the kingdom of heaven,* " that is to say," says Mr. Hallet, " the kingdom of God *belongs to,* or *comprehends* such infants as these." No, Mr. Hallet, to say this, is to say what the passage does not say. It is not said, that the kingdom of God *belongs to* such, or *comprehends* such; but that the kingdom of God *is* of such, that is, such persons constitute this kingdom. If we are not pleased with this paraphrase, Mr. Hallet gives us another, which must be abundantly edifying ; " or," says he, " if any one would have the words so stiffly rendered, *Such's is the kingdom of God,* like, Theirs is the kingdom of heaven, Matt. v. 3." But the latter passage ought to be translated, " of them is the kingdom of heaven." The kingdom of heaven consists of the poor in spirit, and of the poor in spirit only. There is not another in the kingdom. The meaning is not that the poor in spirit will obtain heaven as their inheritance ; but that there is none in the kingdom of heaven but the poor in spirit. Neither of these passages imports that the kingdom of heaven is the property of such persons, but that such persons constitute the whole kingdom. There is not one in heaven but the poor in spirit ; nor is there one in heaven who is not such as the children. However, were it even supposed that the expression was, " the kingdom of heaven belongs to such," the import of the term *such* is not altered. Even *such's is the kingdom,* makes no difference. Every way in which the words can be understood, imports that the heirs of the kingdom are *such as children*— not that they are children. Observe the difference between the expression, Matt. v. 3, from the expression in this place. In the former it is " of them," in the latter it is " of such." The kingdom of heaven is of the poor in spirit, and of them only : but it is not of children only, but of those who *are such* as children. They resemble children in their character. Had *of them* been here used instead of *of such,* it would have imported that none but children are members of Christ's kingdom ; it would have said, that all children are members of Christ's kingdom, and that none but children were included in that kingdom.

Mr. Hallet says, that if we understand the term *such* to refer not to the infants, but to persons resembling them, it will be impossible to make out the force of our Saviour's argument. But let what will be the consequence, this is actually what our Saviour has said; and nothing else can the words import. "The kingdom of heaven *is of such*," cannot possibly mean that the kingdom of heaven *is of them*. The term *such* does not signify identity—cannot signify identity, *but likeness*. Besides, to understand it so, would imply, that none but children could be saved. For if the kingdom of God is *of children*, by consequence none but children are of the kingdom. I am not bound, then, to satisfy Mr. Hallet with a view of the passage that will make out the force of our Saviour's argument. I will show him what concerns this argument, and I will insist that so far the meaning must be what I contend for. After ascertaining what can be definitely and certainly ascertained, let us then endeavour to see the force of the argument. But to see this is not necessary to know the other with the utmost assurance.

"According to these men," says Mr. Hallet, "our Saviour would have said the same thing, if men had brought him *lambs* or *doves*." But if Mr. Hallet would exercise a little discrimination, he would see a difference. The things in which the disciples of Christ are here supposed to resemble children, are not to be found in *lambs* or *doves*. *Lambs* and *doves* are, to a certain extent, fit emblems of the people of God; but for the purpose of our Lord on this occasion, they were totally unsuitable. Children are of the human race, and therefore it is important to know whether they are capable of being blessed by Christ. Now, that they are capable of being brought to Christ, and of being blessed by him, is known from Christ's conduct towards them; though it is not expressed, nor necessarily implied in the term *such*. That term implies only that there is a likeness between his disciples and children. But this likeness is a likeness in rational and moral properties. It is a likeness of temper, disposition, or character of mind. This could not be found in *lambs* or *doves*. In mere harmlessness doves may afford a likeness. Therefore it is said, "Be ye harmless as doves." But the moral qualities here referred to, are not to be found in *lambs* or *doves ;* these are teachableness, humility, &c. That this is the reference, is clear from the fact as recorded by Mark x. 15. "And they brought young children to him, that he should touch them : and his disciples rebuked those that brought them. But when Jesus saw it, he was displeased, and said unto them, Suffer little children to come unto me, and forbid them not: for of such is the kingdom of God. Verily I say unto you, Whosoever shall not receive the kingdom of God as a little child, he shall not enter therein. Is it not evident, that the point of likeness between children and the disciples of Christ, is in their teachableness? Here also it is evident, that the term *such* refers to likeness—not identity. They who receive the kingdom of God must receive it *as* children, but they are not all children. So, then, Mr. Hallet, your *lambs* and your *doves* will not suit this passage. I will receive as a little child anything that the Lord teaches; but your explanation of the term *such*, even a child cannot receive. I must renounce my understanding altogether, before I can admit *such* to import identity, instead of likeness.

The same thing is evident from Matt. xviii. 1.—"At the same time came the disciples unto Jesus, saying, Who is the greatest in the kingdom of heaven? And Jesus called a little child unto him, and set him in the midst of them, and said, Verily I say unto you, Except ye be converted, and become as little children, ye shall not enter into the kingdom of heaven. Whosoever therefore shall humble himself as this little child, the same is the greatest in the kingdom of heaven. And whoso shall receive one such little child in my name, receiveth me. But whoso shall offend one of these little ones which believe in me, it were better for him that a millstone were hanged about his neck, and that he were drowned in the depth of the sea." Here we see that the disciples must be like children in humility. In this sense, the disciples are children. But in humility, lambs and doves could be no figures. That they were capable of being blessed, depends on their being human persons.

"The meaning seems to be," says Mr. Hallet, "of *such* kind of infants *as these is the kingdom of God*, that is, of such infants as have been partakers of the seal of the covenant, of such infants as have been baptized, or, at least, circumcised like these." No, Mr. Hallet, this is a forgery; this is a vile and wicked forgery. Thousands have been hanged for forgery, who have not made such alterations on writings as this makes on the book of God. There is nothing either expressed or implied with respect to the baptism or the circumcision of the infants brought to Jesus; nor does what our Lord says apply to those children more than any other children. It is not, Suffer *these little baptized or circumcised children to come*, but suffer *little children*, any little children, to come to me. Does not the parallel passage, Mark x. 15, apply to children in general? It is the temper of children to which our Lord gives his approbation, and the things referred to are found in all children. Does not the illustration show this? Does not Matt. xviii. 1, confirm this? Why does Mr. Hallet look for a reason of approbation, not only not mentioned by Jesus himself, but different from that which Jesus has mentioned? All children possess what Jesus here approves. But while these dispositions of children are such as to afford a proper figure to represent the teachableness, humility, &c. of the disciples of Jesus, there is no reason to suppose that they are such as are entirely conformable to the law of God. There may be something in them that will need the atonement of the blood of Christ, while they afford a likeness to the character of the disciples. Indeed, the dispositions of children are not considered here in reference to God, but in reference to men. Children believe their parents implicitly; and they are comparatively unambitious. But they are no more ready to believe God than adults are. The approbation, therefore, of infants contained in our Lord's words, does not imply that they are teachable and humble in the things of God. Our Lord may approve of children here, just as he loved the rich young man in unbelief. The young man had lived in such a manner, that in his own view he had kept the law of God from his youth up. To live so, was commendable, though he was in error. Accordingly, "Jesus beholding him, loved him."

But in whatever way the thing may be explained, the ground of our Lord's approbation of children, is their teachableness, humility, &c., and this as it respects all children equally. If Mr. Hallet will not take edification in my way of understanding the force of our Lord's argument, let him look for something to please himself. That the term *such* has the reference for which I contend, does not admit doubt.

That children are capable of being brought to Christ and blessed by him, is clearly established by this passage; and in this light it is of inestimable value. Let every Christian, then, bring his children to Christ. Let him bring them to Christ in his prayers night and day; for their salvation is beyond every earthly consideration. Let him bring them to Christ in his word, and in every thing in which Christ has appointed them to be brought to him. But let not Christians think, that to practise on their infants a religious ordinance of human invention, is to bring them to Christ, but to increase their own sin. Had man appointed an ordinance of imposition of hands on children, from the authority of this passage, it would not have been so strange; but to argue that children must be baptized, because they may be blessed by Jesus, has no colour of plausibility. The whole argument may be reduced to a single sentence. *Children may be blessed without being baptized, therefore the blessing of the children by Jesus is no argument for infant baptism.*

In short, whether our Lord's expression imports that the kingdom of God *consists* of such, or is the *property* of such, the term *such* must necessarily mean not *them*, but persons *like them*—of such as children, not of children such as these. The ground of our Lord's approbation of children is their resemblance to his disciples in certain characteristics of mind, which are to be found only in rational creatures; and they are permitted to come to Christ, because they are capable of being blessed by him.

The fact here recorded, however, instead of affording evidence for infant baptism, affords a presumption against it. If infants were every day brought to be baptized, why did the apostles object to their being brought to be blessed? Mr. Ewing has been aware of this difficulty, and has obviated it by a resource worthy of Ulysses, "for wiles renowned." "The disciples of Christ," says he, "never thought of forbidding the children to be brought to THEM, which they would be, (John iv. 2,) in order to be baptized. They only objected to their being brought also to their Master, that he should put his hands on them, and pray." Now, is this a thought that would ever occur to any simple mind in reading the passage? Is there anything that intimates a double purpose in bringing the children,—first for their baptism to the apostles, and next to Jesus for his blessing? What an eagle-eye must he have that can discover these things! But there is here a distinction never once made in the history of Jesus,—a distinction between coming to him and to his attending disciples. There is no instance of coming to his apostles, for anything in his presence. Jesus indeed did not personally baptize; but he baptized by his disciples. All things were done by his directions, and whoever came for baptism came to Jesus, as much as for anything else. This distinction, however, if admitted, will not serve. Still, it is asked, if children were baptized, why did the apostles object to their coming to Christ to be blessed? Jesus vindicates the propriety of bringing children to him, by arguments that equally apply whether it is to himself personally, or to his apostles acting for him.

But let this passage be ever so finely wire-drawn, it cannot include infant baptism. It applies to children in general, and not merely to the children of believers; and though the children of believers only were included, they may be brought to Christ for his blessing without being baptized.

"The language of the Acts of the Apostles," says Mr. Ewing, " on the subject of baptism, previously to the history of the propagation of the Gospel among the Gentiles, in which family baptism is first mentioned, is always equally comprehensive with that of the Gospels," Acts ii. 38, 39. *On the subject of baptism!* Does the baptism enforced in the passage referred to, at all include any but those who repent? "Then Peter said unto them, Repent, and be baptized, every one of you, in the name of Jesus Christ, for the remission of sins, and ye shall receive the gift of the Holy Ghost. For the promise is unto you, and to your children, and to all that are afar off, even as many as the Lord our God shall call." Does this imply the baptism of any but of those who repent? They who repent, and they only, are to be baptized. "Repent, and be baptized." Can language be more clear? Are they not to be baptized into the remission of sins? Does not this show, that in baptism, repentance and remission of sins are supposed with respect to the baptized? They are not to be baptized, that repentance and remission of sins may follow. Instead of proving infant baptism, this passage proves that none ought to be baptized but such as repent, and have their sins forgiven. Is it not expressly said, that all who are thus baptized shall receive the gift of the Holy Ghost? The promise is indeed said to be to *your* children; but is it not also said, that it is to all that are afar off? And is it not, with respect to both, confined to those whom the Lord shall call? Children denote posterity, and not merely infant children; and the promise of the Spirit is to them and to their posterity, and to all that are afar off, only on their repentance. It is not said, that when a man repents, his children shall receive the gift of the Holy Ghost, whether they repent or not; for this is false. His children, and all that are afar off, shall receive this gift, just as he himself received it, when they repent and are baptized. Does Mr. Ewing believe, that when a man believes the Gospel, his infants, and all the unbelievers of his house, receive remission of sins, and the gift of the Holy Ghost? If not, there is no ground to give them that baptism that implies both remission of sins, and the gift of the Holy Ghost. This promise is to the children, just as it is to the parents; and it is to all that are afar off, just as it is to parents and children, on their repentance: and it is actually communicated only to those whom the Lord calls. Mr. Ewing says, "that when the apostle added, ' To all that are afar off, even as many as the Lord our God shall call,' the meaning plainly is, that the promise which was to the Jews first, and to their children, should be to the Gentiles also, and to their children." No, Mr. Ewing, this is not the plain meaning,—this is a very forced and unnatural meaning. There is no doubt that the promise here spoken of is to the children of the Gentiles, just as it was to the children of the Jews; that is, on their repentance, they shall be made partakers of the gift of the Spirit. But the words referred to have nothing to do with this. The last clause is a limitation of the promise with respect to the three classes mentioned, restricting it to such of each as the Lord shall call. This is as clear as language can make it; and nothing but perverseness can mistake it. The promise is unto you; the promise is likewise to your children; the promise is likewise to all that are afar off. But it is to none of any class, but such as the Lord shall call. The three distinct classes are coupled by *and*—you *and* your children, *and* all afar off. The last clause is not coupled with the rest by *and*, but added to the whole, as a limitation. And does not the whole word of God confirm this view? Do any receive the gift of the Spirit, but such as are called? Do the unbelieving children and servants of a believer receive this gift? It is strange that any Christian should contend for a view of this passage, so unfounded and so forced.

But if Mr. Ewing will be so perverse as to hold to this view, it will profit him nothing as to infant baptism. Whatever the promise here may import, to whomsoever it is made, the baptism here spoken of, is to such only as repent. Besides, even according to his own explanation of the passage, he must view all the infants and unbelievers of a believer's house, as possessing the gift of the Spirit. This is a species of unbelievers unknown to the word of God,—unbelievers possessing the Holy Spirit.

Nothing but perverseness, and an obstinate attachment to a system, could make our opponents rely on an argument founded on the indefinite phrase, *your children.* Does not God promise to "pour out his Spirit upon all flesh?" Might it not be as plausibly argued from this, that the Spirit must be given to every individual of the human race, as that *children* here must mean either all children, or infant children? Even if no explanatory and limiting phrase had been added, the indefinite term must be limited by other known truth. But our opponents are so perverse, as to contend for the unlimited sense of an indefinite term, after it has been expressly limited in the passage itself by the Holy Spirit.

Dr. Wardlaw asks, How would a Jew understand the term children in this passage? I answer, no man of common sense can mistake its meaning, if he takes the meaning from the words. The apostle explains himself, so as not to be innocently mistaken by either Jew or Gentile. Paul says, " Men and brethren, children of the stock of Abraham, and whosoever among you feareth God, to you is the word of this salvation sent." Did not the Jews believe that the blessings of the Messiah's kingdom would be confined to themselves? How then, I might ask, would they understand this language? Would they not have much greater reason to conclude from this, that Paul confined salvation to the Jews, than that Peter extended the gift of the Spirit to the whole offspring of believers, without any respect to their faith? He says nothing here to guard them from this conception. But Peter expressly limits the term children, as applicable only to those called by the Lord. Is the

Gospel sent only to the Jews, and such as feared God? Is it not sent to all? Yet Paul, on this occasion, speaks of it as sent to the stock of Abraham, and such among them as feared God. Just so Peter speaks of the promise to them and their children, but he explicitly limits the blessing to those whom God shall call. The most prejudiced Jew could not innocently mistake this language.

"Are we, then, to suppose," says Dr. Wardlaw, " that this 'holy man of God, speaking as he was moved by the Holy Ghost,' would, without explanation or restriction," &c. *Without explanation or restriction!* How can Dr. Wardlaw use this language? Is not the last clause an express limitation?—" as many as the Lord our God shall call." But even had there been no limitation, it is rash in Dr. Wardlaw to use such language. Jesus himself used expressions that were capable of being misunderstood. Prejudices are no excuse for perverting the word of God. If the Jews took less or more out of the words of the apostles than they express, they were blameable.

Does Dr. Wardlaw believe, that when the head of a family receives the Gospel, all his infants receive the Spirit? If not, why does he baptize them on account of this promise? Even if they did receive the Spirit, they are not to be baptized by this passage, except they repent. Does he say that the promise implies that they will repent? But the promise is, that penitents shall receive the Spirit, and not that the children of such shall repent in time to come. Besides, if there was a promise that all the children of all believers would repent, this would not entitle them to that baptism that supposes repentance.

But if *your children* respects children, without limitation from the concluding clause, then the promise is, that all the children of a believer will receive the gift of the Spirit on his believing. Does this imply that all the children of a believer believe also at the same time? If not, does the promise import that unbelieving adult children will receive the Spirit? According to our opponents, this promise secures the gift of the Spirit to the children of believers, as well as to themselves. If so, except it is a false promise, such children will receive the Spirit. Unless, then, all the children of a believer receive the gift of the Spirit, as well as himself, the gift of the Spirit cannot here be promised to his children, except they believe.

Let it be observed, that the gift of the Spirit, as respects his miraculous operations, was given to their children with the limitation for which we contend. Some of them, indeed, might be children under age, but none of them were unbelieving children. They were old enough to prophesy: "And it shall come to pass in the last days, saith God, I will pour out my Spirit upon all flesh : and your sons and your daughters shall prophesy." This is the promise to which Peter refers, and it was fulfilled, as far as concerned miraculous gifts, in the gift of prophecy conferred on their sons and daughters. Surely these prophesying sons and daughters, were believing sons and daughters,—not unbelieving sons and daughters, nor infant sons and daughters. Now, does not the very nature of the gift promised to their sons and daughters, limit the gift to believing sons and daughters? Nothing can be more clear. But why do we waste time in ascertaining the nature and extent of this promise, or of any other promise? Neither this promise, nor any other promise, respects baptism. For argument's sake, let it be granted that the Spirit is promised to all the seed of all believers; this does not imply their baptism, except it implies faith. The commission limits baptism to believers; and the baptism that Peter here preaches, is limited to those who repent. Whatever a wild fancy may extort from the promise mentioned, it has no concern with baptism. That the promise of the gift of the Spirit is limited to those whom the Lord shall call, with respect to them, their children, and those afar off, is as clear as the light of heaven; but let it be extended as it may, baptism is not attached to it. The passage has no possible bearing on the subject. Our opponents have a popish perverseness in clinging to arguments that have a thousand and a thousand times been shown to be inefficient, and which they themselves represent, not as bearing the weight of their conclusion, but as having merely some favourable aspect toward it. It is a most vexatious thing, that, in the dispute about infant baptism, the greatest part of the arguments brought to support it, have no concern with baptism at all. Is it not evident, on the very face of the business, that infant baptism is not in the Scriptures, when its advocates are obliged to shelter it under such subterfuges? Had they real evidence, they have talents to exhibit it. Had they only one sound argument, they would not degrade their understanding by resting on arguments that have no reference to the subject.

"Precisely in the same strain," says Mr. Ewing, "and almost in the same words, the apostle Paul asserts the interest which believers from among the Gentiles have, in the family promise made to the Jews; and in the same way as Peter does, he connects this family promise with family baptism: Gal. iii. 13, 14, 26–29." *Family promise, family baptism!* How are such things to be found in the passages referred to? Is not the blessing of Abraham, that comes on the Gentiles, justification by the faith of Abraham, in the seed of Abraham? Is it not such only who receive "the promise of the Spirit?" Do any but believers receive the promise of the Spirit? Is it not here expressly said, that the "promise of the Spirit" is "through faith?" Is it not expressly said, that the blessing of Abraham has come on the Gentiles, that "we might receive the promise of the Spirit through faith?" Can this blessing, then, extend farther than the promise of the Spirit connected with it, and to be given through it? This promise is confined to faith, which clearly determines what the blessing is, and strongly confirms our view of the parallel passage from Acts ii. 39.

But Mr. Ewing says that Paul here, as Peter does, connects this promise with family baptism. No, Mr. Ewing, neither of them connects this promise with family baptism; there is not a shadow of foundation for such an assertion. Peter says nothing of the baptism of the children to whom the promise is made. There is no doubt that such children would be baptized as well as their parents, because they were believers, and had received the gift of the Spirit through faith. But this is not said in the passage, nor implied any other way than as, like their parents, they repented, and through faith received the gift of the Spirit. In Gal. iii. 14, even believer baptism is not spoken of as connected with the blessing of Abraham, though it is truly connected with it. In ver. 26, 27, the apostle speaks of the import of baptism, but not as connected with ver. 14. But where is family baptism? How can it be extorted from ver. 27? Mr. Ewing might as well assert that family baptism is connected with the breach of the sixth commandment. Shall any man suffer his understanding to be imposed on, by submitting to believe that family baptism is spoken of in such passages as this? Can a righteous cause require the aid of such support? Give me Scripture for infant baptism, and I will receive it. Give me any reasoning that is founded on a basis of truth, and I will weigh it. But I can have no respect for a mode of reasoning that founds on nothing, or on untrue assumption. A man would read himself blind, before he would find anything like family baptism in Gal. iii. It cannot be truth that requires learned and ingenious men to adopt such a mode of defence. Mr. Ewing, either yield, or give us argument. Do not continue to force and misrepresent the word of God, to sanction the traditions of men. You are floundering in a quagmire,—every plunge to relieve yourself, will only sink you more deeply.

"Unless we admit," says Mr. Ewing, "that infants, nay, every relation, both of affinity and descent, which can be considered as his property, are interested in the privileges of a believer's house, I see not a satisfactory meaning of 1 Cor. vii. 12—14." This is an astonishing avowal. Mr. Ewing believes that all the unbelieving children of a believer, and his unbelieving wife, have from him a right to all the ordinances of Christ. Well, this is extravagant, but it is only consistent. Others have founded an argument for infant baptism on this passage, but they inconsistently refused to admit the argument with respect to the unbelieving wife. Mr. Ewing has perceived that the passage cannot be consistently quoted for the one and not for the other, and that it applies equally to the Lord's supper : he therefore, instead of giving up the argument, as proving too much, boldly adopts all its consequences. The unbelieving wife, then, is to be baptized, and to be admitted to all the privileges of a believer's house. This privilege, it seems, is granted on the right of *property.* The unbelieving wife is to be baptized as the property of her husband. Slaves have a similar claim. To refute so monstrous a position, is anything necessary but to state it? Is this like the kingdom of Christ? Can anything be more contrary to the Scripture accounts of baptism and the Lord's supper? Faith is necessary to entitle to admission into a church ; faith is necessary to eat the Lord's supper without condemnation ; faith is necessary for baptism. How, then, can an unbelieving wife, or unbelieving children, be admitted to such privileges by this passage? Can any passage in the word of God give a warrant to persons to eat and drink condemnation to themselves? Can any passage warrant the admission of unbelievers into a church from which the Lord has excluded them? Can any passage sanction the baptism of unbelievers, when all the accounts of baptism require faith? Can any passage give countenance to persons evidently in their sins, to be admitted to an ordinance that figuratively exhibits their sins as, by faith in the blood of Christ, already washed away? This is an extravagance that, in a person who has any notion of Christian fellowship, and the nature of a church, can never be exceeded.

With respect to the passage referred to, it is usually and sufficiently explained, by an allusion to Ezra x. 3, 44; Neh. xiii. 23, 24. The sanctification referred to, must be *legitimacy according to the law of God.* Such marriages were not lawful to the Jews, and both the wives and their children were put away. It is the duty of the disciples to marry in the Lord; but even if they transgress that law, or are converted after marriage, they are not, like the Jews, to put away their wives and children on repentance. The marriage is to continue, and the relation is sanctified, just as their food is sanctified or blessed to their use. Now this is an important, a most important thing. As Jesus commands his disciples to marry in the Lord, had no provision been made, every marriage contrary to this, must be given up on repentance, just as fornication and adultery; and the offspring of such marriages could not be considered as the children of marriage, according to God's institution. It is said in reply to this, that even the marriages of unbelievers are lawful, and the offspring legitimate. Certainly—because they are according to the law both of God and man. But as Christ commands his people to marry in the Lord, to marry otherwise is contrary to God's law. Neither such marriage, then, nor the offspring of it, would be legitimate according to the law of God, except by this provision. The marriage might be legitimate according to the law of man, and the children legitimate according to the law of man, but neither would be legitimate according to the law of God. This provision, then, is most bountiful and kind. The believer, by remaining in his marriage with the unbeliever, does not continue in sin, as he would by continuing in fornication. His marriage is sanctified to him. I can see no difficulty in the passage; but if any will choose to understand it otherwise, let them have it their own way. In no view of it, can it countenance the baptism of infants or unbelievers. This sanctification, whatever it is, is a marriage of sanctification, and not-the sanctification of the Spirit through the belief of the truth, which is the only sanctification that entitles to any Christian privilege. If such infants were even as holy as the infant John the Baptist, it would not imply their baptism. They may possess the holiness that will fit them for heaven, without entitling them to baptism. Baptism is for believers, and only for believers.

So, then, Mr. Ewing can see no meaning in this passage, unless it is a warrant to give to unbelievers those ordinances that Jesus has provided for believers, and from which he has excluded unbelievers. If this passage will give a right to introduce the unbelieving wife and children of a believer into a church, and to give them the ordinance appointed for believers,—if it will enable such unbelieving wife and children to eat the Lord's supper without eating and drinking condemnation; may it not also introduce them into heaven on the same ground? It is said, "he that believeth not shall be condemned;" but if faith can be dispensed with in the ordinance of Christ, in which it is required, may it not also be dispensed with in this threatening? The same explanation that will baptize an unbeliever, or admit him to the Lord's supper, will introduce him into heaven, in defiance of the condemnation pronounced against him by the Saviour himself. What a wretched thing it is for a Christian to be given up by God to justify the traditions of men, and to fight against the ordinance of Christ! How wide is the range of this error! How much of the word of God does its defence oblige its advocates to pervert!

But this is a new and a strange ground of baptism—baptism on the ground of property! The unbelieving wife is baptized, not, it seems, in virtue of the promises of the Abrahamic covenant, but because she is the property of her believing husband. The promises of the Abrahamic covenant are to his seed, but the wife is included only as property. Can any idea be more abhorrent to the nature of Christ's kingdom? Would not this baptize the whole dominions of an absolute king? I call upon all Christians to reflect on this monstrous avowal. Is it not self-evident that the cause that demands this defence, is not the cause of God and truth? That the baptism of the unbelieving wife is the necessary consequence of the argument for infant baptism brought from this passage, Mr. Ewing sees to be inevitable; and therefore avows the consequence rather than forego the argument. It is, then, utterly vain for more timid minds to attempt to hold the argument and refuse the consequence. Mr. Ewing being judge, the baptism of the infant must be accompanied with that of the unbelieving wife, and the unbelieving adults of the family. Let them, then, choose which they will; they must take all or nothing.

Well, suppose they are all determined to adopt the shocking consequences avowed by Mr. Ewing, their hardihood will show only their disposition—it will not save their cause. This holiness of the unbelieving wife and children, is a holiness not of the *truth* nor of *the Spirit;* and therefore cannot entitle to any ordinance of Christ's kingdom. It is a *holiness of marriage,* which is an ordinance of God for his people, in common with all men. It is a holiness which is here expressly said to belong to *unbelievers;* and therefore can have nothing to do with ordinances that were intended for *believers.* It is a holiness that demands the believing husband or wife to live with the unbelieving, not to baptize such. The question treated of is solely this. There is no reference to any ordinance of the kingdom of Christ. Why, then, should this unbelieving holiness admit to the ordinance of Christ's kingdom, more than it will admit to heaven? All the ordinances of Christ imply, that the partakers of them have the holiness of the truth by the Spirit. If this can be dispensed with as to an avowed unbeliever, the declaration "without holiness no man shall see the Lord," may equally be dispensed with for his salvation. The same reasoning that will baptize the unbelieving wife, will introduce her into heaven as an unbeliever.

But why are unbelievers of this description baptized rather than any other unbelievers? Because, says Mr. Ewing, salvation is come to the house. *Salvation come to the house!* But it seems it has not yet reached the wife; and if it had reached her, it may not have reached the children.

The wife is here said to be sanctified while an unbeliever. Then salvation has not come to her, except the Gospel is false, and she can be saved as an unbeliever. Why, then, should she be baptized, or receive the Lord's supper, which supposes that she has been already made a partaker of salvation? But it may be said, she will yet believe. I reply, although this were certain, it would be no reason to give her an ordinance that implies faith and sanctification of the Spirit through the truth. This, however, is not certain, for the reason by which the husband is urged to live with her as an unbeliever, is, not the certainty that she will yet believe, but the mere possibility of this. "For what knowest thou, O wife, whether thou shalt save thy husband? or, how knowest thou, O man, whether thou shalt save thy wife?" Here the mere possibility of the future salvation of the unbelieving husband, or wife, through the means of the other party, is urged as a reason to continue in the marriage relation. Nothing can be a clearer confutation of the opinion of our opponents with respect to the meaning of the expression, "salvation is come to this house," than this passage. The utmost that the apostle states as a ground of not forsaking the unbelieving partner, is, that it may turn out to the salvation of such; there is not a single promise pleaded. If this is a ground for baptism, we might baptize any person; for we do not know but he may yet receive the truth. What a monstrous prostitution of an ordinance of Christ does this vindicate! It gives the ordinances of Christ to avowed unbelievers, if they will submit to receive them! Am I reasoning with Mr. Ewing? Have I understood him? Will he hold infant baptism at so immense a price? This determined obstinacy reminds one of the desperate perseverance of the Jews in the destruction of Jerusalem. Is Mr. Ewing resolved to overturn the whole spiritual nature of Christ's kingdom, rather than surrender this fortress of the man of sin?

But I appeal to the common sense of all my readers. If it had been the custom to baptize the unbelieving husband or wife on the faith of the believing partner, would there ever have been a question with respect to the propriety of living with such? If the unbelieving husband or wife was admitted to baptism, would it ever be thought that it was contrary to the holiness of marriage to dwell with such a husband or wife? Would they suppose, that a holiness that admitted to the ordinances of Christ's kingdom, was not sufficient for the sanctification of marriage?

Mr. Ewing has had the boldness to carry the principles that justify infant baptism to their proper extent. But he has done no more. Many persons who hold the argument from this passage, will be shocked with his sentiment. It is impossible to vindicate the baptism of infants from this holiness, without affording equal ground for the baptism of the unbelieving husband or wife. Mr. Ewing has the perspicacity to see this, and he has the hardihood to adopt it. He is just like Mr. Hume with respect to the philosophy of his time. Mr. Hume, in rearing a system of universal scepticism, did no more than carry the acknowledged principles of philosophy to their just consequences. Granting him his first principles, which were universally taken for granted, he, with the greatest ease, overturned heaven and earth, matter and spirit. He shocked the world by his conclusions; and thus led, by an examination of his first principles, to the overthrow of his doctrine. Specious or popular error will never be abandoned, till it is driven into extravagance. I hope Christians, who have any regard for the ordinances of Christ's house, and the spirituality of his kingdom, will be led to examine, with more attention, the foundations of a practice that requires such a justification. If the whole ordinances of the house of God must be profaned; if the spiritual fabric of his kingdom must be pulled down, in order to make room for infant baptism, surely enlightened Christians may be expected to renounce it. What an awful sentiment has Mr. Ewing avowed! *Baptism into the name of the Father, and of the Son, and of the Holy Ghost, may—must be given to a professed worshipper of Jupiter, Neptune, and Apollo, with the thousands of inferior gods, if the person is the husband, or the wife, or the slave of a believer, and will condescend to submit to this Christian institution!!!* To refute this, is it not enough to state it?

SECTION II.—Having considered the evidence arising from the commission given to the apostles, and from the practice recorded in the New Testament, I shall now exhibit the evidence that is derived from such allusions to baptism, as may ascertain who were its subjects. In general, it is quite apparent that baptism is not only a figure of the washing away of sin, but that it is always supposed that the sins of those who are baptized are already washed away. Now this can be supposed of none but believers. Infants dying in infancy, if saved, have their sins washed away. But millions of persons who have their sins washed away, have not had them washed away in infancy. With respect to such, then, baptism, that supposes sins already washed away, could have no proper application in their infancy.

From John iii. 5, we see that baptism is a figure of regeneration. They who are baptized are represented as born again. Now this is peculiar to believers. Even if there was a certainty that an infant would believe in future time, it would be no ground to baptize it. The ordinance exhibits the baptized person as at the time born again.

The same thing appears from Titus iii. 5. " Not by works of righteousness which we have done, but according to his mercy he saved us, *by the washing of regeneration*, and renewing of the Holy Ghost." Here baptism is called the bath or laver of regeneration. In the figure, it is the place of birth. The baptized person is represented as born in the ordinance, and is supposed to be already born, or renewed by the Spirit. Now, this cannot belong to infants; because infants dying in infancy are not born of the truth, although they are saved by the blood of Christ; and if they were, how can they be known? The multitude of saved adults were not born again in infancy. To say that it may represent that infants will be born again, is absurd, for the ordinance supposes that they are born again. Besides, it is not certain that they will be born again; their new birth is not a matter of course. It would not be the same ordinance, if, when applied to infants, it represented what might take place in futurity, and when applied to adults, it represented what had taken place. None are represented in Scripture as born again, except through the belief of the truth. "Being born again, not of corruptible seed, but of incorruptible, by the word of God, which liveth and abideth for ever. 1 Peter i. 23.

Agreeably to this Ananias says to Paul, "And now, why tarriest thou? Arise, and be baptized, and wash away thy sins, calling on the name of the Lord." Acts xxii. 16. Here we see baptism figuratively washes away sins, and supposes that they are previously truly washed away. Could our opponents say to the parents of the infant about to be baptized, "Arise, and wash away the sins of thy infant?" The figure supposes that they are washed away, not that they may, in future time, be washed away.

Rom. vi. 3—5, and Col. ii. 12, explain baptism in a sense that suits believers only. They who are baptized, are baptized into Christ's death, as dying with him, and as rising with him to a new life. They are viewed as already risen with him *through faith*. Can any thing be more express than this? Are infants risen with Christ through faith of the operation of God? If not, they are not among the number of those that were baptized.

In like manner, 1 Cor. xv. 29, all who are baptized are supposed, by submitting to that ordinance, to profess faith in the resurrection. Of this faith, infants are incapable.

In 1 Pet. iii. 21, they who are baptized are represented as having a good conscience, which cannot apply to infants.

In Heb. x. 22, 23, baptism is supposed to proceed on a confession of the faith or hope of the baptized persons, which being confessed in baptism, they are exhorted to hold fast without wavering.

That the external washing, or figurative bath, belongs only to believers, is seen in Ephes. v. 26: "That he might sanctify and cleanse it by *the washing of water*, or the laver of the water, *by the word*." Here the bath of baptism is only the figure of that which is done by the word. Believers are washed in baptism only in figure, but the reality of this figure they have had in the belief of the word. Infants are not sanctified by the word, and therefore have nothing to do with that *laver of water* that is appointed for those who receive the word, to their salvation and sanctification.

In 1 Cor. vi. 11, they who were baptized are supposed to be washed, —to be sanctified and justified, in the name of the Lord Jesus, and by the Spirit of our God.

We learn from Ephes. iv. 5, that there is but one baptism. Now, as the baptism of the commission cannot possibly extend to infants, if there is such a thing as infant baptism, there must be two baptisms. If, then, there is but one baptism, there can be no infant baptism.

In 1 Cor. xii. 13, it is taken for granted, all who are baptized belong to the body of Christ. "For by one Spirit are we all baptized into one body, whether we be Jews or Gentiles, whether we be bond or free; and have been all made to drink into one Spirit." They who are baptized are supposed already to belong to the body of Christ; and for this reason they are baptized into it. They are, by baptism, externally united to that body, to which they are internally united by faith. None are here supposed to be baptized upon the expectation, or probability, or possibility, that they may yet belong to that body. They are baptized into the body.

Nothing can be more express to this purpose than Gal. iii. 27, " For as many of you as have been baptized into Christ, have put on Christ." Here, baptism is represented as implying a *putting on* of Christ: surely this is peculiar to believers. Infants cannot put on Christ. Dr. Wardlaw thinks he has entirely overturned this argument, but his reply to it has no just application. He quotes Gal. v. 2–6, as a parallel to the above phraseology. " Behold, I Paul say unto you, that if ye be circumcised, Christ shall profit you nothing. For I testify again to every man that is circumcised, that he is a debtor to do the whole law. Christ is become of no effect unto you, whosoever of you are justified by the law ; ye are fallen from grace." " In the 27th verse of the third chapter of the same epistle, the apostle says, ' For as many of you as have been baptized unto Jesus Christ, (or, ' ye whosoever have been baptized unto Jesus Christ,') have put on Christ.' From this expression," says he, " it has been very confidently argued, that *adults only were baptized*, because of ' putting on Christ,' adults only were capable. Now, let the principle of interpretation, or of inference, be applied to the passage quoted from the *fifth* chapter. It is an address to *adults :* it expresses things of which *adults only were capable*. Are we, then, to infer from this, that *adults only were circumcised?* We certainly ought, on the same principle on which we infer from the other, that adults alone were *baptized*. There is precisely the same ground in the former case as there is in the latter." No, Dr. Wardlaw, the cases, instead of being parallel, are entirely dissimilar. In the one case, the apostle states the import of an ordinance of God ; in the other he is not stating the import of an ordinance of God. He does not allege that their submission to baptism was an evidence of putting on Christ, for it is not such; but it is a figure of putting on Christ. Some of them might not turn out to be real believers, but in their baptism they were taken for such ; and without this, baptism had to them no application. It is taken for granted that all who are baptized have put on Christ. But it is not from the import of circumcision, that the apostle alleges that they were unbelievers who submitted to it. Their receiving of circumcision, as necessary to salvation, was evidence that they were not in the faith, Gal. v. 3. This was decided evidence with respect to every one of them individually, that he was yet in his sins. On the other hand, their baptism was no evidence of their being in the faith ; but this was its import. No two cases, then, can be more dissimilar than the two which Dr. Wardlaw here pronounces to be precisely similar. Let Dr. Wardlaw bring an example of similar phraseology, with respect to the import of any ordinance of God, which yet is divinely appointed for those who are not supposed to " put on Christ," and he will do something to his purpose. Were the Jews ever addressed with such language as this ? Was it ever said, " whosoever of you have been circumcised in your flesh, have been renewed in your hearts by the Spirit of God ?" No, this could not have been said ; for circumcision never imported this.

SECTION III.—THE ABRAHAMIC COVENANT.—As infant baptism cannot be found in the New Testament, its advocates have endeavoured to find a cover for it in the Old. They think they have discovered this in the covenant that God made with Abraham. Of course, that covenant has been much discussed on this subject, and variously explained, to suit the respective sentiments of the different parties. It is lamentable, that the people of God should allow their sentiments on one subject, to influence their decisions, so as to perplex the plainest things. Nothing but the supposed connexion of the Abrahamic covenant with the subject of infant baptism, could produce such a diversity of opinion in explaining that covenant. I have read much that I cannot approve, on both sides of this question; and I cannot but think, that, in many instances, both parties have been more guided by their view of its bearing on the subject of baptism, than by an intense desire to ascertain the import of the documents before them. As I am convinced that truth must be consistent with itself, I have no fear that any real evidence can ever be deduced from the Abrahamic covenant, in opposition to what the Lord has so plainly established in the New Testament. The covenant with Abraham, I am convinced, is, like every other part of the Old Testament, full of instruction to us, and is worthy of the most careful study. But as no view of this subject can have the most distant bearing on infant baptism, I do not think it necessary fully to examine that covenant.

I entirely agree with those who consider this covenant as having a letter and a spirit. For the accomplishment of the grand promise, that all nations should be blessed in Abraham, three promises were given to him. First, a numerous posterity, which was fulfilled in the letter, in the nation of Israel. It was fulfilled in the spirit, by the Divine constitution, that makes all believers the children of Abraham. The unbelieving Jews were Abraham's children as to the flesh, yet there is a sense in which Jesus denies that they were the children of Abraham. The second promise was to be a God to him and his seed, which was fulfilled in the letter by his protection of Israel in Egypt,—his delivering of them from bondage,—his taking them into covenant at Sinai,—and all his subsequent dealings with them in their generations, till they were cast off by their rejection of Christ. This promise is fulfilled in the spirit, by God's being a God to all believers, and to them alone, Rom. iv. 11, 12, in a higher sense than he was to Israel, Jer. xxxi. 33. The third promise was of the land of Canaan, fulfilled in the letter to Israel, and in the spirit fulfilled to the true Israel in the possession of the heavenly inheritance. In accordance with this double sense of the promises of this covenant, the kingdom of God in Israel, with its officers, laws, worship, &c., is a visible model of the invisible kingdom of Christ. The typical ordinances, which exhibited the truths of the Gospel in figure, form one of the most conclusive evidences of Christianity; and present spiritual things to the mind in so definite and striking a manner, that they add the greatest lustre to the doctrines of grace. What a striking emblem of the incarnation have we in God's dwelling in the tabernacle and temple! How clearly do we see substitution and imputation in the laying on of hands on the victim! How blind must they be, who do not see the atonement by the blood of Christ, in the sacrifices of Israel!

This appears to me to be the only view of the covenant of Abraham, that will suit every thing said of it in the word of God. That it has a letter and a spirit is true, and analogous to every part of the Old Testament. But as long as Christians look at this covenant, on the one side to make it a foundation for a New Testament ordinance, and, on the other, to make it as unfit as possible for such a purpose, it need not be expected that the mind of the Spirit will be understood. It will be easy for a little perverse ingenuity on either side, to set it in a light that will perplex the simple. If any one can say with the Psalmist, " I opened my mouth, and panted; for I longed for thy commandments," let him come with me beyond the cloud that has been raised around the Abrahamic covenant, and try what we can discover in the sunshine on the other side. Let them make what they will of that covenant, I maintain that it affords no foundation for infant baptism. They tell us that the covenant of Abraham was the new covenant. Now, for argument's sake, let it be the new covenant, and I deny the result that they wish to draw. INFANTS ARE NOT SAVED BY THE NEW COVENANT, and therefore they cannot be connected with it, in any view that represents them as interested in it. It is a vulgar mistake of theologians to consider, that if infants are saved, they must be saved by the new covenant. There is no such doctrine exhibited in any part of the book of God. Infants must be saved as sinners, and saved through the blood of Christ; but there was no necessity to give a covenant to man to ratify this. Whether all infants dying in infancy are saved, or only some infants, they are saved just as adults, as to the price of redemption, and as to the sanctification of their nature. But they are not saved as adults, by the truth believed. That sacrifice which is the ground of the new covenant, is the salvation of saved infants; but there is no part of the word of God, that intimates that it is through faith in that sacrifice. God, who applies that sacrifice to adults only through faith, can apply it to dying infants without faith,—for faith has no merit more than works. It is only the Divinely appointed medium. Theologians have manifested a great want of discrimination on this subject. That necessity of faith which the Scriptures apply to adults, and adults only, theologians have applied to infants, without warrant, as if God was bound to proceed towards them as he does towards adults. Therefore it is that, even in Dr. Dwight, we find that frightful fanaticism, that speaks of the infant faith of John the Baptist; as if God could not save or sanctify an infant without faith, because none who hear the Gospel can be sanctified without faith. Surely it ought to make every sober mind suspect that there must be something wrong at the bottom of these views, that must consider an unconscious infant as possessing faith.

But this view not only leads to absurdity, it takes its origin in that principle of self-righteousness that is so prone, even in Christians, to work itself into every subject of Divine revelation of which they are ignorant. It supposes that it is so necessary for man to do something as to his acceptance with God, that even the infant who cannot comply with the terms itself, must do it by its substitute. It has its name put into the covenant, or put into the Gospel grant. And who is he that will undertake to put a name into God's covenant? What antichrist will dare to take the throne of Jesus, and put a name into the Gospel grant? Even the most pious men, when ignorant of God's ordinances, will attempt to establish the ordinances of man. Even the pious Henry speaks in this antichristian style. So true it is, that we cannot oppose any part of the Divine counsel, without loss. Every error is in some way injurious to the grand truth of the Gospel itself.

Theologians, justly considering that infants have sinned in Adam, have also justly considered that they must be washed in the blood of the Saviour. But they have, without warrant, and without discrimination, considered that they must be saved by that covenant that was given for the salvation of believers. But they can have nothing to do with a covenant that requires faith for salvation. Were it true that infants could not be saved but by this covenant, none of them would be saved. This would denounce to condemnation all who die before the belief of the Gospel. The new covenant knows nothing of any salvation but through faith. "He that believeth, shall be saved; he that believeth not, shall be damned," is the testimony from which it never for a moment swerves. Such a covenant cannot save an infant, who believes nothing. But there is a covenant in which they are included, and which will save as many of them as are included in it,—the covenant of redemption between the Father and the Son, in which he engaged to lay down his life as a ransom for his chosen, whether infants or adults. Though infants are not saved by faith, they can join in the song of the Lamb in heaven, "Thou wast slain, and hast redeemed us to God by thy blood, out of every kindred, and tongue, and people, and nation."

But let us ask Jeremiah, xxxi. 31,—let us ask the apostle Paul, Heb. viii. 10, 11, who they are that are included in the new covenant? "For this is the covenant that I will make with the house of Israel after those days, saith the Lord; I will put my laws into their mind, and write them in their hearts." "And they shall not teach every one his neighbour, and every man his brother, saying, Know the Lord: for all shall know me, from the least to the greatest." Here we see that all who are included in this covenant, have the laws of God put into their mind, and written on their heart, by himself. Can this be said of infants? The subjects of this covenant know the Lord—all of them— even the least of them. This surely cannot include infants, who know nothing. Is there not a necessity to teach children, as soon as they are capable of instruction, to know the Lord? Are any children found who need not this instruction? If not, there are no infants in this covenant. The sacrifice of the Son of God was as necessary for infants as for adults. But had it pleased God that all the elect should die in infancy, there would have been no need of the new covenant at all. The Gospel would then have never been preached. To keep in mind this distinction, would preserve theologians free from many of their embarrassments. The necessity of faith, and the necessity of atonement, are not of the same kind. Ignorance of this has led to the most frantic extravagance. In order to save infants, some have been led to assert that they have faith; others, that they have *imputative* faith; and others, that they have *habitual* faith. Now, all these opinions are grounded on ignorance of the difference between the necessity of faith, and the necessity of redemption or atonement. The *infant* faith of Luther, the *imputative* infant faith of Calvin, and the *habitual* infant faith of the church of Rome, have a common foundation in ignorance of this distinction, and are all opposed to sound views of the truth. Even Dr. Williams, an English Independent, and a writer of celebrity, makes the most doleful lamentation about cutting off infants from the church *militant*, by refusing to include them in the commission of the apostles. *Militant infants!* What an idea! Might we not as well attempt to cure Bedlam with syllogisms, as reason with persons who speak of believing militant infants? If any general should talk of raising an army of infants to oppose an invading enemy, he would at once be deemed insane, and his sovereign would not one moment longer entrust him to command—no, not though he were the Duke of Wellington. But when doctors of divinity speak like madmen, it is only the depth of their theological learning, and they are only the more admired.

2. My second observation is, that the infants even of Abraham himself, were not saved, when they died in infancy, by Abraham's covenant. He was not the spiritual father of his own infant seed. It is a common opinion, that Abraham, by that covenant, was constituted the head of all the redeemed. But this is a grand mistake. He was the head of believers only. By that covenant he was constituted the father of believers in all ages, but of none else. He was made the father of all them that believe out of every nation; and to his own descendants he was " the father of circumcision to them who are not of the circumcision only, but who also walk in the steps of that faith" which Abraham had. So then he was the spiritual father of none among his own descendants, but of such as believed. There was, then, by this covenant, no spiritual connexion between Abraham and his infant seed. His justification was not the pattern of theirs. He was justified by faith: his infants dying in infancy were not justified by faith. They were saved, as all saved infants were saved from the beginning of the world, and will be to the end of the world, through the *bruising of the heel* of the seed of the woman

Dr. Wardlaw calls on his opponents to show where the spiritual connexion between believers and their infant seed, established by this covenant, is cut off. I cut it off by showing that it never existed.

Abraham himself had no such spiritual connexion with his infant seed. The covenant with Abraham made no new relation between him and his infant seed; and much less did it constitute a spiritual relation between every believer and his infant seed.

But even had this covenant constituted a new relation between Abraham and his infant seed, Dr. Wardlaw is wrong in throwing the burden of proof on his opponents, with respect to the supposed similar relation between every believer and his infant seed. There might have been such a connexion in the case of Abraham and his seed, without involving the necessity of a similar connexion between other believers and their seed. Dr. Wardlaw contends, that if such a connexion existed in the case of Abraham, it lies on his opponents to prove that it was discontinued. But surely it is a self-evident truth, that the burden of proof lies on him who needs as an argument the thing to be proved, for if nothing is proved about it on either side, it cannot be used as an argument. Before anything can be legitimately built on it, it must be proved, if it is not self-evident. To prove such a connexion, then, between Abraham and his seed by this covenant, is not proof that such a connexion exists between other believers and their seed. The latter must be proved before it is admitted. Granting, then, that there was a spiritual connexion constituted between Abraham and his infant seed by this covenant, that such a connexion exists between every believer and his infant seed, is a thing that must be proved. This proof is sometimes rested on Gal. iii., where the blessing of Abraham is said to come on the Gentiles. But that blessing is not the blessing of a spiritual connexion between believers and their seed, but the blessing of having faith counted for righteousness, or of being justified as Abraham was justified. What that blessing is, we see in verse 9: "So then they which be of faith, are blessed with faithful Abraham." None, then, are blessed with faithful Abraham, but "they which be of faith." In verse 7, it is said, "Know ye, therefore, that they which are of faith, the same are the children of Abraham." Abraham, then, has no children spiritually, but such as are of faith. Between him and his infants there was no spiritual connexion.

3. My third observation is, that the covenant of Abraham is not made with all believers. Indeed, it is strange there should be a necessity to make such an observation. The Abrahamic covenant is so evidently peculiar, that it is the most extravagant absurdity to suppose that it is made with every believer in every age. Let us take a look at this covenant, as it is recorded in Gen. xii. 1: "Now the Lord had said unto Abram, Get thee out of thy country, and from thy kindred, and from thy father's house, unto a land that I will show thee. And I will make of thee a great nation, and I will bless thee, and make thy name great; and thou shalt be a blessing. And I will bless them that bless thee, and curse him that curseth thee: and in thee shall all the families of the earth be blessed." Is it not absolute lunacy to suppose, that this covenant is made with all believers? Has God promised to every believer that he will make of him a great nation? Has God promised to every believer that he will make his name great? Is every believer to become as celebrated as Abraham? Has God promised to every believer, that the Messiah shall descend from him, or that in him all the families of the earth shall be blessed? Every believer, indeed, is to be blessed according to that covenant; but it is by having his faith, like Abraham's, counted for righteousness, not by becoming, like Abraham, the father of any of the faithful.

Let us look again at Gen. xv. 5: "Look now toward heaven, and tell the stars, if thou be able to number them: and he said unto him,

So shall thy seed be. And he believed in the Lord, and He counted it to him for righteousness. And He said unto him, I am the Lord, that brought thee out of Ur of the Chaldees, to give thee this land to inherit it." Is every believer to have a posterity as numerous as the stars of heaven? Is every believer to have the land of Canaan for his posterity? It is said that every believer has a provision from God. This is granted, but is that a fulfilling of this promise? This is Canaan; and the whole earth, with the exception of that land, would not fulfil this promise. Every believer has a provision from God, but not in virtue of this covenant, nor at all suitable to the inheritance here promised.— Abraham's posterity must have that land. No other believer has this promise, nor a promise at all corresponding to it. The most of the Lord's people have no Canaan on earth, though every one of them, with Abraham, is by faith heir of that better country typified by Canaan.

Let us read again Gen. xvii. 5 : " Neither shall thy name any more be called Abram, but thy name shall be Abraham; for a father of many nations have I made thee. And I will make thee exceeding fruitful, and I will make nations of thee, and kings shall come out of thee. And I will establish my covenant between me and thee, and thy seed after thee in their generations, for an everlasting convenant, to be a God unto thee, and to thy seed after thee. And I will give unto thee, and to thy seed after thee, the land wherein thou art a stranger, all the land of Canaan, for an everlasting possession ; and I will be their God." Now, can any one think that this covenant is made with every believer? Has every believer a promise that kings shall descend from him? This covenant is indeed everlasting. It is everlasting to the carnal seed, first, as the covenant of royalty was everlasting to the seed of David, and as the covenant of the priesthood was everlasting to the seed of Phinehas. But in all such promises there is a spirit and a letter. The covenant of Abraham is everlasting in the full sense of the word, for by it all Abraham's spiritual seed are blessed with him, by having their faith counted for righteousness to the end of the world. All believers in every age are blessed by this covenant; but to them it is not promised, as it was to Abraham, that God would be the God of their seed, for it does not secure that they shall have any offspring at all. This covenant secured to Abraham that he should have a seed,—that God would be the God of that seed. Had not God provided a seed both carnal and spiritual for Abraham, he would have broken this covenant. When God promised to Phinehas, " And he shall have it, and his seed after him, even the covenant of an everlasting priesthood," Numb. xxv. 13, a posterity is secured by this promise. But believers often have no posterity, therefore they cannot have the covenant of Abraham. Believers have their own place in that covenant, but that is to be blessed in the seed of Abraham, and like him, to have their faith counted for righteousness. The promise to the seed is to Abraham's seed only—not to the seed of all believers. That Abraham's covenant is given to all believers, is not said here, nor any where else. Abraham's covenant is as peculiar to himself, as the covenant of royalty was to David, or the covenant of the priesthood to Phinehas. Even if the covenant of Abraham had promised that every one of Abraham's posterity, by all his wives, to the end of the world, should be heirs of heaven, other believers have no concern in it. What was promised to Abraham's seed, was not promised to their seed. That covenant constitutes all believers Abraham's seed, and secures to them an inheritance as such. But of their seed it says nothing.

4. My fourth observation is, that the covenant of Abraham is not the new covenant, or the Gospel. Dr. Wardlaw supposes that Gal. iii. 8, establishes the identity of the Abrahamic covenant and the new covenant so clearly that it is a matter of surprise that any should doubt it. "And the Scripture, foreseeing that God would justify the heathen through faith, preached before the Gospel unto Abraham, saying, In thee shall all nations be blessed." But this does not make Abraham's covenant the Gospel. It preached the Gospel by promising that all nations should be blessed in Abraham. It might be said also of the Sinai covenant, that it preached the Gospel, because the giving of the law through a mediator was a figure of Christ. Every part of the legal dispensation preached the Gospel, and still preaches the Gospel, Rom. x. 4. Will Dr. Wardlaw say that there was nothing in the covenant of Abraham but the Gospel; and that all its promises are promises of the Gospel, to be fulfilled to every believer? Is it a part of the Gospel, that God will be a God to the seed of believers, as he was to the seed of Abraham? Is this contained in the promise, "In thee shall all nations be blessed?" This is the declaration that is said to have preached the Gospel to Abraham prophetically. But it says nothing to Dr. Wardlaw's purpose.— Many things essential to Abraham's covenant, are not promised by the Gospel to all believers. It is, then, only an abuse of words to call Abraham's covenant the Gospel.

5. My fifth observation is, that the promises of the covenant of Abraham, were not to his seed, either carnal or spiritual, exactly the same as to himself. God promised a numerous seed to Abraham. But this is not promised to his seed, either spiritual or carnal, individually. So far from this, the covenant of Abraham did not secure to any individual of his race, that he should have any descendants, except to Isaac and Jacob, to whom the covenant was expressly given. It would have been quite consistent with all the promises of that covenant, that any other individual should be childless; nay, that the most righteous man of his race might either have no children, or reprobate children. By the covenant, Abraham must have a succession of carnal and spiritual seed; but this is not promised to his descendants. The race of any other righteous descendant of Abraham, except Isaac and Jacob, might have been totally cut off for their sins, without any violation of Abraham's covenant. No Israelite, then, except Isaac and Jacob, had Abraham's covenant. This is a grand mistake in Dr. Wardlaw. He supposes that every believer has Abraham's covenant, whereas no other man ever had it in all respects. Even Isaac and Jacob had it not in all respects: they were not the fathers of all who believe; while in some respects the whole Jewish nation had the covenant of Abraham. Granting, then, that believers now have the covenant of Abraham, even as

his own believing descendants had it till the coming of Christ, this does not give them any promise to their seed. If any man is a believer, God will be his God, according to the covenant of Abraham, or he is by faith one of the seed of Abraham; but that he shall have a spiritual or a carnal seed, is not promised by that covenant. The covenant secures this to Abraham, Isaac, and Jacob only; for to these it was individually given. It is as absurd for a believer to claim the promises to Abraham, as to claim the crown of Great Britain. This is a point as clear as the light of heaven, and it overturns all the elaborate deductions that have been drawn from the Abrahamic covenant.

6. My sixth observation is, that the promise, "I will be a God to thy seed," has a letter and a spirit. It is said, that in this promise God must be a God to Abraham's seed, in the same sense in which he was a God to himself. I acknowledge, that from the words of the promise we could learn no distinction. But this is not absolutely necessary, and other Scriptures demand a distinction. Whether it has not an inferior sense in the letter, must be determined by the history of Abraham's descendants. Now, that it has an inferior sense in the letter, is one of the clearest things in the Old Testament. God is every where considered as the God of the whole Jewish nation, even in the worst periods of their history. This cannot imply that he was their God, in the full sense in which he was the God of Abraham.

Let us take a glance at a few passages that establish this distinction. Exod. xxix. 45, "And I will dwell among the children of Israel, and will be their God." This is spoken of the whole Jewish nation, who never were, as a nation, the true people of God. It might be said that this is spoken with respect to them, as all in the New Testament churches are addressed as saints, though there might be some who were not really such. But this is not an answer. All in the New Testament churches had given evidence that they were believers, though afterwards some of them turned out not to be such. But no such thing was ever supposed with respect to the Jews. They had their privileges, not by evidence of saintship, but by their birth. They were not only born into the kingdom of Israel, but were not afterwards put away for unbelief. There never was a law given them, as it was to the churches of Christ, that none but saints should belong to the nation or church of Israel. In Exod. xxxii. 11, we read, "And Moses besought the Lord his God, and said, Lord, why doth thy wrath wax hot against *thy people?*"—"Turn from thy fierce wrath, and repent of this evil against *thy people.*"—"And the Lord repented of the evil which he thought to do against *his people.*" Here the worshippers of the golden calf are called God's people; and the ground on which Moses pleads that God would not execute vengeance, is, that his promise of their inheriting the land might not be violated.

The same thing is evident from Lev. xxvi. 44, "And yet for all that, when they be in the land of their enemies, I will not cast them away, neither will abhor them, to destroy them utterly, and to break my covenant with them: *for I am the Lord their God.*" Even in Babylon he fulfilled his promise of being unto them the Lord their God.

Agreeably to this, God is every where in the Old Testament con sidered as the husband of Israel; and this relation is acknowledged even in her adulteries. Isaiah iii. 14, "Turn, O backsliding children, saith the Lord; for I am married unto you." But it would be endless to quote passages. Now, God was the husband of Israel only in the letter, which was accomplished in Jesus becoming the husband of his church.

That the covenant of Abraham has a letter and a spirit, is not a theory formed to serve a purpose, but is consonant to every part of the old dispensation, and is the only thing that can harmonise it with the new. The temple was the house of God in the letter; believers are so in the spirit. To call any house the house of God, is as much below the sense which the same phrase has when it is applied to the church of Christ, as to call the nation of Israel the people of God, is below the sense which that phrase has when applied to the spiritual Israel. Besides, there are many things spoken about the house of God in the letter, in terms that can only fully suit the spirit. " I have surely built thee an house to dwell in, a settled place for thee to abide in for ever :" 1 Kings viii. 13. The incongruity of supposing Him, whom the heaven of hea-vens cannot contain, to dwell in a house as a settled habitation, is removed only by referring it to the spirit, or God as dwelling in the flesh. Christ's body is the only temple of which this is fully true. God did not dwell in the temple built by Solomon for ever; but in the spirit, it is accom-plished in its utmost extent. God will dwell in the temple of Christ's body for ever. In like manner, in answer to Solomon, God declares, " I have hallowed this house, which thou hast built, to put my name there for ever; and mine eyes and mine heart shall be there perpe-tually." 1 Kings ix. 3. It is only in Christ that the spirit of this is fully accomplished. In him the name of God is put for ever; and in him is he propitious to his people for ever. His eyes were long ago turned from the house at Jerusalem. The nation of Israel was the kingdom of God as the letter: the church of Christ is the kingdom of God as the spirit. The nation of Israel was a kingdom of priests, and an holy nation: the church of Christ is the spirit of which the other was but the letter. Israel was an elected people; but they were only types of the true election. They were all Jews in the letter; but it is said, notwithstanding, that he is not a Jew who is one outwardly: Rom. ii. 28. There was an Israel after the flesh, and an Israel after the spirit. "For they are not all Israel, which are of Israel; neither because they are the seed of Abraham, are they all children: but, In Isaac shall thy seed be called. That is, they which are the children of the flesh, these are not the children of God: but the children of the promise are counted for the seed." Rom. ix. 6. Here we are furnished with an inspired commentary on this covenant. God was the God of the nation of Israel in the letter; and as such, he gave them an inheritance and laws, and ordinances of worship, &c. Even in that sense, he was not ashamed to be called their God; for he prepared for them a city. But to those who, with Abraham, Isaac, and Jacob, desired a better country, that is, an heavenly, he pre-pared a city fully answerable to the magnificence of the title, PEOPLE OF GOD. Of all the innumerable things which have a letter and a spirit with respect to Christ and his people, there is not one instance in which a magnificence is not given to the letter, which can be fully found *only* in the spirit. So little reason have we to think it strange, that God should call himself the God of a whole nation in a typical sense, when the body of that nation were not his true people.

7. My seventh observation is, that when a promise has a letter and a spirit, it is fulfilled when it is accomplished in either the letter or the spirit. It has two distinct accomplishments, and may be fulfilled in either, or in both. The Scriptures afford many examples to justify this observation. When, then, it is said, that both the temporal promises and the spiritual in the covenant of Abraham are to the same seed, all that can be admitted is, that the words of the covenant do not make the distinction. But the distinction is seen in the history of the fulfilment of the promises, and in the explanation of these promises. Paul, in his Epistle to the Romans, clearly shows the distinction between the two seeds; and the history shows us that the nation in general enjoyed the temporal promises, but only few of them enjoyed the spiritual. Nothing can be clearer than this, and it is useless to reason with any who have so little spiritual discernment, as to think that all who enjoyed the earthly Canaan, were also heirs of the heavenly. The Pharisees and Sadducees enjoyed the earthly rest; while Abraham, Isaac, and Jacob, were strangers in Canaan, and died not having received the promises.

8. My eighth observation is, that circumcision neither signed nor sealed the blessings of the covenant of Abraham to the individuals to whom it was by Divine appointment administered. It did not imply that they who were circumcised were accounted the heirs of the promises, either temporal or spiritual. It was not applied to mark them individually as heirs of the promises. It did not imply this even to Isaac and Jacob, who are by name designated heirs with Abraham. Their interest in the promises was secured to them, by God's expressly giving them the covenant, but was not represented in their circumcision. Circumcision marked no character, and had an individual application to no man but Abraham himself. It was the token of this covenant; and as a token or sign, no doubt applied to every promise in the covenant, but it did not designate the individuals circumcised as having a personal interest in these promises. The covenant promised a numerous seed to Abraham; circumcision, as the token of that covenant, must have been a sign of this. But it did not sign this to any other. Any other circumcised individual, except Isaac and Jacob, to whom the covenant was given by name, might have been childless. Circumcision did not import to any individual, that any portion of the numerous seed of Abraham should descend through him. The covenant promised that all nations should be blessed in Abraham, or that the Messiah should be his descendant. But circumcision was no sign to any other that the Messiah should descend from him,—even to Isaac and Jacob this promise was peculiarly given, and not implied in their circumcision. From some of Abraham's race, the Messiah, according to the covenant, must descend, and circumcision was a sign of this : but this was not signed by circumcision to any one of all his race. Much less could circumcision sign this to the strangers and slaves who were not of Abraham's posterity. To

such, even the temporal promises were not either signed or sealed by circumcision. The covenant promised Canaan to Abraham's descendants, but circumcision could be no sign of this to the strangers and slaves who enjoyed no inheritance in it. Indeed, even to Abraham's seed, it could not sign Canaan individually. For upwards of four hundred years from the institution of circumcision, Abraham's posterity did not enjoy Canaan, and millions of infants died without having enjoyed it. To these, then, circumcision could not be a sign of their enjoyment of that land. If it is said, that though they did not possess it, they had a right to it, I reply, that they had no right to it more than possession, for God would not do wrong in depriving them of their right. What was the ground of their right? Had they a promise or grant? They had not. The land was promised to the seed of Abraham by Jacob, but not to all of them. Had it been promised to them all, they must have all enjoyed it, for God does not break his promises. To Abraham, it was individually promised, as also to Isaac and Jacob; and to them the promise was fulfilled in the spirit, as it was to many in the letter, who enjoyed not the promise in the spirit. They obtained the better country denoted by the promise of Canaan, and so, though they died not having received the promises, they died that they might receive them. When a prediction, or promise, has a letter and a spirit, it is fulfilled when it is accomplished either in the letter or the spirit. What sort of a right is a right to possess what is never designed to be given? A man may have a right to possess what he never possesses, but assuredly he will have no such right from God. God will not withhold any right: Abraham must have enjoyed what was promised. The promise of the land, then, must in the letter have respected Abraham's posterity, while it was accomplished to himself in a higher sense. He died, not disappointed, but looking for the promise. As the promises in the Abrahamic covenant were all unconditional, they must have been fulfilled to every individual interested in them.

But whatever may be said about the right of possessing Canaan, with respect to those who did not possess it, the reply of Mr. Innes is abundantly sufficient. "Even this right to Canaan only belonged to one branch of Abraham's family, while circumcision was to be administered to all. To those who were subjected to it, then, it did not, as individuals, seal temporal blessings. Again, no one will allege it sealed spiritual blessings to every one to whom it was applied, as it was manifest, that many of those commanded to receive it, had no interest in such blessings."

Much stress has been laid on Rom. iv. 11, in which circumcision is called "a seal of the righteousness of the faith which Abraham had, yet being uncircumcised." It is said that it was a seal of spiritual blessings. Undoubtedly it was a seal of spiritual blessings, but not a seal to the individuals who were circumcised, that they were personally interested in those blessings. It seals the truth of the Gospel, namely, that there is righteousness in the faith of Abraham, or that all who have Abraham's faith have righteousness. This is what it sealed when applied to Abraham: this is what it sealed in every instance of its application. But it did not seal, even to Isaac and Jacob, that they had this righteousness. It sealed the same truth when applied to Ishmael or Esau, or the slaves bought with money, as it did when applied to those who walked in the steps of Abraham's faith. It had no individual application to any man but Abraham himself. Words cannot more expressly assert, that the thing of which circumcision is a seal, is *the righteousness of the faith of Abraham.* It was not a seal to others that they possessed the faith of Abraham. Dr. Wardlaw supposes that such a marked reference to Abraham, would be inconsistent with farther trial. But this is a strange observation from an experienced Christian, deeply conversant with the Bible and his own heart. Were we in the morning assured, by a voice from heaven, that God had accepted us, were Satan to be let loose upon us, and we left to ourselves, it would not secure us till the evening from all the horrors of despair. Had God forsaken Abraham for a moment, he might have doubted whether it was God who had spoken to him in these transactions. Trial is not inconsistent with the utmost assurance that the Christian receives in this world. He may hold the truth this moment with the utmost assurance; let him be given into the hands of Satan to sift him, and he may doubt it the next. Christ himself received his Father's testimony by a voice from heaven, before he entered on his temptations, yet they were not less a trial on that account.

That circumcision was not intended to seal anything personally to those who received it, is clear from its being applied to those who have no interest in the covenant to which it was attached. For a full, clear, and satisfactory view of this argument, I refer to Mr. Innes, in his work entitled Eugenio and Epinetus. Dr. Wardlaw alludes to it, but he cannot be said even to have assailed it. Every position of Mr. Innes remains unshaken. Ishmael was circumcised, who was expressly excluded from the covenant. Abraham's slaves were commanded to be circumcised, without any reference to faith. " He that is born in thy house, and he that is bought with thy money, must needs be circumcised." Gen. xvii. 13. " And Abraham took Ishmael his son, and all that were born in his house, and all that were bought with his money, every male among the men of Abraham's house; and circumcised the flesh of their foreskin in the self-same day, as God had said unto him," ver. 23. Dr. Wardlaw supposes that submission on the part of the adult slaves must have been voluntary. But this is not necessary. As a master, he had power to enforce obedience, and this commission authorised him. Abraham would have been justified in circumcising his slaves, had every one of them submitted with reluctance, or had endeavored to resist. If, then, this is the law of baptism, it will justify the Spaniards in compelling the American Indians to be baptized. Nay, it will make it the duty of every master of slaves to have them baptized, whether they have faith or not; for Abraham was bound to circumcise every slave and every person in his house. Dr. Wardlaw speaks of force as being a profanation of a Divine ordinance. To this Mr. Haldane's reply is quite in point. "If in Israel a beautiful woman was taken captive, and an Israelite chose to marry her, it was the *Divine ordinance* that her hair and nails should be cut. Now, why should there be greater profaneness in cutting off the foreskin?" But this objection is founded on an entire mistake as to the nature of the profanation of a Divine ordinance. How is a Divine ordinance profaned? When it is not in all respects applied according to institution. It cannot be a profanation of the ordinance of circumcision, to apply it to those to whom it is expressly enjoined. Had murderers and adulterers been included in the command to baptize, and to eat the Lord's supper, it would have been no profanation of Divine ordinances, more than to preach the Gospel to such persons, profanes the Gospel. Does Dr. Wardlaw mean, that to force compliance to his appointments would be profane in God? Man has no right to use force with respect to Divine appointments, because God has not given that authority. But God is a sovereign in all respects, and may in justice enforce obedience. Accordingly, he commanded the Canaanites to be cut off, and all idolators to be destroyed out of Israel. This is a grand distinction between the Jewish dispensation and the Christian. The subjects of Christ's kingdom are all voluntary. To baptize infants is to profane baptism, because it applies the ordinance to those not appointed to receive it. But to force slaves to receive circumcision is not a profanation, for Abraham's commission warranted force.

But even although the submission to circumcision had been voluntary on the part of the slaves; is a voluntary submission all that is required for baptism? Is every man to be baptized who is willing to submit to the ordinance. Dr. Wardlaw endeavours to obtain some relief from the faithfulness of Abraham, in teaching his family. But whatever may be supposed as to his faithfulness and success in teaching his slaves, their circumcision is not grounded on this, but on their being his property, and in his house. The command will apply to one that had been bought on that day, or to the most profane scoffer, as well as to Eliezer of Damascus. But what an extravagant supposition, that every slave in Abraham's house had Abraham's faith! And if they had not Abraham's faith, they were not such as have a right to baptism. If all Abraham's household were so well taught, Abraham was much more successful with his slaves, than Jacob was with his sons. But we need not waste time in refuting a supposition that is altogether apocryphal. There is nothing said about the knowledge or faith of Abraham's slaves; and they were commanded to be circumcised, not on account of their faith or knowledge, but on account of being the property of Abraham.

The circumcision of the slaves, which destroys the system of our opponents, is not only consonant to our views, but appears as suitable as the circumcision of the natural seed of Abraham by Isaac and Jacob: it is one of the patterns of heavenly things. As natural birth gives a title to circumcision and the earthly inheritance, which was a figure of the title of all who are born of the Spirit, to enjoy the heavenly inheritance; so the circumcision of the slaves bought with money, represented that all who enter into Christ's kingdom are bought with his blood. The circumcision of the slaves is as instructive as the circumcision of Isaac. They had a typical holiness, perfectly the same as the natural posterity of Abraham. The purpose of God in the circumcision of both

Abraham's posterity and of their slaves, was totally independent of personal character.

Such a circumcision, then, could not imply, that the individuals had an interest in the spiritual promises of the covenant. Indeed, the circumcision of slaves did not make them partakers even of the temporal promises. " Servants," says Mr. Haldane, " although circumcised, did not possess the privileges of the children of Abraham, nor were looked upon as the people of God. They had no share of the land, and there was no precept against selling them to another nation, when they would lose all privileges of Israel. This also manifestly appears from many considerations. In many of the laws, the distinction between Israel, who were the Lord's servants, and the stranger, is stated. Thus they might lend on usury to a stranger, but not to their brother, Deut. xxiii. 20. They were not to eat what died of itself; they were to give it unto the stranger that was in their gates, that he might eat it, or they might sell it to an alien ; and the reason given is, ' For thou art an holy people unto the Lord thy God.' Deut. xiv. 21. They might also buy bondmen and bondmaids, not only of the heathen round about them, but of the children of the stranger that sojourned among them, but they could not keep an Israelite a bondman. Lev. xxv. 39—46. Thus it appears, that a person being circumcised did not thereby become entitled to the privileges of the children of Abraham, or of God's peculiar people." The Shechemites, also, as Mr. Haldane observes, were circumcised not only without evidence of faith, but even without a profession of it, which could not have been done with the approbation of Jacob, had it been unlawful. Here, then, persons are circumcised not only who had no evidence of being interested in the promises of the covenant, but who were shut out from its temporal promises most expressly. From the spiritual promises they were excluded as long as they continued unbelievers, but from the temporal promises they were excluded for ever. Persons, then, were circumcised who never could obtain an interest in some of the blessings of the covenant, of which circumcision was the token. How absurd, then, to make this the law of baptism !

But that circumcision, as a seal, had a personal reference to infants, is impossible. Our opponents generally say, that circumcision was a seal of spiritual blessings ; but the spiritual blessing of which it is said to be the seal, is *the righteousness of the faith of Abraham.* Now, of this spiritual blessing infants do not partake—they do not possess the faith of Abraham. Circumcision, then, cannot seal what is not true. To ALL INFANTS IT IS EQUALLY UNSUITABLE AS A SEAL. None of them possess the faith of the righteousness of which circumcision was the seal.— The argument, then, from circumcision, for the baptism of infants, is utterly groundless. The former was applied to those who were manifestly destitute of an interest in the blessings of the covenant of Abraham.

The spiritual or emblematical meaning of circumcision, the change of the heart by the Holy Spirit, is also without personal reference to the circumcised infants. Infants were circumcised in the flesh, but were not circumcised in the heart. Fanaticism itself cannot suppose, that all the male infants of Israel, and of the slaves of Israel, were renewed by the

Holy Spirit before the eighth day. The thing, therefore, that is shadowed by circumcision, is not to be found in the infants who were circumcised. In this it differs from baptism by the distance of heaven and earth.

That circumcision had no personal reference to the individuals circumcised, is also evident from the fact, that when a stranger desired to eat the passover, all the males of his family must be circumcised. " And when a stranger shall sojourn with thee, and will keep the passover to the Lord, let all his males be circumcised, and then let him come near and keep it." Exod. xii. 43. Here there is no faith required in the person who desires to eat the passover, nor in his adult males, whether children or slaves, who are to be circumcised as the condition of his eating the passover. The circumcision of his whole male family takes place as a matter of course. There is, then, no law that requires even a profession of faith in the God of Israel, in order to entitle a stranger to eat the passover. There is no condition of either faith or character ; and had he a thousand unbelieving children and slaves, he has a Divine warrant to circumcise them.

Our opponents are in the habit of insisting that baptism has come in the room of circumcision, or that it is the Christian circumcision. But this is a most groundless figment, for which there is no plausible foundation in the word of God. Yet the thing is so generally received, that it is taken for granted as a first principle. To overturn it, nothing more is necessary than to call for its proof. Col. ii. 11, 12, is usually appealed to as giving some countenance to the idea; and Mr. Ewing is confident that, on any other principle, the apostle's reasoning is inconclusive, and even his language unintelligible. Now, it is very strange how this passage can be made to speak so decisively on this point. Let us hear it speak for itself: "In whom also ye are circumcised with the circumcision made without hands, in putting off the body of the sins of the flesh by the circumcision of Christ : Buried with him in baptism, wherein also ye are risen with him through the faith of the operation of God, who hath raised him from the dead." This passage says not a word about the subject, either expressly or by implication. How, then, does Mr. Ewing extract his notion from it? Why, by the help of a little management. He represents the apostle as saying, " Being buried with Christ by the washing of baptism, they are circumcised with the circumcision made without hands." Ah, Mr. Ewing, can your conscience allow you to put so profane a hand on the word of God? He that can take this liberty with the Scriptures, may prove or disprove anything. Does the apostle say, " Being buried, ye are circumcised?" This makes the apostle assert, that they were circumcised with the circumcision made without hands, by baptism. But this is not the apostle's assertion. He asserts, that they were circumcised with the circumcision of Christ, in or by the putting off the body of the sins of the flesh by the circumcision of Christ. What is said of baptism is something additional. By no torture are the words capable of Mr. Ewing's gloss. The apostle himself minutely explains how they were circumcised in Christ. It is a circumcision made without hands. It cannot, then, be baptism; for it is not without hands. This circumcision consists in putting off the body of the sins of the flesh. The external circumcision cut off a part of the flesh; the circumcision without hands puts off the body of the sins of the flesh. This is the circumcision of Christ; the other was the circumcision of the law. It is the circumcision made without hands, the putting off the body of the sins of the flesh, that is here expressly called the circumcision of Christ. It is called the circumcision made without hands, to distinguish it from its type, the circumcision of the flesh: it is called the circumcision in which is put off the body of the sins of the flesh, to distinguish it from the typical circumcision, which did not cut off sin, but flesh: it is called the circumcision of Christ, to distinguish it from the circumcision of Moses. No language can be more express, or less capable of perversion. The circumcision here spoken of, could not possibly be baptism; because it is a circumcision which Christians are not only said to have without any external operation, but which they have in Christ: *"In whom* ye are circumcised." Christ himself performs this circumcision, and we have it in him.

This passage clearly shows us what came in the room of circumcision. The circumcision made without hands, came in the room of the circumcision made with hands; the putting off the body of the sins of the flesh came in the room of the cutting off the foreskin; the circumcision of Christ came in the room of the circumcision of Moses. All Christians are circumcised in heart, as all Jewish males were circumcised in the flesh. The Christian ordinances do not come in the room of the Jewish ordinances. Were this the case, every Jewish ordinance is equally entitled to a substitute or successor. Circumcision has no peculiar right to a preference. Every Jewish ordinance signified spiritual things, as well as circumcision. They are all fulfilled in their emblematical meaning, not in corresponding ordinances. For anything which we could learn from the Old Testament, there might not have been any ritual ordinance in the New.

Circumcision and baptism correspond in meaning. They both relate to the removal of sin, the one by cutting, the other by washing. The Lord's supper and the passover have a resemblance still more close; yet the one is not said to come in the room of the other. Christ himself has come in the room of the passover; for it is said, " Christ our Passover is sacrificed for us." The Lord's supper is a feast of like nature, but with this fundamental difference, which equally applies to baptism and circumcision,—it does not belong to the same persons. The Lord's supper, as well as baptism, belongs solely to the true Israel of God: the passover belonged to the carnal Israel, without respect to their faith or character. The persons whom John drove from his baptism, had as good a right to all the Jewish ordinances as John the Baptist himself. The scribes, and Pharisees, and Sadducees, with the whole unbelieving body of the Jewish nation, enjoyed all the ordinances of the Jewish dispensation, by as valid a title as the apostles of Christ. Neither Jesus nor his apostles ever forbade this, nor made any observations on it as an impropriety. The ministrations of the priests were never objected to; because they were carnal men, and rejected the Messiah when he manifested himself to Israel. This is the grand distinction between the

Jewish ordinances and the ordinances of the church of Christ. The former shadowed good things to come, and were appointed for the nation in general, which had only a typical holiness; the latter are appointed only for the true holy people, and take it for granted, that all who partake of them, enjoy the thing figured by them.

If baptism came in the room of circumcision, it would not have commenced till the other had ceased; nor would it have been applied to circumcised persons. Why did John baptize the circumcised Jews before the manifestation of Christ? Why did Jesus baptize before the end of the Jewish dispensation? But why shall we labour to overturn a mere figment? There is no need to establish, by arguments, that baptism did not come in the room of circumcision. Our opponents must prove that it did; and for this they have not the shadow of proof. They have the saying of divines, but this is the highest authority. It rests on no better evidence than the doctrine of the Pharisees for the washing of hands before meat; it is a tradition of the elders. Even if it did come in the room of circumcision, this does not import that it must have the same subjects, or be regulated by the same laws. How far they agree, and how far they differ, must be learned from what is said of them respectively. It is impossible to ascertain, from general principles, how far likeness extends.

Our opponents found the right of the child on the faith of the immediate ancestor. But if the law of circumcision is to regulate baptism, the posterity of a believer have a right to baptism, to the remotest generations, if all their intermediate progenitors were atheists. The child of a Jew must be circumcised without any respect to the faith of the parent. If, then, none but believers have a right to obtain baptism for their children, the law of circumcision does not apply to it. Why, then, should it apply in anything else?

It is said, that if the children of believers are not baptized, the privileges of the Jewish church are greater than those of the Christian church. As reasonably may this be said, if slaves are not baptized with their masters, and if we have not all an earthly Canaan. "We have no earthly inheritance like Israel," says Mr. Haldane, "nor are Christian servants entirely exempted from work one day in seven, nor have we a sabbatic year, nor a jubilee when our debts are discharged." As to parents and children, circumcision was no privilege at all. Had circumcision made the children of the Jews heirs either of Canaan or of heaven, it might be considered as a privilege, but it did neither. It was not enjoined, nor ever explained as a privilege to individuals. It was enjoined by the most severe penalty, even death. The females had no loss by the want of it. They enjoyed every spiritual privilege equally with the males; and the want of circumcision did not deprive them even of any temporal privilege, which they would have enjoyed. It is true, indeed, that Paul says that there was much profit in circumcision. Rom. iii. 1, 2. But it is evident that this includes females, and refers to Israel as the circumcised nation. Circumcision is here taken for the whole legal dispensation to which it was attached; for the chief of these privileges was, " that to them were committed the oracles of God."

Now the females had this privilege equally with the males. It was, then, rather a privilege to the females to be freed from this painful rite. Indeed, nothing can more clearly prove that circumcision could not be a spiritual privilege, than that the females were excluded. There never was a spiritual distinction between male and female. Circumcision was a part of that yoke, from which the spiritual Israelites were delivered by Christ. It is strange, then, to hear Christians speaking of it as a spiritual privilege. It arises from the same spirit that in the apostolic age made both Jews and Gentiles so prone to return to the weak and beggarly elements. He must be a babe in Christ, who cannot see how much the privileges of the new dispensation exceed those of the old, without taking into the account any ordinance in the room of circumcision. The church of Israel had the circumcision of the flesh,—the church of the New Testament have the circumcision of the heart. Is not this an immeasurable enlargement of privileges? The child of the Christian is perfectly, as to spiritual things, on the footing of the children of the Jews, for circumcision implied nothing to them individually. It did not mark them as the children of God. The children of believers may be said, in one point of view, to have better privileges, for they have a clearer revelation. They possess the oracles of God in a much greater proportion than the Jews did. *Circumcision secured to the circumcised person no blessing either temporal or spiritual : it was enforced by the penalty of death : it was not enjoined on all Jewish children : it was not enjoined on believers in other nations ; it could not, then, be a spiritual privilege to individuals.* The edification that it contained was as available to females, who were excluded from it, as to the males on whom it was enjoined.

Nothing can more clearly prove that circumcision had no personal application to the circumcised individual, than the circumstance that this ordinance was inapplicable to females,—the one half of the seed of Israel. Had it been of any spiritual advantage, or had it been appointed to mark the character of those to whom it was applied, would females have been excluded? Were they not heirs of heaven equally with the males? Had circumcision, then, been appointed to designate the heirs of the everlasting inheritance, it must have been extended to females. It is said, the Abrahamic covenant contained spiritual blessings : infants had its seal ; why, then, shall not infants have baptism? I reply, the one half of Jewish infants had not the seal, which demonstrates that the seal had no personal application to the individual.

It is said, that there is no better evidence that women should eat the Lord's supper, than there is that infants should be baptized. Now, were this true, what is the consequence? Not that we should baptize infants, to be consistent in admitting females to eat the Lord's supper ; but that females should be excluded from the Lord's supper, as well as infants from baptism. This is the popish argument to induce Protestants to receive the traditions of the Romish church. They tell us, "Ye have changed dipping into sprinkling by the authority of the church ; ye have no better authority for infant baptism itself : why, then, do ye not receive transubstantiation on the same authority?" I always reply, that my

brethren who practise infant baptism, do not ground their practice on
the authority of the church, but on their view of Scripture; and that
the argument is false, because it justifies one tradition by another. They
tell us, also, that we have no authority for the change of the Sabbath,
but the authority of the church; and some pædo-baptists tell us, that we
have no better authority for the Lord's day than for infant baptism. I
give the same reply to both. As soon as I am convinced that this is the
case, I will give up the Lord's day. Much as I value that day, I will
not receive a cargo of Romish trumpery in order to license me to retain
it. If the Lord's day has no better authority than the tradition of the
church, or the arguments that support infant baptism, let it fall. But
this is not the case. The Sabbath rests on pillars as firm as those of
creation, being appointed before the entrance of sin, and grounded on
reasons that are as lasting as the world. And the particular day is
ascertained in the New Testament, as the first day of the week, and the
Lord's day. But I will not here enter into proof, because it has nothing
to do with this controversy. Even granting that it has no better proof
than infant baptism, the latter is not relieved. In like manner, if there
is no better authority for the eating of the Lord's supper by females,
than there is for infant baptism, both must fall together.

But they who make this objection, must have read the Scriptures with
little reflection. That women did eat the Lord's supper, there is the
fullest and most direct evidence. " And upon the first day of the week,
when the *disciples* came together to break bread." Acts xx. 7. Here it
is said of the *disciples* without any exception, that they came together
to eat the Lord's supper. If, then, women are disciples as well as men,
there is here the most direct evidence that they ate the Lord's supper.
Paul delivered the Lord's supper with the rest of the ordinances to the
church at Corinth, without exception, 1 Cor. xi. 23; if, then, there were
females in the church, they are included equally with the males. That
females were members of the churches, is clear from the same chapter;
for Paul speaks of a regulation with respect to them. Besides, from the
whole account, it is evident that all in the church are equally concerned
in eating the supper: " When ye come together, therefore, into one
place, this is not to eat the Lord's supper." This shows that the
primary intention of their meetings was to eat the supper; and that they
partook of it without exception. The word translated *man* also in the
directions, verses 28—34, includes both male and female. Besides, it
is expressly said, that under this dispensation, there is neither male nor
female.

But though I have shown that there is direct proof that women ate
the Lord's supper, I do not consider that this is necessary. Had I no
other evidence than that they were baptized, I should consider this
perfectly sufficient, if no restriction were given in any other part of
Scripture. I do not object to inference; on the contrary, I receive
what is made out by inference, just as I receive the most direct statement. But an inference is not a guess, or conjecture, or probability, or
conceit, drawn at random; it must be the necessary result of the principle from which it is deduced. If it is not, it should not be dignified

with the name of inference. The person who is admitted to one ordinance of a church, is admitted to all, if there is no limitation. Indeed, the person who is admitted into a church, must have all the ordinances of the church, if there is no limitation. Is it not for these ordinances that a church exists. But are we for this reason to infer, that as infants under the Jewish dispensation received circumcision, a rite that supposed no character in the person circumcised, they should under the Christian dispensation receive baptism, which supposes that all baptized persons are washed from sin through the belief of the truth? In giving the Lord's supper, had any directions been added that confined it to males, as the commission confines baptism to believers, then no inference could establish the right of females. There is not the smallest similarity between the cases.

It is often said that the Jewish church was the same with the Christian. There is just such a portion of truth in this assertion, as to enable it to impose on the ignorant. But with respect to every thing which can concern this argument, it is manifestly false. Is the Christian church that rejected the great body of the Jewish nation, the same with the Jewish church, which, by God's own appointment, contained the whole nation? Was the church into which its members were born, the same with the church whose members must be born from above,—born, not of blood, nor of the will of the flesh, nor of the will of man, but of God? Was the church that admitted every stranger to its passover, without any condition of faith or character, merely on complying with a certain regulation that gave circumcision to their males, without any condition of faith or character, the same with the church that requires faith and true holiness in all who enjoy its ordinances? Was the church that contained the scribes, and Pharisees, and Sadducees,—the most cruel, determined, open, and malignant enemies of Christ,—the same with that church into which such persons could not enter without a spiritual birth? The church of Israel was the nation of Israel, and as a whole could no more be called the church of Christ, in the sense of that phrase in the New Testament, than the nation of England can be called the church of Christ. It is said that a similar corruption has taken place in the church of Christ. But this observation proceeds on a fundamental mistake. The very constitution of the Jewish church recognised the membership of carnal persons. It did not make the distinction between those born after the flesh, and those born after the Spirit. There was no law to exclude the Pharisees, or even the Sadducees, from the Jewish church. Their doctrines and practices were condemned by the Old Testament; but it was no corruption of the constitution of the church to contain them. On the other hand, the constitution of the churches of Christ rejects such persons, and provides for their expulsion. It is a corruption of the church that receives or retains them. The distinction between the two cases is as wide as the distance between earth and heaven.

As to the ordinances of the Jewish church, they are all abolished. Christ himself, when on earth, could not be a priest in it, but he is the only priest of the Christian church. " For the priesthood being changed, there is made of necessity a change also of the law." Whatever unity may be supposed to be in the Jewish church and the church of the New Testament, it does not consist in sameness of members, or of ordinances. The one, by its constitution, included carnal members; the other, by its constitution, admits spiritual members only. This, then, is the only point of view in which the subject can have any reference to the controversy on baptism. This difference existing, no number of points of coincidence can avail our opponents.

The church of Israel was the type of the church of the New Testament, containing no doubt the body of the people of God at that time on the earth, and in this point of view, may be called the same. Both are called the kingdom of God, and both were such, but in a different sense. The one was a kingdom of this world; the other is a kingdom not of this world. God's kingdom of Israel contained many who did not belong to his spiritual kingdom; and some belonged to his spiritual kingdom, who did not belong to the typical kingdom. All the believers belong to the church of Christ, but all believers did not belong to the church of Israel.

As the church of Israel was the church of God, typical of his true church, and containing in every successive age a remnant of the spiritual seed of Abraham, according to the election of grace, the New Testament church is spoken of in the Old under the figure of Israel, Zion, Jerusalem, God's holy mountain, the tabernacle of David, &c. &c. This cannot possibly apply literally, and is explained by the apostles as referring to the calling of the Gentiles. In like manner, the book of Revelation speaks of measuring the temple. The reality is spoken of under the name of that which was its type. The restoration of the Jews, also, is spoken of as a re-union into their own olive-tree. A correct view of this peculiarity is of great importance, and I perceive that it is very much misunderstood by our opponents; but as it has no concern with this controversy, I will not enter on any discussion foreign to my subject. As to this controversy, I care not what sameness our opponents may pretend to find between the church of Israel and the church of Christ, as long as they are different in members and ordinances.

9. My ninth observation is, that baptism is not the seal of the new covenant. That baptism and the Lord's supper are seals of the covenant, is a doctrine so common, and a phraseology so established, that it is received without question as a first principle. They who measure truth by the attainments of our ancestors, look upon the questioning of this dogma as a kind of impiety and heresy; and even the modern Independents, who have professed to be guided solely by the Bible, have very generally continued to speak in the same language. While I highly respect and value the ancient writers who speak in this manner, I strongly protest against it as unscriptural, and as laying a foundation for receiving other things on the authority of man. Let our ancestors have all the esteem and gratitude to which they are entitled,—but that esteem is much misplaced, if it leads us to follow them in anything in which they have not followed Christ. In many things their attainments were great, and their writings are worthy of the most careful study;

but in some things they were mistaken, and reverence for them ought not to induce us to receive their errors. It is disgraceful to Christians, that they continue to hold the errors of their unworthy ancestors, and to feel a reverence for the unscriptural phraseology of ancient divines, similar to that of the Pharisees for the traditions of the elders. Is there any Jewish tradition more void of scriptural authority, than that which designates baptism and the Lord's supper *seals of the new covenant?* There is not in the New Testament any single portion that can bear such a meaning. And what can the wisest of men know about these things, but what God has told us? He has not said that baptism is a seal. Circumcision was a seal of the righteousness of the faith of Abraham. This was God's seal to the truth, till the letter was abolished. The Spirit of truth is the seal, and the circumcision of the heart by him is the thing signified by circumcision in the flesh. The circumcised nation was typical of the church of Christ, for the apostle says, " we are the circumcision, which worship God in the spirit;" and " circumcision is that of the heart, in the spirit, and not in the letter." The circumcision of the Jews was the letter, of which the circumcision of the heart in Christians is the spirit. The Christian, then, has a more exalted seal than circumcision—he has the Spirit of God, " whereby he is sealed unto the day of redemption." Ephes. iv. 30. When sinners believe in Christ, they are sealed with that Holy Spirit of promise, which is " the earnest of their inheritance until the redemption of the purchased possession." Eph. i. 13. The seal, then, that comes in the room of circumcision, is the seal of the Spirit. Circumcision sealed God's truth to Abraham, and all who ever shall have the faith of Abraham. It was applied to the typical nation without respect to character; but the seal of the Spirit is applied to none but believers, and to believers of all nations as well as Jews. When the Holy Spirit himself, in the heart of the believer, is the seal of God's truth, there is no need of any other seal. Baptism represents the belief of the truth in a figure, and takes it for granted that they are believers to whom it is applied—but it is no seal of this. They may appear to be Christians to-day, and therefore ought to be baptized; to-morrow they may prove the contrary, and therefore they cannot have been sealed by baptism. He that is once sealed by the Spirit, is secured to eternity.

10. My last observation is, that to place the grounds of infant baptism on the Abrahamic covenant, is to make intelligent obedience impossible to most Christians. If no believer can know what the Lord requires in this matter, till he understands the covenant of Abraham, very many could not act at all. Can any man think that God would leave the grounds of this duty so enveloped in darkness? When the most illiterate heathen, or the most ignorant savage, believes the Gospel, five minutes will be enough to prove to him the duty of being baptized as a believer. But if he has children, when will he be able to baptize them by his knowledge of the covenant of Abraham? The most acute writers who have been all their lives engaged in the study of it, and in defence of infant baptism from it, are not able to keep themselves from speaking in many things like children. And after all their striving, they have

not been able to make out a consistent scheme. It is only the prejudices of the public, which are universally and strongly in their favour,
that screen them from the ridicule of the most childish trifling. Many
of themselves, after wasting perhaps a quarter of a century in adjusting
a scheme, are obliged to tear it down with their own hands. In my
ignorance, I made the attempt, as well as others; but I found I must
either give up the Bible, or give up infant baptism. If, then, it is so
difficult a thing, to make out a plausible case in defence of infant
baptism from the Abrahamic covenant, even with all the advantages
that constant study affords, what must be the situation of the newly
converted pagan! Has God left him in such a condition that he cannot
know whether he ought to baptize his children, till he can penetrate the
deep recesses of the covenant of Abraham? Mr. Ewing complains that
many persons go over from the Independent churches to the Baptists,
before they are thoroughly acquainted with the subject. Now this may
be true, if he means that they are not able to discuss with him the
popping system, or the Abrahamic covenant. But it is not true, as
respects the knowledge of the scriptural grounds for that ordinance.
Five minutes are sufficient to convince any man, who is open to conviction, and who comes to the Scriptures like a little child. I have written
a large book to prove what I believe might be clearly pointed out in a
few minutes, if all the disciples of Christ had in all things the teachableness of a little child. Every believer must be as a little child; he
cannot receive the truth but as a little child. But it is only with respect
to the truth itself, that all Christians are of this character. With respect
to any thing in which we are not taught by the Spirit, we are as un-
teachable and perverse as the world. Christ's institutions, therefore, it
is much to be lamented, are despised and corrupted, even by his own
children. How soon was the Lord's supper corrupted by the church at
Corinth! And by our long sojourning in Babylon, we have been so
accustomed to speak her language, that we have in a great measure corrupted our own. Babylonish words, Babylonish accent, Babylonish
rites, may still be discovered in the school of Christ.

There is not one of all the ordinances of the Lord Jesus Christ, that
has been left untouched by the wisdom of man. Some of them have
been abandoned as worn out by time: others of them have been entirely
new-modelled, so that not a feature of them remains as it came from
his hand: and many things have been added, of which no vestige is
found in the word of God. Baptism has been changed both in its form
and in its subjects; and it is lamentable to observe, with what perverseness even Christians cling to the innovations. In this we see remarkably
fulfilled what our Lord charges on the Pharisees. The commandment
of God requires children to support their parents when destitute, but the
Pharisees delivered men from this commandment by substituting something for it. "Thus," says Christ, "have ye made the commandment of
God of none effect by your tradition." Matt. xv. 6. Now, the like has
taken place with respect to baptism. The ordinance that Jesus appointed
was an immersion in water, as a figure of the death, burial, and resurrection of Christ, and of the believer with him. The wisdom of man

has changed immersion into pouring or sprinkling a little water on the face, without any reference to death, burial, and resurrection. This is the substitute for the Lord's commandment. Is not this the very thing that Christ charges on the Pharisees? The Pharisees told their disciples that the *corban* or gift would be a substitute for obeying the commandment of God; and we are told, that though *immersion* was the original mode of baptism, yet *pouring* or *sprinkling* will answer the same end, and be sufficient for baptism. Others whose principles will not allow them the use of this antichristian liberty, do still greater violence to the Scriptures, by forcing them to speak what they wish. Ah, my fellow-Christians, why will ye follow the Pharisees in making void the commandment of God?

In like manner, the invention of man in baptizing infants has totally set aside the ordinance of God. Jesus commands believers to be baptized; but since the Pharisees have introduced infant baptism, Christ's baptism is not known, so far as the other extends. The baptizing of persons in infancy is made to stand as a substitute for the baptism of believers, which Christ appointed. Christ's ordinance, then, has been totally abolished, and a human invention both in mode and subjects has taken its name. So true it is that every invention of man in the things of God, has a tendency to supplant some part of Divine truth.

Section IV.—Thus have we seen, from the most impartial examination, that infant baptism has not in the word of God an inch of solid ground on which to stand. The apostolic commission commands the baptism of believers, and of believers only. No lawful interpretation can introduce infants into that commission, or give authority to dispense with the baptizing of believers. No instance of the baptism of an infant is to be found among the documents of the apostolic practice. A child may perceive the insufficiency of the argument from the households. The Abrahamic covenant has no bearing on this subject. Baptism, I have shown to be immersion, by a strength of evidence that no true scholar—no sound critic—will ever attempt to overturn. Let the children of God renounce the traditions of men; let them submit with humility and with gratitude to the ordinance of Christ. In the keeping of his commandments, there is a great reward. "He that hath my commandments, and keepeth them, he it is that loveth me, and I will love him, and will manifest myself unto him. This is the love of God, that ye keep his commandments.—Why call ye me, Lord, Lord, and do not the things that I say?"

4

DEFINING GREEK WORDS

REPLY TO REMARKS ON MR. CARSON'S TREATISE ON BAPTISM, CONTAINED
IN A NOTE IN MR. BICKERSTETH'S LATE WORK ON THE SAME SUBJECT

SECTION I.—In religious controversy it is a great advantage to have
an opponent who is under the influence of the fear of God, and who can
be viewed as writing with a paramount regard to the authority of Scripture. With many controversialists the object evidently is, not to ascertain, with exactness and certainty, the testimony of God; but with all
licentiousness to exert ingenuity to defend the cause they have espoused,
and evade the conclusions of their antagonists. The aim is to defend a
favourite cause and put down opposition; not to search for truth, and
exhibit it with evidence. To avoid reprehending such writers with
severity, is neither possible nor warrantable. The artifices of sophistry
are as dishonest as those of pickpockets or swindlers, and they are much
more injurious to the interests of mankind. The delinquents ought not
only to be obliged to restore what they have unjustly taken away; but
to suffer exemplary punishment as a warning to others.
On the present occasion I am peculiarly favoured, in having an opponent whom I respect and love for the truth's sake that dwelleth in him;
and it is my resolution not to sink the probe a hair's breadth more
deeply than the cure of the wound requires. Mr. Bickersteth I believe
to be eminently a man of God. But I must defend truth at every expense.
I shall know no man who opposes it. The word of God is my only standard. It would be much more agreeable to my feelings, and more ad-
vantageous to my interest, to write only on such subjects as would meet
the approbation of the great body of Christians. Yet with the full fore-
sight of all the unpopularity that attends opposition to popular errors, I
have often come forward to the support of injured truth. It is in itself
a grievous thing, that the time and talents of God's people, instead of
being wholly employed against the common enemy, for the advancement
of the common faith, should be employed in opposing each other; but
while error is to be found among them, the thing is unavoidable. It
may be afflictive to us, but the God of wisdom must have some wise purpose to serve by it.
The remarks on my Treatise on Baptism, which are contained in a
note in a work on the same subject by Mr. Bickersteth, he tells us are

from the pen of a friend. But as Mr. Bickersteth has identified himself with his friend, by publishing the remarks in his book, I shall make him accountable for every thing in them. As I have not yet read a line of Mr. Bickersteth's work, except the appendix, I shall confine my observations to the remarks of his friend.

" Mr. C. treats in his work," says the writer, " first of the mode, and next of the subjects of baptism. The choice of this order is itself instructive. The main topic is made secondary to one quite subordinate." I am the most successful author that ever wrote a book. Most authors are very well contented if they yield instruction in the things in which they intend to instruct. But it is my privilege, it seems, to yield instruction utterly beyond the bounds of my contemplation. To express an opinion, with respect to the comparative importance of the mode and of the subjects of baptism, by the order of treating them, never once crossed my mind. I chose this order merely as the most natural. It is surely natural to treat of the meaning of a word, before treating of the persons to whom the thing meant is applicable. I believe it is not unusual for writers on both sides of the question to follow this order. But if any one chooses to follow a different order, I have not the slightest objection. I am just like the preacher, who, in expounding Peter's address to the lame man whom he was about to heal, said, " My friends, this may with equal propriety be translated either silver and gold, or gold and silver." Indeed, many would choose to handle the most important part of the subject last, that it might leave the stronger impression. In oratory, some choose to urge the strongest grounds first, while others prefer placing them last. Had I thought it useful to express an opinion as to the comparative importance of the mode and of the subjects of baptism, I would not have accomplished the thing by insinuation, or indirectly; I have confidence enough to state my meaning in direct terms. Instead of designing to draw peculiar attention to the importance of the mode, I consider both mode and subjects altogether essential to the very existence of this ordinance. If the thing signified by the word, whatever that may be, is not performed on the subjects, it cannot be baptism ; for what is baptism but the thing signified by the word? If the persons baptized are not the persons appointed to be baptized, it cannot be Christian baptism, although in mode it may be perfectly correct; for Christian baptism is not every immersion of persons, but an immersion of certain persons for a certain purpose.

In my turn I shall say, and for the truth of the observation I appeal to every impartial reader, that this assertion of the writer is very instructive. It shows most clearly that he is deeply prejudiced, and that he looks at evidence through a perverted medium. He sees goblins which have no existence, but in his own disordered imagination. Is it to be wondered that such a person should see infant sprinkling in Scripture, when he sees in my work an opinion expressed which never occurred to myself? Had I lived in former times, and had the writer been giving an account of my sentiments on baptism, he would have represented me as holding the opinion referred to. I can believe he is sincere in taking such a meaning from the order of treating the subject;

but verily it is only at the expense of his judgment that I am able to exert so much charity.

"This," continues the writer, "is the common tendency in the vehe-ment advocate of his views." Not only, it seems, is the opinion of comparative importance expressed by the order of treatment, but it is vehemence that originates this opinion. Is this assertion founded on evidence? May not such an opinion be both entertained and expressed by the coolest advocate of the doctrine? The writer has expressed an opinion of the comparative importance of the subjects. Is this to be ascribed to vehemence?

I have on the subject of baptism, the strongest and most decided views; but I have no disproportionate zeal for the mode over that of the subjects, nor for both mode and subjects over other things. I never make them the standard for estimating a man's Christianity, nor even for his advancement in the Divine life. I am sure that Mr. Bickersteth and I are more united in the things which we both believe to be of the greatest importance, than we are with many who may agree with us respectively as to the mode and subjects of baptism. The faith of the Gospel, and that only, I recognise as the bond of union among Christians. Is it, then, in the spirit of a Christian to insinuate that, with respect to my views of baptism, "the ritual prevails over the personal, the tone of the Jew replaces the spirit of the Christian?" Can there be a more ground-less calumny? I set no value on a rite separate from the import of it. Is it wise in the Church of England to tax its neighbours with too great attention to rites? The rites of God's appointment I value most highly: but I value them only as they are applied to the persons for whom God appointed them, and for the purpose for which God appointed them. Were all the people of England to ask me to baptize them, I would not baptize an individual but those appointed by Christ to be baptized. The mere rite could profit them nothing. In urging compliance with the appointments of Christ, I never distinguish between things of a ritual nature and other things. All things commanded by Christ demand equal obedience. It is enough for me to know that Christ has commanded immersion. Were it the very least of all his command-ments, it is to me better than life. This is the spirit with which I read the Scriptures. I never balance the importance of different things, with a view to keep the one and violate the other. Every thing that God commands is important, and bonds and death ought to be endured rather than disobey.

Here, then, Mr. Bickersteth, I charge your conscience as a Christian. You have identified yourself with your friend, by adopting his remarks. I ask you before God, whether you think that the order of handling the subject of baptism, with respect to mode and subjects, indicates an opinion of superiority of importance—whether you believe that such an opinion indicates vehemence, and whether you think it indicates a Jewish tone, and the absence of a Christian spirit? You must give an account of these reckless insinuations. It is a very inauspicious commencement to begin with calumny. "In the former part," says Mr. Bickersteth's friend, "Mr. C. replies to Mr. Ewing and Dr. Wardlaw, two Independent ministers, advocates of pædo-baptism, and the latter of them well known by other works. Mr. Ewing had advanced a strange theory of the derivation of the Greek word *bapto*, from which he inferred that both the word itself and its derivative *baptizo*, apply in their native meaning, alike to dipping, pouring, or sprinkling, or any application of water. He maintained further, that immersion was not commonly, if at all, used in the baptisms mentioned in Scripture. This no sound critic would maintain, and no consistent churchman is called upon to believe. Mr. C. refutes effectively these positions of Mr. Ewing; but the conclusions he establishes, so far from proving his point, that immersion is essential to Christian baptism, really prove the exact reverse. A few words will briefly explain this." However wild and extravagant are Mr. Ewing's criticisms on the origin and use of the word in dispute, they were at the time lauded as triumphant and unanswerable by the reviews and the periodical press. The reviewers now, I am told, are boasting of the exploits performed in this note. If I have refuted effectively the positions of Mr. Ewing, I pledge myself to refute as effectively the positions of this writer. He says, that the conclusions which I have established, so far from proving my point, that immersion is essential to Christian baptism, really prove the exact reverse. Here now my antagonist and I are fairly at issue. If I do not, without stressing a muscle, put him under my feet, I will consent to forfeit all pretensions to critical acumen.

In the mean time, I call on the reader to observe an expression in the above extract. The writer tells us that no consistent churchman is bound to believe Mr. Ewing's doctrine. In their deviations from truth on this subject, there is a great difference among the different sects, and every one is careful to admit no more truth than what is consistent with his sect. It reminds me of the reply of the chief priests and the elders to the question of Christ with respect to the baptism of John. " The baptism of John, whence was it? from heaven, or from men? And they reasoned among themselves, saying, If we shall say, From heaven, he will say unto us, Why did ye not then believe him? But if we shall say, Of men, we fear the people; for all hold John as a prophet. And they answered Jesus, and said, We cannot tell." Now about the meaning of the word baptism, ask the Roman Catholic authorities, and they will at once without hesitation on this matter, freely confess the truth; because their church has power to enact and annul. Ask the church of England the same question, and it comes very near the truth; for it has sufficient power to effect such a change for wise and pious purposes Ask others, whose principles bind them to scripture authority exclusively, and they will force the word to signify *pour*, or *sprinkle*, or *pop*, or *purify*, or *wash*, or *make a wash upon*, or *perform a water ceremony*, or something that will bring the usual mode of practice within the meaning of the word. But ask the Bible Society, which must reconcile the jarring claims of all parties, and they will boldly answer with the chief priests, We cannot tell what it means. It is utterly impossible to translate it; transference is the only means of union.

The numerous and conflicting meanings assigned to this word by persons who in practice are all identified, afford a self-evidence that they are all in error. As their practice is the same, it is evidently their interest to rest it on the same ground; and there is nothing to lead any of them to reject a sufficient foundation, if any such could be found. With all their differences, they are willing enough to avail themselves of common ground, as far as they think it possible. What is the reason, then, that, with a common interest, they cannot agree in a common meaning? The reason obviously is, that no meaning has ever been given by any of them, which is really and perfectly satisfactory even to themselves. They are then constantly on the look-out for something new, and something that will answer more effectually than anything hitherto alleged. Sprinkle and pour have been obliged to retire, and various new meanings successively take their place, and maintain authority for a time. Mr. Ewing's *pop*, however ridiculous it may appear to Mr. Bickersteth's friend and to me, was lauded with loudest acclamations at the time. But poor *pop* has now been obliged to retire in disgrace, branded with reprobation even by the friends of sprinkling. It looked very handsome when it came into life; but Dr. Cox and I applied the dissecting knife, and the skeleton, as it may be seen in the museum, is very hideous. President Beecher, an American writer, has lately found that *purify* is the proper meaning of the term, and I am told that this is looked on as absolute demonstration.

Now, I ask philosophy, what can be the reason of the never-ending variation in assigning meaning to this word? Can it be anything else, but that no meaning can be given which is at once true and suitable? Let it be observed, that it is not variation in the medium of proof, but variation in the very meaning of the term. The sprinklers are evidently like the infidel Jews, who, rejecting the true Messiah, are ever looking out for one, and are deceived with every impostor. *Pop* rises in the secret chamber in Glasgow, and for a time leads away the world : *purify* has spoken from the wilderness in America, and harbingers are found to usher it into Britain. Will the time never come when God's people will submit to his commandments with the docility of little children?

SECTION II.—" First," says the writer, " let us state the exact question in dispute. The Baptist maintains that the word *baptizo*, in its proper classic usage, means to dip or immerse only. He further asserts, that when applied to the ordinance of Christ, this idea of a specific mode remains so essential, that without it the ordinance is void." This is a very circuitous statement of the question at issue. The simple question is, what is the meaning of the word? When this is ascertained, the question is settled. But I will follow the author in his statement. He tells us that the Baptist asserts, that when the word is applied to an ordinance of Christ, the idea of a specific mode remains so essential, that without it the ordinance is void. He should have stated the thing still more strongly. I would not say that without immersion the ordinance of baptism is void. Without immersion it is not the ordinance at all : it may be a very solemn ceremony; but it is a ceremony of human invention. It may be believed by the Lord's people to be an ordinance of Christ;

but this does not make it an ordinance of Christ. If the word signifies immersion, can there be baptism where there is no immersion? This would be immersion without immersion. Grant, as the writer does, that the meaning of the word, when first applied, was immersion, that nothing but immersion is baptism is a self-evident truth. The contrary is a contradiction. Whatever is the meaning of the word at the time of its first application to the ordinance, must be essential to the ordinance; for the ordinance is expressed by the word. If a specific mode was contained in the word when first applied to the ordinance, a specific mode must for ever remain in it; for whatever change may take place afterwards in the meaning of the word, it can have no change with reference to Christ's ordinance. What he enjoined must remain as he enjoined it. Now the word when first applied to this ordinance, not only contained a specific mode, but it expressed nothing but a specific mode. Mode was its very essence.

I may be told, that on my own principles it is possible that the word in the progress of its use might change its meaning. I admit this. I have proved the fact with respect to other words; and what has been effected with respect to others, is possible with this. I do not recede a tittle from what I have taught on the philology of this question. This surely is granting my present antagonist all he can demand. But this question has no concern with any change in the meaning of the word, either possible or actual, *after* its application to the ordinance. As a matter of fact, it never underwent the change for which my antagonist contends. But had it actually undergone such a change, it would not relieve him. Whatever was the meaning of the word, when first applied to the ordinance of Christ, is the thing enjoined by Christ. If at first the command was to *immerse*, the command must still be to *immerse*.

But in the view of this writer, the belief of the Baptist is still more extravagant and paradoxical; for " he believes, that though the minister designs solemnly to administer Christ's ordinance, though the believer designs to receive it,—though the name of the Father, Son, and Spirit be invoked,—though the element of water be used—unless the whole body be immersed beneath the element, the whole is vain and nugatory, and the party remains unbaptized." All true, perfectly true; and no axiom is more evident. However sincere we may believe our opponents to be, still we cannot believe that a person is immersed when he is sprinkled. The minister may design solemnly to administer Christ's ordinance, yet if he sprinkles, we cannot believe that he baptizes, because baptism is immersion. He may be truly washed in the blood of Christ, when, out of ignorance of the will of his Master, he is sprinkled instead of being immersed. Sincerity cannot convert one thing into another, and cannot cause sprinkling to be immersion. Intention to fulfil a command does not fulfil it, if the nature of the command is mistaken. God will forgive the ignorance of his people, but he will not reckon that a person has fulfilled his command, who has mistaken his command. The church at Corinth designed, no doubt, to observe the Lord's supper; yet the apostle Paul would not give their observance the name of Christ's ordinance. A Roman Catholic priest may sincerely design to transubstantiate the wafer into Christ, but notwithstanding his sincerity, he fails. I have no objection to admit, that persons mistaken about the mode and subjects of baptism, may be among the most eminent and the most useful of the servants of God; but to admit that any one is baptized who is not immersed, is self-contradiction. Immersion is the very thing enjoined in the ordinance. The design of both the administrator and the receiver of any rite, can have no effect whatever on the meaning of this word, and cannot at all change into an ordinance of Christ, what is not an ordinance of Christ; neither can the use of the name of the Father, Son, and Holy Spirit, convert sprinkling into baptism. Chivalry creates its knights with this solemnity; but does it thereby make the ceremony a Divine appointment? Is it not a fearful thing, to do in the name of the Father, and of the Son, and of the Holy Spirit, that which the Father, and the Son, and the Holy Spirit have not enjoined? Men may endeavour, by adding a load of ceremonies, to compensate for what they omit, but all is vain. Nor does the use of water make the rite baptism. All use of water is not baptism: it is only as water is used according to Christ's commandment, that it is baptism. The sprinkling of the holy water of the church of Rome is not baptism. To all the things mentioned by the writer, may be added the cross, and the oil, and the spittle, with exorcism, and the honey, and the white garments; yet where there is no immersion, there is no baptism.

SECTION III.—Having given us the creed of the Baptist, the writer of the note next gives us that of the churchman. He does well to restrict it to the churchman; for other denominations of Pædo-baptists would reject it with abhorrence. Here we have the testimony of churchmen, that the meaning of the word when first applied to the ordinance, is that for which we contend, and that the burden of the change must rest on the shoulders of the church; while we have the testimony of the other denominations, that the authority of the church is not a valid foundation. But let us hear the author. "The churchman," says he, "on the other hand, allows that to dip is the primary and almost constant meaning of the word in classic authors. He further admits, that probably, if not certainly, in some of the Scripture instances, and possibly in all, immersion was practised. But he believes that when once the word was regularly applied to the ordinance of Christ, it received a new and more important element of meaning, and that thenceforward the idea of one specific mode was no longer essential. He sees that in Scripture, dipping, pouring, and sprinkling, are all variously used as signs of spiritual cleansing. He knows that in ceremonial observances, Christ has enjoined regard to decency, comeliness, order, and convenience. He is aware that total immersion, in colder climates and tender age, is less convenient. He believes that Christ has given to his church authority in precisely such points of outward order, to appoint, under varying circumstances, as the Spirit of wisdom shall teach and suggest. He, therefore, concurs fully in the arrangement of the church in this land, by which dipping is proposed as the standard mode, the more primitive and fully significant, but in which, for seemliness or safety.

pouring is expressly appointed in certain cases, and sprinkling practically allowed in all." This churchman must know that other churchmen have gone farther. They have not only admitted that immersion is the ordinance of Christ, and that nothing but necessity can justify a departure; many of them have wished that the original practice should be revived. Dr. Johnson, in referring to the change in the eucharist, says, "I think they (Roman Catholics) are as well warranted to make this alteration, as we are to substitute sprinkling in the room of the ancient baptism." Petavius, the celebrated Jesuit, speaking of the power of the church to alter, or impose, says, "And indeed immersion is properly *baptismos*, though at present we content ourselves with pouring water on the head." It is expressly not only on this principle, but on the authority of the very example of changing immersion into sprinkling, that Bossuet vindicates the change in the Lord's supper. Admissions of opponents, however, I entirely disregard on this subject; I can prove the point with evidence sufficient to satisfy any rational creature. If any man will be obstinately ignorant, let him be ignorant. This Lord Jesus Christ will come.

Guarded, however, as this churchman is in his admissions, they are quite sufficient for my purpose. If, as he admits, immersion was the meaning of the word at the time of its appropriation to the ordinance; and if possibly all Scripture instances of baptism conformed to this, I need nothing else to establish my point. The word must be used in reference to the ordinance, in the sense which it possessed at the time that it was first applied to the ordinance. The laws of language absolutely require this. And, according to the testimony of this candid churchman, there is no insurmountable difficulty in supposing that every instance of baptism mentioned in Scripture, was performed by immersion. The difficulties, then, which some have pretended to find on this supposition, the churchman agrees with me, are all surmountable.

"But," says the writer, "he believes that when once the word was regularly applied to the ordinance of Christ, it received a new and more important element of meaning, and that thenceforward the idea of one specific mode was no longer essential." This is a most marvellous doctrine. If the word at the time Christ appointed the ordinance signified immersion, will it lose that signification the moment that Christ enjoins immersion? Does a command to use a specific mode imply that no specific mode is to be observed, but that all modes are equally legitimate? Whatever element it may be supposed is added to the signification of a word on its appropriation, it surely does not lose any element, much less its very essence. The appropriation of a word restricts its application on certain subjects, but it does not divest it of its meaning. The appropriation of this word confines it to the ordinance in question, but it is to that ordinance only as it exists when it is appropriated. Men may change the ordinance, and change the meaning of the word, but such change has no effect on the meaning of the word as used in Scripture for this ordinance. The writer here entirely mistakes the principle of appropriation which I have explained, and which he thinks he can use against himself. Appropriation gave the word a particular direction to a particular subject, but did not divest the word of its meaning. This may be illustrated from every instance of appropriation. When words are appropriated, they are indeed liable to change their meaning with every corresponding change in the thing to which they are appropriated; but as respects the Scriptures there can be a change in neither. The ordinance remains the same there, and the meaning of its name can never, as to Scripture use, be less or more. I care not if it were in actual proof, that pouring or sprinkling was substituted for immersion by those who used the Greek language; and that those modes were actually called by the name of immersion. These facts could avail nothing with respect to the meaning of the word in the ordinance of Christ. It is here that the perspicacity of the writer of the note utterly fails. The possible or actual use of a word in after times, he alleges as its meaning in the ordinance of Christ. "Arise, and be baptized," says Ananias to Paul. Now, if at the time the word signified immersion, is not immersion the thing enjoined? Can this command be fulfilled by being sprinkled? Should the word afterwards change its meaning, does such change avail anything in relieving from obedience to the command?

"The churchman," the writer tells us, "sees that in Scripture, dipping, pouring, and sprinkling, are all variously used as signs of spiritual cleansing." And did not Christ see this as clearly as the churchman? If dipping, pouring, and sprinkling are all equally applicable to this ordinance, why did Christ enjoin one of them only? The churchman's practice is a censure on the Son of God. If the churchman has good reasons, as he says he has, for changing the mode of this ordinance, Christ could not have good reasons for adopting it. Was it not as easy in the time of Christ to pour or sprinkle, as it was to immerse? If he foresaw that there would in future times, and in certain countries, be reasons for a change, why did he not himself provide for this? The churchman makes himself more keen-sighted than the institutor of the ordinance. The Baptist sees as clearly as the churchman, that pouring and sprinkling are in Scripture used for cleansing as well as dipping, and he has no objection to them in any ordinance, if Christ had appointed them. The Baptist cannot presume to use any discretion in altering the commandments of God. Besides, he sees that burial and resurrection, as well as cleansing, are figured in the ordinance of baptism. The churchman himself admits the same thing. Dipping, pouring, and sprinkling, were indeed all used under the law; but had the Jews a right to substitute the one for the other? When they were commanded to dip, did they fulfil by sprinkling? When commanded to sprinkle, did they dip? If indeed the mode in baptism is emblematical, and my opponent admits that it is emblematical, it cannot be changed; to change it would be to destroy the emblem.

The churchman, it seems, knows that in "ceremonial observances Christ has enjoined regard to decency, comeliness, order, and convenience." Here the churchman has undoubtedly the advantage; for he knows what nobody knows but himself and the pope. He knows that he can annul what Christ has commanded, and substitute something more decent, comely, orderly, and convenient, in its stead. On this ground, then, let sprinkling rest, along with all the other trumpery of human invention. But if this writer refers to 1 Cor. xiv. 40, as his sanction for this authority, it will not serve him. This refers not to ceremonial observances, more than other things; and the thing directly spoken of, is not of a ceremonial nature at all. The passage gives no authority to appoint or alter observances of any kind; but directs that all the ordinances or observances of a church, should be attended to in order. This was violated in the church at Corinth, where one had a psalm, and another a doctrine, &c., at the same time. It is the very essence of popery to claim a right to annul or alter the commandments of Christ. A rite appointed by Christ is no more to be tampered with, than any commandment in the decalogue. But with this subject I have nothing to do here. My present business is to prove the meaning of the word baptism in the commandment of Christ. Whether Christ has given any power to men to annul this commandment, and substitute another rite, is a question to be argued on other grounds. In the mean time, I am very well pleased that I have driven sprinkling and pouring out of the Scriptures, and obliged them to take shelter with the figments of popery, in church authority.

The churchman is also " aware, that total immersion in colder climates and tender age is less convenient." All churchmen are not aware of this. With respect to tender age, the Baptist is not concerned to convince his opponents that it is safe to immerse newly-born infants. This he will undertake to prove, when it is proved that newly-born infants are commanded to be baptized. Were it really true, that in any circumstances immersion would be dangerous to health, what would follow? Not that sprinkling should be substituted for immersion; but that the person could not be baptized at all. If the ordinance of Christ is impossible, except at the hazard of life, the law of God does not require it.

The churchman " believes that Christ has given to his church authority, in precisely such points of outward order, to appoint, under varying circumstances, as the Spirit of wisdom shall teach or suggest." Can anything be more provokingly intolerable than this way of reasoning? Way of reasoning! Such a pretence for avoiding reasoning! Is the churchman to foist on us his creed, instead of giving us his arguments? But there is inconsistency in the author's own management of this business. If the church has authority from Christ to alter things of a ritual nature according to its own wisdom, why does the writer strain to sanction the change with the meaning of the word? The writer, then, finds himself in a quagmire, and still as he begins to sink in one spot he shifts with all speed to another. Here we have an express avowal of authority from Christ to change his ritual appointments. If this is not popery I do not know where popery is to be found. Alas, alas! and is this Mr. Bickersteth? But my work is done. When I have driven my antagonist to take refuge among the mummery of the man of sin, my triumph is complete. All I engaged to do was to prove that the word in question signifies to immerse. This writer, instead of fairly meeting me on this, alleges that his church has power to alter the mode, and in certain cases to substitute pouring or sprinkling for immersion. This has nothing to do with the question. This might be true without in the least affecting my doctrine, with respect to the meaning of the word in dispute. Whether it is true or not must be argued on other ground. No wonder that Puseyism spreads in the church of England, when such a sentiment as this can be avowed by such a man as Mr. Bickersteth.

Now I appeal to every impartial reader, whether there can be a doubt as to my victory, when my antagonist is obliged to shelter his practice under the authority of his church? If reasoning on the meaning of the word could have established his point, would he have recourse to church authority? If church authority has changed the mode, why seek a sanction in the meaning of the word? If the meaning of the word sanctions the practice, why admit a change by church authority? This is self-contradiction. Other denominations of pædo-baptists will reject this mode of defence; but ought it not to excite in them a suspicion, that their reliance on the meaning of the word is not well founded? The church of England, by its present practice, is as much concerned as the other denominations of pædo-baptists to vindicate pouring or sprinkling as being baptism. Now, if it was in their opinion possible to do this by an appeal to the word, would they have recourse to the authority of the church, to change the mode? The very claim admits a change. Is not this a tacit confession that, in their opinion, there is no relief for sprinkling, or pouring, in criticism? Does any one doubt, that if criticism could do anything, the church of England is not as able as other denominations to avail itself of its aid? Is all the learning of pædo-baptists confined to other denominations, that they alone attempt to find their practice in the word? If learning could prove that pouring and sprinkling could be brought under the meaning of the word in dispute, would the church of England fail to prove it? I maintain that the church of England is substantially on my side of the question. By resting on the authority of the church to substitute pouring or sprinkling for immersion they have decided the question of criticism against themselves. This certainly ought to bring those denominations of pædo-baptists to reflection, who have no pretensions to church power.

The error of the church of England in its defence of pouring, or sprinkling, is much less hurtful, as regards all passages of Scripture which concern the ordinance itself, than that of other pædo-baptists; but in another point of view it is much worse. It is worse, because it lays a foundation for the alteration of other ordinances, and for piles of mummery to an indefinite extent; but it does comparatively little injury, in explaining passages of Scripture that refer to baptism. The churchman is not obliged to force any of them, or avoid their true import. He can explain them according to their true meaning, and take edification from the mode, as an emblem of the union of believers with Christ, in his death, burial, and resurrection. This is an incalculable advantage, which the church of England possesses over other denominations of pædo-baptists: it contributes much to the production of clear, accurate, and extensive views of the Gospel. On the other hand, other denominations that cannot claim the authority of the church for altering the institutions of Christ, are obliged to find pouring or sprinkling in the meaning of the word; and consequently to torture language with the utmost violence. In this way, also, some of the finest features of the Gospel, which are beautifully displayed in the emblem of baptism, are entirely kept out of view.

It is often thought strange that there should be such a difference, for such a length of time, among good men, on so simple a question as the meaning of a common word. But with respect to persons who hold the views of my present antagonist, the thing is not at all strange. How can there be agreement when the parties do not judge by the same standard? My antagonist builds on the authority of his church, to alter the mode of ritual ordinances: I utterly reject this foundation, and seek authority only in the meaning of the word. The saints in heaven could not agree on any subject, should they adopt different standards of judgment. If Mr. Bickersteth, and his friends, have authority to alter the mode of a ritual ordinance, they may undoubtedly pour or sprinkle in defiance of the meaning of any word. If I do not choose to claim a like authority, I must be contented to observe the ordinance as Christ enjoined it.

Section IV.—" Let us now," says the writer, " produce Mr. C.'s own conclusions, and examine which of these views his critical inquiries confirm. They shall, to avoid all error, be stated in his own words. ' 1st. *Bapto*, except when it signifies to dye, denotes *mode*, and nothing but mode. 2dly. *Bapto* and *baptizo* are exactly the same in meaning, as to increase or diminution of the action. That the one is more or less than the other, as to mode or frequency, is a groundless conceit. 3rdly. There is one important difference. *Bapto* is never used to denote the ordinance of baptism, and *baptizo* never signifies to dye. The primitive word has two meanings,—the primary, to dip; the secondary, to dye. But the derivative is formed to modify the primary only. 4thly. *Bapto* means also to dye. And although this meaning arose from the mode of dyeing by dipping, yet the word has come by appropriation to denote *dyeing* without reference to mode. As this point is of material consequence in this controversy, I shall establish it by examples that put it beyond question. Nothing in the history of words is more common than to enlarge or diminish their signification. Ideas not originally included are often affixed, while others drop ideas originally asserted. In this way, *bapto*, from signifying mere mode, came to be applied to a certain operation usually performed in that mode. From signifying to dip, it came to signify to dye by dipping, because this was the way in which things were usually dyed. And afterwards, from dyeing by dipping, it came to denote dyeing in any manner. A like process may be shown in the history of a thousand other words.' " On this the writer makes the following observations :—" These remarks are distinct and clear. They are also substantially true. But it is most strange the clear-headed author does not see how expressly they overthrow his own theory. He has given us the strongest warrant for extending the meaning of *baptizo*, by showing us the like extension in its primitive, *bapto*, from the very same cause. He has proved that the idea of mode is secondary, and non-essential, when *baptizo* is applied to the sacrament of Christ, by proving the very same of its primitive, *bapto*, when used in the sense of dyeing. The author has left no link wanting in his own refutation. The two words originally signify the same as to mode. *Bapto* acquires the secondary sense of dyeing; *baptizo* acquires the secondary sense of baptizing. *Bapto*, from dyeing by dipping, comes to denote dyeing in any manner. *Baptizo*, from baptizing by dipping, comes to denote baptizing in any manner. What analogy can be more perfect? What justification of the practice of the church can be more complete?"

Here my opponent thinks he has irrefragably refuted me out of my own mouth. He has turned my critical doctrines against myself, and showed that instead of proving my own views of the meaning of the word in dispute, I have unanswerably proved his meaning. But with the utmost ease I shall wrest my weapons out of his hands. I have shown the principles that operate in the appropriation of words, and that words often wander far from their original import, being sometimes restricted in their use, and sometimes most capriciously extended; still, however, even in their wildest freaks, guided by principle, and capable of being definitely ascertained. I exemplified this in the case of *bapto;* and my present antagonist thinks he can turn the force of all that I have said, to demonstrate that there is a like change in the meaning of *baptizo*. There is not, he thinks, a link in the chain wanting. In this, however, he is altogether mistaken. He wants an essential link. *Use has actually conferred the alleged meaning on bapto—use has not conferred the alleged meaning on baptizo.* Now where is his demonstration? He might allege the authority of my philosophy to prove the possibility of such a change in the meaning of the word; but without proof that the process has *actually taken place* in the history of the word, this is of no service to his cause. Here is a poor Jew. I admit that though he is not now worth a farthing, he may, possibly, before his death, be another Rothschild. At the end of thirty or forty years, my antagonist comes to me, saying, "I will prove by your own admissions that the Jew of whom we were speaking is now as rich as Rothschild. Did you not forty years ago admit that it was possible, that this man might in time become so rich?" I admit this, but I want proof that the thing admitted to be possible, has actually taken place. Just so with respect to these words. Give me the same proof that *baptizo*, in the New Testament, has been brought to designate the ordinance of Christ without reference to mode, as there is that *bapto* signifies to dye, and I will at once warrant the change by my philosophy. The gold coin called a sovereign is now worth twenty shillings. I admit that at some future time it may pass for fifteen shillings, or that it may be raised to the value of twenty-five shillings. Will this prove at any specified time that either of these things has actually taken place?

But I shall examine the conclusions of my opponent step by step. Speaking of my proof of the secondary meaning of *bapto*, he says, "He has given us the strongest warrant for extending the meaning of *baptizo*, by showing us the like extension in its primitive, *bapto*, from the very same cause." I have given a warrant that usage has such a power, but I have given no warrant that, in this instance, it has availed itself of that power. On the contrary, I deny that use has ever exercised this power on this word. I have shown a process by which a word may receive a secondary signification, totally excluding the idea that is essential to the primary. But does this imply that any particular word has actually undergone such process, and received such secondary meaning? If the history of the word does not manifest such meaning, it has no warrant.

" He has proved," says the writer, " that the idea of mode is secondary and non-essential, when *baptizo* is applied to the sacrament of Christ, by proving the very same of its primitive *bapto* when used in the sense of dyeing." By what process does this conclusion follow? Because it is proved that *bapto* has come to a secondary meaning which excludes mode, does it follow that when *baptizo* is appropriated to an ordinance of Christ, it excludes mode? He might as well allege, that because *bapto* signifies to dye, *baptizo*, in the ordinance of baptism, must signify to dye. *Bapto* has, without doubt, in its history, taken the secondary meaning of dyeing. *Baptizo*, when applied to the ordinance of Christ, has not laid aside its meaning as to mode. Appropriation produces no such effect. But what does the writer mean by secondary and non-essential? Were it even true that mode is secondary, it does not thereby become non-essential.

" The author," says the writer, " has left no link in the chain wanting in his own refutation." A writer when he speaks thus, should be very sure that he stands on firm ground, and that he thoroughly understands what he is saying. That he speaks at random, I can show in a moment. But let us examine the chain. " The two words originally signify the same thing as to mode." Quite correct. Let this be the first link of the chain. " *Bapto* acquires the secondary sense of dyeing." This is my doctrine. I admit that it has this meaning totally independent of mode. Let this link, then, be made as strong as the smith can forge it; it is made of the very best iron. The next link is, " *baptizo* acquires the secondary sense of baptizing." This link is pot metal; it will break the first snap. What does he mean by the word baptize in these circumstances? Does he mean that it designates the ordinance to which it refers without the expression of mode? If he does, he is wrong: if he does not, it is nothing to his purpose. What can baptize in its appropriated application mean, but to immerse for a particular purpose? Is this anything but the primary meaning of the word with a particular reference? The writer confounds the appropriation of a word, with a secondary meaning acquired by gradual use. When a word is appropriated, it is taken in its proper sense at the time of its appropriation: when a word has acquired a secondary sense by use, it has departed from its primary sense. To make the thing still more plain, let us take another word for illustration, and suppose that *raino*, to *sprinkle*, had been used. According to our author's way of criticising, it would be said, the word primarily signifies to *sprinkle*, but as applied to the ordinance of Christ, it signifies secondarily to *rantize*. Now what can *rantize* mean, in such circumstances, but to *sprinkle for a particular purpose*—to sprinkle with reference to this ordinance? Would there be here any departure from the primary meaning of sprinkle? Let us again illustrate by the passover. The Jews were commanded to *sprinkle* the blood on the door-posts. Now does *sprinkle* in this command lose the idea of mode, and refer to the performance of the rite without reference to *sprinkling*? It is shameful for a scholar to trifle : it is awful for a Christian to cavil. Surely a very child may see, that the appropriation of a word to a particular purpose, does not divest that word of its meaning. The only difference is, that it gives the meaning a peculiar reference to a particular object. The author of this note applies my doctrine to his purpose, only because he does not thoroughly understand it. He has undoubtedly made some progress; and if he continues in this teachable temper, I will more readily acknowledge him to be my disciple, than I will newly-born infants to be called the disciples of Christ.

The next link of the chain is, "*Bapto*, from dyeing by dipping, comes to denote dyeing in any manner." This link is as strong as adamant. I admit that I have taught this; but this chain is like the toes of Nebuchadnezzar's image, partly of iron and partly of miry clay. The next link is of clay of the most brittle constitution. "*Baptizo*, from baptizing by dipping, comes to denote baptizing in any manner." This is mere mud. *Where is the proof that the process has actually taken place?* Had the change taken place, my doctrine would recognise it; but there must be proof of the actual change. Even were it in proof that the change had actually taken place, though my doctrine must recognise it, it would not prove that anything but immersion is scripture baptism.

Any change in the word, *after* its application to the ordinance, is of no authority, as to its use in reference to the ordinance. Had sprinkling been universally adopted at any period, in place of immersion, by those who spoke the Greek language; and had the word which now designates immersion been applied to sprinkling, the fact would have no weight at all, in proving that sprinkling is warranted by the Scriptures. The meaning of the word, in reference to the ordinance, must be determined by its meaning *at the time* of its application to the ordinance. Its meaning in the ordinance must be determined by its sense in the language at the period of appropriation, not by its use in church history in after ages. Does not any one see that a secondary meaning conferred after the institution of the ordinance, can have no bearing on the question? If in its appropriation to the ordinance, it signified *immerse*, as the writer admits, immersion it must be for ever, as far as Christ's authority is regarded. Is it not enjoined in the sense of the word at the time? No after change in the rite, and in the meaning of the word according to the change of the rite, can affect the meaning of the word as it stands in Christ's institution. I am utterly at a loss to conceive how any person of ordinary capacity, can attempt to fasten on a word in Scripture, a meaning which use is supposed to have conferred on the word in after times. This is the same thing as to expound some words in our translation of Scripture by their present use, instead of their old English acceptation. What should we think of an expositor who should expound the word *charity*, in Scripture, agreeably to its present use in the language? To make blindness itself see this truth, let us take an illustration. Suppose that inspiration had recorded the ordinance in *English*, and that the mode had been at first sprinkling; but that in process of time it had been universally superseded by immersion;—how would the secondary meaning of sprinkling in this ordinance, determine the meaning of the word sprinkle in the original institution? Would this be a warrant to neglect the scriptural mode of the ordinance, and to observe it according to after use? Will obstinacy never yield to argument? Will Christians for ever resist the commandments of Christ? And is Mr. Bickersteth the man to sanction such perverted criticism, in order to make void the law of God as to the mode of a Divine ordinance? Sophistry may invent evasions that for a time may impose on the ignorant, the unwary, and the prejudiced; but it is a fearful thing to lead away the disciples of Christ from implicit and universal obedience to his commandments. Jesus has said, that whosoever shall annul one of the least of his commandments, and teach men so, the same shall be called the least in the kingdom of heaven. Reviewers, and periodicals, and prejudiced religious sects, may laud such efforts, but Jesus will at last judge the world, and determine between truth and error. One mode is the same to me as another, had not God interposed his authority; but I cannot force the word of God to sanction human errors. I read the word of God not to find a sanction for the practice of any church—not to find a sanction for my own pratice; but to know what God requires, that to this I may conform my practice.

Section V.—My opponent proceeds next to the subjects of baptism. Here he observes with respect to my treatise, that this part of it is less than half the length of the former. Is this also in his estimation an evidence of my view of comparative importance?

The writer confines his remarks to my view of the import of the commission. " And first," says he, " let us hear Mr. C.'s own statement: ' If our minds were not influenced by prejudice, this inquiry (that is, into the subjects of baptism,) would not be tedious. We have the answer obviously in the words of the apostolic commission. The persons whom it warrants to be baptized, are scholars of Christ, have believed in him for salvation. If this needed confirmation, we have it in the record by Mark. The persons whom Matthew calls disciples, Mark calls believers. None then are warranted to be baptized but disciples or believers. I will risk the credit of my understanding on showing, that, according to this commission, believers only are to be baptized. I would gainsay an angel from heaven, who should say that this commission may extend to the baptism of any but believers. Here I stand entrenched, and I defy the ingenuity of earth and hell to drive me from my position. If infants are baptized, it is from another commission, and it is another baptism, founded on another principle. Even if there were such, when these infants believe the gospel, they must be baptized according to the command, Matt. xxviii., without regard to their baptism in infancy. The commission commands all men to be baptized, on believing the Gospel. Who is he that dares substitute infant baptism for the baptism of believers? Whoever he is, he is the man who by his tradition makes void the law of God.'" I had said that five minutes is sufficient to determine the subjects of baptism from the commission in either Matthew or Luke; this the writer thinks very strange, especially as I allow that so great a majority of Christians do not agree with me on this subject. But I will now reduce the time to half the allowance. I will grant no more than two minutes and a half, and still I may have time to spare. My antagonist should have had the perspicacity to see that I do not rest on the time necessary to examine the foundations of the baptism of analogy and tradition; I have shown that if there is such a baptism, it cannot shelter itself under the commission.

On my statements referred to by my antagonist, he says, " These are hard words and strong charges; and strange to say, they have not a syllable in the text on which to rest; nothing but the bare assertion of the writer." I will make good every syllable in my statement. Let us then hear the grounds of the assertion. " The commission of Christ," says he, " does not contain the words, Go and baptize believers." Does the writer mean that baptism is not in Mark xvi. 16, enjoined on believers? This must be his meaning, or his assertion would have no bearing on the subject. In direct opposition to this, I maintain that baptism is expressly enjoined on believers in this passage, " Go ye into all the world, and preach the Gospel to every creature. He that believeth, and is baptized, shall be saved." Does the writer mean, that because the word relating to the ordinance in question is used as a participle, and not in the imperative mood, there is no command expressed? If he does, I forbear to speak as I think of such an assertion. If anything else could be forcibly taken out of his words, I should think it an insult to a scholar to understand him in this sense; and as a matter of fact, I hesitated so ascribe this meaning to him till I saw that he himself explained it as his meaning in the sequel. Is it unknown to this writer, that what is usually effected by what are called grammatical modes, may be effected in various other ways; and that it is often optional in expressing a command to employ either the imperative mood or a participle? Even in this very commission, the command to go *into all the world* is expressed by the participle. But there is hardly a page of any sort of writing, in any language, from which I could not exemplify this. I wish I had not found this in a writing sanctioned by Mr. Bickersteth; for I cannot avoid saying that it is either gross ignorance or downright cavilling. I will make the most illiterate man in England refute this criticism. Suppose a rebellion had taken place in Ireland, and her Majesty had sent a commission, saying, " Go, and proclaim a pardon to the nation; he that lays down his arms, and takes an oath of allegiance, shall be saved." Would the most illiterate man in the empire say, that this is not a command to lay down the arms of rebellion, and to take an oath of allegiance? What a shame is it for learned men to make themselves ignorant of what is known to the most uncultivated common sense? But how awful is it for Christians to cavil with the language of the Spirit of God, in order to sanction the practices of men with the authority of institutions of Christ! Surely this writer cannot believe that there is no command given by Christ with respect to baptism. And if it is not here, where is it? How astonishing is it that Christians will adopt such means of opposition to the ordinances of Christ! "These are hard words and strong charges." But will any one show me how, with a proper regard to truth, I can say less? I would gladly say nothing; but when I must speak I must designate things by their proper names. When I see perversion so manifest, must I hide my eyes, or pretend to think that it is all legitimate reasoning? No. command in the commission to baptize! And does a. good cause require such a paradox to maintain it? Christians in some things do not see, because they will not see. Lord Nelson when once in pursuit, refused to obey the signal of recall; but to excuse himself he put the telescope to one of his eyes that was blind, and turning it towards the object, swore that he did not see the signal; and Christians sometimes do not see the signal because they put the telescope to the blind eye. I believe Lord Nelson was successful on the occasion, but shall Christians expect success in acting contrary to the authority of their Commander? Such conduct always implies contempt for the skill of Him who gave the orders.

"Still less," continues my antagonist with respect to the words of the commission in Mark, "Go and baptize believers only." Such an addition is not necessary in order to confine baptism to believers. If none but believers are enjoined to be baptized, none but believers are, according to the commission, to be baptized. If there is a baptism for others, it must have other proof. Has my antagonist, then, the hardihood to assert, that there is nothing in the commission on which my assertion can rest? My assertions in every tittle are true beyond the power of the perversions of sophistry.

"The only command expressed on the subject," says the writer, "is to baptize all nations." There is no such command either expressed or implied. The command in Mark is, to preach the Gospel to every creature, baptizing the believers. The command according to Matthew is, to disciple all nations, baptizing the disciples. The phraseology, "disciple all nations, baptizing *them*," necessarily confines the baptism to the persons who shall be discipled. The antecedent to the pronoun is the word disciples, taken, as grammarians speak, out of the verb disciple. The very nature of the thing requires this; it is obviously only disciples that they could baptize. Unbelievers would not submit to baptism. I will undertake to show the greatest bumpkin in England, that the restriction is necessarily in the expression. "Go," says a corn-merchant to his clerks, "buy all the grain in the market, storing it," &c. Does any idiot ask, what grain is to be stored? Is it not the grain that is bought, and not the grain that they could not obtain, or was bought by others? Could there arise a question on this subject? What would be thought of one of the clerks, who should ask, "Do you mean, Sir, that I am to store all the grain in the market, whether I can buy it or not?" Shame, shame, shame! Will the Lord's people trifle in reasoning about the commands of their Master, in a manner that would disgrace idiotcy? Shall they stave off conviction by quibbles, not to be exemplified in the most unprincipled chicanery?

It is evident that the writer's own conscience is no more touched than is mine, in restricting the baptism to disciples instead of extending it to unbelievers in the nations. It is merely a stratagem to bring me to terms. If I allow him to bring in infants as disciples, he will very willingly allow me to exclude adult unbelievers. "The only limitation," says he, "to be learned by inference, is previous discipleship." Now this expressly grants that there is such a limitation, and it is perfectly indifferent how the limitation is made out; it makes no difference whether it is inferential or express. But if it is an inference, it must be a necessary inference, else it has no authority. An inference might exclude unbelievers, but no inference can bring anything into the word disciple, that is not already in it.

"The words in Mark," says my antagonist, "contain no command to baptize at all; they are a promise to baptized believers." I have disproved this assertion; I have shown it to be unworthy of a scholar and of a Christian. It is so utterly unscholar-like, that had not the author himself developed his meaning, I should have ascribed it to him with great hesitation, even when substantially avowed in previous statements. The apostles understood it as a command, for they commanded the disciples to be baptized. Indeed, a promise from Christ to baptized persons implies a command for the institution; for God does not give a promise to will-worship. But to make out a command, I seek for aid from nothing but the words of the commission. "There is no ground in the commission," says the writer, "for saying that St. Mark calls the same persons believers, whom St. Matthew calls disciples. So far from affording an impregnable position, there is not a corner of the passage on which to rest the proof." What does the writer mean by this? Does he mean that the words of the commission in Matthew do not expressly assert, that those called disciples by him, are by Mark called believers; and that the words of the commission in Mark do not assert that those called believers by him, are by Matthew called disciples? This is very true, but for such a declaration we would not seek a corner of the passage. Who would expect such an assertion? Can it never be known that two accounts correspond, except there is an express declaration of the fact? then it could not be known that there is a correspondence in any two accounts in the different gospels. But on whatever occasions the things referred to by the two evangelists in this instance were spoken, can there be a doubt that they refer to the same thing? Are they not both an account of the sending out of the apostles to preach and baptize? Can there be any doubt that the two accounts substantially agree, and that the persons to be baptized are the same in both? Would Mark's account of the commission exclude any whom Matthew's account admits? Can any conscience be so hardened, as to refuse to admit that the disciples of Matthew are the believers of Mark? And does Mr. Bickersteth countenance such an effort to make void the law of God? Is he the man who thus labours to bring darkness out of light? Are the rites of a favourite church to he supported by trampling under foot the commandments of God?

"In fact," says my opponent, "the commission of itself, waiving other arguments, rather implies than excludes infant baptism. Taken in the narrowest sense the words allow, it commands all disciples to be baptized. Now a disciple is simply a learner. And the infants of pious and believing parents are, from their very birth, learners of Christ; they are by Providence placed immediately under the teaching of those who are themselves taught by Christ, and who are his appointed channels for imparting Divine truth to them. They are, in the strictest sense of the word, *mathetai.* Learners they are by the necessity of their age and by the privilege of believing parents, learners of Christ. To shut them out of the ordinance is, then, to reject those whom Christ has himself included." Of all the extravagances that I have ever met with in controversy, this is the most extravagant. Newly-born infants are scholars in the school of Christ!!! Sir, they are not scholars in any school; they know nothing of Christ, and can learn nothing of the things of his kingdom. A disciple and master, or teacher, are correlative terms, and in the very nature of things every disciple virtually recognises the master as fit to teach. Newly-born infants are not fit to understand a teacher on any subject, and cannot be disciples in any sense. But to say that newly-born infants are disciples of Christ, is to outrage common sense. Do they know anything of Christ more than they do of Mahomet? Can the writer produce a single example to justify his assertion? Is there any instance in which newly-born infants are called the disciples of Christ? Is there any instance in which newly-born infants are called the disciples of any teacher? Who were the disciples of Pythagoras, of Plato, and of all the ancient philosophers? Were they not persons who recognised them as their teachers, and received their doctrine? Who were the disciples of John the Baptist? Were they not persons who believed in him as a teacher sent from God, and submitted to his doctrine? Who were called the disciples of Christ when he was on earth? Were they not the persons who believed in him, and who followed him as their teacher? Since the birth of Cain was it ever heard that any newly-born infant was called the disciple of any man? Does this writer suppose that we will take his mere assertions as proof? Why does he not justify the alleged meaning by examples? Another person may as legitimately allege that new-born infants are the disciples of Newton, or any of the philosophers. He might as reasonably allege that they are mathematicians, musicians, or astronomers. I meet the assertion, then, not only as false, but as fanatical beyond the usual bounds of fanaticism. I meet it with indignation, because it manifests a disposition to hold a tenet, not only by forcing Scripture, but by sacrificing common sense; I turn away from it as from the ravings of insanity. Give me argument, and I will answer by argument; but I cannot put down extravagance but by exposing it. I solemnly declare, that it pains me to be obliged to write in this way with respect to a thing recognised by Mr. Bickersteth; but I cannot expose madness but by showing it to be madness. I once met a simpleton, who answered as if he knew every thing that he was asked. After some time, I asked him if he understood Greek. "O ay," was his reply. I then said, "Paddy, were you ever in the moon?" "O ay," said Paddy, with the utmost gravity of countenance. I followed poor Paddy no farther: and what am I to say to the man who asserts that newly-born infants are scholars in the school of Christ? Verily I can see no more sanity in this, than I do in the assertion of innocent Paddy. I hold up this assertion to the reprobation of sober sense in all mankind. Had such an assertion been made in defence of an unpopular truth, the author would be hooted out of society. But great sects screen their advocates in all their wildest conceits. You could not put the Faquirs to shame in the land of the Faquirs; it is only the advocates of unpopular truth who are obliged to stand in awe of common sense.

Were it at all necessary to my purpose, it would be easy to show, not only that the word disciple implies teaching in the correlate, and capability of learning in the disciple, but that it is applied to the followers of Christ as it did to the followers of the philosophers; implying that they have received his distinguishing doctrine, and submit to his laws. A man might have learned much from the philosophers who could not be called a disciple. To be called a disciple of Christ, implies not only to have learned something from Christ, but to have learned the doctrine of salvation, and to have submitted in all things to his teaching. But I do not need this, and therefore will pass it.

Could the writer satisfy my conscience that newly-born infants are disciples of Christ, he would relieve me of a considerable part of the burden of the cross of Christ. Nothing is so offensive in the country in which I reside, as to refuse to baptize infants. Men will not understand it in any other way than as denying infant salvation. I have no pleasure in being odious to the world; still less in being disliked even by the people of God. But I cannot wrest the Scriptures in order to please men, nor to retain popularity even among Christians. I have lost this world: I do not wish to lose both worlds. What Christ has shown me in his word, I cannot conceal or pervert: I must not be ashamed of his word more than of himself. I fight for no church, for no party. I do not make even my past attainments my standard; I am willing to advance or recede, as I am made to hear the word of command. When Christ says "Go," I will go: when he says "Come," I will come. If any man can show me to be wrong in anything, I shall be swift in changing my course. Truth is my treasure.

But the writer himself betrays his own want of confidence in this resource. If newly-born infants are really disciples, what need of any other proof for their baptism but the commission itself? Why is not the battle fought here? Why has he not collected all his force to bear on this part? If he proves that newly-born infants are disciples, is not the battle won? Obstinacy itself would not resist any longer. The newly-born infant is, on this principle, baptized as expressly by the commission, as its parent. But Pædo-baptists do not act on this principle. This writer himself, instead of opening a battery from the commission, aims only to show that they are not excluded by the commission. His chief reliance is an analogy and tradition, which can have no bearing on the commission, more than they have influence on the tides. He endeavours to force me to a compromise on the commission. If I will not allow him to modify it with analogy and tradition, he will force me to baptize the nations, believers and unbelievers. In this he is inconsistent with himself; he does not believe that unbelieving nations should be baptized; and the limitation to the disciples can have no influence in extending the meaning of the term. If disciples only are to be baptized, infants are of necessity excluded. Now this shows that his own conscience is not his own disciple. If newly-born infants are directly and expressly included among the disciples of the commission, why does he seek to modify the disciples of the commission by analogy and tradition? These two modes of defence destroy each other. Indeed, if infants are disciples, what temptation has he to make the baptism literally extend to unbelieving nations? All this management clearly shows that he has not himself full reliance on the discipleship of newly-born infants.

I ask the conscience of every Christian, as a matter of fact, is it as disciples that newly-born infants are generally baptized? Are they baptized because they know Christ, have believed in his salvation and character, and have submitted themselves entirely to his authority? Is not this mode of defence merely a desperate resource, to be employed in dispute, but which has no influence on the conscience? Do they who practise infant baptism believe that the children of Christians know more of Christ when they are born, than do the children of unbelievers, or even heathens?

"Nay," says my opponent, "the argument may be carried still further. We have reasoned as if the words had been, Go, disciple all nations, and baptize the disciples, &c. But these are not the exact terms. Our Lord's command is, Go, and disciple all nations, baptizing them, &c. If we press the force of the letter with Mr. C., setting aside all scripture analogy and argument, and all the testimony of the church, we should be led rather to the compulsory baptism of the ungodly, than to the exclusion of infants. It is reason, scripture analogy, and attention to the spirit of the command, which alone warrant any limitation; and these alike require that the only restriction should be drawn from the previous clause, and that the term disciples should be there interpreted in the largest sense." I have already answered this evasion; I have shown that the grammar of every day's conversation gives my interpretation to the words. Nothing but a spirit of the meanest cavilling would think of extending this command by force to the ungodly. I required neither analogy, nor the testimony of the church, to confine the command to those who are discipled out of the nations. This is the legitimate meaning of the expression. And as I have not been indebted to the testimony of these two witnesses, I will not receive their testimony in extending the meaning of the word disciples to infants. On this they are not competent witnesses; the use of the word alone can determine this. But there is falsehood in the very face of this evasion. The command to disciple all nations expressly excludes force, and it is in connexion with their discipleship that their baptism is enjoined. If they cannot be made disciples by force, they are not to be baptized by force; for it is after they are discipled, and as they are discipled, that they are to be baptized. I ask the conscience of my antagonist, if he thinks that the language of the commission commands the ungodly in the nations to be baptized by force. If not, is it not a fearful thing to handle the word of God deceitfully? Does he say that the principle that I employ to exclude infants from the word disciples, will compel the baptism of the ungodly? This is so false that it has not even a shadow of truth. These two things depend on different grounds of evidence. Whether *disciple* has such an extent in its meaning, depends on the use of the word: the other depends on the grammar of the sentence. Even were it granted, that analogy and tradition establish another baptism, still such baptism could not be brought by interpretation under the commission. No analogy can show that infants are included in a command to baptize disciples; no tradition can witness that a command to baptize disciples includes the baptism of infants. The thing is a matter of interpretation, not of analogy or testimony. Let tradition and analogy have their own baptism, if they will, but it shall have no lodgment in the commission. My antagonist says, that the term disciples should be interpreted in the largest sense: by all means: I will give it the largest sense that he can prove that use has ever conferred on it. But though an Englishman, he is thus like the Irish; no matter how good measure you give him, he must have a *douragh* (that is, something additional). He will not be satisfied with me if I do not throw in the infants as a *douragh*.

The commission, as it is recorded by Mark, commands believers to be baptized. Now if there is an analogical and traditionary baptism in infancy, such analogical and traditionary baptism does not coincide with the baptism of the commission; and as soon as the person is brought to believe to the saving of the soul, he is enjoined by all the authority of Jesus to be baptized into the name of the Father, and of the Son, and of the Holy Spirit. Should a thousand baptisms be proved from other sources, they could not make void the baptism of the commission. But as we are assured that there is only one baptism in the religion of Christ, the baptism of analogy and tradition must be a human figment. This is the ground on which I have placed the subject in my treatise. Many a lever has been employed to move it off the foundation; but it remains like a rock lashed by the waves of the ocean.

It is grievous that Christians are not agreed about the ordinances of Christ; but can union ever be expected as long as they reason on the principles of my opponent? Can that man want proof for anything he wishes to prove, who asserts that newly-born infants are disciples of Christ? Can he be at a loss in justifying the change of any ordinance of Christ, when he justifies the substitution of pouring, or sprinkling, for immersion, by the authority of his church? If such principles of reasoning are not abandoned, the day of judgment will come and find us still divided

That the utmost forbearance ought to be exercised on this and every other subject on which there is a difference among Christians, I not only freely admit, but strenuously contend; but when Christians submit their reasonings to influence others, these reasonings must be tried by the most rigorous test of truth. To our brethren in error we ought to manifest forbearance; to the defence of their errors no indulgence is due. If their reasonings are not only inconclusive, but if they lay a foundation for other errors, they must be exposed in all their deformity for the advantage of the whole Christian brotherhood. We should not judge the individual, but we should unsparingly condemn the false reasoning and the false principles on which his errors rest. Error is more noxious in a Christian than in a man of the world; its influence tends to withdraw believers from the authority of Christ. The salvation of infants I do not question; but their salvation does not depend on their faith and baptism. Faith and baptism are enjoined only on those who hear the Gospel. But I cannot consent to show my faith in the salvation of infants by administering to them a rite which Jesus has not appointed for them. An act of will-worship in the parents will not bring the infants nearer heaven. God abominates all human invention in his service. Let Christian parents pray for their children from their birth and before their birth; let them teach them as soon as they are capable of learning: but who hath required them to baptize them? Too much cannot be said to urge Christian parents to faithfulness to their offspring; but no advantage can be conferred by performing on them a rite which, in their case, Jesus has not enjoined. Could evidence of infant baptism be presented from the Scriptures, I am as ready to receive it as I was before I gave up the practice. Every inducement is on that side; but I cannot do in the name of the Father, and of the Son, and of the Holy Spirit, what Father, Son, and Spirit have not commanded.

5

PHILOLOGY OF BAPTIZO

INCOMPETENCY OF DR. HENDERSON AS AN UMPIRE ON THE PHILOLOGY
OF THE WORD BAPTISM, PROVED FROM THE UNSOUNDNESS AND EX-
TRAVAGANCE OF THE PRINCIPLES OF INTERPRETATION IMPLIED IN HIS
LETTER TO MR. BRANDRAM, WITH REFERENCE TO THAT QUESTION

SECTION I.—FALSE principles of interpretation are the chief source of
the corruption of the truths and ordinances of Scripture. It is not possible that conclusions so very different on almost every question, should
be grounded on the same words, if on all sides the same sound and self-
evident laws of language were employed in the deduction. The meaning
of the word baptism has no difficulties arising from its *use*, or its *origin ;*
and never has been questioned by any of the great masters of Greek
literature. The claims of *immersion* never have been disputed but from
the necessity of shielding present practice; and on grounds subversive
of sound criticism. Immersion can be evaded only by trampling on
first principles, and by establishing false principles. A more flagrant
manifestation of this I have never seen, than in Dr. Henderson's letter
to Mr. Brandram. He grounds on principles of interpretation which,
if admitted, would render all language definitely inexplicable. This
may be supposed a learned question, but I engage to take my unlearned
reader with me. To understand my arguments, and estimate their force,
I demand nothing but a sound and an unprejudiced mind.

"With respect to the Greek word *baptizo*," says Dr. Henderson,
"after having read almost every work that professes to throw any light
upon it, and carefully examined all the passages in which both it and its
derivatives occur in the sacred volume, and a very considerable number
of those in which it is found in classical authors; we are free to confess
we have not yet fallen in with a single instance in which it can be satisfactorily proved, that it signifies a *submersion of the whole body*, without,
at the same time, conveying the idea that the submersion was *permanent*,
i. e. that the body thus submerged, sunk to rise no more.* So far as
has yet been ascertained, the word is never used by any ancient author
in the sense of one person performing an act of submersion upon another;

* "It may be proper to observe, that even if it could be proved that the term was
used in Greek works of classical antiquity, in the sense of plunging a person entirely in
water, this would not determine the meaning attached to it in the New Testament. It
is an acknowledged principle in sacred philology, that numerous Greek words are employed by the writers of the New Testament in an altogether appropriated or religious
acceptation."

yet it is necessary that we bring this idea with us to the reading of the New Testament, before we can affix to *baptizo*, as there occurring, the sense of immersion."

On this single passage I would rest the proof of my charge. It teems with false principles of interpretation.

1. It implies that in order to prove that, with respect to baptism, the word *baptizo* signifies immersion, it is necessary to produce an instance in which it is so applied to the human body. Now, though we can comply with this requisition, it is arbitrary and unphilological. I refuse to admit the principle of interpretation. The immersion of a dog is as good an example as the immersion of a saint. What the thing is which is to be immersed, we are to learn, not from the word *baptizo*, but from the words in connexion.

2. This observation of Dr. H. assumes as a first principle, that no examples can be admitted as proof of the meaning of this word, in reference to the ordinance of baptism, but such as refer to the immersion of the whole body. Now the extent of the immersion has nothing to do with the meaning of the word. The meaning of the word is perfectly the same, whether the action of the verb extends to the whole or only a part of the object. Whether in baptism the whole body, or only a part of it, is to be immersed, we do not inquire at this word.

3. This observation of Dr. H. implies, that when the word applies to cases in which the person or thing immersed remains permanently under water, it is the word itself which imports the permanency of the submersion. This is ridiculously false. The permanency of the submersion must be indicated by something else. The word in question has nothing to do with the after state of the person or thing immersed. Whether the person or thing said to be baptized lies permanently at the bottom, or immediately rises, deponent saith not. Shall the word which signifies to immerse, also signify to emerge? But though we refuse to submit to this principle of interpretation, we could easily comply with it. How could Dr. H. forget the case of Naaman? Did he lie permanently under water? Was he not immersed seven times? Even with respect to Aristobulus, who was eventually drowned, it is obvious from the account in Josephus that he was several times dipped before he was entirely suffocated. If so, the action of the verb was performed on him without destroying him. He might have been saved after having been immersed. It was not the word *baptizo* which destroyed him. It was the keeping him too long under the water after immersion. "Always pressing him down when swimming, and immersing him as in sport, they did not give over till they altogether suffocated him," page 458. This shows that he might have been immersed without suffocation, and that suffocation was the result of several immersions.

4. The observation on which I am now animadverting implies, that in order to prove that the word signifies to *immerse* in reference to baptism, we must produce an example in every thing corresponding to the Christian ordinance. Nothing of this kind is necessary; it is quite enough to prove that the word has this signification in reference to anything. From the word itself we cannot learn that even water is

to be used in the ordinance. An example in which the thing is immersed in oil, or in melted metal, is as good as an example from the water of the river Jordan. Herod, in his last illness, was placed by his physicians in a vessel of oil; and had this been called a baptism, it would have been as good an example, as if it had been done in water, as a sacred ordinance. From the examples of the occurrence of this word, we inquire merely the meaning of the word; from other words we learn what is essential to the rite.

5. The observation quoted from Dr. H. implies, that the application of the word to persons and to things affects the meaning of the word. How is the meaning of the word affected by the objects of its reference? It has perfectly the same signification when applied to persons, that it has when applied to things.

6. Dr. H. here assumes as a first principle, that in order to prove immersion as the mode of baptism, we must give an example in which the word is used by ancient authors, in cases where one person immerses another. Was ever demand more unreasonable? Was ever a law of criticism more monstrously absurd? What has the meaning of the word to do with the persons by whom the action of the verb is to be performed? Is it the word itself that is to determine this? Dr. H. absurdly confounds the meaning of the word that designates this ordinance, with the whole pattern of the rite in all its parts and circumstances. Are we to expect in Greek literature a pattern for the whole rite of Christian baptism? Can anything be more extravagantly unreasonable than this demand? From Greek literature we are to learn the meaning of the word, and from the New Testament we are to learn whether we are to baptize ourselves or be baptized by others! Can sobriety designate such observations as anything but perverse cavilling to avoid the law of Christ? Can such arguments really weigh in any conscience?

7. Dr. H. here demands from ancient authors an example in which one person immerses another, yet an example from ancient authors to determine the meaning of the word he accounts of no value. This is inconsistent and absurd. Ancient authors are competent to determine the meaning of a word in their time, which must still be received as the meaning of the word, except a change is proved; they are no authority, whether in a Christian rite one person is to perform an act of immersion on another, or every one is to immerse himself. The ancients are called in to do what they are not competent to do; and they are refused to be heard in the testimony which they are competent to give. Could any evidence satisfy men who are so unreasonable? Could any kind of proof overcome such obstinacy? Can the man be in search of truth, who will not allow Greek writers to be an authority for the meaning of a word in their own language, while he considers their authority essential for the proof of something enjoined in a Christian rite? Should one rise from the dead, he could not satisfy incredulity so perverse.

8. Were it admitted as a first principle, that in order to prove that *baptizo* signifies to *immerse*, in reference to the ordinance of baptism, an example must be given in which the word is used when one person

performs an act of immersion upon another, followed by immediate emersion, does not Mr. H. perceive that this equally destroys the claims of *purify*, the sense for which he now contends? Can an instance be given from ancient authors in which this is used to designate an act of purification performed by one person on another? In making such a demand, he may have thought himself secure against retaliation, by relying on the rites of purification under the law. But a little perspicacity would have enabled him to see that this is a false refuge. Instances may be produced in abundance in which one person purifies another; but the case requires that such purification shall be designated by the word in question. Can he, then, give one instance from ancient authors, in which the word designates an act of purification as performed by one person on another? Now can anything be more unreasonable than that obstinacy which demands from a meaning which it rejects, a condition which is equally wanting to that meaning which it receives as demonstrably certain? Can that mind be in a proper state for weighing the evidence of truth, that is so partially balanced? This is a suicidal argument. But could President Beecher or Dr. H. produce authority from use proving that the word in question signifies to *purify*, I would make no farther demand in order to admit its competency.

Upon the whole, no word in any language could have its meaning definitely ascertained on the principles involved in the passage quoted. The author demands that the words should determine the objects to be subjected to the action of the verb, the persons by whom the action of the verb is to be performed, and the substance in which the action is performed by the agent or the object of the action. He finds in the verb the baptized person, the baptizer, and the water in which the baptism is performed. The word itself has nothing to do with any of these things, whatever its meaning may be supposed to be. All I require from the word is, the nature of the action imported by it: every thing else I will rest on its proper basis. Persons who do not understand this, are not qualified to enter into the discussion of this, or any other philological question. In reality, the most illiterate men of good sense are better qualified to find out truth, than critics who adopt false principles of interpretation. The man who determines the meaning of Scripture, as he does that of the letter of his friend, is more likely to find it than the man who adopts chimerical laws of interpretation, that will enable him to prove any conceit, however forced; and deny any truth, however obvious. I maintain that on Dr. Henderson's principles of interpretation, there is not a word in language whose meaning might not be evaded. Here, then, the battle must be fought. It is useless to contend about the meaning of words in certain situations, till we have agreed on the great principles which determine the meaning of words. As long as our opponents hold the principles of interpretation on which they now act, it is impossible for them rationally to find truth. They may sometimes stagger on it, but it will be merely at random.

Dr. H. refers us to Mr. Ewing's Greek Lexicon, "where," he says, "the whole philological question is treated with an accuracy and ability which we have not met with in any other work." He gives us in a note, "the admirable classification of meanings which the learned author presents under *baptizo*." Now this will afford us another criterion, by which we may estimate the qualifications of Dr. H. to assume the chair of an umpire on this question.

SECTION II.—It is not my intention in this place to discuss the meaning of the word: this I have done on many occasions. I shall here confine myself to the science of the classification.

The first meaning is, "*I plunge or sink completely under water.* Used only in the passive voice and in a neuter sense." Now here is false philology at the very threshold. The *completeness* of the immersion, as respects the whole of the object, is not expressed by the word at all; but is known from the connexion. The same verb, the same voice, &c., could be used with respect to a person sinking in a quagmire up to the knees. The verb does not express that the whole of the object was subjected to its action, nor does it express that the action was performed in water. This mischievous philology brings into the word things that are not expressed by it, but by other words in the connexion.

2. There is a false principle in supposing that the meaning of a verb in one voice is not authority for its meaning in another. When it is said of a ship that "*it dips*," a foreigner from this example would be warranted in supposing that when he finds the same verb in the active or passive voice, it has the same meaning actively or passively.

3. Nor is it true, as Mr. Ewing thinks it is, that in the examples referred to, the verb has, strictly speaking, a neuter sense. In a free translation it may be rendered *sink*; but the word still has its own proper signification, and some force is supposed to be the cause of the immersion.

4. Mr. Ewing says, "Neither in these examples, nor in any similar passages, does it appear that the *putting under water actively*, as done by a different agent to the object put under water, is meant to be expressed by *baptizo*, but merely the neuter sense of sinking or going down."

In none of the instances referred to by Mr. Ewing, is the thing immersed an agent in its own immersion. A person sinking in water unwillingly, is not an agent. A ship sinking by the winds is not an agent in its own immersion. When the thing is expressed passively, as in immersion, it is the weight of the object, or the force of the storm, that is the baptizer.

But without any regard to this, and granting that the verb is strictly neuter in such examples, can anything be more absurd than to expect that occurrences of a word in which all agency is excluded, should prove a certain kind of agency? If in such cases there can be no agency, we do not look for agency. But is this any reason why the same verb, in an active or passive sense, should not admit the particular agency in question? The verb itself, as I before showed, has nothing to do with the agent who performs its action; and if the verb is used to signify *plunge* in a neuter sense, why may it not signify *plunge* in an active sense? No sound critic would have made this observation. Are not such examples, in every view in which they can be considered, evidence that the word in an active sense signifies to *immerse?*

When a person says, "I fell over the bridge and was immersed in the river," shall a foreigner show his critical skill in the English language by alleging that—"Here *immersed* is used in the passive voice and in a neuter sense; and therefore it does not appear that the *putting under water actively,* as done by a different agent to the object put under water, is meant to be expressed by the word *immerse?*" Would not an Englishman laugh at him? Shall learned criticism for ever trample on common sense?

5. "Ceasing to float," is one of the expressions which Mr. Ewing uses for this sense of the word. This implies that the word imports a floating previous to sinking. Now when this is the case, it is no part of the meaning of the word; it is as applicable when the object sinks immediately, as when it floats long before it sinks.

6. Another expression by which Mr. Ewing characterises this sinking, is, "I cover with water by sinking down." There is neither *covering* nor *water* in the word. All this false philology proceeds on the absurd supposition, that a verb embraces in its meaning every thing in connexion with it, in every occurrence. The adoption of such a principle of interpretation must lead to confusion and error; it is impossible to follow it without being led away from truth. It betrays ignorance of the first principles of language. Not contented with ascertaining what is the action imported by the verb, these philologists embrace in its meaning, the person by whom the action of the verb is performed,—the person or thing upon whom the action of the verb is performed,—the substance in which the action of the verb is performed,—the previous state of the object on which the action of the verb is performed,—the effect produced on the object by the action of the verb,—the extent to which the object of the action of the verb is exposed to the action, &c. They might as well make the word designate the whole Athanasian creed.

The second meaning in Mr. Ewing's admirable classification is, "I cover partially with water." "I am covered with water to a certain degree." Doubtless it is a very scientific classification that gives a different meaning when it is applied to a part of an object, from what it has when it is applied to the whole. What has the word to do with the extent or degree of its application to its object? It is not the word itself that informs us that its action is applied to the whole of an object, or to a part: this is done by words in connexion. The word itself has perfectly the same meaning when it is applied to a part of an object, as when it is applied to the whole. In the examples given by Mr. Ewing, is there not information in express words determining the extent of the immersion? "It happened that their march was in the water the whole day, being baptized or immersed up to the middle." Is it from the word *baptized* here that we learn that the immersion was partial? Is it not expressly asserted by the words "up to the middle?" Where is the difference in the signification of the word *baptize* in this instance, from instances in which it applies to things wholly immersed?

The other example is, "The foot-soldiers passed over with difficulty, *baptized* as far up as the breast." Is it not the expression "as far up as the breast," that informs us of the extent of the immersion? Surely a very child will know that the word *dip* has the same meaning in the expression, "I was *dipped* over the head," and in the expression, "I was *dipped* up to the chin." Is there a man or child in England that would assign two different meanings to the word in these situations? It blasphemes science, it outrages common sense, to call this classification an admirable classification of meanings. Were it not that my friends in England think I am too severe, I would certainly speak strongly here. But I will be as mild as the summer breeze.

I shall enable the unlearned reader to appreciate the merit of this part of the classification, by an example of the use of the English word *immerse*, taken from the Londonderry Sentinel. "On Tuesday morning, about ten o'clock, as his Royal Highness Prince Albert was skating on the spacious water in the grounds of Buckingham Palace, his Royal Highness unfortunately passed over some rotten ice, which immediately broke under him, and he *was immersed* to the chin in water." Now does not every child know that the word *immersed* here has exactly the same signification, as if the Prince had been *immersed* over the head? That he was only partially immersed is known not from the word *immersed*, but from the words "up to the chin." What an admirable classification, then, is it, that would have given a different meaning to the word *immersed* had the water been a little deeper and covered his Royal Highness over the head! I had scarcely copied the last extract, when I read in the next Sentinel, that his Royal Highness "was *immersed* over head and ears in the water." Now would any one who speaks English, think that the word *immersed* has a different meaning in these two extracts? Surely the word *immerse* has nothing to do with the extent of the immersion. Indeed, according to the philology of Mr. Ewing and Dr. Henderson, every line in the length of the Prince's body, and he is said to be five feet eleven inches, would give a different meaning to the word immerse, according to the depth of the immersion. Were I not determined to be extravagantly gentle, I should think it my duty to lash such trifling with the utmost severity.

But there is an absurdity on the very face of this classification, which renders it self-evidently false. It is not possible that the same word can designate both the whole and a part of an object. If one meaning designates that the action of the verb is applied to the whole of an object, how can another meaning of the same word designate that the action is confined to a part? And if it is not the word itself, but something in the connexion, which determines this, then the designation is not in the word.

The above extract will apply to the first meaning in the classification also. The word *immersed*, it may be said, is here used in the passive voice, and in what Mr. Ewing and Dr. Henderson would call a neuter sense. "Neither in this example, then, nor in any similar passages, does it appear that the *putting under water actively*, as done by a different agent to the object put under water, is meant to be expressed by the verb *immerse.*" Can any trifling be more extravagant than this? Will not every man who understands the English language, consider this as determining the meaning of the word? Will any man expect that a neuter sense will also be an active sense? The meaning of the word *immerse* is to be learned from every occurrence of it in the language; whether in a particular rite one màn is to immerse another, or every man is to immerse himself, cannot be learned by the word, but by other information. As long as our opponents allow themselves to trifle so egregiously, no evidence could convince them. On similar principles they might deny every doctrine in Christianity. As far as they have truth, they are not indebted to their laws of interpretation.

The third meaning in Mr. Ewing's classification is, "I overwhelm or cover with water by rushing, flowing, or pouring upon." Science, in classing the meanings of a word, will always ascertain the primary meaning, if it is possible; showing how every secondary meaning flows from this: amidst much diversity it will generally discover a family likeness. It will never ascribe a secondary meaning as long as the primary will serve; and a third or fourth meaning will not be assigned as long as the primary or secondary will apply to all examples. No meaning will be admitted that is not in full evidence from examples which necessarily imply it. These requisitions are self-evidently just; and no sound philologist will question them. Without them, definiteness of expression would be impossible. Had Mr. Ewing attended to them, instead of eight meanings to this word, he would not have found a second.

Nothing is more easy than to reduce to the primary meaning of the word, all the examples which Mr. Ewing brings to justify his third meaning. I have on other occasions disposed of every example of this kind. I shall here teach the unlearned reader to do the work for himself, by justifying my criticism by an example from his own language. Mr. Ewing's first example is, "To arrive at certain desert places full of bulrushes and sea-weeds, which, when it is ebb, are not *immersed*, but when it is full tide, are inundated." Now, even with ourselves, when a part of the country is overflowed by a river, is it not quite common to say that it is submerged by the river? Is it possible to give a more satisfactory justification of any expression?

In the "Pastoral Annals" we have the following sentence: "The peat, the common fuel of the Irish peasant, remained in great part uncut, for the incessant rains of the past summer had exceedingly impeded that important branch of labour. Much which had undergone the first process of sowing, abandoned from the same cause, and *submerged* in the accumulating waters, or drenched by torrents, was irrecoverably lost for all purposes of firing," p. 184. Will the most stupid man in England understand the author as intending to say, that the peat was actually dipped under the water, and not that the water came around it? But what no wise man or fool will say, with respect to the language which he speaks, a controversialist will solemnly allege as decisive evidence with respect to a dead language. Let a foreigner, with a smattering of English, try his hand on the above extract, on Mr. Ewing's principles of interpretation "Here," says the learned critic, "the word *suomerge* cannot signify, as some foolishly contend, to *sink under*, but to *wet, cover with water*," &c. The peat is not put under the water, but the water falls on the peat, or flows over it. The word, then, here properly signifies, I *overwhelm* or cover with water by *showering* down, or *flowing over*." Can anything be more *demonstrative* than this philosophical criticism? It is a truly admirable specimen of classification of meaning.

The other two examples, alleged by Mr. Ewing to justify the third meaning, are real immersions. "Of the land animals, a great part overtaken by the river are destroyed, being *immersed*." The force of the current immersed them in the river. "The river rushing down with a stronger current *immersed* many," &c. There is not a shadow of difficulty in such examples.

But in no view can Mr. Ewing's classification in this point be looked upon as scientific. What connexion is there between *plunge* and *pour upon?* How does the latter rise out of the former? Mr. Ewing may fancy that he connects these meanings by making them both signify to cover with water. But there is no water nor covering in the word. To *pour upon* and to *plunge* have no more relation than any two words in the language. Besides, an object may have something poured on it, when it is not covered with it. Still farther, a word which designates to cover in a certain mode, cannot designate to cover in a different mode. This would render the word unintelligible. If it signifies to cover by plunging in, it cannot signify to cover by pouring on.

Again, this meaning includes three meanings, more different than the first meaning is from the second. *Rushing, flowing*, and *pouring upon*, are all different modes, while there is no difference in the mode, nor in the meaning of the word in any respect, when it is applied to the whole of an object, and when it is applied only to a part. A horizontal inundation is as different from pouring upon, as either of them is from immersion.

Again, this classification makes the same word designate *plunge* and *pour upon*. The same general word may apply in a general sense to both, but no word can designate both.

Besides, what relief do any of these meanings bring to Mr. Ewing and to Dr. Henderson? The thing said to be baptized is, in every instance, even according to their own showing, covered with the water as far as it is said to be *baptized*. Is there anything like this in their mode of baptism? Let it be observed that Mr. Ewing does not here make the word to signify to pour upon, but *to cover with water by pouring upon*. If the object is not covered with water, it comes not under this meaning.

The fourth meaning in Mr. Ewing's classification is, "*I drench or impregnate with liquor by affusion, I pour abundantly upon, so as to wet thoroughly, I infuse*." Here the lexicographer mistakes the figurative for the literal application of the word. Is drunkenness produced by drenching or affusion? Is a man made drunk by pouring wine abundantly upon him? or by wetting him with wine? or by infusing wine into him, as you drench a horse? And I say the same thing with respect to immersion. When a drunken man is said to be *immersed in wine*, there is no literal *dipping*. Whatever may be the meaning of the word, this is a figurative application of it, and not a distinct meaning. It is to me overwhelmingly astonishing that a man like Mr. Ewing should expound such phrases as "drenched with wine," as a literal *affusion, pouring upon, wetting,* or *infusion.* I do not expound the phrase in the original as a literal *immersion;* the *immersion* is only figurative. Now a scientific philologist would first settle the literal meaning of the word, and then understand the figure in conformity to this. The figurative use of a word gives it no new meaning in the language, and consequently is not properly the province of the lexicographer. It needs not to be explained; for a good metaphor contains its own light. There is no need to hold up a candle to enable us to see the sun. Its beauties may be pointed out, but if it needs explanation it would be degraded. Besides, to explain or enumerate all the possible metaphorical applications of a word is impossible. They are innumerable, and every person has a right to issue as many new ones as he chooses, if he does it with good effect.

All the examples under this alleged meaning are evidently figurative. No person, I presume, after the thing is pointed out, will question this. If so, whether they are to be understood in reference to literal *drenching,* or *affusion,* or *pouring upon,* or *infusion,* or *immersion,* must be settled by the examples of the literal meaning of the word. I have no right to understand them in reference to *immersion,* till I have proved that this is the literal meaning of the word; and Mr. Ewing has no right to refer them to *drenching,* &c., till he has by the use of the language proved that this word literally has this meaning. This he has not done: this he cannot do. He has, then, built his house upon the sand.

Mr. Ewing's fourth meaning, I observe also, includes different meanings. Is affusion the same as infusion?

The fifth meaning in the classification is: "I oppress or overwhelm by bringing burthens, affliction, or distress upon." This use of the word, Mr. Ewing himself allows to be metaphorical. If so, why is it a different class of meanings? Why is it distinguished from the fourth class? Surely the fourth class is as really figurative as the fifth. Whether we say "drenched with wine," or "immersed in wine," the expressions are equally metaphorical, and both equally so with *overwhelmed with debt,* or *immersed in debt.* Even if figurative applications are to be considered different meanings, why are not all figurative meanings included in one class? Is every distinct figure to be a distinct class of meanings? Then, instead of one class or two classes of metaphorical meanings, we shall have classes innumerable. *To be immersed in debt,* or *to be overwhelmed with debt,* will be one class—*to be immersed in love* will be another, *to be immersed in trouble* will be another, *to be immersed in business* will be another, *to be immersed in cares* will be another, *to be immersed in pleasure* will be another, *to be immersed in wine* will be another, &c. &c. Each of these is as distinct from the others, as the fifth class is from the fourth. This surely is an "admirable classification."

Mr. Ewing unaccountably takes it for granted, that, in such metaphorical expressions, the likeness is between the objects in the figure themselves. But this likeness is between their effects. I may say with equal propriety of a drunken man, that he is drenched with wine, or that he is immersed in wine; but by neither expression do I intend to show the way in which the liquor was applied to him. Were this the case, I could not use both expressions of the same man at the same time; for the modes are different, and it is only in one mode that the wine was applied. *Overwhelmed with debt,* and *immersed in debt,* are equally good figures, but neither of them is intended to show the way in which debt was incurred by the debtor. We may be *drowned in debt, sunk in debt, buried in debt, burdened with debt,* &c. &c. Surely, then, such figures are not expressive of the way in which debt comes on the debtor. I venture to assert, that there is no instance in which the most unlettered savage of the forest makes the same mistake that is here made by the lexicographer.

But what does Mr. Ewing gain by these his two classes of meanings? Even were it granted that they import a difference of mode, all the examples, even according to himself, unite in showing that the things which are the objects of the action of the verb, are completely covered with water. Has this any appearance of countenancing a baptism by sprinkling a few drops?

"That it is used in the sense of *pouring upon, or into,*" says Dr. H., "every one must be convinced who will be at the pains to consult the important article in Ewing's Greek Lexicon under *Baptizo,* 3, 4, 5." Now I have taken a great deal of pains with these three classes of supposed meanings, and I affirm that there is not one example under any of them that will justify this assertion; and I think all my impartial readers will now have the same conviction. The fourth and fifth classes are figurative, and the third is *immersion.* But even admitting that it is *overwhelming, rushing, flowing, inundating,* it is not *pouring.* The *overflowing* of the tide, the *rushing* of a torrent, the *overwhelming* of a flood, are modes of the motion of a fluid very different from *pouring* a fluid *upon* an object. The examples given, then, to support *pouring,* as one of the meanings of this word, have not even the appearance of yielding their countenance. In every thing I complain of a want of philosophy in this able, accurate, and admirable specimen of lexicography.

Mr. Ewing's sixth class of meanings is, "I wash in general." This meaning is not assigned on sound philological principles. Every example brought to establish it will explain with perfect ease on the ground that the word signifies to *immerse.* If so, such examples cannot be a safe foundation for a new meaning. This I hold to be a self-evident canon, universally applicable to the words of all languages. A new meaning should not be admitted while authenticated meanings will serve. Give up this axiom, and universal confusion and uncertainty will ensue on all subjects. The sixth meaning, then, is dismissed, not on the merits, but for want of proof. The history of the word does not prove that it obtained such a meaning. The proof from 2 Kings v. 10, 14, proceeds on the principle that words which may in any circumstances be interchanged, are perfectly synonymous. After what I have said on this subject to President Beecher, it is useless to give another lesson. The man who grounds on this foundation is not a philologist, though he should speak as many languages as were spoken on the day of Pentecost. But I will enable the most unlearned reader to perceive the fallacy of this argument, by reducing the example to the English language. "Go," says superstition to the devotee, "bathe seven times in the holy well: he went and *dipped* himself seven times in Saint Ronan's well, and returned cured." There we see that our word *dip* is capable of the very use that is here made of the corresponding word in Greek. Now a foreigner, interpreting English on the principles of Mr. Ewing and Dr. Henderson, would, from this example, prove to demonstration that the English words, *bathe* and *dip*, are perfectly synonymous.

With respect to Judith xii. 7, Mr. Ewing says: "In this case, the washing could not have been done by immersion, being done at a spring or a fountain." Why so, Mr. Ewing? Is it not possible to get timber in the forest? Cannot immersion be performed either in or at a fountain? "The Syrians," says Dr. Joseph Wolffe, as quoted by the Baptist Magazine, "baptize the children in the following manner. The child is placed in the fountain, so that a part of the body is in the water; then the priest three times takes water in his hand, and pours it out on the child's head, repeating at each time the name of one Person in the Trinity: after this the body is immersed." Were not the Castalian nymphs said to bathe themselves in the fountain? Can anything be more absurd than to allege that immersion cannot be performed at a fountain?

Mr. Ewing's other example, instead of having any appearance of supporting him, is directly and palpably against him. It is not "wash thyself in the sea," as Mr. Ewing translates, but "dip thyself into the sea." Mr. Ewing builds a bridge on pillars of ice.

The seventh meaning in Mr. Ewing's classification is: "*I wash for the special purpose of symbolical, ritual, or ceremonial purification.*" I have on different occasions disposed of the examples alleged by Mr. Ewing for this meaning. My business here is merely with the science of the classification. Now, even admitting that the word does sometimes signify *to wash*, there is no propriety in making symbolical washing a different class of meaning. The purpose of the washing is not a part of the signification of the word, but is intimated by other words in the connexion. In the phrase, *washed from a dead body*, the word *washed* has the same meaning that it has in the sixth class; and the symbolical or ritual nature of the washing is known from the additional words which express it. That the washing is for a holy or religious purpose, is no part of the meaning of the word. Must a musician, when he designs to perform a sacred tune, put on holy fiddle-strings? Washing is washing, to whatever the word may be applied.

The eighth meaning in Mr. Ewing's classification is: "*I administer the ordinance of Christian baptism, I baptize.*" This gives the word no meaning at all, but merely as the designation of an ordinance, without any reference to anything which that ordinance teaches or represents. On this principle, the rite might as well have been designated by any junction of letters jumbled together at random, without being previously a word in any language. In this sense it has no relation to any of the seven other senses, more than if it had not a letter in common with them. As far as this meaning is concerned, the rite might not only have been performed in any mode, but it might have had any import imaginable. It might have been a symbolical pollution, instead of a symbolical purification. This meaning is self-evidently false.

This principle, however, is the only safe one on which to rest the propriety of transference instead of translation. Undoubtedly, if the word has no meaning in the original, but as the designation of an ordinance, it should have no meaning in a translation but as the designation of an ordinance. How could it be translated if it has no meaning? To give it a meaning significant of anything but of the rite itself, would be to mislead the reader.

But how can Dr. H. agree both with Mr. Ewing and President Beecher? Mr. Ewing gives the word no meaning, but as the designation of an ordinance: President Beecher gives it the meaning of *purify*. How can the same man agree with both?

It is a self-evident truth that any word in a language taken to designate a new rite, must be appropriated according to its meaning in the language. If this word has previously seven other meanings, it must, in reference to baptism, be appropriated in one of these senses. Can any instance be pointed out in any language, in which a word is taken from the language and appropriated to the designation of a rite, when in that rite there is no reference to the meaning of the word in the language?

As an argument for transference instead of translation, Mr. Ewing alleges: "From the various senses in which, from the foregoing examples, it appears that *baptizo* was used among Greek writers, it must be evident that no proper English term could be found when applied to this initiatory rite, to convey a corresponding signification." Here it is supposed that this word in this application has sense enough, if our language could enable us to express it by a single term. This eighth sense is not only not without sense, but it actually has seven other senses implied in its own sense. Yet the definition of the eighth meaning in the classification denies it any sense, but as the name of a symbolical rite.

The difficulty, or rather impossibility, of translation, it seems, arises from the impossibility of finding an English term for this eighth meaning, corresponding to the seven other meanings. Was ever absurdity so absurd, as the supposition, that a symbolical application of a word must embody all the meanings of the word in the language? Is it not enough that it corresponds to that meaning of the word on which it is founded? Should my opponents succeed in showing that the word in question has several meanings, I would not demand that, in reference to baptism, it must have a meaning corresponding to each of their several meanings. I should esteem it quite sufficient, if it corresponded to that one of them on which they pretend to found it. Here, then, this word, which, in reference to baptism, by definition has no meaning, but as the designation of an ordinance, is made to embody seven other meanings. This, surely, is an " admirable specimen of classification."

Here, then, are eight senses of a word, founded on examples, all of which I have, with the utmost ease, reduced to one signification. If simplicity is an essential in science, it is obvious that my view is the most scientific.

But Mr. Ewing should have added another class, in reference to the baptism of the Spirit. This, surely, according to his views, better deserves a distinct place in the classification than some of the meanings which he has dignified with that distinction. He founds this use of the word on its fourth meaning. This is self-evidently false. He might, without absurdity, allege that the meaning of the word in the Christian rite is founded on its fourth meaning in common use. But the word in the phrase, *baptism of the Spirit,* is incontrovertibly founded on the rite of baptism, whatever may be the nature of that rite, and whatever may be the import of its name. *Baptism of the Spirit* is a figurative expression, founded on the rite of baptism.

The figurative baptism, in reference to sufferings, should also, according to Mr. Ewing's classification, have formed a distinct meaning. This is as different from any of his other classes as his fourth class is different from his fifth. Mr. Ewing grounds this use of the word on the fifth meaning. Beyond question, when the sufferings of Christ are called his baptism, the reference is directly to the rite of baptism, and not to the mode either of his sufferings or of the rite.

Dr. H. must add an eleventh meaning to his classification. To *purify* is very different from *wash.* But Mr. Ewing's doctrine will not admit this meaning. This gives a distinct meaning to the word, which may and must be translated. Mr. Ewing's philology utterly forbids and defies translation. Can Dr. H. consistently agree with both?

But we have not yet reached the bottom of the mine of absurdity. Dr. H. declares that it is demonstratively certain that the word in question signifies *to purify,* while with the same breath he pronounces Mr. Ewing's classification admirable, though it does not in all its classes contain the meaning which is demonstratively certain. An admirable classification truly, which does not in all its range include the true meaning of the word in the ordinance of baptism!

Why does Dr. H. attempt to couple Mr. Ewing and President Beecher in the same yoke? Would he have his readers believe that the theory of Mr. Beecher is just the completion of the system of his predecessors, or that it is consistent with it? If President Beecher is right, Mr. Ewing and all the late defenders of *sprinkling* or *pouring* are wrong; and have spent their energies in establishing error. There is no more propriety in Dr. Henderson's identifying himself with President Beecher, than there would be in my identifying myself with the President. Indeed, the difference between Mr. Beecher and me is not so great as is the difference between him and them. Yet, because his doctrine is contrived to allow every one to follow his own accustomed practice, they are willing to have it thought that he and they are perfectly agreed. If Dr. H. now says that President Beecher is right, he must say that Mr. Ewing and all the other defenders of sprinkling and pouring are wrong. President Beecher will not oblige them to alter their practice; but he will oblige them to change their doctrine. Why are the sprinklers so willing to submit to President Beecher? Because they have to change only their view of the meaning of the word, and not to change their old practice. Had President Beecher obliged them to change their practice, he would have found them as restiff with him as they are with me.

My last observation on this classification is, that while the seven preceeding meanings all imply that, whatever may be the mode, the *baptized* object is covered with the water as far as he is said to be *baptized*, the eighth meaning employs but a few drops.

Here, then, are the sources of the error of my opponents. Is it possible that, grounding on such principles, they can come at truth?

Section III.—Dr. Henderson's observation with reference to the Syriac translation abounds with false principles and contradictions. I shall select a specimen. For a full and most satisfactory answer to Dr. Henderson with respect to ancient and many modern translations, I refer to Mr. Gotch's examination.

1. He is as sure as if he had been with the witch of Endor, that our Lord, in giving the commission, used a certain word which signifies *to stand;* yet he is equally sure that President Beecher has given the proper translation of the Greek word, which is to *purify.* Can there be a fairer specimen of contradiction? To *purify* is not to *stand.* If, then, *baptizo* corresponds to the word which our Lord is supposed to have used, it must signify *to stand.* This is a new theory.

2. As President Beecher has attempted to prove that the word *baptizo* signifies to *purify*, with respect to this ordinance; and as Dr. H. has declared that this proof is demonstration, either our Lord Jesus Christ was wrong in the word he employed in verbally giving this commission, and was justly corrected by the Greek Scriptures, or the Greek Scriptures gave a false representation of his commission. It is impossible for any man to agree with both. If Christ, when giving the commission to the apostles, used a Syriac word which signifies to *stand*, and if the Scriptures give a Greek word which signifies to *purify*, the Scriptures, so far from being inspired, are not a faithful uninspired translation. Cease, Dr. H., to pervert the word of God : cease to defend your error at so fearful an expense : cease to massacre the witnesses of God's truth : cease to contradict yourself.

3. It is self-evidently false that the word in reference to this rite signifies to *stand up*, or to *stand erect.* This would correspond to the rite in no view ever given of it, or which can be conceived. This is evidently a desperate resource, which can serve the purpose only of evasion, but which is equally opposed to both the contending parties.

4. Dr. H. says, that "it obviously suggests the idea of a person's taking his station at or in the water, in order to have the act of baptism

performed upon him." Here is another absurdity. If the word suggests the idea of a person's taking his station for baptism, how does it signify the *act* of baptism? According to this, we should have another word to designate the act of baptism, as this designates merely a previous process. Is *standing up,* in order to be baptized, baptism? Should a person *stand up in order to be baptized,* as long as Lot's wife stood on the plain of Sodom, this would not baptize him in any mode. According to this lucid philology, the word does not at all signify the act of baptizing. For that we must have another word. Does the command enjoining soldiers to stand erect call on them to *present* and *fire?*

5. Yet while Dr. H. makes the word designate a process previous to baptism, he makes it again designate the rite itself. Is it not the Syriac term which designates baptism? This is a contradiction.

6. If the word employed by our Lord signifies *to stand erect,* implying that the persons to be baptized took their station in an erect posture, at or near the water, does Dr. H. make his recruits of a few days old take their station at or in the water, and *stand erect* in order to receive baptism? Surely that which is essential to the meaning of the word is essential to the ordinance.

7. If the word signifies *to stand, to stand up, to stand erect,* how does Dr. H. makes it designate the purpose of the standing, and the place of standing? According to his own showing, these circumstances are not in the word.

8. It is assumed that the meaning of the word *baptizo,* in reference to this ordinance, is *purify;* it is assumed also that the version referred to is a translation of *baptizo;* must not the Syriac word, then, signify to *purify,* if it is a just translation? How can it be a translation of the Greek word, if it signifies *to stand?* Can anything be more absurd than to suppose that the word which is the translation of *purify,* signifies not to *purify,* but to *stand erect?*

9. If the Syriac is a just translation with respect to this word, and if the Syriac word signifies to *stand up,* then *baptizo* must signify, not *to purify,* as Dr. Henderson and President Beecher contend, but *to stand up,* or *to stand erect. Pouring* and *sprinkling,* and *popping* and *dipping,* are all impostors. *Standing up* is the true heir to the inheritance.

10. Dr. H. assumes that our Lord gave the commission in Aramaic. I have no objection to this as a possible fact. But it is not in evidence from Scripture, and can be no foundation for a Scripture doctrine. We have nothing to do with the language in which our Lord spoke : we must be guided by the language in which his words and actions are reported. To go to the language which he is supposed so have spoken, is to go beyond first principles. We have no more concern with the language which Christ spoke on earth, than we have with the language which he now speaks in heaven. Our opponents overlook first principles which are as clear as the light, and they bring in first principles which have neither proof nor self-evidence. Here, in order to have a good foundation, Dr. H. attempts to dig to the antipodes.

11. Dr. H. assumes, that if our Lord spoke in Aramaic he must have used the word found in the Peshito Syriac version. If that word signi-

fies *to stand,* there is the most perfect certainty that he did not use it: if he used that word, there is the utmost certainty that in that use it does not signify *to stand;* because in that sense it would not correspond to the word in the New Testament. What reason can we have for saying that Christ must have used either one word or another, but as such word corresponds to *baptizo?* Is it by necromancy that we are to find out what word our Lord used on this occasion? Do we know anything of the nature or mode of this ordinance, but from the New Testament? Dr. H. here absurdly pretends to find out the meaning of the word used for the ordinance in the Scriptures, by the word which Christ is supposed to have used in the language in which he uttered the commission, though the word which Christ used in conveying the commission cannot be even guessed at, but from the word used in the New Testament. This is like another of the author's exploits, in which he pretends to found the doctrine of inspiration, not on the declaration of Scripture, but on the authority of the Son of God, as if the knowledge of the authority of the Son of God did not itself rest on the authenticity of the Scriptures!

12. Dr. Henderson's advice to the Bible Society is inconsistent with his confidence of conviction with respect to the meaning of the word. He believes that it is demonstratively proved that it signifies to *purify.* How, then, can he advise to transfer the word, or translate it by any other word? It is an axiom, as clear as any in mathematics, that every thing in the original, as far as it can be ascertained, ought to be communicated in a translation of Scripture. There can be no reason for withholding anything with respect to one ordinance or doctrine, that will not equally apply to every other. If it is lawful to withhold the knowledge conveyed in one word, it is lawful to withhold the whole Scriptures. If it is lawful to mistranslate one word, it is equally lawful to mistranslate the whole. If any translator believes that the word signifies to *sprinkle,* or to *pour,* he is bound so to translate it. If any one thinks that it signifies *to purify,* as an honest man he must translate accordingly. But to advise concealment, or misrepresentation, of what it is believed God has revealed, is most monstrous. If any translator, after all his study, research, and prayer, is unable to determine the meaning of this word, I am not the person to blame him for transferring it. What can he do but transfer? Every one must act according to his own light. No man ought to be advised to conceal or misrepresent. God is the Almighty, and needs not the assistance of our dishonesty. Jacob would have obtained the blessing without his knavery.

13. Dr. H. scruples to assist a translation which renders the word *immerse,* while he thinks the Baptists very unreasonable because they will not co-operate with the Bible Society; though they not only decline assisting Baptist translations, but also assist translations which the Baptists disapprove.

14. Dr. H. assumes that the opinion of Mr. Greenfield, that the mode of the ordinance is a matter of indifference, invalidates his testimony about the meaning of the word, and of the words employed by ancient translations to represent it. Could any well-regulated mind urge such an argument? What connexion has an opinion regarding the importance

of the mode of an ordinance, with the testimony respecting the meaning of the word which denotes it? A sound mind is better than the gift of tongues.

15. Dr. H. assumes that the objection to the word *baptize*, on the part of the Baptists, is because it is an exotic; and gravely proceeds to show the same thing of the term *immerse*. Was there ever such trifling? The objection to the word *baptize* is not because it is an exotic, but because, as an English word, it is merely the designation of an ordinance, without expressing the mode, which is expressed by the word in the original. *Baptize* has become an English word, but as an English word it has not the sense of the Greek word which it is employed to represent.

Many people were astonished at the verdict of the House of Lords with respect to Lord Cardigan: there is not a man in the empire who can have any doubt with respect to the matter of fact. How, then, could all the noble lords lay their hands upon their breasts and pronounce the words, "Not guilty, upon mine honour!" There is no reason for astonishment. According to the first principles on which their lordships were bound to decide, their verdict could not have been different. The name of the person challenged must be accurately specified in the indictment; and it was not so specified. Just so on this subject. As long as our opponents lay down arbitrary and absurd principles of interpretation, it is useless to present evidence from examples. Were they ever so numerous and clear, the disputant, grounding on his first principles, will lay his hand on his breast and say: "Not proved, upon mine honour." Unless on one side or other our first principles are false, how is it possible that the meaning of this word cannot be settled? It cannot be from any difficulty in the word itself. No word in the language can afford better sources for definite decision. Was ever any word in any language so fully discussed? Is doubt to be eternal? I arraign our opponents as establishing innumerable false principles of interpretation, and as trampling on many of the clearest laws of language. Here, then, let me be met. We need not send the jury into the box, till we have laid down the principles on which they are to decide on the proof that shall come before them on the evidence of examples. I call on the unlearned of both sides to judge for themselves. I engage to make every thing plain to every man of good sense. My rules of criticism may be understood and estimated by men utterly unacquainted with the Greek language. They equally apply to all languages, and to all words of all languages. Let me entreat the studious and prayerful attention of every Christian to this controversy. To suppose that it cannot be decided is to insult the word of God. Were it the least of Christ's commandments, it ought not to be disregarded. But the subject is important in itself: it is important as it regards the peace and prosperity of the churches, the translation and circulation of the Scriptures, and the interpretation of the Word of God on every subject. It is a fearful thing to teach the children of God how to evade his commandments, by adopting laws of interpretation calculated to extinguish every doctrine in Scripture.

6

A FULLER STUDY OF BAPTIZO

SECTION I.—A WRITER in the Congregational Magazine undertakes to prove that *baptizo*, in reference to the ordinance of Christ, signifies to *purify*. Though in answer to President Beecher I have fully refuted that theory, I shall examine, at some length, what is advanced in this series of papers. The writer assumes that we rest on the ancient use of the word, without reference to later usage. Nothing can be more unfounded. We appeal to the practice of the language universally, and admit every sense of a word that usage has established. Our authorities embrace the whole period, from the earliest usage to the times of the apostles.

"If to dip, a dipper, a dipping," says the writer, "be the signification of these words, (*baptizo*, &c.) then, unquestionably, baptism was performed in this manner." This, certainly, is a valid inference. Were all his reasoning equally strong, it would be impregnable. The amount of it is, *if the words have such a meaning, then unquestionably they have such a meaning.* I am not disposed to question this. Had he said, *as the primary meaning of the words is confessedly such,* if a secondary cannot be proved from the usage of the language, then unquestionably baptism was performed by immersion, he would have said something equally unquestionable, and something to the purpose. This is exactly the way in which I proceed, and in which every one in search of truth must proceed, in ascertaining the meaning of words from written documents.

He adds, "If these words have some other signification, then it remains to be considered, whether, from any other source, we can learn how this ordinance was originally administered." This I most fully admit. If, in a single instance in all the history of the Greek language, a secondary meaning can be proved, I admit that such secondary meaning may lawfully compete with the primary, in every case, and that other proof is necessary to decide the preference. Surely this is an admission full enough. But had the word twenty meanings, its meaning in every occurrence must be capable of being ascertained, otherwise there is blame in the composition. "It has been thought enough," says the writer, "by the advocates of dipping, to show that there is nothing in the Bible to make this sense of the disputed term *impossible.*" This is not a fair representation. We do not allege that it is the true meaning, simply because it is not in any case *impossible,* but on the ground that no secondary meaning is in proof. A meaning may be not only not impossible from connexion, but may be entirely suitable to connexion, yet may not be the true meaning,—nay, may be the very opposite of the true meaning. In the expression, " He rode a *black horse," white* is as suitable to the connexion as *black. Suitableness to connexion is a condition of the true meaning of a word, but it is not a criterion.* We are, therefore, infinitely far from saying what this writer represents us as saying. What we say is, that WHEN THE MEANING OF A WORD IS ASCERTAINED BY AN EXAMINATION OF ITS OCCURRENCES IN THE LANGUAGE; AND WHEN NO SECONDARY MEANING IS IN PROOF FROM OTHER PLACES, THEN IN A DISPUTED PLACE NOTHING BUT AN IMPOSSIBILITY CAN FORBID US TO APPLY THE PRIMARY MEANING, OR WARRANT US TO ASSIGN A SECONDARY. In like manner as to a third meaning;—where two meanings are in proof, a third should not be alleged in any case till it is proved. The competition must be restrained to the two meanings in proof. If a third meaning is proved by examples, let it come into competition, but let a fourth be forbidden, except on the same condition. This canon is a first truth, and no candid man of common sense will ever refuse to sustain it. It applies not merely to this word, but to words without exception. For what can forbid the meaning of a word which is in proof, when no other meaning is in proof, and when the passage where it occurs can admit it? If the word is not proved in other places to have a secondary sense, and if in the supposed case it is capable of its proved meaning, where is the difficulty? How can such a passage be proof that the word has a secondary sense, when in such passage it is capable of the primary? If the word in the passage can have such a meaning, can it be said that the passage proves that the word cannot have such a meaning? This is to say that the same thing is both possible and impossible. But if a secondary meaning is in proof, then the *possibility* of the application of the primary, is no evidence that it is the true meaning. The claims of the competitors must be judged on other grounds. So far, then, are we from saying that mere possibility warrants primary meaning in all cases.

" And their opponents," adds the writer, " have been satisfied with proving that, in *heathen literature,* another sense is *possible.*" Now this shows that our opponents do not understand our critical doctrine on this point. They think they stand on the same ground with us, when they allege that, in many passages, the connexion will bear another meaning as possible. But this we admit without the smallest injury to our canon. Indeed, it is the very thing which I have often proved. The connexion may admit many meanings which are false; sometimes as willingly as it admits the true meaning. I do not ground the meaning of the word on the fact that connexion does not make it impossible; but on the evidence of passages which demand this sense. When I have done this, I repel objections by alleging possibility. I deny in this instance a secondary meaning, not because connexion always makes a secondary meaning impossible; but because no secondary meaning has ever been proved in any instance. *My possibility answers objections: the possibility of my opponents, even according to this writer, is the ground of proof.* Now mere possibility is no proof; but it is sufficient to repel objection.

"The principle which has been assumed by those who assert that baptism means dipping," observes the writer, "which has been sometimes, though not always asserted, but which has received little, if any support from fact or reason, is this, that the signification of the root of a word or its signification in classic Greek, is most probably its signification in the New Testament; most probably to such a degree, that no turning from the radical or classic meaning should be allowed, except when these are plainly impossible." This also is a misrepresentation. Instead of confining words in the New Testament to the signification of their roots, we teach, that not only in the New Testament, but in the language of all writers and speakers, many words depart widely from their roots. I have shown this in instances of the most extravagant departure. No writer has ever admitted or proved this to a greater extent than I have done; and I do not confine to classic use in the interpretation of the Scriptures. I admit all use until the very moment in which the document is written. Instead of teaching that no turning from radical meaning should be allowed, except where it is impossible, I teach that, in a multitude of words, there is a departure from radical meaning, without any impossibility from connexion. Where two or more meanings are in proof, which of them is the true meaning in any passage, is to be determined by other evidence. And with respect to classic Greek, if any other Greek has established a secondary meaning, I will admit such meaning as a competition. Can truth require more?

"Accordingly," says the writer, "in discussing the signification of *baptizo,* &c., they first look to the root, and to classic usage." This is our avowed practice. Certainly, with respect to all words, it is the natural process. It is the process followed by all philologists. In tracing the meaning of a word, and its change of signification if it has any, the natural course surely is, to begin with its origin as far as known, observe its first appearance in the language, and follow it through every successive stage in its history. But we have no objection to any process whatever. Let our opponents commence at any stage they choose; we engage to show that in no stage of its existence is there proof that it signifies to *purify,* or anything but to *immerse.*

But the author adds: "And then having fixed in their judgment what is the meaning in heathen writers, they take that meaning to the Bible, and because it is not absolutely *impossible* that the word should have the same meaning there, they declare that it certainly has that meaning, and none beside." In the only sense that this can serve the writer, it is not true. It implies that we carry the classical meaning of the word to the Bible, without regard to a different meaning existing in what they call Hebraistic Greek. Now this is not fact. We appeal to all Greek; and if there is any Hebraistic Greek concerned in the question, we have it, because we have all that the language affords, both from our own industry and the diligence of our opponents. We have not overlooked a single instance. We appeal to all Greek; and if in any Greek we should find another meaning, we would admit it to competition, though the preference might be justly given to the primary. In this case, however, there is no variation among the whole range of Greek writers. Indeed, the question of Hebraistic Greek has no concern in settling the meaning of any word. To the interpreter it is no matter what is the principle which has operated in the change of the meaning of any word. The fact of a change is what he is to ascertain. If this is proved, he is not bound to show the principle, or account philosophically for the change. This is not the business of the interpreter; but of the philologist. It is a matter of great importance to philology, and to the philosophy of the human mind; but interpretation and controversy have no concern with it. If my opponents could prove the change which they allege in the meaning of this word, they need not deign to account for it. Their business is done, when the fact of such change is proved. The difference between the duty of a philologist and that of an interpreter, is like that between the business of a coroner and that of a lawyer, with respect to the sudden death of a person who was the life of a lease. The certainty of the death is all that concerns the latter; the former must investigate the causes of his death. When the interpreter proves a change in the meaning of a word, he grounds on it, without regard to its cause; the philologist endeavours to ascertain the cause. Should I ever find time to finish my work on the canons of Biblical interpretation, Hebraism is one of the things that will demand consideration. But in ascertaining the meaning of any word, opinion of the influence and extent of this principle has no concern. If a word is proved by use to have changed its meaning, the change must be admitted, whatever may have been its cause: if this is not proved, no principle can prove its existence.

"It might be supposed," says the writer, "from the way in which some persons reason concerning words, that they were almost unalterable in their signification; that they were, perhaps, the most immutable things met with in this changing world." Who are the persons to whom this applies? There is no one in existence to whom it can less apply than to me. Have I not, in that which I have written on this controversy, most fully taught that words change their meaning? Have I not given examples showing that words sometimes change their meaning to an extravagant degree? But I have also taught that there are some words which have not changed their meaning; and that the word *baptizo* is one of them. In his second paper this writer endeavours to prove that the word in dispute usually signifies in classic Greek not simply to dip, but to continue for some time under water. The word is not more applicable to water than it is to wine, or oil, or any other liquid. It is not confined even to liquids, but applies to every thing that may be penetrated. And the continuation of the state after immersion is not at all contained in the word, but is learned from the connexion or nature of the thing. Nothing can exceed the absurdity of supposing that the word should designate both the immersion and the state after immersion. Even *duno*, to sink, does not imply continued submersion. It may be applied to a diver who immediately emerges, as well as to a millstone that lies for ever at the bottom. The very words *kill, die,* &c., do not designate a continuation of the state induced. They are as applicable, when there is an immediate re-animation, as if there were no resurrection. None of the examples alleged by him prove his opinion. Cork is said to be *unbaptizable,* not merely because it will not lie at bottom when forced down, but because it will not by its own specific gravity, *dip,* or *sink.* It will no more *dip* of itself, than it will of itself lie at bottom. If as supporting a net it is sometimes covered with water, it does not dip more than it sinks : and if it may be *dipped,* it may also be sunk. If it may be forcibly covered with water at top, so may it be forcibly kept for ever at bottom. If when restraint is removed it will rise from the bottom, surely when restraint is removed it will remain at top. It is said to be *unbaptizable* because it will not *dip* or sink by its own weight.

" It is dipped," says the writer, " but it does not sink." But it does not *dip* more than it does not sink ; and if it is *dipped,* it may be *sunk.* If external force dips it, external force may keep it in continued submersion.

The example from Aristotle, alleged by Dr. Gale, contradicts the doctrine of this writer. The passage asserts that the coast is not baptized at ebb, though completely overflowed at full tide. Does not this imply that the coast was baptized twice every day ? The word, then, cannot import a continued submersion.

The passage from Strabo is not fairly reported : " Things which do not float in other waters, are not baptized in a lake near Agrigentum : they are like wood, which may be *dipped,* but will not sink." Would not any one suppose from this representation, that Strabo had said of the things referred to, that they might be *dipped,* while the verb in question could not be applied to them ? But Strabo says nothing like this. Strabo does not say that " they are like wood *which may be dipped,* but will not sink." He says, " they float like wood." If timber may be *dipped,* so timber may be *kept at the bottom.* Strabo does not say that timber will not continue at the bottom, although it will sink. He says it will not sink. There is no expression of continuation of submersion in any of these passages.

With respect to the baptism of Alexander's soldiers, can there be a better test of the import of the expression, than the fact that it can be literally expressed in our own language? " They marched the whole day in water, *immersed* up to the middle." The continuation of this immersion is not contained in the word, but in the phrase, *the whole day.* The word would have been equally applicable, had it been only a single plunge.

" The same writer states," says the author, " that if a man went into lake Sirbon, owing to the density of the water, he would not be baptized. He might *dip* himself, or be dipped into it, but he would not sink, even if unable to swim." Now this is a strange way of reporting evidence. I appeal to every English reader, if he does not gather from this, that the document makes a difference between *dip* and *sink.* It neither expresses nor implies any such thing. Dr. Gale's translation of the passage is : " The bitumen floats at top, because of the nature of the waters, which admits no diving; for if a man goes into it he cannot sink, or be dipped, but is forcibly kept up." As far as this controversy is concerned, this translation is good enough, though it is not accurate. It is not " admits no diving," but *" requires no swimming;"* that is, the effort of swimming is not necessary to keep above water. It is not, *he cannot sink*, but *he does not of necessity sink*, that is, his own weight does not force him down. The word respects the *dipping* or *sinking*, and has no relation to the continuation of submersion. The same writer speaks of a river whose waters are so dense, that if a dart is thrown in from above, it is with difficulty the dart *dips*. Here the penetration of the water is designated by the verb in question. Nothing can be more decisive. But sound philology would never expect that the same word should express both an immersion and a continuation in that state.

"Lucian," says the writer, "introduces Timon as saying, that ' If a winter storm were to carry any one away, and he should stretch forth his hands, imploring help, he would push down the head of such a person, baptizing him, that he might be unable to rise again.' This person was not only to be dipped, but to be kept under water that he might be drowned."

No doubt the intention of Timon's baptism was destruction; but does this imply, that the intention of every baptism is destruction? Can anything be more ridiculous than to suppose, that the same word should denote both immersion and the intention of the immersion? Does not Lucian expressly declare the purpose of this immersion? Besides, does not Timon say, that he would baptize the person *on his head*, that is, that he would immerse him with his head *downwards*, that he might be unable to rise? Does not this imply, that rising after the immersion was possible? And, after all Timon's efforts, the baptized person might still have risen, as far as either this word or the circumstances were concerned. This is the most astonishing sort of criticism that I ever met with. The writer might as well extract the whole Athanasian creed from this verb, as extract from it that it designates only a continued immersion. It has nothing to do with continuation, or with brevity. Let us try this criticism on our own language. In translating Timon's expression we should say, " I would *plunge* him on his head, that he might not be able to rise again." " Here," says the critic, " the word *plunge* signifies not merely to dip under water, but to dip with the intention of drowning. Timon did not dip the man in order to raise him immediately, but in order to drown him. This, then, is an immersion of destruction—a continued immersion. The word *plunge*, then, cannot be applied to cases in which there is an immediate immersion of the *plunged* object." Would not the most illiterate Englishman laugh at the sapient critic? Yet this is the very criticism employed on the word in the Greek language.

Besides, intention and continuation are two very different things. There may be intention without continuation, and continuation without intention. This writer makes them identical. But this word implies neither continuation nor intention. There cannot be a more appropriate example of the meaning of *baptizo*, with reference to the ordinance of baptism, than this. Timon's baptism for destruction is as good a speci-men of the meaning of the word, as is that of John the Baptist, whose baptism was an emblem of salvation. No critic under heaven would think of extracting the intention or continuation of an immersion from the word that designates immersion.

On the example, "A pilot does not know but that he may save in his ship one whom it were better that he had baptized;" the writer remarks, " the meaning of the word here is obviously opposed to saving; it must, therefore, be not *dipping* but *drowning.*"

Even here the word does not signify *drown,* but has its usual mean-ing. That drowning is the consequence of the immersion is known from the circumstances in which it takes place. Let us try the criticism on the English : "The captain cast one of the sailors overboard." *To cast overboard,* or to *cast into the sea,* does not signify to *drown;* but if it takes place in the midst of the sea, *drowning* is the known consequence. And if we are not informed of his escape, this is the conclusion. Yet a man might be cast overboard, and escape. *To cast overboard,* then, is not the same as *drown.* So with respect to the word in question. If it is said, " Better the captain had *plunged* the fellow into the sea," *drown-ing,* we know, would have been the result, but it is not designated by *plunge.* I have no objection that the word should be here in a free translation rendered *drown;* and our friend Dr. Gale does so translate it : but the word has here its peculiar modal meaning, and nothing more. This is a point which on all subjects I have been continually pressing, but which I cannot get my opponents to understand. Words may, in certain circumstances, be commutable, when they are not at all identical in meaning.

" Most of the land animals, being carried away by the stream, per-ished, being baptized." On this the author remarks, " They would not have been hurt by dipping; they continued under water, and were drowned." The Greek word *baptizo* would not hurt them more than the harmless English word *dip,* were there an immediate emersion; and *dip,* if not followed by an emersion, will be followed by death as its consequence, as well as *baptizo :* and the latter may be followed by emersion as well as the former. The continuation under water is not here expressed by the verb in question. The animals swam for a time, as they were carried down the stream; but at last they sunk, or were completely immersed. The consequence of this was, they perished. Our word *immerse* does not express continuation; yet we could say, " Being immersed, they perished." Indeed, the perishing, so far from being con-tained in this word, is expressly mentioned by another word—" being immersed, they perished."

"As you would not wish, sailing in a large ship, adorned and abound-ing with gold, to be baptized, that is, to be drowned." With respect to this example, I say also, that the word in question does not signify to *drown,* though in this situation this is the consequence. Could we not use our own word *immerse* exactly in the same manner, in the same cir-cumstances?

" Shall I not laugh at the man who baptized his ship by overlading

it, and then complains of the sea for ingulfing it with its cargo?"
Can we not exactly express the same thing in English? "Shall I not
laugh at the man who *immerses* his ship by overlading it?" The continuation of the immersion is not in this word, whether it is *baptizo*
or *immerse*. The author remarks on this example, "He not only dips
his ship, he sinks it." He appears to think that *sink* necessarily implies
continuation; but it does no such thing. A thing may be made to *sink*,
and be immediately brought up. This is the case in the ordinance of
baptism, and in a thousand other things. A thing may even sink by
its own weight, and be immediately brought up. This was the case with
respect to the axe of the prophets, which sank in Jordan. Divers sink,
and rise again. There is no word that has the signification which this
critic confers on *baptizo*.

The same will apply to the ship which carried Jonah. If it was
about to be *baptized*, to be *immersed*, or *to sink*, it was just about to be
lost; yet baptism, and sinking, and immersion, do not express continuation at the bottom of the sea. This is the consequence, if nothing to
the contrary is expressed.

With respect to the death of Aristobulus, the writer says, "He was
not merely dipped, but he was kept under water till drowned." Were
this exactly the case, it is futile. It was not a mere dipping of him
that killed him, but the keeping him under water till he died. But it is
not said that the assassins dipped him, and then kept him under water
till he died. They dipped him again and again, till he was suffocated.
This example is the most complete proof, that the word in question does
not of itself designate continuation. The first baptism did not destroy
him; they repeated the operation till he was suffocated. This shows
that a man may be baptized without being destroyed. The writer
observes, that "This baptism is mentioned as obviously an adequate
cause of death." This, truly, is a very sage observation. If a man is
immersed again and again, till he is suffocated, does it require any other
evidence to prove that he is dead? Suffocation is a very sufficient cause
of death.

"The historian says, that the ship in which he sailed was baptized in
the midst of the Adriatic. It was not only dipped, but it went to the
bottom and remained there." Could we not literally translate this into
English by our own honest word *immersion?* "The ship was *immersed*
in the midst of the Adriatic?" The word has here its usual meaning;
the continuation at the bottom is all inference from situation and circumstances; and will be the result equally from the English word as
from the Greek. Indeed, the expression is perfectly compatible with the
supposition, that after the sinking of the ship it was by miracle raised
immediately. The baptism and the state that follows have no necessary
connexion.

When Josephus says of some persons, that they baptized the city, this
writer asserts, that the expression "means not that they subjected it to any
transient affliction, but that they brought it to complete and final ruin."
In direct opposition to this, I maintain that no such thing is expressed.
The immediate ruin of the affairs of the city is the only thing that is

asserted. Whether they continued in that state, or were retrieved, is not expressed by this figure, though it may be known from other evidence. As far as this figure is concerned, the affairs of the city might have immediately been retrieved. Should the city have been afterwards more prosperous than it was in the time of Solomon, this figure has nothing to object. Can there be anything more absurd than to argue that because a ruined city never recovered, the word which designates its ruin, must be a word that includes continuation of ruin?

"There is one passage," (in Josephus,) says the writer, " referring to purification from defilement by a dead body, where the word accords with the New Testament usage." The passage he translates thus : " Having immersed a little of the ashes and a hyssop branch at a fountain, and having also baptized some of these ashes at the fountain, they sprinkled therewith ' both on the third and on the seventh day, those who had been defiled by a corpse.' The baptizing is here mentioned as something distinct from the dipping, subsequent to it, and applying only to the ashes. Both the ashes and the hyssop branch were dipped, the former only were baptized, *i. e.*, purified."

On this I remark : 1. The writer translates *enientes* by the word *immersed*, and says that the immersion is stated as different from the baptism. This is not correct. *Enientes* is not *immersed*. This is not a modal word at all. It is a generic term, and signifies *to put in*, without any respect to manner. Ashes, when put loosely into water, are not said to be immersed, as they do not immediately sink. A powder is usually said to be *cast into water*, to be *thrown into water*, or to *be put into water* —not to be *immersed in water*. Accordingly, the Greek term exactly corresponds to this idea. It cannot be translated by the word *immersed* or *dipped*. Is it not most perverse to refuse to give its modal meaning to a word which is not, in all the Greek language, proved to have any other than a modal meaning, and to bestow this modal meaning on a word which never has a modal meaning? What are the boundaries of the extravagance employed to set aside this ordinance of God! How easily are our opponents satisfied that a word signifies to immerse, if that word has nothing to do with baptism!

2. The punctuation of the words of Josephus is evidently wrong, and has been made without attention to the rite as described by Moses. The hyssop was not *cast into* the water with the ashes; but the ashes being cast into the water, the hyssop branch was dipped, that by means of it the unclean person might be sprinkled. The comma, then, ought to be before *hyssop*. "Having put a little ashes into the water, and having dipped a branch of hyssop," &c. This is definitely described by Numbers xix. " And a clean man shall take hyssop, and dip it into the water," &c.

3. The comparison of Josephus with the Septuagint determines the meaning of the word *baptizo*. It is used here by Josephus to express the same thing, which the Septuagint expresses by *bapto*, which without controversy is *dip*. It dips the branch of hyssop. Here a Hebraistic Greek writer, even in reference to a sacred rite of purification, uses the word for immersion.

4. The ashes were not to be purified in the water: the ashes mixed with the water, were the means of purification. The water could not have purified without the ashes.

5. It is not " at the fountain," but " *into* the fountain." The ashes were put into the fountain—not put into something else *at* the fountain: the branch of hyssop was dipped *into* the fountain, not dipped into something else *at* the fountain.

6. Josephus here, in what way soever his words may be translated, makes an addition to the account of Moses. He casts some of the ashes into the fountain to make the water of purification; and some of the ashes he dips in such a way that they may be taken out, and sprinkled on the person to be purified. However he is to be understood, his words are to be translated, " and having immersed a branch of hyssop and also a little of the same ashes into," &c. As the ashes that were to be immersed were to be sprinkled on the person to be purified, they must have been put into the water in a bag as in cookery, or in such a way that they could be taken out. This is evidently the meaning of Josephus, though it is not enjoined in the law of Moses.

7. The translation of the words of Josephus by this writer, implies this equally with mine. His rendering is, "having also baptized some of those ashes at the fountain, they sprinkled *therewith*." That is, they sprinkled with those ashes. The ashes, then, according to this, were sprinkled on the unclean, as well as the water of purification by the branch of hyssop.

8. There is also a difference between Moses and Josephus in the preparation of the water of purification. Moses commands the water to be put on the ashes: Josephus puts the ashes on the water. The reason of this difference is obviously that Moses prepares the water in a vessel, while Josephus employs the whole fountain, in which process the water could not be put on the ashes.

" It should be remarked," says the writer, " that not only does it appear in these passages that the object baptized continued under water, but it is also clear that the writers direct attention to this point. This continuance is therefore not only a part of the object referred to, but it is a part of the signification of the term."

1. My philosophy draws a directly contrary conclusion from these premises. If the writers referred to draw attention to the point that the objects immersed continued under water, the continuation under water is no part of the meaning of the word. In all these passages the continuation under water is gathered from the circumstances, or is expressly related.

2. The writer has previously admitted that " an examination of the passages which have been adduced will show that it very rarely has this sense," that is, the sense of dipping without continuation. Now if it never so rarely has this signification, it is enough for me. The nature and intention of the ordinance will show that the persons to be immersed are not to be kept continually under water.

3. If in any instances, however rare, the word applies to cases in which there is no continuation, then continuation cannot be a part of the meaning of the word.

4. If there are some instances in which the verb is applied to cases in which there was destruction, and other instances in which there was not destruction, then destruction is no part of the meaning of the word.

5. The very example brought by this writer from Josephus to prove *purify*, proves immersion to be the meaning of the word. What the Septuagint designates by *baptizo*, Josephus designates by *bapto;* and it is not pretended that *bapto* signifies to *purify*.

6. That *bapto* should signify to *dip*, and *baptizo* to *drown*, would be an odd effect of termination.

7. The case of Aristobulus proves the same thing. It was not one baptism, but a succession of baptisms, that destroyed him. The assassins continued to immerse him till he was suffocated.

8. This doctrine is inconsistent with the hypothesis on which the meaning of *purify* is assigned to this word. Is not the ground on which *purification* is alleged to be the meaning of this word in Hebraistic Greek, the fact that dip was its common meaning; and that from its being so frequently applied to purification, it came at last to signify purification without respect to mode? Here, however, this writer, in direct contradiction to this, assures us that the classical meaning of the word is not *dip* but *drown*, or, continue in a state of submersion. Now if this is true, how will the word come to signify *purification?* Upon what principle could a word whose common meaning is to *drown*, come to signify *purify?* *Pour* or *sprinkle* would be equally suitable to the hypothesis, as the groundwork of the process from mode to purification without respect to mode; but neither of these is the ground on which the *purifiers* build their superstructure. They do not contend either for *sprinkle* or *pour* as the primary signification of the word in question. Could they hope to make good this as the primary meaning, we should never have heard of *purification* as a secondary, from Hebraistic usage. *Purification* has been contrived as a refuge, when they have been hunted from *pour* and *sprinkle*.

On the supposition that the common meaning of the word was *drown*, and that it was employed in reference to this ordinance, in the sense of *purify*, let us try the operation on the English language. Suppose that the ceremony of sprinkling with holy water had lately for the first time been introduced into England; is it likely, is it possible, that it would be designated by the word *drown?* When a few drops of water should be sprinkled on a crowd, would the people be said to be *drowned*, meaning that they were *purified?* And this is the very thing that our opponents do in Greek. They take a Greek word which in its classical meaning they say signifies to drown, or continue in a state of submersion for a length of time, and they employ it to designate purification.

SECTION II.—THE AUTHOR'S GENERAL OBSERVATIONS.—" Our first general observation is," says he, " that the context of the word in the New Testament is never that which is used, both in the classics and in the Scriptures, to connect verbs signifying to dip, with that into which any object is dipped; but on the contrary, the context is always of a kind which proves that, literally, it means some effect produced by water.

Where *bapto* and *baptizo* signify to dip, the context is *eis*, with that into which the object is dipped; as we should say, He dipped into water, &c. But this construction does not once occur in the use of *baptizo* in the Septuagint and the New Testament."

1. This observation is rash and unfounded. *En* is found frequently both in the classics and in the Septuagint, construed with *bapto*, signifying *to dip*. " Dipping but in cold water." Hip. 193. " Thou hast plunged me in filth." Job. ix. 31.

2. *Eis* and *en* are frequently commutative in such cases; and *en* is often used where *eis* might be thought more appropriate. Homer says of Iris, " She leaped *in* the dark sea." We ourselves use both idioms. " He leaped *in* the sea, or *into* the sea." Cowper says, " Eurypylus is shot *into* the thigh"—*in* is more usual. Again, "*into* his throat"—*in* might be substituted. Again, " Either to plunge some Grecian *in* the shades." This is exactly a case in point. To plunge *in* or to plunge *into* are good syntax both in Greek and in English.

3. Yet when *eis* and *en* are commutative, they are not identical in meaning. Each has its peculiar meaning, corresponding to our preposition *in* and *into*—the one implying motion, the other rest. The writer grants in the above extract more than I will receive from him. *En* never has the signification of *into*, though it may occasionally be employed where *into* is more usual, and more appropriate. When construed with *bapto* or *baptizo*, it is not so definite as *eis*. It designates merely the place or substance in which the action of the verb is performed. It will explain as well in English as in Greek. When I say that such a man " was immersed in the river Thames," all I assert is, that the action of the verb was performed in the river. It is the verb *immersed*, and the circumstances, that must prove the mode. This will appear clear to any one who takes an example in which the verb is changed. Such a man " was *killed* in the river." On the other hand, *eis* would express that the action of the verb was *into* the water. Yet I would rely on *en* with the utmost confidence ; because no reason can ever be given why baptism should be performed *in* a river, if there is not immersion. When we say that such a man " leaped in the sea," is it not as obvious that he leaped into the sea, as if the word *into* had been used? Do not we ourselves say " immersed in the water, or *into* the water?" Indeed *immersed in* is more common than *immersed into*. It is always more appropriate when the place or the thing in contradistinction to something else in which the immersion is performed, is designed. This perfectly accounts for the phraseology of Scripture in respect to this ordinance. The verb construes equally with them both : in some cases the design of the speaker will render one of them more eligible than the other ; while in other cases either of them will answer.

4. In the preceding extract the writer asserts that " the context is always of a kind which proves that literally it means some effect produced by water." So far from proving that this is always the case, the context never, in a single instance, proves that the word means *some effect produced by water*. Even if *en* should be translated *with*, " baptized *with* water," or " sprinkled with water," does not express the effect, but

the substance with which the baptism was performed, whatever may be its mode.

5. That *en* construed with *baptizo* signifies *in*, we have the most decisive evidence in the fact that the Christian writers who used the Greek language understood it in this sense. Theodoret, speaking of the baptism of Theodosius, represents him as saying, that he had delayed his baptism, as being desirous of receiving it *in* the river Jordan. The Latin Fathers also understood the preposition in this sense, with respect to baptism, and translated it accordingly. Tertullian writes, " dipped *in* the Lord." Jerome also, in exposition of the language of the commission, says, " *intingunt aqua,*" *they dip them in water.* Indeed this is the very syntax which Greek, Latin, and English would use when place or substance is meant to be expressed.

With respect to Luke iii. 16; Acts i. 5; xi. 16, I admit that as far as syntax is concerned, the verb might be *rantizo,* to *sprinkle,* and the preposition understood might be translated *with.* But even were it translated *with,* the preposition expresses the baptizing substance—not the mode of baptism. This would be quite consistent with immersion, or any other mode. But this solution will not apply to *en Iordane.* This must be *in Jordan—in the river Jordan*—not *with Jordan and the river Jordan.*

The writer tells us, that the common use of the dative case requires that water is referred to as means. No such thing is required. As far as the dative case is concerned, it may or it may not be means, which is referred to. That the preposition *en* is here understood, is clear from the use of it in the contrasted part of the sentence—" *en, in* the Holy Ghost." Now surely no man would say that *en* may not be translated *in.* " It must," he says, " be translated *by* or *with.*" Why so? The other is the more common meaning, and it is so translated here by the best judges.

6. That *en* construed with the verb in question signifies *in,* is evident from Mark i. 4. John was baptizing *in* the wilderness—not *with the wilderness.* If this preposition refers to the place of baptism in reference to a wilderness, why may it not refer to the place in reference to a river?

7. Let the writer say what verb he would use, and what preposition he would construe with it, if he meant in the most definite manner to express that a person *was immersed in the river Jordan.*

8. The writer says here, that the preposition " expresses the means employed for some effect." But has he not said, in the very same connexion, that " it means some effect produced by water?" Is an effect the same thing with the means employed to produce it?

" That *en,*" says the writer, " sometimes has the signification of *into,* is acknowledged." This is an acknowledgment which I do not demand —which I will not accept. It never has the signification of *into,* though it may be frequently used where *eis* is more common.

" The phrase *en hudati,*" says the writer, " is so opposed to *en pneumati* in many passages, that it is clear they are correspondent phrases, and that the prepositions indicate in both the same relation." Nothing can be more evident.

"As the latter cannot be rendered *into* the Spirit," he continues, "for this is unintelligible, it must be rendered *with* the Spirit." Why should it be rendered either *into,* or *with* the Spirit? It can, and must be rendered *in* the Spirit. To baptize in the Spirit is as intelligible as to baptize with the Spirit. The expression is figurative, and must be expounded by the ordinance of baptism, whatever may be its mode. From the admitted correspondence of the two clauses of the sentence above referred to, I draw a directly contrary conclusion from that of this writer. As the preposition must be translated by the same word in both places, and as *en hudati* is in water; so *en pneumati* must be *in the Spirit:* for the figurative expression must conform to the literal, and not the literal to the figurative.

"The word *baptizo* must, therefore," says the writer, "denote some effect produced by water." Archbishop Whately, is this logic? May not the end of using the action denoted by a verb be to produce a certain effect, though the verb itself does not denote the effect? Even were the phrase translated *sprinkle with water,* it would not denote the effect of the sprinkling. Sprinkling may have different effects, but not one of them is denoted by the word itself.

In a note the author gives a number of examples of the verbs in question, with their syntax, implying effect by means of what is associated with the verb. The first is, "Stained with blood:" but the verb here is *bapto* as signifying *to dye,* and in that sense it has the effect in itself. In that sense it has nothing to do with this controversy.

His translation of the next example, "the soul is weighed down by excessive labours," is quite unwarrantable. It is not *weighed down,* but *immersed.* And where excessive labour is the baptizer, the effect is obvious. We do not deny that the syntax in question will express means, and that the means employed may be calculated or intended to produce an effect.

"They wash in warm water." It ought to be, "they immerse in warm water." *Washing* is the consequence of the *immersion.*

"Thoroughly imbued with integrity," ought to be, "immersed in justice to the bottom." The verb is *bapto,* but every scholar will perceive that it cannot here, as the writer translates it, be taken in its secondary sense, *dye.* *Eis bathos, into the depth,* or to the bottom, shows that the verb is taken in its primary sense, and that the primary sense is *dip.* *Imbue to the bottom* would be nonsense. This figurative expression must refer to immersion. When we speak of "going to the bottom of a subject," or "into the depths of science," is there not a reference to immersion?

"I am of those who were overwhelmed by that mighty wave," ought to be translated, "I myself am of those who were *immersed under* that mighty wave." This figure is a most beautiful example to show the nature of baptism. The wave was the baptizer, and under the wave the persons were immersed.

"He who with difficulty has borne his present burden, would be pressed down by a small addition." Not *pressed down,* but *immersed.* The proper translation is, "would be immersed by a small addition."

The small addition to his burden would *sink* him. Do we not say the same thing ourselves? This most definitely implies that baptism is immersion.

"His body was made wet by the dew of heaven," ought to be, "his body was *immersed* by the dew." Why this is called immersion, no person who has a soul to feel will need information.

He concludes the note with the following observation :—"Where verbs denoting to dip, are construed with *en* instead of *eis*, according to a well-known Greek idiom, the sense is, to put *into*, and to leave in —— "mixing myrrh and rosin together, and putting them *in* wine, dip a piece of linen." "I send you forth *to be* as sheep *in* the midst of wolves :" "he put him *into*, and kept him *in* prison." Matt. xiv. 3. This philology I utterly reprobate ; it is not founded either in philosophy or in fact.

1. Verbs of dipping, and verbs of motion in general, may, in certain circumstances, be construed with *en* as well as with *eis*. But in no case is one of these prepositions put for the other, or does it adopt its signification. It is in virtue of its own signification that it fills the situation. No such idiom is known in Greek more than in English ; it is false on first principles. Nothing can be more absurd than to suppose that a word will occasionally give up its own meaning and adopt the meaning of another word ; and fact does not demand the supposition of such absurdity. The phraseology that gives rise to it is explicable on philosophical principles, without departing from the meaning of the word, or assigning it the meaning of another. The usual doctrine of grammarians on this point is unsound and pernicious to philology as well as theology. Examples of the same thing occur as frequently in English as in Greek. I have shown several instances in which *in* and *into* are commutative, without being identical in meaning ; and examples occur every day.

2. In the instances referred to in the above extract, it is not true that the sense of *en* is *into*. The mixture is said to be put *in* the wine, and our language will bear this phraseology as well as the Greek. The thing exactly expressed is, that the mixture after being so put, is now *in* the wine. But to be now in the wine, implies that there has been a previous mixture into the wine. Accordingly, either *in* or *into* will in such cases serve the purpose, while neither here nor anywhere else are they synonymous. Put it *in* the wine, or *into* the wine—your choice.

3. *Dieis, en oino*, literally putting it *through* in the wine ; that is, the mixture was to be not only put in the wine, but through it. There must not only be a mixture of the myrrh and rosin, but this mixture must again be mixed with wine, that the linen may be dipped in it. The writer is here treating of verbs of dipping. Does he consider this a verb of dipping ? It is not a modal word at all, though in its generic meaning it includes mode. The preposition *en* is here connected with *putting through*, not with *dipping*. The regimen, as far as concerns the dipping substance, is to be supplied by ellipsis. The linen is to be dipped in the whole compound of myrrh, rosin, and wine.

4. Nor does *en*, in such instances, express that the thing dipped is left in that state. It might be brought out the next moment after immersion,

for anything that either the verb or the preposition has to say to the contrary. The reader may see instances of this in the examples brought forward in this work. According to the philology of this writer, if a man put his foot *into* mud, he may take it out again; but if, unfortunately, he puts it *in* mud, it must remain in it.

5. Nay more; it not only takes the meaning of *into* while it retains its own, but it does more in this situation than both could do—it leaves the thing dipped in a state of imprisonment.

6. Even in the very example quoted, the thing immersed is not left in that state. The myrrh, and the rosin, and the wine, are indeed left in a state of mixture; but it is the linen that is dipped in the compound, and instead of being left there, it is immediately taken out to be employed. This criticism is guilty of *felo de se*. But I care not that the example implied that the thing immersed was to continue in for ever; the leaving it in that situation is not implied by either the verb or the preposition.

7. With respect to the two last examples I cannot see for what purpose the writer has quoted them. His critical dogma here brought forward respects verbs of dipping. Is *send forth*, Matt. x. 16, a verb of dipping? Is *put* or *placed*, Matt. xiv. 3, a verb of dipping?

8. He is here treating of the preposition *en* when put instead of *eis*. But in translating Matt. x. 16, he does not suppose that *en* is instead of *eis*. He gives it its own peculiar meaning, *in* the midst, not *into* the midst.

9. His critical dogma refers to cases in which *en* is construed with verbs of dipping. But he does not, in this example, construe *en* even with *send*, but with the elliptical verb *to be*—to be *in* the midst, not to *send into* the midst.

10. In the phraseology, Matt. xiv. 3, *put him in prison*, the words *and kept him there*, are neither included in the meaning of the preposition, nor of the verb. The same expression would have been used had John the Baptist been delivered from prison the next moment after imprisonment. It will apply to an imprisonment for half an hour, as well as imprisonment for life. We ourselves use the same phraseology; we say that a prisoner is put *in* prison, or *into* prison, without any design to refer to the duration of imprisonment. But men have great facilities for profound criticism in dead languages. May we not say, "the constable put him *in* prison, but the magistrates immediately released him?" When *in* is used, motion to a place is not expressed, but *position*, when the action of the verb is finished. That *motion into* a place must precede *rest* in a place, is necessary; but this, in the preposition *in*, is understood, not expressed. This always expresses *rest* in the place mentioned.

Thus in every example alleged in this note, I have shown that the philology of the writer is unsound. Let it be observed, also, what a multitude of meanings he is obliged to give to *bapto* and *baptizo*, in these examples. First, to *stain*: *bapto* does indeed signify to dye, but in this sense it has nothing to do with this controversy. Persons are not *dyed* in *purification*. In the second example he makes baptizo signify to *weigh down.* Is this to translate on principle of any kind? The word never has this meaning: the word is here used figuratively, and must in the translation be guided by the literal meaning, which never is what this writer has given. He might as well have rendered the passage by the expression, *the mind is weakened by excessive labour.* On such a principle as this, we might give this word, or any other word, five hundred meanings. His third meaning is *wash:* but *immerse* is the translation—*washing* is inferred as a consequence of *dipping.* The word has perfectly the same meaning here that it has when applied to dipping in mud. The difference of effect is known from the circumstances. Among washer-women is it not often said, in English, "Give that a *dip,*" meaning *wash it?* The fourth meaning is *imbue.* This meaning is palpably false; because the words *into the depth,* construed with the verb, shows most manifestly that *bapto* is here taken in its primary signification. In the fifth example, he gives *overwhelm* as the meaning. The word is used figuratively; but the literal meaning is never to overwhelm, though it will admit this in a free translation. In the sixth example, he gives *pressed down* as the signification. This is entirely different from the second meaning To *press down* is quite a different thing from to *weigh down.* Can any fancy be more wild than to render this word in this manner? This verb is a servant of all work. It is as expert in pressing cheese, and compressing hay for exportation, as in *purifying.* On these principles, what is it that it may not be made to signify? In the seventh example he makes *bapto* signify to *wet.* This is not a meaning of the word, though it may often be substituted for it. To *dip* anything in a liquid will be to *wet* it; still to *dip* and to *wet* are words of quite a different meaning—the one only in certain circumstances is the consequence of the other. Now there is no more reason to make *bapto* signify to *wet,* than there is to make *dip* signify to *wet.* The eighth example gives the verb its own meaning, but entirely mistakes the syntax. Now what a mass of philological confusion is this! Would not definite interpretation be impossible, if all words were to be translated on these random principles? Is it not self-evidently clear, that if I can succeed in giving the same meaning to *baptizo* in every occurrence of it in the language, my doctrine is preferable to that which gives it a useless multitude of meanings? If I can explain on philosophical principles, in perfect accordance with my view, every instance in which the word is used, is it not self-evidently clear that there is no ground to allege a secondary meaning? On the other hand, let the reader try if he can find any philosophy in the assignment of the different meanings allotted to this word by our opponents. They give meaning to the word in each passage—not from the authority of first principles and definitely ascertained usage, but from the supposed exigencies of the place from antecedent probability. They reason as if every passage must independently ascertain its own meaning; whereas in multitudes of instances, every word may be, as far as connexion is concerned, capable of having a word of opposite meaning substituted for it, without detection by context. In such cases, established usage can alone decide. They make the word express, in its own meaning, peculiarities contained or implied only in the context. In this way they can assign to any word as many meanings as there are variations in the connexion. If language could be legitimately interpreted in this way, nothing could ever be proved or disproved; no tongue could ever be learned. I resist such licentiousness in assigning meaning to words, not merely as it affects the subject of baptism, but as it affects every thing revealed in Scripture : I resist it, not merely as it affects the Scriptures, but as it affects every written document that guides the determination of man : I resist it, as it makes all language, either written or spoken, incapable of certain and definite interpretation.

But why does the writer demand *eis* and refuse *en* in construction with *bapto* and *baptizo*, in the signification of *dipping*, when both the classics and Hebraistic Greek afford examples of both? Was not Namaan immersed *in* Jordan? Was not Aristobulus immersed *in* the pond? Did not John immerse *in* Jordan, and *in* water? And the dative without the preposition, we have in Alexander Aphroditus, Problem. lib. 1 : " A power immersed *in* the depth, or most inward parts, of the body ;" with a multitude of others that might be given.

Thus I have proved that the preposition *en* construed with *baptizo*, is evidence in our favour ; and without the occurrence of *eis* in a single instance, would serve our purpose. But the assertion that *eis* is not found in the syntax of this word in the Septuagint and in the New Testament, is not well founded. It is found in Mark i. 9, " Jesus was baptized of John *into* Jordan. The writer admits this in a note; but the note is a contradiction of the text. *A general assertion in the text may be limited, or modified by a note; but a note should not admit what the text universally denies.* This is not explanation or modification, but contradiction, which nothing can justify. The text says, " But the construction does not once occur in the use of *baptizo* in the Septuagint and the New Testament." The note not only contradicts the text, but takes away the ground of the argument which the text employs. The argument is grounded on the supposed *universality* of a fact, which the note admits not to be *universal.* If such syntax is admitted in a single instance, no argument can be founded on its universal absence. It cannot be alleged, that the want of such a syntax evidences a change of meaning, when such a syntax is not wanting. A difference of meaning cannot be alleged from a difference of syntax, if there is not universally such a difference of syntax. The writer, indeed, in his note, endeavours to give another meaning to the preposition, Mark i. 5, but this does not alter the case, even were the preposition capable of the alleged meaning. The complaint is, that such cannot be the meaning, because there is not such syntax. If the syntax exists at all, the complaint is removed. If in such a sense the word *must* have such a syntax, why will you give this necessary syntax another sense, just for the purpose of evading that sense which requires this syntax? But were it a fact, that there is not one instance of such syntax, the fact would not bear the conclusion. If, in common use, any one of two prepositions may equally be used, with a verb in a certain sense, any one of them may be constantly employed with the verb in that sense. With respect to some words there might be but a single example of its syntax in the New Testament. Its syntax, then, must be determined by common usage.

Let us attend to the writer's attempt to set aside the testimony of Mark i. 5. " But," says he, " as this is the only instance in which *eis* is used, and as it is here connected with the name of a place, it is much more probable that it has the common signification of *at*."

1. Here a false first principle is assumed, namely, that one instance may be explained in a meaning, which it could not have in a number of instances. Can anything be more absurd?

2. If it is construed here with the name of a place, that place is a river in which the immersion took place.

3. If in common syntax such a phrase has such a meaning, why should it not have this meaning in the syntax of Scripture?

4. If to produce such a meaning, such a syntax is necessary in common language, why should it be thought probable that where such syntax occurs in Scripture, it has not the same meaning? If the syntax is necessary to the meaning, why is the meaning denied it where the syntax is found?

5. If in common use the same verb is sometimes coupled with *en* and sometimes with *eis*, why may it not in scriptural use be capable, in the same sense, of the same association?

6. This instance does not give, according to our interpretation, a new meaning to the preposition, nor a new meaning to the verb associated with it, nor a new syntax to the regimen. What reasonable pretence, then, can there be for change?

7. The meaning assigned by the writer is not a common meaning of *eis*, as he asserts. Even by those grammarians who give *at* as one of the meanings of *eis*, it is not supposed to be a common meaning.

8. This extravagance is still more aggravated, when it is considered, that the prepositions *para* and *epi* appropriately designate *at;* and that no other prepositions but *en* and *eis* could be employed in expressing an immersion *in* or *into* water. If these are the only prepositions that could be used to express that this ordinance was performed by immersion *in* or *into* water, if there are appropriate prepositions to express *at*, if water or a river is the regimen, what can the meaning be but the common meaning of the prepositions *in* and *into?* Can any reason be assigned for giving another meaning to the prepositions, but an obstinate reluctance to admit the consequence?

9. The thing is still worse when it is considered that this extravagance is employed not only to avoid the common meaning of the verb, but to give it a meaning that in the Greek language is not in evidence from a single example.

10. But this syntax is not confined to *one* instance in the New Testament; it is found in many instances. *Eis* is connected with *baptizo* in the commission. Now, though water is not the regimen, yet it is the meaning of the preposition in reference to the performance of the rite, that must regulate its meaning in all cases.

11. The early Christians who wrote in the Greek language connect *eis* in this sense with *baptizo*. Eusebius construes *baptizontes* with *eis*

onoma—into the name. And Eusebius understood the verb as denoting immersion.

12. The early Latin writers understood the preposition in this sense. Tertullian has not only *tinctus in Domino—dipped in the Lord;* but *tingentes eos in nomen—dipped them into the name.* Now Tertullian knew something of Greek syntax. After this shall we listen to the modern criticism that declares that such syntax is intolerable! As to the soundness, then, of this syntax, there can be no higher authority. Do our opponents pretend to make a discovery in the meaning of Greek verbs and Greek syntax, unknown to the very persons who wrote and spoke Greek?

In fact, the early Christian writers, both Greek and Latin, used both *eis* and *en* in speaking of this ordinance, just as the Scriptures do, and just as we ourselves use the corresponding prepositions. We say immerse *in* or *into,* while we do not confound the prepositions.

But I go much farther. I not only deny that *eis* here signifies *at,*—I maintain that it never has this signification. This is much more than I am bound to prove. I might admit with many that this preposition occasionally has the signification of *at,* while I could successfully exclude it from this place. Grammarians who teach the absurd doctrine, that a word may occasionally desert its own meaning, and assume that of another, confine this privilege to cases in which the word is totally inexplicable in its meaning. The doctrine, then, in their hands is usually harmless; but in the hands of controversialists it does miraculous exploits. They call in its aid on every occasion, when the necessities of their case demand it; and what the grammarians have provided to explain dark passages, they use to make clear passages dark. But I will take away the whole foundation from under this figment. I deny that ever *eis* signifies *at.* So far from being a *common* meaning, as this writer represents it, it is not a meaning at all. Let us, then, examine the examples which the writer alleges to prove this meaning. Luke ix. 61: "Those *at* my house." The proper translation, however, is neither "those *at* my house," nor, with our version, "those which are at home at my house," but "those who belong to my house." *Eis* often signifies *with respect to,* or *in reference to.* The preposition here has no respect to place at all. The whole relations are here included, in whatever houses they might dwell. At all events, it was not *at* but *in* the house they lived. *At* can have no pretensions here.

The second example is Luke xxi. 37. "He lodged *at* the hill." At the hill? Was it not within the verge of what is called the mount of Olives? *At,* then, has no business here. But the preposition has here its own peculiar meaning, and implies motion as well as in other places. The writer has been looking into Matthiæ; why has he not attended to him on this point? He explains this syntax not only as implying motion in the preposition, but as being communicated by the preposition to verbs which do not in their own nature import motion. He illustrates by many examples. His doctrine is, "Various verbs which of themselves do not imply motion, receive this sense by the construction with *eis.*" I agree with Matthiæ as to the fact : I differ from him as to its philosophy. Without doubt, in the cases referred to, there is motion in some verb expressed or understood, according with the preposition that indicates motion. But it is a question whether the motion in the verb, is motion communicated to the verb, which in itself has no motion, or belongs to a verb understood. My doctrine is, that the motion is implied in a verb which is understood, and is not properly communicated to a verb that has no motion in itself. It is absurd to suppose, that the same verb can designate both rest and motion. It is impossible both to stand and move at the same time. What I say is, WHEN *eis* IS CONSTRUED WITH A VERB IN WHICH THERE IS NO MOTION, THERE IS ALWAYS A VERB OF MOTION UNDERSTOOD, AND WHICH IS NOT EXPRESSED BECAUSE IT IS NECESSARILY SUGGESTED.

But whatever is the philosophy of this fact, the fact itself is unquestionable. In all such cases *eis* has motion. It is neither *at* nor *in*, but *into*. Homer represents Achilles as selling Priam's sons *into* Samos; "Agreeing," says Matthiæ, with the English, "*to sell into a place.*" "The Midianites sold Joseph *into* Egypt." Here the preposition has its proper sense, though there is no motion in the verb expressly joined with it. This phraseology is exemplified by Xenophon. Cyrus commanded an officer to "stand *into* the front." Now there must here be motion before standing.

We ourselves exemplify this every day. A soldier not in straight line is commanded to stand *into* his rank. A ship is said to stand *into* land. When Cowper says, "Stand forth, O guest," both motion and rest are expressed.

The writer, however, might have seen in Matthiæ many instances in which *apo*, *ek*, and *eis*, are translated by *in*.

Surely this might teach any one that in such cases the words do not change their signification. Could the word *out*, for instance, assume the meaning of *in?* All such cases are explicable on the principle, that the words retain their own meanings. This critical Mesmerism would stupify an angel, were he to subject himself to its influence.

With respect to the example in question, "he lodged into the mount," the solution is, "he went into the mount to lodge ;" or in whatever other way it may be solved, the preposition *eis* implies that motion preceded the rest expressed in *lodge*.

The third example is, "Wash at the pool of Siloam ;" literally, "wash *into* the pool." He was to go into the pool that he might wash. *At* has no pretensions to demand entrance here, whatever *in* might allege for itself. The blind man might as well have sent to the pool for water, to wash at home, as to take the water out of the pool and wash.

The fourth example is, "She fell down at his feet," John xi. 32. Literally, "She fell unto his feet." The preposition here expresses the motion of the fall. In reference to place *eis* signifies *unto* as well as *into ;* but motion in both. It respects the motion of the falling body, of which his feet were the point of termination. *At his feet* is substantially a very good translation, though *at* is not the meaning of the preposition.

The fifth example is, "to all who are at a distance." Literally, all *unto* a distance, that is, all who are between Judea and the supposed distance, meaning the most distant nations. The author changes the version in order to bring in his favourite *at*. But when he has it, it does him no service. Does *at a distance* signify near a distance? Then they who are *in* the distance, and *beyond* the distance, are excluded. The promise is not to all who are contiguous to a distance, but to all in the most distant places,—all between the speaker and the most distant parts of the earth. Neither *at* nor *in* would exactly suit here.

The sixth example is Acts xviii. 21, " to keep the feast at Jerusalem." Why change *in* of our translation into *at?* Was it not *in* Jerusalem that the feast was kept? Did Paul intend to stop at the edge of the city? Literally, it is neither *in* nor *at*. " It is necessary for me to keep the feast *into* Jerusalem;" that is, on the principle above explained, " it is necessary for me to go *into* Jerusalem to keep the feast." The motion necessary previously to the keeping of the feast, which is not expressed by any verb, is implied in the motion of the preposition. This example is quite similar to those cited by Matthiæ.

The seventh example is, " to die *at* Jerusalem," Acts xxi. 13. Is it not *in* Jerusalem that he is supposed to be willing to die? He did not mean *contiguous* to the city. But in all such cases *at* is sufficiently exact as a translation. However, it is neither *at* nor *in*, that is expressed—it is *into* Jerusalem. The motion from Paul's present position to the supposed place of his death, is not expressed by any verb, but is necessarily implied. This circumstance is expressed by the preposition. The sentiment fully expressed is, " I am willing to go to Jerusalem to be bound or to die."

The eighth example is Acts viii. 40, " Philip was found at Azotus." This proceeds on the same principle. Philip was found after he had gone into Azotus. The preposition does not here signify *at*, more than in any other place, though it is sufficiently exact for a translation. It expresses the motion of the verb that is understood.

The last example alleged by the writer is, " As thou hast borne witness concerning me *at* Jerusalem, so must thou bear witness also at Rome," Acts xxiii. 11. Why does he change the translation from *in* to *at?* Was it not *in* Jerusalem and *in* Rome, that the testimony is supposed to be delivered? Whatever pretentions *in* might have here, *at* can have none. The preposition, however, has here no regard to place, but to the inhabitants of the places mentioned. To bear witness to or into Jerusalem or Rome, is to bear witness *to* the people of those cities. " With the verbs to *say*, to *show*," says Matthiæ, " the reference or direction to the persons to whom anything is said or shown, is sometimes considered as analogous to an actual motion, and this analogy expressed by *eis*." He illustrates by examples perfectly similar to the above, *eis pantas anthropous, before or to all men*, &c.

Reader, have I not redeemed my pledge? Have I not demonstrated that *eis*, in none of the passages alleged by the author, signifies *at?* Have I not shown the philosopical principle which accounts for the peculiarity of the alleged use of *eis?* I have done more than my cause required. I could have defended my point and admitted exceptions. I have proved that there are no exceptions. Mark i. 5, then, itself decides the controversy. It is *into* Jordan; and nothing but *into* Jordan can it be. Were there no other objection to *purify*, this would unseat it. All the electors claimed by it have been grossly misrepresented. They give their vote freely to the other candidate.

The writer, it will be recollected, translated *en* in construction with *hudati*, by *with water*. How does this consist with *en Iordane*, in Jordan? The last phrase is not sufficiently tractable to be translated *with*, and the writer manages to convert it also, as well as *eis*, into *at*. And, indeed, on similar principles, he might convert into *at*, all the prepositions in the Greek language, and of any other language. I appeal to every candid scholar,—I appeal to every sensible man, is not this extravagance? Shall these two prepositions wickedly and feloniously combine to assume the meaning of other prepositions, in passages where they are not only capable of having their own meaning, but where their own meaning is the most natural and obvious, for the purpose of favouring the pretensions of the usurper *purification?*

Nothing can be more evident than that *en hudati* and *en Iordane* use the preposition in the same sense. Each of the phrases refers to baptism,—to the performance of baptism, while each of the words in regimen designates that in which the ordinance may be performed. Why then, shall not the preposition have the same meaning in both places? Is there anything to prevent it? Does the verb refuse its sanction? On the contrary, the common meaning of the verb demands it. Does the preposition refuse to be translated by the same word in two similar places? This cannot be. Does the regimen refuse to dip the baptized person? No, surely, the Jordan will not exclaim, "You cannot be dipped in me." What then gainsays? Nothing but the necessities of this pretender *purification.*

This is so obvious to common sense that some of our opponents translate *en Iordane* by *with* Jordan, that is, with the water of Jordan. Though this is barbarously figurative, it has more consistency. Here, however, we have self-evidence that both of them are wrong. It is palpably evident that if this writer did not think that the expression *purify with Jordan* is absurd, he would not only have avoided giving a various meaning to the preposition in the two cases which are so similar, but would have availed himself of a meaning which he has judged so much to his purpose. On the other hand, it is equally evident that if the persons referred to did not consider that it is absolutely necessary to translate the preposition by the same word in both places, they would not have had recourse to the outlandish figure, *baptize with Jordan.* Each of the parties, then, virtually gives its testimony against the other.

But the author, it seems, has proof for *at* as a meaning of *en*. "Matthiæ observes," says he, "sometimes *en* is used with names of places, when proximity only is implied." Well, granting this for a moment, even in the writer's sense, does Matthiæ teach that a controversialist may avail himself of this resource as often as his exigencies require? Grammarians who teach the above doctrine, confine the use of it to cases that will not explain according to the ordinary meaning of the words. I venture to assert that there is not an illustrious name among grammarians that will sanction the use of their doctrine, that is made of it by this writer. There is not in Europe, there never was in existence a great scholar who would deny that Jesus Christ was immersed in Jordan. Nothing but the confidence of ignorance could ever venture such extravagance.

What are the instances that properly come under the sanction of this doctrine of Matthiæ? Are they not instances in which it is known that the persons referred to, were not actually *in* the place named? What countenance does this give to the extravagance of our author? Is it impossible to give the peculiar meaning to the preposition in this place? Is it known that the baptism could not possibly be *in* the river? Does the common meaning of the verb require another meaning in the preposition? Does not the common meaning of the verb, the common meaning of the preposition, the common meaning of the word in regimen, all unite in demanding the same thing? Can the doctrine of Matthiæ, then, be a sanction to a process that expels the common meaning of the verb, the common meaning of the preposition, and the common meaning of the word associated with them in syntax? The examples, however, referred to by Matthiæ have no need of peculiar solution. It is the territory of Lacedemon, and of Mantinea, to which Xenophon refers. The example from Euripides employs *en* with references to *Dirce*, not as a place, but as a person; and has nothing to do with this subject.

Though in reference to place, this preposition always asserts intusposition, without in the smallest degree verging to the signification of *at*, yet there are situations in which it is used when intusposition does not actually exist. This, however, arises from the latitude given to its regimen, not assumed by itself. This peculiarity I can account for on the most philosophical principles. In writing to correspondents at a distance, I always give my address, Tulbermore; yet my house is more than a mile out of the village. Exact information as to locality is not designed or expected. Now this single fact will explain a great many difficulties conjured up by controversialists to give latitude to explanation. When I am spoken of as residing *in* such a place, *in* has its own meaning most exactly. This I have no doubt may be exemplified in all languages. But let a foreigner, a controversialist, who knows our language from grammars and dictionaries, try his philology on such a use of the English preposition *in*: "Here," he would say, with the appearance of profound learning and critical acumen, "the preposition *in* is used for *at*, signifying not *within*, but *contiguous*." On this foundation he would rest mountains of false interpretation; proving or disproving anything, according to exigency.

My readers will now be prepared to give an answer to the following assertion: "The statement that John baptized *en* the Jordan, and that he baptized *en* Enon, shows that the former no more means within the water of the river, than the latter within the walls of the town. The meaning in both cases is merely that of nearness, and should be translated *at* the Jordan, *at* Enon. In the same manner *en dexia*, at the right hand."

The ingenious writer is most happy in discovering secrets. I could not pretend to take the same information out of this document. How does he know that Enon was a town? How does he know that it had walls? If it had walls, what makes it necessary that the baptizing should have been *within* the walls? Do not the suburbs without the walls belong to a town? How does he know that the baptism was not performed within the walls? Could there not be in a town either much water, or according to him, many fountains? I might confine John to the town, if my case required it, but my philology will give him a little liberty. I care not whether Enon was a town or a district. On the principle above explained, if it was a town, he might be said in English, as well as in Greek, to be baptizing in it, when he was baptizing in the district around it. The extension of meaning is in the regimen, not in the preposition. Should a man from London be baptized by me, he might say on his return, " I was baptized in Tulbermore ;" when he was baptized at my house, or at the river Magola, half a mile from the village. No Englishman would convert *in* here into *at*. The design of such phraseology is not to give exact information as to the spot, but to designate by a name that will be known to those to whom he speaks It is on this principle that we say, that such a man fell *in* Waterloo, &c.

In the phrase *en dexia*, the preposition *in* does not signify *at*, but has its own meaning,—*in the right-hand place*. Indeed, instead of designating *nearness*, it may extend to any distance : it indicates merely, that the situation of the object is in the space to the right. A bird appearing at any distance to the right, is said to be *en dexia*. Where it is applied to the closest juxtaposition, this is not the thing expressed.

SECTION III.—THE WRITER'S SECOND GENERAL OBSERVATION.— " In all cases where the word occurs in the New Testament," says the writer, " it is applied to things connected with religion, generally to a sacred rite significant of the purifying of the soul. Whatever may be supposed to be the symbolical meaning of Christian baptism, that of the Jews, to which reference is made in the epistle to the Hebrews, that of the Pharisees, and that of John, were unquestioned rites of purification : this was the meaning of them all, and their only meaning. Now the meaning of a rite being of more importance than the mode, would be more frequently referred to when the rite was mentioned."

There is here some truth, but false conclusions are drawn from it. It is true that Christian immersion, and Jewish immersions, and, he might have added, heathen religious immersions, are all emblematical of purification, or supposed to be effective of it. But does this imply that the word by which these purifications were designated must signify purification? This is grossly unfounded. Was not circumcision a rite of purification? Did the name designate purification? How often must I ask this question? Rites of purification may have names that do not express purification. What does the writer mean by the meaning of a rite being more frequently referred to than its mode, when the rite is mentioned? Can this say anything with respect to its name? And is not its mode an essential part of the meaning of the rite? If a rite has a name from mode, can it be spoken of as to its meaning, without indication of mode?

"If, therefore," he continues, " a term at first descriptive of mode was employed, it might be expected that it would, as an appellative for the rite, sometimes lose its reference to the manner of action, and denote merely the end."

1. This observation is founded on an admission that destroys the writer's theory; it admits that the disputed word was at first applied to the ordinance in its modal meaning. But the author's theory is, that the word had, in Hebriastic use, dropped that meaning, and assumed that of purification.

2. *This admits all we want. If baptizo was employed to designate this ordinance at first, in its modal meaning, in that meaning it must be for ever understood as to the ordinance.*

3. That a modal word, given as the designation of an ordinance, will apply to the rite with respect to every thing asserted of it, is the very thing which we teach. That many things may be contained in its nature, or import, which are not pointed out by the mode, we not only admit, but contend. The ordinance of baptism is an emblem of cleansing, but this emblem is in the water, not in the mode; the mode is an emblem of death, burial, and resurrection; but whether the ordinance is called *immersion*, or *purification*, or *sprinkling*, every thing spoken about it may be referred to it under its peculiar name. This is manifestly the case with respect to the word *circumcision;* every thing said about it in the Old and the New Testament, is applied to it under the name, when there is no reference to *cutting around.*

4. But when this is the case, the word does not lose its reference to manner of action, and does not " denote merely the end;" it still retains its modal meaning. Whatever may be said about *circumcision,* the word still has the same signification.

5. Even when the meaning of a word is not understood, and it is known only as the name of a rite, it is not correct to say that it there denotes only the *end.* It does not denote the end at all; it denotes the rite itself, without reference either to mode or end. Thus, with respect to the word *baptism;* this is an English word, used merely as the name of an ordinance, without reference either to *end* or *mode.*

6. To suppose that a word assigned as the name of a Divine ordinance, from the mode of that ordinance, as emblematical of something in its nature, would be changed in its meaning in Scripture, so as to lose its reference to mode, denoting merely its end, is as absurd as it is impious. After ages might change the meaning of the name of the ordinance; but such a change could not take place in its Scripture use.

7. The principle of appropriation is entirely different in its nature from that which the writer supposes to operate in the meaning of this word. When words are appropriated, they receive a peculiar application, but do not lose their former meaning. It is on the ground of that meaning that they are appropriated. Along with their own meaning, appropriation supplies by ellipsis that which is necessarily understood. Had *sprinkling* or *pouring*, for an emblematical purpose, been the mode of

this ordinance, the name might have been *sprinkling* or *perfusion;* and these terms would have been appropriated so as to designate the ordinance, without expressing either water or end. These would be elliptically supplied; but the word would retain its modal meaning. Things relative to its end, or relative to it in any view, may be referred to it under its appropriate name; but appropriation and change from progressive use, are as different as any two principles that operate in language.

8. The writer adds, "Words always change in their meaning with modes of thought." This is an impious remark in regard to the meaning of words in Scripture. Do the writers of the New Testament change the meaning of this word, in reference to the same ordinance? Change of modes of thought may operate in changing the meaning of words in different ages; but what relation has this to the use of words by the inspired writers of one period? Let it be observed that the question is not about the change of the meaning of the word, after the times of the apostles, but respects its meaning in the New Testament. Now, in this point of view, can anything be more absurd than, for a purpose of establishing a different meaning, to appeal to change in modes of thought?

The writer alleges that the words *rantismos, sprinkling, circumcision,* and *anointing,* underwent his process. It is not so. *Sprinkling* is applied to the mind only figuratively; *circumcision* is an appropriated word; and *anointing* is not a word of mode at all.

"It will scarcely be pretended," says the writer, "that the words, the Messias and the Christ, retained, in the common usage of the Jews, any reference to the pouring out of oil." That it had reference to *pouring* is not pretended, for there is nothing of pouring in the word; but that the name had always a reference to *anointing,* is most confidently asserted. That the word Christ does not suggest this to us is, because in its original sense it is not an English word. The *anointed* would always refer to *anointing.*

But the writer supposes, that according to our view, we must hold that the exhortation to the Jews, to circumcise their hearts, directed them to make circular incisions on that organ, or to do something similar to that with their minds. It is painful to be obliged to spend time in noticing such reasoning. Is not this a figurative expression? To the heart it does not apply literally; but the word circumcision, whether used literally or figuratively, has always the same meaning. "Crucified with Christ," refers to crucifixion as really as when applied to the death of Christ.

The Jewish rite had the name *circumcision,* not from process or change of modes of thought, but by appropriation; and every thing that was ever included in it in the Scriptures, was in it from the first moment of its appropriation. A better example could not be chosen to illustrate our doctrine. This rite, according to the writer himself, received a modal meaning: *purification,* he says, is its meaning; yet the word first and last has its modal meaning, and does not designate *purification.* When it is said that the sword of the Lord is *bathed* in heaven, must we either admit a change in the meaning of the word *bathe*, or hold that there is in heaven a literal bathing of a sword?

"The common tendency to use," says the writer, "in speaking of sacred things, words significant of their design, rather than of their mode, appears in our own language. The terms *christen, commune, ordain, consecrate, worship*, are of such a nature that neither their etymology, nor their ordinary signification, would give the least clue to the *manner* in which the service thus named was performed." Now what trifling is this! What bearing can it have on the question at issue? Does this show, that in giving a name to an ordinance, with a view to designate something in its meaning, a word of mode might not be employed by its author? Does this show that Christ did not appoint an ordinance emblematical in its mode? Shall every man be allowed to give names to his inventions, and shall not Christ be allowed to give names to his ordinances, and give such modes to his ordinances, as he pleases? Must we confine him to the common tendencies of human nature on such occasions? We do not argue from antecedent probability, that a word of mode must be appropriated to this ordinance: we do not argue that an ordinance must have a modal meaning. We do not argue from the nature of things, that a word indicative of *end* would have been improper. *We argue that it is a matter of fact that the word employed is a word of mode; that the syntax of the word indicates the same thing; and that the Scripture explanation of the ordinance declares that its mode is emblematical.* Does it follow, that because certain words, neither in their etymology nor ordinary signification, give any intimation with respect to the *manner* in which the service thus named was performed, no indication of this can be given in an ordinance of Christ? How could we expect indication of manner ˙n words which have nothing of manner in their literal meaning? Because *christen* gives no clue to its mode, since there is no mode in its origin; shall *baptizo*, which the author himself in this connexion admits to be given to the ordinance at first in its modal sense, and changed only by change in modes of thought, give no clue in its etymology or ordinary signification, to the manner in which baptism is to be performed?

Some of the words referred to by the author, do indeed indicate the tendency of the human mind both to change the ordinances of Christ, and give them new names. *Christen*, to make a Christian, is a very happy Puseyite name for a Puseyite rite. But we cannot forget that Paul, when the Lord's Supper was abused, would not give it the Scripture name.

But the fact of giving names to ordinances from modes or circumstances is not singular. Does the writer forget that *breaking of bread* is among the inspired designations of the Lord's supper? Is not *laying on of hands* a similar expression? What about the name of the rite of circumcision?

"The designation of the Lord's supper is retained by us," says the writer, "though that ordinance is no longer observed as a meal."

No longer observed as a meal!!! Was it ever observed as a meal?

Was it a meal in its institution? Was it not instituted immediately after a meal? That it never should be a meal, are we not taught in the indignant question, " Have ye not houses to eat and to drink in ?" It is called a supper from the time of its institution, and this circumstance is still imported in the name, as much as on the evening when it was appointed. To retain it is not optional—to change it is an invasion of the prerogative of the Son of God. The ordinance has in Scripture other names ; but to give it the name of *sacrament* or *eucharist* is as unwarrantable as to change the name assigned by her Majesty to the Prince of Wales. The name of the ordinance has no respect to the time at which we observe it, but to the time at which it was instituted. There is neither a change in the term, nor in the meaning of the term. *Supper* does not now mean *breakfast* or *dinner :* the tendency in the human mind to change the meaning of words, can have no bearing on this question. The inquiry is not whether certain words afterwards changed their meaning ; but what is their meaning in the New Testament? This must still be their meaning to us.

" And in many countries," says the writer, "where terms expressive of dipping were first used for baptism, because it was thus administered, the same terms continue to be used when the mode is no longer in accordance with their primary signification."

Whatever may be the case with respect to the fact here referred to, the principle I have not only always admitted, but from the beginning I have pointed it out. But my opponents make a very unjustifiable use of it. Because a word designating mode, appropriated to an ordinance of Christ, will continue to be applied to the ordinance, even when the mode is changed, does it follow that in the New Testament either the mode or the meaning of its name will be changed? Changes of mode and meaning of name in the usage of ages, have nothing to do with this question. Had the mode been universally changed even in the second century, it would not disturb my philology. Whatever change men may make in this ordinance, its name, its mode, and its nature, must remain the same in Scripture for ever. What has the meaning of the word in Scripture, to do with after-changes in its meaning? According to this writer, every change in the meaning of Scripture words made by after ages, must produce a similar change on the meaning of Scripture itself. On this principle, language would be incapable of conveying a revelation.

But does not the writer see that this admits all we want? If many countries employed to designate this ordinance, terms expressive of dipping, because it was thus administered, and afterwards, changing the mode, continued the name, does not this imply that dipping was their original mode? Now this is all we want with respect to *baptizo*. If immerse was its meaning in its first application to baptism, we care not how many changes may be afterwards made in its meaning.

In his reasoning in this general observation, there are no less than four theories involved in his arguments, as the ground of his conclusions. 1. The grand theory is, that this word, by frequency of application to purification, came at last to designate purification without reference to mode : that such was its use in the time of John the Baptist, and consequently that it was so used in the New Testament. 2. A second implied theory is, that at first a word of mode, it would lose that meaning, adopting that of *end*. 3. That from the tendency of the human mind to give names from *end* rather than *mode*, the word when first assigned to this ordinance, must have been a word designating *end*, not *mode*. 4. That it was *dipping* at first in mode, and dipping in name; but change of mode made a change in the meaning of the name. Besides, the author asserts that certain countries gave the ordinance a dipping name, from its dipping mode. Does not this contradict his theory from the tendencies of human nature to give names from *end* rather than from mode? Can anything more clearly indicate a desperate cause, than that men of ingenuity, employing the most extensive research, are not able to write a page in defence, without plunging into confusion and contradiction? Ah, my fellow Christians! cease to torture the word of God. You have taken in hand what an angel could not perform.

SECTION IV.—AUTHOR'S THIRD GENERAL OBSERVATION.—The third general observation of the writer is: " In many passages the word is applied to the minds of men ; their spirits are said to be baptized. That when thus used it is employed properly, and not figuratively, is probable, from the frequency of its occurrence, and from the simple, unpoetic character of the style."
1. And does the writer seriously assert that frequency of the occurrence of a word, in application to mind, makes it probable that the word is used literally, and not figuratively? Is this one of the characteristics that distinguish between figured and unfigured diction? Has any rhetorician ever alleged this as a criterion? Could such an observation suggest itself to a philologist?
2. How could it escape the writer, that this frequency does not respect the mind only in one view of it, but includes infinite variety? It includes every affection of the mind in excess. A proper term designating one affection of the mind, cannot designate another. A word used figuratively, may apply to all in which likeness can be found.
3. Our term *immerse* may be used figuratively as frequently, and with the same variety of application. What should we think of a foreign critic, who, on this ground, should allege, that in all such occurrences the word *immerse* is used, not figuratively, but literally, and without any allusion to literal *immersion* ?
4. Are not *pour* and *sprinkle* capable of the like figurative application ? Pouring is used figuratively in Scripture much more frequently than *immersion*. It is applied both with respect to Divine blessings and judgments. 5. *The simple, unpoetic character of the style!* Does not the writer know that the diction of the Lord Jesus abounds in figures? The strongest figures found in language are found in him. Mr. Fuller, we are told, after examining an ingot of gold in the Bank of England, said to his friend, " How much better to have this in the hand than in the heart!" Must we say, in order to make the diction of Mr. Fuller simple and unpoetic, that the word *heart* is to be understood literally, and that

the observation respected the danger of having the ingot literally in the heart? Would any child expound on such a principle? In that view Mr. Fuller might as well have referred to the liver or to the kidneys, and to a leaden bullet. 6. As the writer, with frequency of occurrence with regard to mind, joins the simplicity and unpoetic character of the style, he must, by frequency, mean frequency not as to general use, but in the New Testament. I do not recollect any figurative application of the word in the New Testament, except that with respect to the baptism of the Spirit, and that with respect to the sufferings of our Lord. Both refer to body as well as mind. The word is indeed very frequently, in good use, applied figuratively; and so must corresponding words in all languages.

"If *baptizo*," says the writer, "when applied first to a body, meant to dip; when applied to mind, it must necessarily have a different sense." This is not philosophically correct. Words do not change their meaning when used figuratively. The whole advantage of the figure depends on the word's retaining its literal meaning. When Homer calls wheat *the marrow of man*, *marrow* does not lay aside its own meaning, and become another name for *wheat*. This would destroy the figure. The figure asserts that one thing is another, without any alteration in the signification of words. When Christ calls Herod a fox, he gives no new meaning to the word *fox*. The doctrine of rhetoricians on this subject is erroneous and absurd. This I have proved at great length in a treatise on the Figures of Speech, now out of print, but which may shortly be re-published. Indeed, when a metaphorical application of a word becomes one of its meanings, then it ceases to be a figure.

With respect to the point in which the likeness consists, between the primary and secondary object in a figure, there never can be any question. Every good figure has its own light. As the immersion of a body is the complete covering of it in the thing in which it is immersed, so the baptism of the Spirit must imply the sanctification of the believer in mind and body. No one needs to ask the difference between a *sprinkling* of learning, and an *immersion* in it. When Cowper, in his translation of Homer, speaks of a *hide drunk with oil*, will any child need an explanation of his meaning? When, again, he speaks of being *drunk with joy*, his meaning is equally intelligible. Were the term *drunk* used figuratively in respect to a thousand different things, every instance would explain itself. *Drunk with oil* refers to the quantity absorbed by the hide—*drunk with joy* is excess of joy : *drunk with blood* refers to the quantity of blood shed by the woman in the book of Revelation, and to the effect of it on herself. Why, then, should there be any doubt as to the reference in the phrase *immersion in the Spirit?* Could any man really doubt as to the meaning of such expression, his case would indeed be pitiable. He would have more need of medicine than of logic.

Three effects, the writer tells us, have proposed themselves as candidates for this likeness. Let us for a moment attend to this award with respect to their claims. The first is, that of *colouring*, which he dismisses on the merits. "It is enough," says he, "to say that this signification is without any support from profane or sacred literature."

Now while I agree in this award, I differ utterly with respect to the ground on which it is rested. He treats a figurative application of a word as if it were literal. He calls on it to justify itself by examples. A figurative application of a word has no need of justification by similar use. The first application is the best; and it declines in value, every time it is used. It requires nothing to justify it but likeness and agreeableness. While a writer has no right to use a new word, or an old one in a new signification, he is perfectly at liberty to use any word in a new figurative application.

"In respect to the second, which," says the writer, " is the classical usage of the word, it should be remarked, that when in the classics the mind is said to be baptized, (*i. e.* overwhelmed or oppressed,) never is reference made to an abundance of *good*, but always and only to an abundance of evil."

1. The classical meaning of the word is in no instance *overwhelm*.

2. Has not the writer admitted *immerse* as one of its meanings? Why, then, confine the figurative application to one literal meaning, when the word is admitted to have many?

3. The word, neither in its literal meaning, nor its figurative application, has anything to do with the nature of the thing to which it is applied. It denotes excess, and nothing but excess; the nature of the thing must be known otherwise. In the word itself there is no expression of either *good* or *evil*.

4. Admitting that the classical meaning of the word is *overwhelm*, this would destroy the writer's theory. How would he contrive to get *purify* out of *overwhelm?* Is it not admitted that purify comes from immersion, by process of usage?

5. All the instances of classical usage in a figurative application, do not confine this word to evil. As to immersion, *bapto* and *baptizo* are the same; and *immersed in justice*, a classical phrase, is not an immersion in evil.

6. The English corresponding word *immerse*, is figuratively applied to both *good* and *evil;* and all corresponding words in all languages must be equally capable of such an application. Homer speaks of ambrosial sleep, which Cowper translates, "Immersed in soft repose ambrosial."

7. But with respect to figurative application, I am not bound to rest on examples. On this point, as I have already intimated, I disregard the authority of use. All I want is likeness, and likeness I have. The author's allegation is the very ground on which Dr. Wiseman rests his proof of transubstantiation from the words of our Lord. He admits that the words themselves are capable of a figurative interpretation. How, then, does he deny the consequence? He denies that the phrase, *eat flesh*, is ever used figuratively, except as denoting destruction; and as this cannot be the meaning in our Lord's address, the words must be literal. I deny the critical dogma as firmly as I do transubstantiation itself: it is grounded on ignorance of philology; it confounds the laws of literal and figurative expression. *The sanction of use is necessary in assigning the meaning of words; but no sanction, except likeness, is neces-*

sary to justify its figurative application. Any word may be figuratively used as no man ever used it before.

But even admitting that *overwhelm* is the meaning of the word, and that figuratively, in classical usage, it always applied to calamity, the philosophy of the writer is unsound. The manner might designate what is in itself an evil, while the ordinance designated by the word might indicate a blessing. Was not circumcision, as to the thing in itself, an evil? Was it not emblematical of a blessing? Is not the serpent an animal accursed of God? Was not the brazen serpent indicative of the greatest of all blessings? Were not *sin offerings* emblematical of a blessing? Is crucifixion no evil? Are not believers said to be *crucified with Christ?* Is such a crucifixion no blessing? Sprinkling with blood is in itself defilement; yet it is emblematical of a blessing—even the blessing of purification.

" Baptism," says the writer, " having been long used by the Jews as a symbol of the purification of mind, would be closely associated with mind by this idea. It would, therefore, be most unnatural to speak of the baptism of mind, except in the sense of the purifying of mind."

1. What does he here mean by baptism? Does he mean immersion in water for a symbolical purpose? If so, this is all we want. Does he mean by baptism all the rights of purification? The word never had such an application. Does he mean purification by the word baptism? This his theory demands. Then the assertion is, that " Purification, having been long used by the Jews as a symbol of purification of mind, would be closely associated with mind by this idea."

2. Immersion in water, both among Jews and heathens, was always a symbol of purification. Will men ever learn that this does not imply that the word designates purification?

3. As all applications of the word to mind are figurative, no number of applications having one figure, will prevent its application to another —even to the very opposite. The emblem of purification is in the pure water—not in the mode of its application; defilement might equally be referred to by immersion in a defiling substance. How could the writer overlook the fact, that the Septuagint says, "Iniquity baptizeth me?" When iniquity is the baptizer, purification cannot be the effect.

4. Figurative baptism respects both body and mind. This criticism is mere speculation, founded neither on principle nor on observation of facts.

But is the writer aware of the consequence resulting from his assertion, that the word baptism, in the phrase, *baptism of the Spirit,* is used in its literal, not in a figurative acceptation? If the baptism in the Spirit is a literal baptism, then must also the baptism *in fire* be a literal baptism, for the same persons are to be baptized in the Holy Spirit and fire. Now, as the writer, being a Protestant, can have no claim on purgatory, I cannot see where he will get the fire. " The simple, unpoetic style" must forbid a figurative baptism *in fire,* as well as in the *Holy Spirit.* In like manner, " salted with fire" must employ literal salt and literal fire. Yet, after all, I cannot see how literal salt will salt with literal fire. Ah, my brethren, it is at a fearful expense that you can resist this truth and defend your error. You must trample on all the laws of language. Your ingenuity may devise innumerable schemes, but you will never devise one that may not be dispersed as gossamer by the breath of the morning.

SECTION V.—AUTHOR'S EXPOSITION OF THE WORD IN THE PASSAGES IN WHICH IT OCCURS.—In his exposition of the different passages in which the word occurs, the writer commences with 2 Kings v. 14. " Now," says he, " what is it likely that he did ?" It is not likely, but certain, that he did what he was commanded. Likelihood has nothing to do with the question—it is a matter of testimony, and testimony must be expounded by the ascertained meaning of the words employed to convey it. He asks another question, " How is his action described?" Why it is described as an *immersion*. Nothing can be plainer. Then, is the matter at an end? Not so fast; stop a little, friend. " To reply to these questions, it is proper to ascertain what was the washing required by the Mosaic law in cases of leprosy." What has such an inquiry to do with an answer to either of these questions? To know what the prophet commanded, and what Naaman did in obeying, is any reference necessary but what is contained in the record? This was not a Jewish purification. What had Naaman to do with the law of leprosy?—Even after he became a believer in the God of Israel, he had nothing to do with the law of Israel. Much less, then, could he have to do with that law, when he was a heathen. The author asserts of the law of leprosy, that one part of it was ceremonial, the other sanative. There was nothing sanative in it. The leper was healed before the purification.

He asserts also that the washing and shaving of the leper were designed to remove the danger of infection. Who told him so? The preventive of infection is spoken of in the previous chapter. Can any Christian be at a loss to know the emblem of the washing of the leper? " Such were some of you, but ye are washed," &c.

Had it been a legal purification of a leper, it would have been performed after his cure.

Had it been a legal purification of a leper, the whole ritual, with respect to the cleansing of the leper, would have been observed. Here the thing commanded was to effect a cure, and nothing but washing was commanded.

The writer says, that the command to wash seven times is a command to sprinkle seven times. A command to wash, however, is very different from a command to sprinkle. Seven *bathings* cannot be effected by seven sprinklings.

This is still more absurd in reference to Naaman. Would that Syrian understand a command to *wash*, as importing Mosaic sprinklings?

The word *louo* signifies to *bathe*, and except when a part is mentioned, it refers to the person in general. This I have proved at large in my dissertation on the word in reply to President Beecher.

In the law of leprosy, with respect to purification, there are seven sprinklings with blood, and two washings with water. Our author thinks it more probable that the word *wash* in this command should correspond to the seven sprinklings with blood, than to the two bathings in water! But the command refers to neither.

" The law," the writer says, " did not enjoin dipping; and it is most improbable that not being enjoined it should be generally practised." If the law required bathing, or washing the body all over, how is it improbable that they immersed? But the command of the prophet was most certainly obeyed by *dipping*, though neither the command nor the performance had anything to do with the law of Moses.

Seven bathings of his person were enjoined on Naaman for his cure; which was performed by seven baptisms. If, then, baptism is purification, there were seven purifications instead of one. The seven sprinklings of blood, with two washings, constituted only one purification.

The author thinks it improbable that Naaman dipped himself, and gives four reasons :—

First, " He was only required to wash;" this requirement was performed by immersion. He bathed, and consequently he immersed. Probability has nothing to do in this matter ; we have testimony. That Naaman was immersed is as certain as that the word of God speaks truth.

The second reason is, that " what he was commanded to do is represented as a small thing." And is it a great thing to dip seven times in a river, in order to be cured of one of the most loathsome and disgusting diseases that ever afflicted the human body? If this is a great thing, what is small? He was enjoined to *bathe*—can there be any easier way of bathing than by dipping?

The third reason to make it probable that Naaman was not dipped, is, that " his temper of mind was not that which would lead him to do more than was enjoined." Nor did he more than was enjoined; a dipping is not more than a bathing.

The fourth reason is, that " his action is stated to have been in accordance with the prophet's command." Doubtless; and was not his *dipping* a fulfilment of his command to bathe? Reasons! Were there ever four such reasons alleged for or against anything? How easily are our opponents satisfied with reasons for one side of the question! On the other, Naaman himself, compared with them, was yielding in his obstinacy. If I produce any such reasons, let them be treated with the scorn they merit.

" But," says the writer, " whatever may have been the mode in which Naaman obeyed the prophet's order, that his action is not described as *a dipping*, is evident from these considerations." Let us hear the author's considerations. " If so common a signification was to be expressed, *bapto*, or some common word might be expected, and not a word whose rare occurrence indicates that it had already some peculiarity of meaning, like what it is found to have possessed afterwards."

1. Is not this extravagantly unreasonable and inconsistent? The action the writer has himself declared to be not only a religious rite, but the Jewish rite of the purification of a leper, yet this word is too solemn to designate the immersion performed in it! He demands the little wicked word *bapto*, to express a holy immersion. Had *bapto* been

actually used, I have no more doubt than I have that the pen is in my hand, that he would have objected that *baptizo* was not used—the word on which the controversy principally rests. "We have piped unto you, and ye have not danced: we have mourned, and ye have not lamented." We give you *bapto*, and you require *baptizo:* we give you *baptizo*, and you require *bapto*. Can it be expected that in each passage we shall have both words? I cannot, I will not, suppress my indignation at such unreasonableness. The meaning of no word could ever be settled with certainty, if such reasoning is allowable. Availing myself of like liberties, I will undertake to show that there is not a word in the Greek language whose meaning can be ascertained with certainty.

2. What does the writer mean by *so common a signification?* By a common signification, I understand a common meaning of the word. But if this is a common meaning of the word, why does he object to its use on this occasion? Does he mean so common an operation as dipping? Why should not the same operation have the same name, whether common or infrequent? Does he mean common in contra-distinction to sacred? How can he consistently call this a common dipping?

3. If a common word is employed in the command, may not a common word be employed with respect to the performance? *Louo* is a common word, yet it refers equally to things common and sacred. Why may not *baptizo* do the same?

4. *Baptizo* is not a more sacred word than *bapto;* the latter is applied to Jewish rites more frequently than the former. If this gives holiness, it is the holier of the two. It is indeed a little word, but it is often as full of the odour of sanctity as Homer's ox hide was of "slippery lard." It applies to the dipping of a flea's foot, yet it equally applies to the Jewish immersions for purification Whether either of the words in any instance refers to sacred or common things, ıs not known from them-selves, but from connexion and appropriation.

5. *Baptizo* is applied to common things. Is it not applied to the immersion of Aristobulus in bathing? It applies to the dipping of a person in the sea—to the dipping of a man's hand in blood, for the pur-pose of writing—to the dipping of the head of a crow, &ι. &c.

6. But I resist the ground of this criticism. If a word is proved to dip one object, it may dip another. It might as well be said that though the word will apply to dipping in the Jordan, this does not prove that it will apply to dipping in the Thames ; or that though a word may be used to designate killing as to a nun, this is no proof that it will kill a friar. Did I meet such criticism with respect to the meaning of a word in the classics, I would not give it an answer.

7. That the Greek word signifies *dip,* is clear from the fact that this is the meaning of the word in the original.

8. Has not the term sprinkle been used in the church of Rome for hundreds of years, in reference to the performance of the most solemn rites? Yet they can use the same word in reference to the most common things. It is a most unfounded and ridiculous conceit, to suppose that when a word is applied to solemn things, it is disqualified for service

with respect to things that are common or trivial. This is philological Puseyism.

The second reason from which, according to the writer, "It is evident" that this word cannot here signify *dipping*, though *dipping* had been the action performed, is that "there is nothing to show that dipping was in the thoughts of the writer; for there is no word in the context, and nothing in the scope of the passage, having the least relation thereto. On the contrary, while apart from the signification of the word itself, there is nothing to lead to the supposition that Naaman was dipped, we know that he was cleansed. The action, however performed, was a purification."

1. Does the fact that there is nothing in the context to ascertain the meaning of the word, make it evident that it has not such a meaning? This is lame logic. Evidence from context is of the greatest importance; but the want of it cannot prove an objection—much less disprove. In many instances context can afford no evidence, but will be as favourable to a false meaning as to the true. It is strange beyond measure that the writer should rest on such arguments.

2. We have evidence from context that the word cannot mean *purify*. The action prescribed as the means of purification was performed by seven baptisms, or by seven times performing the thing imported by the word. There was then only one purification, by means of seven baptisms. If the meaning of the word is purify, then there would be seven purifications.

3. This is still more absurd, because the purification spoken of was the *healing* of the leper. Was he seven times *cured*? Though the action performed was the means of purification; yet it was neither ceremonial nor spiritual purification. It was purification from disease. Naaman, though cleansed from his leprosy, was still, in the sense of the Jewish law, equally impure as an uncircumcised man. His cleansing did not fit him for the ordinances of Israel. When our Lord cleansed the lepers, it was healing that was meant—not ceremonial cleansing; as all the cleansed lepers who were Jews, would afterwards be cleansed by the law of Moses. The writer confounds the healing of disease with legal purification.

The third reason, according to our author, which makes it evident that dipping is not here expressed by the word, even though dipping had been the mode in which Naaman obeyed the prophet's order, is, "on this occasion Naaman became a worshipper of Jehovah." What has Naaman's conversion to do with the meaning of the word? Just as much as with the era of the Chinese empire. Every thing would have been the same had Naaman continued in his idolatry. Even had his conversion preceded his cure, he could not have received any Jewish ordinance without circumcision. In this affair Naaman can be considered in no other light than that of an unclean heathen and idolator. He was not in any point of view entitled to any of the legal purifications of the law of Moses.

To turn away the testimony of the original in this passage, the writer alleges that the Hebrew word signifies to *stain* and to *moisten*, as well as to *dip*. Now granting this to be a fact, how utterly unreasonable is the allegation! How can this serve his purpose here? Did the prophet command Naaman to *stain* himself seven times in Jordan? Did he command him to *moisten*? If the command is to *bathe*, must there not be bathing in the performance?

In Lev. iv. 17, *moisten* will not serve. The blood was to be sprinkled from the finger; and to do this, *dipping* is necessary. The finger might be *moistened*, when the blood will not drop from the moistened finger. "And the priest shall dip his finger in some of the blood, and sprinkle it seven times before the Lord." Who would substitute *moisten* in this place? So also Lev. xiv. 16, with respect to the oil. A finger might be very moist with oil, when the oil would not drop from it.

The writer alleges the authority of the Syriac and the Vulgate, which render both the word in the command, and the word expressing the performance, by *wash*. In a free translation this is often done; but it is not faithful. *The readers of a translation ought to have as far as possible all the distinctions of the original.* But this is no proof that the authors of such translations considered the words as perfectly identical. Besides, this does not serve our author. He makes the word signify not *washing*, but purification by seven sprinklings, as the whole purifying process of the law of Moses.

SECTION VI.—AUTHOR'S INTERPRETATION OF THE WORD IN THE SEPTUAGINT, ISAIAH xxi. 4.—In interpreting the word in the Septuagint, Isaiah xxi. 4, the author alleges that, according to Schleusner, *anomia* here has the sense of *terror*, as well as *iniquity*. Were this the assertion of all the lexicographers in existence, it is false and extravagantly foolish. It never signifies *terror*, nor anything but want of *conformity to law*, or *transgression of law*. No matter in what way the Septuagint is to be reconciled with the text of the original; "iniquity immerses me," is the only allowable translation.

With respect to this passage, the writer says, "There is no reference to dipping—nothing even to suggest the idea." Whether there is a reference to dipping depends entirely on the pre-established meaning of this word. If the word literally, as it does, signify *immerse*, the figurative reference must be immersion. If, with respect to the English expression, "iniquity immerses me," it should be alleged, "there is no reference to dipping—nothing even to suggest the idea," what would be our answer? Why it would be: Every one who knows anything of the English language, knows that *immerse* signifies to *dip*. The same say I, with respect to this allegation. What better reference can there be to a mode, than to use the most definite word that signifies that mode?

"But its common classic signification," says the writer, "when applied to mind, to press down or overwhelm, is exactly suited to it." Neither *overwhelm*, nor *press down*, is the classic meaning of this word, nor any meaning at all. But is it not admitted that *immerse* is the primary meaning, or at least one of the meanings of the word? What then disqualifies it here, even if *terror* is the baptizer? Cannot *terror* immerse as easily as it can *press down* or *overwhelm*? Schleusner's interpretation of the word *anomia*, has nothing to do with the meaning of the word *baptizo*. It was not to accommodate any theory with respect to the meaning of the word, that induced Schleusner to commit this violence on the word *anomia;* but a desire to reconcile the Septuagint with the original. This lexicographer, as well as others, gives *immerse* as the classical meaning of *baptizo*.

The writer speaks of the word as applied to mind, as if it were applied to mind literally. This is not so. When applied to mind it is always figurative. Besides, *press down* or *overwhelm* is figurative, as well as is *immerse*, when applied to mind. Is the mind *pressed down* on, or *overwhelmed* literally?

But why does the writer bring the classical meaning of a word into Hebraistic Greek? He perceived this inconsistency, and attempts in a very unsatisfactory manner, to account for it. "That *baptizo*," says he, "though it had in the Hebraistic Greek another meaning, should be once used by a translator in its ordinary classic sense, is what might be expected." *Just what might be expected!* Why should it be expected to be used in a sense which to those who made the translation, and those for whom it was made, it would not convey? Why once, rather than a million of times? If it may once be used, it may so be used any number of times. This admission shows that the word never received a Hebraistic sense. Even if it had the two meanings, might it not be appropriated to the ordinance of Christ, in the sense of *immerse?*

The author comes next to the case of Judith at the fountain of Bethulia. "Then Holofernes commanded his guard that they should not stay her: then she abode in the camp three days, and went out in the night into the valley of Bethulia, and washed herself in a fountain of water by the camp."

It is perfectly incomprehensible to me how any one can find a difficulty in this instance. The most scrupulous and even romantic delicacy is provided for in the retirement of the lady to a fountain in a valley. It is evident that though in a camp, she was in such a part of it as afforded her the necessary seclusion. Had she been the wife of the general, she could not have greater security for privacy, nor better means of effecting it. I must think that this plea of delicacy is unreasonable and affected. Had not the ordinance of baptism been supposed to be affected by this matter, I believe we should never have heard of a complaint against the lady for indelicacy. But I care not, in the least degree, how any one may decide as to views of delicacy in this matter. However indelicate any one may choose to consider the conduct of Judith, the fact is in proof, and I will not suffer views of delicacy to question it.

The writer gives us a number of authorities for purification, by washing of hands and sprinkling with water. What has this to do with the question? We do not deny such purifications. *Sprinklings are purifications*, but they are not *baptisms*.

He tells us, that if we *imagine* that Judith was immersed in water, we *assume* what is highly improbable. What sort of reasoning is this?

We neither *imagine* nor *assume* as to this fact; we rest on the testimony of the word. It is from the established meaning of the word, not from views of independent probability, that we must derive our knowledge of the fact. Even were the fact improbable in itself, the testimony of the word would establish it. Were an English traveller to relate that in a certain city he saw the people bathing in the street, we must believe either that the persons referred to actually so bathed, or that the narrator falsifies. The plan of this writer, however, would be to explain the word *bathe*, as signifying to sprinkle a few drops of water, on the ground of improbability.

But it is physically impossible, he tells us, that the fountain was sufficiently deep. This shows that the writer does not understand the fundamental laws of controversy. Does not the burden of proof lie on him? Is it not the objector who must prove? I care not if there had not been a fountain at all in Bethulia; she might have been immersed without it. If from other places I prove that *immerse* is the meaning of the word, this in every situation will provide the water. We refuse, then, to be gauger of the fountain of Bethulia; let them dip it who need the evidence. But to allege that it is improbable that the fountain was of sufficient depth, is perfectly captious. Do we not know that it is still customary to bathe in sacred wells? According to the philosophy of our author, when an historian relates that an army forded a river, we cannot believe him till it is proved by other evidence that the river was in some part fordable. If it was *forded*, it must be fordable. If Judith was baptized in the fountain of Bethulia, it must have been deep enough for immersion.

Though I care not whether it be supposed that she was immersed in the fountain, or in a cistern or bath beside it, yet it is plain that the historian understands that it was in the fountain. The preposition, indeed, does not designate this, but it is often used when *in* might have been used. We do the same thing—we speak of bathing *at* a river or *in* a river. But that the historian meant that she was immersed *in* the fountain is plain, from his speaking of her praying immediately on *ascending*. The English translation also understands it in this sense, for it renders it, " when she came out."

The delicacy of our author is so very romantic, that it is not enough for him that the guard of Holofernes were forbidden to hinder her—he complains that they were not forbidden to watch her. He might still require security from the Man in the Moon, for who could say, but, like peeping Tom of Coventry, he might be awake while all others were asleep? Can there be a greater instance of trifling than this? Could the meaning of any word ever be determined if such a mode of reasoning were admitted?

"If still it should be asserted," says the writer, " that she did dip herself, this will not prove that to dip is the sense of the word." Here again the writer mistakes the burden of proof. Our business is merely to answer objections. But what does he mean by saying that, " if it should be asserted that she did dip herself, this will not prove that to dip is the sense of the word?" Surely he does not mean to say that such an assertion will not prove the fact; for no one could allege that an asser tion is proof. If he has any meaning, it must be that though she were dipped, this would not prove that *dip* is the meaning of the word. This admission, however, destroys his cause: for what is the ground on which the admission can rest, but on the meaning of the word? If she was *dipped*, this word must have dipped her. It cannot be known or rationally admitted that she was dipped, but on the testimony of this word. To admit that she was dipped, on the evidence of the passage, is to admit immerse to be the meaning of *baptizo*.

He tells us that, " in whatever way it was performed, the historian wished to represent it as a religious purification, and consequently that this is the meaning of the word." Who doubts that it was a religious purification? What sort of logic is it to say, " consequently this is the meaning of the word?" How many times must I prove that purification may be the nature of a rite, while it has not purification as its name?

The Syriac also, he tells us, agrees with this—" lavabat se," *she bathed herself.* As a free translation I can have no objection to this. But it is not exact. A preacher expounding the words of Peter, " silver and gold have I none," remarked very profoundly, that this might be translated *gold and silver*, or *silver and gold.* So if the lady dipped herself in the fountain of Bethulia, she was bathed: if she was bathed in it, she was dipped; but dip and bathe are not therefore synonymous. The passage in Sirach, xxxi. 25, is the next that comes under the consideration of the writer. The English translation is: " He that washeth himself after touching a dead body, if he touch it again, what availeth his washing?" Literally it is, " He that is immersed from a dead body and again touches it, what avails his bath or bathing?" The writer says, " It is impossible that *baptizomenos* here means *dipped.* 1. Because if there were any immersion, it is unlikely that this rite should be characterised by a part not named in the law." Is a thing impossible, because it is unlikely? If immersion is not named in the law, it is implied in what is named—bathing. This is the way that the law was fulfilled. Why, then, may it not be so designated? It is perfectly the same thing that takes place in the case of Naaman—*bathing* was commanded; *dipping* fulfilled the command. As immersion was the completion of the purification after the touch of a dead body, the concluding rite alone is referred to. This supposes all the rest. But whatever may be supposed the reason, the immersion only is meant.

The second reason alleged why the word cannot here signify immersion, is, " It is construed with *apo*, which is not suited to that signification, for such an expression as to dip *from*, could not be used in any language." What if I could show him the very expression? " Dip it in the blood," Exod. xii. 22, and many other places, is literally, dip it from the blood. But though the expression is the same, it does not proceed on the same principle. Here to *immerse from a dead body* is an elliptical expression, and means to *dip in order to purify from the touch*, or after the touch, of a dead body. The thing was so common, that all persons at once understood and could supply the ellipsis. All common processes are usually expressed elliptically.

A third reason alleged by the author is: " The question shows that the attention of the writer was directed, not to the manner in which a rite might be performed, but to its end. Without doubt purification was the thing in the mind of the writer; but might not this be the case though he referred to it as an immersion? "A man once dipped," says the writer, " could not be undipped." Very true; but could not his dipping become unavailing, which is the thing that is said? Even were the word purification used, it is in this respect perfectly the same thing. A man purified becomes defiled by touching a defiling object after purification.

A fourth reason is, "The correspondence which exists between *euchomenos, he who prays*, in the 24th verse; *baptizomenos*, in the 25th verse; *nesteuon, he who fasts*, in the 26th, makes it probable that as the first and the last are religious terms, and are applied to those who are seeking the favour of God; that *baptizomenos*, also, has a religious sense, and is peculiarly appropriated to those who, by ceremonial purifications, would prepare themselves for the worship of the Most Holy."

Euchomai is not exclusively a religious word; *nesteuo* is not a religious word; and *baptizo*, signifying *immerse*, can be as religious as either of them, without renouncing a tittle of its meaning or adopting anything in addition. May not an immersion be performed for a religious purpose, without making it signify anything but immersion? It is most extravagantly absurd to suppose, that if a word is at any time applied to religious things, it is thereby incapacitated for serving generally, and must become a religious term.

But that *baptizomenos* here means *immersed*, is demonstratively evident from the fact that *loutron, bath*, is given as a corresponding word. The question is not, what avails his purification? but, what avails his bathing? Baptism, then, and bathing, refer to the same thing. They are not the same in meaning, but they reciprocally imply each other. This determines, beyond controversy, that the word does not signify purification. Instead of extending to all the rites of Mosaic purification, it applies only to the bathing. Even were it identical with *bathing*, it cannot designate purification; for *louo* and *bathe* apply only to the washing of animal bodies. *To bathe from a dead body* requires the same ellipsis as to immerse from a dead body. And if it is *bathing*, it will equally serve our purpose. A person is buried in *bathing*, as well as in *immersion*.

What the author says upon Mark vii. 3, is mere conjecture. The meaning of the word in this place must be determined by its meaning where there is no controversy. In all controverted cases, let the meaning be settled independently of them, and bring the result to settle the controversy. If the Rabbins say, that in the time of our Lord there was no such custom as immersion on the occasions mentioned, I will reply, I believe the evangelist rather than you. What do you know of the matter more than others? Have not others had access to all the documents accessible to you? The evangelist declares, that on certain occasions it was then usual to baptize themselves; and baptize, in all the Greek language, signifies nothing but immerse. What difficulty is there in this matter?

But the writer tells us, " That copper vessels and couches should be immersed in water, is another great improbability; with regard to many of the latter, it would hardly be practicable, with regard to all it would be difficult and injurious." A radical error pervades the whole of this writer's criticism. He founds the meaning of words on views of probability, without reference to their use in the language. On such a first principle nothing could ever be known from history. We make the historian express what we think probable, independently of his testimony; and whatever may be his testimony, we force it to renounce a meaning that seems to us improbable. A principle more absurd, fanatical, and mischievous could not be adopted. We are not left to determine the question by views of probability or improbability, independently of the testimony of the words employed to convey the testimony. The question must be decided by the legitimate meaning of the language, whatever may be the result. However improbable any person may choose to consider the matter, if it is attested by suitable evidence, it is to be believed. If the thing is not true in the legitimate meaning of the testimony, the reporter must be branded as a falsifier. His language is not to be forced in order to harmonize with his veracity. Even profane history commands our belief with respect to many things that, independently of the testimony, are improbable. But to me there is nothing improbable in anything here related. The things said to be baptized are all capable of immersion. Why should we force and falsify the word of God to save the character of the Jews of our Lord's time from the imputation of gross superstition? It would not disturb me in the least if such immersions were even injurious, difficult, and disagreeable, though not one of them is really such. The words of the Holy Spirit must not be tortured to make superstitious practices easy to the devotee. Should an English traveller relate that he had lately discovered a colony of Jews who *immersed* all the things mentioned in Mark vii. 3, should we say either that he is a liar, or that by *immerse*, he means *purify* by sprinkling? No truth could stand on such a ground of interpretation. Give it to the Socinian, and he will overturn orthodoxy without any trouble. Were I to make a selection of the false principles of interpretation employed by our opponents, admitting their validity, I would undertake to prove or disprove anything.

In a note the writer edifies us with an account of the different ways in which the Jews washed their hands: he might as well inform us of the way in which they ate their breakfast. The question is not about purification in general, nor about the way in which the Jews washed their hands, but about something that was done under the name of baptism.

" That it was not the writer's design," says the author, " to speak of these baptisms as immersions, appears also from the train of thought which the passage exhibits. He wished to explain the reason why the disciples of Jesus were censured for not washing their hands. It was not likely that for this end he would refer to the practice of dipping the whole body, even if it were customary; but it is likely that he would refer to purifications similar to what they had neglected."

Now, what is the use of such airy speculation? The evangelist wished to do whatever he did; and what he did can be known only from what he has said. Why should he be confined to the instance of superstition respecting washing the hands? Why should he not proceed to give instances of more extravagant superstition? He tells us that the water-pots, John ii. 6, will not serve us. I care not that those pots would not hold as much as an egg-shell ;· we have no need of them. We care not where water was found; superstition will be at no loss to procure it.

The most illiterate person may perceive the absurdity of translating the word by *purify* in this place. What nonsense would it be to say, "They eat not unless they wash their hands; and coming from market, they eat not unless they *are purified!*" Is not the washing of the hands a purification?

"How this purification was performed," he says, "is not expressed; probably by washing and sprinkling combined." And are we to take his dreams, rather than the testimony of the word itself? Another person may as warrantably allege, that the ceremony was performed with holy oil, salt, &c. It is to me unspeakably astonishing that Christians will permit themselves to sport so wantonly with the word of the living God. Expositions of Homer on this ground would be of no use in ascertaining the customs referred to by him. Conjecture and probabilities have no just authority in history either sacred or profane. To attempt to ascertain a custom by conjecture, is not only to communicate no knowledge, but to deceive the unwary, who sometimes feed voraciously on the husks of conjecture.

But *purify* is not entitled to compete here, or anywhere else, as a meaning of this word. It is like a person proposing himself as a candidate for a seat in parliament, who is not qualified by possessing the landed income required by law. It nowhere can be shown to be the meaning of the word; if not, why should it be a competitor as the meaning in a disputed passage? It is in proof that the word signifies *immerse;* no meaning can compete with this that is not also in proof. He who will not admit such laws of interpretation, cannot be worthy of being reasoned with. He refuses to admit self-evident truth.

"The next passage for consideration," he tells us, "is Luke xi. 37." He tells us "that nothing is said of the retirement of the host, or of any invitation given by him to his guests, to retire to the bath." No such information is necessary. It is evident that there must have been means of performing the thing meant by the word; but whether these were in the Pharisee's house, or elsewhere, is of no consequence. The Pharisee was with Jesus in the multitude, and accompanied him to his house. Whether, then, the bath was in his house, or elsewhere, he must have known that Jesus did not use it. A thousand means of immersion might have existed, of which we can know nothing; and common sense should teach the most ignorant that such information is not necessary. Is it to be expected that the whole conversation of the host with his guests is to be recorded?

How differently would an antiquarian reason from this passage! "Here," he would say, "it is palpably evident that bathing for religious purposes was exceedingly common among the Jews at this period; and that there must have been many baths, both public and private. Most probably every house had one or more." How differently do men reason, when an ordinance of Christ must be made to conform to the practice of man!

The writer tells us, that in his reply, Jesus did not refer to immersion, but to purification. What wonder is this? Was not the immersion for the purpose of purification? Is it strange, then, that in his reply, Jesus should refer to the thing, and not to the mode in which it was effected? Does this imply that immersion was not the mode of performing the purification?

"The last passage referring to Jewish baptisms," says the writer, "is Heb. ix. 9. During which time offerings and sacrifices are presented, which are incapable of making perfect, in respect to the conscience, him who does service only with things to be eaten and to be drunk, and with various baptisms, services of the body, imposed until the season for reformation."

The writer here translates for himself. If, then, I can answer him on the ground of his own translation, the refutation must be unsuspicious and satisfactory. Even this translation is in perfect accordance with my view of the meaning of the word. It is substantially the translation of Macknight; and Macknight even here translates the word *immersion*, —"both gifts and sacrifices are offered, which cannot, with respect to conscience, make him perfect who worshippeth only with meats and drinks, and divers *immersions*." Even according to this translation, the service or worship respects not only the gifts and sacrifices offered in the tabernacle, but every act of service in the whole law of Moses. It must respect the services performed in their own houses, as well as those performed at the tabernacle. The meaning is, that the gifts and sacrifices offered in the tabernacle could not perfect persons whose worship consisted in the things mentioned, which had no excellence in themselves. No translation could suit me better. The baptisms, then, must apply to every rite performed by immersion.

Should Professor Stuart's view of the connexion between the ninth and tenth verses be preferred, it is equally suitable to my view of the meaning of this word. He understands the meats and drinks, as exclusive of the gifts and sacrifices. "*Meats* and *drinks*," says he, "have respect to that which was clean and unclean, under the Jewish dispensation ; and not, (as some critics interpret the word,) to the meats and drinks offered to the Lord." He makes the baptisms refer to the ceremonial ablutions of the Jews. Doubtless they include every thing that was performed by immersion.

"The baptisms here mentioned," says the writer, "were a part of the service of the tabernacle." By this he seems to assert, that all the things here referred to were performed in the tabernacle. There is no foundation for this, even in his own translation, more than in that of Professor Stuart, who as to baptism is on the same side. The two dispensations are contrasted in general. He might as well confine it to the tabernacle, to the exclusion of the temple; or confine it to the things done in the tabernacle, to the exclusion of things done elsewhere. The service of the worshipper, or the person who does the service, must respect all the things included in the law, which is the rule of his service. Indeed, in the thirteenth verse, the cleansing by the rite of purification, with the ashes of a heifer, which was not done in the tabernacle, is expressly mentioned.

" We may learn what they were," says the writer, " by referring to the Old Testament, Exod. xxix. 4 : ' And Aaron, and his sons, thou shalt bring unto the door of the tabernacle of the congregation, and shalt wash them with water.' Exod. xxx. 19 : ' For Aaron and his sons shall wash their hands and their feet thereat : when they go into the tabernacle of the congregation, they shall wash with *water*, that they die not; or when they come near to the altar to minister, to burn offering made by fire unto the Lord, so they shall wash their hands and their feet, that they die not.' " Now from what source do we learn that the things referred to in these passages were baptisms ? They are not here called baptisms. We can therefore learn that they were baptisms, only from our previous knowledge of the word, and from the fact that the thing signified by the word, whatever that may be, takes place in the performance of the thing here mentioned. If then they were not *immersions*, I would permit no man to call them *baptisms*. I am, however, quite willing that they should be called *baptisms :* the first as an immersion of the whole body ; the second as an immersion of the hands and feet.

But I will not extend this act of grace to the next examples, Numb. viii. 5 : " And the Lord spake unto Moses, saying, Take the Levites from among the children of Israel, and cleanse them ; and thus shalt thou do unto them to cleanse them : sprinkle clean water of purifying upon them." Numb. xix. 20 : " But the man that shall be unclean, and shall not purify himself, that soul shall be cut off from among the congregation, because he hath defiled the sanctuary of the Lord. The water of separation hath not been sprinkled upon him; he is unclean." Where did the writer learn that these were baptisms ? Are they called baptisms here ? Are they called baptisms anywhere else ? He might as well assert that they were circumcisions. They are purifications : but all purifications are not baptisms.

" Such," says the writer, " were the principal, if not the only baptisms alluded to by the apostle." It fills me with astonishment beyond what I can express, that any person could make such an assertion. Is there a man of common sense in England who in reading, or hearing these passages, would understand them to be called baptisms ? If this passes for proof, anything may be proved : I call the attention of the unlearned to this. If our opponents can misrepresent evidence, in a case so palpable, can they be trusted in cases of profound criticism ? If such things are the baptisms referred to by the apostle, it is not because they are called baptisms in the law of Moses, nor because of any explanation in this passage, but from the meaning of the word independently ascertained.

" There is," says the writer, " nothing to show that one immersion of the whole body was ever required." If bathing was required, does not this imply immersion? An immersion of any part, and of anything, is as good in proof of the meaning of the word, as the immersion of the whole body. Besides, it is not the command, but the performance, that is here referred to; and the case of Naaman shows us that *dipping* is the performance of a command enjoining *bathing*. Justin Martyr also speaks of dipping in reference to bathing, as prescribed by the law of Moses. But it is quite enough for us, that the law of bathing may have been fulfilled by immersion.

"It is superfluous to remark," says the writer, "that even if there had been many immersions, these could not be styled *diaphoroi*. The dipping of various things could not be various dippings." Why does he say so, when examples in contradiction occur every day in every language? In Deut. xxii. 9, it refers to different sorts of seed; and instead of implying a great variety of difference, a single variety is sufficient. It applies to two seeds that differ, as well as to a thousand sorts. Do not our opponents say, that John's baptism, and our Lord's baptism, were different baptisms? They were different in neither form nor emblem, and the difference was confined to two. This passage, then, supposed to be so unequivocally against us, gives us no disturbance.

Indeed we require no more than the repetition of the same act to exemplify this difference. The word is *baptismos*, not *baptisma;* and the different baptisms might refer to different acts of immersion of the same object. In 2 Mac. xiv. 21, the word is applied to two different seats of the same kind. The only difference here was that Nicanor and Judas, instead of sitting on the same throne or chair of state, when they sat in conference, had each a chair for himself, a *different seat.* Every one of my opponents has brought this word against me as if it were utterly irreconcilable with my doctrine; but it is the most harmless word imaginable. Their criticisms are founded on mere speculation— not on either observation of the various occurrences of the word, or in its philosophy.

"Baptisms," says the writer, "were rites performed in the Jewish temple in connexion with the worship of God. Immersions were never performed in the Jewish temple," &c.

Where is it said that all baptisms were confined to the temple? All baptisms were not in the temple. *Immersions* of some things were constantly performed in the Jewish temple. "But his inwards and his legs shall he wash in water, Lev. i. 9." Did not this imply immersion? "He made also ten bases, and put five on the right hand, and five on the left, to wash in them; such things as they offered for the burnt offering, they washed in them; but the sea was for the priests to wash in." Are not these immersions? Are not these different immersions even in the temple? But we are not, as we have already seen, confined to the temple, even by the author's own translation; we have the whole range of Jewish practice both public and private.

But why does the author say that baptisms were rites in the Jewish temple in connexion with the worship of God? Is not this as inconsistent with his own doctrine as with mine? Does he not make the cleansing of a person defiled by the touch of a dead body, a baptism? Was this performed in the temple? Was this in connexion with worship? It was a part of the service of God, but not an immediate act of worship —much less of worship in the temple.

"The apostle states," says he, "that these baptisms were appointed by God." This is not the thing which the apostle states; he states what the worshipper did in performing what the law of God required. If immersion fulfilled the law, and if immersion was the way in which the law was usually fulfilled, it is quite enough for us.

"Immersions of the person," says the writer, were not appointed by God." Bathings were appointed by God, and bathings imply immersions. But it is enough if the *bathings* were usually performed by immersion. Besides, there is no reason to confine these immersions to the persons. It may include every thing in which there was immersion, whether of persons or things. Indeed it is quite sufficient if we can show different immersions of anything. Neither the word nor the connexion restricts.

"They were," says he, "purifications with water." Jewish baptisms were not all purifications with water. They were in many different things, blood—blood and water, fire, &c.

"Only in one instance in the whole Mosaic law," says he, "is there a direction to put the object to be purified in water: Lev. xi. 32." And were this the only one, it would serve us. There were different immersions in several different respects; and that they were not performed in the temple, and were not immersions of persons, is of no importance. It is quite enough that they were immersions.

But why does he refuse immersions in other things? Are not immersions in other things equally worthy of the name? "Every thing that may abide the fire, ye shall make it go through the fire." Numb. xxxi. 23. Here is a baptism in fire, and as good a baptism as one in water. It is added, "and all that abideth not the fire shall go through the water." Here is a different baptism in water. We are at no loss to make out different baptisms under the law.

In every view of this passage it is in harmony with our doctrine; in no view of it does it demand any other meaning in the disputed word. But let it never be lost sight of, that the burden of proof lies on our opponents. We stand on the defence. We do not allege this passage as proof; our duty is merely to reply to objections. Our opponents, almost in every instance, overlook this. They think if by new translations, and suppositions not founded on the passage, they can make the passage suitable to their purposes, they succeed. We demolish all their batteries, the moment we show that the passage does not necessarily import what they teach. There is nothing less understood than the burden of proof. Controversialists usually bandy it from one to another; as if it were a matter of mere etiquette It must always depend on self-evidence.

But I can carry the field with respect to this passage, even if all I have said on it were to be given up. Admitting that the many *baptisms* must include all Jewish *washings*, the word may still have its primary meaning, in reference to the Christian ordinance. In excluding from this passage all purifications but such as were done by immersion, I defend my own doctrine with respect to the word as being univocal. But the doctrine of immersion, with respect to the Christian ordinance, may stand independently of this.

Besides, *washing* and *purification* are very different. The latter is a generic word of which the former is a species. All washings are purifications, but all purifications are not washings. Washing is performed by means of water; purification may be performed by means of blood, fire, sulphur, &c.

Even on the supposition that the word here signifies *washing*, and that in the ordinance of Christian baptism it has the same sense, if the person to be baptized must be washed, it will be quite as objectionable to our opponents. I think immersing a person is the easiest way of washing him.

One of the most romantic exploits of this champion, is that at the Red Sea. The hosts of Pharaoh did not attempt anything more fanatically daring. The baptism here is the mere *separation* of the children of Israel from their enemies by means of the cloud and the sea *intervening* between them and their enemies. There is neither dipping nor sprinkling, washing nor purifying, in this baptism. But let us hear himself: "There is one passage," says he, "which, though it does not refer to rites of baptism, speaks of a baptism of the Jews, and may properly be noticed here. 'I am unwilling that you should be ignorant, brethren, that our fathers were all under (the guidance of) the cloud, and all passed through the sea, and all were baptized for Moses by the cloud and by the sea.' 1 Cor. x. 1."

It is always a suspicious thing in a controversialist to be obliged on all occasions to translate for himself, and form his version for serving his purpose. The best version may occasionally admit improvement; but if on the subject of controversy, a party can find nothing right in a translation made by those, as to the point in question, on the same side with himself, every impartial judge will receive his translations with the utmost caution. In my observations I shall advert to nothing but what concerns the point in hand.

1. In rendering the phrase *under the cloud*, by *under the guidance of the cloud*, where does the translator find the supplement? It is not implied in the text; it is not warranted by any supposable ellipsis. This figure always grounds on the fact, that the elliptical matter will be suggested by frequency of the use of the phrase, so that it cannot be either wanted or mistaken. If it does not necessarily and obviously present itself, it is essentially vicious in rhetoric, and utterly unworthy of revelation. I am bold to assert that such an ellipsis as the writer here supposes, does not exist in our language. *Under the cloud* cannot signify *under the guidance of the cloud*. There is not a rhetorician in existence who would warrant such a figure. This is downright forgery —forgery as palpable as to add a cipher to a one pound note, to make it ten. Controversialists who are not acquainted with the philosophy of figurative language, imagine that they may in explication avail them-

selves of their service as often as an exigency requires. This enables ignorance to do miracles. But the operations of figurative diction are as subject to law, as are those of words used literally.

2. The thing here supplied by the authority of ellipsis, is never once literally expressed in the Scripture accounts of this cloud. It is a strange ellipsis that supplies to a word or phrase an idea never elsewhere expressed. Now not one of the references to this cloud calls it the guide of the Israelites, or declares that the Israelites were under its guidance. So far from this, God is said to lead them by the cloud. He was in the cloud, and was himself their guide and leader. This was a mere signal. It might as well be said, than an army is under the guidance of the trumpet.

3. This exposition takes away all emblematical meaning from the cloud, and considers it merely as a signal by agreement. It might as well have been a flag as a cloud.

4. But it is evident that the cloud is here considered not merely as a signal, but as an emblem similar to that of baptism, whatever baptism is.

"The cloud," he says, "did not cover them, so that they might be said to be immersed in it." Can it be more clearly said that the cloud covered them? Is it not expressly said that they were all *under the cloud*, and *in the cloud?*

"We are expressly told," says he, "that they were not *immersed* in the sea." I say we are expressly told that they were immersed in the sea—the apostle directly asserts that they were all *baptized in the sea.* Where are we told, either directly or by implication, that they were not so immersed? "The sacred historian," adds the writer, "says that the Egyptians were immersed and overwhelmed, and that the Israelites were not. 'For the horse of Pharaoh went in with his chariots and with his horsemen into the sea; and the Lord brought again the waters of the sea upon them; but the children of Israel went on dry land in the midst of the sea.'"

I have no objection that the descent of the Egyptians into the sea be called an immersion; but this immersion was to them a dry dip, as well as to the Israelites. When they went in, the water was removed, and they, as well as the Israelites, at first stood on dry ground. When the water returned, they were overwhelmed, which was not the case with the Israelites. Both armies are said to go down into the sea. On the very same principle that they are said to go into the sea, when the place where they entered was dry land, they may be said to be immersed in the sea, while the water surrounded them walking on dry ground. The man who asks, how could they be immersed in the sea, when the water was removed? may ask, how could they go into the sea, when the place where they walked was dry? No rational man can need information on such a point. We talk familiarly of plunging into a forest, and of being immersed in a valley. The going down into the sea is the immersion—the overflowing of the waters was the overwhelming of the Egyptians.

"St. Paul," says the writer, "declares that the Israelites were baptized both by the cloud, and by the sea; but from the history of Moses, we learn that they were neither dipped, nor immersed, nor overwhelmed, by either the one or the other." They were not overwhelmed, and they are not said to be overwhelmed. They are said to be baptized, and they were immersed in the sea, as they went down into the sea. They were immersed in the cloud, as they were said both to be *under* it, and *in* it. If on the top of a mountain I am suddenly involved in mist, shall any one misunderstand me, when I say that I was suddenly *immersed in a cloud?*

But how were the Israelites purified by the cloud, and by the sea? Why, by being through this means separated from the Egyptians. Upon this I remark, 1. *Separation* is no *purification* of any kind, either real or emblematical. Does the author ever find mere separation called purification? Was ever extravagance more extravagant than this? I suppose he confounds *purification* with the original idea in the word that signifies *holiness.* But *holiness* and *purification* are as distinct as *sin* and *duty.*

2. In this view of the matter, the things that *separated,* might as well have been anything else as the *cloud* and *sea.* A *curtain* would have served as well as a *cloud;* and a *mountain* as well as *the sea.* The wall of China would purify as well as the Red Sea.

3. Even were the passage translated *purified by the cloud* and by the sea, it would imply that the purification was something done by means of the cloud, when they were in it; and by the sea, when they were passing through it. The cloud and sea could not have been mere separation; but must have been means of purification by application to their bodies. Would any reader understand *purification by a cloud,* as expressing separation from something, by intervention of the cloud; or *purification by the sea,* as expressing separation from idolaters, by intervention of the sea? The application of the purifying substance to the thing purified, is essential to purification.

4. The baptism was not *by* the cloud, and *by* the sea, but *in* the cloud, and *in* the sea. The primary meaning of the preposition, all must allow, refers to place; and to employ a word in a secondary meaning, in a situation where the primary is not only suitable, but where it most obviously suggests itself, would be a very essential fault in style. The preposition is often to be translated *with,* but in the sense *by,* grammarians themselves acknowledge it to be rare. Why then desert the obvious meaning for one rare, and in this place the cause of obscurity, or rather of necessary misunderstanding?

Again, the preposition *en,* with the verbs in question, always, in other cases, signifies *in.* Why another meaning on this occasion? Must all words desert their usual meaning, and all phrases their syntax, to favour the claims of this pretender purification? Further, the connexion demands *in,* as the meaning of the preposition. *In* the cloud, refers to *under* the cloud; in the sea, to *through* the sea. It must then have been when they were under the cloud, that they were baptized with respect to the cloud; and while they passed *through* the sea, that they were baptized with respect to the sea. For what purpose does the apostle so solemnly call their attention to the fact, that their fathers were *under* the cloud, and passed *through* the sea, if their baptism, which is connected with this, did not take place while they were under the cloud, and while they passed through the sea? According to the writer, the baptism of the Israelites by the sea, was accomplished after they passed the sea; according to the apostle, the baptism was by passing through the sea.

5. There is in the passage a reference to the ordinance of baptism, and something is said to take place in the passage through the Red Sea, that is called a baptism unto Moses. There must be, then, some similarity between Christian baptism, and what took place with respect to the Israelites. But purification as a mere separation, without respect to the nature of the things that purified, cannot be this baptism. In this, there is no emblem at all. The sea and the cloud are not considered as emblematical : it might as well have been a volcano, or a morass. There is no baptism at all; the sprinkling of the cloud, and the spray of the sea, are less extravagant fancies than is this *purify*. Even though this could be called a purification, it could not be called baptism, for every purification is not baptism.

Immersion and nothing but immersion will suit this passage. Did I choose to stand here on the defensive merely, I might content myself with answering objections. It would be enough for me, on that ground, to show that the common version is warrantable, even though I should admit that this passage is capable of the translation of my opponent. If it is also capable of mine, it cannot stand as an objection against me. If the word can have its ordinary meaning here, without any force, it is all my case requires. But I do not stand here, merely on the defensive; I found proof on this passage, and maintain that no view of the meaning of the word will suit this passage, but that of our version. On this ground, the burden of proof lies on me, and I will sustain it. I refuse nothing to my opponent that in my turn I demand from him. Truth is my only object, and sternly just reasoning, grounded on self-evident principles, is my only reliance, both in defence and attack.

The author comes next, to the consideration of the passages that relate to the baptism of John, Matt. iii. 1. The first thing he quarrels with is, the meaning of the word in our view of it, as it regards the title of the Baptist. "*The dipper*," he says, "is offensive, not merely because it is strange, but especially because it has no apparent fitness to his work, as the great predicted reformer of the day." On this I remark,

1. This is a most unjustifiable foundation of evidence in a matter that must be decided solely by the testimony of language, according to the legitimate laws of interpretation. The meaning of what is said, is to be determined solely on the authority of the meaning of words, ascertained by the occurrences in the language of the documents. Our business is to examine what is the meaning of his title, not to speculate on what would have been the most suitable title. I am quite contented to learn from the word of God. I never presume to dictate to it : our view of fitness is no ground on which to rest faith.

2. This is a most hazardous way of attempting to settle the question

If it shall be found in the day of judgment, that the meaning of this title is what this writer represents as so unsuitable and improper, is it a light thing to find folly in the Divine wisdom? The Spirit of wisdom calls him John the Baptist; if this is John the *dipper*, then this writer rebukes the Spirit of God, as employing an unsuitable title to designate the office of John. Is it becoming, is it wise, to risk such observations? Will men never cease to teach the Almighty?

3. This observation is as absurd as it is impious. How is it that the writer did not perceive that even had John been called the purifier, the title must refer to the rite, and not to spiritual purification? It was as a baptizer, not as a great reformer, that John had his title, whatever may be supposed its import. Did John purify any man from sin? This is as rank Puseyism as ever proceeded from the cave of the Pythoness in Oxford.

"It is surely more likely," says the writer, "that John and his disciples would select a name that would express what was spiritual, than one that would express only what was sensible." Is it not strange to astonishment that he could venture such a speculation, with the word *circumcision* before his eyes? Did this word express what was spiritual, or what was sensible? A volume of such assertions would not form the shadow of an argument.

How John's title was originally conferred, we are not informed; but whatever way he got it, we know it only is the title by which he is designated by the Spirit of inspiration. But whether the title is Divine or human, the argument from the word is perfectly the same. The title is from the ritual service.

It is most lamentable that a dissenter should speak of *the spiritual portion of John's work.* Did the spiritual work belong to John? If John was a spiritual purifier, then baptism is salvation.

4. But did the writer forget that Tertullian, and a multitude of translators, have designated John by the very title supposed to be so unsuitable and offensive? Here fact refutes theory. Can demonstration be stronger? *John the dipper* was the usual title of the prophet.

"The term baptize," says the writer, "is used alone, and in connexion with the names of places. Why dost thou baptize? John was baptizing at the downs, at Bethany, at Enon. Now terms denoting a definite end may with propriety be thus used, but not terms denoting a general mode of action."

This has an appearance of profound philology; but it is an appearance only to those who are unacquainted with the effect of the principle of grammatical appropriation. When a word is appropriated to a rite, the frequency of its application when speaking on the subject enables us to use it with an ellipsis of the words usually connected with it in other cases. The thing is of so frequent occurrence in the conversation of every day, that I am surprised that any one who has paid any attention to the philosophy of language, should overlook it. Should any person but a priest anoint a sick person with oil for the good of his soul, every Roman Catholic would ask him, Why do you *anoint*? He would not think it necessary in order to be intelligible, to say, Why do you anoint dying persons with oil, for the salvation of their souls, as you are not a priest? Indeed every trade and every workshop exemplify this process every day, though it is so strange to this Biblical critic. But it is strange that the writer did not perceive that the word *circumcise* can be used in the same way. Can we not say, Why do you circumcise? *Why do you cut around?* Here the philosophy of this critic would object, " terms denoting a general end may with propriety be thus used, but not terms denoting a general mode of action." The word *circumcision*, then, cannot signify to *cut around*, but it must signify to *purify*.

The word, *baptize*, whatever may be supposed its signification, was appropriated to the Christian rite, and in that meaning it may be used in the manner objected to, with the strictest propriety, and with the most lucid perspicuity. Indeed even *purify* itself, had it been appropriated to this ordinance, would be subject to the same law. In the question, Why dost thou purify? there is an ellipsis of " thy disciples with water, as an emblem of the washing away of their sins."

" This word," says the writer, " is so associated with the terms belonging to religion, that it is highly probable the accordance of signification was such as to favour the union. Jesus having been dipped and praying, is felt at once to be incongruous."

Here again *circumcision* destroys the philosophy of the critic. Could it not be said of a proselyte of Judaism, " having been circumcised he prayed?" Whenever a modal word is appropriated to a rite, it designates that rite in every reference, and the appropriation supplies what is necessary. When it is said, " Jesus having been immersed, prayed," it is as well known that the immersion relates to the rite, as that prayer was offered to God.

" The contrast made between the baptism with water," says the writer, " and the baptism with a holy influence and with fire, would alone indicate the meaning of the word. Fire is commonly employed in the Bible as emblematical of the means of destruction."

1. This observation is founded on the same erroneous view of figurative language, on which Wiseman rests his defence of transubstantiation. A figurative application of a word needs resemblance only to justify it : it disdains the sanction of precedent.

2. Even when fire is to burn, the thing subjected to it may not be destroyed, but rendered more valuable. Were not some things under the law purified by passing through fire? And when Christians are immersed in the fire of affliction, they are not destroyed ; they lose nothing but their dross.

3. I care not what the writer may understand by the baptism of fire. Let it be the fire of persecution, of affliction, even of hell, the emblem is suitable. Immersion in fire is intelligible, both literally and figuratively.

" The words of John," says the writer, " were addressed to an assembly of those who would believe in Christ, and of those who would reject him. It was not true that all would be baptized with a sacred influence. It is more likely, therefore, that the two baptisms had a corresponding reference to the two classes of which his audience, and the whole Jewish nation, consisted, than that both should relate to the one smaller portion."

1. John's saying, I baptize *you*, addressing the people in general, did not imply either that he baptized the whole nation, or the whole of the present audience. Therefore, when he says of Jesus, *he shall baptize you*, it is not implied that Jesus baptized, in any sense, either the whole Jewish nation, or the whole of John's present audience.

2. This phraseology imports merely that John baptized those of the Jews who became his disciples; therefore the same phraseology implies when spoken of Jesus, that he baptized those among the Jews who became his disciples. This corresponds both with fact and with phraseology.

3. The author's exposition is inconsistent with itself. He makes Christ's baptism one baptism, and two baptisms. If it refers to the whole nation, purified by the destruction of his enemies, it includes both classes. In this light, it has no reference to baptism in any view. Baptism does not represent the purification of the Jewish nation, nor of any nation; but the purification of sinners individually, from their own sins.

If there are two baptisms, one for one class, and another for another, then how can it be the one baptism that purifies the nation? The class that has the baptism of this *sacred influence*, has not the baptism of fire; yet it is the baptism of fire that separates the pure from the impure; and both must be immersed in the trying fire.

4. There are not two classes in these baptisms. The baptism of the Spirit, and the baptism of fire, belong to the same persons. " He shall baptize you in the Holy Spirit and fire." Every person who has the one baptism, has the other.

" The collecting the wicked," says the writer, " and the burning of the chaff, are described as the *purifying* of the threshing-floor." Even this is not a correct explanation of the figure. It is the separation of the chaff from the wheat; not the collecting of the wheat, and the burning of the chaff, that is the purification. The collecting of the wheat, and the burning of the chaff, do not take place even at the same time with this purification. But what has this figure to do with baptism? The separation of Israel after the spirit, from Israel after the flesh, was a purging of the threshing-floor; but this is quite a different purification from that which is represented by the ordinance of Christ. So far from being the baptism of Christ, this purification has not the same emblem with the baptism of Christ. Besides, it is not the destruction of the unbelieving Israelites that is the purification of the figure. There is nothing right in this explication of the figurative language of John the Baptist. The purgation of the nation might have taken place, had there been no such ordinance as baptism; and baptism would have been the same, had Israel been all believers, and needed no national purgation.

" The baptism of a number of persons," he continues, " is confined to the cleansing of a threshing-floor." Now where is the comparison to be found? The baptism of a number of persons is not compared to a threshing-floor. Nothing like this is said. The separation of the natural and spiritual Israel, is compared to the winnowing of grain;

but there is no comparison at all between baptism and the cleansing of a threshing-floor. It is astonishing that writers will leave themselves open to detection and rebuke, by such reckless assertions. Would any lawyer, even on a case of life and death, put it in the power of his opponent, to charge him with so serious a misrepresentation, in reasoning from a written document? I would let the honour of revelation itself suffer, rather than undertake to protect it by such an asseveration. Let baptism be reasoned out of the world, rather than uphold it by such reasons

The question put to John, has no reference either to the mode or to the nature of the ordinance. Whatever had been the thing done by him, which was not in obedience to the ceremonial law, would equally have given occasion to the question. They questioned his authority, on the ground that he was not one of the persons whom they expected. Had he been such a person, whether he dipped, or sprinkled, or poured, would never have been questioned. If he was not one of the persons expected, why did he introduce among the Jews anything not enjoined by the law of Moses?

" But dipping the multitudes into the Jordan," says he, " would be an act of itself requiring explanation." If the person were recognised or commissioned by God, would his mode of practising a rite be questioned? If he were not recognised, not the mode of the rite, but the rite itself, would be questioned.

The difficulty found in the number baptized by John, is not worthy of a moment's consideration. It is capable of many solutions.

1. If John requires more time for his work, I shall lengthen his commission. How long he entered on his work before our Lord entered on his, I will allow nothing but inspiration to determine. I care nothing for human conjectures and probabilities.

2. There is no necessity to suppose that John baptized all personally. He might have employed the instrumentality of others along with himself. Indeed, without any reference to the difficulty, I perceive no reason to believe that John declined assistance in the work of baptism. Christ's baptism is surely equally important : Christ baptized none ; Paul baptized but few ; and if the converts made by the brethren scattered by the persecution, at the death of Stephen, were baptized at all, they must have been baptized by unofficial brethren. That Puseyism, which is now so general, even among dissenters, has not a vestige of authority in the practice of the first churches. Every man has a right to preach the Gospel, which is a higher privilege than baptizing; and every Christian man has a right to baptize believers.

This writer, indeed, tells us that, " It should be remarked that it is expressly stated, that the people were all baptized by him; not by his disciples." No such thing is expressly stated. Where is it expressly stated, " not by his disciples?" I am astonished at such assertions. We are told that " Herod laid hold of John, and bound him, and put him in prison." Did Herod do this himself? Did he perform the work of a constable? The conversation of every hour exemplifies this phraseology.

3. It is not necessary that the number of those baptized by John should be so great, as stated by this writer. The language of hyperbole is not capable of arithmetical calculation. The writer, with great candour, admits that the language " need not be understood as meaning every individual; but it must be interpreted in reference to the larger portion of the population." Now, if the bankrupt put himself into my hands, I will oblige the creditor to compound for a much smaller sum. This is a new law of hyperbole. Where is it found? On what is it grounded? It is a mere figment, unauthorised by any principle. To justify a hyperbole, I maintain, it is not necessary that truth should extend to the larger portion. When the evangelist says, " And there are also many other things which Jesus did; the which, if they should be written every one, I suppose that even the world itself could not contain the books that should be written," must fact extend to the larger portion of the literal amount?

4. Every hyperbole must be limited by impossibility; it cannot, in any case, be extended beyond what is possible. It cannot oblige John, then, to baptize in a certain time, more than can in that time be baptized.

5. Were the thing asserted admitted, according to the modal meaning of the word, to be impossible, to assign another meaning, not in proof, would not relieve Christians from the difficulty. The infidel might justly object to such a solution. " I deny," he might say, " that the word has the meaning that you allege. The assertion, then, is a falsehood." This objection, then, is the objection of an infidel. Were it a just objection, it would not give the word another meaning. It bears on the truth or falsehood of the Scriptures, not on their interpretation. Should a man report that in Roman Catholic chapels, all the people are *immersed;* and when challenged, should defend himself by saying, that he meant that they were sprinkled with holy water; would his interpretation relieve him from the charge of falsehood? And immerse does not more uniformly signify *dip* in English, than does *baptizo* in Greek. The evangelist, then, cannot be justified by such interpretation. If John did not immerse his disciples, the narrative of the evangelist is false.

6. At this distance of time there may be in Scripture records many difficulties apparently incapable of solution, that after all may be perfectly true. We never give up the truth of the Scriptures for such difficulties, and we never solve them by denying the authenticated meaning of words.

7. The great difficulty in performing immersion is altogether unfounded. Any way of putting the person under water is equally an immersion, and equally an emblem of the death, burial, and resurrection of Christ and his people with him. There is no need of dramatic representation. Indeed there is no uniform way of burial. There can be, then, no propriety in endeavouring to imitate the custom of any nation in committing the body to the earth. Whether the person is immersed on his back, or his face, or by sinking directly downwards, is perfectly the same as to baptism. The easiest way is preferable; and in deep water to press the person down, or forwards, may be done with the greatest convenience. Instead of keeping John the Baptist ten hours every day in the water, I will not oblige him to go into the water at all: he might have stood on the brink. Philip and the eunuch, indeed, went both into the water, and in many cases this may be still necessary; but it is not essential to the ordinance of baptism. This case, however, has, in the Divine wisdom, been recorded to confound obstinacy.

With respect to delicacy, it would be easy from the law of Moses to make a comparison with this rite; but I do not design to defend an ordinance of God from such a charge. I prove God's law from his own word. He who charges it with indelicacy, charges God himself.

The author thinks that an immersion with garments on is inconsistent with the idea of purification. Does he forget that in their purifications, the Jews were sprinkled on their garments? Is he not aware that Josephus represents the female Essenes as bathing with their garments on; and the males as covered with a veil or girdle round the waist? Does not Herodotus represent the Egyptian, after touching a swine, as plunging immediately into a river with his garments on? Do not Roman Catholics continually purify by sprinkling on the people with their garments on?

The writer has an argument from the probable want of conveniences for immersion. Does he really think that the Scripture history must give an account of such things? Must we go back eighteen centuries to find a change of raiment, &c.? We have nothing to do with inquiries of this kind. I prove that they were immersed,—I care not from what sources they had suitable conveniences. Would any one think of making such an objection, if the narrative respected even modern times, and asserted immersion?

SECTION VII.—PREPOSITIONS CONSTRUED WITH THE VERB.—The author comes next to the consideration of the prepositions construed with this verb. He tells us, "that, according to the testimony of most critics, *en* has the signification of *at*, and *apo* of *from*. *Apo* rarely has the sense of *out of*, but *en* very frequently has the sense of *in*. A few instances of the signification of *at* and *from* are given below."

Whatever may be the testimony of critics, I deny that *en* ever signifies *at*; and it never has been argued by me that in the cases that refer to baptism, *apo* must signify *out of*. When the writer, then, grants that the preposition rarely has this signification, he grants me more than I will accept. I deny that it ever signifies *out of*. I shall not force the word to do more for me than what it can do honestly. But let us first attend to the preposition *en*. In a note the writer gives us a number of examples, in which he alleges that it signifies *at*. Now I dispute this with respect to every instance that he has alleged. *En* in Greek no more signifies *at*, than does in English the preposition *in*. We can as often convert *in* and *at* as the Greeks could *en* and *para*, or *epi*. We may often say indifferently, *at* a place or *in* a place; but this does not imply that in such cases *in* signifies *at*, or that *at* signifies *in*. The prepositions have always their own characteristic meaning; while in cases innumerable they may be substituted for each other.

The first instance which he alleges of *en* in the sense of *at*, is in the phrase *en Troie*, which occurs several times in Homer. *At Troy*, says the writer,—*in Troy*, say I. But I shall be asked, How was it *in Troy*? Did they fight within the walls of the city? No, but every one who knows anything of such matters, knows, that the district around a city was always spoken of by the name of the city. The name of the city was given to the whole adjoining country. I can demonstrate this, even with respect to this instance, as clearly as ever a mathematical proposition was demonstrated. Does not Homer call the city " the fertile Troy?" Was it within the walls that it was fertile? Was it not the country about the city that was fertile? The Grecian heroes, then, who fell near wind-swept Ilium, fell *in* Troy. Now this criticism will apply to his examples from every city.

The next example is from Homer also—*en proto rumo*, literally, "*in* the first pole." The place where the pole of the chariot snapped, was in the first part of it. I think the phraseology implies that there were two poles joined together, as the topmast is joined to the mainmast of a ship, or like the different parts of a fishing rod. But whatever may be in this, it is most certain that it is *in the first pole* that the chariot is said to have been broken. Besides, it must necessarily have been within the pole that it was broken. Could the pole be broken outside the pole? It is *in the first pole*, not *at* the first pole. *At* the first pole would be *near* the first pole, and would be in the second pole, or second part of the pole.

He gives another example from Homer—the spear was broken—*eni kaulo, at the top. At* the tip, or *at the point*, would be a very good translation, according to our idiom. But *kaulos* does not signify *top;* it denotes the whole blade, or metal part of the spear, like the top of a halbert. Now it was not *at* this part, but *in* this part, that the weapon broke. The breach may have been in any part of the blade, from the utmost extremity of the point to the wooden shaft. The preposition is used altogether in its own primary meaning.

The next instance is the ambuscade represented on the shield of Achilles. The ambuscade is represented as placed *en potomo*, " *at the river*," says the writer,—*in the river*, say I. It was within the banks of the river that the ambuscade lodged. This is a much better place for an ambuscade than the bank of a river,—especially as they lay in wait for the cattle which were driven to drink at that place. Cowper and other translators have entirely missed the meaning of this passage. The ambuscade was not on the banks of the river, but within the banks. Accordingly we find that the ensuing battle, in driving away the cattle, is not *en potomo*, but *para ochthas*,—not in the river, but *at the banks of the river*. That an ambush should be laid in such a place, will not startle any one who considers the account given by Ulysses, of an ambuscade in which he was concerned at Troy :—

> " Approaching to the city's lofty wall
> Through the thick bushes and the reeds that girt
> The bulwarks, down we lay, flat in the marsh,
> Under our arms. Then, Boreas, blowing loud,
> A rueful night came on, frosty and charged
> With snow that blanched us thick as morning rime,
> And every shield with ice was crystall'd o'er."—Cowper.

The next passage cited by the author is that which in the Iliad represents the stopping of the mules and horses of Priam to drink *en potomo*—*in the river*, as he went to the Grecian camp to redeem the body of Hector. The preposition has here strictly its usual meaning—it was *in* the river that the horses drank. According to our idiom we may say either *at* the river, or *in* the river ; but *in* the river is the idiom of the original, and it is literal fact.

The passage next cited by the author is that which refers to Ulysses escaped from shipwreck, and lying on the bank of a river. He has only the choice whether to watch all the rueful night *en potomo*—*in the river*, or to ascend the acclivity. But why *in* the river ? Is he not out of the river ? Why does he suppose a necessity of going into it again ? The reason is obvious. If he does not choose to ascend the acclivity and go into the wood for shelter, and make a leafy couch, he must lodge in the river under the cover of its banks. It is not *at* the river, but *in* the river that he supposes himself to watch. On the bank he could have no shelter; in the river he would have the shelter of the bank. He might be in the river, yet not in the water: all within the banks is the river.

The daughter of the king of Phæacia is said to have stopped her car, *en prothuroisi*, *in* the vestibule. The word includes the whole court before the gate. It is not *at*, but *in*.

The next instance brought forward by this writer to prove that *en* sometimes signifies *at*, is *en prochoes potomou*, translated by him, "*At* the mouth of the river." But it is better translated by Cowper, "*Within* the eddy-whirling river's mouth."

The next is from Herodotus, translated by this writer, " A city *at* the Euxine sea." But this translation misses the whole spirit of the phrase. The city is said *en Euxino ponto malista kakeimenon*, the city lay almost, or very much, in the Euxine sea.

The sea-fight *en Krupo*, *in* Cyprus, is to be understood like the phrase, " in Troy." The sea about Cyprus may be called Cyprus. We could employ the same idiom. In like manner, the Greeks are said to conquer the Persians *in* Salamis. Overthrown *in* Drebescus—not *at* Drebescus ; though our idiom may prefer this in translation. The use of the word in reference to towns and islands may be, in every instance, accounted for by what has been observed with respect to the use of the name of the city of Troy. The example from Xenophon, *in the Euxine sea*, may be accounted for on the same principle with that from Herodotus. Nothing is more common than to speak of a town situated in a bason of the sea, as *lying in the sea*. A promontory is even said to *run into the sea*. Homer speaks of the tomb of Achilles as *prochouse*, on a tall promontory, *shooting far into* the spacious Hellespont. Odys. xxiv. 82.

Why does he say *at* Gilgal, 1 Sam. xv. 4 ? Is it not in Gilgal ? Does not our version render it, *in* Telaim ? Why does he say *at* the brook, verse 5 ? What forbids the place of the ambush to be *in* the brook ? Why, *at* the brook, 1 Kings xvii. 5 ? Could not the prophet take up his residence within the banks of the brook ? Why, *at* the corners of the streets, Matt. vii. 5? Does ever our idiom forbid *in* the corner of the streets? Why, tower *at* Siloam, Luke xiii. 4? What objection can be to *in* Siloam? Why, *at* the treasury, John viii. 20? Why not, *in* the treasury? *On the right hand* is as suitable to our idiom as *at* the right hand. *In* the right hand, is in the region or place to the right.

Schleusner adds other examples of this signification, which are not more to the purpose. *Standing in the holy place*, Matt. xxiv. 15, he understands as referring to the Roman army brought forward to the city and temple; but this conceit deserves no attention. Whatever may be the *holy place* referred to, the thing referred to is represented as standing *in* it. *In* the temple, John x. 23, he understands *nigh the temple*, namely, in the porch of Solomon. But this whim is not only wanton, but absurd. The porch of Solomon is here considered as a part of the temple. Jesus walked in the temple, in that part of it called Solomon's porch.

In short, though this preposition may, according to our idiom, be frequently translated *at*, such cases are always capable of analysis according to the proper meaning. *When there is latitude in any phrase in which this preposition is used, the latitude is always in the régimen.* This is a point which all the grammarians seem to have overlooked.

But even where lexicographers and grammarians allege AT as one of its primary meanings, they never apply it, when the common meaning will serve; it is reserved for cases which are supposed not to admit the strict signification of the word. This forms no apology for those who apply it in the exigency of a favourite cause, when the usual meaning would apply. Does any one who deserves the name of a lexicographer or grammarian, understand *en* as signifying *at* in reference to the phrase *en Iordane?* Here the preposition is not only capable of its primary meaning, but it is in this sense that it is always construed with the verb in question. Why should it be otherwise in this instance?

The writer proceeds next to give some examples in which the preposition *ek* signifies not *out of*, but *from*. He should understand that in this controversy we are concerned with no examples except such as *imply the motion of an object from one place to another.* Now, of such cases, I still maintain what I taught on this subject from the beginning, that there is no instance in which the preposition signifies *from*—it always means *out of.* In Acts viii. 39, the phrase is capable of no translation but *out of* the water, and necessarily implies that they were *in* the water.

But though it does not concern this controversy, I dispute the philology of this writer, in every instance which he has alleged. Even in the first example, *ek* has not the sense of *from*. "He cut the hairs *out of* the heads of the lambs" is the Greek idiom, which we would express by *from*. Every sound philologist, in expounding the Greek phrase, would observe that *out of* is the exact meaning of the original. He would also show, that this is as agreeable to philosophical principle as our idiom *from*. *Out of* respects exterior space considered horizontally, as well as contrasted with *interior*. When we say a man comes down *out of the hill,* we do not mean that he was in the bowels of the earth. Just so with the hairs out of the heads of the lambs. All the hair of the heads of the lambs was not cut, but some of it was cut *out of* the remainder. Indeed, to *cut from* the head is as difficult in a philosophical analysis. *From* respects not the *cutting,* for that was *at* the head; but the removing of it after the cutting. It was cut *at* the head, and then removed *from* the head.

Though I am going farther than the cause I have undertaken requires, yet I the more willingly follow the writer here, for the sake of pointing out to my readers the source of much false criticism, which affects every subject. Critics usually proceed upon the principle, that the phrase which our idiom requires in a translation, corresponds exactly to the idiom of the original. But idioms are really different, so that this cannot be the case. An idiomatic phrase in one language cannot be exactly rendered by an idiomatic phrase in another; and neither of them ought to be obliged to conform to the other. We may say, to *cut from,* when the Greeks would have said, to *cut out of;* but we are not on that account to explain *out of* as signifying *from,* more than we are to explain *from* by *out of.* A Greek, for instance, criticising on the principle of this writer, in comparing the English translation with the original, would say, "Here *from* signifies not *apo,* but *ek*—it is not from the head, but out of the head." Why should he say so? Because he makes the English idiom conform to the Greek, just as this writer makes the Greek idiom conform to the English. Now neither idiom conforms to the other; each of them explains on a different principle, and has a different signification, while they both are fitted to fill the same place.

This is illustrated by the next example alleged by this writer. We say, from head to foot; but the Greek says, out of the head *into* or *unto* the feet. Homer represents one of his slain heroes as lying on the field, covered with dust and filth, *ek kephales.* Now, we translate this *from his head;* and from this the writer argues, that the preposition signifies not *out of,* but *from.* This I maintain is not only false as to this instance, but is founded on the false principle above explained. It obliges the idiom of one language to conform to that of another, when each of them has a distinct meaning, while they are fitted to fill the same place in their respective languages. A Greek might as well argue from this example, that *from* signifies *out of,* as this writer argues, that *ek* signifies *from.* Neither idiom is to conform to the other, while each of them must be used in such cases for the other in translation. And with respect to the philosophy of the English and the Greek idioms, the latter is, in this instance, the most exact. *From* head to feet exactly begins at the head, without including any part of it; *out of* commences within the head. The Greek idiom covers the fallen hero, *head and feet;* our idiom literally leaves *head and feet* uncovered.

The phrase *ek genees,* we translate according to our idiom, *from his birth,* but it is in Greek idiom *out of* his birth. The disease commenced within the period mentioned. The Greek idiom is more philosophical than ours. The phrase *ex hou egenonto Athenaioi,* is literally, "*out of* the time the Athenians existed." The point of time referred to is any point within the period. The Greek idiom is here also more philosophical than ours. Such examples prove a different idiom, not that the preposition in the one language is the exact equivalent of the other. When a mountain is said to extend *out of* one sea *into* another, its extremities are supposed to reach into each sea. Though we should say from sea to sea, this does not imply that the Greek phrase is exactly equivalent. We would say, from Byzantium to Heraclea; the Greeks said, out of Byzantium into Heraclea. We commence the distance *at* the town, the Greeks commence it *within* the town. This does not imply that the English preposition is the exact translation of the Greek. In the same way, with respect to what the writer translates, "*from* the distant streams of Ethiopia." "*Go from* my presence;" the Greek is, "Go out of my presence." And our idiom will bear a literal translation. "They descended from the hill;" Greek, "out of the hill." They were within the horizontal space called the hill. The Greek is more philosophically exact. " Gather figs *from* thorns;" Greek, *out of* thorns. Is it not literally *out of* the bush that they were gathered? A Greek, considering *from* as the translation of the preposition in this phrase, agreeably to this writer's philology, might allege, that the English preposition *from* here signifies *out of*. "A hair *from* your head;" Greek, " a hair *out of* your head." And we can say the same thing. Do we not say, that " She tore the hair *out of* her head?" " Hanging *from* his hand;" Greek, " *out of* his hand." The Greek is philosophical, the English is not. The hanging object is partly within the hand. Is it like a philologist to argue from different idioms, that the original must conform to the translation? " Ships come *from* Tiberias;" Greek, " *out of* Tiberias." " I come *from* God;" Greek, " *out of* God." " He arose *from* supper;" Greek, " *out of* supper." He rose and came *out of* the place *in* which he had supped. "*From* the chief priests;" Greek, " *out of* the chief priests." The officers referred to were those who were in attendance on the chief priests. " His chains fell *from* his hands;" Greek, " *out of* his hands." The chain must have been fastened somewhere within the part of the body which the word hand designates. An antiquarian, instead of making the Greek idiom conform to the English, would here gain some information with respect to the chaining of criminals. " They cast four anchors *from* the stern;" Greek, " *out of* the stern." And our idiom would exactly translate the Greek. " We have an altar *from* which they have no right to eat;" Greek, " *out of* which." And is it not within the table that the meat is placed for eating? Must it not, then, be *out of* the table that they are supposed to take the food laid on it? Every example, then, of this kind, I can easily solve, on philosophical principles, in perfect uniformity with the proper meaning of this preposition. Even the secondary meanings of the preposition, which have no respect to either motion or place, may generally, with ease, be reduced to the primary meaning. An effect, for instance, is supposed to proceed *out of* its cause, and the thing formed is supposed to proceed *out of* the matter of which it is formed. But, in reference to the present controversy, I have nothing to do with any examples, except such as express the motion of an object from one place to another. The other examples I have noticed for the sake of overturning a false principle of interpretation, namely, the assumption that the idiom of our language must be a perfect equivalent to every idiom which it translates.

The author grants that *apo* rarely signifies *out of*. But I will not avail myself of this admission, because it admits what is not true. Had he said that *apo* is sometimes used where *ek* is more usual, or that there are cases in which either may be used, I would unite in the affirmation. But in all such cases each of the prepositions has still its own peculiar meaning. I may say, I came *from* town, or *out of* town. Does this imply that *from* and *out of* are perfectly equivalent in any instance in English? Perfectly the same is the case, when *apo* and *ek* may be substituted for one another. Grammarians and lexicographers, as far as I have observed, are far from being decisive authorities for secondary meaning. Schleusner gives *dum, whilst,* as one of the secondary meanings of the preposition *en;* and *si, if,* for another. The preposition never has any appearance of such signification. It is the multiplication of meanings, grounded on loose views of the laws of language, that has enabled controversialists to prove anything they choose to undertake.

According to this way of assigning meanings to words, *en* may be said to signify the very opposite of its own signification. The signification of *ek* may be given to *en,* and that of *en* to the opposite *ek.* The Greeks speak of drinking *in* a cup, and *out of* a cup. Here, then, we may say that *ek* signifies *en,* and *en* signifies *out of.* But the two Greek phrases do not express the same idea, though they may be used for the same actions. In the one case the drinking refers to the liquor as contained within the cup, in the other to the liquor as proceeding *out of* the cup. Now if two so different phrases are used for the same action in the same language, in accordance with the distinctive meaning of the words, much more may this be the case with respect to two idioms of different languages employed to express the same thing.

I have met the encounter of Socinians, who, without the least scruple, degraded anything from the Scriptures which they could not manage to their satisfaction. But criticism so licentious as that which is employed to evade the mode of this ordinance, I have never witnessed in the most reckless Socinian. The word itself is so obviously univocal, that an instance of its use cannot be produced, irreconcilable with this view; yet a meaning is arbitrarily assigned to it, which it cannot, in a single instance, be proved to have, on the ground of difficulties and impossibilities with respect to its established meaning. The prepositions *en* and *ek,* which are quite decisive in their testimony, have been forced to become lax, that their testimony on this subject may be evaded. But even if the authority of lexicographers is relied on as asserting a rare use, why should a rare use be forced on any of the words in this situation? Why should a rare use be forced on both of them? Why should they have this rare meaning in combination with a word which usually signifies immersion, and in combination with what they usually signify, *in* and *out of?* Why should there be supposed such a wicked conspiracy in all the words in combination, to deceive the reader by leaving their usual meaning, and assuming a rare meaning?

In the following extract we have one of the most astonishing declarations that I ever saw on paper from the hand of a disciple of Christ. "If it were asserted," says the writer, "that persons went *into* the water, and came *out of it,* it could not be justly inferred that they went in to be dipped. Where shoes were not worn, the necessity of frequently washing the feet, might naturally make that a part of a ceremonial or symbolical washing. It was so used by our Lord when he washed his disciples' feet. In eastern countries it is common to walk into the stream to wash their feet." If any man who trembles at the word of God, and thirsts for the knowledge of it as to this ordinance, does not see the condemnation of this observation in its very face, I should never think of presenting him with evidence. I cannot conceive how it can satisfy any conscience. If in performing the ordinance of baptism, we have both the baptizer and the baptized in the water, the man who cannot see proof in this that there was an immersion in the ordinance, appears to me to be far beyond the reach of evidence. Jesus raised the dead, and did not convince his enemies. It is very true that persons may go into the water to wash their feet, and for a thousand other purposes. But here the going into the water was for the purpose of the baptism. But is any washing of the feet mentioned? Baptism is the only thing that can here be the reason of their going *into* the water. But the washing of the feet is no part of the ceremonial, because it is neither here nor any where else enjoined as a part of the ceremonial of baptism. Should it, however, have been a part of the ceremonial of baptism, it must still be a part of the ceremonial. Can either Pope or Puseyite abrogate what Christ has made a part, a symbolical part of this ordinance? Such an argument has no force on my conscience. I am willing to observe this ordinance in any way that can be proved to be the original mode; but I could not think of looking Jesus Christ, my Master, in the face, and say to him at the same time, that I am satisfied with this argument. If it really convinces any of Christ's disciples, I leave them to the judgment of Christ.

What has the washing of the feet of the disciples to do with this subject? Was this connected with baptism? Was this a part of any ceremonial? Was it not a particular symbolical action to represent a general principle? Besides, did our Lord take the disciples to a river in order to wash their feet? Can such reasoning merit any other denomination than that of evasion, as weak as it is wicked? If it is lawful, no ordinance or doctrine of Christ could afford sufficient proof. What proof would satisfy the mind that can allow itself to rest on such arguments? Again and again we demand, what is wanting to the proof that baptism is immersion? Is there any more definite word to denote immersion? Are there any more definite prepositions to denote, *in, into,* and *out of?* Can it be shown with respect to any word in the Greek language, that there are more numerous and decided proofs of its meaning, than those exhibited in proof of the meaning of the word in question?

To the argument from John iii. 23, the author replies: " First, that the name Enon, which means *the wells*, and also the nature of the country, favour the opinion that *polla hudata* denotes many streams, rather than one large connexion of water." Let the origin of the name be what he alleges, it bears not his conclusion. All the springs might unite in forming one collection.

His second reason is, " That the water was necessary, not for baptizing, but for drinking, ordinary washings, cooking, &c."—necessary not only for men, but for asses and camels. " The statement," he says, " that John was *preaching* at Enon, because there was abundance of water there, would be perfectly proper."

On this I observe, 1. Not a single well—not a single bowl of water was necessary for preaching. Had the whole of Judea been present at one sermon, there was no absolute need for a drop of water. Our opponents seem to think that the people who attended John, encamped, and remained with him for a considerable time. There is no reason to believe that they remained with him a single night; there was no necessity to remain a moment after they were baptized. As for the asses and camels, they exist only in the imagination ; they might as well allege that the people came to John in steam carriages. We know that the people followed our Lord on foot. But had as many asses and camels attended John as were possessed by Job in the land of Uz, there was no necessity for a single fountain ; they could have watered by the way. Every candid person must perceive that these are forced reasons ; they never would suggest themselves to any one who had not a purpose to serve by them.

2. Jesus preached every where without any respect to the convenience of water, and to greater multitudes than came to John. When they came to Jesus to the most distant places without a supply of food, it is evident that they did not intend to make a long stay. Why should they stay longer with John ? Jesus usually dismissed the multitudes in time to go to their lodgings ; and on an occasion of staying later than usual, it was food, not water, that they required. John's peculiar work was baptizing, and for that purpose he frequented such places as afforded the best facilities for performing immersion with convenience. It could not then be said that John was *preaching* at Enon on account of the water, because preaching does not need water.

3. The use of the water here is not left to conjecture ; it is specifically mentioned : it was for the very purpose of baptism. It is added, also, by the evangelist, " and they came and were baptized." Here their coming was not for the purpose of hearing, but of being baptized. Shall we, then, overlook the reasons which the Holy Spirit alleges, and allege reasons from our own fancy ? Were this a point of heathen antiquity, there never would have been a question on the subject. Ah, my brethren, why will you, by your traditions, make void the word of God ?

With respect to the words in the original, much controversy has taken place whether they ought to be translated *much water* or *many waters*. Either of these will serve my purpose well enough. Neither *much water* nor *many waters* could be necessary for either *preaching* or *sprinkling*.

The argument alleged by Baptists from the performance at rivers, the author answers in a very strange way. "First," says he, "that the use of running water was expressly enjoined in the law for the purifications performed by sprinkling, &c." What has this to do with Christian baptism? Are we to be guided in the ordinances of Christ by Jewish rites? Is it not monstrous to allege that it was the practice, both among Jews and other nations, to go to large collections of water, such as rivers in the sea, to observe purifications which needed very little water? Are gross superstitions to be a model for Christ's ordinance? If the author chooses to imitate either Jewish or heathen superstitions, let him follow his guide; but let him not allege these as a model for Christian baptism. We have nothing to do even with the law of Moses. Yet even the Mosaic law that required *running*, that is, spring water, did not require to perform the rite either at the river or at the fountain. Is it possible that this writer can allege that the inspired messengers of God practised baptism as a sprinkling in the neighbourhood of rivers, from a view of the sacredness of the place? No wonder that the Oxford divines are paving a holy way to the altar, when the English Independents speak of rivers as *sacred places* for the performance of sacred sprinklings on their banks. Why not come to Lough Dergh, where they can be made drunk with sanctity?

But if the banks of rivers were at first chosen by the inspired servants of Jesus for the performance of sprinkling in this instance, why is not this still observed? I have never heard that the London Independents go even to Old Thames to perform their sprinklings on its banks. I declare solemnly that if I met this allegation in a detached form and unauthenticated, I should fear to ascribe it to any friend of infant sprinkling; I should strongly suspect that it was to expose the cause that it pretended to defend. It is Popery and Puseyism to suppose that any place on earth is more holy than another.

If ever perverseness was perverse, it is here. If we drag them down to the water, they will do nothing but sprinkle on the banks from their view of the sacredness of the place: and if we force them even into the water, they will do nothing but ceremonially wash their feet. Can anything be more calumnious with respect to the kingdom of Christ, than to allege that any part of the sacredness of an ordinance should consist in the place where it is performed? Jerusalem itself is not more holy than Mount Gerizim.

SECTION VIII.—The author makes some observations on the difference between *baptisma* and *baptismos*. There is a difference in words of this different formation; and the constant use of the former for the ordinance of Christ, shows that the Scriptures recognise the difference. But this writer has not been so fortunate as to hit the difference in the centre of the mark: he has hardly struck the hill on which the target is fixed. With respect to *baptisma*, he says that this form "indicates that its signification is some effect." It does not designate an effect. *Baptisma* is not the effect produced by *baptismos;* it is the *rite* performed by this act. "The two words," he says, "differ in their meaning, as do the English words, an immersing, an immersion, a purifying, a purification.'

The words, I maintain, do not differ as the English words referred to. Immersion, instead of corresponding to *baptisma,* corresponds to *baptismos.* It is for want of an appropriate English formation that *immersion* is used as the translation of *baptisma;* and when the participle is used as a substantive, it can translate *baptisma.* If the rite is spoken of by the word dip, as we have no *diption,* we must say *dipping.* We have no word to correspond to *baptisma,* whatever may be the mode or the nature of the ordinance. *Sprinkling* is a similar formation to *dipping.* *Perfusion* would correspond to *baptismos,* not to *baptisma.* *Purification* itself designates the act as well as does *immersion.* The complaint against the one word stands equally against the other : *immersion* is the act of immersing, and for want of an appropriate formation, we must apply to the rite the word that denotes the act. And if the rite should be called *purification,* the same process takes place. No philologist would bring such a complaint against the word *immersion* as the representative of *baptisma.*

It may be observed also, that though in this instance the Greek language affords us a distinct formation for the rite, yet it does not so in all cases. Besides, even in that language, which has the advantage of having one formation for the act, and another for the rite, the rite may be designated by the formation that signifies the act. Josephus employs *baptismos,* the word that signifies the act for the rite, in reference to the baptism of John.

But were it a fact, that the formation of the word *immersion* is not an adequate representative of the Greek formation, and that the term *purification* were free from this objection, what would this prove? Nothing to the purpose : it would affect only the English term, and not the meaning of the Greek word. It would prove the poverty of our language, and its inadequateness to translate the Greek, but would not in the slightest degree affect the proof about the meaning of the word.

" The difference," says the writer, " between *baptismos* and *baptisma* is, that the former denotes an act that is transient, the latter an effect for a time permanent." How can this be, when Josephus employs *baptismos* where the other form is used in the New Testament, and by the Greek Christians? Was not Christ's baptism as permanent as that of John? Was not John's as transient as that of Christ? But *baptisma* is not an effect either permanent or transient—it is the rite. *Immersion* also, is not an effect either transient or permanent, but an act, or a rite. *Immersing* and immersion do not differ as to permanency.

" If the subject," he tells us, " were left for a while in the water, then the effect would be rightly called an immersion." What sort of philology is this? Is not the *immersion* the act of *immersing?* What has it to do with the length of time that the subject continues in the state of immersion? The *effect* of *immersing* is not *immersion.* The effect of immersion must be something of which immersion is the cause. How can he say that immersion applies to the effect of a continuation in the state of immersion, when every one knows that we apply the word immerse to the most transient act, as well as to cases in which the subject continues in a state of immersion? The word has nothing to do with the effect produced by it, or the state of the thing immersed. "The sense of *purifying*," he continues, "agrees with the peculiarity of sense belonging to *baptismos;* and that of *purification,* with the peculiarity of sense belonging to *baptisma.*" *Purification* corresponds both to *baptismos* and *baptisma.* We have no other word for the rite of purification, but that which signifies the act.

"When it is said that the Pharisees and Sadducees came to his baptism," says the writer, "reference obviously is made to what he did. But in other places it appears, that this word is used, not for what he did, but for what he taught." Can a word ever be used without a reference to the thing signified by it? What is the thing signified by the word baptism? Is it the name of the rite? If it is the name of the rite, can the name be used without reference to the rite? Even if the name is *purification,* it must have a reference to the rite. The author, if I can venture to expound his meaning, seems to think that the word *baptism* is sometimes used not with reference to the rite, but to the doctrine connected with the rite. It appears to me absurd, to suppose that the name of a rite should be used without reference to the rite. But as soon as a word is appropriated as the name of a rite, every thing included in the rite will be referred to it under its appropriated name, whatever the name may signify. The writer every where, seems not to be aware of the nature and effects of grammatical appropriation. Are not the doctrines implied in circumcision, referred to circumcision? Perfectly the same thing applies to every appropriated name. This determines nothing as to the meaning of the name itself. Now we are inquiring not about the doctrines implied in this rite, but about the meaning of its name. Can anything, then, be more useless than the assertion, that corporeal purification was not the great subject of John's preaching? What has this to do with the rite which he practised? "The great doctrine," he continues, "taught by him was, the necessity of a spiritual purification." Well, does this say that the name of the rite which he practised was *spiritual purification?* Does this forbid that the name of the rite should be *immersion?*

The writer brings out his point even by mathematical demonstration, in the following words: "If baptism was the chief theme of John's preaching, and it is so described, then, because repentance also was the chief theme, baptism and repentance coincide." 1. Now I ask, what does he understand by the word baptism here? Is it the Christian rite? If so, this rite is repentance and salvation. If it is not the Christian rite, we have nothing to do with it in this controversy, for we are inquiring about the Christian rite. 2. John did not preach repentance as a baptism, nor baptism as a repentance; but baptism as implying repentance. He preached the *baptism of repentance.* This shows that baptism and repentance are different things. 3. How do baptism and repentance coincide? It must be in a sense of baptism—which excludes the ordinance of baptism, otherwise the rite is a part of repentance. If it is in a sense that excludes the ordinance, then we have nothing to do with it in that sense: our inquiry is about the meaning of the word, as the name of the rite. If a person will give the name of baptism to repentance, he must be left with other fanatics to enjoy his own whim 4. Repentance may be imported in a rite, though the name of the ordinance may not be repentance. 5. *Repentance* and *purification* are not the same thing, though they are essentially connected. If baptism signifies purification, it does not signify repentance; if it signifies repentance, it cannot signify *purification*. 6. With much better reason it might be said, that the words repentance and faith, and repentance and sanctification, coincide: they all imply each other, yet they are all different. But the word *repentance*, and the word *baptism*, do not coincide in name, and they do not necessarily imply each other. Repentance may exist without baptism, and baptism without repentance.

"Repentance," says the writer, "is not a *dipping*, nor an immersion, but it is a purification." The words *dipping, immersion, purification*, must be taken as the names of the rite, otherwise the observation is nothing to the purpose. Now repentance is not a purification, as that term is the name of a rite, more than it is immersion, as the name of the same rite. "The phrase *baptisma metanoias*," says he, "might mean either the corporeal baptism, connected with repentance, or the spiritual baptism, consisting of repentance." 1. The phrase *baptism of repentance*, most evidently means the rite which is performed on those who profess repentance. No one can mistake this, who looks for truth. But if any one will be ignorant, let him be ignorant. The baptisms under the law were for ceremonial purifications; but the baptism of John, and of our Lord, imply spiritual purification in those who receive them. 2. The writer makes repentance and spiritual baptism coincide; the spiritual baptism, then, of repentance, is the repentance of repentance. 3. This exposition excludes the rite of baptism altogether from the preaching of John. He preached only repentance, if the baptism of repentance is nothing but repentance.

But even granting that the phrase "baptism of repentance" has no reference to baptism as a rite, does this imply that the word baptism, in reference to the rite, must signify purification, or that it cannot signify immersion? This has nothing to do with the question in any point of view. "Apollos," he tells us, "taught diligently the things of the Lord, being acquainted only with the baptism of John. If only acquainted with the dipping of John, he would have been little fitted for the office of a religious instructor." Would Apollos have been a more competent religious instructor, on the supposition that the rite had been called *purification?* Is it not evident that the word baptism here refers to the rite of baptism, whatever may be the meaning of the word? But the writer, as usual, errs from inattention to the effect of appropriation. The baptism of John includes every thing included in John's commission, and implied in the rite which he practised. Does not the apostle Paul speak in the same way about preaching circumcision? The baptism of John must surely be the baptism which John preached. The rite, then, must be referred to, whatever may be its name.

Section IX.—Author's Explication of the Passages which refer to Christian Baptism.—The author comes next to the examination of the passages which refer to Christian baptism. The first to which he refers is John iii. 25, 26. "What is called a *purifying* in the twenty-fifth verse, is called a *baptizing* in the twenty-sixth verse." The lesson which I gave to President Beecher on this allegation, seems to have had its proper effect on this writer; for he grounds no argument for identity of meaning on this fact. But he derives evidence from the passage on another ground. "Neither in this passage," says he, "nor in one of all the passages which mention Christian baptism, is the word construed with the preposition *in*, or with any other word that accords with the sense of dipping. In no single instance are we told that persons were baptized *into* the water, which would be the proper phrase, if to baptize meant to dip. The word is here used alone, and as many other passages, both the noun and verb are similarly situated. From this, it is probable that the object signified by them was commonly and properly regarded alone, and was in some measure complete in itself."

It is to me astonishing, beyond what I can express, that any person accustomed to reflect on language, were he even unable to read, should make the observation with regard to the defect of the regimen of the verb. Every ear is familiarly accustomed to such grammatical deficiency of expression; and every hearer and reader can instantaneously supply the ellipsis: it is a common case with all grammatical appropriations. The expression of the regimen would be quite useless. I have already, again and again, illustrated this by examples; and every hour's conversation will supply instances. Can we not say, "Was the child sprinkled?" Can we not say, "Was such a person immersed?" Would any child need the regimen to be expressed? Try the experiment on an idiot, and I venture to say, he will not ask for the regimen of the verb. Critics should be ashamed of having recourse to such philology. Is it not strange that the ghost of our old friend, the word *circumcision*, does not rise up to their imagination, and frighten them, when they make such observations? Should a modern Jew be asked if he was circumcised; would he need the grammatical regimen to be expressed, before he would answer? It might as well be said that the English word *immerse* cannot signify *dip*, because it is used in reference to the ordinance, without any regimen. Let us try this criticism on a sample of English. Let the critic be a foreigner, knowing the English language through grammars and dictionaries, and determining meaning according to the canons of this writer. Let the text be, *Were you immersed since you believed?* "Nothing," says the critic, "can be more evident than that the word *immerse* cannot here signify *dip*, because there is no regimen to the verb." With respect to the preposition *eis*, I have shown that it is construed with the verb, with respect to John's baptism; and in this respect there can be no difference between the word in reference to the baptism of John, and that of Christ. Besides, it is used by the early Christians, which is as good an authority as to syntax, as is the Scripture itself. Inspiration does not give law to syntax, but must use the syntax of the language which it employs; otherwise it could not give a revelation. Besides, *en* is construed with the verb, as well as *eis*, when immerse is spoken of; and in English, we use *in* much more frequently than *into*. Indeed, when we wish merely to designate the place of baptism, we always use *in*.—They were baptized in the Thames. I might add, that the preposition *eis* is in the Scriptures construed with the verb, in reference to Christian baptism; and as to the syntax, there is no difference whether the regimen be water, or anything else. But I do not recognise the demand; I will not plead on the ground of its authority. A phrase might occur only once in Scripture; and on the ground of the author's criticism, it could not have its common meaning, without alleging at least one instance of every variety of its syntax. I denounce this canon as unsound and unauthoritative.

But what does the writer mean, when he says that the object signified, is regarded alone and complete in itself? Must not every active verb have a regimen, either expressed or understood? *Purify* must have its regimen, as well as *immerse :* the thing or means used to effect purification must be supplied, either in expression or by ellipsis. He says, indeed, "the term to *purify*, exhibits a particular end, on which the mind naturally rests, and from which accessory ideas are fitly removed." It expresses *purification ;* but it expresses neither the end nor the means of purification, more than does *immerse.* Whether the purification is for the end of natural, emblematical, or spiritual cleansing; and whether by means of water, or fire, or sulphur, or anything else, deponent saith not.

"The term to dip," says he, "exhibits a general mode of acting, and could not so well be used alone." Here, again, he overlooks the effect of the principle of grammatical appropriation. Either *immersion* or *sprinkling* could be used alone in appropriation, as freely as *purification.* The Baptists can use the word *immerse* in this way; though from the usual custom of speaking of this ordinance, under the name baptism, the word *immerse* is more seldom used in an appropriated way. The harshness and abruptness which the author fancies, arise solely from the want of constant appropriation. It is really irksome beyond expression, to be obliged to notice reasoning so totally without application. When there is a real difficulty presented to us, the mind rouses to exertion; and from the pleasure of discovery, is insensible of fatigue. But to be obliged to reply to arguments which have not even plausibility to recommend them, is an intolerable grievance.

"It may be asked," says the writer, "Why was *baptizo* ever used, if *katharizo* would express the same meaning? We reply, that though they both convey the sense of purifying, they do not exactly agree in signification. We have no English words corresponding to the various Greek words, *agiazo, baptizo, katharizo, rantizo,* &c., because we have not rites of purification corresponding to the various rites to which these words were applied; and they may all, in some cases, be translated by the one word *purify.* While from the passages examined, it appears that *baptizo* does mean to purify, it also appears that when used in reference to the body, it is applied especially to the more solemn purifications, by means of water; and we shall find that in its application to mind, it has a corresponding intensity of meaning."

The writer here endeavours to avoid the absurdity of the view of

President Beecher, who makes *baptizo* and *katharizo* identical. But he has plunged into numerous absurdities to avoid one.

1. Nothing here alleged unfits *katharizo* from being applied to designate the ordinance, if it was designed to name it by a word signifying purification. It is not necessary that the peculiarities of purification should be specified in the name of a rite of purification. *The water of purification* was of a peculiar kind; yet the term *purification* designates it. If the ordinance is called *sprinkling*, it is a sprinkling of water, not of blood; yet sprinkling applies to every fluid equally. If *immersion* is the name of the ordinance, it is immersion in water; yet immersion equally applies to all substances in which anything can be dipped. I still ask, then, why was not *katharizo* employed, if the name of the ordinance is to express purification?

2. Does not the writer call the ordinance purification? Yet the term *purify* is as general as *katharizo*. If in English, a purification of a particular kind is named by the general word *purification*, why may not the same thing be done in Greek? There is not the smallest apology for *baptizo*, to thrust itself into office; nor is there the least ground for its adoption on any occasion of the meaning purification. Its services can never be required.

3. We have English words to represent the Greek words specified.

4. The ground on which it is asserted, that we have no words to translate the words specified, is unsound. Similarity of rites in two languages, is not necessary to translate all words employed in one of them, to designate religious rites. The word *rantizo* could be translated equally well into our language, if there never had been a sprinkling rite in use amongst us.

5. The words specified, are not always applied in Greek to religious rites. Why then should similar religious rites be necessary to translate them?

6. So far from its being true, that all the specified words may be, in some cases, translated by the one word purify, not one of them, but *two* can, in *any case*, be translated by the word *purify*. *Rantizo* cannot be translated *purify*, though purification is effected by sprinkling. The phrase *sprinkling of the conscience*, is not translated by *purification of the conscience*. This might give the general meaning, but it would not translate the original. The Holy Spirit, by this phraseology, designs not only to designate the purification of the conscience, but to show us that the sprinkling of the blood of the sacrifice was emblematical of this. A version that would here substitute *purification* for *sprinkling*, I would renounce, as inadequate and corrupt. I say the same thing with respect to *agiazo* —it never is *purify*. *Holiness* and *purification* are quite different ideas.

7. Even when there is a rite in the language of the original, without any similar rite in the language of the translation, the words that designate the rite, are capable of translation, as far as the language of the rite employs words that also apply to common actions.

8. And in all such cases the common words of the translation are as capable of assuming an appropriated meaning as the original itself. The word *passover*, is as much appropriated in English as is the word in the original. The word *circumcision* has received a similar appropriation; yet we have no similar rite. In like manner *sprinkling*, and *perfusion*, and *immersion*, may be applied to the ordinance, according to different views of the import of its name. Though from the more common usage employed by all parties, of speaking of the rite by the name baptism, the other terms are less used in an appropriated way; yet they are occasionally used both with propriety and perspicuity. A religious rite of immersion previously existing, is not necessary in order to translate the word which signifies immersion in the original. *Immersion* itself is known to all nations, though some of them may have no religious immersion previously to the introduction of Christianity.

9. The Greek word specified by the writer, and words in general, have the same meaning, when applied to religious rites, that they have when applied to common things. It is from their meaning as applied to common things, that they are fitted to apply to religious rites. The writer, with many others, seems to think that when a word is applied to a sacred rite, it must itself become sacred. This is philological Puseyism. A word may apply to common and sacred things perfectly in the same meaning. The word sprinkle has the same meaning when applied to the sprinkling of the streets to lay the dust, as when applied to sprinkling with holy water.

10. Even had *katharismos* itself been used as the designation of this rite, *immersion* might have been its mode, for an emblematical purpose. In this sense it is explained in the Scriptures.

11. The author tells us that we have no word corresponding to *katharizo*. Will he tell us in what respect purify fails ?

12. When *baptizo* is used in reference to the body, it applies to other purposes as well as ritual purification. Aristobulus was drowned by it, and Naaman was bathed by it.

13. When *baptizo* is used in reference to the body, it applies to other things as well as to water. Nothing was more common than to speak of a baptism in blood. It is quite different as to the means which it employs, provided it can penetrate.

14. In reference to ritual purification, it applies to every thing as well as to body. It was applied to the pots and cups and vessels of the kitchen, as well as to the persons of the Pharisees.

15. It applies to common washing as well as to sacred washing. It is altogether, in reference to cleansing, as general in its application as is *katharizo*, though it does not itself in any instance signify to cleanse . while it equally refers to defiling as to cleansing.

16. The applications of the word in reference to mind are all figurative. In such instances the word has always its proper meaning; and they are all not only in perfect harmony with our view, but many of them absolutely require it.

17. It is absurd to speak of the word as having a different meaning in reference to the body, from what it has in reference to other things.

18. It is equally erroneous to speak of a word as being used with different degrees of intensity, though some hermeneutical writers employ this distinction in their laws of exegesis.

19. The author seems to think that a word derives a portion of its meaning from its situation with respect to other words. Connexion may sometimes be absolutely necessary to determine which of two or more meanings is the meaning in the passage; but connexion never bestows a particle of meaning.

20. By the hypothesis of our opponents, this word, from the fact that immersion was so much used for cleansing, came at length to signify cleansing, as the parent word came to signify *dyeing*. Had this been the case, *washing*, not *purification in general*, would have been the secondary meaning. *Purification* has no pretensions to competition on any ground whatever.

With respect to John iv. 1, 2, the author says, "Remarks similar to those already made, may be repeated here. The verb has not the context appropriate to the sense of dipping." And to these similar observations I give the same answer; they are founded on the same inattention to the effect of grammatical appropriation, that meets us every where in this writer. Even had the word *katharizo* itself been used, it must be supplied with its regimen by ellipsis. The thing with which a purification is performed, is as necessary as the thing in which an immersion takes place. When the Lord's supper is designated by the phrase *breaking bread*, there is a perfectly similar ellipsis: the eating of the bread for a particular purpose, and the drinking of the wine for a particular purpose, are to be supplied elliptically. How could the writer overlook facts so glaringly conspicuous, and so decidedly opposed to his doctrine!

The author next refers to the supposed improbability of immersion with respect to the three thousand baptized on the day of Pentecost. Had it been related in the word of God that every man and woman in Jerusalem were baptized on the same day, it would not, in the estimation of any sound and candid mind, form the slightest objection to the meaning of this word as *immersion*. There could be no difficulty in the business. Comparatively few of the Jews, either from the requirements of the law of Moses, or the traditions of the elders, could be a single day without immersion. But even without reference to this point, that the thing alleged Acts ii. 38, 41, was practicable, is sufficiently attested by the fact that it was practised. What that thing is, must be learned from the testimony of the word employed to convey the testimony, ascertained by its occurrence in the language. I will not suffer my opponents to call on me to gauge the fountains and ponds that were in Jerusalem eighteen centuries back. Whether they used baths or cisterns, is quite alike to me: the word provides every thing necessary for me. They must have been *immersed*, for the word has no other meaning. Should an English traveller inform us that in a very distant country, on a certain great festival, there were three thousand persons *immersed* in observance of a religious custom, should we either refuse to believe him, or explain the word *immerse* in the sense of purification by sprinkling? Why then do we find a difficulty in regard to three thousand Jews, who were as familiar with the water as water fowls?

In Acts viii. 12, 13, 16, he brings the same complaint as to the regimen, which surely I have answered often enough. He thinks it very improbable, also, that the great number of believers on that occasion should be immersed. Especially he is overwhelmed with astonishment that, if they were immersed, there should be no account of the inquiries of the Gentiles about the new rite. Does the author really expect a detail of every thing that happened on such occasions? What sort of a book would the Bible be, had it been formed on this gossiping principle? But from the conduct of Philip in preaching to the eunuch, we may learn that the new rite would be sufficiently explained, both to Jews and Gentiles.

The author thinks that *immersed into the name of Christ,* is unsuitable phraseology. The Baptists, and millions of others, have found this phraseology very intelligible and edifying. But does not the author perceive that, except he has taken out a patent for his translation of *eis* in this place, we can have the benefit of it? We may be immersed *for* the name of Jesus, as well as he can be purified *for it.* I reject this translation, however, though it is no part of my duty to refute it.

With respect to Acts viii. 38, I have already shown that *ek* is decisive evidence that Philip and the eunuch were in the water. It never, in a single instance, designates merely *from;* it is always *out of.*

I admit that *eis* means *unto* as well as *into.* I will not take a particle of evidence from a word but what it legitimately contains. I write not for a party, but for the people of God without exception—not for the praise of reviewers, but for the judgment seat of Christ. But while I admit this variety of meaning in this preposition, I will not give up its testimony in this place. A word that has two meanings may be definitely ascertained, and all good composition must afford evidence to ascertain it, where it is used. That *eis hudor* here is not *unto* the water, but *into* the water, appears evident from the fact, that the persons to whom the fact refers, are previously brought to the water by another verb and another preposition. *Epi* is the preposition that gives them their station *at* the water. When, then, after coming to the water, they are said both to go down *eis hudor,* what can it be but *into* the water? Let this be coupled with the fact which our opponents themselves cannot deny, that immersion is frequently the meaning of the verb which designates the action which they are about to perform. Let the testimony of *ek,* which I have shown never wavers, and which this writer himself must admit to be its usual meaning, be viewed in combination with all this, and what doubt can remain on the mind of any man who really wishes to come at truth on the subject?

"If it were stated," says the author, "that both these persons went *into* the water, this would be very different from the statement that one *dipped* the other *into* the water."

These two statements are indeed very different, but it must be obvious to any child that the first was in order to effect the last. Can any man think that they would go both into the water, when a few drops would serve in any place? Every candid mind must see that going into the water was here necessary for the performance of baptism. Such obstinacy can never be cured by argument. Were this a matter of heathen antiquity, is there a man in existence, who would question the meaning?

With respect to Acts ix. 18; xxii. 16, the author thinks that Paul being a sick man, it is not probable that he was immersed. I see nothing in Paul's case to prevent his immediate immersion : I consider such reasoning as the most egregious trifling. Can anything be more unreasonable than to attempt to evade the established meaning of a word, and confer on it a meaning that cannot plead the authority of a single example, on the pretence of such improbabilities? I object to this, not merely as it affects the point in question, but as it establishes a false principle of interpretation.

If a similar document came from the Baptist missionaries in any very distant country, would there be any hesitation as to the meaning? Would any one allege that it was probable that sprinkling was used instead of immersion, or that the word immersion signifies sprinkling or purification? Were we to admit, as a canon of interpretation, that difficulties and views of probability ought to set aside the usual meaning of words, and give them meanings for which there is no other sanction, what facts in history could stand their ground? Every fanatic, every religionist, every heretic, would give words whatever meaning they pleased. In all cases of contested meaning, we must proceed on the authority of ascertained examples, without any deference to the authority of previous probability. If Paul was baptized in a state of exhaustion, before partaking of refreshment, we are not from this to deny the meaning of the word, but to learn that baptism ought to be attended to immediately on believing. It is connected with the faith that saves the soul, and ought as closely as possible to be connected with it in practice.

" It was either performed," says he, " while the person stood up, or it so quickly followed his rising from a couch, that it might be said, He rising up was baptized."

I care not that it was expressly said that he was baptized in the very room where he was then sitting, immediately after the address of Ananias. This would not create the smallest difficulty. Yet I am utterly astonished that a literary man should interpret such forms of expression in this manner. They are quite consistent with the supposition that some time might intervene between the command and the execution; and at some distance from the place. When Ulysses returned to the ship with a stag, throwing it from his shoulders, he called on his hungry companions, saying, *Rise* and *eat*. Yet the stag must be skinned, spitted, and cooked, before it was eaten; and it was eaten in a different place from that in which the address was made. In the Battle of the Frogs and Mice, the herald that proclaimed war against the frogs, says :—

> " Leaders of the host of frogs, put on
> Your armour, and draw forth your bands to battle!"

The frogs were now in council, and some time must intervene before the bands could be led forth. God says to Moses, " Rise up early in the morning, and stand before Pharaoh." There was some time before his rising and his standing before the king; and some space between the place where he rose and where he afterwards stood. "Now rise up, said I, and get you over the brook Zered." There was some time between the command and the performance of the thing commanded; and some space between the place of rising and the place where they were commanded to go. "Rise, go up, take your journey, and pass over the river Arnon," &c. &c.

The author tells us that the word has here "that connexion with terms of religion which favours the supposition that it had a sacred meaning, such as to purify, and not a common meaning, such as to dip,—"Dip and cleanse away thy sins, invoking his name." Upon this I remark:—
1. What does he mean by terms of religion? Does he mean words that are used in religion only? There are no such terms here. All the words referred to are used in common as well as in sacred things. Does he mean words that are often used in religion? Any word may be used with respect to religion when its meaning is suitable. 2. Do we not find a similar connexion with respect to the words *wash, cleanse, sprinkle?* yet they are common words. 3. A word does not become a religious word by being applied to religion; to *wash,* to *cleanse,* to *purify,* are common words. A common word may apply to a sacred object without becoming sacred. The hog and the devotee are cleansed by the same word. 4. If *immersion,* as a mode, is employed by God to designate a rite, is it not as holy as any word in the language? I make no such objection to *sprinkling* or *pouring,* as the appointed mode of this ordinance. 5. What are the consecrated terms with which *baptizo* is here associated? The first of them is *wash away.* Is *louo* a consecrated word? *Invoking*—the word calls on man as well as on God. 6. The word is indeed associated here with a word that determines its meaning. It is coupled with *louo,* to bathe, which always respects the person in general when no part is named.

"The additional clause, cleanse away thy sins," says he, "is to be regarded as additional in sense, and not as merely explanatory. Baptize is the first injunction; Cleanse away thy sins, that is, repent, is the second; Become a worshipper of Jesus Christ, is the third."

This is a very pure specimen of Puseyism. It is incontrovertibly evident that the command, "*Wash away thy sins,*" respects what was to take place in baptism. If then it was not symbolical washing, it must be Puseyite regeneration. It is equally evident that this washing is performed by the rite itself, and not by the Holy Spirit, for the command about it is given to Paul. There is a place in the north of Ireland, called the Holestone, named from a certain stone with a hole in it sufficient, with difficulty, to allow a man to pass through it. In ancient times, it is said, that there was a ceremony of passing through this hole by which persons were *born again.* Now I think it might be expedient to revive this ceremony; for I cannot perceive any respect in which the Holestone regeneration is inferior to baptismal regeneration.

This theology is very different from that of our Lord and his apostles. It commanded them to make men disciples, and then to baptize them and they said, Repent and be baptized, or, Believe and be baptized

Where does the writer learn that *cleanse away sins* and *repent* are the same? They are always connected, but they are perfectly different. *Repentance* is the duty of man; *washing away of sins is solely* the work of the Spirit. Paul had already repented; his sins also were already washed away. In baptism this was to be exhibited in a symbolical washing. Paul had already become a worshipper of the Lord Jesus; he had previously called on the Lord Jesus. Why is it supposed that this was the first time in which he called on him?

But the author is not contented with making *cleanse away sins* to be *repent*. By a second process in the manufacture, he converts it into "let there be in your heart that purity which, commencing with repentance, is by regeneration perfected in those that trust in the Lord Jesus," &c. What a bright specimen of theology!

On Acts x. 47, 48, the author remarks, "The word here used in connexion with water is, in the New Testament, always construed with the object whose action or movement to any place is hindered or forbidden."

Profound philology! This surely will settle the question. What can stand against such a battery of metaphysics? But let us examine it, and we shall find that it is metaphysical only in form, and profound only to those who have not a rule to dip it. I remark, then, 1. Were it perfectly correct, it is quite consonant with immersion. I have no objection at all, that the water should be brought into the room. I have no doubt that, whatever may have been the case on this occasion, the thing was often practised. 2. There is here no movement of the water expressed, nor does the verb require movement at all. It is frequently used when there is no motion of an object from one place to another 3. It is not philosophical, but absurd, to speak of *action* here with respect to the water. Water is not considered as an agent, but as the thing employed by the agents. 4. In whatever way the phrase *forbid water*, is understood, no person can suppose that the command is given to the water, and that it was the water that was forbidden to come into the room. If the prohibition respects the bringing of water into the room, it must be directed to the persons, and not to the water. This is as necessary in the sense of the phrase, according to this writer, as it is in ours. 5. The writer says, "It is most properly employed, if the water for baptism was brought into the room in which the persons were." Granting this for a moment, what is the ellipsis? Would it not be: "Who can forbid water *to be brought into the room?*" Now is not a like ellipsis warrantable on our side? Who can forbid water *to be brought for immersing these persons?* 6. The conversation of every day exemplifies the phrase in our meaning. The physician *forbids wine*, &c. &c. Does not this mean, he forbids the invalid the use of wine? 7. *Forbid water* has not, even to a child, the appearance of relation to the question whether water was to be brought, or they were to go to the water. Common sense at once declares the meaning to be, *Who can forbid baptism? Who can forbid the external rite, when the thing of which it is an emblem, is verified? If they have received the Spirit, what ordinance should be denied them?* 8. We have in Luke vi. 29, the very same word similarly construed. " *Forbid not the coat.*" Was this command to the coat? Was it the *action* or the *movement* of the coat that was forbidden? Can we not ourselves say, can any forbid the Lord's supper? The phraseology of this passage will equally suit every mode of this ordinance, and any ordinance that employs water. With respect to Acts xvi. 15, I certainly can have no objection to the opinion of the writer, that Lydia was baptized in the place where Paul preached: the sooner the better. As to her dress, and anything that is not matter of Divine prescription, I leave to the descretion of those concerned on the occasion. I shall neither be the master of the ceremonies myself, nor allow my opponent to undertake that service. The author, as usual, complains of the want of regimen. It cannot be necessary for me to return to this subject. He tells us that "It cannot be inferred from the mention of the river, that a large quantity of water was necessary for Christian baptism." I admit this most fully, and most cheerfully. I have no doubt that the river would have been in that place, and that it would have contained as much water, had sprinkling been the mode of the ordinance of Christ. But the writer forgets that this is the very kind of proof the burden of which he demands from us. Does he forget that he calls on us to gauge the fountain of Bethulia? I shall take on me no such burden. When a word requires water, it must have it, wherever it may find it. Had Lydia been said to be baptized on the spot where she believed, without the mention of fountain or river, I should have perfectly the same confidence in the mode of her baptism. Little value, however, as the writer sets upon the river here, had Lydia been said to be baptized in the place where Paul preached, without any evidence that a river or fountain was near, I am fully convinced he would have loudly complained of want of water. Still the river would have been there.

Taking it for granted, then, that she was baptized at the river, and that her house, as the author seems to think, was in the city, does not the phraseology annihilate the distance as much as that in Acts x.? When she was baptized she said, "Come into my house, and abide;" or, "Having entered into my house, abide." Similar phraseology occurs in verse 40, "They went out of prison, and entered into the house of Lydia." Here the time and distance, according to this writer, are annihilated.

Let the unlearned reader here take notice, that the place of preaching is said to be *para*, *at*, or near the river—not *en*, *in* the river, as it might be, according to the criticism of our author.

The author comes next to the baptism of the jailer. He usually translates for himself, as if the common version were in every thing wrong. I am not to be supposed as approving his version, as often as I pass it without censure. I notice no errors, but such as concern the point in hand. What our version calls " *washed their stripes,*" he translates, " made them clean from their wounds." The author's translation is inferior, both in elegance and in correctness. The original is *stripes*, not *wounds*: the term wounds is too generic. The original is *bathed*, not *made clean*: the latter is generic, the former is specific. *Bathing,* and *making clean,* are not equivalent. Homer represents Jupiter as giving directions to Apollo, to cleanse the body of Sarpedon, slain in battle, and afterwards to bathe it in a river.

> "Phœbus, my son, delay not: from beneath
> Yon hill of weapons drawn, cleanse from his blood
> Sarpedon's corse; then, bearing him remote,
> Lave him in waters of the running stream."—Cowper.

The jailer, then, might have cleansed them from their wounds without bathing them; but the original imports, that they were cleansed by bathing. All cleansing is not washing; and all washing is not bathing. When Achilles sends out his friend Patroclus to battle, he took out his goblet of exquisite workmanship to make libation to Jupiter. But first he purified it with sulphur, and then washed it in running water.

> "That cup producing from the chest, he first
> With sulphur fumed it, then with water rinsed
> Pellucid of the running stream."—Cowper.

Cleanse, or *make clean,* is, then, quite a different thing from bathe. It may here be observed also, that this was a sacred rite, yet the same words are used for ritual purification, that are employed for common purification.

The author is of opinion, that there is an apparent connexion between the washing of the wounds and the performance of the rite. Be it so; why might they not immerse the jailer and his family in the same bath in which they were washed from their stripes? But there is no such connexion as this writer fancies. The baptism and the bathing, as far as the passage is concerned, might not have been at the same time, or the same place. Had there been no conveniences for immersion in the prison, what would prevent them from going to the Strymon, on which the city was situated? But where they were baptized, I neither know nor care.

It is of importance, however, to consider the intimate connexion between baptism and the faith of the Gospel, as it is exhibited in this transaction. Notwithstanding the miserable plight of Paul and his companion, the baptism was performed before they partook of refreshment in the jailer's house. Can anything more clearly indicate the importance of this ordinance?

The author speaks of " the assumption of the axiom, that *baptizo* must mean to dip." Who is it that assumes this as an axiom? I assume nothing but what is self-evident, which the meaning of no word is. As far, then, as I am concerned, this representation is calumnious; I never assume the meaning of any word: I assign no meaning till the occurrences of a word are ascertained and examined. Whether a word has one meaning, or several meanings, I determine by this examination on philosophical principles. When I have ascertained the primary meaning of a word, I apply it to every case where it will serve, admitting no new meaning till occurrences prove it. When I have ascertained a second meaning, I will not admit a third as long as the first or second will serve.

Thus I proceed with respect to any number of meanings, never admitting a new meaning without proof. Submission to these principles I demand on the ground of self-evidence. Submission to them, I yield with respect to every opponent. These laws are for truth—not for party. Perverseness may reject them—perverseness has rejected every first principle; but I have no doubt that all candid persons will acquiesce in them. Without first principles interpretation is impossible. Mathematics may as well demonstrate without axioms. The criticism of our opponents is altogether without science: instead of leading to sound conclusions, it introduces universal confusion and uncertainty.

Now, let us for a moment compare the assumptions of this writer with mine. Let us take an example from the very case in hand. Having enumerated a great number of his improbabilities, he concludes: "But if this was not Christian duty and practice, then *baptizo* does not signify to dip." Now, does not the writer here assume the very point in debate? He assumes a view of Christian duty and practice; and on that ground determines the meaning of the word totally without reference to its use in the language. What is Christian duty and practice, we must learn from the words of Scripture,—not from a crazy imagination. Whether this word signifies to immerse, we must learn, not from our own views of probability, but from the examples in which it is found in the language. Had Abraham used this principle of interpretation, he never would have submitted to circumcision—he never would have consented to kill Isaac. I refuse to listen to any testimony but that of the word itself, speaking in the instances in which it is found in the language. All persons who attempt to settle the question on any other ground, I denounce as fanatics in criticism.

With respect to Acts xviii. 8, and 1 Cor. i. 13—17, the author says, "In both of these passages the verb is used alone; and that the special and sacred sense of *purify*, is more suitable to such a usage, than the general common sense of dip, is immediately obvious. On the one supposition, we have the strange sentences, They believed and were *dipped*," &c.

Here, again, our author's error arises from his inattention to grammatical appropriation. I have, again and again, shown that even where purify is applied to a sacred rite, it acquires no sacred or special signification. It is just the common signification, applied in reference to a sacred thing; and in like manner dip, in its common signification, applies to the most sacred things. As to the sense of the word there is no difference between the common and sacred.

What the author calls strange sentences, are exemplified in all languages every hour : it is what must happen with respect to all appropriations. It is strange beyond conception, that the author did not perceive that the very same thing takes place with respect to the word *circumcise*. This word can be used alone: "Ye on the sabbath-day circumcise a man." What a strange sentence! *Cut a man around!* But I need not waste time in proving what must be familiar to every reader.

"That baptizing," says the writer, "was regarded by St. Paul as a purifying or consecrating to the service of Him for whom the rite was administered, agrees exactly with the train of thought exhibited in tne latter passage," &c.

Might not baptizing be viewed as a purification, though its name is not purification? Purifying may be the emblem of the rite, as well when it is called immersion, as if purification were its name. It is strange that the author brings this so often forward, without perceiving its fallacy. One would think that he never heard of circumcision. It is not my object to discover the errors of the writer on any other subject than that of the meaning of the word in question; but I strongly suspect that he had some Puseyite view of the nature of this rite. It is no *consecration;* it is no ceremonial purification; it is only an emblematical cleansing.

The question, Acts xix. 4—7, has to the writer the same appearance of strangeness in our view of the meaning of the disputed word. I hope I have, by this time, made him a little more familiar with this style, from circumcision and other appropriations. His *anointed king or priest,* would be familiar to every one; *an oiled king,* would appear strange. I could bear such criticism from the vulgar; but it is intolerable from a man of letters. Did the writer ever hear of *dubbing a man a knight?* To *dub,* means to strike; and knights were constituted by the blow of a sword. Let us try the writer's criticism on this expression : " On the supposition that *dub* signifies to *strike,* we have this strange question, Were you *struck* a knight? *Dub,* then, cannot signify to strike; but *purify* will suit to admiration. *Were you purified a knight?* is most natural and appropriate."

On the supposition that the persons referred to in this passage were baptized in the first interview, the author complains with respect to a change of raiment. Such inquiries show more perverseness than wisdom. I hold such things as utterly unworthy of mention. The meaning of the word can never be affected by such scruples. As they were baptized, they were immersed. I care not how they were provided on the occasion.

I have now gone through this series of papers, and examined every thing that has the appearance of argument with a minuteness that must appear tedious to most readers. Two ways suggested themselves to me for my procedure. The first was, to detect the false principles on which both the arguments and objections rest, and leave the reader to make the application. The second was, to follow the writer, and refute every thing in detail. The first would have been more suitable to my general undertaking; but the second is the most satisfactory for most readers, especially as the controversy immediately concerns the interpretation of so many passages of Scripture, and so vast a range of Greek literature. Had I contented myself with showing that when he takes out of the word in question *continuation, effect, intention,* with many other things that the word itself does not contain, I might have done enough for the learned world; but readers in general, will wish to have the principles unfolded by illustration. At first, I determined to dismiss the consideration of the prepositions concerned in the controversy, with a few observations; but I afterwards considered that, however tedious the task, it would be more satisfactory to give a particular account of every passage in Greek literature, to which the writer appeals for his doctrine, as to the testimony of the prepositions. This I thought the more necessary, as some of the most essential principles on this subject have been overlooked, or mistaken, by the most distinguished grammarians; while their doctrine has been used for purposes they never contemplated.

The fundamental error of my opponent, with regard to the prepositions concerned in this controversy is, that in ascertaining their testimony, he makes the English idiom the standard to which the Greek must conform. I have shown, that with as good reason the English might be made to conform to the Greek; but that neither should be obliged to conform to the other. It is not certain that a Greek preposition has such a meaning in such a place, because in such a situation we should use such a preposition; for the idioms of the two tongues may be, in this respect, different. We may sometimes use an English preposition to translate a Greek one, when the two prepositions are by no means coincident in meaning. This is a canon of great importance. My opponent, so far from being aware of it, interprets the Greek prepositions by whatever English prepositions would be used by us in the same situation. Can anything more strongly show the necessity of sound principles as the foundation of sound interpretation.

7

EARLY NEW TESTAMENT BAPTISMS

OBSERVATIONS ON THE VIEW OF DR. MILLER, OF NEW YORK, WITH
RESPECT TO THE MEANING OF THE WORD BAPTISM

Section I.—" If I know my own heart," says Dr. Miller, " it is my
purpose to exhibit the subject in the light of truth, and to advance
nothing but that which appears to rest on the authority of Him who instituted the ordinance under consideration, and who is alone competent
to declare his will concerning it." Though this is of no value as to his
argument, yet it is of infinite value as to himself; and the expression of
such a sentiment cannot fail to be satisfactory to his opponents, while
it entitles him to that " candid and patient hearing" which he requests.
If I forget it in any of my observations on his work, it is far from my
intention in the commencement. My design is to examine his reasoning fairly, candidly, and patiently. If he has a single particle of truth,
which I have not yet discovered, I will accept it with gratitude. Truth
is my riches: to contend for it in the sight of God, is my highest glory.
Men of sincerity and men of God may be in error as to the meaning of
Scripture, yet in no instance is error either innocent or harmless. We
should know, and it must be in all cases important to know, what God
has revealed for our belief and practice. If attachment to a favourite
view makes its evidence appear stronger than it really is, or makes us
view as evidence that which is not of the nature of evidence; if it prevents opposite evidence from having its due weight, our sincerity is no
security for arriving at a just conclusion.

Notwithstanding the favourable impression made on me by the declaration quoted above, I am greatly impressed with a conviction that in
announcing his very design, he manifests symptoms of distrust in his own
cause. He seems to me hardly to know with precision what he is to
state as his belief on the subject, and what he is to prove. " Sprinkling or affusion," he tells us, " is a method of baptism just as valid and
lawful as any other." And while he announces it as his object to prove
this, he says, in the same breath, " or rather to maintain, from Scripture, and from the best usages of the Christian church, that baptism by
sprinkling or affusion, not only rests on as good authority as immersion, but that it is a method decisively more scriptural, suitable, and
edifying."

Here then is an utter want of precision. He does not tell us what is the meaning of the word; and throughout his whole work I have not learned what he makes its meaning in the ordinance of Christ. He confounds sprinkling and affusion, which are different modes, and which are expounded by their friends as being different emblems. He supposes that several modes, or all modes, are equally lawful, yet that sprinkling or affusion is more scriptural, suitable, and edifying, than any of them. If it is more scriptural than the rest, how can all modes be included in the meaning of the word? If all modes are included in the meaning of the word, no mode can be more scriptural than any other. If sprinkling is decisively more suitable and edifying than any other mode, does he not bring a charge against the Institutor for not restricting the observance to this mode?

"Now we contend," says Dr. M., "that this word does not necessarily, nor even commonly, signify to immerse, but also implies to wash, to sprinkle, to pour on water, and to tinge or die with any liquid; and therefore accords very well with the mode of baptism by sprinkling or affusion."

You contend, Dr. M.! Where do you thus contend? Say rather you assert, for there is not even an attempt to prove this diversity of meaning. I have gone through a vast range of Greek literature; and from all the examples I could meet, I have shown that the word has but one meaning, and that this one meaning is immersion. Dr. M. meets me by an objection that he contends that the word has not only a secondary meaning, but a variety of meanings that no word in any language could have; and all this without even an attempt at proof by examples and criticism. If Dr. M. and his friends think that this is evidence, they may be sincere in believing anything. Dr. M. not only asserts what he has not attempted to prove, but what is contrary to self-evidence. There is not in any language a word that signifies the three modes in question, or any two of them. If a word extends to all of them, it can signify none of them. It might as well be said that the word *immerse* in English signifies to *dip*, to *pour*, to *sprinkle*, as that the Greek word has such significations; or that *pour* signifies to dip and to sprinkle; and that sprinkle signifies to *pour* and to *dip*. I would dispute the point with every confidence, if it respected a language of whose very alphabet I am ignorant.

But what shall I say to the assertion of Dr. M., that this word signifies to *tinge* or to *dye*? Have I not, on the authority of every example of the alleged occurrences of this word, proved that it is never used in the sense of the primitive word signifying to *dye*? Has he met any instance proving the contrary? If he has, why has he not produced it? If he has not, why has he made such an assertion?

SECTION II.—There is a peculiarity in Dr. M.'s reasoning, which I do not think I have ever met in any controversial writer. He substitutes his own solemn assertions for proof. "I can assure you," says he, "that the word we render baptize, does legitimately signify the application of water in any way, as well as by immersion." This he never attempts to prove. Surely they who can be convinced by this, may believe anything to which their prejudices incline them. To rebut this, it would be enough for me to say, "I assure you that Dr. M. is quite mistaken." Why has Dr. M. entered the field at all, when he has never fired a shot, but only blank cartridge?

I demand the proof of this solemn assertion. Where are the documents that warrant it? So far from signifying every application of water, the word has no essential connexion with water at all—nor even with fluids. It is applicable to every thing that is capable of being penetrated. But if it is a word so various in its meaning, as to common things, why has not Dr. M. told us whether it has all these meanings in the ordinance of baptism, or which of them it has?

"The evangelists," says Dr. M., "tell us that the scribes and Pharisees invariably washed (in the original, baptized) their hands before dinner." Where are we told this? The common reading is not *baptized*. But were it adopted, is it not quite suitable? What hinders the hands to be immersed? Does Dr. M. think that if the word can refer to the hands as a part, it cannot refer to the body as a whole? May we not dip the hand as well as the body? This argument is so inapplicable, that I can hardly trust myself to state it in order to refutation. To whom does it need refutation?

"When we are told," he continues, "that when they come from the market, except they wash, (in the original, ' except they baptize,') they eat not." What difficulty is here? Why should not this be immersion? What they did on this occasion is known from the signification of the word; let that be determined by the authority of the language in general, and it will then be known what they did on coming from market.

"When we read," says Dr. M., "of the Pharisees being so scrupulous about the washing (in the original, the baptizing) of cups, pots, and brazen vessels, and tables, &c.; it surely cannot mean in any of these cases, to immerse or plunge." How does the reading of this prove that baptism is not immersion? If these things were baptized, they were immersed, because this is the meaning of the word in the language. What would hinder the Pharisees from immersing these things? Every thing mentioned is easily capable of immersion. Must we give a new meaning to a word in order to save trouble to superstition? If such arguments weigh in the mind of any man, I will not deny that he may be very conscientious, but I cannot avoid believing that he is more easily satisfied with proof than a sound mind ought to be.

Dr. M. next refers to the baptism of the Holy Ghost; but this is a figurative baptism, in which there is no literal *immersion, pouring,* or *sprinkling,* nor any likeness as to any mode. There is no mode in the operations of the Spirit.

Next, he brings us to the Red Sea, and denies that the Israelites in their baptism there, were immersed. If he means that the water did not touch them, it is very true; but can candour refuse to admit that what took place on that occasion may, both emblematically and beautifully, be called an immersion, or a burial in the sea? He says, that the cloud did not touch them. The Scripture says, that they were *in* the cloud, and *under the cloud.* He knows that they were not immersed, though the narrative expressly says that they were immersed, using the most definite word in the language; yet he is very willing to believe that they were sprinkled by the spray, though there is no such thing mentioned. If persons will be so unreasonable in rejecting evidence on one side, and so credulous on the other, they may be very conscientious, but we must be allowed to say, that they are very confident in error.

He next refers to the case of Judas dipping his hand in the dish, at the passover. He says, that "no one can imagine that this implies that the whole hand was immersed in the gravy." Surely, this is egregious trifling. Has this anything to do with the mode expressed by the word? Might it not as well be alleged that the English word *dip* does not signify to immerse, because the English version says of Judas, that he *dipped* his hand in the dish? Does not the same objection apply equally to the translation as to the original? It is astonishing that any degree of perspicacity could not discover this. Besides, the whole hand might be immersed in the dish: it is *in the dish,* and not *in the gravy.* Surely, it is unworthy of such a man as Dr. M. to quibble in this manner. The word has its mode here, as well as if the object had gone to the bottom of the Baltic.

With respect to the above cases he says, "It surely cannot mean, in any of these cases, to immerse, or plunge." It surely does mean to dip, in each of the cases.

"If a man is said, by the inspired evangelist," says Dr. M., "to be baptized, when his hands only are washed." I must believe that Dr. M. states evidence conscientiously. If I must, what am I to think of his accuracy? Is it not awful to report evidence from the testimony of the Holy Spirit in this manner? Millions of people will rely on this representation, as on an oracle; and believe that the Holy Spirit says that the persons are baptized, who have only their hands washed. This is not the testimony of the evangelist. As long as the leaders of parties will allow themselves to take such freedom with their documents, they teach their followers to pervert the word of God.

"If couches," he says, "are spoken of as baptized, when the cleansing of water was applied to them in any manner." When it was applied to them in any manner! Is this an honest way to report facts? Where did he learn that the water was applied in any manner, when it is spoken of, as the baptism of couches? This is to assume the thing in dispute. How the water was applied, we can learn only from the word. Now can this be reasoning? What is the use of such assertions? Can it serve any purpose but to deceive the ignorant and the credulous?

He adds: "and when the complete immersion of them is out of the question." Here again he assumes as a thing impossible, that which is not only possible, but of easy performance. Couches may be immersed without any difficulty; and if the Holy Spirit reports truly, couches were immersed, as they are said to have been baptized. I cannot sufficiently express the surprise I feel, that this distinguished writer should allow himself to make such assumptions. If he counted on the credulity of his own party, did he think that we should allow him to assume the point in debate ? Indeed the palpable fact that among all the instances in which this word is applied, there is not one in which the thing said to be baptized is not capable of immersion, is an irrefragable argument in favour of immersion. Had it any other signification, it must sometimes be found applied to things incapable of immersion. Did it, for instance, signify to *purify,* or to *pour,* or to *sprinkle,* it would often be found applied to things that could not have been immersed, as houses, &c. Houses are said to be purified,—never to be baptized. If we allow Dr. M. to assume the point in debate, and take his solemn assurances for proof, there is not on earth a more convincing reasoner. But if this is not granted to him, there is nothing of argument in his work.

Let us suppose that the question respects a modern custom of some foreign nation, and that from the report of a traveller, there is a different judgment formed as to the action performed on the couches. One party says they were dipped; another says they were merely sprinkled; another, that water was poured on them; another, that they were washed in any manner; another, that they were fumigated; another, that they were scoured, &c. How is the controversy to be settled? Is it not by the testimony of the word employed to designate the action ?

With respect to Heb. ix. 10, Dr. M. says: "Now we know that by far the greater part of these 'divers washings,' were accomplished by sprinkling or affusion, and not by immersion." Do we so, Dr. M.? How do we know that these *divers baptisms* were accomplished by sprinkling or affusion? We cannot know this, unless we take Dr. M.'s solemn assurance as proof of the fact. Here, again, he assumes the point to be proved; he assumes that these baptisms are washings in general, and that *sprinklings* are *washings.* We know, indeed, that there were a great number of sprinklings and affusions under the law; but how do we know that all these sprinklings and affusions, or any of them, are called baptisms? How do we know that what are here called *divers baptisms* were performed by sprinkling and affusion? This passage does not assert this. Can this be known in any other way than by ascertaining the meaning of the word baptism, by the usage of the language? Where does he learn that what is done by sprinkling or affusion, belongs to those divers baptisms? Can he know this from any other source, than from the meaning of the word itself? "The blood of the paschal lamb," he tells us, "was directed to be sprinkled on the door-posts of the tabernacle." Nothing can be more incontrovertible. But was this sprinkling of blood a literal washing? Was it a baptism? It was an emblematical purification; but it was a literal defilement. Sprinkling is not washing; and washing is not baptism. Is the sprinkling of the blood on the door-posts called a baptism here, or anywhere else? Is the sprinkling of the book, and of the people, Heb. ix. 19, called a baptism? Is the sprinkling of the consecrated oil called baptism? Is the sprinkling of the blood on the day of atonement called baptism? Why assume all these points as facts? Can this be called reasoning from principles, or expounding from the ascertained meaning of words? Dr. M. might as well solemnly assure his readers of the truth of his doctrine, on the authority of his dreams. This is worse than dreaming; for thousands of readers will take this for satisfactory proof. To what purpose is it to refer us to the sprinkling of Aaron and his sons with blood, with other sprinklings? There were *divers purifications*, but they were not *divers baptisms*. Yet, after enumerating these sprinklings, he gravely tells us: "Now these are the divers baptisms of which the apostle speaks." Who told him this? The passage does not say so: we have not even the authority of a dream. Nothing but assumption, assumption, assumption. Why does he not identify these sprinklings with the baptisms? This has never been effected; this cannot be effected. Dr. M. is like a lawyer, who is very strong in proof that the son of such a man is entitled to a particular estate, but utterly fails in proving the identity of his client with the person who is the heir. This he merely assumes.

But Dr. M. will give us proof at last. "Happily," says he, "the inspired apostle does not leave us in doubt what those divers baptisms were, of which he speaks." Well, I will ask no better authority than that which he proposes. I will bow with implicit submission to the decision of the inspired apostle. If Paul tells us that certain sprinklings are baptisms, I will believe that they are such. But the inspired apostle says nothing like this. Dr. M. tells us that the inspired apostle "singles out, and presents sprinkling as his chosen and only specimen." Does the apostle give sprinkling as a specimen of baptism? He does no such thing. In showing us how the apostle gives sprinkling as a specimen of baptism, Dr. M. says, "'For,' says he, in the 13th, 19th, and 21st verses of the same chapter, explaining what he means by 'divers baptisms,' 'if the blood of bulls, and of goats, and the ashes of an heifer, *sprinkling* the unclean, sanctifieth to the purifying of the flesh; how much more shall the blood of Christ,'" &c. Now how is this a reason for what he alleges? How does this explain what the apostle means by *divers baptisms?* Does this identify sprinkling with baptism? The argument of this passage is, that if the sprinkling of blood under the law served to purify ceremonially, much more would the blood of Christ purify from sin. There is here nothing that looks like an identification of the sprinklings under the law, with the baptisms under the law. How can any man say, that the sprinkling in the 13th verse is one of the "divers baptisms" previously mentioned? The verses referred to, give no specimen of the "divers baptisms," but contrast the efficacy of the blood of Christ with that of the sprinklings under the law. Instead of explaining what the inspired apostle means by the *divers baptisms,* the verses referred to preach the atonement.

But in addressing Jews, it is absurd to suppose that it was necessary for the apostle to explain what was meant literally by the *divers baptisms.* Did they need an explanation of the meaning of a word employed to designate a practice of their own law?

That the word signifies every application of water, Dr. M. again and again asserts; but he never enters into proof by an actual appeal to the occurrences of the word in the language. Of what use is such a work as to controversy? Can anything but the usage of the language, proved by examples, determine the question? There is in his work, nothing like criticism. He alludes to my bold assertion, that the word is perfectly univocal, yet he never grapples with my reasoning and examples. The work may be a very good confession of his faith, as to the meaning of the word; but it never enters into the discussion of the question.

The next point which Dr. M. professes to prove is, that "there is nothing in the thing signified by baptism which renders immersion more necessary or proper than any other mode of applying water in this ordinance."

Were this a fact it would not deliver from the obligation of immersion. If a mode is commanded, that mode ought to be observed. If Jesus says Go, we should go: if he says Come, we should come, without stopping to inquire the reason of the command. Whether there is anything emblematical in the mode of the rite, depends not on the word, but on the inspired explanation of the ordinance. Nothing can be more clearly taught than that the mode is emblematical. Rom. vi. 1, is most express.

Dr. M. gives us a number of examples in which *pouring* and *sprinkling* are used with respect to Divine blessings. Did any one ever deny this? Does this show that immersion cannot be used for an emblematical purpose?

Does Dr. M. believe that *pouring* and *sprinkling* are emblematical in baptism? If so, which of them is the mode appointed? Pouring and sprinkling are modes as different from one another, as each of them is from immersion. If so, no other mode but the one appointed can be true baptism. How can he admit that the other modes can be valid? Assuredly, if any mode is used for an emblematical purpose, that mode is essential, as really as the water. He appears to me, however, to believe that Christ has affixed no emblem as to mode, but that we may adopt a mode that will be suitable and edifying by its emblem. If this is his meaning, then he may compete either with Pusey, or the Pope. If he has a warrant to create emblems, he may also create ordinances.

The improbabilities and difficulties of immersion are the next objections. How could three thousand be immersed in one day? Would to God that he would put it into my power to make the experiment; I have no doubt that I could accomplish the matter in the third part of a day. The difficulties and improbabilities are all grounded on superstitious views of the ordinance. The performance of baptism is not confined to office—this is the mummery of Babylon. In baptizing the three thousand on the day of Pentecost, I will trouble neither the twelve nor the seventy, if they have more important work. But he has another difficulty as to the water. I can do miracles about the water; I will make the word find it for me, even in the deserts of Arabia, if it is asserted that there was a baptism there. This writer, like our opponents in general, mistakes the burden of proof. It does not lie on us to show that there is any evidence of water, except the evidence implied in the word. Many writers on our side have shown that there is independent evidence of the sufficiency of water in Jerusalem. This is highly useful, with a view of putting obstinacy to the blush; but it is not necessary to prove the fact by direct evidence in any instance. I trample on such objections. If it be asserted by credible testimony that a man was shot, are you to refuse belief, unless you are informed where the powder and ball were purchased, in order to kill him?

SECTION III.—The following observation appears to me to be both unchristian and unphilosophical. " The man, therefore, who can believe that the three thousand on the day of Pentecost were baptized by immersion, must have great faith, and a wonderful facility in accommodating his belief to his wishes." Must have great faith! Is this a becoming way of speaking of the belief of a Scripture statement? To have any propriety, this must imply that the thing is asserted, but that it is highly improbable. If the thing is not supposed to be asserted, there cannot be great faith in believing it. I can find no other consistent meaning in the expression, than that, although the word did testify the fact, it is too improbable for rational belief. Now I will make myself still more credulous, and had it been testified by the inspired writer that three hundred thousand were baptized in one day, I would not scruple to believe that the thing was true in the proper meaning of the word. Let God be true, and all men liars. If the word is supposed to have other meanings, and that the testimony of the Spirit in this place has not the alleged meaning, then it is absurd to speak of faith in that alleged meaning as great faith. It is faith in a thing that is not testified.

It is utterly unphilosophical as well as unscriptural to reject testimony on views of probability: on this very ground all the doctrines of the Gospel have been rejected. Another may as reasonably say, " The man that can believe that a guilty creature can become righteous by faith in Jesus, must have great faith." When we believe that three thousand were immersed in one day, we rest on the Divine testimony, ascertained by the meaning of the words which the Spirit uses. Whether they were immersed depends on the meaning of the word, not on any view of probability. To speak of a facility in accommodating our faith to our wishes, is speaking not only without evidence, but contrary to self-evidence. How many thousands of those who are the most zealous for immersion, have received it not from their fathers, nor their sect, nor from their temporal interests, but in opposition to all these! What advantage can it be in this world to any man? To oppose infant sprinkling is the heaviest part of the cross of Christ. Why, then, should we wish it true, when it is our interest to be convinced that it is false? All temptations to tamper with evidence lie obviously on the other side. Were Sir Isaac Newton at this moment alive, and a Baptist, I really believe that in Great Britain or Ireland it would be difficult to procure him the situation of a parish schoolmaster.

But so far from being an insurmountable difficulty at all, except to superstition, what could prevent any number to be immersed on the same day? Could there be any difficulty in finding water in Jerusalem and its neighbourhood? Had he nothing but human testimony for the fact, to reject it on the ground of improbability would be unwarrantable.

SECTION IV.—The next point which Dr. M. approaches is John's baptism. This, he tells us, was not Christian baptism. Well, what does this say on the meaning of the word? What is baptism in one case is baptism in another. Whatever difference in any other respect there may be between the baptism of John and the baptism of Christ, there could be no difference in the mode: there could be no difference in the meaning of the word.

He appeals to Acts xix. 1—6, as proof that some of John's disciples were afterward baptized in the name of the Lord. I know this is disputed; but for my part I never doubted it, I cannot see how this can be denied without torturing the word of God, which I will never do for any cause whatever.

"There is no evidence," says he, "and I will venture to say no probability, that John ever baptized by immersion." What evidence could he expect but the testimony of the word? If that signifies to immerse, then there is express evidence that the very action designated by the name of the ordinance is immersion. He might as well venture to say that there is no evidence, and no probability, that Jesus rose from the dead. He might allege that the word resurrection has another meaning. On the same principle, when we read that such a person was *killed* in the field of battle, there is no evidence that he is dead. Is not this imported in the word *killed?* And if it is not proved by this, it is not proved at all by the document. Now there is no man who would reason with obstinacy so foolish in reference to our own language. Yet this is the very thing that Dr. M. and almost all our opponents do with respect to this word. In ascertaining the evidence of its meaning, they receive not its own testimony. Nothing can be more purely fanatical. There may be additional evidence and corroborating circumstances, but the direct proof of what John did in baptizing, or any other man did in baptizing, must be the testimony of the word itself. Men who do not understand this are not fit to enter the field of controversy. Besides, as the ground-work of his allegation of improbability, he assumes what is not in evidence, that John must have baptized all his converts personally, and all in the space of two years and a half. The very improbability is mere assumption.

At Enon he makes the abundance of water necessary for an encampment of men, women and children around John the Baptist. Is this interpretation, or is it romance? Is there any among the fairy tales more a work of fancy than this? Is there evidence that any of the crowd remained on the ground a single night? I must believe, and I will try to believe, that Dr. M. thinks he is fairly representing the evidence of the inspired documents : but if he does, he must be to a wonderful extent under the influence of imagination. He creates a fact in order to create a difficulty. What is it that men may not fancy that they see in Scripture, when, under all the pledges he has given us, Dr. M. reports that this passage informs him of an encampment around John the Baptist? No wonder that historians like Gibbon, vitiate their facts by additions from imagination, when they are opposed to truth! But of all extravagances, the following is the most extravagant :—

" John, as a poor man, who lived in the wilderness, whose raiment was of the meanest kind, and whose food was such alone as the desert afforded; it is not to be supposed that he possessed appropriate vessels for administering baptism to multitudes by pouring or sprinkling. He, therefore, seems to have made use of the neighbouring stream." If any man can believe this reason, I will not envy his faith. On the ground of improbability he refuses the testimony of the word, yet here he can believe his own fiction, for which there is neither testimony nor probability. Why the hoof of an ass would be perfectly sufficient.

But this allegation is not only absurd and fictitious, it is also inconsistent with the reason which he has alleged for John's taking up his abode at Enon. Has he not told us, that the supply of water for the necessities of men, women, children, and beasts, directed to this locality? Surely I may retort his own observation. He must have great faith and a wonderful facility in accommodating his belief to his wishes, who can believe this!

I have still another complaint against this fiction. Were it ever so plausible, were it ever so probable, it is utterly valueless, *unless it is in proof from Scripture.* The writer mistakes the burden of proof. If it is not proved that the water was necessary for other purposes, there lies no objection to the assertion, that it was necessary for baptism. If an objection is not proved, it is no true objection.

SECTION V.—With respect to the accounts of the baptism of Christ, Matt. iii. 6, Mark i. 9, 10, he rests on the fact, that the preposition is *from,* not *out of.* Of what use is this, when we have *out of,* in the case of the eunuch? When he translates Mark i. 9, by *in* Jordan, he mistranslates. Jesus was baptized *into* Jordan. This shows not only that the action of the verb was performed in the water, but that the performance of it was a putting of the baptized person *into* the water. Besides, if the ordinance is performed *in* the water, what relief does the writer get from the preposition *from,* more than *out of?* If Jesus was *in* the water, might it not be said that he came up *out of* the water, as well as *from* the water?

" Laying aside his sandals," says Dr. M., " he might only have stepped a few inches into the river." What could take him into the river at all, if he was only to be sprinkled? What could take him to the edge of the water? What could take him to the river? No rational answer can ever be given to this, on the ground that sprinkling a few drops of water is baptism. Is there no misgiving of conscience, as to the sufficiency of this answer? I could not believe this, should I gain the whole world by my faith. But the account of the evangelist not merely asserts that Jesus went *into* the water, but that, when in the water, he was baptized or immersed *into* it.

SECTION VI.—" The baptism of Paul," Dr. M. asserts, " affords not the smallest hint or presumption in favour of immersion." If he means, that the account affords no evidence, unless it is in the word, he says only what might be true in a thousand instances, without affecting the question. No other evidence but that of the word is necessary in any instance. If he means, that without evidence, independent of the word itself, the question cannot be determined, he entertains views of evidence fundamentally erroneous. When the meaning of a word is ascertained, by an examination of its occurrences in the language, it may be applied with the utmost confidence, without a tittle of additional evidence from context. Very often context affords no confirmation of the true meaning. No word in language affords, in every occurrence of it, evidence of its meaning from context. I will make this intelligible to every child, if men will shut their eyes. In reading the expression, "Arise, and be immersed or dipped," would any Englishman hesitate as to the mode expressed, because the context affords no evidence, additional to that of the word? And what evidence would a person who understood Greek have needed, in addition to that of the word itself? However, in the present case, it is not fact that there is no additional evidence from the context: there is most satisfactory proof, even if the word itself had been used but once, in all that remains of the Greek language. Baptism is here said to be a bathing of the person.

"There is no hint that Paul changed his raimant." No more is there any account from what point the wind blew on the occasion. Shame, shame, to trifle in this way in opposing the ordinances of God! How many thousand accounts of immersion in modern times, when there is no mention of changing of raimant! Does Dr. M. really expect, that in case immersions were practised, the Scriptures must record the changing of dress? Where did he find the laying of the sandals aside, which he lately mentioned? Is there no evidence that such a man was hanged, because there is no account whether he wore his ordinary dress, or obtained one for the occasion? There may be honesty in this sort of reasoning, but there is no logic.

But our author has not yet done with this species of logic. "There is no account," it seems, "that Paul and Ananias went out of the house to a neighbouring pond or stream." What need of such information? When I hear that Dr. M. is immersed in New York, I shall never inquire whether it was in a river, in a pond, or in a bath. Dr. M., let us have every thing like evidence; but let us have no trifling with the word of the living God.

Adverting to Paul's situation, he asks, "Can it be imagined that a wise and humane man, in these circumstances, would have had him carried forth and plunged into cold water?" The wisdom and humanity of Ananias had nothing to do in the matter; he had the express command of God. If Dr. M. has any charge against the wisdom and humanity of the institution, no doubt its Author, in due time, will give him a sufficient answer. I can, however, see nothing in Paul's situation that would render immersion either dangerous or disagreeable. But Paul was immersed, whatever Dr. M. may choose to suppose to be the consequence. I draw a different conclusion. If Paul, in such a situation, was immersed, clinical sprinkling, the invention of human wisdom, is never to be a substitute for baptism.

SECTION VII.—The account even of the baptism of the eunuch, does not convince Dr. M. that immersion was the mode. He tells us, that "they were travelling, and probably destitute of any convenient vessel for dipping up a portion of water from the stream; they both went down to the water, probably no farther than to its margin, far enough to take up a small portion of it, to sprinkle or pour on the eunuch."

How can he assert, that probably they went only to the edge of the water, when the Holy Spirit expressly asserts that they came *out of* the water? Does Dr. M. intend to give the lie to the word of inspiration? How could they come *out of* the water, if they were not in it? This fact is beyond controversy. But is it not extravagant to suppose that such a man as the eunuch, on his journey, had no vessel fit to carry as much water as would sprinkle him with a few drops? One of his attendants might have brought enough in the hollow of his hand. Such evasions are ridiculous.

While I admit that the preposition *eis* may convey to the edge of the water, as well as into it; yet I cannot but feel surprised that Dr. M. is so unfortunate in his proofs. "Jesus went down to Capernaum," surely does not mean, that he stopped at the edge of the city. He entered into Capernaum. "Jacob went down into Egypt," does not mean that he stopped at the borders of the country. "He went down to Antioch," is a similar example. Instead of proving for the writer, these examples show the unreasonableness of his doctrine. Would he deserve the name of a critic, who should argue, that because the preposition in question is sometimes used when the object in motion goes only to the edge of the object approached, therefore in the example there is no evidence that Jesus entered Capernaum, that Jacob went into Egypt, or that Paul entered Antioch?

Dr. M., I am surprised to find, repeats the objection, that "there is the same evidence that Philip was plunged, as that the eunuch was." This was a very shallow observation. There is the same evidence that both were in the water, but only one of them is said to have been immersed. Their being in the water may be proof that immersion must have taken place, without proving that both were immersed. It is strange that wise men will risk the credit of their understanding by such allegations.

Dr. M. concludes his observations on this example, by asserting that the confidence of the Baptists, in the account of the baptism of the eunuch, "must be regarded as amounting to a gross imposition on popular credulity." Dr. M. has done nothing to entitle him to speak so arrogantly. He has done nothing to diminish our confidence in this example. He has not entered into the criticism of the question. Our proof that they were in the water is not only unrefuted, but unassailed by criticism. We can afford to leave imposition and credulity to those who need them.

SECTION VIII.—The baptism of Cornelius comes next under the review of our author. Here again he complains of the absence of hints, with respect to the "candidates for baptism being led out of the house, to a river or pool, for the purpose of being dipped." Such information is altogether unnecessary. If they were baptized, they were immersed. Whether in the house or elsewhere, is nothing to the purpose. But he can find not only hints, but full evidence on his side. "Who can forbid water?" he interprets, "Can any man forbid water being brought in a convenient vessel, to be applied by pouring or sprinkling?" Can anything be more arbitrary and unfounded than this interpretation? Can the man who will take this liberty with his documents ever be at a loss for proof? I will not say, that this is imposition on credulity; but I will say, that this is not interpretation. Might I not as well interpret the passage thus? "Can any man forbid water to be brought in to fill a bath for the purpose of immersion?" But I scorn such a mode of interpretation to suit a purpose. The expression has no concern at all with the mode of the ordinance. The meaning most evidently is, "Can any one forbid baptism with respect to these persons?" The passage determines nothing as to what baptism is, only that water is employed in the ordinance. If we take the liberty of forging an addition to our documents, in order to suit our purpose, we cannot pretend to ground on the Scriptures.

But if this passage affords evidence that the mode of this ordinance is pouring or sprinkling, and that, too, for an emblematical purpose, how is it that the author allows that immersion is also a valid mode of the ordinance? If this is true, immersion cannot be baptism.

SECTION. IX.—The immersion of the jailer Dr. M. pronounces not only to be improbable, but impossible. Here now we have an assertion that gives us an opportunity of estimating Dr. M.'s perspicacity in weighing evidence, or his candour in representing it. On what ground does he allege immersion to have been here impossible, or even improbable? "Paul and Silas," he tells us, "were closely confined in prison when this solemn service was performed." Your documents have not told you so, Dr. M. They were not now closely confined, nor confined at all, even although the baptism had been performed in the prison. What makes immersion impossible, even in the very cell in which they were closely confined? The man who asserts impossibility as to immersion even on that ground, I charge as unfit to weigh evidence.

Again, when he expounds the bringing of them *out*, as respecting the outer part of the prison, and not the outside of it, granting this to be true, what makes immersion impossible in that place? No thinking being can allege impossibility. But if my cause required it, I would not grant this. Dr. M. must prove it before it can serve him. The burden of proof lies on the objector. If it is not proved that *out* refers to the *outer* prison, and not to *outside* the prison, it cannot stand as an objection. If the word *out* will explain as referable to either, I am at liberty to explain it in the way that the word employed to designate the ordinance demands.

But that *out* refers to outside the prison is evident from the fact, that we find them immediately in the jailer's house. Paul preached the Gospel to all in the jailer's house before any of them were baptized. There is not a particle of evidence that the baptism was in the jail. It was after this they were bathed; the bathing, then, must have been done in the house: and if they could be bathed in the house, could not the jailer and his family be bathed in baptism in the same bath? The performance of bathing implies the existence of a bath.

But had the jailer been as destitute of baths as John the Baptist was of vessels for sprinkling, what could prevent them from going to the Strymon? Must they wait for permission from the magistrates? Not a moment. In civil things Christians are to obey, but in the things of God they are to have no respect to the authority of man. Dr. M. speaks of Paul and Silas as not being " *dishonest* enough to steal out of prison by night!" Is so slavish a sentiment worthy of an American citizen? Is so Erastian a sentiment worthy of a Christian, even in Turkey? No man can carry the duty of civil obedience farther than I do; but I would frown defiance in the face of Majesty were it to presume to dictate in the things of Christ. According to Dr. M., Peter was guilty of stealing out of prison, when he was released by the angel, and the angel was guilty of a treasonable rescue.

The refusal to quit the prison next morning was not out of obedience to civil authority, but from a just and indignant sense of their own violated rights. How could it be for conscience' sake that they refused to quit the prison, when the magistrates sent an express order by their officers, urging them to go? It is astonishing that any writer should venture such observations.

Equally astonishing it is that Dr. M. should allege the jailer's alarm on account of his own responsibility. Was not this alarm previous to his faith and baptism? Had he any such fears afterwards? Besides, if it was contrary to Paul's duty to baptize the jailer's family at the river, it was equally contrary to his duty to accept hospitality in the jailer's house. If they had a right to quit the prison, they had a right to go to the river. What a scrupulous conscience has Dr. M.! I suppose if the government of the United States were to forbid him to preach, he would never open his mouth to proclaim the glad tidings of salvation. Am I to believe that any man really feels these scruples, or am I to think that they are mere evasions? Were I to use such arguments, I must confess it would be from a design of *imposing on popular credulity.*

With respect to the possibility of immersion in the prison, Dr. M. says, " He who can believe this must be ready to adopt any supposition, however extravagant, for the sake of an hypothesis." This shows the distinguished writer to be unacquainted with the fundamental laws of controversy. We have neither to prove nor suppose anything with respect to the way in which immersion was possible. If the word is proved to mean immersion, whenever there was a baptism, there must have been a way of immersion. Any objection that is alleged against the possibility of this must be in proof. Granting that the baptism was performed in the jail, without any mention of a bath, I should have every confidence of immersion, equally as if I had been told that there was a bath, or a reservoir. Suppose we read in English that the Baptists immersed a person in a jail, would any man act so ridiculously as to deny the immersion unless the bath were spoken of? Why, then, should the mention of a bath, or a pond, or of a river, be necessary as to the examples in Scripture? However, I can prove that there was a bath in the jailer's house, because that Paul and Silas were bathed; but I refuse to give proof as a matter of right: it is all mere grace. I will never consent to prove, when proof lies on the other side. What does this writer mean by an hypothesis? We interpret language by its fundamental laws: we do not invent hypotheses. If the word does not signify immerse, we will invent no hypothesis to provide for immersion. But while I have provided a bath in the house, I am inclined to think that the document proves that the baptism was without. Paul preached in the jailer's house, and, after the baptism, was brought back to the house, which appears to show that the baptism was either at the Strymon, or some other place out of doors. But I care not where the baptism took place, and I will pledge myself for nothing on this head.

SECTION X.—Dr. M. complains of the Baptists, that they consider their mode as essential to the ordinance. This complaint, surely, is absurd. If the meaning of the word is *immerse*, is not *immersion* essential to *immersion?* Can *pouring* or *sprinkling*, fulfil a command to *immerse?* Especially if immersion is emblematical, must it not be essential to have the emblem? We grant that our opponents are sincere; that they believe that they are fulfilling the command of Christ; but, if our view of the meaning of the word is just, we should be palpably self-condemned, were we to say that *pouring*, or *sprinkling* is baptism. In like manner, if any man believes that the word signifies to *pour*, or *sprinkle*, and that the ordinance is emblematical in such a sense, he cannot consistently admit that any other mode is baptism. Of all the writers I have ever met, Dr. M. is, on this point, the most inconsistent. He makes the mode emblematical, yet he allows that any mode is baptism. He has two favourite modes, yet he does not say that either of them is appointed. He makes the word signify immerse, pour, sprinkle, dye, wash, and every application of water; yet I cannot gather from him what meaning he gives it in this ordinance. He tells us that "The inspired writers did not deem the mode of applying water in baptism an essential matter; and did not think it necessary to state it precisely." What, then, is the meaning of the word? It cannot be *pour*, or *sprinkle*, for this is as precise as *immersion*. If it expresses no mode, why does he make the mode emblematical? Has he got a patent to manufacture emblems for the ordinances of Christ? Here he avows the authority of will-worship, and considers it lawful and edifying to conform Christian rites to emblematical representations, not annexed to them by the Head of the church. This is as pure a specimen of Popery as ever was manufactured at Rome.

As, in its common use, Dr. M. makes this word signify every mode, and every application of water, without saying what is its meaning, I must believe that in reference to this ordinance he gives it the same extent. Now, nothing can be more extravagant than this. Whatever number of meanings the word may be supposed to have, it can have only one in reference to this ordinance, whether that may be general or specific. If it has a general signification in reference to baptism, it cannot also have a specific signification. If it has one specific signification, it cannot have another. I really think criticism wasted on such reasoning as this.

SECTION XI.—The following extract shows that the clearest and most overwhelming proof of the original mode of this ordinance, even when admitted, would not change the practice of our opponents. Dr. M. arrogates the anti-christian authority of changing the mode of the ordinances of Christ, according to expediency. " Even if it could be proved (which we know it cannot be) that the mode of baptism adopted in the time of Christ and his apostles was that of immersion, yet, if that method of administering the ordinance were not significant of some truth, which the other modes cannot represent, we are plainly at liberty to regard it as a non-essential circumstance, from which we may depart when expediency requires it, as we are all wont to do in other cases, even with respect to positive institutions." Popery, I see, is not confined to Rome. But the church of Rome is the only consistent body that claims the authority of changing the laws of God. If the author believes his own doctrine, why has he employed so much straining and torture on the documents that respect this ordinance? The church of Rome claims a right to change the mode, and it boldly confesses that it has done so. Dr. M. alleges that we are all wont to do the same thing. For myself, I deny the charge in every instance. I would as soon attempt to regulate the changes of the moon, or alter the course of nature, as make the smallest modification on an ordinance of Christ. This principle is the very foundation of the anti-christian system : this principle I abhor with the most perfect abhorrence. Dr. M., no doubt, is conscientious in this; but is not the Pope equally conscientious, while, with more grace, he exercises the same privilege to a greater extent?

" For example," says he, " the Lord's supper was, no doubt, originally instituted with unleavened bread," &c. Now the cases are not at all parallel. Unleavened bread was never appointed. It was used merely on the occasion because it was the bread that was present. Indeed, it is not even said that it was unleavened bread; we know that it was so, because there was no other. Is that anything akin to a command to baptize? If this word signifies to immerse, then immersion is the very thing commanded. A good conscience is a good thing; but the best conscience is the better for a little discrimination. Nothing that was at first a part of the Lord's supper can ever cease to be a part of it. Had unleavened bread been here enjoined, unleavened bread must be used to the end of the world. The same observation applies to the posture at the Lord's supper. Had Christ enjoined kneeling or sitting, reclining or standing, that posture would be always binding. As it is, posture is no part of the institution, and it is anti-christian to make it necessary.

Dr. M. next considers the difficulties attending immersion in many cases; and contrasts with this the ease and convenience of sprinkling, or pouring. This might be very much to the point, after a proclamation from heaven that we might choose what pleases us best. But, in determining what is the law of Christ, such speculations are worse than useless: they are an exhortation to disobedience and rebellion. To be immersed every day in my life would be no sacrifice to me; shall I complain about one immersion in my whole life?

He speaks of some districts so parched that it would be difficult to find a natural stream or pool. What makes either a stream or a pool necessary. There is no inhabited country in which a disciple of Christ may not procure as much water as will immerse him once in his life. He speaks of a siege. If a man cannot get bread, is he guilty in dying of hunger? If a disciple cannot get water, is he guilty for not attending to baptism? Baptism is an ordinance of Christ—an edifying ordinance of Christ, but it is superstition that makes it essential to salvation. He speaks of cold countries, where rivers are locked up with ice. Is there any habitable country where the water is all turned into ice? Is there any country in which ice may not be melted by fire? How perversely opposed is the human mind to the mind of God, when the disciple of Christ can allege such evasions to relieve him from his commandments!

He speaks of health. When medical skill pronounces it dangerous, I will not urge it: nor will I urge a sick man to go to the assembly of the saints. He speaks about *old, feeble ministers*. This is *young, strong superstition*. If ministers are old and feeble, let them do what they are fit to do; let others take the water. The churches planted by the apostles were not Puseyites. No wonder that the Oxford pestilence has spread so rapidly: there is almost in all men a predisposition to the disease.

SECTION XII.—Dr. M. tells us, that in the third, fourth, and following centuries, the custom was to baptize naked. Where is the logic of this? It is Satan's logic to deter the disciples of Christ from following their Master. Although this logic will have no effect upon a sound head, it may not be without its effect upon a corrupt heart. Dr. M. does not pretend to say that the apostles baptized naked. Of what use, then, is his observation? Is church history a ground of proof to us? Let him admonish the Puseyites on this subject, and they will very likely return to the old edifying practice. This practice was a human invention, as Dr. Hall himself confesses, to make the ordinance of Christ more edifying, just as Dr. M. annexes an edifying emblem to pouring and sprinkling, while he confesses that Christ has not appointed the emblem. The above practice, then, has no charms for us, but it must be very edifying to Dr. M.'s turn of mind. The Christians who practised this " thought it better represented the putting off the old man, and also the nakedness of Christ on the cross." A perfect parallel to Dr. M.'s edifying emblems of *pouring* and *sprinkling*. For a like edifying purpose the early Christians practised trine immersion. Is this proof that trine immersion is proper? A good conscience is a good thing; but a good conscience may be married to very bad logic.

"Besides," says Dr. M., "if the principle for which our Baptist brethren contend be correct; if the immersion of the whole body be essential to Christian baptism; and if the thing signified be the cleansing and purifying of the individual by an ablution which must of necessity extend to the whole person; it would really seem that performing this ceremony divested of all clothing, is essential to its emblematic meaning." To this I reply: 1. The principle here represented is not the ground on which we rest immersion. We rest it on the command of Christ; not on views of peculiar fitness for emblematic representation. Its emblematic meaning affords us edification, but is not the ground of our obedience. 2. The immersion of the whole body is essential to baptism, not because nothing but immersion can be an emblem of purification, but because immersion is the thing commanded, and because that, without immersion, there is no emblem of death, burial, and resurrection, which are in the emblem equally with purification. Had no emblem but that of purification been intended in this ordinance, we do not say that immersion would be either essential or preferable. In a partial ablution there might be an emblem of purification, but no emblem of death, burial, and resurrection. If the whole person must be buried, the whole person must, of course, be washed, when the burial is in water. 3. Dr. M. ought to know that nakedness is not necessary for emblematical purification. Were not the Israelites sprinkled with their garments on? Besides, are not Christians said to wash their garments, as well as themselves, in the blood of the Lamb? Even in bathing for health or cleanliness, it is common to use a bathing dress. Nakedness is necessary neither for the emblem nor for obedience to the command. It was the invention of the same spirit that has changed all the ordinances of Christ.

He speaks of the propriety of applying the water " to that part of the body which is an epitome of the whole person." Who has commanded this? Has Christ given authority to add to his ordinance by human wisdom? This is the prerogative of the man of sin. Is not this manufacture from the same factory that applies the holy unction to certain parts of the body for emblematic purposes? Nothing can be more evident than that, as no part of the body is by inspiration spoken of as having the water of baptism applied to it, the whole body must be immersed.

" Besides," says the author, " let me appeal to our Baptist brethren, by asking, if they verily believe that the primitive and apostolic mode of administering baptism was by immersion, and that this immersion was by entire nakedness, how can they dare, upon their principles, to depart one iota from that mode?" I will not say that there is anything intentionally unfair in this; but I will say, that the reasoning is unfair. He here speaks as if he had proved, and that the Baptists believe, that naked baptism was an apostolic practice. Neither of these is true. He stated merely the practice of the third, fourth, and immediately succeeding centuries. And why does he assume that the Baptists believe that naked baptism was the practice of the apostles? Why urge them on this ground? Is the practice of the third, fourth, and immediately succeeding centuries, to be taken as the primitive and apostolic practice? I can see no way to vindicate both his sincerity and his logic.

From these difficulties he is convinced that immersion "cannot be of Divine appointment; at any rate, that it cannot be universally binding on the church of God." Whether it is a Divine appointment depends on evidence, and is not at all influenced by the existence of difficulties. But what a sentiment is here expressed! A Divine appointment, yet not universally binding!!! Then we cannot have a pope too soon. If Divine appointments may be annulled, infallibility is necessary to annul them. Who can put a limit to the extent to which this principle may be carried? May it not set aside the ordinance of baptism itself, and all other ordinances? May it not appoint as many other ordinances as it may think fit? Let Dr. M. reflect on the denunciation against those who take on them to abrogate any of God's appointments. "Whosoever, therefore, shall *abrogate* one of these least commandments, and *teach men so*, he shall be called the least in the kingdom of heaven." Great Jesus, enable me to suffer martyrdom, rather than give me up to utter a sentiment so dishonourable to thy sovereignty! Dr. M. avows a right to change ordinances of Christ, and to confer on them an emblematic meaning, not in the appointment of the Institutor. What is popery, if this is not popery? To practise immersion conscientiously, even although a Divine appointment, he designates as *servility* and *superstition. Servility* and *superstition!* What a prostitution of language! *Servility*, to obey a Divine appointment! *Superstition*, to practise what God commands! This is so monstrous in sentiment, so paradoxical in phraseology, that I dare not trust myself to say more on it.

"We may say of this ordinance," says the author, " as our Lord said of the sabbath, *Baptism was made for man, and not man for baptism.*" I adopt the language with my whole heart. We may say this with respect to every ordinance. But does this imply that we may abrogate, alter, or modify, either baptism or the sabbath? Let us apply this principle, then, to the sabbath, which Dr. M. applies to baptism. "The keeping of the sabbath has great inconveniences in many places: either, then, it is not a Divine appointment, or, at any rate, it is not universally binding." Is this Dr. M.'s theology? Many persons will shudder at it, when applied to the sabbath, who may not be frightened when it is applied to an ordinance against which they are prejudiced. How is it, that such a man as Dr. M. can assume it as a principle, that if an ordinance is made for the good of man by Divine appointment, men must have the right of changing it? Is man fitter than God, to judge what is best for man? Is not the fact, that God's ordinances are all designed for the good of his people, the strongest reason to abide strictly by them? I complain, that in this work there is a want of accurate thinking, of just reasoning, and of sound principles. In justice to truth, I must say so, while it grieves me to be obliged to give it expression.

"Where," says he, "a particular mode of complying with a religious observance would be, in may cases, ' a yoke of bondage,' and one, too, for which no Divine warrant could be pleaded, it would argue the very slavery of superstition, to enforce that mode of the observance as essential to a regular standing in the visible family of Christ." Here my complaint of a want of accurate thinking is renewed. If a yoke is of God's making, must it not be worn? If it is not of God's appointment, does any one require it to be put on? Was not circumcision a yoke? Had any man a right to abrogate or neglect it? We are commanded to give our lives for Christ, rather than deny him. Has any man a right to refuse this yoke? But there is no yoke in baptism, although my defence of it will not deign to repel the charge. It is God's appointment: I call on Christians, on their allegiance, to obey.

That immersion is a Divine appointment this argument assumes, for it pleads for a right to change a Divine appointment. Now is it the slavery of superstition to obey a Divine appointment? Superstition and slavery must respect such religious ordinances only as are of human appointment. It is absurd—it is monstrous—it is blasphemous, to speak of obedience to a Divine appointment as the slavery of superstition.

But if it is a Divine appointment, how can it be also "a yoke of bondage," "for which no Divine warrant could be pleaded?" If no Divine warrant can be pleaded, it cannot be a Divine appointment. But there is still another absurdity in this. On the supposition that no Divine warrant can be pleaded for immersion, does any one make it essential to baptism? Surely it is only on the ground that there is a Divine warrant, that it is deemed essential, or even in any degree obligatory. Why, then, does this learned writer beat the air? Why does he reason with people who never have existed?

SECTION XIII.—Dr. M. comes now to Rom. vi. 1. He observes, that we believe and insist that baptism and immersion are synonymous terms. We believe and insist that immersion is the meaning of the word translated baptism, but we do not believe that baptism, as an English word, is synonymous with immersion. As an English term it respects not mode at all, but refers to what is considered the rite, apart from the mode. In English, baptism and immersion are anything rather than synonymous.

Believing and insisting as above, we are represented by him as taking for granted that the phrase, "buried with him in baptism," refers to the resemblance between baptism and burial. Now we believe that this phrase implies this resemblance, not by taking it for granted, but as the necessary import of the expression. When our Lord says, "This cup is the new testament in my blood," is it taking anything for granted, to assert that the expression implies that there is a resemblance between the wine and the blood of Christ? We take nothing for granted but what is either in proof, or is self-evident.

He observes, that "in the general interpretation of the figure, many pædo-baptists are agreed with us, and have thus not a little confirmed the confidence of anti-pædo-baptists in their cause." Is not this a hint, that even though pædo-baptists should agree with us in this, it is bad policy to acknowledge it? On the other hand I ask, are there no pædo-baptists, who, from a fear of increasing the confidence of their opponents, are willing to dispute every thing? Excessive candour is not, as far as I have observed, the fault of any of the late writers on the subject. It would hardly surprise me if some of them would call on us to prove the existence of the river Jordan. It is quite true that all eminent scholars, whatever may be their practice, if they speak at all on the subject, will confess as plainly as prudence will permit them, that we have both the meaning of the word and the inspired explanation of the mode in our favour. But even this we produce not as a confirmation of our own faith, but as a proof that our view of the emblem is irresistible to our candid opponents. Who is it that does not perceive that Dr. M. feels this affliction? But the thing is so plain in itself, that if all the men on earth should deny it, I could not think of it otherwise than as I do. And if all pædo-baptists should be convinced by myself, I could not receive the smallest additional confidence. Dr. Campbell, indeed, observes, that in a long process of abstract reasoning, even in matters of demonstration, a person will find additional confidence by the agreement of others whose judgment he respects. With this I fully agree. But there is here no intricate or tedious process of thought. Any one who understands the words, will be able to discern the assertion as clearly as Newton or Locke. *Buried with Christ by baptism,* must mean that baptism has a resemblance to Christ's burial. Were the angel Gabriel to hesitate, I would order him to school. In many cases of error I can see the plausible ground on which it rests; but here I can perceive no *den* in which deception can be concealed.

"The apostle," says the writer, "then adverts to the significance of baptism, which being the ordinance which seals our introduction into the family of Christ, may be considered as exhibiting both the first principles of Gospel truth, and the first elements of Christian character." Now what a mass of lumber is this! Does the apostle say anything about baptism as being the ordinance which seals our introduction into the family of Christ? Does he say anything about it as a seal of introduction, exhibiting an emblem of first principles? Baptism is not here spoken of as a seal of introduction, nor as a seal of anything; it is spoken of as importing in its nature an emblem that believers cannot continue in sin that grace may abound. The emblem shows them to be dead, buried, and risen with Christ. How, then, can they continue in sin? This death, burial, and resurrection, take place in baptism: if so, they take place emblematically.

"He then infers," says the author, "that since baptism has so immediate a reference to the death of Christ, it must, by consequence, be connected also with his resurrection." Immediate connexion with his resurrection! This cloud of words is to hide the sun. What connexion has baptism with Christ's burial? Is it not because it is a burial with Christ? What other reference is either stated or hinted? But there is no such reference in the language of the apostle, as Dr. M. represents. The apostle does not infer that since baptism has an immediate reference to the death of Christ, it must, by consequence, be connected also with the resurrection. It is a fact that baptism actually refers as well to the resurrection of Christ as to his death. But the apostle states the two things as facts, and does not infer one of them from the other. There might have been an ordinance having reference to the burial of Christ, without having any reference to his resurrection. The language of the apostle does not infer, but it asserts. "For if we have been planted," &c.

"The obvious design of the apostle," says Dr. M., "is to illustrate the character and obligations of believers, from the circumstance that they are in a certain respect conformed to Christ's death; that as he died for sin, so they are dead, or are under an obligation to be dead *to* sin, that is, they are holy, or are by their profession obliged to be holy." If any man is now ignorant of the obvious design of the apostle in this passage, he would not deserve pity were he not to see the sun at noon-day. Yet after reading, and reading, and reading, I am so far from knowing the obvious design of the apostle better than I did before, that I can hardly venture to say that I understand the writer himself. He adds explanation to explanation, till his meaning is *buried* in explanation, if he himself will not be buried in baptism. In what part of the passage does the writer find the apostle illustrating the character and the obligation of believers? My eyes are so bad, that I cannot discover it any where in the documents. The apostle himself states, that the believer cannot live in sin; from something that is implied in his baptism. Nor is the believer's conformity to Christ merely a conformity to his death, but to his death, burial, and resurrection, as they are exhibited in baptism. Believers are buried with Christ by baptism, and it is by baptism also they die with him. The very reference that is here made to death, depends necessarily on burial. Death, burial, and resurrection, are all expressly in the emblem. And what, according to this writer, is the conformity to Christ's death? Why, Christ died *for* sin, and believers die *to* sin. What sort of conformity is this? There is no likeness at all in this conformity; it is only a mere play upon words. But what is this dying *to* sin? Why, it is "being under obligations to be dead." Under obligations to be dead! What sort of security is this that they will not continue in sin? Do obligations to duty afford a security of performance? Writers who take on them to direct the public, are surely under obligation to reason connectedly. But what sort of an explanation of death is an obligation to be dead? To die, and to be under obligation to be dead, are surely very different things. Surely it must be a desperate cause that puts wise men under the necessity of employing such interpretations of the word of God. The sense in which they were dead to sin, must insure their not living in it, otherwise there is no meaning in the apostle's reasoning.

Having expounded the death to sin as being under obligation to be dead, he expounds both as being *holy;* and holy he further expounds as being by their profession, obliged to be *holy.* Is an obligation to be holy the same as *holy?* The one does not even presuppose the other. But death to sin, and holiness, are two distinct ideas, though they always co-exist. Every thing is wrong in this most unhappy commentary. To what shifts are men driven, who will force the word of God, to silence its testimony in condemnation of their errors!

Speaking of the death to sin, he says, "This is what was signified by baptism." How does baptism signify death, but as it is an emblem of it? And how is the emblem of death in baptism, but as baptism is a burial?

"And so," he continues, "believers were baptized *into Christ's death:* not that baptism was a symbol of *death,* or the state of the dead; for water, or a washing in water, never was a symbol of this." This explanation palpably contradicts the text. The apostle expressly says that believers " are buried with Christ by baptism into death." But Dr. M. gives a reason why baptism cannot be a symbol of burial. Now what is this reason? Let all the ends of the earth hear it. Because water, or washing with water, was never a symbol of burial! May not a man be buried in water as well as washed in it? How many millions are actually buried in the seas? There are two distinct emblems in baptism: one of purification by water, another of death, burial, and resurrection, by immersion. It is shameful for such a man as Dr. M. to allege the impossibility of there being in baptism an emblem of burial, because washing in water is not an emblem of burial. Why, Dr. M., will you blind your own eyes? Why will you teach the disciples of Christ to disannul the commandments of God by your forced explanation?

"Now," says he, " being *dead,* or in a state of *death to sin,* is the same thing as to be *spiritually purified,* or made *holy.*" Here it is obvious that the writer has no definite views of this passage. The Christian's death to sin he had formerly expounded as " being under obligations to be dead:" now it is "being in a state of death." Which of these is the writer's real sentiment? But to be dead to sin is not the same thing as holiness, or spiritual purification: it respects our union with Christ in his death for our sins, and has no reference to personal holiness. But whatever this death is, it is a death that is exhibited in baptism, of which immersion in water is the emblem. Believers are here said not only to be dead, but to die, to be buried, and to rise in baptism. No sophistry about the kind of death meant, can disturb this.

" And this is the very thing," says the writer, "that baptism, coming in the place of ablutions under the former economy, is exactly adapted to signify." No doubt that the application of water under the law and under the Gospel has the same emblem of purification. But does this imply that a burial in water might not, in the new dispensation, be an emblem of Christ's burial, as well as of purification? Shall I be obliged to teach this lesson again? But the fact is that baptism, as far as it is here expounded, refers to death, burial, and resurrection, without any mention of purification, or allusion to it. In other places, it is referred to as emblematic of purification, without any reference to the emblem of death, burial, and resurrection. Baptism is here spoken of, not with respect to the water, but with respect to the mode. In this there are death, burial, and resurrection.

"The sum of the apostle's illustration," says the author, " so far as the point before us is concerned, is simply this;—that in baptism, as a rite emblematical of *moral purification,* Christians profess to be baptized *into the death* of Christ, as well as *into* (or into the hope of) his resurrection; that they are dead and *buried* in respect to sin, that is, in a moral and spiritual sense."

As a rite of moral purification! How can such an idea be contained in the sense of a passage in which purification is not even mentioned? Baptism is, indeed, a rite emblematical of moral purification, but it is not as emblematical of this that it is here considered: it is here an emblem of burial. When baptism is considered with respect to purification, it is referred to as a washing—not a death, or burial. Even as respects the change in the mind of a believer, the emblem of dying with respect to sin, and that of purifying, are quite different. Death considers sin as destroyed; purification considers it as washed away. In this passage, we have death, burial, and resurrection, and they are all in emblem in baptism. We are buried with Christ *by means of baptism*. This burial, surely, is a burial in emblem. The writer never attempts to expound the phrase "buried with him by baptism into death." Can we be buried *by* baptism and *in* baptism, if in baptism there is no burial?

But our exposition of this passage, it seems, has another fault. "The burial of Christ was by no means such as the friends of this exposition commonly suppose." Commonly suppose! What is this to the purpose? Does he deny that Christ was buried? Does he think that an emblem of burial must perfectly correspond to Christ's burial? He might as well require us to eat literal flesh and blood in the Lord's supper, in order to have a better emblem. This is as foolish as it is perverse. A dramatic representation, and an emblem, are things of a very different nature. Christ was buried; and the believer is, by baptism, buried with him. There is no need that there should be a closer resemblance between the mode of the rite, and the entombing of Christ, than that each should be called a burial. Dr. M. has not profited by the lesson I gave Mr. Ewing on this subject. Why, then, has he not answered me? Was not Jonah in the whale's belly an emblem of Christ in the heart of the earth? And is not a believer's baptism as like Christ's burial, as was Jonah's in the belly of the fish?

"The Gazette de France," says one of our newspapers, "contains the details of a frightful accident to fifty workmen employed on the fortifications of Mount Valerien, who had been buried by the falling in of a large bank of earth." Here, says the critic, there can be no likeness to interment. The bank fell in of itself, and the persons on whom it fell are covered as they stand at work. *Buried* here does not signify *interred*, but merely killed. All that the Gazette means to say, is, that the falling bank *killed* the workmen.

With respect to Col. ii. 12, the author says, that in baptism the "putting away of the sins of the flesh" is "emblematically represented : as a man dead and buried is cut off from all temporal connexions and indulgences." But how can baptism, as a washing, be considered *as a death* and burial? Besides, it is in baptism that this burial takes place. *Buried in baptism.* There must, then, be an emblem of burial.

SECTION XIV.—Dr. M. crosses the Red Sea a second time; but as I do not find that he has made any additional discoveries, it is scarcely necessary to give him a second dip. He finds no immersion. Well, I have found what I have justified as being called an immersion, by the common usage of language. In order to get an immersion in the passage referred to, I am not obliged to make the smallest addition to the text. Dr. M., however, is very willing to allow that there may have been spray from the sea, and a few straggling drops from the cloud, though the text says nothing of either. Is it not strange partiality that will not accept an explanation according to the meaning of the word, justified by similar usage, and will avail itself of things that exist only in imagination? Why does not Dr. M. tell us what is the thing that is here called baptism in the cloud and in the sea? My way on every subject of interpretation, is first to ascertain the meaning of the word employed to designate the object, then to see how this meaning can apply.

Section XV.—Dr. M. dismisses the argument from 1 Pet. iii. 20, 21, on the ground that there was no immersion of Noah and his family. With as great propriety the learned gentleman may deny that a man in a tomb is buried, because he is covered with a coffin. What! Noah not immersed, when buried in the waters of the flood? Are there no bounds to perverseness? Will men say every thing rather than admit the mode of an ordinance of Christ, which is contrary to the commandments of men? "Further," says the author, "that immersion is not necessary in baptism; and that to insist upon it, as indispensable, is superstition, appears from the indisputable fact, that *both the significance and the effect of baptism are to be considered as depending, not on the physical influence of water, or upon the quantity of it employed, but on its symbolical meaning, and on the blessing of God upon its application as a symbol.*" Here, as almost every where else, I find this writer remarkably deficient as a reasoner. There are, in this extract, almost as many faults as there are lines. 1. He grounds the non-essentiality of immersion, on the fact that "the significance of baptism depends not on the physical influence of water." This implies that God could not make immersion, or any other mode, necessary to an ordinance, without making the significance of the ordinance depend on the physical influence of the water. This is absurd. The mode of the application of water has nothing to do with its physical influence. 2. This supposes that we contend for mode, as it respects quantity of water. We hold that there is nothing in quantity, if it is sufficient to immerse. What will bury the believer is as good as the Southern Ocean. The dispute is not about the greater virtue of a large quantity of water, but about the mode as a command of God, and an emblem of burial with Christ. 3. This directly asserts that the significance of baptism depends not on the physical influence of water; but a part of its significance does depend on the physical influence of water. Water is an emblem of purification from sin, because its physical influence is to purify. 4. The author here tells us, that the significance of baptism depends on its symbolical meaning! What is the amount of this? It is, that its significance depends on its significance. Is not its significance its symbolical meaning? Is not its symbolical meaning its significance? 5. This supposes that immersion cannot have a symbolical meaning. We practise immersion because it is commanded; but we hold it to be commanded because of its symbolical meaning. This makes it still more essential. 6 This supposes that it is not necessary to obey God in the manner of doing anything, except that manner is symbolical. This is teaching rebellion against God. 7. This designates strict obedience to the forms that God prescribes as being superstitious, unless these forms are symbolical. This is an odd kind of superstition. 8. This mistakes the nature of superstition. A mistake in interpreting a law of God, with practice accordingly, is not superstition, though it is error. 9. What does the author mean by the effect of baptism? I wish to know what amount of Puseyism the writer holds. Is there anything to be expected from the performance of any rite, but the blessing of obedience and the edification conveyed by the Spirit through it? 10. Have we any right to expect the blessing of obedience, when we do not obey? Have we any right to expect the blessing of edification through the Spirit, when we reject the symbol appointed to convey it? If Christ has appointed immersion, can we look for his blessing on a different observance? If immersion is a symbol, can we expect a blessing on a rite which rejects the symbol? Water, no doubt, is a symbol, but it is only a part of the symbol of this ordinance. God, no doubt, will pardon the ignorance of his people; but I have never seen the Scripture which warrants us to expect the blessing of obedience to the commandments of God, on the observance of the ordinances of man. When the Lord's supper was abused, Paul would not give it the name of the ordinance. To alter or modify the ordinances of Christ, is anti-christian arrogance; though great divines may think it not only harmless, but a praiseworthy thing.

Section XVI.—Dr. M tells us that Protestants consider the stress that Roman Catholics lay on rites, "as superstitious and dangerous." There is great confusion of thought in this observation. To lay *stress*, as to salvation, even on the ordinances of God, is to turn away from the Gospel; but to observe them most strictly is the duty of every Christian. To observe rites not of Divine appointment, is an abomination to God : this is the thing in which consistent Protestants blame Roman Catholics, as superstitious. They are never charged as superstitious for the most exact observance of any of the laws of God. To make the observation applicable, the parallel must run thus : As we call Roman Catholics superstitious, because they rigidly practise all the rites of the church, and lay on them the stress of salvation, so if any one will scrupulously practise every ordinance of God, he is superstitious, and lays on them the stress of his salvation. Is this a just parallel? If Roman Catholics are superstitious because they observe as doctrines the commandments of men, are we superstitious because we most scrupulously observe the ordinances of God? Must we show our liberty by plunging into licentiousness? Must we sin, that we may prove that grace abounds? This is the spirit of the reasoning of this author. Shall we take the liberty of disobeying what God commands, in order to show that we are not saved by our obedience to his commands? There are very many of the observations of this writer which have this dangerous tendency. "We believe," says he, "that no external ordinance has any power in itself," &c. I believe the same thing. What then? Shall we teach Christians to neglect the external rites appointed by God, or to alter or modify them at pleasure, in order to show that we believe that there is no power in the ordinances themselves? If this is not antinomianism, I have never met a specimen of it. If immersion is of Divine appointment, to argue that it is not necessary, because to make it necessary is to lay stress on ordinances, is directly to turn the grace of God into licentiousness. If it is not of Divine appointment, then it is absurd to oppose it on the ground that no external ordinance has any power in itself. Nothing can relieve Dr. M. He tell us again, "There is no disposition in depraved human nature more deeply inwrought, or more necessarily operative, than the disposition to rely upon something done by us for securing the Divine favour." I most cordially agree with this statement; nothing can be more true. But, as it stands here, it is most dangerously erroneous. It stands as a warrant to neglect what God has appointed, in order to avoid a legal spirit. Must I plunge into antinomianism with Dr. M. to show that I do not look for salvation by my exactness in following the ordinances of Christ? What other tendency can this observation have, than to induce the disciples of Christ to neglect the commandments of God, that they may show that they do not depend on works of law for their salvation? I have never read any work of a more dangerous tendency than this, from a professor of the true Gospel of God.

On the supposition that the benefit of the ordinance depended on the physical influence of water, he says, that it would "be wise to insist on a rigorous adherence to that form." Pray, Dr. M. is it not enough that God has commanded that mode? And, on the supposition that he has not commanded that mode, it is not insisted on.

But Dr. M. does not here draw the proper inference. He argues, that as the benefit depends not on the mode, the mode may be changed. In like manner, if the benefit depends not on the physical nature of water, the water may be changed. So Sir Walter Scott's Moslems in the desert observed their ablutions with sand. "In an instant each Moslem cast himself from his horse, turned towards Mecca, and performed with sand an emblem of their ablutions, which were elsewhere required to be made with water." Christians, then, in changing the water in baptism for sand, in a case of necessity, are justified by the followers of the prophet of Mecca!

"The benefit," he says, "is the result solely of a Divine blessing on a prescribed and striking emblem." Do we teach otherwise? Do we teach sacramental efficacy? Do we hold that the benefit of immersion depends on the mode without the blessing of God? This is idle reasoning. But what is the prescribed emblem? It is both water and mode—purification and burial. Shall we look for a blessing while we trample on the mode through the observance of which the blessing is to be given? But he adds, "and as the word of God has nowhere informed us of the precise mode in which the emblem should be applied." Is not this to assume the very point in dispute? If this is taken for granted, there is no controversy. Does any man insist that immersion is essential, while he grants that the word of God is silent as to mode? What sort of reasoning is this? But let it be observed that the author here admits that the mode is not fixed by scripture, while he prefers *sprinkling*, or *pouring*, for an emblematical purpose. Has he a license from Rome for this popish manufacture?

Section XVII.—Dr. M. adverts to the conduct of Peter, on the occasion of Christ's washing the disciples' feet. A finer or more appropriate condemnation of his own party could not be found. Peter, influenced by his own wisdom, would not submit to this, as it appeared a degradation to his Master. "Jesus answered and said unto him, What I do thou knowest not now; but thou shalt know hereafter." Is not this enough for thee, Peter? No, replies the arrogant fisherman, "Thou shalt never wash my feet." What petulance under the guise of humility, though mingled with sincerity! Who does not see in Peter the opposers of Christian immersion? From their own view of decency, propriety, &c., combined with a number of forced improbabilities and difficulties, that are mere phantoms, they cry out against immersion, though Jesus has positively enjoined it. Peter's obstinacy at last gave way; but his own wisdom is still his guide, instead of the wisdom of his Master; and he cries out, *Not my feet only, but my hands and my head.* Will nothing restrain the arrogance of thy wisdom, Peter? Will you never learn that true wisdom teaches submission in all things to the wisdom of God? When Peter saw that it was a good thing to be washed by Christ, he must have more washing than Christ commanded. Just so with our pædo-baptist brethren. Christ commands believers to be baptized; they cry out, Not ourselves only, but our little ones. In like manner, in early times, naked baptism, trine immersion, &c. &c.

Section XVIII.—"Another, and in my view," says the writer, "conclusive reason for believing that our Baptist brethren are in error, in insisting that no baptism, unless by immersion, is valid, is, *that the native tendency of this doctrine is to superstition and abuse.*" Here again I charge the writer as being unphilosophical in his principles, and illogical in his reasoning. He assumes the point in debate, by taking it for granted that God had not appointed immersion: for if God has appointed it, would it tend to superstition to insist on obedience? Again, if the thing is believed to be of Divine appointment, even although this should be a mistake, it has no tendency to superstition. If any one believes that Christ has appointed sprinkling, I know he is in error; but to charge him with superstition, or his practice as having a native tendency to superstition, would be an abuse of words. But while they who practise infant sprinkling, believing it to be an ordinance of God, are not superstitious, they are superstitious who practise it as a human tradition.

How can the native tendency of the doctrine, that nothing but immersion is baptism, be to superstition? Would the native tendency of the doctrine, that water is essential to baptism, lead to superstition? And how can one of those tend more to superstition than the other, if they are both commanded? If God has not commanded immersion, then it is foolish to talk of it as tending to superstition: it is itself superstitious, if practised on that ground. Nothing can be superstitious which God has appointed. When God appointed circumcision, would it have tended to superstition to insist on the thing commanded, and that paring the nails was not valid circumcision?

What does Dr. M. mean by saying, that the native tendency of the doctrine is to abuse? Is this philosophy? Is it Scripture? Is it common sense? If the native tendency of a doctrine is bad, bad must be the doctrine itself. If the bad consequence is not in the doctrine, but in its abuse, the consequence is not native. If Christ appointed immersion, to hold that it is essential to the ordinance cannot have a bad tendency. If he did not appoint it, the bad tendency is not an abuse. It is foolish to argue against the abuse of a thing which has not been divinely appointed. To argue against the abuse of any observance, takes it for granted that the observance is duty : to argue against it as natively tending to superstition, takes it for granted that it is not divinely appointed. Here, then, Dr. M., in the very same sentence, in the immediate junction of two words, considers immersion to be both true and false.

If Dr. M. has met with any who believe that there is some inherent efficacy in "being buried under water," and that those that have submitted to it "are, of course, real Christians," I give them up to his unmitigated reprobation. But when he contends that this is the natural tendency of the Baptist doctrine, I must affirm that this is downright misrepresentation. Our doctrine is that the word signifies immersion, and consequently nothing but immersion can be a fulfilment of the command. This is saying no more than that nothing but immersion is immersion. Sprinkling cannot be called baptism with more propriety than sand can be called water. This I do not leave as an inference from my doctrines : I wish to proclaim it to all my brethren. Does this import that I lay on it any stress for salvation? Does it import that I deny the Christianity of those who will not receive it? Does it say, that I cannot consistently unite with every Christian in every thing in which I am agreed with him? It imports none of these things. I can say with the utmost sincerity, *grace be with all who love our Lord Jesus Christ in sincerity.* The Christian who denies baptism altogether is not excluded from my recognition.

SECTION XIX.—" Finally," says Dr. M., " that immersion cannot be considered, to say the least, as *essential* to a valid baptism, is plain *from the history of this ordinance.*"

1. Here Dr. M. grounds on a false principle. He assumes the opinion of antiquity as authority. This is Popery, or Puseyism. He assumes, that if Christians in early church history considered affusion as a valid substitute for immersion, it must be a valid substitute. I deny the position : this is an unprotestant foundation.

2. Because antiquity sanctioned affusion, as a substitute for immersion in some circumstances, even were its opinion authoritative, does it follow that it is a lawful substitute in all circumstances? Does it imply that the mode is optional?

3. The Fathers were led to this by an opinion that baptism was necessary to salvation.

4. They did not consider affusion to be baptism, but only a valid substitute for baptism. Dr. M. misrepresents Eusebius, when he says, that he "states that Novatian was baptized in his bed." Eusebius says nothing like this. He does not say that Novatian was baptized on his bed, or that he was baptized at all; but that, falling sick, he had water poured around him in his bed. The word used by Eusebius is *perichutheis*. He received *the grace* usually conferred by baptism, though he was not baptized, but only *perichysed*. There is an ellipsis both of the word water and of the word grace. He was *poured around*, namely, with water; he received, namely, *grace*. That it is the word *grace* that is to be supplied by ellipsis is evident from several parts of Cyprian's letter, and the phraseology usual on such occasions. This affords the most irrefragable proof that they did not consider *affusion* as *baptism*, but that affusion in a case of necessity will serve instead of baptism. The superstition both of Christians and Mahomedans has, in cases of necessity, substituted sand for water, as well as sprinkling for immersion. It is very merciful in the *two churches* to make so needful a commutation.

5. Nor is Dr. M. correct in reporting the testimony of his documents when he says, "And although some questioned, whether a man who had been brought to make a profession of religion on a sick bed, and when he considered himself as about to die, ought to be made a minister; yet this doubt arose, we are assured, not from any apprehension that the baptism itself was incomplete, but on the principle that he who came to the faith not voluntarily, but from necessity, ought not to be made a priest, unless his subsequent diligence and faith should be distinguished and highly commendable." Eusebius says nothing at all about the completeness or incompleteness of Novatian's baptism. He does not represent him as baptized at all. The question was, whether a man having water poured about him on a sick bed could be said to have received *the grace*, and more especially whether he could be fit for an office in the church. Though he was *perichysed*, he was neither *baptized* nor *confirmed*. The words of Eusebius expressly state, that it was not lawful that a man having water *poured around* him in his bed should have any ecclesiastical office conferred on him. If he might by such a substitution be allowed to go to heaven, this might not be sufficient to make him a good Puseyite clergyman. And, to make the matter still worse, he had not, after this substitution for baptism, received the confirmation of the bishop, without which a man could not receive the Spirit, even though he had been born of water. How can Dr. M. say that the affusion, instead of baptism, was no part of the complaint against Novatian, when the very words quoted by himself imply this most decidedly? Cyprian's answer shows that the question was, "whether they are to be accounted lawful Christians because they have not been *washed all over* with the water of salvation, but have only some of it *poured on them?*" After quoting this, how could Dr. M. say that the complaint did not respect the want of immersion, and the substitution of affusion?

Dr. M. tells us that Origen was contemporary with Cyprian, and that he, in commenting on 1 Kings xviii. 33, tells us that "Elijah baptized the wood on the altar." This proceeds on a principle I have often explained and illustrated. Every child knows that our word immerse may be used in the same way.

Dr. Miller's work can have no pretensions, as a work of controversy, founded on criticism. He merely asserts the meaning of the word by solemn declaration, or rests it on the testimony of others without producing their proofs. If I have paid him the compliment to notice him as a controversial writer on the meaning of the word in question, he is indebted to his fame on other subjects. In his reasoning he either assumes false first principles, or from sound principles deduces false conclusions.

8

FURTHER STUDY OF MODE

EXAMINATION OF THE VIEWS OF MR. HALL OF AMERICA, ON THE MEANING OF THE WORD BAPTISM

SECTION I.—WHILE Mr. Hall thinks that pouring and sprinkling are "the only modes for which we have any clear scriptural example, or even clear scriptural authority," he also thinks, that the mode of the application is a "matter of entire indifference," and that "immersion is a valid baptism." Here Mr. H. and I differ fundamentally, with respect to the obligation of scriptural example and authority. If there is clear scriptural example, and clear scriptural authority, for pouring and sprinkling, and neither scriptural authority, nor example, for immersion, I cannot admit that immersion is baptism. Can anything be valid, which is not scriptural? Can a thing be scriptural, which has no scriptural authority? This is a VALID *invalid*. If the word in question is so extensive in its meaning as to include immersion, then how can it be said, that there is no scriptural authority for the mode? On that ground it has the clearest proof, though not to the exclusion of other modes. It is evident that the author has no clear conception of his own meaning of the word that designates this ordinance. He cares not what the meaning is, provided it has sufficient extension for pouring and sprinkling.

The command to baptize, he thinks refers to the *thing done*, rather than to the *mode* of doing it. But what is the *thing done?* As far as respects the word, *mode* is the very thing in command; the water itself is usually supplied by ellipsis. When Mr. H. asserts of himself and others, that "they would as soon throw their bodies into the fire, as refuse to be immersed, were they convinced that immersion is essential to baptism," I give him full credit, and rejoice in the belief of his integrity. At the same time, I must say, that as long as he grounds on the rules of interpretation adopted by him, overlooking the fundamental laws of language, I can see no reason for his changing his convictions on any subject.

SECTION II.—He commences with some observations on the laws of interpretation. This is as it should be. On the soundness of the philosophy of this procedure, the whole question must for ever depend. It is hardly ever named by the generality of our opponents. I am, then, much pleased to find this writer commencing so auspiciously. Even though here in error, he may, by the habit of pursuing first principles, find the truth at last. With a view, by one stroke, to set aside all the authorities on our side, for the meaning of the disputed word, he alleges the use of the word *provisions*. All the dictionaries, he says, give *victuals* as the meaning. Yet in a law of Edward III., forbidding all ecclesiastical persons to purchase *provisions* at Rome, it means *nomination to benefices by the pope*. But how does this example stand in my way? Is it by the authority of dictionaries that I determine the meaning of any word? The language, and not lexicons, is my authority; and the language in the alleged example, gives the word *provisions* a secondary meaning, which is of equal authority with the primary. Nothing can be in more perfect accordance with my doctrine. It is just an example that I would select to illustrate my views of the laws of language. The English language gives *nomination to ecclesiastical benefices by the pope*, as one of the meanings of the word *provisions;* and when used in reference to ecclesiastical things, it is self-evidently clear that this, and not *victuals*, is its meaning. How does this apply to my doctrine with respect to the word in question? In what department, in what author, Jew or Gentile, is it used in any sense but that of immersion? Here Josephus and the Septuagint agree with the heathen poets; the latest writers agree with the earliest. If one decided example, in any author, of any age or country, gives a secondary meaning, I will admit such meaning to a fair competition. Mr. H. thinks he has here the strength of demonstration, yet he proves nothing that I will not assert. It is my own doctrine.

Mr. H., with my other opponents, represents me as resting the proof on the classics alone. This, as I have again and again showed, is a gross misrepresentation. I begin with the classics, I end only with the hour of the institution of the ordinance. If Josephus and the Septuagint established a secondary meaning, corresponding to the meaning of the word *provisions* in the canon law, I would admit it with the greatest promptness; but if ancient authors establish but one meaning of a word, a secondary should not be supposed in later writers, except in proof of its existence. A good deal of unsound observation has been employed by the learned, on the subject of the distinction between classic and Hellenistic Greek, and torrents of nonsense and of ignorance have been poured forth by those who adopt their conclusions. I may yet have an opportunity of stating my views on the subject. But here, the question has no concern. The fact to be ascertained is the *change* —not the *cause of the change*. If a change is proved, I will admit it, whatever may be supposed the cause.

He alludes triumphantly to the case mentioned Ecclesiasticus xxxiv. 30. The baptizing here, he thinks, was done by sprinkling. Demonstrably it was not; it was a *bath*. As the words *baptize* and *louo* here refer to the same thing, Mr. H. thinks that this is evidence that they are *synonymous*. I have often been obliged, gratuitously, to teach my opponents that WORDS MAY REFER TO THE SAME THING WITHOUT BEING SYNONYMOUS. I bestow on him this canon. If he looks through what I have written on the subject, he will see it proved. When words refer to the same thing, they must be consistent in what they express; but one may express more or less than the other. As Mr. H. appears to have a turn for the philosophy of first principles, I hope this will not be lost on him.

I had said that, " When I have proved the meaning of a word by the authority of the whole consent of Greek literature, 1 will not surrender it to the supposition of the strict adherence of the Jewish nation, in the time of writing the Apocrypha, to the Mosaic ritual." I have no need of availing myself of the aid of this observation ; but I still rigorously adhere to it as a sound principle. A change in a rite is frequent; and a change is rather to be admitted than to disregard the authority of language.

" The question, then," says Mr. H., " comes to this dilemma; either the Jews had abandoned the mode of purifying from a dead body, as specifically and minutely pointed out by God; or, here was a baptism by sprinkling." The question has not come to this; for I can do without this supposition altogether. In fact, I have no need of it: I give it merely as an ultimate possible resource, or a proof beyond what is necessary. And if it did come to this, where is the improbability, especially where is the impossibility of such a change? The Jews made greater changes in their religion than this. Surely our opponents should not think this an unjustifiable change.

He speaks of me, as " driven *to assume*, and that without the least shadow or pretence of authority, that when God had commanded a purification by *sprinkling*, the Jewish nation had turned about and made an immersion of it." Why does he say, I am *driven?* Does he not perceive, that I have pointed to this as a possible resource? Have I not proved the thing without this? Why does he say, that *I assume?* Does he not perceive that I do not assume it as a fact? I assume it merely as a possibility; and while I assume it as a possibility, I do not believe it to have been a fact. The writer's observations show that he is not acquainted with the philosophy of the burden of proof. He supposes that it lies on me to prove that there was actually such a change as I suppose possible, before 1 can avail myself of the argument. But I am here only answering an objection—not establishing an affirmative; and a bare possibility is perfectly sufficient. Let Mr. H. acquaint himself with the philosophy of evidence, before he ventures to criticise my reasoning. He is strong only from his ignorance of the grounds of proof. He supposes that I must have felt great difficulty in Mark vii. 4. I can assure him, that I never felt a moment's embarrassment : it is as plain to me as any point in history. If I believe the evangelist, I can have no doubt of the fact reported. Either the persons referred to, were immersed on the occasions mentioned, or the inspired writer testifies a falsehood. Between these alternatives my faith cannot hesitate. But my opponent not only frequently tramples on self-evident first principles; he here adopts an unsound and arbitrary first principle, as the foundation of his argument. He assumes that *every Scripture historical fact must be authenticated by uninspired history.* This is not a sound first principle: it is not essential even to an uninspired historian. But the Scriptures disdain it. But even were the canon admitted in this instance, what would it prove? It might serve the infidel, but could not affect the question as to the meaning of the word. Grant to the infidel, that no historical fact in Scripture can be admitted as truth unless it is authenticated by the history of the time,—he will triumph in his unbelief. In vain will you allege that the word may not here signify immersion; he defies you to bring an instance, in which it has another meaning. If they were not immersed, he will say, the evangelist asserts a falsehood. What is meant by the word, must be proved by the usage of the language. If the word signify to immerse, then there is the best of all historical proof: there is inspired proof that the persons referred to, immersed themselves before meat, after market.

But here, Mr. H. is confident that he takes away my foundation. "The meaning of the word," says he, "is the very thing in question here. We cannot allow him to prove a matter in question, by first assuming it as true." To this point, I invite the rigorous exercise of discrimination in all my readers. Assume the point in question! I would almost as soon be convicted of high treason. Sound and fair reasoning is with me the point of honour as a controversialist. Let truth itself fall, rather than uphold it by falsehood. But I do not assume the meaning of the word here; I rest it on the proof previously alleged. Have I not found the meaning of the word, by the testimony of the whole range of Greek literature? When, from this authority, I have found that it signifies immerse and nothing else, have I not an unquestionable right to allege this proved meaning in any place where the connexion itself does not decide? Had I alleged that the word in Mark vii. 4, must signify immersion, without having submitted any previous proof, then I might be charged with assuming the point in question. But when in a disputed passage, I allege that the word must have the meaning which in other passages it is proved to have, I rest on a self-evident first principle; I assume merely, that the meaning of the word in the language must be the meaning of the word here. Is there any one possessed of a sound mind, who will dispute this? This assumption, I grant equally to my opponents. Had they a meaning in proof, as the only meaning of the word, I would grant that they might apply this meaning to every passage that did not decide its own meaning. Is it not on the ground that I have proved the meaning of the word, and not by assumption, that I assert that it must be immersion in this place? Suppose for instance, that we interpret the expression, "*Her Majesty took an airing yesterday in her pony phaeton:*" and that we dispute about the meaning of the word *pony*. "*Pony*," says one, "is a small horse;" "*Pony*," says another, "cannot be a small horse, for I saw her Majesty yesterday, driving with very large horses. Pony, then, must signify a large horse" "I care not what you saw," says the first, "pony is a small horse, for the use of the word in the language is nothing else. Either then, the account is false, or her Majesty did yesterday take an airing with small horses in her carriage." "Assumption, assumption!" cries Mr. H.: "the fact must not be determined by the word, but by other proof." Would not this be ridiculous? It is the very soul of Mr. H.'s objection to my doctrine on this point. In any particular passage where my opponent may choose to dispute the meaning of the word, I rest on the meaning of it as already in proof. The word in question, signifies to immerse, as certainly as *pony* signifies a *small horse.* If it is not in proof that the word signifies to *immerse,* then I allow that the meaning cannot be assumed here. Surely, this is very far from assuming its meaning. As I would not charge Mr. H. with a want of candour, I must charge on him a want of perspicacity, in not being able to discriminate between resting on previous proof, and mere assumption of the point in question. This is the only point in which Mr. H. is plausible; and here he is plausible only to persons who have as little discrimination as himself.

"What," says Mr. H., "is the historical fact, as to what the Jews did before eating, when they came from market? Settle this, and you settle the meaning of the word baptize in this connexion." This is not the question to be settled. Uninspired testimony might say nothing on the subject. The question is not, what history says on the subject; but what the evangelist says? Can this be known, but by the meaning of the word he employs? I do not say that it must be the meaning that I attach to it, but its meaning in the language, whatever that may be. You must know the meaning of the word baptize, before you can know what the Jews did on the occasion, according to the evangelist. History might be silent, history might be lost, history might speak of other things done, while the thing asserted by the evangelist might be omitted. Nothing but a contradiction on the part of history, could place history in opposition to the evangelist; and even in that case the evangelist is better proof than history. Whatever history may or may not say, it is the meaning of the word baptize, in the Greek language, that must inform us what the evangelist means on this occasion. When we go to history, is it not by the meaning of the word in the language, that we are to know its meaning, in any particular case?

On the ground that the fact must be settled by the meaning of the word, he asserts, that "the thing in dispute should be proved by itself." This is an amazing want of discrimination. What is the thing in dispute in this place? The meaning of the word in this passage,—the meaning of the assertion with respect to the Jews. Now, is the assertion, that the thing which they are said to do must be known by the meaning of the word used by the evangelist, the same thing as to prove the thing in dispute by itself? It is not from this passage that I prove the meaning of the word : I bring the proved meaning, to show what must be its meaning here. I do not argue from the passage, that the word must signify to immerse : I argue that it must signify here, what it signifies elsewhere. My reasoning on the point, so far from proving the thing by itself, is perfectly consistent with the supposition that the word signifies *fumigation.* I argue, that if the word is proved, from its use in the language, to signify *fumigate,* and nothing but *fumigate;* fumigate it must be here, and nothing but *fumigate.* In determining the meaning of a word, in passages in which connexion does not decide, we must be directed by the use of the language. Can anything but the wildest fanaticism deny, that the meaning of every assertion is the meaning of the words employed to express it? And if the meaning of any word is not determined by the passage in which it is used, must it not be ascertained by its use in other places? Whether other history confirms this, or contradicts it, is to me a matter of perfect indifference. If an English traveller relates, that on a certain occasion a particular people *immersed* themselves; and another, that on the same occasion they fumigated; instead of reconciling them, by making immersion coincide with fumigate, or fumigate with immersion, I will say, " either they did both, or one of the travellers relates a falsehood." I will not allow any man to defend them by tampering with the English words.

I find as little trouble in immersing the *couches*. Whatever might have been their size, they might easily be immersed in a pond. But even on the supposition that they were too large to be immersed entire, I have contrived to take them to pieces, and immerse them in parts. This excites Mr. H.'s great admiration. I have not the smallest need for the supposition; nevertheless I will retain it carefully, as a safe last resort. " Indeed," exclaims Mr. H., " what shall we not allow him to suppose might have been the case, rather than grant the possibility that the Jews might have used the word baptize in a different sense from that of the old heathen Greeks?"

I will make this supposition, Mr. H., without waiting for your allowance: it is my right to make it. Here, again, I must discipline him on first principles. In answering an objection, anything possible may be supposed; in proof, nothing can be admitted without evidence. The greatest part of my trouble is, to teach my opponents the laws of reasoning. Not one of them knows when proof lies upon him, and when it lies upon me. They call for proof from me, when they should prove themselves. When I answer objections by possible and even probable solutions, they call on me for absolute proof. No man is entitled to appear in the field of controversy, till he has studied the laws of the combat. It is ignorance of this, with the adoption of false first principles, that makes some ingenious men think it possible to bring immersion into doubt. Let a man once know on which side, in every case, the burden of proof lies, and let him adopt no principle of interpretation but what is self-evident, and he will never, for a moment, consider immersion assailable.

But Mr. H. here supposes that I consider it impossible for a word to be used by later writers, in a sense different from its earliest use. This is not truth. Many words have changed their meaning; but in all cases of alleged change, I demand proof of the change. What say you to this, Mr. H. ?

Mr. H. is pleased to say, that it would seem to make no matter to me, " how often people had been baptized in other modes than immersion, I would still maintain my ground." On what ground does he venture this assertion? Do I admit that people may be said to be baptized in other modes than immersion, while I contend that nothing but immersion is baptism? If one instance of sprinkling was called immersion, I would give up the point of univocal meaning. The above assertion of my antagonist is grounded on the following passage in my work : " I care not if there never had been a human being immersed in water since the creation of the world : if the word denotes immersion, and if Christ enjoins it, I will contend for it as confidently as if all nations had been daily in the practice of immersing each other." Now does this language give any ground for Mr. H.'s observation? What I say is, that I care not if there never had been one immersion previously to the institution : Mr. H. represents me as saying, that I care not how many people had been baptized in other modes besides that of immersion. Is this a want of discernment, or a want of honesty? What I have said, I still say ; does Mr. H. pretend to refute it? Does he not say, "True, if the word means immersion, and never means anything else?" And is it not on that ground solely, that the assertion is rested?

" But I humbly suppose," says Mr. H., " that the common practice of a people who called a purifying, by sprinkling or pouring, a *baptism*, would have some little weight upon the question, what the people did in fact understand by the words baptize and baptism." A people who called a purifying, by sprinkling or pouring, a *baptism !!!* Where is such a people? Not under the heavens. The facts alleged to prove this, are all mere assumptions. Were they admitted, then due weight would cheerfully be given them.

Section III.—Mr. H. represents me as esteeming it as nothing, " that the Scriptures represent the baptism of the Spirit uniformly under the mode of pouring, 'coming down like rain,' and shedding forth." Is this truth? Do I admit *pouring, coming down like rain, shedding forth*, to be the thing that is called baptism, while I make no account of it? I do not, Mr. H.; I admit that the gift of the Spirit is spoken of under every mode of the motion of water, but I contend that this is not the thing that is called baptism. Is it not self-evident, that if the gift of the Spirit is spoken of under every mode of the motion of water, no mode can really belong to it? It cannot, then, be from mode called sprinkling or pouring. But if in baptism it is a *pouring*, it cannot be a *sprinkling ;* and if it is a *sprinkling*, it cannot be a *pouring*

He quotes from me the following sentence : " It is a fixed point that baptism means immersion." That with respect to the baptism of the Spirit, " nothing can be admitted inconsistent with this;" and that " the baptism of the Spirit must have a reference to immersion, because baptism is immersion." Mr. H. represents me as, in these sentences, taking the thing for granted, and replies, " That is the very thing to be proved." And, Mr. H., is it not on the ground that I have proved it, that I have made the above assertions? Why do I call it a fixed point? Is it not because I had fixed the point? Is there a child, in the whole range of the American continent, who can read my book without perceiving that I used all these assertions on the ground of previous proof? I must charge Mr. H. as having so little perspicacity, for I am convinced it is not a want of integrity, as not to perceive the nature of an assumption without proof. I will make this plain even to the most obtuse intellect.

If any of my opponents attempt to prove that the word in question signifies to *pour*, or to *sprinkle*, or to *purify*; afterwards, on the import of
the phrase, *baptism of the Spirit*, I will allow him to make use of the
result, and adopt the language that I have used. If he has found that
the word signifies to *sprinkle*, or to *pour*, or to *purify*, then he has a
right to explain the phrase, baptism of the Spirit, accordingly. The
figurative meaning, it is self-evident, must have a reference to the literal,
and be explained in accordance with it. The man who disputes this is
not worthy of castigation.

With respect to me, he adds, "But he *insists* upon it directly in the
'ame page, and puts his words in italics, '*Pouring cannot be the figura-
ive baptism, because baptism never literally denotes pouring.*'" Here
again, I suppose, he thinks I beg the question, or rest it on mere asser-
.jon. Has he not the perspicacity to perceive that I rest this assertion
on the ground which I had already gained "with my sword and my
bow?" Do I not here found on the proof which I had previously given
for the meaning of the word, and on the self-evident principle, that the
meaning of a word in a figurative use must be known from its literal
meaning? After all my proof of the meaning of the word, does my
assertion of its meaning rest on this assertion? I can give argument;
but I cannot give my opponents discernment.

In my treatise on baptism I had said, that "Pouring could not represent the pouring of the Spirit, because the Spirit is not literally poured."
This is a fact that common sense will never question. It is so obvious,
that I am astonished that it could be hid from any. Yet, obvious and
self-evident as it is, I believe I am the first who pointed it out. On this
I rest as on the pillar of heaven; it is an axiom that never can be questioned by a sound mind. Is there any pouring in the Godhead? It is
blasphemy to suppose it. But Mr. H. very coolly answers me, "Does
not God himself say, I will pour out my Spirit?" Yes, Mr. H., God
himself says, I will pour out my Spirit; so does God himself say, that
he has hands and heart. Has he hands and heart? To make pouring
emblematic of pouring in the Spirit, makes the Godhead material. I
say the same thing with regard to *immersion*. Immersion as a mode can
be no emblem of the Spirit. But if it is *pouring* in baptism, as an emblem of the pouring of the Spirit, how can *sprinkling*, or *immersion*, or
any other mode, be baptism?

Nothing can be more evident than that the phrase, *baptism of the
Spirit*, refers to the abundance of the gift of the Spirit. It is perfectly
similar to the phrase, "arrows drunk with blood." Deut. xxxii. 42
Arrows drunk with blood, means arrows that have shed much blood.
What would be thought of the writer who should allege that there must
be in the arrows something like drunkenness? The Holy Spirit asserts
the very same sort of baptism with respect to Asher, Deut. xxxiii. 24:
"He shall dip his foot in oil." This does not mean that he was literally
to dip his foot in oil; it means that the tribe was to have abundance
of oil. He was not to be all immersed in oil; but his foot was to be
immersed. He was immersed up to the ankle. This is entirely the
same figure with *baptism in the Spirit*. It denotes plenty—not mode.

To be baptized in the Spirit, is to have abundance of the gifts of the Spirit. I rest fully satisfied that no man of sense will ever question what I have written with respect to *pouring* and *sprinkling*, as emblematical in baptism.

Section IV.—Mr. H. disputes some of my examples from the classics. *Soldiers baptized up to the middle*, he thinks, could not be said to be immersed or buried. They could not be said to be wholly immersed or buried : but they are not said to be immersed or buried as to the whole person. Is not the baptism expressly limited? *Up to the middle*. This example is as good as if the soldiers had been actually buried in the sea. It is to me unaccountably astonishing that men will risk the credit of their understanding by such observations; keeping out of sight altogether, that it is the law of our God that we are handling. What can the words give us but mode? Would a child imagine that the word of mode should determine the extent of an object subjected to that mode? In determining the meaning of the word, the immersion of a joint of the little finger is as good as the immersion of the whole body.

With respect to the Roman general who baptized his hand in blood, to write an inscription for a trophy, he says, " Suppose we grant it. My pen is the instrument of writing, and I *dip* it in the ink when I write; surely I never immerse it in ink when I write. When will our Baptist brethren cease this play upon the word *dipping*, when they are to prove a total immersion?" Must I tell you again and again, Mr. H., that we never pretend to prove the extent of the immersion from the word itself? I wish to treat my antagonist with respect; but it is difficult to avoid an expression of contempt in repelling such allegations. We can prove a total immersion ; but we are not to prove it from the word itself. He makes a distinction in dipping a *pen* in ink, and *immersing* it. But there is no difference as to totality between *dip* and *immerse;* both may refer either to a part or to the whole. In the expression, *dip the pen in the ink*, there is an ellipsis of the part of the pen dipped, understood from the commonness of the operation. Besides, dip is used as a more familiar word than immerse. What idea has the writer of the meaning of the phrase, *playing upon a word*, when he calls this a playing upon the word *dipping?* Has it not the same meaning here that it has every where else? How, then, is this playing upon it? If we choose to be stiff and stately, can we not also say, *immerse the point of the pen?* This is egregious trifling.

With respect to the sinner represented by Porphyry, as baptized up to his head in Styx, he says, " He is not immersed ; he is not buried in water." Is he not immersed as far as he is baptized? Would Mr. H. have him immersed farther than he is said to be baptized? What more can be required than proof that the word immerse corresponds to the word baptize? Does he expect that if the word will extend to the whole person, it cannot also be capable of restriction to a part? Was ever nonsense so nonsensical? But is not the express restriction here subjoined, evidence that, without such restriction, the baptism would be understood as extending to the whole person?

In reference to Alexander's soldiers baptized in the tide up to the middle, he says, that if this was immersion, "then, when our Baptist ministers *wade* out into the river with their candidates, then *both* the minister and the candidates are immersed without being put under water at all." Not so fast, Mr. H. Is this a fair representation? Are Alexander's soldiers said to be immersed? They are not : they are said to be immersed up to the middle. Is it, then, Mr. H., consistent with your ideas of truth, to represent, that either of those things was an immersion generally? Alexander's soldiers are expressly said to be immersed only in part : and in the situation supposed, the minister and the candidate may be both said to be immersed up to the middle. In that situation, the candidate is *immersed* without reference to a part; that is, he is wholly immersed. Cease trifling, Mr. H.; it is about a law of Him who shall judge the world, that we are contending. Could you not say, *the woman carried the child into the river, and dipped him three times?*

SECTION V.—Mr. H. proposes three inquiries, which I notice merely as a specimen of his reasoning.

1. "What would the immediate disciples of our Lord understand as the meaning of the command, baptize?" What could they understand as the meaning of the command, but the thing meant by the word? The answer is self-evident. If the word signified to sprinkle, they would so understand the command; if it signified to pour, they would understand the command accordingly : and if immersion was the meaning of the word, they would understand the command to be to immerse. The true question is, what was the meaning of the word?

2. Mr. H.'s second question is, "Is there satisfactory evidence that they always administered the ordinance by immersion?" To this I reply, had there been no account at all of their practice, it is evident that they performed the rite in the manner commanded. We know from the word itself, what must have been their practice, had there been no account of that practice. If the word signified to immerse, must not inspired practice correspond with a Divine command? Had the word signified to *pour*, the apostolical practice must always have been *pouring*. As it was to *immerse*, it must have been always *immersion*. No evidence is essentially necessary, but that of the word itself. Apostolical practice independently proves the same thing.

Mr. H.'s third question is, "On the supposition that they did so, is there evidence that they considered that one mode essential?" To this I reply, if the command was to immerse, is not the command the same thing to us as it was to them? Besides, if the apostles always practised immersion, when other modes were not only practicable, but more easy, their practice is equal to a command. Would they have practised immersion, if sprinkling would serve?

With respect to the *divers baptisms*, Heb. ix. 10, he says that Paul "specifies here, what washings (baptisms) or purifyings he speaks of; and the only ones which he specifies are here performed with blood, and with the ashes of an heifer *sprinkling* the unclean." Paul specifies no such thing. None of the things referred to are a specification of the baptism. Does he refer to the baptisms, what was done with the sprinkling of blood? There is not the semblance of truth for the assertion. The apostle does not call the sprinkling of blood a baptism, nor even a washing of any kind. He does not speak of washing with the ashes of an heifer. The blood of bulls and of goats, and the ashes of an heifer, sprinkling the unclean, are said to sanctify to the purifying of the flesh, but are not said to be baptisms. "These sprinklings," says Mr. H., "Paul calls *baptisms*." It is not so, Mr. H. Paul does not call these sprinklings, baptisms. Why will men again and again assert what has not a colour of truth? It is painful to be obliged to give so strong a contradiction to men who are, as Christians, worthy of esteem; but it is not from inadvertence that such assertions are made; on that ground, it would claim indulgence: but the assertion continues to be made, after being a thousand times contradicted. The subtilty of Satan himself cannot plausibly contrive to force these sprinklings into *the divers baptisms*.

With respect to the opinion of the Baptists that the *bathing* (Numb. xix. 17, 18) may be one of the divers baptisms, (Heb. ix.) Mr. H. observes, "I am glad of the objection, because it distinctly recognises the fact that Paul refers to those purifyings as among his *divers baptisms*." The Baptists do not allege this as an objection; they bring it as an example. But how does it serve Mr. H.? He says, "It recognises the purifyings as among the divers baptisms." It makes no such recognition; it recognises one of the purifications as a baptism. Does that import that all the purifications were baptisms? This is an amazing want of perspicacity. If a man presents to a banker twenty notes, does the banker recognise them all as his, because he recognises one of them?

" But the objection," says Mr. H., "is idle; as Paul *does not specify the bathing* as any part of what he means, but he does specify the sprinkling." Baptists do not allege that Paul specifies the bathing as a baptism. It is enough for them that it may have been an immersion; they need no information from the apostle on the subject. The apostle tells them, that there were under the law *divers baptisms*. He tells them nothing more about these baptisms; but they are entitled to include among them every thing that can come under the meaning of the word. Here, Mr. H. shows himself deficient as to first principles. He assumes that the bathing, in Numb. xix. 17, 18, cannot be among the baptisms; because Paul does not express this. Every thing must be included among the divers baptisms that comes under the meaning of the word, without any explanation of the apostle. Paul specifies none of the *divers* baptisms; but if there was a bathing in any of the Old Testament rites, which was performed by immersion, then such bathing was a baptism. That the sprinklings referred to are a specification of the *divers baptisms*, is a most unfounded assumption. On similar grounds, he assures us, that ver. 15 and onward speak of baptisms. He might as well assert, that the apostle speaks of the thing referred to, as belonging to the Eleusinian mysteries.

" Another of those baptisms," says Mr. H., "is mentioned, Numb. viii. 7." As I cannot think that the author wishes to impose on his readers, I must say that an argument more childishly weak, I have never found in controversy. The leper was cleansed by sprinkling; but is that sprinkling ever called baptism? Are such assumptions to be continually reiterated? " As it is the sprinkling of the blood of Christ," says Mr. H., "that does the cleansing, surely it should be the *sprinkling* of the water in baptism, that *signifies* the cleansing." Here, the author conveniently overlooks what I have said on the phrase, *sprinkling of the blood of Christ*. There is no actual sprinkling of the blood of Christ on the believer. The application of the blood of Christ is called a sprinkling, in allusion to the type,—the sprinkling of the blood of the sacrifice. No man of sense has ever questioned this, since I pointed it out. The man who does not acknowledge it, I cannot think worthy of being addressed by argument. No axiom can be more self-evident. Neither *pouring* nor *sprinkling* can be emblematical, for the reasons alleged. But it is strange to astonishment, that the author did not see, that if baptism is a sprinkling as an emblem of the sprinkling of the blood of Christ, it cannot be a *pouring* as an emblem of the *pouring* of the Spirit. Yet, the writer and many of my opponents are so extravagantly inconsistent, that they take both emblems out of the ordinance. Dr. Miller takes both emblems, while he acknowledges that Christ has appointed neither.

With respect to Mark vii. 3, 4; Luke xi. 38, he says: "The fault of the Lord Jesus and of the disciples, in the eyes of the Jews, was, that they had not first *been baptized* before eating; *i. e.*, they had eaten with unwashed hands." Now, with respect to facts that interest the passions and prejudices, who can trust historians who report documents that never see the light, when a man of God makes such a representation of documents that are in the hands of all his readers? Mr. H. tells us, that the fault of the Lord Jesus, in the eyes of the Jews, was, that he had eaten with unwashed hands. It is not a fact. Mr. H. tells us, that the fault of the disciples was, that they had not first *been baptized* before eating. Neither is this a fact, Mr. H. The disciples are charged as eating with *unwashed hands;* the Lord is charged as eating *unbaptized*. These are the facts, however baptism may be explained. How is it consistent with integrity to confound these facts, for the purpose of drawing the following conclusion: "The washing of the hands, therefore, was a baptism?" The washing of the hands is neither here nor anywhere else said to be a baptism of the person.

In reference to my assertion, that the baptism after market *before* eating is immersion, he asks, "What does he bring to prove it? The word baptize!" Here we have a note of admiration. Well may we wonder that any intellect is so obtuse as not to perceive that the proof objected to, is the only proof that the case admits. What other proof could be given, than that such is the meaning of the word in the Greek language? Should I say that the man is *stupid* who cannot see this, how is Mr. H. to know what I here mean by the word *stupid?* Is it not by its meaning every where else? If it signifies *dull of apprehension* in the English, is it not so to be understood as here used? Yet, Mr. H. would call this proving a thing by itself, or assuming the point in debate. When the meaning of a word is proved, and when a secondary meaning is not in proof, it is self-evident that in every situation it has its proved meaning. This is as certain as proof in mathematics.

Mr. H. tells us that there is no evidence that the Jews had such a practice. There is no need of such evidence; the testimony of the evangelist ought to be sufficient. It is a false first principle to assume, that a fact in Scripture cannot be believed, unless it is proved by the history of the times. This is not essential even to civil history. He refers with astonishment to my assertion, that "even an inexplicable difficulty could not affect the certainty of my conclusions." Is he so little conversant with the nature of evidence, as to think this a bold assertion? The Bible itself could not stand without the assumption of its truth. But in the question at issue, there is not one inexplicable difficulty—indeed, to learning and skill there is not a single difficulty at all. I make the observation for the sake of truth in general, rather than its bearing on this point.

"To my mind," says Mr. H., "here is, so far, *demonstration*—proof which puts it beyond my power to doubt—that *sprinkling* and *pouring* are scriptural modes of baptism." Here we have a specimen of what, in the estimation of Mr. H., is demonstration. Because the Jews were displeased with the disciples for not washing their hands before eating, and with Jesus, for not baptizing himself before dinner, therefore, sprinkling or pouring is a mode of baptism! Demonstration, admirable demonstration! Because the Jews had water-pots for purification, therefore, *sprinkling* and *pouring* are modes of baptism! Such demonstration is not to be found in Euclid. Even were immersion out of the question, Mr. H. and the rest of my opponents, who allege an improbability from this passage, assume a false principle. They assume, that if it is not immerse, it must be what they mean. It might be neither sprinkle, nor pour, nor purify; it might be any one of many other things. This is another instance in which they assume what they ought to prove.

With respect to Acts ii. 17; xi. 15, 16, he says, "the mode of baptism here spoken of, is under the figure of pouring and shedding forth." The gift of the Spirit is spoken of under the figure of *pouring* and *shedding forth*, but the *pouring* and *shedding forth* are not called baptism. The gift of the Spirit may be figuratively spoken of under any mode of the figurative object. But there is no mode in the operations of the Spirit. The likeness of the figure is always in the effects. The gift of the Spirit is spoken of under all the modes of the motion of water. Does this imply, that any one of these motions is the same as any other? or, that there is any real motion in the Spirit like the motion of water? Surely any portion of discernment may perceive that the same object may be figured under different modes. Moses says, "My doctrine shall drop as the rain, my speech shall distil as the dew." Is the dropping of rain the same figure with the distilling of dew? And is there any likeness in mode, between doctrine and the thing referred to? Nothing but ignorance of the philosophy of language could embolden our opponents to use such arguments. May not a child perceive, that if the gift of the Spirit is spoken of, both as a *pouring* and a *shedding forth*, the likeness in the figure cannot be in mode, as the same motion cannot have two modes? Shall I never be able to teach my opponents, that whenever mode is ascribed to the Spirit, the phraseology is accommodated to the emblem—instead of mode being employed as an emblem?

Speaking with respect to *pouring, sprinkling,* &c., he says: " I cannot but wonder that those who insist so much upon the words, ' *buried with him in baptism,*' are not able to see in these also an equal authority for proper modes of baptism." A very little penetration would entirely relieve the patient from this malady. His wonder, as in most instances, would cease, with a little more knowledge. Baptists cannot but see immersion in the phrases " *buried in baptism,*" and " *buried by baptism ;*" because believers cannot be buried in baptism without being immersed in the water of baptism. They cannot see a mode of baptism in *sprinkling, pouring, shedding forth, falling as rain,* and because none of these are ever called baptism. Cannot Mr. H. see, that if *pouring* and *sprinkling* are both applied to the gift of the Spirit, without implying that they are the same mode, *immersion* may likewise be applied to the same gift, while it is a mode different from both?

SECTION VI.—Mr. H. thinks it strange that Baptists dwell so much on the *much water* at Enon, while they find enough in Jerusalem to baptize three thousand converts in a small part of one day. Here he thinks he has shut us up in a dilemma, from which there is no escape. We must either give up a sufficiency of water in Jerusalem, or we must set no value on the abundance of it in Enon. But a little discrimination would have prevented this observation. There is not the slightest inconsistency in our sentiments on this subject. The writer assumes that we think that John the Baptist declined Jerusalem for want of water. This is not the fact: he chose the wilderness for other reasons, and in the wilderness he chose the place most fit for his purpose of baptism. Had there been a lake at Jerusalem, John would have chosen the wilderness as the station of his labours. He thinks it strange, also, that if the *much water* in Enon was necessary for the purpose of baptism, we never hear a complaint about the want of water with the apostles. The apostles, however, did not confine themselves to the wilderness ; and, wherever they went, they could find as much water as would immerse their converts. For the multitudes baptized by John at the same place, much water was necessary ; no such thing was necessary for the immersion of a few.

Much water, he says, was necessary for supplying John's hearers with drink, as he wrought no miracle. Our Lord had as great crowds to hear him, yet he did not supply them miraculously with drink. John is not said to have preached at Enon, because there was much water there. Not only is the *drink* apocryphal, but the use of the water is expressly stated. He baptized at Enon because there was much water. It is also stated, that it was to be baptized the people went.

He quotes from travellers an account of the destitution of water in the wilderness of Judea. Well, was not this the very reason why John baptized in Enon? He could have sprinkled any where. He thinks it might be necessary for purification. But there is no purification in the narrative. Perhaps it was for swimming, or sailing, that the much water was necessary. Is there no end to extravagance? But for purification it could not be necessary, as they need not delay a moment after baptism. The Spirit of God assigns the use of the much water; dare arrogant mortals give another and a different use?

SECTION VII.—With respect to our Lord's baptism, Mr. H. tells us, that "the original language here is such as can have no reference to *emerging* from under water." He alleges a concession of mine with respect to the preposition *apo;* but he does not, it seems, understand the criticism. *Apo* commences its motion *from* the object: the edge of the object, then, is a fulfilment of its meaning. But it is obvious that it may commence in any part of the object, while its commencement is still equally from the object. Accordingly, it is frequently used when the motion commences within the object: but for the reason alleged, it cannot definitely express this. To express this definitely, *ek* is necessary. But to say, with Mr. H., that the Greek language forbids the idea of emerging from under water, is unwarranted by the use of the word. It does not decisively express that idea, but it may be used when the motion commenced in any point in the water.

As to the verb, I suppose Mr. H. rests on the authority of Professor Stuart, of Andover. But I tell both these gentlemen, that the verb does not forbid *emersion.* On the contrary, the verb, compounded with *kata,* is used by Æsop as signifying to *dive.* When Mercury, compassionating the woodman who let his axe drop into the river, dived three times, one of the dips was by *kataduo,* and the other two by *katabas. Anabas,* then, would be the exact word for emerging, corresponding to the word that expresses the *diving.*

I will tell Mr. H. another secret. Justin Martyr uses the word *anaduntos* (emerging) instead of *anabainontos,* in relating this transaction. Did not Justin know, as well as Mr. H., what is consistent with the original language? We have Justin's authority that this account of the evangelist refers to the immersion and emersion of Jesus. He understood the passage as asserting that the Spirit of God descended on Jesus as he emerged from the water; and he uses the very preposition *apo,* which Mr. H. represents as precluding the idea of emersion. After all, I freely admit that the phrase itself is not decisive. It would be amply verified if the motion commenced at the edge of the water. Instead of being a partisan to force evidence it will ever be my purpose to represent evidence as in the sight of God Let my opponents take this concession also. I am too strong in truth, to be afraid of conceding anything that truth requires. But is it not absurd to ground anything here on the difference between *apo* and *ek,* when we have *ek* in the case of the eunuch?

He alleges that the phrase, *coming up out of the water,* "does not necessarily imply that one has been under water." Very true; but if persons are represented as going into water for the performance of a certain rite, there must be something in the nature of the rite that obliges them to go there, in order to perform the rite. Perverseness may cavil, but no fair answer can ever be given to this. If the answer usually given can satisfy any conscience, I do not envy that conscience.

SECTION VIII.—Mr. H. thinks that Jesus was baptized as a priest, and, therefore, that he was purified by sprinkling. He was not baptized as a priest. This is extravagantly absurd. 1. John's baptism did not belong to the old dispensation. It made no distinction between priests and the rest of the Jews. 2. Jesus could not be baptized as a priest, because he was not of the priesthood to which the Levitical ceremonies belonged : these belonged only to the priesthood of the tribe of Levi and of the house of Aaron. 3. Had he been consecrated as a Levitical priest, all the ceremonies of consecration would have been employed as well as sprinkling. 4. John had nothing to do with the consecration of priests. 5. It was the baptism that others received from John to which Jesus submitted. 6. Justin Martyr had a better view of the necessity of baptism with respect to Jesus. He was not baptized, he said, for his own sins, but for the sins of the human race, which had fallen under death by the seduction of the serpent. There was in Christ's immersion the same figure as in that of his people. They are cleared of sin by fellowship with him in his death, which is figured in their burial with him by baptism. He took their sins off them, and cancelled them by his death : the blood of his death washed them away. His own baptism, then, had as much propriety in the figure as the baptism of his people.

SECTION IX.—Mr. H., as well as Dr. Miller, adopts the silly evasion, with respect to Philip and the eunuch going into the water, which alleges that it equally proves that they were both immersed, if it proves that either of them was immersed. He entirely mistakes the argument. No man reasons so foolishly as to assert that every one who is in water must be totally immersed. The argument is, that nothing but the necessity of immersion, as to one of them, could take them both into the water. Indeed, what can be the use of telling us that they went into the water, if it is not for our instruction ?

He tells us, that it is not certain "that they went farther than to the river." What! Not certain that they went into the river ? How, then, could they come out of it ? If I have admitted this as to *apo*, I have not admitted it as to *ek*. He gives us a number of passages in which *eis*, the preposition signifying into, signifies *unto*. This is no news to us; it needed no proof. Our proof is independent of this.

"Who will prove to me," says Mr. H., "that the stream was a foot deep ?" If he means proof independent of the passage, there is no need of such proof. A controversialist that knows his business will never attempt this; nor will he demand it. The proof is, that Philip and the eunuch went into it in order to the performance of the rite, and nothing but immersion could make it necessary to go into the water. If the baptism was an immersion, I suppose that it may be taken for granted that the water was deep enough for immersion. Had pouring or sprinkling been used, they would neither of them have gone into the water.

"Who," says Mr. H., "will prove it a stream at all?" Wisdom will never undertake the proof—wisdom will never ask the question. Whether it was a fountain or a pond, a river or a lake, makes no difference. Could any fact in history afford proof on such a principle? Indeed, had there been no mention of water, and had it been in a desert, the word baptize proves that there must have been water for immersion. What folly is it, then, when the water is mentioned, to demand proof that it was a stream!

"Who will prove," he asks, "the quantity of water there was sufficient to render an immersion possible?" If they went into the water for the purpose of performing the ordinance, *pouring* or *sprinkling* a little water could not have been the thing performed. If, then, immersion is the only thing that will give a reason for their going into the water, there is proof that the water was deep enough for immersion.

"If it was," he continues, "who will prove that the eunuch was immersed?" The passage proves it. He was the person baptized, and to perform the baptism they went into the water.

Mr. H. thinks that there is some probability in favour of sprinkling on this occasion. Philip expounded the chapter of the prophecy which the eunuch was reading: in that chapter there is something about sprinkling: this would naturally bring on a conversation about baptism, which is sprinkling, &c. &c. Am I to refute dreams and visions? But the dream, like other dreams, is inconsistent. It supposes that *sprinkling* is the meaning of the word *baptism*, which is inconsistent with the author's theory. He gives it a general meaning, though I cannot discover exactly what that general meaning is. Whatever it is, it must include all modes, and therefore it cannot be modal at all. Here he makes it one precise mode.

Section X.—With respect to Rom. vi. 1, and Col. ii. 12, he says, "There is just as much reason to argue from them that believers are literally *put to death* in baptism, as that they are literally buried under water in baptism." To this I reply, that they are literally immersed, but the burial is equally figurative as the death; and they die in baptism as well as they are buried in baptism. Indeed, it is *by being buried* that they die. That this figurative burial is *under water* is not in the passage: this is known from the rite, and is here supplied by ellipsis.

"They are planted together," says the author, "in the likeness (not of his grave or burial) but in the likeness of his death." This is exquisite criticism. He here confounds *burying* and *planting*. Are not these two different things, and have we not here two figures? Believers are said to be *buried* with Christ by baptism, and to be *planted* with him in the likeness of his death. The burying and the planting both refer to baptism, but they are not the same figure, but exhibit the object in a different point of view.

"If," says Mr. H., "we are to infer the mode of baptism from these figures, the evidence is strongest for drawing a resemblance for the mode of baptism from hanging on the cross, for that was the mode of his dying; and the passage says, we are crucified with him." How extravagantly absurd is this! We are, indeed, said to be crucified with Christ, but are we said to be crucified *in baptism?* But we are said to be buried in baptism. Besides, crucifixion is still a different thing from both planting and burial. Does he expect the same likeness in all? Are we said to be crucified in baptism in the likeness of Christ's death? There is no criticism in these observations.

"The argument," says the writer, "is, We are *dead* with Christ, and we must no more live to sin than a dead body must live." I am not sure that I understand this commentary. What is meant by the phrase, "than a dead body *must* live?" I suppose, by the phrase, *must not live to sin*, he means the duty of not living to sin. But in the contrast he cannot mean the duty of a dead body. A dead body cannot live; the contrast, then, would be that believers cannot live in sin more than a dead body can live. This supposes that the security against being in sin is the total extinction of sin in the Christian. I do not understand this theology.

"We are dead," says Mr. H., "and more—we are buried; as we often say, to express strongly the fact that a person has ceased from living, He is dead and buried." But, Mr. H., this is not the apostle's phraseology; he does not say that believers are dead and buried, but that they are *buried into death,* and that burial into death is *in* and *by* baptism. Believers are not merely said to be dead and buried, but to die and to be buried in baptism. They are buried by baptism into death. Twist and twist as you will, still there is burial in baptism. There must be something in baptism to emblematize death and burial; no sophistry can evade this. "The burying," says he, "is the conclusive token of his being dead." But, I ask, how is the token found in baptism, if it is not in its mode? There is no token of death in *pouring* or *sprinkling*. "So," continues Mr. H., "the baptism is a token—not of the burying —but of the death." Why does he so directly contradict the apostle? Does not Paul expressly say, that we are buried *in* baptism and *by* baptism, which necessarily imports that there is a burial in baptism? But how is baptism a token of death, if there is no figurative death in baptism? How is baptism a token of death, but by its being a burial? The death here spoken of takes place in the burial. Believers are *buried into death.* It is not, they die and are buried, but, they are *buried* and *die.*

"It is not," says Mr. H., "the mode of the baptism that is referred to, but the effect of the baptism." What! the mode of baptism not referred to in the phrase, *buried in baptism!* Can there be any figurative burial, without something to represent the body as buried? But what is the effect of baptism? Mr. H., as plainly as Dr. Pusey could do, tells us that it is the crucifixion of the old man. No wonder that this leprosy of Oxford has spread so widely in the Church of England. But Mr. H., it is not the effect of baptism, whatever that effect may be supposed to be, that is here referred to. Our old man is indeed here said to be crucified with Christ, but not in baptism. There is in baptism no crucifixion.

The argument which we draw from 1 Cor. x. 1, and 1 Pet. iii. 21, Mr. H. understands to be rested on the quantity of water in the Red

Sea, and in the deluge. I can see neither wit nor refutation in this. He knows well, what we have said on these passages. But he tells us, that the eight souls "were in the ark, and neither buried nor immersed." What could be a more expressive burial in water than to be in the ark, when it was floating? As well might it be said that a person is not buried in earth, when lying in his coffin covered with earth. May not persons in a ship be said figuratively to be buried in the sea? They who were in the ark were deeply immersed.

"Moses," Mr. H. tells us, "walked on dry ground." Yes, and he got a dry dip. And could not a person, literally covered with oil-cloth, get a dry immersion in water? Are not the Israelites said to go into the sea? Was it sea where they walked? It is called *sea* on a principle similar to that on which it is called baptism.

Mr. H.'s charge of failure in making out an immersion in the case of the ark, and of the passage of the Israelites through the Red Sea, shows a total inattention to the processes of thought in language.

> "Few, few shall part, where many meet;
> The snow shall be their winding sheet;
> And every turf beneath their feet
> Shall be a soldier's sepulchre."

Would any Goth object that the snow cannot be a winding sheet, because it does not wind round the whole body of the dying soldier? As the soldier, says the critic, was uncovered above, the snow cannot be his winding sheet. And is he not a Goth, who says that the Israelites could not be buried or immersed in the sea, because they were not covered with the water? But our critic must proceed. As the soldier lies on the turf without any covering from it, it cannot be said to be the soldier's sepulchre. What sort of criticism is this?

"Look into my face, dear cousin," said one pitted by the small-pox, "and tell me, are there not pit-holes deep enough to bury a million of Cupids?" The critic replies, with triumph, "However deep the pits may be, no one can be buried in them, seeing they are open at top." This is the very criticism of our opponents.

If Mr. H. is unreasonably obstinate in not finding an immersion here, he makes ample amends by his facility in finding *spray* for sprinkling. But not only is the spray a creation of the imagination, it is a creation unsuitable to the occasion. It would have been an annoyance; and the wind that blew the water from them could not blow the spray on them. Yes, and the very tempest that God sent on their enemies for their destruction, Mr. H. employs for the baptism of the host of Israel, Psalm lxxvii. On the Israelites there was neither spray, nor rain, nor storm. Will Mr. H. say, what is the baptism of the Red Sea?

Mr. H. comes next to the consideration of a number of passages in which he alleges that we are compelled to take the labouring oar, and render that certain or probable, which in the face of it seems impossible. Here, Mr. H. manifests that he has insufficient skill in the fundamental laws of controversy. I tell him, that in these instances, proof does not lie on us: we are not bound to prove, independently of the word, that there was a sufficiency of water in any of the situations referred to. If we have proved the meaning of the word, the word commands the water, in opposition to any number of improbabilities. The proof of impossibility lies on him. Go, then, Mr. H., and study the principles of reasoning. You should know when it is your duty to prove, and when you have the privilege of calling on your antagonist to prove.

I tell Mr. H. that I can immerse the three thousand on the day of Pentecost, without the assistance of the brook Kedron, or any proof from history. I will not take the trouble even to gauge the ponds and reservoirs in Jerusalem. There may have been many conveniences on that occasion in Jerusalem, of which we can know nothing. This is enough for me, had it been situated in a desert. I have been formerly too good-natured in making faith easy to my opponents, by putting the water before their eyes: I shall, henceforth, oblige them to go and look for it.

" Now," says Mr. H., " what do those who make John take Jerusalem and Judea out to Enon, to immerse them, because there is much water there? All at once, and very conveniently, there is discovered a number of *reservoirs* and *baths.*" Here, surely, he has got us into a net; but it is a weak fish that cannot break the meshes of this net. The author founds on a false assumption: he assumes that John avoided Jerusalem for want of a sufficiency of water. This is not the fact. Had there been a lake in Jerusalem, John would have chosen the wilderness; and in the wilderness he chose the place most convenient for the immersion of great multitudes. If we refer to the number of reservoirs, and baths, and pools in Jerusalem, it is out of compassion for the weakness of our opponents. In a city where purifications by bathing were every day so numerous, with respect to both rich and poor, there could be no want of conveniences for immersion. But I care not if there were not in proof a single pool in the city: I will force water out of the word, *as used in the ordinance*, although there is no water in the word itself.

But " a simple mathematical calculation," says Mr. H., " will show that the eleven apostles could hardly have immersed three thousand persons in so short a time."

Here again Mr. H. grounds on a false assumption. He assumes that none but the apostles baptized. Where is this taught? I promise, in the name of Dr. Pusey, to offer him a premium if he will prove this What a great evil is superstition? To make anything necessary in religion, that God has not commanded, is to lay a foundation for Babylon the Great. Mr. H. thinks he has here the certainty of mathematical calculation, when his reasoning is founded on his superstition.

Next comes the jailer. Mr. H. thinks that he makes out a strong point of inconsistency on our part, when he observes that we find means of immersion even in a prison, while we are obliged to send John to Jordan and Enon. But I have shown that the appearance of inconsistency here, is in the false conceptions of those who allege it. We did not send John out of Jerusalem for want of water: he chose the wilderness as the theatre of his labours, and chose such places in it as suited the immersion of such multitudes as came to his baptism. Does this imply that water may not be found in any inhabited part of the country sufficient to baptize individuals? Shame to common sense if it stumble here!

He tells us with an air of triumph, that there is not a "scrap of evidence in the history, to show that an immersion was possible." Here, again, I arraign my antagonist as ignorant of his duty as a controversialist. He comes into the arena, without a knowledge of the laws of the tournament. He calls on us for proof, when proof lies on himself. We are bound to prove the meaning of the word. If an objector alleges the inapplicability of such a meaning in any case, he is bound to prove that it is inapplicable. An unproved objection is no objection. Is there in the passage any proof of the possibility even of sprinkling? It may be alleged that there is no need of this. I admit the truth of this; but this shows us that there is no need of proof from the passage, that the thing asserted was possible. That it was possible, is assumed in the word, whatever the word may signify. If we read that a sportsman was drowned in crossing a certain district, are we obliged to prove the existence of a river or pond, before we know the meaning of the word *drowned?* Were we even certain that in that district, there was not as much water as would cover him, we should discredit the report, but never question the meaning of the word. The meaning of no word could, in every instance, be proved, if it is not lawful, in cases in which context does not decide, to rest on previous proof: the meaning of no word could in any case be proved, if it is necessary, in every case, to prove the possibility of the alleged meaning by historical evidence. The confidence of our opponents rests entirely on the assumption of false principles. Instead of thinking myself obliged to prove the existence of a bath in the jailer's house of Philippi, or the possibility of going to the Strymon, I utterly refuse to be called on for proof. I prove the possibility of immersion, by the fact that there was an immersion.

Mr. H. thinks he finds an inconsistency in us in flying from the bath to the river. Here, again, he has demonstration. "Now," says he, "this is to give up the baptism in a bath within the prison; for I take it as a point not to be debated, that he was not baptized both *in* the prison and out of it, in one and the same baptism." This has, to superficial thinkers, an appearance of acuteness, but it really manifests a want of discernment. In holding the possibility of an immersion, both in the jail and in the river, are we bound to hold that it was actually performed in both? Can any intellect make such an assertion? We might prove the probability of immersion in a third different place, while we believe that it actually takes place only in one. I believe that the passage affords evidence that the immersion takes place without, yet I shall strenuously contend for the possibility of immersion in the jail.

With respect to Paul's baptism, Mr. H. asks, "What pretence for a bath in the chamber?" What pretence, I reply, for denying the possibility of a bath in this chamber? And a possibility is all I want, to enable me to work the miracle. I ask in return, what is the necessity of confining the baptism to this chamber? Where did you learn that they did not go to another chamber? Where did you learn that they did not go out of the house altogether? Where or how the immersion was performed, I neither know nor care. All I know is, and that I thoroughly know, Paul was immersed; for the word tells me this. Will my opponents learn when they are to prove, and when they may demand proof? But I refuse to give proof, though I have proof. Paul was *bathed* in *baptism*, therefore he was immersed. In Judea, where the law forced them so often into the water, baths must have been as common as ovens in English farm-houses.

In the account of the baptism of Cornelius, Mr. H. thinks that the idea of Peter "seems to be, not that they might be carried and applied to the water, but that water might be brought and applied to them." Whether they were to go to the water, or the water was to be brought to them, is not in evidence from the document. And the water might have been brought for immersion as well as sprinkling, even had it been implied that the water was brought. "The Spirit's mode of baptism," he tells us, "was by falling upon." The Spirit is indeed said to fall upon them, but that falling is not called baptism. There is no mode in the operation of the Spirit. Whether the Spirit is said to fall on persons, or to be poured on them, or they are said to be immersed in the Spirit, there is no mode in the working of the Spirit.

"That immersion," says Mr. H., "was early and extensively practised is certain. That it was not considered essential is also certain." It is true that very early in cases of necessity, pouring water around persons on a sick bed, was admitted a substitute for immersion; but it is not true that they called the substitute by the name of baptism. Now it is only with the meaning of the word in the writings of the earliest fathers that we have any concern. Their opinion as to the effect of baptism, or as a substitute, I despise as much as I do the opinions of Dr. Pusey.

The following extract he quotes from the Rev. William T. Hamilton: "For any one to *assume* that one mode only was employed, and then demand that all should comply with that mode, while they can produce neither express command nor an undeniable example of baptism by immersion in the Bible, is rather a bold stand to take, especially for those who insist that in a positive ordinance, the law of the ordinance must be our guide."

Who is it, Mr. Wm. T. Hamilton, that assumes this? Did any Baptist ever ground the meaning of the word on assumption? The Rev. Wm. T. Hamilton may dispute their proofs, and has a right to express his opinion of the sufficiency of their proofs; but he should know that to allege insufficient proof is not to *assume* the point at issue. This writer appears to have a loose random way of speaking; and perhaps he has not asked himself what he means by the charge of assumption. If he really understood what he was saying, can there be a greater misrepresentation of Baptists than to charge them with *assuming* that there is but one mode of this ordinance; and on the ground of this *mere assumption*, calling on all Christians to comply with it? Do they not pretend express command and example? If the command is not proved, and the example not satisfactory, let this be shown; but let them not be represented as grounding on assumption, and forcing their assumption on their neighbours.

SECTION XI.—Mr. Hall asserts that Justin "uses such language as renders it certain that he by no means considered immersion essential, and such as renders it doubtful whether he meant immersion at all." Justin uses the word in the sense of immersion, whenever he does use it—never in any other sense. Mr. H. tells us that in writing to the Emperor, Justin "invariably describes the baptism, and does not use the word baptism at all." Well, if this were so, how can his use of the word prove that he did not consider immersion essential? If in a certain case he did not use the word at all, how can the word in that case prove that he used it in a certain meaning? Very true, in writing to the Emperor, Justin describes the ordinance, without using the word: but that description, so far from being inconsistent with immersion, adds to the proof of immersion: it proves it by other words. Is not this necessarily implied in the fact that the candidates for baptism were led to a place where there was water? Is it not necessarily implied in the assertion that they were there *born again* in that ordinance? Is not this a reference to their issuing out of the water of baptism?

Another of Mr. H.'s proofs is, that Justin applies *louo* and *loutron* to the ordinance. I maintain that this is proof of immersion. These words apply to the bathing of the whole person. When Mr. H. speaks of *louo* as signifying *washing* in general, he speaks not in knowledge. Baptism is represented by Justin as *a bathing of the body*. Yet I tell Mr. Hall, that though *louo* is applied to the same ordinance as *baptizo*, the words are by no means synonymous. I have given a thousand proofs of this.

The author's own quotation from Cyprian, might show him that even that Father, who makes *perfusion* a valid substitute for baptism in case of necessity, does not consider perfusion to be baptism. "Perfusion," says he, "is of like value with the salutary bath." Does not this import that perfusion is not the same thing as the salutary bath? Perfusion, then, is not baptism, in the estimation of this Father, although he made it serve the same purpose.

Mr. H. quotes the case of the Jew, who, falling sick while travelling with Christians, was sprinkled with sand, for want of water. Yes; and if this is proof that *sprinkling* will serve for *immersion*, it equally proves that *sand* will serve for water. This trash will find no purchasers except the Puseyites.

SECTION XII.—Mr. H. inquires, "On the supposition that the early disciples always baptized by immersion, is there evidence that they considered that mode essential?"

To this I reply: 1. This supposition is not fully and fairly stated. It ought to be included in the supposition that the word in the command signifies to immerse. If we are right as to the meaning of the word, the thing commanded is in all ages the same.

2. Even on the defective supposition stated, the answer must be in the affirmative. If they who practised according to the command of the apostles, always observed the ordinance in one mode, while several other modes were practicable and were much more easily observed, it is evident that the mode cannot be indifferent. Besides, the apostle Paul fully teaches this : " Now I praise you, brethren, that ye remember me in all things, and keep the ordinances as I delivered them unto you." Even the covering and uncovering of the head in public worship, and the wearing of short or long hair, are things thought worthy of Divine regulation. Should any be contentious with respect to the forbidden practices, it was deemed a sufficient answer, that " neither the apostles nor the churches had any such custom." This establishes the customs of the apostolical churches as firmly as if all those customs were in all the formality of an act of parliament.

3. Mr. H.'s supposed case in answer to his question is not parallel to the case put by himself. The case put is example; the case in illustration is command. " Suppose," says he, " the command had been, ' *Let every believer go down to Jericho.*' Suppose that the Saviour and his early disciples all went by one particular way, and always rode on ass colts, must we always go in that road?" &c.

To this I reply : The way by which they are to go to Jericho not being included in the command, can never by any example be brought into it. To go to Jericho in any way to the end of the world, is a perfect fulfilment of the command. If they always go to Jericho by one way, while that way is fifty times as long as others, it cannot be without design. But this has no bearing on the question at issue. The command is to immerse, and immersion must ever continue to be obedience to the command. As they always actually immersed, it shows that they understood the command as an immersion. To make the supposed case in point, the command should be to go to Jericho, while it is obeyed by going to Damascus. This is the principle on which our opponents act. They justify a change of the mode on the principle of expediency.

SECTION XIII.—" The thing is commanded," says Mr. H., " the mode is not commanded." I have proved a thousand times that mode is the very thing directly commanded. But what is the meaning of the command, according to Mr. H.? I can understand those who say that the word in this command signifies neither to pour, nor to sprinkle, nor to immerse, but that it signifies to *purify*, and may be fulfilled in any mode. This is bolder extravagance than that of Mr. H., but it is consistent extravagance: I cannot find that Mr. H. has any definite idea as to the meaning of the word in the command. It is with him sometimes one thing and sometimes another, as it suits the occasion. Here it is pouring—there it is sprinkling; while on some occasions he appears to favour the supposition that it signifies to purify. These views are perfectly inconsistent. If it is pour, it cannot be sprinkle : if it is either, it cannot be purify : if it is purify, it cannot be mode at all. Mr. H. illustrates, by six examples in a note, with respect to the Lord's supper, none of which have any application to the subject. *It was at night.* This fact has no feature of an example. Every fact is not an example. When a thing could not be otherwise, it cannot be an example. But it does not even suit the case put by him. Does not the case put suppose universal practice ? Is not this a solitary fact, evidently without an intention of being an example ? I need not waste time by running over the six examples : they are all of the same stamp.

"So here," says Mr. H., "we are to be baptized, and simply baptized." Certainly : but what is this to the purpose of the argument alleging universal practice as an insufficient proof? All we want is, that our opponents should comply with the command. "But I have shown," says he, "that the words baptized and baptism were in common use among the Jews of that time to denote ritual purification by sprinkling or pouring." You have shown no such thing, Mr. H. : but had you shown it, what has this to do with universal practice ? This extract shows that the author has no definite view of the meaning of the word. Had he understood and adopted the theory that makes the word signify to *purify,* he would not have spoken of proof with respect to *sprinkle* or *pour.* All modes on that supposition are indifferent. When he speaks as if the word designates both purification and different modes, he speaks most unphilosophically.

On the subject of the variety of baptism, under different modes, Mr. H. tells us, with respect to the difference between John's baptism and that of our Lord, "Here were two baptisms, while doubtless there was but *one* mode." Thank you, Mr. Hall, I never could get an antagonist to confess this honestly on Heb. ix. 10. There may then be *divers baptisms ;* while doubtless there is in them all but one mode. But though there may be two or more baptisms in one mode, this does not prove that there may be two or more modes in one baptism.

In another publication, Mr. H. asserts, with respect to my views of Mark vii. 4, that I see and feel the difficulties. There is no truth in the assertion ; I neither feel a difficulty in the passage, nor see one. I believe God on his own testimony, without the slightest wish for other proof to confirm his statement. His testimony I cannot but understand in the sense of the language which he employs. Instead of feeling difficulty, I am more inclined to feel contempt for the understanding that hesitates in believing the fact without the co-operation of uninspired history. This lays down, as a first principle, that nothing in Scripture is to be received, but what is proved by the history of the times. This is a false axiom : this is not essential even to uninspired history. If a modern traveller relates that a certain nation *immerses* before meat after market, we shall not think of giving a meaning to the word immerses, to suit our view of probability.

As some who make the word signify immersion, understand this passage of the immersing of the hands, Mr. H. thinks he makes us destroy each other. Now this is a species of argument which has its use, and if well used it is very powerful. Baptists have often used it with great success against their opponents. But the ground of it is not well understood, and Mr. H. entirely mistakes it. I shall not, however, at present enter into the subject, farther than the refutation of the writer in the present instance demands. Let us see, then, with what skill Mr. H. wields this sharp and powerful weapon. It is the sword of Goliath, but with Mr. H. it is in the hands of an infant : he is not able to raise it above his head. The fact on which he grounds is, that while I contend for a total *immersion* before dinner; others, on the same side, are satisfied with *immersing* their hands. How do we destroy each other ? With respect to the subject at issue we never clash. The same common truth as to the mode of baptism equally stands, whichever of us is correct as to the baptism of the Jews. We differ only about the extent of a certain Jewish baptism. As to the mode, there is no difference between us; and mode is the point at issue, and is the only thing signified by the word itself. On the meaning of the word there is no difference between me and Dr. George Campbell, whom, as to the extent of the baptism, I refute. Whether, according to him, the hands only were immersed, or, according to me, the whole body, the word itself does not testify; this must be decided by connexion.

In the same way he makes us strangle one another on Rom. vi. 1. Some Baptists, it seems, do not perceive the force of the argument which others ground on this passage. Well, is this a difference as to the meaning of the word ? At the very worst, it is only the loss of a single argument—an argument, however, which I would hold, were an angel to reject it. Must a cause fall, if all its supporters do not support it with all the same arguments ?

In like manner many Baptists contend strongly that Acts xix. does not prove that they who are spoken of as baptized into John's baptism, were on that occasion baptized into Christ, while I admit this without hesitation ;—what then ? Has this anything to do with the mode of baptism ? With respect to the points at issue, namely, the mode and subjects of baptism, there is no difference between Baptists; and these are the only essential points of unity on this question. But we can bring the charge home to our opponents with tremendous effect. Their differences are such that they really destroy each other. I have no time at present to pursue the subject, but it has been done by many. The different grounds on which a deviation from immersion is defended, effectually destroy each other. If it is *pour*, it cannot be *sprinkle;* if it is *purify*, it can be neither. The different grounds of infant baptism in like manner destroy each other. If the baptism of the one is truth, the other is falsehood.

9

SPRINKLING? POURING? IMMERSION?

REMARKS ON MR. MUNRO'S WORK, ENTITLED "MODERN IMMERSION,"&c.

SECTION I.—IN reference to my denial that in Heb. ix. 10, the *divers baptisms* include sprinklings, Mr. Munro exclaims, "Which are we to adopt,—Mr. Carson's bold denial, or the apostle's explicit affirmation?" The apostle's explicit affirmation! Does the apostle explicitly affirm what I deny? Does he, in the 13th verse, affirm that sprinklings are included in the baptisms of the 10th verse? The man who takes this for proof, need never want proof for anything which he chooses to assert.

Mr. M. denies as explicitly as I do that the word in question signifies *washing*, or *sprinkling*, or *pouring*, or *purifying;* but in all his work I cannot find that he gives it any meaning at all. He tells us, that it is applied to designate a sprinkling ordinance; but its own meaning he leaves in mystery. Surely, if it was applied to designate an ordinance, it must have had a meaning in the language which fitted it for such a designation. Of all that I have found advanced with respect to this word, this is the most rational.

SECTION II.—Mr. M.'s exploits at the Red Sea surpass every thing attempted by his predecessors. It seems, the Red Sea had no concern with the baptism spoken of 1 Cor. x. 2. The baptism took place at Mount Sinai, after the giving of the law. This extravagance is so extravagant that I am convinced it needs no refutation with respect to pædo-baptists themselves. That the people of Israel were baptized *in the sea*, is the explicit assertion of the Holy Spirit. Could sobriety of judgment assert that what is described Exod. xxiv. 3–8 is the baptism of 1 Cor. x. 2? What must be the strength of evidence on our side, when men are driven to suppositions so extravagant, to explanations so forced, in order to evade it! Ought not this to rouse pædo-baptists to inquiry? Can it be truth that requires such a defence?

The baptism 1 Cor. x. 2, Mr. M. alleges, cannot have taken place on passing the sea, because no part of the covenant had been published at that time. What had the covenant to do with the baptism?

In reference to Exod. xxiv. 3—8, Mr. Munro says, that "Moses sprinkled, baptized, or purified the altar." Where it is said that he baptized the altar? and why does he assume that sprinkling is baptizing? Is there any reasoning in this?

He tells us also, that " with that half of the blood which Moses had put in basins for the purpose, he baptized the great congregation." Where is this called a baptism? Is not this an assumption of the point in debate? Not one of the sprinklings which this writer calls baptisms is ever so designated in Scripture. A thousand folio volumes of such reasoning could not produce the smallest degree of evidence to a rational mind.

We are told by this writer, that " the baptisms and the washings included in the law were perfectly distinct ordinances." What he calls baptisms are, no doubt, perfectly distinct from the washings. But what he calls baptisms are never so called in Scripture. All he advances, then, on this head, is without reference to the point, till he proves that the sprinklings are called baptisms.

In replying to the argument, that the Holy Spirit is said to be poured out, and therefore to represent the pouring out of the Spirit, baptism must be pouring, I used very strong language. I still adhere to my argument in the strongest language in which it can be expressed. No man of common sense will ever call it in question : it is self-evident. On this point, I have satisfied all rational pædo-baptists. It requires nothing but to point out the fallacy. My argument is, THAT, AS THERE CAN BE NO MODE IN THE OPERATIONS OF THE SPIRIT, SO NO MODE IN ANY ORDINANCE CAN BE AN EMBLEM OF MODE IN THE SPIRIT ; AND THAT WHEN MODE IS ASCRIBED TO THE OPERATIONS OF THE SPIRIT, IT IS IN ACCOMMODATION TO THE EMBLEM—NOT A REPRESENTATION OF THE THING SIGNIFIED. Accordingly, different modes, and all the modes of the emblem, are ascribed to the work of the Spirit, which implies that none of them can be intended to represent mode in the thing expressed. In like manner I disposed of sprinkling as an emblem of the sprinkling of the blood of Christ. It cannot be an emblem of this, because the blood of Christ is not literally sprinkled on the believer; it is said to be sprinkled in reference to its emblem, the blood of the sacrifices. With all sober men this point must be settled for ever. All the language of Scripture referred to by this writer, ascribing mode to the Holy Spirit, is suited merely to the emblem.

Mr. M. disclaims the imputation of holding that the spirit is literally poured out. This is all I want to prove that pouring in baptism cannot be an emblem of mode in the operations of the Spirit. If there is no mode in the work of the Spirit, there can be no emblem of mode. No axiom is clearer than this. To hold that mode in baptism is emblematical as to the operations of the Spirit, necessarily makes the Godhead material. I care not whether my opponents avow or disclaim the imputation; it is necessarily contained in their doctrine. But what does the author mean when he says, that " sprinkling or pouring is the only mode which can properly represent the thing signified?" Does not this avow the very thing he disclaims? Does not this imply that there is mode in the thing signified which can be represented by a certain mode in the emblem, and properly by that mode only? If there is no mode in the thing signified, how can pouring and sprinkling, as modes, be necessary to represent it?

He tells us, that "in Scripture language sprinkling and pouring are terms of the same import." Neither in Scripture nor any where else are the terms of the same import: they express modes essentially different—as different as either of them is from immersion   But it is idle to reason with persons who can make such assertions.

Mr. M. alleges, that any "definition of the baptism of the Spirit supposes the subject to be put into the Spirit; whereas the Spirit is invariably represented as poured out, so as to be put into them." I give no definition of the baptism of the Spirit; I merely explain the figurative expression. The fact that the Spirit, in allusion to its emblem, is spoken of under other modes, does not prevent the application of the mode of immersion. Pouring, and sprinkling, and distilling, and immersing, &c., may all be applicable, because they are all suited to the emblem, and mode in the thing signified is not designed to be represented.

He says, also, that I confound the baptism of the Spirit with the effects of it. To this I reply in like manner, that I do not define the baptism of the Spirit, but explain the expression as a figure.

Mr. M. is persuaded that Rom. vi. 3, refers to the baptism of the Spirit, and not to water baptism. Baptism into Christ, he says, cannot be done with hands. As well might he say that Ananias did not speak of water baptism in addressing Paul, because he calls on Paul to wash away his sins. As well might he say that Peter does not refer to water baptism, because he says that it saves us. This conceit is perfectly groundless. When the disciples at Ephesus declared that they had not heard of the Holy Ghost, Paul asked them, "Into what then were ye baptized?" This implies that water baptism is baptism into the Spirit.

He grounds another argument on the parallel passage, Col. ii. 12. As their circumcision was not literal, he thinks their baptism could not be literal. But there is no force in this argument: they might be said to be spiritually circumcised, while they are said also to be literally baptized. The same persons might be said to be both literally and spiritually circumcised. Why, then, may they not be said to be spiritually circumcised, and literally baptized? The baptism here must be literal, because in no other is there a burial. They are not only said to have been baptized, but to have been *buried* in baptism. This must for ever settle the point, both that literal baptism is meant, and that baptism is immersion. Even were the phrase *buried in baptism*, supposed to be figurative, it equally implies that literal baptism is a burial.

That it is a literal baptism is evident also, from its having a likeness to Christ's resurrection, and implying, with respect to us, a new life. It is only in the ordinance that such likeness can exist. That it is a literal baptism is also clear, from its being called a planting in the likeness of Christ's death. Indeed, whether it is planting or anything else, still there is likeness, and likeness implies something external.

Mr. M. tells us that the word likeness is not applied to baptism, but to planting. But it is baptism that is here called a planting. Between planting, then, and baptism there must be a likeness. This baptism, or figurative planting, has a likeness to Christ's death, by its likeness to burial. Baptism is both a planting and a burial. But whatever the word *likeness* may be supposed to respect, still it equally implies that the baptism is literal.

Mr. M. tells us that the likeness is not to the burial, but to the death of Christ. But the likeness to Christ's burial is a likeness to his death; it is a likeness to him in the state of death. Besides, the phrase *buried with him in baptism*, shows that the likeness to death respects burial. But whatever the likeness respects, still it equally implies literal baptism. When he says the likeness is to the death of Christ, what is the thing that has the likeness to Christ's death? Is it not baptism? How can it have this likeness unless it is literal baptism? How can it have this likeness, but as death is implied in burial?

Like others, Mr. M. insists on the want of resemblance between baptism and burial. The resemblance is perfectly sufficient as an emblem; and it was not intended to be a dramatic representation. But what does he mean when he tells us that Joseph did not dig a pit in the rock, nor cover the dead body of Christ? If this has any bearing, it must be to prove that Christ was not buried, and that there is no burial in baptism. For the purpose of this figure, it is quite enough that baptism is a burial in any way. Does not the experience of every day show us that being covered with water, in any way, may be called a burial? In an account of a shipwreck it is said, "Boils appeared on all the seamen's legs at once, and they were benumbed by being continually *buried* in water." Here is a burial in water, when the water rose on the baptized from a leak. The seamen did not dig a pit in a rock, for this burial.

With respect to Enon, Mr. M. alleges that much water was as necessary for dipping as for sprinkling. This observation is not very profound. Much water is not necessary for the immersion of a few persons; but for the immersion of multitudes very important. The water of a fountain would soon become unfit for baptism, if used for the multitudes baptized by John. Whether the phrase denotes one collection or many collections of water, is quite immaterial.

He asks: "If baptism must be administered by immersion, why did not Christ or the apostles ordain the construction of baptismal cisterns?" What an argument! We might as well ask, if sprinkling had been appointed, why was not the construction of basins ordained by the apostles? Why ordain the construction of baptisteries, when all means of immersion are equal? What must be the degree of prejudice and blindness in the mind, that sees an argument in this!

He tells us, that the much water was necessary for other purposes to the multitudes who attended John. To this I reply: 1. The cause assigned is not known to exist. It is not in evidence, that the multitudes remained with John any length of time. 2. Had the cause existed, it is insufficient to produce the effect. The multitudes might have remained with John days and nights, though there had not been a single fountain. Might they not have brought their water as well as their victuals?

3. The cause alleged by us is expressly mentioned in the passage: John was baptizing in that place, *because there was there much water.* The much water, then, was for the baptism. **4.** It was also for the purpose of being baptized, that they came to this place of water.

With respect to the eunuch, he says, "Among the myriads of baptisms of which we read in the Acts of the Apostles, with the single exception of that of the eunuch, there is not a hint about going to or from any pool or river." Does any rational man expect that every account of baptism will record every circumstance in the transaction? One example is perfectly sufficient. He demands an example of going from any chapel or house to the river, or of going to any font of water in a house. Such an example is not necessary. If they went to the water, in any case in which a few drops of water could be brought to them, sprinkling could not have been the mode. But they not only went to the water, but both of them went into the water, for it is on record that they came *out of* the water. I have, again and again, proved that the preposition signifies *out of,* not *from.*

I had said, that there is not a spot in which a human being can be found, in which a few drops of water cannot be found. Mr. M. alleges the fact of great tracts of country being totally destitute of water. Is this an answer to me? Does any human being reside in a country, where a few drops of water cannot be found? If the eunuch travelled through such a country, it is self-evident that he had a supply of water with him.

I speak of the retinue of the eunuch. That such a man as the eunuch took a retinue, needs not to be proved by record; it is self-evident. But for my purpose, there is no need of a retinue. One servant will suffice; and it is expressly on evidence that he had attendants: he commanded to stop the chariot. Yet both Philip and the eunuch went not only to the water, but both of them into the water, which lunacy itself would not allege as necessary for sprinkling.

Mr. M. says that "they went down to the water, because they needed water, and because the water would not come up to them." There is neither wit nor strength in this remark. Do all men go to the water who need water. The water would have come up to them, had a few drops been sufficient. The eunuch could have commanded the water to come up, as well as the chariot to stand still.

He says, that "I would persuade my readers that my opponents maintain that the Greek word signifies to pour, but that I know they do no such thing." I do not represent all my opponents as maintaining that the word signifies to pour, for I have shown that some of them think that it signifies to sprinkle; and that there is an endless diversity of opinion among them, as to the meaning of the word. But is there any one who does not know that many of them make the word signify to pour? But what does he make the word signify? This he does not tell us. Of all the absurdities that I have met in criticism, this is the most absurd— a treatise to ascertain the meaning of a word in an ordinance; yet in all the treatise there is no meaning assigned to the word!

He says, that he can assign a probable reason for the selection of this word, as the designation of the ordinance. The reason is, "Dipping is included in any scriptural baptism." Does not this take for granted that the word signifies to dip? But if the word signifies to dip, the person baptized must be dipped. The baptism is not the dipping of the head of the baptized, or water made to sprinkle the baptized; but the dipping of the person who receives the ordinance. The priest, indeed, dipped his finger in the blood of the sacrifice, in order to sprinkle it; but this was not called the dipping of the altar.

Mr. M. asks where I got the information, that the eunuch did not ask for baptism till he saw the water in which it might be performed? But is it not obvious to the smallest degree of discernment that I speak from the testimony of the documents, and not as regards abstract possibility? Besides, there is positive evidence from the passage, that the eunuch considered baptism impossible, till the appearance of this water. It is equally evident that this is the first time he asked for baptism; for had he asked before, he would have got an answer that would have prevented this question. In every point of view, then, the author's objection manifests as great a degree of captiousness, as want of penetration.

10

IS IMMERSION BAPTISM?

REMARKS ON MR. THORN'S "MODERN IMMERSION NOT CHRISTIAN BAPTISM"

THE work of Mr. Thorn discovers very great industry, and an extensive acquaintance with books on both sides of the question, as to the meaning of the word in dispute. He manifests that, if the cause which he has espoused is not successful in proof, it has not failed for want of zeal and study. He has raked together all that lexicons, concordances, and the other usual resources of second-hand critics, could afford; and he has enriched the treatise by long contributions of original trifling. There is no science in his criticism, no philosophy in the principles on which he assigns meaning. His interpretation is extravagant and wild beyond almost any of his fellow-labourers. Yet there is one thing in him with which I am well pleased;—he appears perfectly convinced of the truth of the point which he labours to prove. He does not, like some, labour to produce confession; as if the object were gained when decision is rendered doubtful or impossible. He writes like a man in earnest, and I cannot but respect sincerity even in its errors. As a defender of sprinkling, it is fortunate for Mr. Thorn that he was not acquainted with the philosophy of language, and the laws which operate in varying the meaning of words. The sounder a writer's first principles are, under the greater necessity will he be to give evidence when he defends error. Where a Porson would fail, a Thorn would triumph. His examples are fully met in my work, and I need not waste time in running over the same ground in reference to his interpretations.

As a specimen of his criticism, I shall produce a few short examples.

As an objection to our meaning of the word in certain passages, he alleges (p. 124) that it is "partial dipping." Would any critic speak thus? Would any man who knows anything of language, expect that the word itself was to determine whether the dipping were total or partial?

He tells us in the same page, that "the moistening of the bread and wetting of the finger are the ultimate intentions of the several expressions, and not the present mode of doing it." When I say, *Dip* your pitcher in the fountain, is not filling of the pitcher the intention of the *dipping*? Is such an objection to be dignified with the name of criticism?

He tells us (p. 128) that "it cannot be asserted, that it is expressive of one person dipping another." Would any writer, would any man of ordinary acquaintance with language, expect that any word should express this? Whether in baptism the believer is to dip himself, or to be dipped by another, is not to be known from any word signifying immersion, but from other criticism.

He makes the same complaint with respect to the twofold action of sinking and raising. Does any one pretend that the raising is expressed by the word?

He alleges, (page 139,) that according to us, the verb with the preposition in its syntax must express a double dipping. Was ever ignorance so consummate under the guise of knowledge? Will not the objection apply equally to the English phrase *dip in* or *into?* Does it not apply with greater plausibility to *immerse in* or *into?* There is *in* accurately expressed in the verb, while it is repeated in the preposition. Are we obliged to meet such objection as criticism? Are writers of this stamp worthy of our rebuke?

11

PURIFICATION OR BAPTISM?

BAPTISM NOT PURIFICATION; IN REPLY TO PRESIDENT BEECHER

SECTION I.—Mr. Beecher, President of the College of Illinois, America, has lately written on the import of the word *baptismos*, undertaking to prove that it refers not to mode at all, but signifies purification in general. Consequently, while we are on both sides of the question wrong, we are still right. We are wrong in believing that mode is designated, but we are on both sides right, because any mode of the religious application of water is baptism. This is the happy theory by which harmony is to be effected on this much and long-controverted subject.

To much of the former part of the work I can have no possible objection, because it is a mere echo of my own philological doctrines, illustrated with different examples. In a work controverting the conclusions which I have drawn in my treatise on baptism, it surely was very unnecessary to prove that words may have a secondary meaning, wandering very far from their original import. Can any writer be pointed out who has shown this more fully than I have done? I do not question this principle: I have laid it down for him as a foundation. All I require is proof of the existence of the secondary meaning, and proof of the existence of the secondary meaning which he alleges. Had he given this, I would admit such secondary meaning; but would still show that the word in reference to the rite appointed by Christ, has its name from the primary meaning of this word. Mr. B. has done nothing of all this. He has not proved that the word, in reference to the ordinance of Christ, signifies *purification;* he has not proved that in any reference it signifies *purification;* he has not proved that it has any secondary signification at all. His dissertation is no more to critical deduction than Waverley or Kenilworth is to history. Indeed the relation is not so true: it wants that verisimilitude which is to be found in the novels of the illustrious Scott. To the ignorant there is an appearance of philosophy and learning; but sound criticism will have little difficulty in taking the foundation from under the edifice which he has laboured to erect.

The first argument which he alleges to prove that *baptismos* signifies purification, is drawn from John iii. 25. "In John iii. 25, *katharismos* is used as synonymous with *baptismos;* and the *usus loquendi*, as it regards the religious rite, is clearly decided. The facts of the case are these,

ver. 22, 23. John and Jesus were baptizing, one in Judea, the other in Enon, near to Salim, and in such circumstances that to an unintelligent observer there would seem to be a rivalry between the claims of the two. The disciples of John might naturally feel that Jesus was intruding into the province of their master: they might even believe John to be the Messiah, and thus give rise to the sect that held that belief. On this point a dispute arose between the disciples of John and the Jews, (or a Jew, as many copies read) verse 25. They come to John and state the case, verse 26: ' Rabbi, he that was with thee beyond Jordan, to whom thou barest witness, *behold, the same baptizeth, and all men come to him;'* plainly implying that in so doing he was improperly interfering with the claims of John. John in reply, verse 27—31, disclaims all honour except that bestowed on him by God, of being the forerunner of the Messiah, and rejoices to decrease in order that he may increase—thus justifying the course which was so offensive to his disciples, and settling the dispute in favour of the claims of Christ. The argument from these facts is this : The dispute in question was plainly a specific dispute concerning baptism, as practised by Jesus and John, and not a general dispute on the subject of purification at large; so that *zetesis peri baptismou* is the true sense; and if it had been so written, the passage would have been regarded by all as perfectly plain. But instead of *baptismou,* John has used *katharismou,* because the sense is entirely the same. In other words ' a question concerning baptism,' and ' a question concerning purification,' were at that time modes of expression perfectly equivalent; that is, *baptismos* is a synonyme of *katharismos.*"

To this I reply, 1. Mr. B. says, "On this point a dispute arose." On what point? As I understand the author, it is with respect to the conflicting claims of John and Jesus. This is the obvious reference, and this is confirmed as his meaning, by his afterwards saying that John settled this dispute in favour of the claims of Christ. Now this is not at all the point to which the question at issue between the disciples of John and the Jews had reference. That question was about *purifying,* and not at all about the claims of John and Jesus. For anything that appears in the document, the Jews might never have heard of Jesus.

2. The author says, " They come to John and state the case." They did not state to John the case concerning purification; they stated another case quite different. What they stated to John was an expression of surprise that another person was baptizing, and especially that he was more successful than John himself. As this statement was for the purpose of eliciting a reply from John, I have no objection that it shall be called a question, though not so in form. But if it is a question, it is one different from that at issue between the disciples of John and the Jews. John replies to this question, but says nothing about purification, because nothing with respect to it was submitted to him.

3. Mr. B. says that " the dispute in question was plainly a specific dispute concerning baptism as practised by John and Jesus." The dispute had no relation to the baptism of John and Jesus; the dispute does not imply the existence of the baptism of Jesus, nor of himself.

4. The author tells us that it was not "a general dispute on the sub-

ject at large." The dispute was a dispute on the subject of purification generally. This does not admit dispute with respect to any who submit to the assertion of the document. *Katharismos* is not a species of purification, but purification without reference to species. Mr. B. assumes that *katharismos* is the appropriated name of the rite of baptism. This is not only a groundless, but a false assumption. In early church history, it came with a multitude of other words and phrases to be applied to baptism, but at this period of its history it had no such application. At this period, to speak among the Jews of baptism under the appropriated name *katharismos*, would be to speak unintelligibly. Mr. B. mistakes the meaning of *katharismos* as well as of *baptismos*. It could not come to designate baptism specifically on any other principle than that of appropriation, by which, though general in its original extent, it might be limited by use If assumption would do the business, Mr. B would prove his point.

5. The writer tells us here that the phrase *a question about purification*, is in sense the same as if it had been said, *a question about baptism*. I have shown that this is false. But in addition to this I remark, that even if the word *baptism* itself had been used instead of *purification*, it would not have referred to a dispute concerning the conflicting claims of John and Jesus. A question about baptism, and a question about the conflicting claims of two persons engaged in baptizing, are surely two very different questions. This confusion of ideas does not argue well for the perspicacity of the antagonist with whom I am now about to engage. Even on this supposition the dispute between the disciples of John and the Jews about baptism, would have been a different matter from that submitted to John, and to which nothing in philosophy at all applies.

6. Mr. B. makes the general word *katharismos* specific, in conformity to the word *baptizo*, and the specific word *baptizo* he makes general, in conformity to the word *katharismos*, so that in fact he makes each of the words both general and specific. Why does he consider *katharismos* specific? Because it here, he thinks, refers to the specific rite of baptism. Why does he make *baptizo* here signify purification in general? Because he thinks it to be a synonyme of *katharizo*. Does not this make each of the words both general and specific, at the same time? Is this philological? This is critical legerdemain.

So confident is the writer that he has succeeded on this part of the subject, that he adds, "The only mode of escaping this result is to say, that as immersion in water involves purification, and is a kind of purification, so it may have given rise to a question on the subject of purification at large : but to this I reply, that the whole scope of the passage forbids such an idea. The question was not general, but specific, being caused by the concurrence of two claims to baptize ; and so was the reply of John."

It is no part of my duty to show the process which led from one of those questions to the other ; this it might be impossible to ascertain without any injury to my cause. But nothing can be more natural than that a question about purification should be suggested by a rite that was an emblem of purification, and that this should lead to a comparison of the baptism of John and of Jesus. But I will not deign to allege this in argument: my business is with the document before me. Anything expressed or necessarily implied, I will meet; but I sternly refuse to know anything but what is in evidence.

But what sort of a reply is this which the author gives to the argument which he professes to meet? The question, he says, is not general, but specific. The question is expressly stated as general, and not specific; for it is a question about *katharismos*, which is *purification* without regard to species. The word is as general as is purification, the corresponding word in English. "It was caused," he says, "by the concurrence of two claims to baptize." It was not caused by the concurrence of two claims to baptize; for these claims are never mentioned with regard to the dispute. If we had not the document in our hands, we should be led to think, from Mr. B.'s representation, that the dispute was between the disciples of John and the disciples of Jesus, with respect to conflicting claims between their masters.

"Moreover," continues Mr. B., "to assume a general dispute on purification renders the whole scope of the passage obscure; as is evident from the fact, that those who have not seen that in this case *katharismos* is a synonyme of *baptismos*, are much perplexed to see what a dispute on purification in general has to do with the facts of the case."

Assume! Who is it that makes assumptions? We assume nothing in the whole controversy. That the dispute was about purification, and not about a specific rite of purification, is in express evidence from the word. And what necessity is there to show how the statement to John, and John's answer, bear on the subject of purification, when that statement and that answer never glance at the question of purification?

"The origin of the dispute, from the concurrence of two claims to baptize," says the author, "is obviously indicated by the particle *oun*, in ver. 25, showing undeniably that the events just narrated gave rise to the question." How can any particle in the twenty-fifth verse indicate the origin of the dispute, from the concurrence of two claims to baptize, when previously to that verse there is no mention of such concurrence? If the question arose from the events just narrated, how could it arise from a concurrence of conflicting claims? No doubt the dispute about purification originated in the baptism of John; but this does not imply that baptism signifies purification, nor that purification signifies baptism.

"And what reason is there," says Mr. B., "for denying this conclusion? None but the fear of the result." It is not so, President Beecher: fear of the result never in a single instance prevented me from admitting a sound argument. I do not fear the result; for truth is my object, wherever it may lie. But in this instance I can have no temptation to fear the result, because I could admit that *purification* here refers to baptism specifically, and still defeat President Beecher. He has laboured in vain; he builds on a false first principle. He assumes that if two words refer to the same ordinance, they must be identical in meaning. Nothing is more unfounded—palpably unfounded. There are situations in which two words may be interchanged at the option of the writer, while they are not perfectly synonymous. They may so far agree that they may be equally fitted to fill a situation, while each has a distinct meaning. This is so obvious a truth, that I am perfectly astonished that it should lie hid from the President of the College of Illinois. This is a fact that lies on the very surface of philosophy; there is hardly a page of writing in which it might not be illustrated. The varied designations given to the ordinance of baptism by the ancients, fully manifest the truth of this observation. Baptism they called *regeneration*, yet they did not consider that the word *baptism* and the word *regeneration* were identical in meaning. *Baptism* was the name of the rite from its mode, *regeneration* was the effect produced by the observance of the rite. They called baptism *renewing, renovation*, or *restoration*, for a like reason; but they did not understand the word baptism to signify any of these. Without exception, they all considered the word to mean immersion, while they gave it other names from its nature, effects, &c. They called baptism *sanctification*, because they supposed persons to be sanctified by it; not because they considered the two words as synonymous. They called baptism *illumination*, and the baptized they called *the illuminated;* yet they did not understand the word baptism as signifying *illumination*. Illumination was the effect of the rite. They called baptism *consecration*, yet they did not do so because they considered the word to have this meaning, but because the rite had this effect. They called baptism *initiation*, because *initiation* was effected by the rite, not because it was signified by the word baptism. They called baptism the *laver* or *washing;* not because they considered the word to signify this, but because washing was effected by immersion in pure water. They called baptism *the anointing;* because, in their view, persons are anointed with the Spirit in baptism; not because baptism signifies *anointing*. They called baptism the *gift* or *grace;* yet they did not suppose that the word baptism denoted *gift* or *grace*. They spoke of baptism as the seal, yet they did not understand the word baptism as signifying *seal*. They called baptism *purification;* yet they did not on that account, with President Beecher, understand the word baptism as signifying *purification*. Baptism was an immersion which produced *purification*. Would he deserve the name of a philologist, who would say, that the word baptism is identical in signification with all these words, and that all these words are identical in signification with each other?

I might illustrate my doctrine by the various names which are given to the followers of Christ. They are called *Christians, disciples, believers, saints, &c.* Are these words identical in meaning? Does not each of these names designate the persons in a different manner?

The very case in hand may be verified in our own language. When it is asked, what is the name of the child? it may sometimes be answered, " it is not yet baptized." Are we from this to conclude that the word baptism is supposed to mean *the giving of a name?* This is not implied; the thing implied is that the name is given in baptism. In like manner, a vast variety of names is given to the rite of baptism, not implying that they are synonymous with the word, but that they are designations of the same ordinance.

The English word *immerse* itself, according to Mr. B.'s philology, may be made to signify *cleanse*. The surgeon, after an operation, says, "cleanse the instrument." The assistant immerses it in water. Immerse, then, signifies to cleanse.

Sprinkle may on the same principle be made to signify *to purify*. Purification is effected by sprinkling, therefore sprinkling signifies purification. In Heb. ix. 22, the same thing that is called purging with blood, is in the preceding case called sprinkling with blood. Does it not follow from Mr. B.'s philology, that sprinkling means purging? But is it not obvious to every child, that sprinkling designates the *mode* of applying the blood, and purging the *effect* of the blood so applied? Mr. B., then, has failed in every point. He has laboured to prove that *katharismos*, John iii. 25, refers specifically to baptism, as practised by John and Jesus. His proof I have demolished. He assumes that if *katharismos* here refers to baptism, the words must be identical in meaning. This I have shown to be a gross fallacy.

SECTION II.—The next argument by which Mr. B. endeavours to prove that *baptismos* signifies *purification*, is taken from Malachi. "This view alone," says he, "fully explains the existing expectation that the Messiah would baptize. That the Messiah should immerse, is nowhere foretold; but that he should *purify*, is often and fully predicted: but especially is this foretold in that last and prominent prophecy of Malachi, (iii. 1—3,) which was designed to fill the eye of the mind of the nation, until he came. He is here represented to the mind in all his majesty and power, but amid all other ideas that of purifying is most prominent. He was above all things to purify and purge, and that with power so great, that few could endure the fiery day. Who may abide the day of his coming, and who shall stand when he appeareth?

This is so destitute of all appearance of a bearing on the subject, that it deserves no attention. It is answer sufficient to this allegation that this prophecy could have been perfectly fulfilled, had no rite of purification, in any mode, ever been appointed. It requires more than the patience of Job, to be able to mention such an argument without expressing strong feelings. Could not Christ have been a *Purifier*, though he had instituted neither baptism nor the Lord's supper? His being said then to be a *Purifier*, does not imply that a certain rite implying purification, must be called *purification*. May not a rite import purification, though *purification* is not its name? Even if it had been foretold by Malachi that the Messiah should appoint a rite of purification, that rite might have been designated, not *purification*, but have had its name from its mode, or a thousand other circumstances. It might have been called *immersion*, or *sprinkling*, or *effusion*, according to the mode appointed; as it might have been designated from any one of a multitude of other relations. Circumcision denoted purification, yet it had its name from the external operation. The passover had its name on the same principle. This argument manifests such a want of discrimination, and a confusion of things which differ, that the mind on which it has force, must be essentially deficient in those powers that qualify for the discussion of critical questions.

"Suppose, now, the word *baptizo* to mean as I affirm," says the author, "the whole nation are expecting the predicted purifier; all at once the news goes forth that a great purifier has appeared, and that all men flock to him and are purified in the Jordan. How natural the inference! The great purifier so long foretold, has at last appeared, and how natural the embassy of the priests and Levites to inquire, Who art thou? And when he denied that he was the Messiah, or either of his expected attendants, how natural the inquiry, 'Why purifiest thou, then? It is his work—of him it is foretold, why dost thou intrude into his place and do his work?'"

I might with perfect safety admit that on John's appearance, the report went forth that a great purifier had appeared. For if he was a great *immerser*, he was a great *purifier*, as immersion was for the purpose of emblematical purification. He might, from the administration· of this ordinance, have been called a great purifier, while the name of the ordinance was *immersion*, or *sprinkling*, or anything whatever. As a matter of fact, however, the news did not go forth that a great *purifier*, but a great *immerser* had appeared; and it is not said that all men came and were purified by him in Jordan, but that they were immersed. The question of the priests and Levites was as apposite, on the supposition that the word *baptizo* signified to *immerse*, or *sprinkle*, or *pour*, as if it signified to *purify*; because whatever was the mode and whatever was the name, the nature of the ordinance implied purification. There is no evidence that a general expectation prevailed that the Messiah should baptize, or use any rite of purification; and had there been such an expectation, and even a prophecy on which to found it, the fact could make no difference. The question put to John, on the supposition that he was not the Messiah, was not founded either on the name or the nature of the rite, but on his employing a new rite. If he was not the Messiah, or at least Elias, or the prophet, they judged it improper for him to introduce a new baptism. It was not with the name of the rite they quarrelled. Does Mr. B. imagine that had the name of the rite been immersion, the question of the priests and Levites would have been precluded? Such reasoning is perfectly an astonishment to me. I have greater difficulty in conceiving how it can have force on any mind, than I have in refuting it. How can any discriminating person think that the priests and Levites objected to John's baptism on the ground that to use this rite was to intrude into the work of the Messiah, when on the very question it is admitted that the thing might be done by Elias or the prophet? Is it not astonishing that gentlemen in eminent situations, will risk the character of their understanding by pouring forth such crudities? It is painful for me to use the knife so freely : but I must, for ·the sake of the Christian public, find out the disease under which my patient labours. It is better that one delinquent should suffer, than that a multitude should be drawn into error by his transgression.

"In view of these facts," says the writer, "I do not hesitate to believe most fully, that the idea which came up before the mind of the Jews when the words *Ioannes o Baptistes* were used, was not John the immerser, or John the dipper, but John the purifier, a name peculiarly appropriate to him as a reformer—as Puritan was to our ancestors, and for the same reason."

In view of these facts! Shall he by sleight of hand be allowed to convert his suppositions into facts? What are the facts? Are we with the child to take his dreams for realities? There is not in all the references one fact that will bear the conclusion.

But there is an inconsistency in this specimen of philology: it makes the title of John originate in the administration of a rite of purification, yet its adaptation to him is grounded on his being a reformer, for the same reason that our ancestors were called Puritans. Now, if John was the *purifier* as the administrator of a rite, he was not a *purifier* as a reformer. If he was a purifier as a reformer, he would have been a purifier had he administered no baptism at all. There is great confusion in the ideas of this writer. If John was called *the purifier* on account of the rite which he administered, he was not so called as a Puritan. This is my philology.

SECTION III.—Mr. B.'s next argument is, "The contrast made by John between his own baptism and that of Christ, illustrates and confirms the same view."

Without adverting to Acts ii. 1, which is evidently a fulfilment of John's declaration referred to, the phrase *immersed in the Spirit*, as referring to the ordinary work of the Spirit, is perfectly analogous to *steeping the senses in forgetfulness*, with which all are acquainted; and the contrast between the immersion of the rite, and the sanctification of the Spirit, is exactly on the same principle with " Be not drunk with wine, but be filled with the Spirit." The abundance of the Spirit in sanctification is contrasted with the abundance of wine in the drunkard. If we may be said to be *filled with the Spirit*, in contrast with the drunkard filled with wine, may we not be said to be *immersed in the Spirit*, in contrast with the immersion in water in the rite of baptism? The contrast is obvious and just. Is it not sometimes said of persons distinguished for humanity and kindness, that their souls are steeped in the milk of human nature? There is no more incongruity in *immersing* a person in the Spirit, than there is in steeping a soul in milk. Such arguments and such objections are mere trifling.

" This sense," continues Mr. B., " is never transferred to the mind, in any language, so far as I know, to indicate anything like the effects of the agency of the Holy Spirit.

Were this true, it is nothing to the purpose; but having by the use of the language found that the word has this meaning, and no other, the example in question is an instance in which it is applied to the Holy Spirit. Mr. B. has adopted some of my philological doctrines. I will give him another lesson, which will prevent him from again alleging such an objection. It is this: Metaphor is not bound to find examples to justify its particular figures; but may indulge itself wherever it finds resemblance. It gives words a new application, but does not invest them with a new meaning. It is not, then, subject to the law of literal language, which, for the sense of every word, needs the authority of use.

This I have established in my Treatise on the Figures of Speech, in opposition to the common doctrine of rhetoricians. With respect to the point in hand, I would maintain my ground, if a single other example of the figurative use of this word could not be produced. Any word may be used figuratively in any view in which there is likeness. This argument of Mr. B. is perfectly the same with that of Dr. Wiseman in proof of transubstantiation. He admits that the phrases, *this is my body*, and *eat my flesh*, may be used figuratively; but if they are used figuratively, they are always used in a bad sense He challenges his opponents to show an instance in which it is otherwise. Now this sophism has, in my doctrine of the metaphor, a complete answer. Metaphors are not bound by the law of literal language : they need not the sanction of use. A writer may use as many as are just in resemblance; and the more original they are, they are the more meritorious.

But what shall we think of the philologist, who says, "When the agent is spiritual, the object spiritual, and the means spiritual, and the end purity, immersion is out of the question?" Must I dignify such trifling with refutation ? When God says, *I will pour out my Spirit*, is not the agent spiritual, the object spiritual, and the means spiritual, and the end purity ? Shall we, then, blaspheme the word of God, and say, *pouring* is out of the question ? Literal *pouring* and *immersing* are out of the question, not figurative *pouring* and *immersing*. If one mode of employing water may be figuratively applied to the Spirit, what will prevent another mode from being applied ? Ignorant persons in reading Mr. B.'s work will think that he is a deep philosopher, and that he is a profound philologist. But the smallest degree of perspicacity will enable any one to see that his philosophy is very shallow sophistry. I have no wish to be severe ; but no man ought with impunity to be allowed to trifle so egregiously with the disciples of Christ, and with the awful commandments of the eternal Jehovah.

The author thinks that his view is confirmed by comparing the language of John with the passage from Malachi, and refers to the word *diakathariei*. But how could it escape him that *the purging of the floor* refers not to baptism at all in any view ? Indeed, it refers not even to the work of the Spirit in sanctification, but is the separating of the chaff from the wheat. But I will for a moment indulge him in his whim. Let this *purging* be baptism ; may it not be *immersion* in mode, and *purging* as an emblem ? The language of Malachi and the purification of John would equally accord with any meaning that may be assigned to the word baptism. I have never found a greater want of discrimination in any writer.

Section IV.—Mr. B. deduces another argument, from 1 Cor. xii. 13. In this passage he tells us, "The Holy Spirit is directly said to baptize, and in this case all external acts are of course excluded, and purify is the only appropriate sense: 'For by one Spirit are we all baptized into one body, and have been all made to drink into one Spirit.'" Now can anything be more extravagantly idle than this? When the Holy Spirit is said to be *poured out* by God, are not all external acts equally

excluded? Are we, then, to say that *cheo* does not signify to *pour?*
Believers are said to have their hearts *sprinkled* from an evil conscience.
All external acts are out of the question. Shall we, then, say that
rantizo does not signify to *sprinkle?* Believers are said to wash their
robes, and to make them white in the blood of the Lamb. All external
acts are out of the question. Are we, then, to say that *pluno* does not
signify to *wash?* Am I to war eternally against nonsense? Even the
very examples alleged by himself from Chrysostom, p. 23, refute him.
Is there any literal immersion in the phrases *immersed in cares, immersed
in sins, immersed in business?*

" But this baptism," says Mr. B., " is as much a real work of the
Spirit, as the causing to drink into one Spirit, which is not external, but
internal and real." Who doubts it? But how can he be so blind as
not to perceive that though " causing to drink of the Spirit," is an internal work of the Spirit, yet *drink of the Spirit* is as much a figure
relating to an external action, as is *immerse by the Spirit?* If believers
are here said to be *immersed by the Spirit,* they are also said to be made
to *drink* by the same Spirit. Is not *drinking* as much an external
action as *immersing?* If we may figuratively *drink,* may we not figuratively *be immersed?* The writer has so little perspicacity as to argue
against a figurative meaning with respect to the word *immerse,* by the
very authority of a like figurative meaning with regard to drink. If
there is *spiritual drinking,* may there not be *spiritual immersing?* But
we have not yet done with Mr. B.'s exploits in figurative language. He
says that the *drinking* here referred to is not external, but internal and
real. According to this philosophy, *literal drinking* is not *real drinking.*

" To immerse in water," he tells us, " is not the work of the Spirit."
Where is it said, Mr. B., that the Holy Spirit baptizes in water? And
is it the work of the Spirit to *pour himself* out on believers literally?
Is it the work of the Spirit literally to *sprinkle* the heart? Such cavilling is unworthy of a candid mind and a sound understanding.

Mr. B. founds another argument on the relation which the words
baptize and *purify* have to the forgiveness of sins. " *Baptizo* and
katharizo," says he, " are so similarly used in connexion with the forgiveness of sins, as decidedly to favour the idea that they are in a
religious sense synonymous." This is philological mathematics; and if
there is no error in the statement, or in the process, it is the evidence of
an axiom.—Two quantities that are equal to a third are equal to one
another. But a mere breath will destroy this mathematical bubble. It
is not as words that *baptize* and *purify* agree with *forgiveness of sins:*
for neither *baptism* nor *purification* is as a word identical in meaning
with forgiveness of sins. Baptism is connected with the forgiveness of
sins, not from its name, but from the nature and import of the rite. If
baptism in its import is essentially connected with forgiveness of sins, it
will have the same relation to purification, whatever be its name.

Faith is essentially connected with the forgiveness of sins, as well as
purification. Is *faith purification?* *Holiness* is essentially connected
with the forgiveness of sins, as well as faith. Is *holiness faith?* *Repentance* is essentially connected with the forgiveness of sins as well as

purification. Is *repentance purification?* On the same principle Unitarians allege that forgiveness of sins, in reference to Christ, is synonymous with *healing diseases.*

But it is strange to astonishment that President Beecher has not perceived that baptism would have the same connexion with the forgiveness of sins, whatever might have been the word employed as its designation. If the nature of the rite imports purification, though its name is *immersion,* has it not perfectly the same relation to the forgiveness of sins, as if its name were *purification?* Take any of the names assigned to it by the ancients, and you will still have the same connexion with the forgiveness of sins. But does each of these words signify purification? If baptism is called *regeneration,* it is connected with the forgiveness of sins. Must the word *regeneration* on that account signify *purification?* This argument proceeds on an amazing want of discrimination. Many things essentially connected with the forgiveness of sins are entirely different from one another. Baptism is a rite emblematical of purification; but this does not imply that its name must signify purification. The passover was a rite which was an emblem of atonement through the blood of Christ, or if you will, of purification. Does this imply that the word passover signifies purification or atonement? Whether the rite of baptism is called *pouring,* or *sprinkling,* or *immersing,* or *popping,* or *purifying,* or *consecrating,* or *initiating,* or *regeneration,* &c. &c., it has the same relation to the forgiveness of sins. The blood of Christ cleanses from all sin: baptism emblematically cleanses from sin: the blood of Christ, then, and the emblematical meaning of baptism, have the same relations to the forgiveness of sins. Does it follow that the phrases, blood of Christ and the word baptism, are synonymous?

Mr. B. gives us a dissertation on purification, which is no more to the purpose than a treatise on logarithms. He then tells us, " between immersion and the forgiveness of sins no such associations had ever been established." Does not the writer here take for granted the very thing in dispute? He set out with saying that *baptizo* and *katharizo* are similarly used with respect to the forgiveness of sins: now he says that immersion has no such connexion. But if *baptizo* has such a connexion, *immerse* must have the same connexion, as it is the only proper translation of the word that has this connexion. Whatever connexion *baptizo* has with the forgiveness of sins, *immerse* has the same connexion.

There is another false principle at the bottom of this remark: it supposes that if baptism is connected with the forgiveness of sins, its name must denote this connexion. It supposes also, that if a word has the same connexion with the forgiveness of sins with another word, it must have the same meaning with that word. This is another false principle. Circumcision was connected with the forgiveness of sins in the same manner as purification; but did the word circumcision denote either purification or forgiveness of sins? It was the nature of the rite of which circumcision was the name, which indicated purification, and was connected with the forgiveness of sins. It is the water in baptism that indicates purification, not the name of the rite. Immersion is an emblem of the believer's communion and oneness with Christ, in his death, *burial*, and resurrection. If mere purification was designated by baptism, *sprinkling* or *pouring* might have been used as well as *immerse.* But immersion represents the whole spiritual body of Christ as *dying* with him, *buried* with him, *risen* with him. As members of the body of Christ, they have done and suffered whatever Christ has done and suffered for them. True views of the import of baptism are essentially connected with clear views of the Gospel.

"Now if any word," says Mr. B., "is found to sustain the same relations as *katharizo* to the same idea, forgiveness of sins, we have reason to think that it is used in the same sense." Here is a philological axiom; but it is a philological sophism. First, it assumes that it is *baptismos* as a word, that is, that it is the meaning of the word, that has the supposed relation to the forgiveness of sins. But *baptismos* has this relation only as designatory of an ordinance, which in its nature implies purification. *Baptismos* has this relation to the forgiveness of sins, only as it refers to the rite of baptism.

Secondly, the conclusion is false, even on the ground on which it proceeds. Two words may have the same relation to the forgiveness of sins, yet not be identical in meaning. *Faith, repentance, regeneration,* &c., have the same relation to the forgiveness of sins, yet they are very far from being identical. If each of the words signified forgiveness of sins, they must all indeed have the same signification; but none of these signifies forgiveness of sins. This is a childish fallacy.

He concludes this argument with the following deduction: "Hence, as *baptizo* has the same extent of application with *katharizo*, and as it stands in the same relations with it to the forgiveness of sins, it is highly probable that it has the same sense." Here, again, he assumes the point in debate. Has he found that *baptizo* has the same extent of application with *katharizo?* If this is in evidence, what is the dispute? It has not the same extent of application; for it applies to no purifications but such as were immersions. His business is to prove that it has such an extent of application—not to assume this as a ground of argument.

But the author is very modest; having assumed that *baptizo* has the same extent of application with *katharizo*, instead of bearing down on me with all the force of an axiom, he is contented with claiming a high probability. What! highly probable! If the words are of the same extent in application, they are perfectly identical in meaning. What is sameness of sense, but sameness of extent of application? Not only has Mr. B. failed in proving his point by this argument, but I maintain that on such ground it is impossible to prove the meaning of a word. No sound philologist would ever think of availing himself of such are source.

Mr. B.'s next argument is, that "the account of baptism given by Josephus, a contemporary Jew, is perfectly in accordance with this view."

The account which Josephus gives of the baptism of John in no respect confirms the view of President Beecher. Why did he not produce his document? Is he to decide as a judge? Ought he not as a lawyer to exhibit his documents and his statutes, reasoning from their necessary import? Josephus represents John as exhorting the people, practising justice towards each other; and piety towards God, to come to *immersion;*

declaring that the immersing would be acceptable to God, when done, not in deprecation of the punishment of any sins, but for the *purification* or *lustration* of the body,—the soul being previously purified by righteousness. Josephus, as might be expected, gives a very false view of the object of John's baptism; but with respect to the meaning of its name he could not be mistaken. Instead of representing this name as signifying purification in its meaning, he represents the object of it to be purification. They come to baptism for the lustration (*epi agneia*) of the body. Does not this imply that *baptism* is one thing, and *lustration* another? Mr. B. confounds a thing with its effect. Baptism is the name of the rite from its mode : lustration is its effect from its nature, being an immersion in pure water.

This is confirmed by the contrast which Josephus states, denying it to be the proper object of baptism—namely the deprecation of punishment (*epi paraitesei*). This is an object which he supposes some might have, but which would not be acceptable to God. Here purification of the body is the lawful object of baptism; deprecation of punishment is a wrong object. Now we might as well confound *deprecation of punishment* with the meaning of the word *baptism*, as confound purification with it; for both are supposed to be its object—the one a lawful object, the other an unlawful one. Does baptism, then, signify deprecation of punishment, because it may be used for that purpose? It is this excessive deficiency in perspicacity that has emboldened Mr. B. to undertake to prove that *baptismos* signifies *purification*. He every where confounds things that are different. From this he thinks he has succeeded, when he finds baptism spoken of as a purification; not distinguishing between the name of the rite and its object. If one word can supply the place of another in a certain situation, he thinks they must be synonymous. If Josephus speaks of baptism as performed on account of purification, he states that he has proved the word baptism signifies purification. By this philology he might prove that the word *bapto* signifies to *draw water*, or to *fill*, because these words could sometimes be substituted for it. In one of the examples of the occurrence of this word, which I gave in my Treatise, the translation is : "the youth held the capacious urn over the water, hasting to *dip* it." Here *fill* might be substituted for *dip*; but does *dip* signify to *fill*? *Dipping* is the mode by which the vessel is to be filled. The filling of the vessel was the effect of the dipping; just so with the case in hand. Immersion is the mode—purification is the object. They were two things as different as *dipping* and *filling*. One of the scholiasts, in expounding my next example, actually substitutes the words *aruomai* and *chemizo*, I *draw water* —I *fill*. " Take a vessel, ancient servant, and having *dipped it* in the sea, bring it hither." On Mr. B.'s principles of criticism, this would be sufficient authority to say that *aruomai* and *chemizo* are synonymous with *bapto*. Even our own word *dip* might be made synonymous with *fill*. We may say either *dip the bucket*, or *fill the bucket*. The writer who confounds distinctions on account of such facts, has not a soul for philological discussion.

But were we at a loss, on this occasion, to know in what sense Josephus here uses the word in question, where can we learn this with such authority as from his own use of the word in other places? In every instance in which he uses the word, he employs it for *immersion*, and never for *purification* or anything else.

SECTION V.—Mr. B. passes next to Heb. ix. 10. But this passage cannot afford him any proof. For argument sake, I will first admit that the word here is used for purification in general. As it does not refer to the rite of baptism, it may have a secondary signification here, without affecting its modal meaning in the Christian ordinance. Had a word twenty significations, they must in every instance be capable of being definitely ascertained; otherwise language would be unintelligible. That it is used here in a religious application, makes no difference. *Bapto* even in the art of dyeing may be used in the same page for *dyeing* and for *dipping;* and though it has a secondary signification of *dyeing*, it is often used with respect to religious *dipping*. The admission, then, that the word here signifies *purification*, does not at all affect the question at issue. I have undertaken to prove that the word has not a secondary meaning; but I have not done so on the ground that this is necessary for the proof of its modal meaning, in reference to the ordinance of baptism. Now, how can this prove that the word in reference to Christian baptism signifies *purification*, when I can admit all that Mr. B. attempts to prove from the passage, without admitting his conclusion? The proof which I have adduced for the modal meaning of the word in reference to the ordinance of Christ, remains still unaffected.

But instead of surrendering this passage, I utterly refuse to admit that the word has here a secondary signification. It is *immersion* here as well as every where else. Let us now examine my antagonist's reasoning.

1. " Those things only are spoken of in the whole discussion," says he, " which have a reference to action on the worshippers; that is, the whole passage relates to the effects of the Mosaic ritual entirely on *persons*, and not on *things*. The gifts, the sacrifices, the blood of sprinkling, the ashes of a heifer sprinkling the unclean, all relate to persons."

To this I reply,—1. Whether the word here signifies *immersion* or *purification*, it must extend to all the immersions or all the purifications under the law. I am under no concern to separate between action on persons, and action on things. If things were commanded to be immersed, which had no reference to persons, they must be included here, if the word signifies *immersion*. And if the word signifies *purification*, and if things are commanded to be purified which have no reference to persons, they must be here included. This distinction can bring no relief: for whether the word signifies *immersion* or *purification*, it must extend to all things immersed or purified.

2. The things admitted by Mr. B. to be immersed, had an equal relation to the person, as " the gifts, the sacrifices, the blood of sprinkling." Every thing immersed, or sprinkled, or in any way purified, had a reference to the worshippers. The vessels which they used, the garments which they wore, the utensils which in the service they employed,

had all a reference to their persons as much as the things which they offered.

3. Are not meats and drinks among the things referred to in this chapter? And had not their vessels, sacks and skins, a reference to their persons, as well as the meats and drinks?

4. Was not the blood of sprinkling sprinkled on other things beside their persons, and as little connected with their persons, as the things admitted to be immersed? Was not the water of separation sprinkled on the tents and all the vessels, as well as all the persons?

5. But I care not that every purification referred to in the whole chapter, referred to persons solely and directly, except in this instance. I am not disturbed with the supposed fact. Whatever be the meaning of the word, it must extend to every thing it includes, whether it signifies *immersion* or *purification*.

6. Even if the word here signified *purifications*, it must include the very things which Mr. B excluded. If certain things are admitted to be immersed by the law, are they not purified by that operation? Then, though immersion should not be the only purification here denoted, it is at least included among the *purifications*. This refutes the assertion that the things admitted to be immersed, cannot be included here among the things said to be purified.

Mr. B. proceeds: "The *baptismoi* are spoken of as enjoined, as well as the other rites. But of persons no immersions at all are enjoined under the Mosaic ritual." I have already shown that it is not necessary that immersion of persons should have been practised under the law, in order that the word should here signify *immersions*. There is no evidence that the baptism here spoken of must refer to persons. They are not said to be the baptisms of persons, nor are they said even to include the baptism of persons. It is enough for my purpose that there were *various immersions* under the law. There were immersions in blood, immersions in blood and water; immersions in water, immersions in water and the ashes of a red heifer; immersions in oil, and immersions in fire. But even if the word were admitted here to denote *purifications*, it must include all purification, and extend to the immersion of things.

But though it is not essential to the defence of my cause, to prove the immersions of persons under the law, I will undertake the task with all its supposed impossibilities. I admit that the Hebrew modal verb is not used with respect to persons, yet other circumstances imply that the mode of washing was immersion. How did they wash Aaron and his sons at the door of the tabernacle? Exod. xxix. 4. Must there not have been an immersion? Was there not constantly an immersion of the hands and the feet of the priests, before engaging in the service? Exod. xxx. 18—20. Now, an immersion of the hands, or the feet, is to me as good as an immersion of the whole body fifty feet under water. Let it not be forgotten that we are not discussing a passage for an example of Christian baptism, but one that speaks of Jewish baptism: and an immersion of a part is to me as good as an immersion of the whole. All I want is an immersion of any part of the person.

Solomon made ten lavers for the washing of such things as they offered for the burnt-offering. This was one of the baptisms under the law. But he made a sea for the priests to wash themselves. 2 Chron. iv. 6 Was not this washing performed by immersion?

Let it be observed that the apostle is here speaking of the Jewish baptisms as *practised* under the law, and not giving an account of their institution. It is certainly implied that the baptisms referred to were agreeable to the law, and a fulfilment of it; but it is not necessary that they should have been presented specifically as the only mode of fulfilling the law of washing. If *immersion* was the usual mode of washing the person, and if that mode fulfilled the law, may not a writer in giving an account of the practice, include the immersion of the person among the immersions under the law? Was it not a fact that under the law there was an immersion of the person, when it is admitted that the washing of the person commanded by the law was usually performed by immersion, and that this immersion was a proper fulfilment of the law? It is not necessary that immersion should be the only mode in which the law of washing the person could possibly be fulfilled; it is quite enough that it was the usual way, and a lawful way. This may be proved by a similar fact. The immersion of Naaman was a fulfilment of the command of Elisha, yet it was a specific way of fulfilling a command to wash without specification of mode. Is it not said that in obedience to the command of the prophet, Naaman *dipped* himself seven times in Jordan? Now, if the thing prescribed to Naaman had been a rite enjoined on all the Jews, which in every age they usually fulfilled by *dipping*, would not an historian speak of this as an immersion under the law? I think no sound understanding can hesitate a moment to receive this solution. This is confirmed by the fact that Trypho in Justin Martyr, p. 228, speaks of ablution after touching any of the things forbidden by the law of Moses, as *baptism;* and Justin Martyr every where uses the word for *immersion.*

"Nor is the washing of the clothes," says Mr. Beecher, "so often spoken of, enjoined by a word denoting *immersion.*" Very true, but are clothes washed without immersion? In speaking, then, of the practice under the law, was not the washing of clothes the immersion of clothes? But are not clothes and all other things that cannot endure the purification of fire, *to pass through water?* Can they pass through water without being immersed? Numb. xxxi. 23.

SECTION VI.—The argument from Tobit vi. 2 is utterly valueless.—
1. This is not ceremonial purification, or fulfilment of the law of Moses. The young man went down to the river to bathe, not to cleanse himself from ceremonial defilement. The object of the writer in bringing his hero to the river, was to bring about the exploit with the fish.

2. That complete washing of the person without immersion is possible, we are not obliged to deny. No other washing, however, is called *baptism.* If a man washes himself without *immersion,* he washes without *baptism.*

3. This washing is not called *baptism.*

4. Mr. B. here mistakes the argument of the Baptists, which he here

represents. When he asks for what purpose the young man went down to the river, he answers: "to immerse himself of course, the advocates of immersion will reply." This is not fact. *Bathing* or *washing* is the object: immersion is the mode in which that object is effected. But as the mode implies the effect, the mode may be substituted for the object, and instead of saying he went down to bathe, it may be said he went down to *dip himself*. The Baptists will not say that immersion was the object, but that immersion was the mode of effecting the object. If he went down to bathe, of course he was *dipped*.

5. But Mr. B.'s criticism on the Greek word *kluzo*, here employed for washing, is entirely false. He expounds the word as signifying a washing all around, "just as a man stands in a stream and throws the water all over his body, and washes himself by friction." Mr. B. criticises from imagination—not from knowledge of the language. Has he justified his criticism by a single example? He seems better acquainted with the different circumstances in the operation of bathing, than with the occurrences of the word on which he undertakes to criticise. The simple word signifies to deluge, to overwhelm, to inundate, or flow over anything, and is generally applied to water flowing or rolling in a horizontal manner. It is much employed in the medical art, and occurs in Hippocrates times without number. It is compounded with almost all the prepositions, and is accordingly modified by them. It is applied to the waves of the sea rolling over the shores, or running in high currents or billows in the ocean. It is with *kata* applied to the general deluge. With *peri*, the preposition with which it is here compounded, (*periklusasthai*) it is applied to the earth which is all around, as to its shores, washed or overflowed by the waves of the ocean; and the adjective as an epithet is given as a characteristic of islands. It has no application to the throwing up of water about himself by a man standing in a river. There is no friction nor hand-washing in this word. It performs its purpose by running over, either gently or with violence. The word does not signify that the young man in bathing splashed about like a duck, or rubbed himself like a collier; but that he threw himself into the river that the stream might flow over him. He was then *baptized* indeed, and much more than *baptized*.

6. Even according to his own showing, the argument which Baptists found on *going down to a river* is not refuted, nor weakened. The young man went down to the river to wash his whole person by friction. Does this countenance the opinion that persons usually go down to a river, to sprinkle a few drops of water on the face? He admits that it is probable that the young man immersed himself also. This, then, was not less than baptism, but more than baptism. Indeed, if the rite of Christ required a whole hogshead of water to be poured on the person, there could be no necessity to go down to the water. But in performing the rite of baptism, persons went not only *down to the water*, but *into the water*, which to every candid mind must ever prove immersion. From the manner in which the author ushers in his observations on this subject, one would think that he had made a discovery that would silence the argument for ever. "Whole volumes," says he, "of argument,

as we all know, depend *on going down to the river.*" Whatever are the number of volumes that have been written to enforce this argument, it remains in full force for anything this author has done. But it requires only a naked statement, to make it irresistibly evident to any mind not jaundiced by prejudice.

"The only immersions enjoined in the Mosaic law," says Mr. B., " were immersions of things to which no reference can be had here—as vessels, sacks, skins, &c. In this case no act was performed that had any tendency to affect the *worshipper,* but only the thing immersed." What! Does Mr. B. assert that the purification of vessels, &c., had no relation to the worshipper? Was it for the sake of the vessels, sacks, and skins, that they were purified? Was it not because the things immersed were used by the worshipper? Were not their vessels purified for the very same reason that their persons were purified? Had not the vessels, &c. been purified, the worshipper using them would have been defiled. What had God's law to do with the purification of the vessels, &c. of the Jews more than of the heathens, but from the connexion of those things with the worshippers? Did ever so monstrous an idea enter the mind of man, as that God commanded a rite to be performed on vessels, &c. which had no reference to the worshipper, but only to the things immersed? I should not have thought that there could have been found a Christian child, who would make such an assertion. Had not the vessels, &c. the same relation to the worshipper, as the meats and drinks here specified? What nearer relation had a pure sacrifice to the worshipper, than had a pure vessel? Are not vessels, &c. ordinances of the flesh as well as meats and drinks? In fact, every thing enjoined or forbidden in the ritual ordinances of Moses, had a reference to the flesh; they are all carnal ordinances.

What does Mr. B. mean when he asserts, that " no reference can be had to the immersions of *inanimate things,* but only to the purification of *persons?*" Are *meats* and *drinks* persons? Are gifts and sacrifices persons? Are the various things mentioned belonging to the tabernacle, persons? Had not the vessels which a man used the same relation to his flesh, as the meats which he ate? Why must the *baptisms* be confined to persons? The inanimate things immersed, had the same reference to the persons of the worshippers, as had the gifts and sacrifices, as had the meats and drinks, as had all the things specified in this chapter.

"What could any one think," says Mr. B., " that the immersion of vessels, of earth or wood, had to do with the purifying of the conscience or the heart of a worshipper?" The immersion of those things had just as much to do with purifying the conscience, as had the purification of the person. Neither of them could purify the conscience : both of them purified ceremonially as types of that which truly purifies ; and the purification of all our services is as necessary as the purification of our persons. If men, mistaking the meaning of the rites, might think that the purification of the body cleansed the conscience, so might they think of the purification of vessels. Did they immerse the vessels, sacks, and skins, to purify the conscience of the vessels, sacks, and ɛkins? Can anything be more plain than that the true relation, and the falsely supposed effect of the Jewish rites to the persons of the worshippers, were the same with respect to what was to be performed on inanimate things, as to what were to be performed on the person itself? For what purpose were inanimate things *purified*, if they had no relation to the persons of the worshippers?

For a full answer to the objection from the epithet *divers* or *different*, I refer to my reply to the Presbyterian Review. I shall here merely observe, that though immersion is always the same as to mode, there may be innumerable different immersions. An immersion of the body is a different immersion from the immersion of things. An immersion of a variety of different things is in each a different immersion. An immersion of every different substance is a different immersion.

Why *immersions* are mentioned rather than *purifications* in general, it is not my business to declare: all I have to do is to show that *immersions* and not *purifications* are mentioned. It is to me quite obvious that there is no necessity to mention purifications universally in this place: the apostle is not professing to exhaust the subject of purification, but to give a specimen of the things practised under the law, to point out their insufficiency to purge the conscience; and other purifications are mentioned in other parts of the epistle. But I observe not this as a controversialist. In that character I do not give an opinion, nor undertake to satisfy an opponent. There may be reasons which we cannot perceive. Our business is not to account for God's reasons for not saying what he has not said, but to discover what he has said. I act on this principle in every instance, as well as in this. I endeavour to find out the meaning of the Holy Spirit, by the words which he has used; not by speculations and opinions with respect to what he should say.

"No man," says Mr. B., "who had not a theory to support, could bring himself to do such violence to all the laws of interpretation in a case so plain." I think I am entitled to ask, with indignation, the ground on which my antagonist presumes to make this assertion. I have no theory to support. I never use theories in ascertaining the truths and the ordinances of Christ; I interpret by the laws of language. Neither have I any philological doctrine which demands my denial of such a secondary signification of this word. How can I have a theory to support in denying such a secondary meaning, when it is my doctrine that words might receive such secondary meanings? The process by which, in various instances, such secondary significations are imposed on words, I have exemplified in some of their wildest caprices. Mr. B. himself is in this doctrine merely my pupil. As far as he is right, he has adopted my philology; and has illustrated it merely by different examples. Must I, then, in opposing his conclusion, have a theory to support in opposition to my own doctrine? Mr. Bickersteth's friend, in proof that the word in question, from signifying baptism by *immersion*, came to signify baptism in any way, alleged the authority of my own doctrine against myself. There was, however, a trifling deficiency in his reasoning. He proved from my doctrine that the word *might* come to have such a meaning; but he forgot to prove that it actually underwent the supposed process. Perfectly on the same principle Mr. Beecher shows, from my doctrine, that the word might come to signify *purification;* but he has not proved that, in the history of the word before the time of Christ, it actually received such a meaning. The principle I do not dispute; it is my own principle. What temptation, then, can I have, from any theory of mine, to dispute this secondary meaning?

Again, I can have as little temptation from interest or popularity, to do violence to any passage in order to prove a particular mode of any religious ordinance. Have I made a fortune by immersion? Would *purifications* destroy me? Should I become less popular among Christians, or with the world, by returning to *sprinkling?* If emblematical purification by *sprinkling* or *pouring* were optional, as well as by *immersion*, I would most assuredly never *immerse*. Besides, why should I do violence to this passage, in order to reject *purification* as its meaning, when I could admit this meaning here, and still, with the utmost ease, prove immersion to be the mode of Christ's ordinance? Were I ever so partial to water, Mr. B.'s good-natured doctrine will indulge me, and allow me to immerse as freely as to sprinkle. I can have no possible reason, then, for confining the word in this passage to *immersion*, but the innumerable proofs that it has this meaning, and the absence of all proof that it ever has any other. I should act perfectly in the same way, if the dispute were solely of a literary nature, and the question were the mode of a heathen rite.

But should it be admitted that the word here is confined to persons, and that it includes washings of the person in every mode, still this would not countenance the opinion that it signifies *purifications.* All ceremonial washings were purifications; but all purifications were not washings. *Washings* and *purifications* are not synonymous.

SECTION VII.—Mr. B. next presents us with the usual objection from Mark vii. 4, and Luke xi. 38. "In Mark vii. 4, 8, and in Luke xi. 38, *katharizo* is the natural and obvious sense of *baptizo*, and *katharismos* of *baptismos*." Let us hear the proof. "1. This sense," says the writer, "fulfils perfectly all the exigencies of the passages." And if it did, I care not. Many a false sense may fulfil all the exigencies of the connexion. This false sense, however, has not even this merit; whereas, *immersion* is quite suitable to the connexion, and *immersion* is the only meaning of the word in every instance in the whole compass of the language.

"I know, indeed," says the writer, "that it is said by some, that in Mark there is a rise in the idea from the lesser washing of the hands, which was common before all meals, to the greater washing implied in the immersion of the body after coming from the market. But, on the other hand, there is simply a rise from the specific to the general and indefinite. They always *wash their hands* before meals; and when they return from market they also *purify themselves* (as the nature of the case may require) before they eat." A rise from the specific to the general and indefinite! This indeed is a new climax. This is Gothic rhetoric. A rise from the washing of the hands to the immersion of the whole body, or the washing of the body in any mode, is a rise which all can understand; but a rise from the washing of the hands to indefinite purifications is a fall. Mr. B.'s own phraseology is nonsense: "They also purify themselves." Does not *also* imply that the washing of the hands is not purification? This is not an advancement from a species of purification to purification in general, but an advancement from what is supposed not to be purification to purification. But such an advance might be an *advance backwards.* The washing of the hands is a species of purification; if the advance is to purification indefinitely, then it may be fulfilled by something less than washing the hands, by dipping the finger, for instance, or by touching the body on any part with a drop of water, or even without water, with blood, &c.

If any reader has a conscience at all, I ask nothing more than common sense in him, to perceive in this passage, that the persons referred to usually washed their hands before eating; and that when they came from the market they did something more than this. What that something more was, depends on the meaning of the word. "In the latter case," says Mr. B., "Mr. Bloomfield remarks, it denotes a washing of the body, but not an immersion." Now, as far as the passage itself is concerned, it is fully admitted that it does not determine; and the climax would be the same to Mr. Bloomfield as to me. But I determine the meaning of the word here, by its meaning as established by the use of language: I never press an argument a hair's breadth farther than it can go. I tell Mr. Bloomfield that the word never signifies to *wash*, as I tell Mr. Beecher that it never signifies to *purify*. My authority is the practice of the Greek language.

But why does Mr. Beecher appeal to Mr. Bloomfield? Mr. Bloomfield is as much opposed to him as he is to me. If the word here signifies to *wash the body*, then it does not here signify to purify in general. Mr. B.'s artifice is just that of the Socinians, when they explain the words "Before Abraham was, I am," in the sense of the Arians. It is a dishonest and uncandid way of escaping. He does what he is able to make it *purify ;* but as he cannot make it *purify*, even to his own satisfaction, he will give it over to Mr. Bloomfield for washing the body without immersion. This is not my way of handling the word of God. Purification, then, cannot be the meaning of the word here, because it is not suitable to the phraseology in which it is employed. But let it be observed that this is more than I am bound to show. Were it suitable to the context, I would equally reject it. I dismiss it *on the ground of* want of a title from the use of the language. I am not here grounding a proof, but obviating an objection. It is quite sufficient that I can show that the meaning which I assign to the word is suitable to the passage: I am not bound to show that either *wash* or *purify* is unsuitable. The title of my client to the whole estate is already in evidence : my opponents must show that some part of it has been alienated. This passage will not prove such alienation.

Mr. B.'s second proof is, "Nothing in the context demands the sense immerse, and powerful reasons forbid it. All must confess that purification is the only idea involved in the subject of thought. Now it is no more likely that a want of *immersion* offended the Pharisee, Luke xi. 38, in the case of Christ, than it is that this was the ground of offence in the case of the disciples, Mark vii. It does not appear that Christ had been to the market; nor is it likely at all that an immersion was expected, as a matter of course, before every meal, even on coming from a crowd. The offence in the case of the disciples was, that they had not washed their hands. An immersion was not expected of them, though they had been in crowds. Why should it be of Christ?" It is not necessary that the context should demand the true meaning of a word; it is enough that the context does not forbid it. The usage of the language demands this meaning without any additional demand from the context. The context, however, forbids *purification*, though this is not necessary to me. The reasons alleged, as forbidding it to signify immersion, have no force. Might not the Pharisees expect more sanctity in the Messiah than in his disciples, or than even they themselves professed? But I have nothing to do with conjectures. Whatever might be their reasons, they did expect that Christ would have immersed before eating. To deny this is to give the lie to the inspired narrator. The word used by the Holy Spirit signifies immersion, and immersion only. A thousand reasons might influence the Pharisees in the expectation referred to, which may not be at all known to us. To know their reasons is not at all necessary to the knowing of the meaning of the word. Mr. B. rests this argument on a false principle of interpretation, namely, that to know that a word is used in its established meaning, it is necessary to know that there are sufficient reasons to warrant its truth in such an application. This we are to take on the authority of the narrator. His meaning we are to know from his words, and his veracity we must rest on his character.

" Rosenmüller, on this passage," says Mr. B., " well remarks, that the existence of any such custom of regular immersion before all meals, cannot be proved." This is another false first principle. What makes it necessary that a practice should be proved by foreign evidence, before the testimony of the Holy Spirit is received in its proper meaning? Is every thing recorded in Scripture to be denied, except it is proved by history? Am I to suspend my faith in the resurrection of Christ, till I find it proved by uninspired records. This is a Neological canon, well worthy of its author. It tends to sap the very foundations of Christianity. Is not the testimony of the Spirit of God sufficient to prove this fact? And what word could he have used more decisively to assert immersion? The custom referred to as regards immersion after market, rests on the evidence of inspired history. Is not this as valid as the testimony of uninspired historians?

" But above all," says Mr. B., " the immersion of the couches on which they reclined at meals is out of the question." I most freely admit that the word ought to be translated *couches*, and not *tables*. It designates not only the couches on which they reclined at table, but even the beds on which they reposed at night. It applies also to the *litters* on which persons of distinction were carried on the shoulders of men. I will never hesitate to recognise anything in evidence, whatever bearing it may have on my views. "Mr. Carson," says my antagonist, "seems to feel this point keenly, and yet manfully maintains his ground." Mr. Carson does indeed feel with regard to this objection something that he does not wish to express. But he can assure President Beecher that he never felt it as a difficulty: in the strongest light in which it can be viewed, it is futile. There is no furniture in a house that could not be immersed. I have said that the couches might have been made to be taken to pieces, in order to their more convenient immersion; and were this necessary, it is a valid solution. The supposition is perfectly allowable. The couch on which rested the urn containing the ashes of Cyrus, is said by Arrian, p. 144, to have had feet of solid gold; and those on either side of the throne of Alexander, for his friends to sit on, had feet of silver, p. 165. Now what could be more easy than to have the feet of the couch, of whatever materials composed, to be taken out at pleasure for the purpose of immersion? The immersion of the couches would be a thing of little trouble. But I care not that they were baptized all of a piece: the thing could be very easily accomplished. Ingenuity is very idly expended in making will-worship easy to superstition. The couches were immersed, because the word which is employed to express the operation has this signification, and no other.

Mr. B., throughout his whole work, mistakes my doctrine as *to a possible sense* of a word; and labours under a fundamental error as to the difference of founding an argument on any passage, and answering an objection from it. When we found an argument on any passage, we must prove that the passage has our meaning, and no other: for if this is not proved, the argument can have no weight. But when we answer an objection from any passage, it is sufficient that a particular word may have the sense for which we contend; because, if it may have such a sense, the objection which supposes that it has not this sense, but another sense, is unfounded. It is a contradiction to say that a word *may* have such a sense in such a place, yet that it *cannot* have this sense. If, then, the answer to the objection is *possible*, it is valid. Were not this so, Christianity itself could not withstand the attacks of the infidel. Many objections must be answered by the authority of merely possible solutions. This is what I mean by a *possible sense*. I never extend this to cases in which I found an argument: I confine it resolutely to cases in which I answer objections. With respect to the passage now under discussion, Mr. B. is bound to proof; because on this he founds proof that the word in question signifies to *purify*. I stand only on the defence; for I do not allege the passage as proof, but repel the objection which pretends that the passage is irreconcilable with immersion. In this point my antagonist proves himself ignorant of one of the fundamental laws of controversy. He demands proof from me, when he himself is bound to prove. He asks, "What has Mr. Carson proved? Why, truly, that in other instances *baptizo* means immerse. But does this prove that it means it here?" Could any man who understands the self-evident laws of controversy, look for proof on my part from this passage? Is it not enough for me to show that there is nothing to prevent the word from having its established meaning in this passage? If this is possible, his objection is removed. My antagonist is bound from this passage to show that the word signifies to *purify*. How can he do this, if he has not proved the word to have that signification in any other place; and if even in this it may have its usual meaning? If, as he admits, I have found that *baptizo* in other instances signifies to *immerse*, there is a certainty that it has this meaning here, except it is proved that it has another signification somewhere else. If another signification is found, I will not insist that immersion *must of course* be the signification here. In such a case as this, the meaning must be settled by additional evidence. When a word has two or more meanings, actually in proof, which of them may in any passage be the true meaning, is a question; but if no secondary meaning is in proof, there can be no question on the subject. *Now there is not in all Greek literature a single instance, ever alleged, in which this word* MUST *have a secondary meaning.*

Mr. B. admits that I have proved that the word signifies immersion in other places; but asks, " Does this prove that it means so here?" I answer most decidedly that it does prove this, if the word is not proved to have another meaning. If but one instance prove a word to have a certain meaning, it is proof that every other instance has the same meaning, except a secondary meaning is proved. If a secondary meaning is proved, then the claimants must rest their suit on their respective peculiar resources.

" The probability," says Mr. B., " is all the other way." Here there is a want of discrimination and a confounding of things that differ. I am not speaking of what is *possible, probable,* or *certain,* independently of the testimony; I am speaking of the testimony of the word known by its use; I am saying that a word in a certain place must have the meaning which it is found to have in other places, when no secondary meaning has ever been proved. Mr. B. alleges not the testimony of the word, but imposes a testimony on the word. He forces it to take a meaning which use has never given it, on the authority of what he thinks probable, utterly independent of the authority of the word. He tampers with the witness, and tells him what he must say. I allow witness to tell his own story, and believe him implicitly on his own authority, without regard to what I might think independently probable. Mr. B.'s conduct is just the same with that of a jury who, having heard the testimony of a number of competent eye-witnesses, with regard to the way in which a man was killed, decide in opposition to their evidence, on the authority of the conjectures of a surgeon. This word declares that couches were purified by immersion. Mr. B., on the authority of what he thinks probable, declares that it was not by immersion. He dictates to the word what it must say, instead of receiving its testimony. On the contrary, my decision is, that the way in which the couches were purified, is to be known from the testimony of the word, and not from what, independently of that testimony, is probable; and that from this testimony they were immersed, because the word has no other meaning.

" Hence," says Mr. B., " the demand to prove an impossibility of immersion is altogether unreasonable." If a secondary meaning had been proved from use, then, in any instance to demand an impossibility of the primary meaning, before the secondary is admitted, would be unreasonable. But is it unreasonable that a word should be understood in this passage as it is proved to signify in other passages, when no secondary signification has ever been proved? Instead of being unreasonable, the demand is founded on self-evident truth. Why should the word have a meaning here, which it is not proved to have in use, when its own established meaning will serve? How can a meaning which is not known to exist, dispute with the only established meaning? Views of probability, independently of the testimony of the word, are not a competent witness; for they are often mistaken. What we might, previously to the hearing of evidence, judge probable, might, on the hearing of evidence, be proved most satisfactorily to be false. The meaning of this word must be known from its use—not from views of probability independently of this use. When we hear that a certain person has *killed* another, we may think the thing very improbable; but shall we on that ground assert that *kill* does not *signify* to take away life? In fact, to allege that the *couches* were not immersed, is not to decide on the authority of the word used, but in opposition to this authority; to give the lie to the Holy Spirit. Inspiration employs a word to designate the purification of the couches, which never signifies anything but *immerse*. If they were not immersed, the historian is a false witness. This way of conferring meanings on words is grounded on infidelity. It dictates to inspiration instead of interpreting its language. It would be improper in ascertaining the meaning of words even in a profane historian. Are we to deny the meaning of words established by use, as often as, independently of the testimony of the words, we may think a thing improbable? This would destroy the faith of history: it would destroy every doctrine of Scripture. This is a usual way with some in interpreting the Bible; but is not the way that any interpret the language of the profane historian. When the profane historian narrates what is thought improbable, his veracity is questioned, but his words are not tampered with. When the Holy Spirit employs words whose meanings are not relished, critics do not say that he lies, but they say what is equal to this, that his words mean what they cannot mean. If a word may have in any instance its established meaning, when it cannot be proved in any instance to have another meaning, it cannot be probable that it has in that instance a meaning which it cannot be proved to have anywhere else. Surely this is self-evident.

"And it is," continues my antagonist, " against his own practice in other cases. Does he not admit that *bapto* means to dye, or colour, when it is applied to the beard and hair?" Here I am caught at last: surely my feet are entangled in my own net. But let the reader see with what ease I can extricate myself. The assertion of my antagonist arises from his want of discrimination. I admit that *bapto* has a secondary signification, because such secondary signification is in proof, and instances may be alleged in which its primary meaning is utterly impossible. When applied, for instance, to the lake, the immersion of a lake in the blood of a frog, is beyond the bounds of possibility. Show me anything

like this with respect to *baptizo,* and I will grant a secondary meaning;
and as soon as a secondary meaning is ascertained on sufficient grounds,
I do not demand in every instance a proof of impossibility of primary
meaning before the secondary is alleged. The competition between the
rival meanings must then be determined on other grounds. This law i
apply, not to *baptizo* only, but to every word of every language. The
immersion of the couches, in no light in which it can be viewed, has
the smallest difficulty. From an excess of good nature I made faith
easy to the weak, by fixing the couches so as readily to be taken to
pieces; but if obstinacy will not avail itself of this help, I will force it
to carry the couches to water wherever it may be found.

"The fact is," says Mr. B., "that the whole reasoning against the
sense claimed for *baptizo* in these passages, rests on false principles."
False principles! What now are our false principles? Is it a false principle to rest on the ascertained meaning of a word, and not on probabilities independently of the word? Is it a false principle to refuse a word
a meaning in a disputed passage, till it proves itself to have such meaning in an undisputed passage?

"It assumes," says my antagonist, " a violent improbability of the
meaning in question, and resorts to all manner of shifts to prove the possibility of immersion, as though that were all that the case required."
What shall I say of this? Is it calumny, or is it want of perspicacity?
Assume! I assume nothing, Mr. President Beecher, but self-evident truth.
My reasoning does not at all rest on assumptions. The meaning which
you assign to the word, I reject, because it wants evidence, not on any
assumption of its violent improbability. *All manner of shifts!* I repel
the charge with indignation. I never used a *shift* in all the controversy
I ever wrote. Does it require a shift to prove that in all the cases
referred to, immersion was possible? Will any man of common sense
question the possibility? If the possibility is unquestionable, why shall
I be supposed to employ all manner of *shifts* to prove it?

But my opponent asserts also that I consider that the *possibility* of
immersion in the cases referred to, is all that is required to prove it. Is
this a *shift?* It is worse than a *shift:* it is not a fact. The proof that
immersion was used in the cases referred to, is that the word has this
meaning, and no other. The *possibility* of immersion only removes
objection. But for argument's sake, I will for a moment admit that *immersion* was in these cases impossible: even then I will deny the title of
purification. *Washing* is a meaning which would come previously to
purifying. These passages, then, cannot in any view, ground the title
of *purification.*

SECTION VIII.—His next argument, Mr. Beecher grounds on a passage in Ecclesiasticus. "In the case," says he, "so often quoted from
Sirach xxxiv. 25, *baptizo* requires the sense *katharizo.* The passage is
this : *Baptizomenos apo nekrou kai palin aptomenos autou ti ophelese to
loutro autou.* 'He that is cleansed from a dead body, and again touches
it, of what profit to him is his cleansing?' " No such thing is required
But let us hear his proof.

"1. The sense, *katharizo,* purify," says he, "suits the preposition *apo ;*—immerse does not." The preposition, I assert, equally suits immersion. *Immersed from a dead body,* is an elliptical expression, for *immersed to purify from the pollution contracted by the touch of a dead body.* And on this principle it is translated into English, in the common version, though the translators were not *immersers.* " He that washeth himself after the touching of a dead body, if he touch it again, what availeth his washing ?" But it is strange beyond measure that President Beecher did not perceive that even if the word *purify* itself had been here used, there would have been a similar ellipsis. To *purify from a dead body,* is to purify from the pollution contracted by touching a dead body. This is school-boy criticism, Mr. President.

His second observation on this example is : " No immersion, in the case of touching a dead body, was enjoined, but simply a *washing of the body.*" It is not necessary that an immersion should be enjoined : it is quite sufficient that the injunction of washing the body was usually performed by immersion. The writer is alluding to practice, and is not relating the words of the injunction.

Mr. B.'s third observation on this passage is, that " the rite of purification from a dead body was complex, and no import of the word *baptizo,* but the one claimed, is adapted to include the whole." The writer is not describing the whole process of the rite of purification according to the law of Moses. Why, then, should the word include the whole? He is referring to a part of that rite merely as an illustration of another subject. Priests were *anointed* to their office, but there were other things included in the rite of inauguration, besides *anointing.* Might it not be said, " If a priest is anointed, and afterwards render himself unfit for his office, of what avail is his anointing?" The washing completed the process of purification. Another touch of a dead body defiled again, and rendered the washing, consequently the whole process, useless.

But in the word *loutron* there is the most decisive evidence that the whole process of purification is not included in *baptizo.* The word *loutron* here refers to the thing done to the person by his baptism. But *loutron* cannot refer to purification in general, but only to washing. It cannot include the sprinkling of the water of separation. This is purification, but not washing.

On this view, Mr. B. asks : " How then is it consistent to apply it to the blood of Christ, which is spoken of as the blood of sprinkling?" This to Mr. B. appears an unanswerable question : to me it has not the smallest difficulty. We are said to be *washed* in the blood of Christ, and we are said to be *sprinkled with* the blood of Christ. But the *washing* and the *sprinkling* are never confounded; we are not said to be washed by being sprinkled, nor is *sprinkling* called *washing.* These two forms of speech refer to the application of the blood of Christ under figures entirely different. When Christ's blood is said to be sprinkled on us, there is an allusion to the sprinkling of the blood under the law ; when we are said to be washed in the blood of Christ, there is an allusion to the *washing* under the law. Does not Mr. B. know what a difference there is between a mixture of metaphors, and a succession of distinct metaphors? Careless readers will imagine that there is wonderful acuteness in Mr. B.'s observations. But the eye of the philosopher will perceive that they are subtle without discrimination. A little more perspicacity would have saved him from undertaking the impracticable task of proving baptism to mean purification.

But were we to grant that the word here signifies *purification*, this would not be proof that it has this signification in the rite of Christian baptism. It would give ground to send the case to the jury; but would not decide the controversy. Still we would most satisfactorily prove that baptism must be by immersion.

"The case of Judith, also," Mr. B. alleges, "sustains the same view." But what appearance of difficulty does this occurrence of the word present? Is it a thing impossible, or even difficult, to be immersed near a fountain? Might she not have had attendants with her to provide her with a bath at the fountain, had this been necessary? From the civilities and attentions of the governor, could she be supposed to want anything that would not be most cheerfully supplied? Was it not usual to have stone troughs at fountains, for the purpose of watering cattle? "Haynes informs us," says Mr. Whitecross, in his Anecdotes Illustrative of Scripture, "that having arrived at Nazareth, at the end of December, about five in the evening, upon entering the town, he and his party saw two women filling their pitchers with water at a fountain he had described, and about twelve others waiting for the same purpose, whom they desired to pour some into a trough which stood by, that their horses might drink; they had no sooner made the request than the women complied, and filled the trough, and the others waited with the greatest patience." p. 83. Yes, but Mr. B. will say, *Mr. Carson has not proved that there was such a trough at this fountain. Mr. Carson will reply, This is not necessary, Mr. President; it is sufficient for my purpose, if it may have been so.* I am answering an objection, and if the thing *might* be as I suppose, the objection is invalid.

But what should prevent her from bathing in the fountain, even if we were assured that there was no other way of bathing? This is quite usual to superstition. Charlotte Elizabeth, speaking of a holy well at the top of Slieve Donard, a lofty mountain in Ireland, says, "Many a diseased creature had dragged his feeble, perhaps crippled limbs and exhausted frame, to the top of Slieve Donard, to plunge them in the so-called holy well, hoping to find a healing power in its spring:" shall less be expected from Jewish superstition? In fact, the English version, which was not made by immersers, actually translates the passage, "and washed herself *in* a fountain of water by the camp." Judith xii. 7. It is true that the exact rendering is, *immersed herself at a fountain*, not *in* a fountain. The immersion is proved not by the preposition, but by the verb; and though *at a fountain* does not signify *in a fountain*, yet it is consistent with it. A person may be said to be *immersed at a fountain*, when he is *immersed in it*. A person coming from Palestine may say, I was baptized at the Jordan, when he was immersed in it.

I have said all this, however, only to put obstinacy to the blush, and overwhelm it with confusion. Not a word of it is essentially necessary. Had Judith been most rigorously treated, and confined to her tent, when she is said to be baptized for purification, I will make the word find her water. Can anything be more unreasonable than for persons at the end of thousands of years, to allege difficulties as in certain cases insuperable? Could not innumerable circumstances render a thing practicable, which to us are now unknown?

"We are told," says Mr. B., "of her courage, and faith, and of possible bathing places near the spring, and all for what? To avoid so obvious a conclusion as that the writer merely means to say, that she purified or washed herself, without reference to the mode." To avoid such a conclusion, it is not necessary to allege any of the things mentioned. The immersion would be secured by the word, though he could see no way of its accomplishment. It is enough that nothing is seen to render it impossible. When we take the trouble of showing how the immersion might be accomplished, it is a work of supererogation. How is the conclusion obvious that the historian means only that she purified or washed herself, without reference to mode, when the word that he employs designates mode in the most decisive manner? What is the ground of the supposed obvious conclusion? Is it that it would have been sufficient to tell us that she washed or purified herself, without telling us the mode? This is no ground for such a conclusion; this does not imply that she did not purify in the mode of immersion, or that the historian should not mention the mode employed. But can anything be sufficient ground for a conclusion as to this point, but the import of the word itself? How do we conclude that she purified herself at all? Is it not from the word used by the historian? Ought we not, then, to ground our conclusion, as to the mode of that purification, on the same word, and not on independent probability? We have no testimony on the subject, but that contained in the word *baptizo*, and that testimony asserts immersion. How can it be concluded that the historian speaks of purification without expressing mode, when he employs the word that most definitely expresses mode?

"What reason is there," says Mr. B., "for all this?" Astonishing demand! What reason is there for giving a word the only meaning it is known to possess! When a person says, *I dipped myself in the river*, shall we say, "what reason is there to suppose that the word *dip* here signifies to *immerse?* Is it not here intended to tell us that *he bathed himself?* What reason, then, is there to suppose that *dip* does not signify to bathe, without reference to mode?" Our reason for believing that Judith was *immersed* is, that the historian tells us that she was *immersed*. Is not this a sufficient reason?

"Is not the sense *purify*," continues Mr. B., "*à priori* probable?" Whether in giving an account of the performance of a rite of purification, a writer will mention the process in the rite to be performed without specification, cannot be previously known: it must be learned from the words of the narrative. That Mr. President Beecher will be immersed in one of the great American rivers, is now very improbable; but should I ever read that, in obedience to Christ, he was *immersed*, I certainly will not attempt to discredit the account by alleging that *immerse* does not here signify to *dip*.

" Does it not," continues Mr. B., " fulfil all the exigencies of the case ?"
This is no criterion. A word might fulfil all the exigencies of the case,
and yet another word, either more general or more specific, might be
used. When a person says, I *dipped* myself in the river, either *washed*
or *bathed* would fulfil all the exigencies of the case. Does this prove
that *dip* signifies to *wash* or *bathe* without referring to mode ?

" Was it of any importance," says Mr. B., " to specify the mode ?" If
it is truth, the importance is not to be weighed. My last reply will serve
equally here. But is it a thing of no importance to specify the mode in
which a rite is performed ?

" Do the circumstances of the case," continues my opponent, " call
for immersion ?" The word calls for immersion ; it is enough that no
circumstances forbid it. If this was the usual mode of performing the
rite of washing in purification, which is admitted, why is it not demanded ? Such objections are unworthy of an answer. Suppose it is said
that an army on its march *forded* a river near such a place. Suppose again that I know that in that neighbourhood there is a bridge
over the river ; is it not probable that, if there is a bridge, the army
will pass by the bridge ? Am I then to say, that *ford* signifies *to pass
a river by a bridge ?* Whitecross relates the following anecdote : " Very
near Columbo is a school built in a beautiful and romantic situation, on
the high bank of a noble river, across which a bridge of boats had
recently been thrown for the convenience of the public. A number of
fine little boys residing on the side of the river, opposite the school, were
exceedingly anxious to enjoy the benefits of the instruction which it
afforded, but were utterly unable, from their poverty, to pay the toll for
passing this bridge four times every day, to and from school. In removing this serious difficulty, the little fellows showed at once their eager-
ness to obtain instruction, and their native ingenuity. Wearing only
a light cloth around them, according to the custom of the country,
they were accustomed to assemble on the bank in the morning, and
the larger boys binding up the books of the smaller ones, which they
had home with them to learn their tasks, to tie them on the back
of their heads, and swim over, the little ones following them ; and this
inconvenience they constantly encountered, rather than be absent from
school."

Now, if instead of this particular narrative, which explains every circumstance, it had been recorded only that the boys passed the river
by *swimming*, while we knew that a bridge of boats was near, what
would be the sense in which, according to Mr. B.'s philology, a foreigner
should understand the language ? " *Swim*," says the writer, " must undoubtedly be here taken to signify to walk over *a bridge of boats*. It
is true, in many books in the English language, the word *swim* has
another meaning, but there is the highest probability that it has not
this signification here. Is it to be believed that the boys swam, in
the primary sense of the word, across a great river, when there was a
bridge at the place ? Incredible, utterly incredible ! My opponents,
it is true, may plead the authority of classical English ; but I rely
on Columbine English. The word *swim*, then, must here have the

secondary signification for which I contend." Every child who speaks English will laugh the critic to scorn; but to his own countrymen, as little acquainted with the English language as himself, he would appear to be a very profound philologist. I maintain that this is exactly Mr. B.'s criticism, and that it can satisfy nothing but ignorance.

Is it not evident, on the face of the document, that Judith went out from the camp to the fountain at Bethulia for the purpose of bathing, or washing her whole person? This the law of purification required, and no other reason made it necessary for her to go to the fountain. Even then, supposing that it were allowed that the word signifies to wash without reference to mode, this gives no countenance to Mr. B.'s opinion that the word signifies *to purify*. *To wash* and *to purify* are not identical. On this supposition, the passage would favour those who think that the word signifies to *wash*—not those who think that it signifies to *purify*.

Again, if the washing of the person in any manner was the way in which the law was fulfilled, why did she go to the fountain? Why did she leave the tent? Could not a small basin of water have served the purpose of successive washing?

Again, even had it been said that she washed her person at the fountain, was not immersion likely to be the mode? Is it not the usual and the most convenient way of washing her person? Why then shall it be supposed that it was not the mode employed here, even though the word of mode had not been used? But especially when the word of mode is used, why should supposed difficulties make it incredible? The alleged difficulties, however, are no difficulties. Mr. B. cannot find a tree while he is in the forest.

But even were it admitted that the word signifies *purify* in this place, this would not prove that it has this signification in the ordinance of baptism; we could still prove immersion to be the mode of the Christian rite. Mr. B. fails in every thing which he attempts to prove; yet were he successful, it would not prove his position.

Throughout his whole work, my antagonist labours under an essential error. He reasons on the supposition that every instance of the occurrence of the word must be treated independently of its established meaning, and its meaning assigned according to views of probability, without reference to testimony. He understands not the difference between answering an objection and founding an argument; and calls upon me for proof, when he himself is bound to prove. In answering objections, a merely possible supposition is as good as demonstration: in proof, probability, even the highest probability, avails nothing against testimony. If Judith is said to have been baptized, she must have been immersed, though a thousand difficulties may occur in providing the water. My opponents are more unreasonable with me than the Israelites were with Moses: they murmured when they had no water. Must I bring water out of the rock, when there is enough in the fountain? Such a mode of disproving the established meaning of a word, and of giving a new and unauthorised meaning, I cannot dignify with any other designation than that of perverse cavilling.

Mr. B. alleges as another argument, that " no contrary probability, or usage, can be established from the writers of the New Testament age, or of the preceding age, who used the Alexandrian Greek." With probability we have nothing to do in this question; we are inquiring about a matter of fact, namely, whether a certain word had a secondary meaning. We admit proof from writers of all classes to the time of Christ. Mr. B. tells us that to refute a secondary meaning, it is of no use to appeal to the earliest writers. This also we admit. If in all the history of the word, till its appropriation to the ordinance of Christ, he brings one instance in which it *must* have a secondary meaning, we admit that a secondary meaning is fully proved. An example from Alexandrian Greek would prove the fact, though it should not be owned by any writer of antiquity. Is not this admission sufficiently liberal? Candour requires no less: it cannot require more. I have no object but truth; and I am so strong in truth, that I fearlessly grant every thing that candour can demand.

But what does the writer mean when he asserts that no contrary usage can be established from the writers of the New Testament age, or of the age preceding? Does he mean that during this time the word is not used in its primary sense? If he does, the assertion is palpably false. Does he mean that during the specified time, there are examples of this secondary meaning? Is not this the very point in dispute? To assume it, is to assume the question at issue. There is not one instance to prove this.

Here, however, Mr. B. labours under his usual mistake—he puts proof on his opponent, when it lies upon himself. Why should we prove a contrary usage in the times of the New Testament, or the preceding age? Does not proof lie upon him? If I prove that in its early history a word has a certain meaning, it must in every age be supposed to have the same meaning, till a contrary usage is proved. If the possessor of an estate proves that he has hitherto possessed it by a good title, his possession cannot be disturbed till alienation is proved. It is possible that he may have sold it, but this is to be proved, not taken for granted.

" I do not deny," says my antagonist, " that these writers do also use the word *baptizo* in other circumstances, and in a secular sense, to denote immersion, sinking, overwhelming, or oppression. But this only proves that the two usages did co-exist; just as Mr. Carson proves that the two usages of *bapto* did co-exist in Hippocrates, and that the existence of the one did not disprove the existence of the other."

But is there not a great difference between Mr. Carson's *proving*, and Mr. Beecher's *asserting*, and supposing, and alleging *probabilities*, independently of the word? All my opponents endeavour to take advantage of my candour in proving the secondary meaning of *bapto*, taking it for granted that this equally applies to *baptizo*. Let *baptizo* show as good evidence of a secondary meaning, as I have shown on the part of *bapto*, and I will without controversy admit the fact. But when Mr. B. has done this, he has not succeeded; even then I am perfectly able to prove that the word applies to the ordinance of baptism in its primary meaning. A primary and a secondary meaning may co-exist, while each of them must be capable of being definitely ascertained. I deny a secondary meaning, not because it would disprove immersion in the ordinance of baptism, but because it wants the countenance of use. I give my opponents the whole range of Greek literature till the institution of the ordinance of baptism. I have never met an example which I cannot reduce to the one meaning.

SECTION IX.—Mr. B.'s explanation of Acts xxii. 16, is not a little singular. On the strength of this single example, I would undertake to refute his meaning of the word in dispute. Let us hear his explanation of it. " Here," says he, " we have faith in Christ, the washing away or pardon of sins, and a purification intended to symbolise it. *Baptisai*, purify thyself, or be purified bodily,—*apolousai tas amartias*, wash away thy sins, as to the mind, by calling on the name of the Lord." On this I remark, 1. This makes the pardon of sins to be conferred at the time of baptism. It is the very error which he reprobates, p. 42. If the distinction is, that purification is emblematic, and pardon of sins real, then the pardon of sins takes place in baptism. In fact, this is what he expressly says. He makes *purify* refer to the body, and *wash away thy sins* refer to the mind. Could Mr. B. more clearly avow the doctrine which he stigmatises?

2. This makes the external rite of baptism purify the body from sin, while the mind is purified not by baptism, but by calling on the name of the Lord. If the body is not purified from sin by the rite, it is not, according to Mr. B., purified at all. It is the mind only, as distinguished from the body, that is purified by calling on the name of the Lord.

3. This represents the mind as purified at the time of baptism, by calling on the name of the Lord. Is it not by faith in the blood of Christ, that both soul and body are purified? And does not this take place at the moment when the sinner believes in Christ.

4. It is not said that he was to wash away his sins by calling on the name of the Lord, but that he was to be baptized, *having called* on the name of the Lord.

5. *Purify* and *wash* are not indeed synonymous, but they are too nearly related to be both applied *together* with reference to the same thing. The one is the genus, and the other is a species under it. *Be purified*, and *wash away thy sins*, would be intolerable English. Is not *washing* contained in *purifying*? What need is there for both the genus and the species?

6. Mr. B. has felt this consequence ; and to avoid it, he has invented a distinction, not suggested by the words, but inconsistent both with truth and with the passage.

7. The emblem in baptism refers to the soul as well as to the body, though the body only is washed ; and the thing signified by the emblem refers to the body as well as to the soul. The body is washed from sin as well as the mind. The distinction, then, is not between the baptism of the body and the washing of the soul.

8. "*Be baptized*," evidently refers to the rite as designated from its

mode; and "*wash away thy sins*," to its emblematical meaning. *Baptism* is the name of the rite; the *washing away of sins* is its emblematical import. Sins are washed away by the blood of Christ, the moment a person believes on him. This is exhibited in emblem immediately after believing the truth, by being immersed in water. Sins are emblematically washed away in baptism, just as ceremonial sins were washed away by ceremonial purification. In like manner the Lord's supper represents that which has already taken place, and not that which is done during the ordinance. The blood was previously shed, the atonement was made, and the sins of the worthy partakers were remitted. But in the ordinance of the supper all this is exhibited in emblem.

9. This phraseology shows that baptism is a *washing* or *bathing :* then it cannot be a purification by sprinkling a few drops of water. This is no washing; the whole person was bathed.

10. Yet though there is a washing in baptism, the word baptism cannot signify washing, for this would be to say, " Be *washed*, and *wash* away thy sins." Two words with exactly the same meaning could not be thus conjoined. No criticism will ever be able to reconcile this passage with either *washing* or *purifying* as the meaning of the word *baptism*. It is suitable only to its modal meaning, *immersion*.

Mr. B. thinks that 1 Pet. iii. 21, proves his view. The apostle, he tells us, " seems to think that, if he left the word *baptisma* unguarded, he might be taken to mean the external purification of the body." Is not this reason of caution as applicable to *immersion* as to purification? Whatever might have been the name or mode of the ordinance, it is an ordinance of emblematic purification, and as such was liable to perversion. Have not Baptists as much need to caution ignorance against supposing that the external rite is salvation, as those who make the word signify *purification?* The *immersion* is an emblematical *washing*, and it is necessary to guard against the universal proneness to superstition, in substituting rites for the things signified by them.

Mr. B. seems to think that the word baptism in the passage does not at all refer to the Christian rite, but to purification or atonement by the blood of Christ. This conceit is unworthy of notice. 1. Immerse is the meaning of the word, whatever the immersion may represent. 2. It is the appropriated name of the ordinance, and to the ordinance it must refer here, whatever the word may signify. 3. That it refers to the ordinance of baptism is evident on the whole face of the document. No man could deny this who had not a purpose to serve. 4. Mr. B. does not, as he ought, show the consistency of the meaning alleged, with the phraseology of the passage. 5. The ordinance of baptism, and the salvation of Noah by water, have the most lively resemblance. Noah and his family were saved by being buried in the water of the flood; and after the flood they emerged as rising from the grave. There is no correspondence between *purification* and the water of the flood. 6. We are saved by baptism, just as Paul washed away his sins by baptism—just as the bread in the Lord's supper is Christ's body, and the wine his blood—just as the rock was Christ—just as the joint participation in eating the bread and drinking the wine in the supper, is the communion of the body of Christ, and of the blood of Christ. There is no difficulty in this phraseology to any who have not some heresy to support by perversion. The author refers next to the authority of Josephus. I have already disposed of the testimony of Josephus, with regard to the baptism of John : it is completely in accordance with our views of the mode of the ordinance of Christ. "To denote baptism," says Mr. B., "he uses the word *baptesis*, and to denote its import he states that they are to use it, *eph agneia tou somatos*," &c. Josephus does not use *baptesis* to denote the rite of baptism, but for the act of baptizing. To denote the rite, he uses *baptismos*. The *e baptesis* is the immersing—*baptismos* is the rite of *immersion*. And the words of Josephus, quoted by the author, are the import of the rite as to its nature or object, not the import of its name. This manifests a great want of discrimination in my opponent. Except this were the import of the name of the rite, it cannot serve him. The import of the rite, as given by Josephus, instead of serving my opponent, refutes him. If the people came to John's baptism on account of purification, then baptism is the name of the rite, and *purification* is its object. They came to be *immersed* in order to be purified by that immersion. Surely a very child will understand this.

"Now here I remark," says my antagonist, "that there was nothing to cause Josephus or any other Jew to think of the mode, or to attach any importance to it." What trifling is this! What necessity for Josephus to think anything of the mode? Does this say that a certain mode was not employed, and that Josephus did not mention the purification by the name of the mode employed? Does any one expect Josephus to attach importance to the mode whatever it might be? Does this imply that Jesus attached no importance to the mode? I never met so great and so constant a want of discrimination. Suppose an infidel to give an account of the performance of this rite by immersion, would he not speak of it as an immersion?

"No idea," continues the author, "of a fancied reference, in the rite, to the death of Christ, could bias his mind to the sense immersion." Was it necessary that Josephus should understand the reference of the mode of this rite to the death of Christ, in order to his knowing it to be an immersion; and in order to his giving it the modal appropriated name? I am not sure that John the Baptist understood this. Did Josephus understand the emblem of the burial of Christ, that was contained in the figure of Jonas in the belly of the whale? Did all men know what was the import of the rite of circumcision, who spoke of it by its appropriated name; and who knew what was performed in the rite? How many people know that the Baptists immerse in the performance of the ordinance of baptism, who do not know that in that mode they have a reference to the death, burial, and resurrection of Christ? I am weary of replying to childish trifling.

"To him, it is plain," continues the author, "that it meant nothing but purifying the body," &c. It may be very true that the rite was understood by Josephus to mean nothing but purifying the body, without implying that its name signified purification. As usual the author does not distinguish between the name of the rite and the object of the rite. Though Josephus might see no emblem in the mode, does this imply that immersion was not its mode; that it had not its name from the mode; and that Josephus spoke not of it by its appropriated modal name? It is sickening to be obliged to notice such arguments.

"Now," says the writer, "although I would not rely on such places for proof, against a strong contrary probability, yet when I find them so perfectly coincident with all other facts; when all shades of probability so perfectly harmonise and blend in a common result, I cannot hesitate, for I see no good reason for doubt." Whatever may be supposed the probability with regard to the mode in the facts referred to, independently of testimony, the moment competent testimony gives its evidence, it decides the matter. Instead of a probability, there is a certainty that immersion was the mode, because the word used by the historian signifies immersion, and has no other meaning. Is not the meaning of a word testimony? The author here admits the possibility of immersion in each of the cases referred to. What, then, should prevent it, when it is testified by a word that has no other meaning? This is testimony against previous improbability, which in all courts is competent evidence. That cannot be a safe principle, which, it is admitted, may possibly fail. Now the author himself here admits that the principle on which he interprets this word, will not universally hold good.

Mr. Beecher proceeds on an axiom that is false, fanatical, and subversive of all revealed truth, namely, that meaning is to be assigned to words in any document, not from the authority of the use of the language, ascertained by acknowledged examples; but from views of probability as to the thing related, independently of the testimony of the word. He learns not facts from history; but he dictates to history. The historian he will not allow to use his words in the sense acknowledged by the language, because that sense is, he thinks, unsupported by the previous probability of the fact.

If a word is found to have two meanings, it is lawful in every instance of its occurrence, to bring their respective claims to the test. But if a secondary meaning is not in proof, previous probability as to the fact has nothing to do; because a thing previously improbable may be received as truth, with perfect confidence, on sufficient testimony. To allege probability against the ascertained meaning of a word, is to deny testimony as a source of evidence; for the meaning of testimony must be known from the words used. This is a Neological canon, and is the very principle on which Neologists interpret the Bible. It is very improbable, they say, that such a thing was the case, therefore the words of the historian do not mean this. It is very improbable, some say, that Samson killed so many people with a jaw-bone of an ass; therefore the word does not here signify the jaw-bone of an ass, but the *tooth of a rock*, which being loosely attached, was pulled down on his enemies by the hero. This canon would not leave a miracle in the Bible, nor a doctrine in revelation.

On the same principle, should a foreigner read in English, that a prisoner was immersed in jail, on the belief of the Gospel, he might say, " as it is improbable that there was water for the *dipping* of his person, it is to be concluded that *immerse* here signifies to purify without reference to mode." Yet *immerse* does not more decidedly mean to *dip*, than does *baptizo;* and there is not in all Mr. B.'s examples, a higher probability than this. Such previous probabilities give place to testimony, as darkness gives place to light.

Mr. B. alleges that " it is not a solitary fact on which the argument rests." This can mean no more, as to the examples alleged, than that there are several instances of improbability, considered previously to testimony. But this is not a combination of evidence. Each of the cases considered separately is nothing; all taken together, then, must be nothing : it is the addition or multiplication of ciphers. The *Columbine bridge* will solve a thousand such difficulties.

There is no word, whose meaning is not liable to the like objections, as are here alleged with respect to the word in dispute. What word is there, which in the whole history of its use, does not sometimes occur in circumstances, in which the thing which it attests is previously as improbable as immersion in the cases referred to by Mr. B.? Yet this never shakes our confidence as to the meaning of any word, when it testifies. There are some islands in which it is very improbable that horses would be found; yet if a traveller tells us that he saw a horse, we shall believe either that he really saw a *horse*, or that he deceives us. We never think of solving the difficulty, by alleging that *horse* here signifies a *leopard.*

With respect to the relation between the name of this ordinance and purification, the reason is quite obvious. That a coincidence and harmony should exist between a word which is the appropriated name of an ordinance, and the thing emblematically meant by the ordinance, is a thing that can strike no philologist with surprise. This is altogether necessary, instead of being a thing unexpected. There cannot be an instance of a similar connexion without a similar result. If *baptisma* is the name of the ordinance, whatever may be supposed its meaning ; and if purification is the emblem of the ordinance, there must be such a coincidence. Any man of ordinary understanding will perceive the ground of the connexion, without any recourse to identity of meaning in the terms *baptize* and *purify.* Was not the ordinance of circumcision so connected with purification? Yet the word *circumcise* does not signify to *purify.*

But if all these examples were admitted to imply this meaning, it would not prove that the rite of baptism is not an immersion. These examples refer not to baptism. Even on that supposition we should fight the battle with success.

" The argument," says my antagonist, " from the usage of the writers of Alexandrine Greek, is now at an end." Would not any one from reading this conclude that he had brought from these writers, examples in which the word is used without reference to mode? But has he alleged one such? All he has done is to allege that the word is sometimes used, when, without reference to the testimony of the word, immersion is improbable. Does this imply that the thing is improbable, after the word gives its testimony? Have I not exemplified this by an instance from Columbine English? He need not go to Alexandrine Greek for such instances; they might occur in the oldest Greek without affecting the question

SECTION X.—Mr. B. next professes to find proof in the Fathers. Proof from the Fathers that *baptizo* signifies to *purify!* As well might he profess to find in them proof for the existence of railroads and steam-coaches. There is no such proof; there is not an instance in all the Fathers in which the word, or any of its derivatives, are so used. Without exception, they use the word always for immersion. Now a reader not acquainted with the Fathers, may ask himself, how it is possible that two persons can give a directly contradictory account of the testimony of the same documents. Without any reference to the veracity of either of the combatants, he may say, the fact must be so easily decided, that it is strange that any of them should be rash in his testimony. Let such a reader attend a moment to me, and I will ask no learning in him, in order to enable him to decide between us: all I demand is a little common sense.

Well, how does Mr. B. bring out his proof? If the writings of the Fathers prove that they understood this word in Mr. B.'s sense, must not Mr. B. prove this by alleging examples of the use of the word in this sense? Common sense, what do you say? But Mr. B. attempts no such thing; he does not appeal to the use of the word by the Fathers, but to other words applied by the Fathers to the same ordinance.

Now I do not charge my opponent with dishonesty in the use of this argument: I do him the justice to believe that he is the dupe of his own sophistry; but it is a sophistry childishly weak. I have already disposed of this argument. It assumes as an axiom, that words that apply to the same ordinance are identical in signification. Every child may see that this is not fact. The same ordinance is called by different persons, *the Lord's supper, the communion, the ordinance, the sacrament, the eucharist,* &c. Does this imply that each of these words is identical in meaning with the term *Lord's supper,* or that they are identical in meaning with each other? Every one of these words has a meaning of its own, while they all agree in designating the same ordinance. *Baptism* itself is by some called *christening.* Does this imply that the word *baptism* signifies christening? I could produce examples at will; but no reader can need more. The Fathers called baptism *regeneration;* but they never supposed that the word baptism signified regeneration. Both the words referred to the same ordinance, but they referred to it under a different view of it. Baptism was its appropriated name from its mode: regeneration was its name from its supposed effect. When I say *William the First,* and *William the Conqueror,* I refer to the same man, but I do not mean that *the first* signifies *the Conqueror.* William the First, is the designation of the man as king of England—the Conqueror, is a designation of the same man from the way in which he became king. Even if *katharizo* itself had been the appropriated name of the ordinance of baptism, it would not be identical in meaning with the word regeneration. In fact, this is one of the words which the Fathers employed to denote baptism, yet this did not make it identical in meaning either with baptism or with the other words by which they designated this ordinance. When baptism is called *purification* by the ancients, it is considered as it was supposed to purify : when it was called *regeneration*, it was considered as a new birth. *Purification* is baptism under one view of it : regeneration is the same ordinance under another view. *Purification* does not signify *new birth ;* nor does *new birth* signify *purification.* A hundred words or terms might be used to denote the same ordinance, without implying that any two of them were perfectly identical in meaning. In fact, a great multitude were actually employed, while each designated the same ordinance in its own peculiar manner. The Fathers employed a great multitude of terms to designate baptism; but they did not make the word baptism designate the same idea with each or any of these terms.

'What is it to purify the spirit," he asks, "but to regenerate?" It is true that they who are purified are regenerated, and they who are regenerated are purified. Still, however, the terms have quite different meanings. *Regeneration* is a new birth : *purification* is an effect of this.

I might now dismiss this part of the subject ; but our author gives us such a delicious morsel of his philosophy, in accounting for the fact that baptism came to be considered as regeneration, that I am tempted to take a look at it for a moment. Nothing enables us with greater certainty to estimate the powers of an author, than his attempt at philosophy.

" Now," says the writer, " in a case where analogical senses exist, one external and material, and the other spiritual, it is natural that they should run into each other, and terms applied to one be applied to the other. Thus, if *baptizo* means to purify, then there is natural purification and spiritual purification, or regeneration, and there would be a tendency to use *anagennao* to denote the latter idea, and also to transfer it to the external rite ; and, at first, it would be so done as merely to be the name of the rite, and not to denote its actual efficacy."

Upon this I remark : 1.—The author here mistakes what he calls the external and material sense, for the emblematic sense. It is of the emblematic sense, as distinguished from the proper sense of the word, he is speaking ; and not of an external or material sense as distinguished from a spiritual sense. Purification, for instance, first applied to external things, and afterwards by analogy was transferred to the mind. But it is not of *external,* or *material,* or *natural* purification, as distinguished from spiritual purification, he is speaking ; but of emblematic purification, as distinguished from the purification of the soul and body from sin. Every external, or material, or natural purification, is not the purification of which he is speaking, namely, baptism. It is only when the purification is emblematic, that it is the purification of which he speaks. The relation, then, which subsists between what he calls the external or material sense, and the spiritual sense, is not the same with the relation that subsists between the emblematic sense and the proper sense of the word. *Purification* applies as properly to mind as to matter, and designates neither of them separately, but includes both of them. To apply to either of them separately, the word has not to give up its meaning, or to run into a different meaning.

2. *The running of two senses into each other* is philological transubstantiation. Two senses cannot run into each other, nor can one sense run into another sense. This language is paradoxical. Not only does the whale swallow Jonah, but Jonah at 'the same time swallows the whale. Whatever change may take place in the application of words, one sense cannot become another: this would imply that a thing is different from itself.

3. The author here supposes that purification in baptism is natural purification. But is the design of baptism to wash away the filth of the flesh? Is not the purification of baptism an emblematic purification?

4. He tells us that on the supposition that *baptizo* signifies to purify, with reference to both material and spiritual purification, there would be a tendency to use the word *anagennao* to denote the latter idea. What is the latter idea? Is it not spiritual purification, or regeneration? What is this but to say, that, on a certain condition, there is a tendency to use a word in its own sense? There is a tendency to use the word regeneration for regeneration; and a tendency to use a word that signifies spiritual purification for spiritual purification. A wonderful tendency indeed! Does not the author himself explain regeneration as signifying spiritual purification? He must be a hardy sceptic who will deny this.

5. He tells us here, that if *baptizo* signifies to purify, with reference to both natural and spiritual purification, there will be a tendency to transfer the word *anagennao* to the external rite. Now would not this tendency be the same, on the supposition that the purification was to be found in the nature of the rite, as if it were found in the name of the rite?

6. If *baptizo* signifies both natural and spiritual purification, and *anagennao* signifies only the latter, what tendency is there to transfer *anagennao* to a rite designated by *baptizo*, in that part of its signification which *anagennao* does not possess; abandoning that part of the meaning of *baptizo* which it does possess? Surely if from the partial agreement of *baptizo* and *anagennao*, the latter is transferred to a rite designated by the former, it must be in that part of their meaning in which they agree—not in a meaning in which they differ. This is a very perverse and capricious tendency. Can the author illustrate this tendency? He affirms it, but does not show it.

7. He tells us that in the first application of *anagennao* to baptism, it would be as the name of the rite without reference to its effect. This is absurd and self-evidently false. How does *anagennao* come to be applied to the rite of baptism? Is it not, even on the author's theory, because it agrees with *baptizo* in a part of its meaning? If then it is applied to the rite, from its agreement with the appropriated name of the rite in a part of its meaning, it must be applied to the rite in that part of its meaning in which it agrees with *baptizo*, and not in that part of the meaning of *baptizo* with which it has nothing common. No axiom is more clear than this.

8. Of all the terms by which the Fathers designated baptism, there is not one of them conferred on it on the principle supposed by the author. Even *katharismos* is not given to this ordinance on the principle of the connexion between analogical meanings; but as the nature of the rite is supposed to be a purification. The various names are conferred on it, not from their relation to the word *baptizo*, the appropriated name of the ordinance, but from the supposed nature of the ordinance. Any child may understand this. It is called *initiation*, for instance. Has initiation any relation to the meaning of the word *baptizo?* It is called *illumination*. Has the word illumination any relation to the word *baptizo*, whatever may be the meaning of *baptizo?* The author's philosophy is false, absurdly and extravagantly false. He gives us eight lines of philosophy. I will give a premium to any one who will produce me a greater quantity of absurdity in the same compass, under the appearance of wisdom. The only merit this nonsense can claim, is that it is original nonsense. No one these seventeen hundred years has ever thought of accounting for the opinion that baptism is regeneration, on the principle of President Beecher. It grieves me to be obliged to write in this manner; but I cannot avoid it. Half-learned people will think that this account of the phenomenon is an unparalleled effort of philosophy; and thousands will rely on it who cannot pretend to fathom it. They will conclude either that he is right, or that the subject is so deeply involved in obscurity, that it is utterly impossible to bring the truth to light. I cannot avoid showing that there is neither learning nor logic in the attempt to unsettle the meaning of the word in question.

But the source from which baptismal regeneration springs is not left to philosophical investigation. The ground on which the Fathers considered baptism to be the means of regeneration, and to be essential to salvation, is clearly attested by themselves. The very passage which Mr. B. quotes from Justin Martyr fully explains this: it was their view of John iii. 3. In giving an account of the dedication of Christians to God, Justin Martyr tells us, that after a certain process, the candidates were led by the Christians to a place where there was water, and were *regenerated* as they themselves had been *regenerated*. Here I observe that President Beecher is mistaken in supposing that *anagennao* here describes the rite. It does not describe the rite; but tells us what is effected by the rite: the persons baptized were regenerated by baptism. Justin then tells us the reason why he says they were regenerated by baptism. "For," says he, "they are *washed* or *bathed* in the water, in the name of the Father," &c. Does not this imply that the *washing* was the baptism; and that by that washing they were regenerated? It is because they were so washed, that he considers them to have been born again. Regeneration is not here considered as the name of the ordinance, nor as synonymous with its name; but as an effect of the rite, which consists in a certain washing.

Justin Martyr next expressly refers to John iii. 3, as their authority for considering that regeneration was effected by baptism. He then refers to Isaiah i. 16, to prove the same thing. Justin subjoins an account which he alleges they had from the apostles, of the necessity of this second birth, by a contrast of it with the first birth; and in this he expressly asserts, that they obtained remission of former sins " in the water." Here is a foundation for all the towers of Babylon.

Now if President Beecher had this document before him, as his quotation leads us to believe, how could he give such a philosophical account of the origin of the belief of baptismal regeneration? How could he doubt that baptism was understood by the Fathers to be a washing of the whole body? Is it not described as a washing of the person? On what account are candidates led to places where there was water? Are not baptized persons considered as having their former sins remitted *in the water?* What is the hardihood of men who can presume to allege the Fathers on the other side!

I may observe also that the editor of Justin, in a note, refers to Clemens Alexandrinus, who says, that " the same thing is often called *gift,* and *illumination,* and *initiation,* and *bathing.* Bathing, because through it we are cleansed from our sins; *illumination,* because through it that holy light which is salvation is beheld," &c. Justin himself says that this *washing* is called *illumination,* because the minds of those who learn these things are *enlightened.* Is it not obvious to a child that every one of these names is given to the rite on a different ground? Not one of these is given as a synonyme of *baptismos.* It is *washing* for one reason, it is *illumination* for another, and *initiation* for another. Even in this very passage, Justin commences by referring to baptism as a dedication. See Justin Martyr, p. 89, Thirlby's Ed.

It is strange to astonishment that President Beecher did not perceive that each of the words applied by the Fathers to the rite of baptism, has the same right to force its meaning on the word baptism, as the word purification has, from the fact of this application. If any one chooses to adopt the theory that the word baptism signifies *illumination,* or *initiation,* or *dedication,* &c. &c.; may he not allege that the Fathers called baptism by this name? The answer to all is, the Fathers did call baptism by all these names; but they did not make the word *baptism* signify any of them. It was baptism from its mode: it was each of all those other things from its nature. He who cannot perceive this, is not fit for the discussion of a deep philological question.

" This view," says Mr. B., " explains not only the early prevalence of the idea of baptismal regeneration, but also the other extreme, the entire denial of water baptism." There is no philosophy in this observation. Will a rite be more likely to be perverted from its name, than it will be from its nature? Is it not obvious that whatever may be the meaning of its name, if it implies purification in its nature, or import, the supposed tendency will be the same? And as to the latter part of the argument, whatever may be the meaning of the name, or even the import of the rite, when it is grossly perverted, there will be the same tendency for one extreme to produce another. Some in flying from the perversion of the ordinance, will relieve themselves by denying the ordinance altogether. Whether the name of the rite signifies immersion, or pouring, or sprinkling, or purification, or initiation, or dedication, &c. &c., if purification is implied in its nature, there will be the same tendency to pervert it; and when the perversion is perceived, there will be the same tendency to get rid of the perversion, by freeing themselves from the rite.

"Besides this general reasoning from well-known facts," says Mr. B., "there is also philological proof that the word was often used by the Fathers in the sense *katharizo.*"

1. Now how does he prove this. I am fond of philological proof. His first philological proof that the Fathers often used the word in the sense of *purify,* is taken from the passage in Justin Martyr already considered; in which he refers to baptism by the phrase *loutron poiountai,* "they wash or purify them;" that is, there is proof that the word is here used in a certain sense, when the word is not here used at all!

2. He here assumes that wash and *purify* are the same. They are not the same; and they are distinguished in the very passage quoted from Justin Martyr. The words which he cites from Isaiah are *lousasthe, katharoi genesthe,* "wash ye, make you clean." Washing is the action performed—purification is the effect of this action. Will President Beecher never learn to distinguish things that differ? Even if the word baptism signified washing, this would not make it signify purification in general. Even this, instead of proving, would overturn Mr. B.'s theory.

3. The phrase *loutron poiountai* in Justin Martyr, as I have already showed, does not designate regeneration, but the action by which regeneration was supposed to be effected, or as President Beecher himself here says, "the mode of regeneration."

4. Baptism is a washing, and is so called by the Scriptures as well as by the Fathers; but this does not imply that the word baptism signifies washing. I think by this time I must have made this distinction clear to my opponent.

5. This phrase is not only not inconsistent with immersion, but immerse is the only thing that will explain it. A purification performed by sprinkling or pouring a few drops of water, would not be a *loutron.*

Mr. B.'s second argument to prove that the Fathers used the word as signifying purification, is, that Chrysostom says, that Christ "calls his cross and death a cup and baptism; a cup, because he readily drank it; baptism, because by it he purified the world." But is it not obvious that Chrysostom refers not to the name of the rite, but to the rite itself in its import? Whatever may be supposed the meaning of the name of this rite, it is in its nature a rite of purification. The meaning of Chrysostom is perfectly the same, whatever may be supposed the meaning of the word baptism. It is quite immaterial whether the idea of purification be found in the name, or in the nature, of the ordinance. Shall I never be able to force this into the mind of my antagonist? If he would allow himself to perceive this distinction, he would be delivered from much false reasoning. I will then try to make the thing plain to every child. When it is said that "Christ our passover is sacrificed for us," it is implied that the passover was a sacrifice. But does this imply that the word *passover* signifies *sacrifice?* The phrase *circumcision in heart,* signifying purity of mind, implies that circumcision denoted purity. But does this imply that the term circumcision means purity? Will Mr. B. need another lesson?

But there must be in my antagonist a most astonishing want of persp.cacity, else he would have perceived that he was making a snare for his own feet, out of which he could not possibly escape. If the calling of Christ's cross and death a baptism, because it purifies, implies that the word baptism signifies purification, then, for the same reason, does not the calling of his cross and death a cup, because he readily drank it, imply that the word cup signifies *drinking?* Try now, Mr. President, to escape out of this snare. Is it not obvious to every man of common sense, that Chrysostom refers to baptism in its import or nature, and not to its name? There is nothing in the name that signifies either *purification* or *drinking.* The same answer serves for the quotations from Theophylact, and for all others of a similar kind. The purification is in the nature, not in the name of the rite.

Mr. B.'s third argument to prove that the Fathers used the word as signifying purification, is that they "sometimes, in describing the rite, use *purify* alone;" that is, a great number of passages in which the Fathers did not use the word at all, prove that they used it in a certain sense! This fact proves that the Fathers used purify in reference to the ordinance of baptism, not that they used the word baptism as signifying purification. I have already fully explained the principle on which this word and all the other names were given to this ordinance. None of them are of the same meaning with the word baptism.

Mr. B. seems quite aware that the authority of the Fathers for the use of this word is against him; and endeavours to escape from this argument. "It would be of no use here," says he, "to say that the Fathers did in fact immerse; this could not decide that purify was not the sense."

1. If the Fathers immersed, it proves that they considered immersion as the proper mode of the ordinance.

2. The authority of the Fathers on this question is not their practice, but their use of the word. They not only immersed in baptism, but they use the word always for immersion. They knew the meaning of the language which they spoke. On their practice I should not have the least reliance on any question.

3. If there is a single instance of immersion, it is evidence of a conviction of its necessity. Would any one go to a river to plunge, if he could be sprinkled in a parlour?

4. Why does Mr. B. doubt as to the practice of the Fathers, when Justin Martyr shows him what was the usual practice?

"And even if it could be shown," adds the author, "that some of them use the word *baptizo* to denote the act of immersion in baptism, it would avail nothing; it would only prove inconsistent usage."

1. "Could it be shown that some of the Fathers used *baptizo* for the act of immersion in baptism!" Might he not as well say, could it be shown that the sun shines at noon-day? Can the man who will not concede this, be in earnest in the search of truth? Can any man who has read the Fathers consider it as a matter of doubt whether any of them use this word in this sense? No fact in history can be better ascertained. Most of the best established facts on record have not as

clear evidence. If the words in which they are recorded were to be interpreted on Mr. B.'s principles, not a fact of them could remain in evidence.

2. This assumes that the author has proved a contrary practice. But he has not proved this in a single instance.

3. If it is admitted that some of the Fathers used the word in the sense of immersion, all the arguments alleged by Mr. B. will be quashed. They can prove nothing against an admitted fact.

4. If I can explain all his alleged facts in accordance with my sense of the word, and if it is admitted that some of the Fathers use the word in this sense, is it likely that his sense of the word is the just one, when it makes the Fathers inconsistent with one another and *themselves* in the use of a common word?

5. Inconsistent usage can never be fairly alleged, if any way of reconciliation is possible. Only on this principle could the Scripture itself be freed from the charge of contradiction; and I have shown the reconciliation.

6. Inconsistent usage cannot be charged till each of the alleged meanings is in full proof. Our meaning is in proof that candour can never question : the other meaning is not in proof.

7. Is it on the authority of such arguments as are produced by Mr. B. that we are to charge inconsistency of usage with respect to a common word, on writers who lived at the same time, and derived their knowledge of the ordinance from the same sources?

8. Were we for the sake of argument to admit that the word had a secondary meaning, and were we to indulge Mr. B. in supposing that it was in that signification applied to designate the ordinance of Christ, this would not produce an inconsistency of usage in the use of the word with respect to that ordinance. The sense in which it was used by the apostles must have been known most assuredly to all that either heard them, or read their writings. To suppose that persons who spoke the Greek language might understand their words in a sense different from that in which they used them, would be to charge the Scripture as not being a revelation. Whatever was the sense in which the apostles used the word, must have been known to all who heard them or read their writings. To talk of "two currents" is to speak without thinking.

9. Can any other such inconsistency of usage be found? The cause that produced this inconsistency must have produced many others.

10. This Alexandrine Greek is a perjured witness. When it is brought into court by the sprinklers, it most solemnly swears that the word received a secondary meaning of sprinkling or pouring, and in this sense it is applied to the rite of baptism. When it has been tampered with by Mr. B., it as solemnly on oath renounces such a meaning ; and deposes that its true secondary meaning in this ordinance is *purify*. May it not with equal propriety be brought into court by *initiate, dedicate, illuminate*, and by every one of all the numerous claimants? What is it that this witness ever refused to swear, when solicited by a sufficient temptation? If President Beecher should turn into Greek letters, a document in any of the languages of the Indian tribes, I have no doubt that this

witness would swear in an English court that it is good Alexandrine Greek.

11. Where is this Alexandrine Greek to be found? If it exists at all, must it not be in the Septuagint? Yet no such usage prevails in that translation. The word is used here, and by the other Jewish writers, perfectly in the same sense as it is used by classical Greeks. The case of Naaman the Syrian presents this fact in the strongest light. Instead of *baptizo* having the sense of *katharizo*, it took seven *baptizos* to make one *katharizo*. And even a child may here see that the washing and the cleansing are different ideas. " Wash in Jordan seven times, and thou shalt be clean." Washing is the means of effecting the purification.

12. If *baptizo* signified *purify* in Alexandrine Greek, why is it that in all the numerous passages in which purification is spoken of, this word is not once to be found in the Greek translation of the Old Testament? Is it possible that a word in its primary sense signifying to *dip*, should, from its constant application to the rights of purification among the Jews who spoke the Greek language, come to signify to *purify;* yet in all the translations used by those Hellenistic Jews, the word should never occur in that sense, when speaking of their different purifications? I confidently affirm that this observation must appear convincing to every one who is capable of weighing it. Is it possible that a word could get a secondary meaning, from being so constantly applied to certain rites, when, in speaking of these rites, it is never used in that sense? Now let any one who knows only so much Greek as to enable him to trace the two words *baptizo* and *katharizo* in a Greek concordance of the Old Testament; and I pledge myself that, if he has a spark of candour or honesty, he will be convinced.

Nay, I will make the matter plain even to the most unlearned. Let them take an English concordance, and trace the word purify; and when they are assured, on sufficient testimony, that *baptizo* is not used in any of the places, will they ask any other evidence that *baptizo* did not, in the estimation of the Greek translators. signify to *purify?* The " Englishman's Greek Concordance" will show this at a glance.

13. Even the Jews who lived in countries where the Greek language was spoken, would use their own language in their worship. There could be no ground for their giving a Greek word a secondary meaning, from their frequent use of it in religious matters. There is no philosophy in this philology.

14. If a secondary meaning was likely to be given to this word from its frequent application to purifying rites, would not this principle operate more powerfully on the Hebrew word which was always used for immersion by the Jews? Yet the Hebrew word that signifies to dip, never obtained the secondary meaning of *purify.*

15. If frequent application of a modal word to rites of purification, would confer a secondary meaning, *rantizo* would have been more likely than *baptizo* to receive the meaning of *purify.* It is more frequently applied to purifying rites than the other.

16. *Baptizo* is by no writer, either with respect to things sacred or

civil, ever applied to any object but such as may be immersed. To things palpably too great for immersion it was never applied. To the purification of a house, of the city Jerusalem, of the temple, it is applied by no writer. Now, if it signified purification as definitely as *katharizo* itself, how is it that it is never used to designate the purification of any object too large to be immersed? If it signified *purification*, we should certainly, on some occasion, find it applied to the largest objects that were purified, as well as the smallest.

17. Had it been intended that the word to be appropriated to designate this rite should signify *purification*, *katharismos* itself would, without doubt, have been the word. This suited in every respect. Why, then, should another word be employed, which certainly was not so suitable for the supposed purpose? What should prevent *katharismos?* What should give the preference to *baptisma?* Was *baptisma* employed in order to create confusion?

18. Though the rite of baptism is an emblematical purification, yet purification is not the only thing represented by the emblem. The communion of the believer with Christ in his death, burial, and resurrection, and his salvation by that union, and only by that union, is also represented. *Katharismos*, then, was not suitable as the appropriated name of the ordinance.

19. Is there any Scripture rite in which the way in which the things appointed are to be used, is not also appointed? Now, according to Mr. B. there is no specific way appointed for the performance of this rite. We may plunge the person once, or three times; we may pour water all over him, or pour a little on any part of him; we may sprinkle him all over, or sprinkle a few drops on any part of him; we may rub a little water on any part of him with our finger, as in the eucharist the ancients rubbed the child's lips, or we may rub him all over. Any application of water, according to Mr. B., will be equally sufficient for this ordinance. Can sobriety of mind receive this doctrine? Could sobriety of judgment have suggested it?

I have now examined Mr. B.'s arguments, and there is not the shadow of evidence that the word *baptism* signifies *purification*. I have met every thing that has even a shadow of plausibility; and completely dissected my antagonist. Am I not now entitled to send *purify* to the museum as a *lusus naturæ*, to be placed by the side of its brother *pop?*

SECTION XI.—FACTS WHICH DISPROVE MR. BEECHER'S THEORY.- Having fully refuted every argument presented by Mr. Beecher, I shall now, as briefly as possible, state a number of facts which dispute his theory.

PASSAGES OF SCRIPTURE WHICH EXPLAIN BAPTISM AS AN IMMERSION

Not only do occurrences of the word in question prove that it signifies *immersion* and not *purification*, but the Scriptures themselves explain it as an immersion. No candid mind can read these passages without being impressed with this conviction.

Rom. vi. 4, for instance, must bring conviction to every mind not shut against evidence. All attempts to explain it otherwise are unnatural,

forced, and perfectly unsuccessful. The same may be said with respect
to Col. ii. 12. The apostle in these passages reasons on immersion as
the mode of this ordinance, and draws conclusions from its import.

Is not this the most satisfactory way of bringing the truth of criticism
to the test? The phraseology of 1 Peter iii. 21, gives the same testimony Baptism is explained here in a way that will coincide with no
view of this ordinance, but that of immersion.

PASSAGES WHICH IMPLY THAT IMMERSION WAS THE MODE OF BAPTISM

Baptism is not only explained by Scripture as *immersion*, but many
passages imply that this was its mode. Of this kind are the passages
which represent the persons as going to the water, being baptized in
the water, and after baptism coming up out of the water. Could madness itself allege any other reason for this, than that baptism was an
immersion of the body? Even if it should be supposed a washing of
the body without reference to mode, it is equally fatal to *purify*. It
could not mean purification in general, or purification by a few drops
of water, if the whole person must be washed. It must be a purification by washing the whole body.

The reason alleged for John's baptizing in Enon, John iii. 23, implies
that baptism was immersion. Had any mode of purification by water
been sufficient, there would have been no need for *many* waters, or
much water.

Christ refers to his death as a baptism in a figurative sense; but if
the word in a figurative sense signifies afflictions, the literal sense cannot be anything but immersion. Neither purify, nor sprinkle, nor any
other supposed meaning, will admit the figurative meaning, of afflictions,
or calamities. This is the figure also by which the calamities of the
Saviour are figuratively designated in the Psalms. He is represented
as overwhelmed with great waters.

PASSAGES WHICH ALLUDE TO BAPTISM AS AN IMMERSION

There are many passages of Scripture which allude to baptism in such
a way as to show that immerse was its mode. Of this kind is John iii.
5, a passage the misunderstanding of which has laid a foundation for the
grossest superstitions of nominal Christianity. *To be born of water*
most evidently implies, that water is the womb out of which the person
who is born proceeds. That this is the reference of the figure, whatever
may be supposed to be its meaning, cannot for a moment be doubted by
any reflecting mind. Here the figure must signify the washing of the
believer in the blood of Christ, which is figuratively represented by the
water in baptism. This our Lord stated in a figurative manner, as he
did other things, which were more clearly to be exhibited in the teach
ing of his apostles. Who can doubt that it is the blood of Jesus Christ
that washes away the sins of the believer?

Many persons on both sides of the question are unwilling to allow any
allusion to baptism here, in order to avoid the supposed consequence,
that it would imply the necessity of baptism to salvation. It has always
appeared to me that candour cannot deny that there is an allusion to

baptism; and I will never, for fear of the consequences, refuse to admit anything that appears to be in evidence. But no such consequences can flow from this admission. In whatever way its reference may be explained, it cannot possibly imply that baptism is essential to salvation. Were this the case, then it would not always be necessarily true that faith is salvation. Were this true, it would imply that an external work performed by man is necessary to salvation. I need not state the thousandth part of the absurdity that would flow from this doctrine. Whatever is the truth of the matter, this cannot be true; it is contrary to the whole current of Scripture. One fact will by example prove that baptism is not necessary to salvation: the thief who believed on the cross was saved without baptism. This single fact will for ever forbid such a meaning to be taken out of this passage.

Having, then, in the most satisfactory manner ascertained from Scripture that baptism cannot be essential to salvation, we may next examine what is the figurative import of this expression, *born of water.* To be *born of water*, then, as a figurative expression, signifies to be washed or cleansed from our sins. In what we are to be washed we must learn from other parts of Scripture, which teach us that we are to be washed in the blood of Christ.

The objection which naturally presents itself to the considering of the water, in reference to the thing signified by the water, is, that this is supposed to be immediately added—"*and of the Spirit.*" It is supposed that *born of the Spirit* is the thing signified by *born of water.* But this is not the case; to be born of the Spirit is not the thing signified by the figure *born of water.* The water in baptism is not the emblem of the Spirit, but of the blood of Christ. The Spirit washes us, not as being himself like water, but as the agent who uses the water by which we are cleansed, that is, the blood of Jesus Christ. Let a man understand this, and he will cease to feel difficulty on this passage. To be *born of water*, and to be born of *the Spirit*, are expressions which do not refer to the same thing. The one refers to the blood of Christ, and the other to the Spirit who is the agent of the spiritual birth, and of the washing away of sins through the application of Christ's blood. We must be born both of the blood of Christ and of the Spirit. It is in the blood of Christ that the Spirit washes us. There is the washing in Christ's blood, and also the renewing of the Spirit.

Let it be observed, that though this passage alludes to baptism as the foundation of the figure which it employs, yet baptism is only alluded to—not mentioned. It is not said that except a man is baptized he cannot be saved; but, except he is *born of water.* Now figuratively considered, a man may be *born of water* without having water literally applied to him. He is born of water when he is washed from sin, in whatever way sin is to be washed away. There are many figurative expressions of this nature—and on this fact I will venture to rest the whole solution of the difficulty. When poets are said to drink of the Castalian springs, the figure is perfectly the same: there is no real drinking: it is the supposed reception of the spirit of poetry. So in being *born of water*—the thing meant is the being washed in the blood of Christ. If a person presents us with a specimen of his poetry, which we do not approve; may we not answer that except a man drink of the Castalian springs, he will never be a poet? Do we mean literal drinking at the place?

That this is the true explanation of the passage, we have infallible evidence. I can produce an inspired commentator to warrant my solution of this difficulty. Christ gave himself for the church, "that he might sanctify and cleanse it with the washing of water by the word." Eph. v. 26. Here it is expressly said, that the washing of water is by the word. The word is the means by which the believer is washed in the blood of Christ. The whole church is supposed to be washed in this way. The believer, then, is washed by the word, even although, from ignorance of his duty, or from want of opportunity, he has never been washed in water. I may observe, also, that this is another passage of Scripture which alludes to baptism as a washing of the whole person. A purification with a few drops of water would not suit the phraseology. Here I observe, also, that *sanctification* and *cleansing*, or *purification* and *washing*, are considered as different from each other. Sanctification and purification are not exactly coincident; nor is either of them coincident with washing; they are all effected by the instrumentality of the word.

" But ye are washed, but ye are sanctified, but ye are justified, in the name of the Lord Jesus, and by the Spirit of our God." 1 Cor. vi. 11. Here also *washing* and *sanctification* are distinguished; and both are effected in the name of the Lord Jesus, and by the Spirit of our God. Faith in Christ is that through which they are washed; and the Spirit of our God is the agent who washes them by this means. This washing is represented in baptism, to which this passage refers.

In Rev. i. 5, Christ is said to wash us from our sins in his own blood. Christ washes us by his Spirit in his blood; but his blood is the cleansing element in which we are washed. This shows that to be born of water is to be washed in the blood of Christ.

When Paul says: " My little children, of whom I travail in birth again until Christ be formed in you," Gal. iv. 19, is there any literal travailing in birth? " I bare you on eagles' wings," Exodus xix. 4, is a similar figure. Would a child understand it literally? Gill shows very bad taste, when he supposes that it is necessary to supply *as*, the note of similitude, to prevent it from being understood in the literal meaning. Why then should there be a literal washing with water in the phrase *born of water?*

Is not the phrase *born of God* figurative, referring to that spiritual birth of which God is the author, and in which he is our Father? So *born of water* is that birth which is represented by being immersed in water.

The heart is said to be purified by faith, Acts xv. 9. Now, if faith purifies the heart, the water in baptism cannot be essential to the purification. It must be an emblem—not a means. The purification is effected without it, and before its application.

It is on a good conscience produced by faith in Christ, as distinguished from the external washing, that Peter places the value: 1 Peter iii. 21

" Seeing," says Peter, " ye have purified your souls in obeying the truth through the Spirit." 1 Peter i. 22. It is the belief of the truth, then, that purifies the soul—not the water of baptism. This purification is effected by the Spirit: he is the agent, and the truth is the instrument. The water is an emblem; but whether it has place or not, it has no share in the effect, either as an efficient, or as an instrument. " Being born again," says he, " not of corruptible seed, but of incorruptible, by the word of God." In the whole process of the spiritual birth the word of God is the only means, as the Spirit is the only agent. In Heb. x. 22, believers are said to have their bodies washed with pure water. This must be an allusion to baptism; and what could answer to this but immersion? It is a bathing of the whole body. Purification could not correspond to this. No application of water but a washing of the whole person could suit this language.

" Not by works of righteousness which we have done, but according to his mercy he saved us, by the washing of regeneration, and renewing of the Holy Ghost." Here the washing of regeneration is expressly distinguished from the renewing of the Holy Ghost. What in John iii. 5, is called *born of water*, is here called the *washing of regeneration;* and what is there called *born of the Spirit*, is here called the *renewing of the Holy Ghost*. *Born of water*, then, and *born of the Spirit*, are two distinct things; and born of the Spirit is not, as many suppose, the explanation or meaning of *born of water*. The *washing of regeneration* is the washing that takes place when we are born again of the incorruptible seed of the word, or by the belief of the truth. We are washed by faith in the blood of Christ. This washing takes place before baptism, and there must be evidence that it has taken place, before any person is entitled to be emblematically washed in baptism. The person who is thus *washed* is also *renewed* by the Holy Ghost. We are regenerated by faith, and not by the rite of baptism. Baptism is an emblem of this washing and regeneration.

Those who would reduce the conversion of sinners unto God, to a sort of religious manufacture, understand the *washing of regeneration* here, to be the rite of baptism. But though they have the support of the superstition of the Fathers, they have not the authority of the doctrine of the apostles. The Scriptures never speak of baptism as regeneration: regeneration is the act of God—not the effect of a rite performed by man. The apostle is, in this passage, asserting salvation by mercy, in express opposition to works of righteousness of our own. In asserting, then, that we are saved by the *washing of regeneration*, he cannot mean we are saved by a work performed on us by human hands.

But if it is a truth, that in this passage the washing of regeneration is the rite of baptism, and not the doctrine of which baptism is the emblem, it is a very melancholy truth with respect to most of those who believe it. They are not baptized. No person is *baptized* who is not *immersed;* and no person is baptized with Christ's baptism, who is not baptized as a believer. The great multitude, then, of those who speak of the necessity of baptism to salvation from the authority of this passage, are, according to their own view of it, condemned by it. But although every believer ought to be urged with all the authority of Jesus, to submit to all his commandments, yet neither ignorance of them, nor want of opportunity to observe them, will exclude them from his favour. No ordinance of Christ ought ever to be put in the room of Christ. I will fight the battle of baptism with all zeal; but I will acknowledge, in the greatest heat of my zeal, the worst instructed of all the disciples of Christ. To set at nought the very least of them, is to insult Christ himself.

The reference to baptism in this passage is decisive of its mode: it refers to the washing at the birth of an infant. Both the things referred to, and the word translated washing, imply that the whole body is covered with water in baptism.

DISSERTATION ON *LOUO*

SECTION XII.—The philosophical linguist, Dr. Campbell, of Aberdeen, in distinguishing the words *louo* and *nipto*, makes the first signify to *wash* or *bathe* the *whole* body, the last to wash or bathe a *part*. This distinction has been generally recognised since the time of Dr. Campbell. Mr. Beecher calls it in question, yet he does not touch the subject with the hand of a master. He merely alleges an objection which he thinks calculated to bring confusion into what is thought to be clear; but he gives no additional light by any learned observation of his own. I shall endeavour to settle this question by evidence, founded on the practice of the language, as well as the practice of the New Testament. I shall as much as possible avoid the technicalities of criticism, and as little as possible disfigure my page with Greek quotation. I request the merely English reader to understand that I intend to carry him along with me. There is very little real criticism which may not be made obvious to good sense, without the knowledge of the language which the criticism respects. All that my unlearned reader will be obliged to take on trust, is the fairness of my references to my authorities; and for this he has the security that I am open to the assault of all my enemies, if I unfairly represent.

Dr. Campbell's distinction in the use of the two words referred to, is well founded on fact, but he has scarcely reached the exact truth. It is this that lays his doctrine open to the objection of Mr. Beecher. That this distinction in the use of these words is fairly made out by the examples alleged by Dr. Campbell, and by the practice of the New Testament and Septuagint, is a fact that cannot be overturned. That it is a fact established by classical authority, I will show afterwards. But the reason alleged for this usage by Dr. Campbell is not the true reason. It is not because one of the words *signifies* to wash or bathe a *part*, and the other *signifies* to wash or bathe the *whole* body: the difference is in the action of the verbs; they are not the same *washing*. One of them may most generally be translated by our word *wash*, though *wash* is rather general for it; and the other may almost always be translated by our word *bathe*, though we sometimes translate it also by *wash*. In the one, the *washing* is by the pressure and motion of the water without manual operation, as in our word bathe, yet this bathing may also be accompanied with washing by the hand, though it is not signified by it. In the other, the action of the hand in the washing is almost always necessary. Now this is the reason why the one is generally applied to the bathing of the whole body, and the other to the washing of a part; because the body is generally bathed in this manner, and the hands or the feet are generally washed with the operation of the hands. One plunge in a river is a bathing; but when the hands are washed, friction is generally necessary; a mere bathing is not sufficient. Now, while this accounts for the fact asserted by Dr. Campbell, it will also allow the possibility of the application of *nipto* to the whole body, if it must be all successively washed; and it will allow the application of *louo* to a part, if the part is specified. Accordingly, we find in the first Idyl of Bion, that when Adonis was wounded by a boar, some bring water in golden caldrons—others *bathe* his thighs, one of the parts in which he was wounded. It is evident, however, that even here they must have put him in a bath for this operation. Yet this does not at all disturb the fact as to the practice alleged by Dr. Campbell, had he placed that fact on its true foundation. The criticism is this, and if I mistake not, the criterion will suit every occurrence : the verb, when it has no regimen supplied by the context, always refers to the bathing of the whole body; when it refers to a part, the context must supply the part. This observation will guide the reader through the whole practice of the Greek language. If every part of the body requires the washing that this word imports, there is nothing to prevent the application of *nipto*.

We make the same distinction in the use of our word *bathe*. When the physician directs his patient to *bathe*, without giving the verb any regimen, every one understands it to be a bathing of the whole body. Yet we also speak of bathing the feet

There is another distinction between these verbs, to which I have observed no exception. *Louo*, like our word bathe, applies to animal bodies only : we do not speak of bathing cloth.

Now to confirm this doctrine by examples. Nothing but the authority of the practice of the language, can be of any weight. If I have not thought it too laborious to collect my examples, my readers must not think that I call them to hard duty, when I demand their patience to attend to them. No labour can be too much to settle the meaning of the commandments of God. This can be known only from the meaning of the language in which they are revealed.

Let us begin with Hesiod. The distinction which Dr. Campbell points out in the New Testament and Septuagint is as strongly marked in the second book of the Works and Days. Several examples occur between lines 343 and 371. He forbids to pour out black wine to Jupiter in the morning with *unwashed hands*. He enjoins the washing of the hands before passing through a stream of running water, and speaks of the danger of *unwashed hands*.

On the other hand, when speaking of the whole body, he forbids to bathe in vessels not purified, and men he forbids to wash their bodies in a woman's bath. The word used is *loutron*. What, then, is the *loutron* when applied to baptism? Let the most unlearned judge from this.

In the beginning of the Theogony, Hesiod speaks of the Muses of Helicon, as bathing their tender bodies in the fountain of Termessus, *loessamenai.*

Let us now examine the testimony of Herodotus. He tells us, p. 54, that Cyrus commanded the Persians to assemble on a particular occasion, *leloumenois, bathed.* Here the verb has no regimen, yet its regimen is perfectly understood. The distinction, then, is as clear in Herodotus, as Dr. Campbell asserts it to be in the New Testament and Septuagint.

Speaking of the Egyptians, p. 104, he says they *lountai* (bathe) twice each day, and twice each night. Here the distinction is also marked, the verb having no regimen. If Mr. B. would bring this to the test of his probability, by which he would force its meaning from the word baptize, he would doubtless have much better reason to deny that they were actually bathed twice each day and twice each night. A baptism before dinner after market he thinks incredible in the superstition of a Jew. What shall we make of this purification of the Egyptians? Many people think it a great yoke for Christians to be obliged once in their lives to take the trouble of immersion : the devotees of superstition are contented to be baptized twice every day and twice every night.

Speaking of the Scythians (p. 248) he says that they use a certain fumigation instead of the *bath, loutrou;* adding, that they never *bathe the body with water;* but the women pouring out water and making a certain preparation, daub themselves all over with it.

Heraclides, as cited in the Appendix to Herodotus, (p. 594,) observes that the attendants on the king of Persia, at supper, ministered after being *bathed, leloumenoi.* Here the same distinction is recognised. The verb without a regimen refers to the washing of the person.

Ctesias, as cited in the same Appendix, (p. 664,) asserts that the wives of the Cynocephali, or dog-headed Indians, *lountai* (bathe) once a month; and that the men do not bathe at all, but only wash their hands, *aponizontai.* Here the distinctive use of the two verbs is clearly and strongly marked; and the verb which refers to bathing has no regimen.

The same writer (p. 666) mentions a fountain in which the Indians of distinction, men, women, and children, *lountai,* bathe, for the purpose of purification, and the expulsion of diseases. Here we see that the word refers to the bathing of the person; and that people bathed not only at, but in, the holy well. He tells us also that they all swam in it, as they could not, on account of the nature of the water, sink in it.

Hippocrates affords us many examples which definitely ascertain the distinctive meaning of this word; and precision of meaning is nowhere so exact as in medical language, with respect to words which designate the application of fluids. He tells us, (p. 26,) that in summer it is necessary to use many *baths,* or frequent bathings; in winter, fewer; and that it is more necessary for the morose to be bathed, than for the corpulent. Here *loutron* and *louesasthoi,* without any regimen, refer to the bathing of the whole body.

In a certain case he directs (p. 159) to *bathe* twice or thrice each day, *except the head.* Nothing can be more decisive than this exception. The word itself is supposed so definitely to refer to the whole body, that it is thought necessary to except the part that should not be bathed. After this, who can doubt that this word, when used without a regimen, refers to the bathing of the person? And would any one, in fulfilling this medical prescription, rub a little water over the body, instead of putting the body in the water, as Mr. Beecher fulfils the law of Moses?

That the word may, contrary to the doctrine of Dr. Campbell, be applied to the bathing of a part, the two following examples leave no doubt; and I conceal no part of the truth. For pains in the head, Hippocrates tells us that it is profitable to warm the head thoroughly, *bathing* it with much warm water, &c. In the same passage he says, " If the pain falls into the ears, it is profitable to *bathe* them with much warm water." Here, however, the regimen is supplied by the connexion; and the part which is the object of the action of the verb is all covered with the water. Even in such cases as this, the complete covering of the object by the fluid is as clearly seen as when the whole body is the object of the bathing.

In the case of tenesmus, (p. 184,) he orders to *bathe* with warm water, except the head. Here the word *louein* without any regimen refers to the body; and as there is a part which must not be *bathed*, that part must be expressly excepted. Surely this is decisive of the distinctive meaning of this word. In the same passage he speaks of " softening the body with *warm baths*, except the head."

In page 376, he gives us a whole treatise on bathing, referring to almost every thing in the process, and showing when it is useful, and when injurious. The vat, or vessel, in which the bathing is effected, is called *puelos;* and to this the verb *louein* and the noun *loutron* are constantly applied without any regimen.

The usage of Homer makes the same distinction in these words; and *louo*, without a regimen supplied by the connexion, always refers to the person. His baths for his heroes after battle, and after death, are well known, and uniformly conform to this distinction. It is so clearly marked in the tenth book of the Iliad, that were there not another passage, this is sufficient to establish it. In the beautiful language of Cowper it is—

> "Then, descending to the sea,
> Neck, thighs, and legs from sweat profuse they cleansed,
> And, so refreshed and purified, their last
> Ablution in bright tepid baths performed.
> Each then completely laved, and with smooth oil
> Anointed, at the well-spread board they sat,
> And quaffed, in honour of Minerva, wine
> Delicious, from the brimming beaker drawn."

Here the heroes, returning from slaughter, go down into the ocean and wash off the sweat, *apenizonto*. A mere bathing would not be sufficient; the gore must be washed off by rubbing—much rubbing; and in my judgment, the adverb *pollon* ought to be joined with the verb, as designating *much washing*, and not with the word sweat, according to Cowper. This, however, is not material to the point which I have now in hand. It is evident that the poet, in designating the action of cleansing the person by hand-washing, uses the verb *nipto*. Neck, thighs, and legs are specified, because these are the parts defiled. But there is no reason to allege, according to Dr. Campbell's ground of the distinction, that if every part of the body had been so washed with the hand, the same verb could not have been used. Indeed the wave is expressly said to *wash the body from its filth, nipsen apo chrotos.*

In the next place, after this washing in the sea, they went into the *baths,* and were bathed, *lousanto.* Nothing can more clearly manifest a distinction in the use of these words, and prove that the distinction is what I have alleged.

In the twenty-third book of the Iliad he applies the word to the horses of Achilles. Speaking of Patroclus, the poet, according to the translation of Cowper, says—

> "Who many a time hath cleansed
> Their manes with water of the crystal brook,
> And made them sleek himself with limpid oil."

Here the translator applies the word to the manes of the horses; but I think it ought to be applied to the horses themselves. Literally it is, "he poured limpid oil on their manes, having bathed in pure water." Now the regimen to bathe may be either the manes of the horses, or the horses themselves; and there is every reason to make it the horses. The horses appear first to have been bathed in the river; and after this their manes were anointed with oil to make them shine. I have no objection that the word should be applied to a part; but I think it would hardly be applied to the washing of hair. This interpretation is confirmed by a passage in the fifteenth book, in which, referring to Hector, the poet says—

> "As some stalled horse high-pampered, snapping short
> His cord, beats under foot the sounding soil,
> Accustomed in smooth-sliding streams to lave
> Exulting."

Here we see it was usual to bathe horses in rivers

In the third book of the Odyssey the word is used with respect to the bathing of Telemachus in a bath. When he had bathed, he is represented as *going out* of the bath.

In the sixth book, both the words are employed with respect to Ulysses washing in the river after his shipwreck. This was both a bathing and a hand-washing. Here the *apolouo* is applied to his shoulders, which shows that it may be applied to a part: and *nipto* is applied to the body in general. *He washed the brine from his body.* This shows that the distinction is not what it is made by Dr. Campbell, though that, in every instance, there is a distinction cannot be doubted.

In the eighth book, Ulysses is bathed at the house of Alcinous. *Louo* is the word several times used, and he is represented as *going into* the bath, and *coming out* of it.

In the tenth book, in the house of Circe, the hero is again led to the bath; and warm water is plenteously poured on his head and shoulders, until he is completely refreshed; and after he was clothed and seated on his throne, a nymph brings water for his hands. Here *nipto* is used without the regimen—the word hands being understood in the use of the verb, as Dr. Campbell observes on John ix. 7.

In the seventeenth book, Telemachus leads Piræus, the messenger of Menelaus, into his house, and they bathe before the banquet. Water was also ministered for the washing of the hands after they were clothed and seated. If Cowper, when he translates the passage thus,—"And plunged his feet into a polished bath," means that only the foot-bath was used, he is undoubtedly in error. They are represented as themselves going into the bath, and coming out of it; and the word *louo* without a regimen implies this. Perhaps the translator takes this way to express their going into the bath.

In the nineteenth book, the command of Penelope with respect to Ulysses as a beggar, which Cowper translates, "Give him the bath, my maidens; then spread his couch," it is undoubtedly the foot-bath that is meant. The verb is *aponipsate* without a regimen. "Attend him also at the peep of day with bath and unction." This refers to the bathing of the whole body. He was to be bathed and anointed before breakfasting with Telemachus. That it was the foot-bath that was meant in the first part of the sentence, is clear from the reply of Ulysses:

> "Nor me the foot-bath pleases more ; my feet
> Shall none of all thy minist'ring maidens touch,
> Unless there be some ancient matron grave
> Among them, who hath pangs of heart endured
> Num'rous and keen as I have felt myself;
> Her I refuse not. She may touch my feet."

It was actually the foot-bath that was used on this occasion, and his feet only were washed by his nurse, for which *nipto* is the verb used.

Simonides, concerning women, represents one as *unbathed* and *unwashed* in garments, *aloutos, aplutos*, with characteristic reference. He speaks of another as *bathed* twice and sometimes thrice every day. Here the verb has no regimen, yet definitely refers to the whole body.

Ælian, in the beginning of the third book of his Var. Hist., speaks of certain springs in Tempe, whose waters are good, *lousamenois*, to those who are bathed in them. He speaks also, in the thirteenth book, of an eagle snatching the slipper of Rodope the Egyptian, while she was *bathing*, carrying it to Memphis, and dropping it on the bosom of Psammitichios sitting on the judgment seat. The word *louomenes* is twice used without a regimen to designate the bathing of the person.

Nicolas of Damascus tells us that the king of Babylon ordered one of his eunuchs to bathe a certain person twice a-day. He uses the word *louo* without a regimen, as definitely importing the bathing of the whole body. He tells us also of a certain usurer, who ordered Crœsus to wait at the door, until the usurer should *bathe* himself. Here also the same verb is used with reference to the whole body, without any regimen. He speaks of the Dardani, an Illyrian nation, as being bathed only three times in their lives—when they are born, when they are married, and when they die. Here the word is used without any regimen ; and nothing can more definitely show its distinctive meaning.

Arrian, (p. 165,) giving an account of the last illness of Alexander the Great, uses the word ten times in conformity with the distinction I have assigned. After his debauch he bathed and slept. Again he supped, drank till far in the night, and afterwards *bathed,* ate a little, and slept. He was several times bathed during his fever, and usually bathed before sacrifice. Homer's heroes sometimes wash their hands before prayer, and before meat. Telemachus walking along the beach, having washed his hands in the hoary sea, prayed to Minerva. Odys. ii. Ulysses and his companions, having washed their hands, feasted on the stag. Odys. x.

The Essenes, Josephus informs us, (p. 728,) after working for some hours in the morning, assemble in one place, and girding themselves with linen veils, bathe before dinner. Here we see a daily baptism by a whole sect of the Jews. Mr. Beecher thinks a baptism after market incredible in Jewish superstition.

Justin Martyr not only always uses the word conformably to this distinction, but, speaking of the pagan purifications invented by the demons in imitation of baptism, he showed that they used the washing of the whole body as the most complete purification, p. 91.

Eusebius, speaking of Simon Magus, represents him as continuing his hypocrisy even to the bath, *mechri loutron,* p. 12; and the places where the Christians usually baptized, he calls *loutra,* bathing-places.

Lucian, in the dialogue of Micyllus and the Cock, uses the word *louo* without a regimen for bathing in a bath. He was invited to come to a feast, having bathed himself. He speaks also of his impatience in waiting for the time of the bath, *achri loutrou.* This determines not only the use of the word, but also shows that it was customary even for Gentiles to bathe before dinner. The bath was a luxury, not a penance.

On these grounds, then, there can be no hesitation in maintaining a distinctive use of the word *louo.* There are situations in which either of the words may be used, because both of them are in their peculiar meaning applicable. According to my view of the distinctive meaning of this word, there is nothing to prevent it from being applied to the vessels in the vestibule of ancient churches, for washing the hands of the worshippers. These might be called either *louteres* or *nipteres,* because the hands might be either bathed or washed. I have shown that the essential distinction has no reference to the whole and a part; though from circumstances the one is usually applied to a part of the body, and the other to the whole. And that the word does not necessarily express mode, I readily admit. This must be determined by circumstances; though, as a matter of fact, immersion is almost always the way of bathing. All I contend for from this word is, that the object to which it is applied is covered with the water, and that when used without a regimen in the context, it refers to the whole body. The application of this word to baptism shows that the rite was a bathing of the whole body; and as immersion is the usual way of bathing, baptism must have been an immersion, because, when it is called a bathing, the reference would be to the common way of bathing, not to a merely possible way. I claim, then, the evidence of all those passages in the New Testament which by this word refer to the ordinance of baptism. I make a similar demand with regard to the use of the word by the Fathers. Baptism, then, is immersion, and nothing but immersion is baptism.

12

CHURCH FATHERS SPEAK

REPLY TO PRESIDENT BEECHER'S ARTICLE IN THE AMERICAN BIBLICAL
REPOSITORY

PRESIDENT BEECHER, in an article of the American Biblical Repository, complains loudly of the severity of my attack on his theory of the meaning of the word *baptizo*. He has paraded a great number of extracts as evidence of a bad spirit. Now, every one of these extracts I recognise, and I make the charge of incompetence against him more strongly than ever: but, in those extracts, I deny the existence of the smallest degree of bad spirit. I act upon principle solemnly and deliberately. My design is to show my unlearned readers what account they are to make of his discoveries in a balloon above the clouds, from a specimen of what he has done before their own eyes. In questioning a decision of a court of law, is it not proper to show that they who made the decision are men without discrimination, and without accurate knowledge of the law? If such a case is made out, has it not the nature of evidence? In like manner, when we ask who are our opponents, and assert that all the illustrious scholars of all ages and countries are on our side, our design is not wantonly to wound. There is in this fact a species of self-evidence. If a judge is at once competent, and incontrovertibly disinterested, is not the greatest weight to be attached to his decision? Now, the illustrious scholars referred to are not only disinterested, but they decide against their own practice. How great, then, must be the weight of their testimony on this question!

I have charged President Beecher as deficient in discrimination, and as employing false principles of interpretation. For proof of this I refer to the work entitled "Baptism not Purification," sold by Mr. Burton, of Ipswich. I shall give my readers a sample of the grounds on which I found my charge.

He makes the words *baptismos* and *katharismos* synonymous, on the ground that they both in a certain place refer to the same rite. This is an error into which no philologist could fall: it shows a remarkable deficiency in discrimination. This I have frequently exemplified. The same error is to be found in most of the writers on that side of the question.

He makes *baptismos* a word designating purification in general, because it is a synonyme of the general word, *katharismos* · and the general word *katharismos* he makes specific, as it corresponds to *baptismos*. I have called this legerdemain. Here, also, I might offer a premium for a purer specimen of nonsense.

That the disputed word signifies *purification*, he proves from Malachi iii. 1—3. Does not even a child see that the prophet does not refer to ritual purification, but to the separation of the chaff from the wheat; and that the prophecy could have been equally fulfilled had no ritual ordinance of purification ever been instituted?

He makes the title of John the Baptist originate in the administration of a rite of purification, and he finds proof for this in John's being a moral reformer. May I not offer another premium here?

He proceeds on the principle, that every occurrence of the word must prove its own meaning. No philologist could fall into such an error. The meaning of no word could submit to such a test.

With respect to the testimony of Josephus, Mr. Beecher tells us, that "There was nothing to cause Josephus to think of the mode, or to attach any importance to it." This observation assumes, as a principle, that Josephus had a share in giving this rite its name. Can anything be more unlike a philologist? Can any observation be more destitute of common sense? Josephus speaks of the rite by the name already given to it.

As a proof that the disputed word is *often used* in the sense for which he contends, he alleges a passage in which the word is not used at all. Is this philology? Must this be dignified as criticism? Can the author possess that discrimination which is necessary to determine such a question?

This is but a small specimen of the author's qualifications as a critic, yet it clearly manifests his incompetency.

Nothing alleged by Mr. Beecher at all affects my view of the testimony of the Fathers on this subject. I still equally admit that testimony in a proper view of the subject. It is their testimony as it regards the meaning of the word at the time of the institution or commencement of the rite. I have expressly mentioned this: "I give my opponents the whole range of Greek literature till the institution of the ordinance of baptism." It is only as far as the Fathers can testify as to this fact, that they are competent witnesses. They might also testify to a secondary meaning without at all affecting this subject. I have said, "I deny a secondary meaning, not because it would disprove immersion, but because it wants the sanction of use." Notwithstanding all the examples alleged by Mr. Beecher, I am still of the same opinion. But, though a secondary meaning were fully proved, it would not in the smallest degree affect the question. Mr. Beecher's confidence is an additional proof of his want of discrimination. He ought to perceive that the Fathers might prove a secondary meaning, while, at the same time, they prove that, in reference to the original institution, the word is used in its primary meaning.

That the Fathers understood the word as immersion in reference to the institution of baptism, no scholar ever questioned. To prove this at any length would be totally unsuitable to my present work; but I shall submit two or three arguments that I hesitate not to say will produce conviction on the mind of every unprejudiced reader. I shall rather suggest them than urge them.

1. The Fathers not only practised immersion, but considered it essential except in cases of necessity. This could not have been the case, if they considered any purification to fulfil the meaning of the word.

2. The question about the validity of Novatian's perfusion never could have originated, had they considered that any purification was a fulfilment of the meaning of the word. On that supposition, how could any object to perfusion?

3. Even when writing on the subject of Novatian's perfusion, and defending the validity of it, Cyprian considers it not as baptism properly, but as a valid substitute for baptism.

4. Cyprian, even in the letter in which he defends the validity of perfusion as a substitute for baptism in cases of necessity, calls it an abridgement or compend of the ordinance.

5. In the same letter Cyprian uses the word *baptizo* in the sense of immersion, in reference to the ordinance, in contradistinction to perfusion. He argues the validity of perfusion from the fact that the persons who were perfused in their sickness, were never afterwards *baptized*, or immersed, which they must have been had not perfusion been accounted valid in such cases. If, as he reasons, the grace usually conferred by the ordinance has not been received by perfusion, let them be baptized or immersed when they recover: but as this is not the custom of the church, why do they object? No evidence can be more conclusive than this. This Father uses the word in its proper sense of immerse, in reference to the ordinance.

6. Cyprian calls perfusion the *ecclesiastical baptism*, as distinguished from baptism in the proper sense of the term. The persons perfused in their beds on account of sickness were not supposed to be properly baptized; but they received the ecclesiastical baptism—that is, what the church, in such cases, admitted as a valid substitute for baptism. This fact is conclusive, and will afford an answer to all the passages referred to by President Beecher to prove a secondary meaning in the use of the word among the Fathers. It was not a secondary meaning, because it never went into general use; but it is called a baptism, because it served the same purpose. It would not in the smallest degree affect the subject in question, had the word really received such a secondary meaning; but no such secondary meaning is in proof from the alleged examples.

7. Tertullian understood the word in reference to the ordinance as signifying immersion. He translates it by *tingo*. Mr. Beecher thinks he has silenced this testimony, by translating the word by *purify*. But the disproof of this is as certain as it is short. What Tertullian designates by *tingo*, he designates by *mergito*. And if he says *ter mergitamur*, he says, also, *ter tingimur,—We are thrice dipped.* It was only one purification, though it was performed by three immersions. Mr. Beecher, then, cannot, by all his torture, force *tingo*.

8. It appears to me self-evident that Christ would not appoint a rite, without appointing the way of its observance.

9. If the word signifies to purify, and if all may purify as they please, then, all the mummery of superstition is a fulfilment of Christ's command in the performance of the ordinance.

10. If the word denotes purification in general, then we may purify with fire, or sulphur, or salt, or oil, or anything we please, and water will not be essential. We may dispense with water as well as the mode.

11. If the water is known to be essential from the practice recorded in Scripture, this will not serve Mr. Beecher. He cannot reason on this principle. According to his principle, the first Christians might choose water in their purification ; but that others were not bound to their example.

12. The Greek translation of the Old Testament and Josephus have innumerable occasions to use the words designating the rites of purification. I have them all drawn out, though they cannot be inserted on this occasion. In not one of them is *baptizo* used for purification. Can anything more fully show that the word had not such a signification ?

Justin Martyr not only describes the performance of the rite as an immersion, but he speaks of it in a way that shows he considered the mode as emblematical, and, therefore, essential to the rite in its proper import. When he says, that in this rite they are born again, the reference, without doubt, is to their being in water and coming out of the water. Besides, he says, that it is *in the water* they have the remission of sins. This shows that to be in the water, and to come out of it, is the true meaning of the rite. He tells us that the demons, hearing of this washing from the prophet Isaiah, induced their worshippers to imitate it ; in the first step by sprinkling, and in the end using a complete washing of the body. In the first step they imitated it as a purification by water : in the last they imitated it not only in the water, but in the manner of using the water. In another place he speaks of baptism as cleansing *the flesh* and *the body* only : this shows that the water was applied to the body in general. He speaks of it, also, as referring to cisterns, or pits, as trenches that are *dug*. It must, then, have been an immersion. He sometimes, also, speaks of circumcision as a baptism, or agreeing in the emblem, though altogether different in the things and in the words that designate them. Let President Beecher study this, and it will show how the Fathers can call various things by the name of baptism, without importing that they are included in the meaning of the word. All his examples may be solved by this single fact. In like manner Justin speaks of Christians as having the spiritual circumcision, of which Greeks and those like him were partakers, though they had nothing that literally resembled what was imported by the word. Justin speaks, also, of certain washings prescribed by Moses as being baptisms. Now purification in general would not suit this, for every purification would not fulfil the injunction. But the passage in which he brings the literal and the figurative applications of the word to bear on each other, puts Justin's testimony on this subject beyond controversy. He considers the prophet's bringing up the immersed head of the axe out of Jordan, by casting in a piece of wood, as corresponding to men immersed in the greatest sins, yet brought out by the crucifixion of Christ and the purification of water. What can be more decisive than this? We are supposed to be *baptized* in the most grievous sins. What can baptism, then, be but immersion? Are we purified by sin? We, like the head of the axe, are immersed in sin: as the axe was brought up by the wood cast into the river, so we are brought up and purified by the baptism or sufferings of Christ. Besides, when Justin speaks of purification, he never employs any word that signifies baptism. If the word had this signification in his time, why did he sometimes use it in that sense?

In like manner, from a figurative application of the word by Origen, it is decisively evident that he understood it as meaning immerse. He speaks of persons totally given up to sin, as being entirely immersed or sunk down under wickedness.

From a figurative application of the word by Clemens Alexandrinus, it is evident that he understood it as literally signifying immersion. He speaks of persons baptized by drunkenness into sleep. All language must recognise this figure: it is an immersion or burial in sleep. It is utterly impossible that purification should be the ground of this figure.

Gregory Thaumaturgus speaks of drawing baptized persons up as fish are drawn out of water by a line. Now, when a figure can be definitely ascertained as to its secondary object, it is the most unexceptionable way of ascertaining the literal meaning of a word.

That Tertullian understood immersion to be part of the nature of the rite, is evident from his saying, that " in baptism we die through a likeness." There is no death in purification except when it is performed by immersion.

Chrysostom most definitely shows that he attached this meaning to the word by coupling it with the word *sink*, and making the action designated by both an emblem of burial and resurrection. " *To be baptized and to sink down*," says he, " then to rise, is a symbol of the going down into the grave, and of the coming up from it." Here he not only couples *baptizing* with *sinking down*, but makes both words, as to the ordinance of baptism, designate an idea which is an emblem of going down into the grave. He not only uses the word in the sense of immersion, but in that sense he applies it to the ordinance of baptism. No evidence can be more decisive than this. Even had the word obtained a secondary meaning by use, it is in its primary that the Fathers apply it to baptism; but, though the Fathers called many things baptism, the word never obtained a secondary meaning. Besides, Chrysostom expressly expounds Rom. vi. as asserting an emblem of burial and resurrection in baptism. This not only proves that immersion was the usual practice at the time, but that they considered this as the appointed mode of the rite.

The three immersions used by the ancients in the performance of the rite are called *tria baptismata, three baptisms*, that is, *three immersions*, for it could not be *three purifications*: it was only one purification. I am well aware that the three immersions may be called also one baptism. *My philosophy* can account for this. When they are said to be three baptisms, the word is used in reference to the act of immersion; when they are called one baptism, the word is used in reference to the rite in its appropriated sense. The three immersions are, in the estimation of those who used them, only one rite, which was designated by the name baptism.

That Cyprian, and those concerned in the case of Novatian, understood the word as signifying immersion, is clear to demonstration, from the fact that the justification of perfusion was not rested on the meaning of the word, but on other grounds. Had the word signified purification without reference to mode, would they not have appealed to the meaning of the word? Would Cyprian have employed so much trifling in vindicating the sufficiency of perfusion, if he could have found a complete vindication in the meaning of the word, and in the essential nature of the ordinance? Jerome also translated the word in the commission by *intingo*, to *dip into*, which shows that in his time the Greek word was understood to signify *immersion*.

Mr. B does not understand my canon as to impossibility. He says, that my doctrine is " that we cannot admit a secondary sense unless we can prove that the primary sense is impossible." He leaves out an essential part of my canon. Impossibility is required only when a secondary meaning is not in proof. If in any occurrence in the language a secondary meaning is in proof, impossibility of primary meaning is not essential to warrant the application of a secondary meaning. I have again and again explained this doctrine.

He complains that I assume universal use, though all the occurrences of the word are not produced. On this ground, universal use could not be assumed with respect to any word, for all the instances in which any word has been used can never be produced. It is quite enough, that after all the researches of all writers on both sides of the question since the birth of the controversy, a refractory instance, till the time of the institution, cannot be produced.

The passages which he quotes from the Fathers are all explicable on the principle which I have pointed out in the sentence from Cyprian; but, were it true, which it is not, that the word in process of use, after the institution of the ordinance, received a secondary meaning, it has no bearing on this subject; it does not at all stand in my way.

The passages from Clemens Alexandrinus in which the word occurs, are entirely misunderstood. Where did the President learn that *koite* is a dinner couch? It is a bed for sleeping on. It is not, "this was the custom of the Jews that they often should be baptized upon their beds." This passage refers to the nightly pollutions after which bathing was prescribed by the law of Moses. They were immersed " on account of the bed ;" that is, pollution contracted there.

The instance from Nicephorus is perfectly explicable from the passage in Cyprian's letters. Cyprian, while he uses the word *baptizo* for *immerse*, calls the perfusion of Novatian an ecclesiastical baptism, because it was used by the church as conveying the same grace with baptism. Indeed, had the custom of immersion been universally changed into any other mode, the rite would still have continued to be called immersion. This, which the President thinks must prove so refractory to me, has not the smallest difficulty ; it is quite in accordance with my doctrine.

Mr. Beecher represents the preposition *ek* as "a preposition at war with the idea of immerse." This is an error that no philologist could hold. Any person who has ever passed the threshold of the temple of philology must know that such combinations of prepositions, both in composition and in syntax, are quite common. Prepositions the very reverse of each other, are often combined and prefixed to the same word. I cannot pursue this subject here: I shall merely suggest it to literary men. Even *apobapto* itself is used in the same way in the Septuagint; and though it should be supposed to mean *wet* or moisten, still the result is the same. Even wetting or moistening implies that the wetting or moistening is effected while the object is in union with the wetting or moistening substance. Yet *from*, or *apo*, signifies *separation*, not *union*. Had I no other evidence that the President, however great a man he may be in other respects, is not a philologist, I could take his measure from this single observation. I will make this plain even to my most unlearned readers. Dr. Miller, I think, somewhere in his treatise, speaks of dipping *up* a bucket of water. Let a foreigner interpret this on the principle of President Beecher. *Up*, says the critic, signifies ascension; dipping, then, cannot denote immersing, for this implies sinking. The preposition is at war with immerse as the meaning of the word *dip*. Dip must, then, signify to raise, or draw, or lift—not to immerse; and this critic would know English as the President knows Greek. All languages must admit such combinations as President Beecher supposes to be in this case incongruous.

The examples produced by Mr. Beecher prove that *louo* sometimes applied to other things besides animal bodies; but none of them prove that the thing so washed was not covered with the water. This is all we want: the water might be applied by sprinkling, or by pouring, or in any way. Indeed it would be enough for us if this was its usual signification. Why should it on this subject be supposed to assume a rare meaning?

With respect to the baptism of the Spirit, after admitting my assertion that metaphor may indulge itself wherever it finds resemblance, he says, "But my objection is, that *there is no resemblance* between the operations of the Holy Spirit and immersion." Is not the resemblance in the effects?

With respect to my illustrations, "steeping the senses in forgetfulness," "steeping the soul in the milk of human nature," "be not drunk with wine, but be filled with the Spirit," he says,—"How, I ask, are the words to steep, to be drunk, and to fill, verbs denoting the mode of an action, and that alone? or are they words denoting an effect?" This is a strange observation for a man of letters. It is no matter what the verbs signify if they can be figuratively applied with regard to their effects. Words can be used figuratively where the resemblance is not in their literal signification, but in their effects. Besides, would any philologist—would any intelligent child say, that *steep* denotes an effect? Steep denotes a certain action which has a certain effect.

The metaphysical nonsense, for the exceeding of which I offered a premium, Mr. Beecher ascribes to several of the Fathers. I find nothing like it in his quotations; and notwithstanding the modesty of the President, I must still think that the union of *meanings running into one another* is all his own.

He complains that I unjustly represent him as founding on probability independently of the meaning of the word. I reiterate the charge. Does he not perceive that by *the meaning of* the word I understand a previously ascertained meaning? To this he does not even pretend. I found all on meaning previously ascertained: this is a fundamental difference between him and me.

The characteristic meaning of the word *klizo* is exactly what I have represented; and all the examples accord with this: but the example to which he refers has no bearing on the subject. When he alleges proof that persons may go to a river for other purposes than the immersion of the whole body, he manifests a want of discrimination. Our argument is grounded on the fact that the going to the water was for the purpose of baptism. When our opponents triumph, and tell us that if our argument is conclusive, Philip was baptized as well as the eunuch, their triumph is in their want of discrimination.

In defending the combination of his probabilities, he makes a distinction as to the nature of the subjects; but, on all subjects, nothing is nothing; and if I have proved that the probabilities are *nothing* separately, nothing must they be in combination. Besides, the probability that, independently of testimony, a thing was done in a certain way, is a very different thing from the probability that a word has a certain meaning. That A killed B may be very probable from many circumstances; but the moment A proves an *alibi*, or that it is proved that C is guilty of the murder, all the previous probabilities are of no account.

After all his complaints about a bad spirit, it is amusing to consider the gross manifestations which he affords of this himself. In all I have ever written I defy my adversaries to point out one particle of a bad spirit. My severity respects the execution of the work before me, and my censures are preceded by proofs of the thing condemned. Justice to truth demands the exposure. But what spirit is indicated by such expressions as " the guise of zeal for the glory of God?" " Being determined not to admit the truth, he did the only thing that remained, first to misrepresent, and then to deny it?" If this is not a bad spirit, what will indicate a bad spirit? But in the field of battle I never murmur. I never pronounce on the motives of my opponents; but I always, as a matter of duty, measure their talents. This they are pleased to call a bad spirit, while they have poured out whole torrents of the most virulent abuse: this never moves me,—I write for eternity.

I had charged President Beecher with using a Unitarian canon. How does he repel the charge? He tells me that a good canon is not the worse for being employed by Unitarians. I redouble the charge. A Unitarian canon is not a sound canon employed by Unitarians as well as others. A Unitarian canon is one which, if admitted, will prove Unitarianism. What a want of discrimination is in this defence! A canon that is sound ought to be used by all. A Unitarian canon cannot be sound, unless Unitarianism is true.

To enable my readers to estimate the qualifications of my antagonist as a controversialist, I shall slightly notice the several particulars which he states in recommendation of his view of the meaning of the word in dispute. To judge on this matter requires nothing but a sound intellect and an unprejudiced mind. He tells us, for instance, that to adopt his conclusions "takes nothing from any one but the right to think others wrong," &c. Now was there ever a purer specimen of absurdity than this? Were it as true as it is false, it could not take from any man the right to think another wrong. Must not every one who thinks his own view on any subject right, think all others wrong who differ from him? Does not the writer think that I am wrong?

Six special advantages, as recommendations of this view, are enumerated by the writer. "1. It is more adapted to the varying conditions of men, and to all change of climate, times, seasons, and health." Immersion is not injurious to health in any climate: but should the physi-cian, in any case, recommend the warm bath, there is nothing to prevent it. If the believer is on a sick bed, or death bed, the rite is not a duty. Clinical perfusion could never have been introduced as a substitute for baptism, had not Puseyism been previously introduced. Is there as much danger in immersion as there was in circumcision? Had the matter been left to himself, I doubt not but the ingenuity of Abraham would have found that shaving the head would have been better adapted to the comfort of himself and his posterity.

But it is perfect absurdity to talk of recommendations on one side or the other, on such a matter. Whatever God has appointed must be observed. Had God appointed two modes, giving us a discretionary power to observe which of them should be most pleasing to us, we might make a choice: but whatever recommendations a thing may have to us, God may have good reason for appointing a different.

"2. It is more accordant," says the writer, "with the liberal and en-larged spirit of Christianity, as a religion of freedom, designed for all countries and all times."

Does the writer mean that the prescription of mode, as emblematical in a Christian rite, is inconsistent with the practice of religion? Another may as well say, that the prescription of water, or of wine, or of any-thing else, is equally inconsistent with Christianity. What a notion this writer must have of religious freedom!

"3. It better agrees," says the author, "with our ideas of what is reasonable and fit." And will the writer take on him to say that it is not reasonable and fit in God to appoint immersion as the mode of this ordinance, as an emblem of the burial of Christ? If this is not blas-phemous, I know not what blasphemy is.

"4. It offers," says the writer, "no temptations to formalism, nor does it tend to foster arrogance and exclusion." Here is the very spirit of philosophy. How does immersion, or any other mode appointed by God, offer a temptation to formalism? Is it formalism to observe a mode which by the very supposition is appointed by God? Is it formalism to observe Divine forms? As to arrogance, is it arrogant to say that immersion is the only mode, if it is the meaning of the word? As to exclusion, the meaning of the word is not concerned in settling the question of church fellowship.

"5. It is perfectly adequate," says the author, "to harmonise the church." What a recommendation! Is it not obvious to every human intellect, that any view of the meaning of the word, if it is universally received, is equally calculated to effect harmony? The advocates of pouring, of sprinkling, of immersing, &c. &c., may all equally allege this recommendation. Even if a man should say that the word signifies to *tattoo*, he may say that, if all parties receive this meaning, it would harmonise the church. Was ever such a specimen of reasoning committed to the types?

"6. It is susceptible," says the author, "of any necessary degree of proof." This confounds evidence with recommendation. If it is capable of proof, it should be received without any recommendation. If it is not proved, no recommendation can entitle it to reception.

Now I call the attention of my plain, unlettered readers to this brief specimen of my antagonist's reasoning powers, that they may judge what confidence they are to place in his criticism. If in matters of common sense he stumbles at every step, can he be trusted in matters of the most profound metaphysics? My antagonist may be a very ingenious man, and a very pious man, and in many respects a very clever man, but he has not a head for the philosophy of language : and I say this with as little bad feeling as I say that the three angles of every triangle are equal to two right angles.

SCRIPTURE INDEX

AUTHOR INDEX